Black
American
Colleges
&
Universities

Virgin Islands

NATIONAL ADVISORS

D. Kamili Anderson
Associate Editor, *Journal of Negro Education*
Washington, D.C.

Deborah J. Carter
Associate Director
Office of Minorities in Higher Education
American Council on Education
Washington, D.C.

Patricia Deveaux, Ph.D.
Senior Advisor, Diversity Programs and Educational Initiative
Department of Energy
Washington, D.C. 20585

Vonita W. Foster, Ph.D.
Library Director
Virginia Union University
Richmond, VA

Courtney H. Funn
Thurgood Marshall Library
Bowie State University
Bowie, MD

Beverly Guy-Sheftall, Ph.D.
Anna J. Cooper Professor of Women's Studies
Director of Women's Research & Resource Center
Spelman College
Atlanta, GA

Frances K. Hall
Retired Assistant Deputy Director
Buffalo & Erie County Public Library
Buffalo, NY

Aloma D. Johnson
Guidance Counselor
Grover Cleveland High School
Buffalo, NY

Alan H. Kirschner
Vice President of Programs and Public Policy
United Negro College Fund
New York, NY

N. Joyce Payne, Ph.D.
Director, Office for the Advancement of Public Black
  Colleges
National Association of State Universities and Land-Grant
  Colleges
Washington, D.C.

Jessie C. Smith
Director of Library Services
University of Maryland Eastern Shore
Princess Anne, MD

Levirn Hill, Editor

Gale Research Inc. Staff

Peg Bessette, Developmental Editor
Kelle S. Sisung, Associate Developmental Editor
Lawrence W. Baker, Senior Developmental Editor

Christine Nasso, Acquisitions Editor

Mary Beth Trimper, Production Director
Evi Seoud, Assistant Production Manager
Mary Kelley, Production Associate

Cynthia Baldwin, Art Director
Barbara J. Yarrow, Graphic Services Supervisor
Pamela A. E. Galbreath, Cover and Page Designer
Willie Mathis, Camera Operator

Benita L. Spight, Data Entry Supervisor
Gwendolyn S. Tucker, Data Entry Group Leader
Frances E. Hall, Data Entry Associate

Library of Congress Cataloging-in-Publishing Data

Hill, Levirn, 1942–
    Black American colleges and universities / Levirn Hill.
       p. cm.
    Includes bibliographical references (p.).
    ISBN 0-8103-9166-X: $55.00
    1. Afro-American universities and colleges–Directories.
    [1.Afro-American universities and colleges–Directories. 2. Universities and colleges–Directories.]   I. Title.
    LC2781.H54 1994

           378.73'08996073–dc2094-3898
                       CIP
                        AC

Gale Research Inc.
835 Penobscot Bldg.
Detroit, MI 48226

Printed in the United States of America

Published simultaneously in the United Kingdom by Gale Research International Limited
(An affiliated company of Gale Research Inc.)
10 9 8 7 6 5 4 3 2 1

Black American Colleges & Universities:

PROFILES OF TWO-YEAR, FOUR-YEAR, & PROFESSIONAL SCHOOLS

Levirn Hill, Editor

Introduction by
Reginald Wilson, Ph.D.,
Senior Scholar,
American Council on Education

Gale Research Inc. • DETROIT • WASHINGTON, D.C. • LONDON

This book is dedicated to my mother, for roots and wings—

My husband, who is my hero—

My identical twin sister, who is my better half—

My three sons, two engineers and an audiologist,
who are products of black colleges and universities—

My grandchildren, who motivate me to keep my spirit alive—

And Virginia Union University, which awakened the God in me
by helping me realize that I could do anything I set my mind to
by listening to that still, quiet voice within me

CONTRIBUTORS

Gladys Smiley Bell, M.L.S.
Assistant Professor, Kent State University
Libraries and Media Services
Kent, OH

Helen Bush Caver, Ed.D.
Associate Professor and Assistant Librarian
Jacksonville State University
Jacksonville, AL

Sarah Crest, M.L.S.
Coordinator of Library User Instruction
Townson State University
Townson, MD

Jeannie Gex, M.L.S.
Retired Librarian
State University of New York at Buffalo
Buffalo, NY

Glen McWilson, B.S.
Computer Specialist
Buffalo, New York

Cynthia Maxwell, M.S.
Educator
Olmstead Elementary School
Buffalo, NY

Lut Nero, M.L.S.
Library Director
Cheyney University
Cheyney, PA

Hilary Sternberg, M.L.S.
Senior Assistant Librarian
Buffalo State College
Buffalo, NY

Betsy Strother, M.S.
Consultant
Dimensions Unlimited, Inc.
Buffalo, NY

Mira Venkataraman, M.L.S.
Assistant Librarian
Medaille College
Buffalo, New York

INDEXERS

Katherine Hill, M.L.S.
Assistant Librarian
Erie County Community College (North)
Buffalo, NY

Marsha Moses, A.S.
Community Relations Assistant, Office of the President
Buffalo State College
Buffalo, NY

Willa Spivey
Retired Secretary, Business Department
Buffalo State College
Buffalo, NY

CONTENTS

PREFACE xix

ACKNOWLEDGEMENTS xxiii

HISTORICALLY BLACK COLLEGES AND UNIVERSITIES:
AN ACADEMIC EVOLUTION xxv

FEATURES: HOW TO GET THE MOST OUT OF THIS BOOK . . xxviii

SCHOOLS-AT-A-GLANCE xxx

FINDING THE SCHOOL FOR YOU 1

ROOM, BOARD, AND DEBT: HOW TO FIND THE FUNDS 7

ALABAMA 19
Alabama Agricultural & Mechanical University 21
Alabama State University. 28
Bishop State Community College. 35
Concordia College 40
J. F. Drake State Technical College. 44
Lawson State Community College 48
Lomax-Hannon Junior College 53
Miles College 56
Oakwood College 61
Selma University 67
Stillman College 71
Talladega College 77
Trenholm State Technical College 83
Tuskegee University 86

ARKANSAS 95
Arkansas Baptist College 97
Philander Smith College 100
Shorter College 106
University of Arkansas at Pine Bluff 110

CALIFORNIA 117
Charles R. Drew University of Medicine & Science . . 119
Compton Community College 123

DELAWARE 129
Delaware State University 131

FLORIDA 139
Bethune-Cookman College 141
Edward Waters College 147
Florida Agricultural & Mechanical University 152
Florida Memorial College 160

GEORGIA 167
Albany State College 169
Clark Atlanta University 175
Fort Valley State College 181
Interdenominational Theological Center 187
Morehouse College 192
Morehouse School of Medicine 198
Morris Brown College 204
Paine College 211
Savannah State College 217
Spelman College 223

ILLINOIS 231
Chicago State University 233
Kennedy-King College 240

KENTUCKY 245
Kentucky State University 247
Simmons University Bible College 254

LOUISIANA 255
Dillard University 257
Grambling State University 263
Southern University and Agricultural
    & Mechanical University at Baton Rouge 269
Southern University (New Orleans) 276
Southern University (Shreveport) 280
Xavier University of Louisiana 284

MARYLAND 291
Bowie State University 293
Coppin State College 299
Morgan State University 306
Sojourner-Douglass College 314
University of Maryland Eastern Shore 318

MASSACHUSETTS 327
Roxbury Community College 329

MICHIGAN 335
Highland Park Community College 337
Lewis College of Business 341
Wayne County Community College 345

MISSISSIPPI 349
Alcorn State University 351
Coahoma Community College 357
Hinds Community College 362
Jackson State University 368
Mary Holmes Community College 375
Mississippi Valley State University 380
Rust College 386
Tougaloo College 392

MISSOURI 397
Harris-Stowe State College 399
Lincoln University 404

NEW YORK 411
LaGuardia Community College 413
Medgar Evers College 419
New York City Technical College 424

NORTH CAROLINA 429
Barber-Scotia College 431
Bennett College 437
Elizabeth City State University 442
Fayetteville State University 448
Johnson C. Smith University 454
Livingstone College 459
North Carolina Agricultural &
   Technical State University 465
North Carolina Central University 471
Saint Augustine's College 477
Shaw University 482
Winston-Salem State University 487

OHIO 493
Central State University 495
Cuyahoga Community College 501
Wilberforce University 506

OKLAHOMA 513
Langston University 515

PENNSYLVANIA 521
Cheyney University of Pennsylvania 523
Lincoln University of Pennsylvania 529

SOUTH CAROLINA 537
Allen University 539
Benedict College 543
Claflin College 548
Clinton Junior College. 553
Denmark Technical College 556
Morris College 561
South Carolina State University 566
Voorhees College. 572

TENNESSEE. 577
Fisk University 579
Knoxville College 585
Lane College. 589
LeMoyne-Owen College 594
Meharry Medical College. 600
Tennessee State University 606

TEXAS 613
Huston-Tillotson College 615
Jarvis Christian College 620
Paul Quinn College. 626
Prairie View Agricultural & Mechanical University . . 630
Southwestern Christian College 636
Texas College 641
Texas Southern University 645
Wiley College. 652

VIRGIN ISLANDS 657
University of the Virgin Islands 659

VIRGINIA. 663
Hampton University 665
Norfolk State University. 671
Saint Paul's College 677
Virginia Seminary and College 681
Virginia State University 683
Virginia Union University 689

WASHINGTON, DISTRICT OF COLUMBIA 695
Howard University. 697
Howard University School of Law 706
University of the District of Columbia 709

WEST VIRGINIA 717
Bluefield State College 719
West Virginia State College 725

NOTABLE ALUMNI CHART 733

APPENDIXES
Church-Affiliated Schools 759
Land-Grant Schools 760
Public or State-Supported Schools. 760
United Negro College Fund (UNCF)
  Member Schools 761
Two-Year Schools 761
Four-Year Schools 761
Professional Schools 762
Historically Black Colleges
  and Universities (HBCUs) 763
Thurgood Marshall Scholarship Fund
  Member Schools 764

BIBLIOGRAPHY 765

PHOTO CREDITS 769

COMMON ABBREVIATIONS AND DEFINITIONS 773

SCHOOL PROFILES INDEX 779

MASTER INDEX 783

PREFACE

Scope: Covering the Territory

Black American Colleges and Universities: Profiles of Two-Year, Four-Year, and Professional Schools (BACU) is a comprehensive guide to 118 historically and/or predominantly black colleges and universities. *BACU* includes 22 two-year community colleges, 91 four-year colleges and universities, and five professional schools.

Purpose: Providing Options

BACU provides greater access to these 118 schools than any other single source. Many students, parents, counselors, and information specialists are not aware of the majority of the schools covered in this title. This comprehensive source focuses solely on black colleges and universities, which typically get lost in the larger college guides. Profiled schools range from the well-known, selective schools, such as Spelman and Morehouse, to the lesser-known, open admission schools, such as Simmons Bible College and Coahoma Community College.

Because institutions of higher education such as those featured in *BACU* have played such a critical role in the education of blacks throughout history, the guide also serves as a historical document on these ecumenical institutions as they continue to expand their programs and grow demographically.

Primarily a search tool for the prospective student, *BACU* is easy to use (*See* **Features: How to Get the Most Out of This Book,** later on page xxviii) and was written for students, parents, high school guidance counselors, college admission counselors, and librarians, as well as for alumni of these schools.

Arrangement: Where Would I Find . . . ?

BACU is arranged by state, with schools profiled alphabetically within their states. State maps open each chapter, denoting school location, state capitol, and major cities within the state. An alphabetical list of schools featured in the map serves as its key.

Selection Process: Shaping the List

A school was selected for inclusion in *BACU* if it was either historically or traditionally black, or if it was a school with a predominantly black enrollment. For example, West Virginia State University's present student enrollment includes 4,000 caucasians and 300 blacks, but as an historically black college, it is included here. *BACU* also covers schools that are not historically black but currently have a predominantly black enrollment, such as Highland Park Community College and Kennedy-King College.

Schools were selected from several independent lists of historically black colleges and universities (HCBUs), including those of the National Association for Equal Opportunity in Higher Education (NAFEO), the Minority On-line Information Service (MOLIS), *The Black Resource Guide* (Black Resource Guide, Inc.), *Black American Information Directory* (Gale Research Inc.), and the United Negro College Fund member list. Of the 140 black colleges and universities on the above-named lists, 120 appeared on four out of five and therefore were selected for this guide. However, two of those schools are not profiled in *BACU*. In the case of Natchez Jr. College, too little information was available to provide a true profile on the school. The other school that was eliminated from the 120, Atlanta Metropolitan College, will close in August, 1994. Other schools not selected were primarily two-year institutions. In the next edition of *BACU,* additional schools will likely be included.

Compilation Method: Getting the Facts

To ensure a high degree of accuracy, a survey and a letter explaining the project were sent to each school requesting detailed information. Each school was contacted at least four times in an attempt to get a high return rate on the surveys. Sixty-five percent of the surveys were completed and returned. Additional information was obtained from school catalogs or brochures. Other sources consulted included MOLIS, Gale Research Inc. references, and other college guides. Where discrepancies in the sources existed, the information provided from the schools themselves was used.

Content: Defining the Data

BACU contains the following information for almost all schools:
    address
    phone numbers
    total enrollment (undergraduate and graduate)
    level of selectivity
    history
    major accreditation

estimated yearly college cost

financial aid deadline and contact

admission policy for high school graduates, GED, international, and transfer students

admission deadline and contact

graduation requirements

grading system

school calendar

degrees offered (arts or science degrees if available)

special programs

athletic program

intercollegiate and intramural sports

library holdings

student life (including special regulations, student services, campus activities, handicap services, and housing availability)

Information on the following was provided when available:

toll-free and fax numbers

photo of school

school motto

specialized accreditation

institutional and governmental financial aid

profile of students and faculty

number of degrees conferred

notable alumni

Academic years for various types of information may differ. *BACU* aims to provide the most current information available on the school calendar, costs per year, and financial aid.

Level of Selectivity

This ranks the degree of competitiveness for admission to each school. Competitive schools require four to six elements for admission such as: minimum SAT/ACT, GED, or GPA; class rank; college preparatory units; high school recommendations; personal essay and statement of intent; and completion of 18 or more units. Moderately competitive schools require three of the above, slightly competitive schools require two of the above, and non-competitive schools require one of the above and/or have an open admission policy. All schools require either graduation from high school or a GED and proof of a physical, while some schools want proof of immunizations against measles and rubella. Most require a non-refundable application fee of $15 to $25. The level of selectivity information is also summarized in the **Schools-at-a-Glance** chart, for easy comparison.

Financial Aid

Federal financial aid is available at all schools and therefore was not included. The U.S. Department of Education makes the following student financial aid programs available: Federal Pell Grants; Federal Supplemental Educational Opportunity Grants (FSEOG); Perkins Loans, Stafford Loans, Supplemental Loans for Students (SLS), Parent Loans to Undergraduate Students (PLUS); and college work-study. Information on financial aid is summarized in **Room, Board, and Rent: Finding the Funds,** *BACU's* financial aid chapter.

Trends at Black American Colleges and Universities: Where We Are Going

As Dr. Reginald Wilson points out in his guest introduction, black American schools continue to evolve. Listed below are current trends.

- Female-male ratio is 2:1
- Enrollment is up at all black American colleges and universities
- Non-black faculty positions and student enrollment are on the increase
- More faculty are securing terminal degrees
- Publications about these schools are on the increase
- Philanthropic gifts from celebrities, corporations, and alumni are on the increase
- More schools are facing the possibility of merging or closing
- Recently, four public schools have been granted university status

Comments and Suggestions Welcome

Black American Colleges and Universities was compiled between September, 1992 and February, 1994. Although all address and telephone information was verified in the first two months of 1994, costs, profiles, and calendars often change. For further information, use *BACU* to contact the college of interest to you. While considerable care has been given to keeping errors and inconsistencies to a minimum, invariably some may have occured. Corrections or suggestions for the improvement of future editions will be greatly appreciated. Please direct them to:

Editor
Black American Colleges and Universities
Gale Research Inc.
835 Penobscot Bldg.
Detroit, MI 48226-4094

Levirn Hill, Editor

ACKNOWLEDGEMENTS

The completion of this guide on black American colleges and universities involved many people I would like to acknowledge. First I would like to acknowledge my husband, Edward Hill, who provided a shoulder to lean on when I felt weary and who was a sounding board when I needed to vent; I also thank my three sons, Edward, Daryl, and Talbert, who gave me practical advise on how to persevere—as did my mentors, Jim and Mamie Crawford.

My colleagues at E.H. Butler Library, Buffalo State College are a special group of people. On whatever project I have undertaken, they have provided both the cheers and encouragement for me to stay focused. I acknowledge Dr. Newman and Carol Richards who supported this librarian's study leave, allowing me to complete the project in a more timely manner; Maureen Lindstrom for her computer assistance; Sandy Colucci for covering the Curriculum Lab while I was out on study leave; Marjorie Lord and Betty Plewniak for sharing the fax machine; Peggy MacDonald for microfilm support; Hilary Sternberg for teaching my classes; Randy Gadikian and Maryruth Glogowski for editorial advise and support; and the rest of my colleagues in Information Services for being good listeners and supporters as well as covering the reference desk for me. Thanks also go to Kathy Babcock for research assistance and Shirley Posner for mail support.

I would like to thank the New York State United University Professions Professional Development and Quality of Working Life (NYS/UUP PDQWL) Committee for the Librarian's Study Leave grant they provided to enable me to complete part of *BACU*. I would also like to thank Buffalo State College for approving the study leave.

My sisters Willa Spivey and Marsha Moses provided invaluable back-up support as contributing editors, indexers, or whatever I needed when I felt overwhelmed. My other sisters Melvina Davis, Zayeekah Talib, and Ayvonne Luchey assured me that if I needed their help they were waiting in the wings for me to ask for their assistance. Other family contributors included Constance Sparks-Clark who contributed one entry and Carolyn Holder who made sure I took time to relax. Thanks to Deborah Curry (SUNY at Albany) and Dr. Lorna Peterson (SUNY at Buffalo) who contributed one entry each. Loving thanks to graduate student Sherry McDuffie who provided research assistance.

A special thanks to Reginald Wilson, Ph.D. for honoring the project with his introduction. Dr. Wilson is Director of the Office of Minorities in Education, American Council on Education (ACE), ACE scholar, and author of several articles on black colleges and universities. N. Joyce Payne, Director, Office for the Advancement of Public Black Colleges served as a national advisor and provided more than 30 photographs needed to complete the guide as did Alan Kirschner, Vice-president of Programs and Public Policy, United Negro College Fund (UNCF). Thanks also to Deborah Carter and Patricia Deveaux for promptly faxing pertinent information. The other national advisors listed in the guide provided editorial advise and guidance whenever necessary.

Many thanks go to the 11 contributing editors and 3 indexers who assisted in the completion of this manuscript, as well as Michael Woodruff and Deborah Jones of Buffalo State College who wrote the financial aid chapter and admissions chapter respectively; I am eternally grateful to all of you for time, effort, and support of the project.

I would like to thank the staff at Gale Research Inc. for their confidence in me and invaluable guidance in my first major publishing project, especially Christine Nasso for her belief in my ability to complete such an undertaking, and Lawrence Baker and Kelle Sisung for their editorial support. I am particularly indebted to Peg Bessette, Developmental Editor, for her patient guidance, gentle nudging to meet deadlines, and her loving support in the completion of *Black American Colleges and Universities*.

Finally, I would like to thank all the colleges and universities who provided photographs and information on their schools.

Levirn Hill, Editor

HISTORICALLY BLACK COLLEGES AND UNIVERSITIES: AN ACADEMIC EVOLUTION

by Dr. Reginald Wilson

For more than a century and a half, the historically black colleges and universities (HBCUs) have played an extraordinary role in the history of education in this country. During more than one hundred years of strict—and legal—racial segregation, they were, ironically, islands of integration throughout the dark period of American *apartheid*. Their primary mission was, of course, to provide higher education for black citizens, which they did nearly exclusively from 1865 to the 1950s. But they also provided jobs for hundreds of white faculty and administrators who, in some instances, allowed their sons and daughters to attend these institutions as well. They were models of what America could be during a time when the nation's racial practices were far from its ideals.

Although the first college for African Americans was started before the Civil War, the overwhelming majority opened after 1865 in response to two concerns: the need to quickly establish institutions to educate the newly freed slaves, and the segregationist sentiments of southern educators who opposed integrating blacks into already-existing white schools and colleges. The Freedmen's Bureau—established by Congress in conjunction with northern church missionaries and philanthropies to assist the newly freed slaves—began to establish primary schools and some colleges under the constraints of the exiting Jim Crow laws.

Under these inauspicious circumstances and despite monumental restrictions and obstacles, more than 120 public and private collegiate institutions were developed. Most public black colleges in their early years were true colleges in name only. They typically began as primary schools and added upper grades and collegiate divisions as students progressed over the years. For example, as late as 1917, Florida Agriculture and Mechanical College enrolled only 12 students at the collegiate level. All other public black colleges combined enrolled 7,500 students in elementary and secondary grades, and only 24 students in the collegiate curriculum. Until well into the twentieth century, private black colleges carried the substantial responsibility of educating blacks at the college level, accounting for 72% of black student enrollments in 1926. However, by 1935, public black colleges accounted for 46% of black student enrollments and shortly thereafter surpassed the private black colleges. Currently, nearly 80% of the students who attend HBCUs attend public black colleges. Today these institutions enroll more than 250,000 students, their highest enrollment in history. The total number of HBCUs now stands at 102, as a few marginal institutions have closed and others have succumbed to financial difficulty.

The HBCUs have produced some of the most illustrious black leaders in the United States and the world:

W.E.B. DuBois, eminent sociologist, writer, and teacher
Ralph Ellison, recipient of the National Book Award
Leontyne Price, opera and concert diva
Ronald McNair, physicist and astronaut
Kwame Nkhrumah, first president of Ghana
Alice Walker, award-winning author
Damon Keith, Federal Appeals court justice

and thousands more. Indeed, 65% of black physicians now practicing are graduates of HBCUs, as are 35% of the lawyers and 50% of the engineers.

With the Supreme Court decision in *Brown v. Board of Education* (1954), which declared segregated public schools unconstitutional, and the subsequent federal court decision in *Adams v. California* (1973) ordering the dismantling of segregated state college systems, the future of publicly funded, racially exclusive higher education institutions becomes problematic. However, the HBCUs have consistently done a better job of welcoming ethnic diversity than predominantly white institutions. Of their enrollment, 17% consist of non-black students and they have an average of 35% non-black faculty and administrators. Indeed, five of the HBCUs now have a majority of white students. There are currently three state higher education desegregation cases—in Louisiana, Alabama, and Mississippi—making their way through the federal courts. These outcomes will profoundly affect the future of public HBCUs, causing a rethinking of their mission and focus. These cases may have some peripheral impact on the private HBCUs as well.

Whatever the restructuring of the HBCUs, they will continue to play a critical role in the education of African Americans and offer higher education opportunities to diverse others. These issues make the timing of *Black American Colleges and Universities* particularly important as the historically black colleges and universities enter a new era in their development. You will see, described here, institutions of various types, sizes, and missions—from community colleges to large comprehensive universities, from highly selective institutions with Phi Beta Kappa chapters to ones with open admission. Historically black colleges, in their variety, can meet the needs of every student whatever their previous level of academic preparation. They have attracted students throughout the African diaspora, from the continent and the Caribbean, as well as from Asia and Europe. They are truly ecumenical institutions.

I especially recommend this excellent volume to all students, high school guidance counselors, teachers, and administrators, as well as to college staff, faculties, and educational researchers. It is a valuable addition to any library or historical collection.

Reginald Wilson, Ph.D.
Senior Scholar
American Council on Education
April 30, 1993

FEATURES: HOW TO GET THE MOST OUT OF THIS BOOK

Below is a list of the valuable features found in *Black American Colleges and Universities* and what they can do for you.

Schools-at-a-Glance

Organized by state, just like the book itself, this section conveniently provides—in a table format—critical information on the schools profiled in *BACU,* including: total enrollment, type of school (4-year, 2-year, etc.), coed or single sex, estimated total cost per year (in-state), incoming freshman GPA, teacher/student ratio, and the level of selectivity. Use it to look up key elements about schools you are considering.

Finding the School for You
The Admissions Chapter

Immediately following the **Schools-at-a-Glance** section, the admissions chapter provides you with helpful tips on identifying the schools you are interested in and applying to them, including useful advice on narrowing your search and writing the personal essay.

Room, Board, and Debt: Finding the Funds
The Financial Aid Chapter

This chapter addresses college costs and discusses eligibility for different types of financial aid. It includes sample financial aid forms, information on federal aid programs and other sources of financial aid, and provides statistics on average family contribution.

118 School Profiles

Organized by state, this is the bulk of *BACU. See* the **Preface** on page xix for more information on what you can expect to find in the individual school entries.

Notable Alumni

Immediately following the 118 profiles is the Notable Alumni chart. It consolidates the notable alumni listed in the individual school profiles into one convenient alphabetical listing for easy browsing. Find out your hero or heroine's alma mater!

Appendixes

Lists all of the schools profiled in *BACU* that fit into the following categories.

- Church-Affiliated Schools
- Four-Year Schools
- Historically Black Colleges and Universities (HBCUs)
- Land-Grant Schools
- Professional Schools
- Public or State-Supported Schools
- Thurgood Marshall Scholarship Fund Member Schools
- Two-Year Schools
- United Negro College Fund (UNCF) Member Schools

Common Abbreviations and Definitions

A quick glossary of acronyms and terms found in *BACU*.

School Profiles Index

The 118 schools profiled in *BACU* listed in alphabetical order for quick searching.

SCHOOLS-AT-A-GLANCE

UNIVERSITY OR COLLEGE NAME	TOTAL ENROLLMENT	4-YEAR, 2-YEAR OR PROFESSIONAL	COED OR SINGLE SEX
ALABAMA			
Alabama Agricultural & Mechanical University	5,215	four-year	coed
Alabama State University	5,490	four-year	coed
Bishop State Community College	2,144	two-year	coed
Concordia College	383	two-year	coed
J. F. Drake State Technical College	979	two-year	coed
Lawson State Community College	1,738	two-year	coed
Lomax-Hannon Junior College	60	two-year	coed
Miles College	751	four-year	coed
Oakwood College	1,334	four-year	coed
Selma University	287	four-year	coed
Stillman College	822	four-year	coed
Talladega College	615	four-year	coed
Trenholm State Technical College	704	two-year	coed
Tuskegee University	3,598	four-year	coed
ARKANSAS			
Arkansas Baptist College	291	four-year	coed
Philander Smith College	640	four-year	coed
Shorter College	120	two-year	coed
University of Arkansas at Pine Bluff	3,709	four-year	coed
CALIFORNIA			
Charles R. Drew University of Medicine & Science	140	four-year	coed
Compton Community College	5,700	two-year	coed
DELAWARE			
Delaware State University	2,882	four-year	coed
FLORIDA			
Bethune-Cookman College	2,301	four-year	coed

ESTIMATED TOTAL COST PER YEAR	INCOMING FRESHMAN AVERAGE GPA	STUDENT/ TEACHER RATIO	LEVEL OF SELECTIVITY
$4,675	2.41	19:1	slightly competitive
$4,333	2.49	21:1	noncompetitive
$1,730	n/a	15:1	noncompetitive
$6,362	n/a	28:1	noncompetitive
$1,825	n/a	n/a	noncompetitive
$1,550	n/a	20:1	noncompetitive
$3,974	n/a	18:1	noncompetitive
$7,150	n/a	18:1	noncompetitive
$10,940	2.81	12:1	noncompetitive
$6,265	n/a	11:1	noncompetitive
$8,064	n/a	15:1	noncompetitive
$7,444	n/a	13:1	slightly competitive
$2,029	n/a	16:1	noncompetitive
$10,655	2.7	13:1	slightly competitive
$4,715	n/a	14:1	noncompetitive
$5,660	n/a	16:1	noncompetitive
$4,081	n/a	5:1	noncompetitive
$3,885	n/a	19:1	slightly competitive
$15,739	n/a	20:1	competitive
$645	n/a	24:1	noncompetitive
$5,696	2.49	15:1	moderately competitive
$9,145	2.45	16:1	slightly competitive

SCHOOLS-AT-A-GLANCE

UNIVERSITY OR COLLEGE NAME	TOTAL ENROLLMENT	4-YEAR, 2-YEAR OR PROFESSIONAL	COED OR SINGLE SEX
FLORIDA			
Edward Waters College	634	four-year	coed
Florida Agricultural & Mechanical University	9,200	four-year	coed
Florida Memorial College	2,172	four-year	coed
GEORGIA			
Albany State College	3,106	four-year	coed
Clark Atlanta University	3,507	four-year	coed
Fort Valley State College	2,368	four-year	coed
Interdenominational Theological Center	383	three-year	coed
Morehouse College	2,992	three-year	all-male
Morehouse School of Medicine	140	four-year	coed
Morris Brown College	2,030	four-year	coed
Paine College	790	four-year	coed
Savannah State College	2,656	four-year	coed
Spelman College	1,906	four-year	all-female
ILLINOIS			
Chicago State University	8,648	four-year	coed
Kennedy-King College	3,137	two-year	coed
KENTUCKY			
Kentucky State University	2,500	four-year	coed
Simmons University Bible College	103	four-year	coed
LOUISIANA			
Dillard University	1,700	four-year	coed
Grambling State University	6,485	four-year	coed
Southern University and Agricultural & Mechanical University at Baton Rouge	8,941	four-year	coed
Southern University (New Orleans)	3,734	four-year	coed

ESTIMATED TOTAL COST PER YEAR	INCOMING FRESHMAN AVERAGE GPA	STUDENT/ TEACHER RATIO	LEVEL OF SELECTIVITY
$7,466	n/a	12:1	noncompetitive
$4,874	2.5	24:1	moderately competitive
$7,900	2.5	17:1	slightly competitive
$4,020	n/a	16:1	slightly competitive
$11,252	n/a	19:1	slightly competitive
$4,657	n/a	14:1	slightly competitive
$6,695	n/a	13:1	moderately competitive
$12,910	n/a	17:1	slightly competitive
$25,962	n/a	4:1	competitive
$11,298	2.5	13:1	slightly competitive
$8,707	2.66	12.8:1	noncompetitive
$4,375	n/a	22:1	slightly competitive
$12,571	3.0	16:1	moderately competitive
$1,528	2.39	30:1	slightly competitive
$1,653	n/a	19:1	noncompetitive
$4,702	n/a	13:1	slightly competitive
$1,345	n/a	n/a	noncompetitive
$9,815	2.5	15:1	slightly competitive
$5,037	n/a	21:1	noncompetitive
$4,747	n/a	17:1	noncompetitive
$2,090	n/a	19:1	noncompetitive

SCHOOLS-AT-A-GLANCE

UNIVERSITY OR COLLEGE NAME	TOTAL ENROLLMENT	4-YEAR, 2-YEAR OR PROFESSIONAL	COED OR SINGLE SEX
LOUISIANA			
Southern University (Shreveport)	1,067	two-year	coed
Xavier University of Louisiana	3,330	four-year	coed
MARYLAND			
Bowie State University	4,437	four-year	coed
Coppin State College	2,816	four-year	coed
Morgan State University	5,034	four-year	coed
Sojourner-Douglass College	441	four-year	coed
University of Maryland, Eastern Shore	2,100	four-year	coed
MASSACHUSETTS			
Roxbury Community College	1,800	two-year	coed
MICHIGAN			
Highland Park Community College	2,335	two-year	coed
Lewis College of Business	346	two-year	coed
Wayne County Community College	11,123	two-year	coed
MISSISSIPPI			
Alcorn State University	3,526	four-year	coed
Coahoma Community College	1,373	two-year	coed
Hinds Community College	934	two-year	coed
Jackson State University	6,203	four-year	coed
Mary Holmes Community College	745	two-year	coed
Mississippi Valley State University	1,691	four-year	coed
Rust College	1,129	four-year	coed
Tougaloo College	1,003	four-year	coed
MISSOURI			
Harris-Stowe State College	1,881	four-year	coed

ESTIMATED TOTAL COST PER YEAR	INCOMING FRESHMAN AVERAGE GPA	STUDENT/ TEACHER RATIO	LEVEL OF SELECTIVITY
$1,455	2.0	17:1	noncompetitive
$10,950	2.78	16:1	moderately competitive
$4,595	2.49	20:1	slightly competitive
$5,483	n/a	25:1	moderately competitive
$8,280	n/a	18:1	moderately competitive
$3,930	n/a	10:1	noncompetitive
$6,731	2.4	19:1	slightly competitive
$2,080	n/a	25:1	noncompetitive
$1,620	n/a	21:1	noncompetitive
$2,875	n/a	13:1	noncompetitive
$1,639	n/a	25:1	noncompetitive
$2,762	2.495	20:1	slightly competitive
$2,962	n/a	22:1	noncompetitive
$3,367	n/a	19:1	noncompetitive
$5,621	n/a	16:1	slightly competitive
$8,300	2.495	20:1	noncompetitive
$4,814	n/a	18:1	slightly competitive
$6,100	2.5	18:1	slightly competitive
$6,810	2.50	19:1	slightly competitive
$2,253	n/a	18:1	slightly competitive

SCHOOLS-AT-A-GLANCE

UNIVERSITY OR COLLEGE NAME	TOTAL ENROLLMENT	4-YEAR, 2-YEAR OR PROFESSIONAL	COED OR SINGLE SEX
MISSOURI			
Lincoln University (MO)	4,101	four-year	coed
NEW YORK			
LaGuardia Community College	9,000	two-year	coed
Medgar Evers College	4,400	four-year	coed
New York City Technical College	10,426	two-year	coed
NORTH CAROLINA			
Barber-Scotia College	708	four-year	coed
Bennett College	568	four-year	all-female
Elizabeth City State University	1,762	four-year	coed
Fayetteville State University	3,903	four-year	coed
Johnson C. Smith University	1,256	four-year	coed
Livingstone College	654	four-year	coed
North Carolina Agricultural & Technical State University	7,119	four-year	coed
North Carolina Central University	5,385	four-year	coed
Saint Augustine's College	1,900	four-year	coed
Shaw University	2,149	four-year	coed
Winston-Salem State University	2,655	four-year	coed
OHIO			
Central State University	3,913	four-year	coed
Cuyahoga Community College	6,200	two-year	coed
Wilberforce University	758	four-year	coed
OKLAHOMA			
Langston University	3,323	four-year	coed
PENNSYLVANIA			
Cheyney University of Pennsylvania	1,607	four-year	coed

ESTIMATED TOTAL COST PER YEAR	INCOMING FRESHMAN AVERAGE GPA	STUDENT/ TEACHER RATIO	LEVEL OF SELECTIVITY
$4,885	n/a	18:1	noncompetitive
$2,704	n/a	18:1	noncompetitive
$1,960	n/a	19:1	noncompetitive
$1,600	n/a	10:1	slightly competitive
$7,212	2.5	12:1	noncompetitive
$8,924	n/a	10:1	slightly competitive
$4,172	2.68	15:1	noncompetitive
$4,125	2.85	18:1	slightly competitive
$8,922	n/a	15:1	slightly competitive
$9,100	n/a	15:1	slightly competitive
$4,560	n/a	14:1	moderately competitive
$5,119	n/a	13.5:1	slightly competitive
$8,200	n/a	16:1	slightly competitive
$9,146	n/a	16:1	slightly competitive
$4,641	2.56	15:1	slightly competitive
$7,493	n/a	21:1	noncompetitive
$1,782	n/a	14:1	noncompetitive
$10,838	2.5	20:1	slightly competitive
$3,850	n/a	24:1	noncompetitive
$6,813	n/a	16:1	slightly competitive

SCHOOLS-AT-A-GLANCE

UNIVERSITY OR COLLEGE NAME	TOTAL ENROLLMENT	4-YEAR, 2-YEAR OR PROFESSIONAL	COED OR SINGLE SEX
PENNSYLVANIA			
Lincoln University of Pennsylvania	1,458	four-year	coed
SOUTH CAROLINA			
Allen University	223	four-year	coed
Benedict College	1,469	four-year	coed
Claflin College	900	four-year	coed
Clinton Junior College	200	two-year	coed
Denmark Technical College	725	two-year	coed
Morris College	792	four-year	coed
South Carolina State University	5,145	four-year	coed
Voorhees College	600	four-year	coed
TENNESSEE			
Fisk University	867	four-year	coed
Knoxville College	1,200	four-year	coed
Lane College	562	four-year	coed
LeMoyne-Owen College	1,297	four-year	coed
Meharry Medical College	867	professional	coed
Tennessee State University	7,500	four-year	coed
TEXAS			
Huston-Tillotson College	536	four-year	coed
Jarvis Christian College	592	four-year	coed
Paul Quinn College	517	four-year	coed
Prairie View Agricultural & Mechanical University	5,590	four-year	coed
Southwestern Christian College	244	four-year	coed
Texas College	400	four-year	coed
Texas Southern University	10,777	four-year	coed
Wiley College	406	four-year	coed

ESTIMATED TOTAL COST PER YEAR	INCOMING FRESHMAN AVERAGE GPA	STUDENT/ TEACHER RATIO	LEVEL OF SELECTIVITY
$6,702	2.50	15:1	moderately competitive
$8,902	n/a	12:1	noncompetitive
$7,776	n/a	17:1	slightly competitive
$7,260	n/a	14:1	moderately competitive
$3,710	n/a	17:1	noncompetitive
$3,914	n/a	16:1	noncompetitive
$7,170	n/a	14:1	noncompetitive
$5,411	2.50	19:1	slightly competitive
$6,628	n/a	15:1	moderately competitive
$9,415	n/a	14:1	slightly competitive
$8,595	n/a	n/a	noncompetitive
$7,460	n/a	14:1	slightly competitive
$6,825	n/a	18:1	noncompetitive
$15,906	n/a	6:1	competitive
$4,633	2.50	25:1	moderately competitive
$8,639	2.50	13:1	slightly competitive
$7,395	2.85	14:1	noncompetitive
$6,275	n/a	12:1	noncompetitive
$2,626	2.50	20:1	slightly competitive
$6,093	n/a	10:1	noncompetitive
$7,225	n/a	16:1	noncompetitive
$4,985	2.50	18:1	slightly competitive
$6,494	2.49	15:1	noncompetitive

SCHOOLS-AT-A-GLANCE

UNIVERSITY OR COLLEGE NAME	TOTAL ENROLLMENT	4-YEAR, 2-YEAR OR PROFESSIONAL	COED OR SINGLE SEX
VIRGIN ISLANDS			
University of the Virgin Islands	2,176	four-year	coed
VIRGINIA			
Hampton University	5,161	four-year	coed
Norfolk State University	8,624	four-year	coed
Saint Paul's College	750	four-year	coed
Virginia Seminary	40	four-year	coed
Virginia State University	4,585	four-year	coed
Virginia Union University	1,511	four-year	coed
WASHINGTON, DISTRICT OF COLUMBIA			
Howard University	11,222	four-year	coed
Howard University School of Law	380	three-year	coed
University of the District of Columbia	11,153	four-year	coed
WEST VIRGINIA			
Bluefield State College	2,907	four-year	coed
West Virginia State College	4,986	four-year	coed

ESTIMATED TOTAL COST PER YEAR	INCOMING FRESHMAN AVERAGE GPA	STUDENT/ TEACHER RATIO	LEVEL OF SELECTIVITY
$6,415	n/a	15:1	slightly competitive
$10,626	2.3	18:1	competitive
$6,655	n/a	22:1	noncompetitive
$9,218	n/a	17:1	slightly competitive
$5,145	n/a	n/a	noncompetitive
$8,749	n/a	18:1	noncompetitive
$10,152	2.3	16:1	slightly competitive
$11,300	n/a	15:1	competitive
$12,730	n/a	8:1	competitive
$1,589	n/a	10:1	noncompetitive
$2,351	2.5	25:1	noncompetitive
$2,906	2.0	21:1	slightly competitive

FINDING THE SCHOOL FOR YOU

Deborah Jones

So you're ready to apply to the school of your choice—or are you? Applying to a college or university can be a costly and time-consuming venture—but it does not have to be. If you do enough digging, you can eliminate illogical choices, and spend your time and money wisely.

The key is to honestly evaluate your interests, strengths, and needs. The best person to do this is yourself; nobody knows you better.

ASK YOURSELF THE TOUGH QUESTIONS

The first thing you'll want to do is ask yourself the following questions to pinpoint exactly which schools are in the running:

- Do I want a 2-year or a 4-year degree?

A 2-year—or associate's—degree is often a stepping stone to a 4-year—or bachelor's—degree. It's a good place to start if the field you plan to enter requires only an associate's degree or if you plan to earn a four-year degree, but need a firmer academic foundation before you are accepted into a four-year school. While a four-year bachelor's degree may be a bit more competitive in the job market, it requires more academic stamina and will cost you more money. Consider this when deciding whether you will attend a 2-year or 4-year school.

Talk with people who work in the professions you are interested in. Find out what kinds of people they want to hire, and what the academic requirements are for that field. Once you determine whether you will pursue a 2-year or 4-year degree, you will have eliminated a considerable number of schools from your search.

- Do I want to attend a school that is in-state or out-of-state?

Although this seems simple, it is a critical piece of information. Attending school in-state is often much less expensive than going out-of-state because schools tend to charge higher tuition to nonresidents. You'll also want to factor in the travel expenses you will incur going between home and school for breaks. If money is tight, you might want to limit your list of potential schools to in-state institutions. On the other hand, if your budget isn't so limited,

> *Talk with people who work in the professions you are interested in. Find out what kinds of people they want to hire, and what the academic requirements are for that field.*

then you might as well consider out-of-state institutions as well.

- Do I want to attend a small (2,500 or less), medium (2,500–8,000), large (8,000–15,000), or very large (more than 15,000) school?

If you don't mind the prospect of being in a class with more than 150 other people and perhaps never getting a chance to really have a chat with the instructor; if choosing from a wider range of course offerings and getting lost in a larger crowd is appealing, perhaps the larger institution is for you. On the other hand, if you feel you would thrive in an environment that would afford you more one-on-one attention, then a smaller school may be right for you.

- If I am attending school within-state, will I live at home and commute to school, or live on campus, away from home.

Again, if you are trying to go to college on the tightest budget, you should seriously consider commuting to a local college, if there is one that meets your needs. You could save yourself costly room and board expenses.

However, if you plan to commute from home, you need some mode of transportation in order to do so. Find out if you can reach your school of choice by public transportation or if you will need a car. Be sure to factor in the various expenses of running a car, including insurance, maintenance, and parking fees on campus.

THE TOUGHEST QUESTION: WHO AM I?

- What kind of degree am I interested in?

Once you have answered the broadest practical questions, listed above, and have targeted your search accordingly, ask yourself who you are. What do you hope to accomplish with your degree? Although you probably won't know exactly what you want to do with your life just yet, you should have a fair understanding of what you enjoy and what you do well, or at least what you want to do well. Focus your energy there and explore the careers related to your interests and talents.

Your high school counselor should be able to help you with this decision. Now is the time to take inventory of your extracurricular activities, and your special skills and talents. Ask for evidence of your strengths from sources such as standardized tests, academic records, and other data in your school's counseling office, such as the Holland Self-Directed Search or the World of Work section on the ACT.

- What special needs do I have?

If there are specific features that you require in a school, such as excellent handicapped services, a large fra-

If you feel you would thrive in an environment that would afford you more one-on-one attention, then a smaller school may be right for you.

ternity/sorority network, a sprawling green campus, or an excellent pre-veterinary medicine program, eliminate the schools that do not qualify immediately. Ask yourself if there is a special need that you have, and decide if it is important enough to drive your decision.

Once you know which schools you are interested in, you need to know how to apply. Below are requirements and some tips for freshmen, transfer students, and international students on the application process.

PAPERWORK: PULLING THE PIECES TOGETHER

Freshman Students

What you need:

- graduation from an accredited high school or a passing grade on the General Education Diploma examination (GED)

- completed applications to the schools of your choice. You can get blank applications from your high school counselor or contact the prospective schools' admissions department.

- the nonrefundable application fees

- scores for either the Scholastic Aptitude Test (SAT) or the American College Testing Program (ACT)

Tips for Freshman Applicants

- You can begin applying to schools as early as the latter part of your junior year in high school. Sometimes, applying early will allow you a better chance at being admitted.

- Your high school academic preparation should be balanced, and should emphasize the five major academic areas, including English, history, mathematics, science, and foreign language.

- SAT or ACT scores are used both for admission and for placement counseling. Let these tests work for you.

- Once you're admitted, you might also need to submit the following: housing forms, physical examination forms, and proof of immunization.

Transfer Students

What You Need:

- potentially, all of the above items listed under "Freshman Students: What You Need"

- transcripts of all credit earned

- often, if student has attended another institution for less than one year, she or he must submit a high school transcript along with a college transcript

Tip for Transfers

- Upon acceptance, a transfer evaluator will assess previous college credits to be transferred. If you are dissatisfied with the evaluation, you may often request a review

International Students

What You Need:

- completed application
- proof that you have received 12 years of elementary and secondary education
- an English Proficiency Report, which should be completed by a person who can verify that you have the ability to speak English
- Teaching of English as a Foreign Language (TOEFL) scores (only if your native language is not English)
- nonrefundable application fee
- foreign student financial aid statements

LEVEL OF SELECTIVITY: EXACTLY HOW CHOOSY ARE THEY?

One of the most important pieces of information in making your decision is a college's level of selectivity. Be realistic about your qualifications and know which schools you are qualified for. To help you with this, *Black American Colleges and Universities* ranks the degree of competitiveness in the admissions' policy for each school profiled. Each school is ranked according to the number of requirements needed for admission which may include: minimum SAT or ACT scores, GED score or GPA; class rank; college preparatory units; high school recommendations; personal essay and statement of intent; and completion of 18 or more units. Competitive schools request four to six of the above requirements; moderately competitive schools require three to four; slightly competitive schools require two to three; and noncompetitive schools ask for only one or two of the above requirements. Look for a handy breakdown of each school's level of selectivity and other key pieces of information, such as coed vs. single sex school and two-year vs. four-year, in the **Schools-at-a-Glance** section in this book. The chart will help you quickly identify key facts about schools of interest to you, and help you to narrow your search.

At some schools, conditional admissions are sometimes available to students who do not meet regular admission requirements. In this case, students are placed on probation for the first year while completing developmental courses to make up for deficiencies. Other admission policies include early admissions, early decision, advanced placement, and deferred entrance (*See* **Common Abbreviations and Definitions** section at the back of this book).

At some schools, conditional admissions are sometimes available to students who do not meet regular admission requirements.

A WORD ABOUT THE PERSONAL ESSAY

The best advice you can get when you are preparing to write an essay for college entry is this: know what the assignment is. Read the instructions on your applications and ask yourself the question "what are they asking me to do here?" Then, do it. And do it well. In some cases reviewing your instructions will leave more questions than answers for you. For example, you might be instructed to write a 1,000-word personal essay. If that is all the guidance you are given, then it is your job to fill in the details of your discussion. Review your acheivements, your academic and professional goals, and seize this opportunity to reveal to an admissions officer what is not evident on a college application, just what makes you unique, an asset to his or her school. You might start with what you discovered about yourself when you asked "the tough questions" in deciding what kind of a degree you were looking for.

Read the instructions on your applications and ask yourself the question "what are they asking me to do here?"

Start by writing a quick draft of whatever first comes to mind, if only to have something to rewrite. Write several drafts, and try setting your complete draft aside for a day, then go back and refine it. Once you have all of your thoughts down, reread your essay to ensure that it flows from beginning, to middle, to end.

Technology is Your Friend

No matter what people tell you to the contrary, neatness counts. Unless the application stipulates that you handwrite it, type your essay, preferably on a word processor or computer so you can spell check it. Then proofread it again for those errors that only the human eye can detect. (Most software packages don't know enough to choose between to, too, and two for you.)

Lastly, ask someone—a professional writer, editor, or English teacher— to proofread it and give you their comments. It's better to know at this point—while it's still in your hands—if you have made some ugly grammatical snafu. While it is acceptable to get this type of technical advice on your essay, remember that this is your essay, and must be your work.

And while we're on the subject of outside help, a word of advice when you ask an adult to complete a teacher recommendation form or write a letter of recommendation: GIVE THEM AT LEAST TWO WEEKS' NOTICE. Even if the people you are asking to recommend you are not terribly busy, they will certainly appreciate your respect for their schedule. If they agree to write a letter on your behalf, send them a note of thanks after about a week. This will also serve as a tactful reminder to them of their commitment to you. And, if you want better letters of recommendation, do your letter-writers a favor by supplying them with a brief list of your achievements, special projects or activities, or anything that might help them write a more specific letter for you.

Do your letter-writers a favor by supplying them with a brief list of your achievements, special projects, or activities.

Finally, apply to more than one school; give yourself options. And, if you possibly can, make an effort to visit your prospective schools. If you call in advance you can even sit in on some relevant classes. Really explore the campus, and see if it feels like you.

ROOM, BOARD, AND DEBT: HOW TO FIND THE FUNDS

Michael Woodruff

You've lived through four years of high school, you've taken your SATs, you're about to embark on that great adventure called "college." So, again, you do your homework: you graze through college catalogs and you finally find "the one"—the perfect school for you. But how do you make it happen? Pursuing an education is a major investment of time, energy—and money.

According to a recent *Fortune* article, tuitions increased 9% annually during the 1980s and are expected to grow at an annual rate of 7% throughout the 1990s. What does this mean in real numbers? Well, according to national averages, a student entering college in the fall of 1993 will pay $77,000 for four years of tuition, room, and board at a private college; $36,000 for four years at a public university. Traditionally, tuitions at black colleges and universities are about half the national average, yet they are not immune to the average tuition hikes. For example, at Stillman—a private four-year college—tuition, room, and board for 1990–91 was $5,404. For 1993–94, college costs rose to $7,214, an increase of 33%.

Don't panic! These figures aren't meant to discourage you, they are only offered to make you aware of the reality of college costs. Although the primary obligation for college expenses lies with the family, keep in mind that at most schools almost all students receive some sort of financial aid. In addition, a number of other options exist to make your financial road a little less rocky. The following chapter is designed to let you know of viable alternatives and to help you devise a feasible financial aid plan.

Tuitions increased 9% annually during the 1980s and are expected to grow at an annual rate of 7% throughout the 1990s.

WHAT IS FINANCIAL AID?

You may be eligible to receive three types of financial aid:

- grants or scholarships (outright gifts that do not have to be repaid)
- loans (money that must be repaid at low interest after graduation or after leaving school)

- work-study programs/internships (employment opportunities that help defray tuition costs)

FINANCIAL NEED: AM I ELIGIBLE?

The majority of colleges receive financial aid from the federal and state government. The various grants, loans, and work opportunity funds are provided to assist those students demonstrating the greatest need. For financial aid, need is defined as the difference between the amount of money a family may be expected to contribute and the total cost of education. Financial need is expressed as an equation:

$$\begin{aligned} &\text{Cost of Education} \\ -\ &\text{Expected Family Contribution} \\ =\ &\text{Financial Need} \end{aligned}$$

While cost may vary from school to school, the expected family contribution generally does not, since it is derived through a national formula. *(See* the Estimated Family Contribution chart located at the end of this section.)

Financial need is expressed as an equation:

Cost of Education
− Expected Family Contribution
= Financial Need

COST OF EDUCATION

The cost of education includes expenses that are reasonably related to education:

- Tuition and fees
- Room
- Board
- Books
- Supplies
- Transportation
- Personal Expenses

Cost may also include other expenses such as childcare for dependents; disability expenses not covered by other agencies; or participation in a program of study abroad. If you believe that you will incur extra expenses in order to attend college, write a letter explaining your circumstances to your college's financial aid officer.

HOW DO I APPLY?—
IT ALL STARTS WITH THE CORRECT FORM!

First, contact your high school guidance counselor or the financial aid director of the college that you are interested in attending. He/she will make sure that you know exactly which forms to complete, and the dates by which these forms must be returned. Do not wait for an admissions decision to apply for financial aid. Start your search early.

To apply for federal aid, all students must complete the Free Application for Federal Student Aid (FAFSA). No fee is charged in accordance with filling out the FAFSA (see example on page 11).

To be considered for non-federal aid, you may be required to fill out the following, all of which require a fee for each college that you list on the application:

- Financial Aid Form of the College Scholarship Service (FAF) (see example on page 10)
- Family Financial Statement of the American College Testing Service (FFS)
- Application form of the Pennsylvania Higher Education Assistance Agency (PHEAA)

In addition to the above, you may be required to complete individual state scholarship or grant program applications. Some colleges may require a campus application as well.

Complete the forms as soon as possible after January 1. (You will be required to file financial aid forms for each year of college that you attend.) You may file your applications using estimated income figures in order to meet the application deadlines. The records that you will need from the previous year to complete your FAFSA are:

- W-2 forms; income tax forms for you, your parents, and your spouse, if married
- records of social security benefits, veteran benefits, and other nontaxable income
- bank statements
- business/farm records
- statements of trust funds, money market funds, stocks, bonds, certificates of deposit, and similar assets

Save all your records after you have completed the applications in case you have to prove that the information is correct. Keep a copy of the applications you are filing for your records. For additional information about federal student financial aid, call the Federal Student Aid Information Center at 800-4 FED AID.

Dependency Status

Income and asset information is used to determine eligibility for financial aid. The information you will be asked to provide is contingent on whether you are dependent or independent. If you are considered dependent, you must report your parent's income and assets, as well as your own. If you're independent, only your income and asset information (and that of your spouse) is needed. The definition of an independent student has changed.

SAMPLE FAF

FAF® Financial Aid Form — 1993-94 □□ □

This form is not required to apply for Title IV federal student aid. However, information from the FAF is used by some colleges and private organizations to award their own financial aid funds. CSS charges students a fee to collect and report this information. By filling out this form, you are agreeing to pay the fee, which is calculated in question 44.

Section A — Student's Identification Information — Be sure to complete this section. Answer the questions the same way you answered them in Section A of the Free Application for Federal Student Aid (FAFSA).

1. Your name

Last   First   M.I.

2. Your permanent mailing address (Mail will be sent to this address.)

Number, street, and apartment number

City   State   Zip Code

3. Title (optional)

1 ☐ Mr.   2 ☐ Miss, Ms., or Mrs.

4. Your date of birth

Month   Day   Year

5. Your social security number

Section B — Student's Other Information

6. If you are now in high school, give your high school 6-digit code number.

7. What year will you be in college in 1993-94? (Mark only one box.)

1 ☐ 1st (never previously attended college)
2 ☐ 1st (previously attended college)
3 ☐ 2nd
4 ☐ 3rd
5 ☐ 4th

6 ☐ 5th or more undergraduate
7 ☐ first-year graduate/professional (beyond a bachelor's degree)
8 ☐ second-year graduate/professional
9 ☐ third-year graduate/professional
0 ☐ fourth-year or more graduate/professional

8. a. If you have previously attended any college or other postsecondary school, write in the total number of colleges and schools you have attended. ☐

b. List below the colleges (up to five) that you have attended. Begin with the college you attended most recently. Use the CSS code numbers from the list in the FAF instruction booklet. If more space is needed, use Section M.

Name, city, and state of college	Period of attendance From (mo./yr.)	To (mo./yr.)	CSS Code Number

9. During the 1993-94 school year, you want institutional financial aid

from   Month   Year   through   Month   Year

10. Mark your preference for institutional work and/or loan assistance.

1 ☐ Part-time job only
2 ☐ Loan only
3 ☐ Will accept both, but prefer loan
4 ☐ Will accept both, but prefer job
5 ☐ No preference

11. If it is necessary to borrow money to pay for educational expenses, do you want to be considered for a Stafford Loan? (optional)

Yes ☐ 1   No ☐ 2

(If you mark "Yes," your information may be sent to the loan agency within your state.)

12. a. Your employer/occupation _____

b. Employer's address _____

c. Will you continue to work for this employer during the 1993-94 school year?   Yes ☐ 1   No ☐ 2

13. If you have dependents other than a spouse, how many will be in each of the following age groups during 1993-94?

Ages 0-5 ☐   Ages 6-12 ☐   Ages 13+ ☐

14. 1992 child support paid by you $ .00

Section C — Student's Expected Summer/School-Year Income

	Summer 1993 3 months	School Year 1993-94 9 months		Summer 1993 3 months	School Year 1993-94 9 months
15. Income earned from work by you	$ .00	$ .00	**17.** Other taxable income	$ .00	$ .00
16. Income earned from work by spouse	$ .00	$ .00	**18.** Nontaxable income and benefits	$ .00	$ .00

Page 1

SAMPLE FREE APPLICATION FOR FEDERAL STUDENT AID

Free Application for Federal Student Aid

1993-94 School Year   CCCCC 1

U.S. Department of Education
Student Financial
Assistance Programs

WARNING: If you purposely give false or misleading information on this form, you may be fined $10,000, sent to prison, or both.

"You" and "your" on this form always mean the student who wants aid.

FORM APPROVED
OMB. NO. 1840-0110
APP. EXP. 6/30/94

Section A: Yourself

1. Your name

Last | First | M.I.

2. Your permanent mailing address
(Mail will be sent to this address. See page 2 for State/Country abbreviation.)

Number and Street (Include Apt. No.)

City | State | ZIP Code

3. Your title *(optional)*

❑ Mr.   ❑ Miss, Ms., or Mrs.

4. Your State of legal residence ____ State

4a. When did you become a legal resident of the State you listed in Question 4? *(See the instructions on page 2.)*

Month | Day | Year

5. Your social security number

6. Your date of birth

Month | Day | Year

7. Are you a U.S. citizen?

1 ❑ Yes, I am a U.S. citizen

2 ❑ No, but I am an eligible noncitizen. *(See the instructions on page 3.)*
[A]

3 ❑ No, neither of the above. *(See the instructions on page 3.)*

8. Will you have your first Bachelor's degree before July 1, 1993?

❑ Yes   ❑ No

9. As of **today**, are you married? *(Check only one box.)*

1 ❑ I am not married. (I am single, widowed, or divorced.)

2 ❑ I am married.

3 ❑ I am separated from my spouse.

9a. • If married or widowed, date married or widowed.
• If currently divorced or separated, date separated.

Month | Year

Section B: Student Status

		Yes	No
10.	**a.** Were you born **before** January 1, 1970?	❑	❑
	b. Are you a veteran of the U.S. Armed Forces?	❑	❑
	c. Are you a graduate or professional student?	❑	❑
	d. Are you married?	❑	❑
	e. Are you a ward of the court or are both your parents dead?	❑	❑
	f. Do you have legal dependents (*other than a spouse*) that fit the definition in the instructions on page 3?	❑	❑

• If you answered "**No**" to **every** part of question 10, go to Section C, and fill out the GREEN and the WHITE areas on the rest of the form.

• If you answered "**Yes**" to **any** part of question 10, go to Section C and fill out the GRAY and the WHITE areas on the rest of the form.

Section C: Household Information

PARENTS

11. What is your parents' current marital status?

1 ❑ single   3 ❑ separated   5 ❑ widowed

2 ❑ married   4 ❑ divorced

12. What is your parents' State of legal residence? ____ State

12a. When did your parent(s) become legal resident(s) of the State you listed in Question 12? *(See the instructions on page 4.)*

Month | Day | Year

13. Number of family members in 1993-94

(Always include yourself [the student] and your parents. Include your parents' other children and other people only if they meet the definition in the instructions on page 4.)

14. Number of college students in 1993-94

(Of the number in 13, write in the number of family members who will be in college at least half-time. Include yourself – the applicant. See the instructions on page 4.)

STUDENT (& SPOUSE)

15. Number of family members in 1993-94

(Always include yourself and your spouse. Include your children and other people only if they meet the definition in the instructions on page 4.)

16. Number of college students in 1993-94

(Of the number in 15, write in the number of family members who will be in college at least half-time. Include yourself. See the instructions on page 4.)

ED FORM 255

You will be considered independent if you meet one of the following:

- you turn 24 by December 31 of the school year for which you are applying for financial aid (e.g., applying for aid for 1994–95, you must be born before January 1, 1970)
- veteran of U.S. Armed Forces
- graduate/professional student
- married
- orphan or ward of court
- have dependents other than a spouse

If you think you have some unusual circumstances that should be taken into consideration regarding your dependency status, contact your financial aid officer. Be prepared to document your case.

FEDERAL FINANCIAL AID PROGRAMS: WHAT IS AVAILABLE?

Federal Pell Grant

Depending on financial circumstances, undergraduate students from families with annual incomes of up to about $40,000 may qualify for a Pell Grant. For 1993-94, Pell Grants range from $400 to $2,300. Eligibility is based on financial need as determined by a national formula that takes into account total income; net assets, such as savings/checking accounts and real estate investments (not including your home); family size; and number of family members in college. Grant payments may be made for the period of time required to complete the first bachelor's degree.

FEDERAL CAMPUS-BASED PROGRAMS

The three programs listed below are called "campus-based" programs because they are administered by individual colleges. Availability of funding is different at each institution.

Federal Supplemental Educational Opportunity Grant (FSEOG)

The FSEOG is available for undergraduates with exceptional financial need. Priority is given to Pell Grant (*See* Federal Pell Grant above) recipients. The college determines award amounts based on the funds available at that college. Awards range from $100 to $4,000 and do not have to be repaid.

Federal Perkins Loan Program

Under the guidelines of the Perkins Loan Program, undergraduate students may borrow up to $3,000 per year for a total of no more than $15,000 for undergraduate programs; up to $4,000 per year for graduate study; and up to $30,000 total for all years of study. This loan is interest-free while the student is enrolled at least half-time. Eligibility is based on exceptional financial need and availability of funds at each college. Repayment of interest and principal begins six to nine months after the student is no longer enrolled at least half-time. The interest rate is fixed at 5%.

Federal Work-Study Program (FWS)

The FWS program provides job opportunities for undergraduate and graduate students to earn minimum wage or more. Eligibility is based on student's financial need. Students usually work 10 to 20 hours per week.

FEDERAL FAMILY EDUCATION LOAN PROGRAMS

Some banks, credit unions, or savings and loan associations offer low-interest education loans that are insured by the federal government. Forms may be obtained from your lender, your college, or your state guaranty agency. For a list of lenders in your state, contact your state guaranty agency.

Federal Stafford Student Loan (Subsidized)

As of July 1, 1993, the subsidized Stafford Student Loan limit for a new undergraduate student is $2,625 for the first year, $3,500 for the second, and $5,500 per academic year for the third through fifth years. Graduate students can borrow up to $8,500 a year. The total loan amount for undergraduate studies is $23,000. The total debt for graduate or professional study is $65,000, including any Federal Stafford Loans received as an undergraduate. The college certifies enrollment and loan eligibility on the loan application. Loans are subject to a origination fee and an insurance fee. The interest rate is variable and will change each year on July 1, but is capped at 9%. Repayment of interest and principal begins six months after the student is no longer enrolled at least half-time. Eligibility is based on need by completing the FAFSA.

Federal Stafford Student Loan (Unsubsidized)

The terms and conditions of the unsubsidized loan are the same as for the subsidized loan (above), except that: 1) interest on the loan is due while the student is in school or the interest can be deferred, and 2) loan limits cover the cost of education minus any aid received up to the limits of the subsidized Stafford Loan. Accrued interest may be paid against or added to the loan (capitalized) as agreed by the borrower and the lender.

Federal Supplemental Loans for Students (SLS)

Independent undergraduate students as of July 1, 1993, may borrow $4,000 per academic year for the first two years and $5,000 per academic year for the third through fifth years. The total loan amount for undergraduate studies is $23,000; for graduate students it is $10,000 per year with the total debt for graduate or professional study not to exceed $65,500 including Federal SLS loans made at the undergraduate level. An insurance fee of up to 3% and an origination fee of 5% are deducted from the amount borrowed. The interest rate on SLS loans is variable and will change each year on July 1—but is capped at 11%. Repayment begins within 60 days of receipt of the loan. Full-time undergraduate students may defer the principal but are responsible for the payment of interest while in school.

Federal Parent Loans for Undergraduate Students (PLUS)

Parents may borrow up to the cost of education, minus any other aid received, per academic year on behalf of each dependent student. Eligibility is not based on need. PLUS loans can be used to meet all or part of the calculated family contribution. For new borrowers, the interest rate is variable, with a 10% cap. The interest rate is recalculated on July 1 of each year. An insurance fee of up to 3% on the amount borrowed and an origination fee of 5% are deducted from the amount borrowed. Repayment begins within 60 days of receipt of the loan. A credit check is required for loans disbursed after July 1, 1993.

OTHER FEDERAL PROGRAMS

Military Service Scholarships

The Army, Air Force, and Navy offer Reserve Officer Training Corps (ROTC) Scholarships and Armed Forces Health Professions Scholarships. Contact the appropriate military service recruiting office for specific information and a directory of participating colleges.

National Science Scholars Program (NSSP)

This program awards funds to graduating high school seniors (or those who will obtain the equivalent of a certificate of graduation), who have demonstrated excellence and achievement in the physical, life, or computer sciences; mathematics; or engineering. The award is $5,000 per year for undergraduate study, or the cost of education, whichever is less, and is awarded to two students from each congressional district. For 1993-94, funding is expected to be $3,300. To obtain an application and additional information, contact your high school guidance counselor or your college's financial aid officer.

Office of Vocational and Educational Services for Individuals with Disabilities (VESID)

Disabled students pursuing higher education may be eligible for assistance through the State Office of Vocational and Educational Services for Individuals with Disabilities (VESID). Criteria and funding vary. Applications and eligibility requirements may be obtained at the local VESID office.

Paul Douglas Teacher Scholarship Program

This scholarship awards up to $5,000 per year for up to four years of full-time undergraduate study. To be eligible, students must be in the top 10% of their high school class or have high GED scores, and be matriculated in a degree program leading to certification in teaching. Students must teach two years for each year of aid received. To obtain an application and additional information contact your high school guidance counselor or your college's financial aid officer.

Robert C. Byrd Honors Scholarship Program

The Byrd Program was established to recognize students with outstanding academic achievement who show promise of continued excellence. Students may receive $1,500 a year for up to four years at a college. At least 10 scholarships are available per state. To obtain an application and additional information, contact your high school guidance counselor or your college's financial aid officer.

State Student Incentive Grant (SSIG)

These federal funds are allocated to states to encourage scholarship/grant assistance to college students who demonstrate need. Further information may be obtained from your high school guidance counselor or your college financial aid officer.

Veterans Educational Benefits

Eligible veterans and children or spouses of eligible deceased or service-connected disabled veterans may be able to receive aid for approved college study. Information and application forms are available at all Veterans Administration Offices.

INSTITUTIONAL GRANTS AND SCHOLARSHIPS

Thurgood Marshall Scholarship

The Thurgood Marshall Scholarship fund provides a four-year scholarship to one entering freshman at each of the 37 historically black public college and universities including the University of the District of Columbia and the University of the Virgin Islands. To qualify, students need a high school GPA of 3.0, and a SAT score of 1000 or a ACT score of 24 or more. Students must be recommended by their high school counselor as exceptional or exemplary in the creative or performing arts. Students should contact the Thurgood Marshall Coordinators at each of the 37 historically black public colleges and universities listed in Appendix IX of *BACU*.

United Negro College Fund (UNCF)

The United Negro College Fund program awards 300 scholarships through its 41 member schools. To be eligible students must attend one of the 41 UNCF schools listed in Appendix IV of *BACU* and must demonstrate financial need. UNCF scholarships range from $500 to $7,500 per year.

COVERING THE BASES

Don't limit your search for financial aid to the federal and state levels. Explore all your options. Many grants and scholarships are available through individual colleges and universities. Some are based on academic achievement; others could be based on creative talent or athletic ability. Contact the financial aid office at the colleges where you are applying to find out:

1. What institutional grants and scholarships are available?

2. What are the eligibility requirements?

3. What is the criteria for selection?

4. What are the range of awards?

5. How and when can I apply?

Not-So-Obvious Sources

- Companies that you or your parents are associated with may provide some type of assistance for pursuing post-secondary education.

- Contact local clubs, fraternal organizations (such as Elks, Kiwanas, etc.), and civic leagues. Community-based associations often have scholarships available.

- The local library or bookstore has myriad sourcebooks that provide information on locating funds for college.

Many private sector resources often go untapped because prospective students are simply not aware of them. All sources cited in the bibliography following this chapter are readily available at your local library.

FINAL NOTE

It is important to note that it is never too early to begin your search for financial aid. In fact, it is not uncommon to begin two years prior to entering your freshman year in college. The search for financial aid should be an aggressive one, and although it may be an arduous journey, it is one that definitely pays off in the long run.

ESTIMATED FAMILY CONTRIBUTION CHART

The following estimated family contribution chart provides an idea of what colleges expect families to contribute at various income levels. This is an estimate based on averages. The chart is also based on the following assumptions:

- Two-parent family
- Assets estimated at $20,000
- One family member in college

Many private sector resources often go untapped because prospective students are simply not aware of them.

ESTIMATED FAMILY CONTRIBUTION FOR A DEPENDENT STUDENT FROM A TWO-PARENT FAMILY 1993-94

Total 1992 Family Income	Number of Family Members			
	3	4	5	6
$15,000	0	0	0	0
20,000	483	0	0	0
25,000	1,203	651	172	0
30,000	2,045	1,419	905	315
40,000	4,065	3,173	2,525	1,803
50,000	7,015	5,863	4,799	3,501
60,000	9,858	8,628	7,292	6,049
70,000	12,000	11,747	10,545	9,358
80,000	15,615	14,458	13,116	12,039
100,000	21,630	20,193	19,070	18,145

Bibliography

Ballen, Kate. "Paying for your kids' college." *Fortune* 126 Special Issue (fall 1992): 107–8.

The College Cost and Financial Aid Handbook 1993–94. College Scholarship Service. New York: College Entrance Examination Board, 1993. (Annual)

Paying Less for College. 11th ed. Princeton, N.J.: Peterson's Guides, 1993. (Annual; formerly, *Peterson's College Money Handbook)*

Scholarships, Fellowships and Loans, 1992–93: A Guide to Education-Related Financial Aid Programs for Students and Professionals. 9th ed. Debra M. Kirby and Eric G. Carlson, eds. Detroit: Gale Research, Inc., 1992.

"Tuition at black colleges is a bargain, survey shows." *Jet* 70 (August 25, 1986): 27.

United States Department of Education. *The Student Guide: Financial Aid from the U.S. Department of Education, 1993–94.* Washington, D.C., 1993. (Free; available from U.S. Department of Education, U.S. Government Printing Office, Washington, DC, 20402)

Alabama

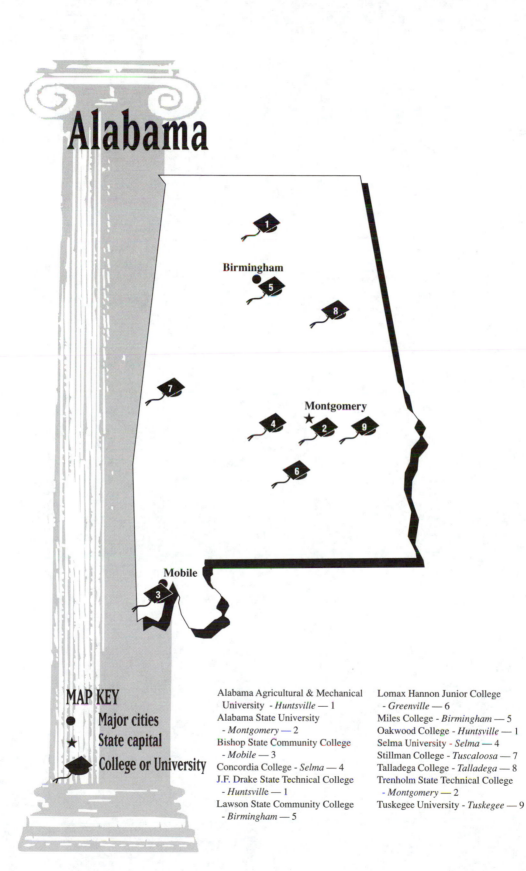

Birmingham

Montgomery

Mobile

MAP KEY

● Major cities

★ State capital

College or University

Alabama Agricultural & Mechanical
  University - *Huntsville* — 1
Alabama State University
  - *Montgomery* — 2
Bishop State Community College
  - *Mobile* — 3
Concordia College - *Selma* — 4
J.F. Drake State Technical College
  - *Huntsville* — 1
Lawson State Community College
  - *Birmingham* — 5

Lomax Hannon Junior College
  - *Greenville* — 6
Miles College - *Birmingham* — 5
Oakwood College - *Huntsville* — 1
Selma University - *Selma* — 4
Stillman College - *Tuscaloosa* — 7
Talladega College - *Talladega* — 8
Trenholm State Technical College
  - *Montgomery* — 2
Tuskegee University - *Tuskegee* — 9

ALABAMA AGRICULTURAL AND MECHANICAL UNIVERSITY

Normal, AL 35762
Phone: (205) 851-5000
Toll-free:
800-553-0816
Fax: (205) 851-9747

Total Enrollment:
5,215

Level of Selectivity:
Slightly competitive

Motto:
Service is Sovereignty

HISTORY

Alabama A&M is a four-year, state-supported, coed, liberal arts institution. Organized through the passage of a bill by the Alabama State Legislature, Alabama A&M opened as the Huntsville Normal School in 1875. The first president was William Hooper Councill, a former slave. The name was changed to State Normal and Industrial School at Huntsville in 1878.

An appropriation from the Morrill Act, the second land grant act that passed Congress in 1890, gave the school the status of a land grant institution. It was renamed The State Agricultural and Mechanical College for Negroes in 1891, and its present campus was established at Normal, Alabama, where it has grown from 200 acres to more than 2,000.

The attainment of junior college status in 1919 resulted in a new name, The State Agricultural and Mechanical

Institute for Negroes. Authorized to offer senior college work in 1939, the first bachelor's degrees were conferred in 1941. The name changed again in 1948 to Alabama Agricultural and Mechanical College, and the present name, Alabama Agricultural and Mechanical University, was established in 1969.

Alabama A&M University's mission is to serve as a land grant institution, providing a setting for the formation of scholars, leaders, and others who can contribute to society. "It operates in the three-fold function of teaching, research, and public service, including extension."

The spacious hillside campus has 30 major buildings made of red brick and 11 dormitories. The city of Huntsville is serviced by bus lines and airlines. Located in a suburb just two miles from downtown Huntsville and 100 miles from Birmingham, a major metropolitan center, students have access to a wealth of cultural and recreational experiences.

ACCREDITATION

Alabama A&M University is accredited by the Southern Association of Colleges and Schools (SACS) to award the Bachelor of Arts, Bachelor of Science, Master's, and Ph.D. degrees.

Other Accreditation

Accreditation Board for Engineering and
  Technology
Alabama State Department of Education
American Dietetic Association
American Home Economics Association
American Library Association
American Planning Association
Council on Social Work Education
Institute of Food Technologists
National Council for Accreditation of
  Teacher Education

COSTS PER YEAR

1992–1993 Tuition: $1,600 (in-state);
  $3,150 (out-state)

Room and board: $1,108 (room); $1,242
  (board)
Special fees: $25
Books: $700
Estimated total cost: $4,675 (in-state);
  $6,225 (out-state)

FINANCIAL AID
1991–92 Institutional Funding
Number of scholarships and grants: 823

Total amount of scholarships and grants:
  $1,484,565

Range of scholarships and grants:
  $1,393–$2,093

1991–92 Federal and State Funding
Number of scholarships and grants: 2,195

Total amount of scholarships and grants:
  $3,747,012

Range of scholarships and grants:
  $1,504–$1,721

Number of loans: 1,628

Total amount of loans: $3,800,776

Range of loans: $2,335 (average)

Number of work-study: 355

Total amount of work-study: $1,189,626

Range of work-study: $1,008–$1,766

Financial Aid Specific to the School
80% of the student body received financial aid during 1991–92.

The Alabama Emergency Secondary Education Scholarship Program provides scholarships/loans to students interested in the teaching profession in the state of Alabama. Student awards range from $1,998 per semester to $3,996 per year.

Alabama GI Dependents Educational Benefit Program pays tuition, fees, and books for dependents of Alabama Veterans who attend higher educational institutions in Alabama. Contact the Alabama State Dept. of Veterans Affairs, PO Box 509, Montgomery, AL 36102.

The Alabama Scholarship for Dependents of Blind Persons pays instructional fees and tuition for children from families with one or more blind parent. Applicant must also demonstrate financial need.

Alabama Student Assistant Program provides incentive grants ranging from $300–$2,500 a year for residents of the state of Alabama.

The American Legion and Legion Auxiliary Programs pay tuition, fees, and board for families of veterans of World Wars I or II, the Korean War, or the Vietnam War who attend college in Alabama. Contact the American Legion, PO Box 1009, Montgomery, AL 36192.

The Army ROTC program provides two-year and three-year scholarships. ROTC scholarships pay tuition, fees, books, and other expenses, as well as provide a monthly stipend of $100.

Athletic scholarships are awarded in football, basketball, swimming, soccer, tennis, track & field, and volleyball.

Performance grants are available for musicianship in choir and band.

Police and Firefighters' Survivors Educational Assistance Program pays tuition, fees, books and supplies to dependents and eligible spouses of Alabama police or firefighters killed while on duty.

The Robert C. Byrd Honors Scholarship Program provides entering students with a one-time scholarship of $1,500.

Thurgood Marshall Black Education Fund provides a four-year scholarship at this black, public college. Qualifying students must have a high school GPA of 3.0 or better, and an SAT score of 1,000 or ACT score of 24 or more. Students must be recommended by high school counselor as exceptional or exemplary in the creative or performing arts. Scholarship pays tuition, fees, room, and board not to exceed $6,000 annually.

Wallace Folsom Prepaid College Tuition Program guarantees four years of fully paid tuition for Alabama undergraduate students. Contact the State Treasurers' Office, 204 Alabama State House, Montgomery, AL 36130.

Work-related programs, including work-study, provide employment in offices and departments of the university.

Financial Aid Deadline
April 1 (fall and spring)

Financial Aid Contact
Mr. Percy N. Lanier, Director of Student Financial Aid, Alabama A&M, Normal, AL 35762; (205) 851-5400

ADMISSION REQUIREMENTS
Open admissions; SAT or ACT required.

Entrance Requirements
A high school graduate with a 2.0 GPA and completion of the following 20 units: 4 English, 2 mathematics, 2 science (including biology), 3 social science, and 9 electives; history, and political science required. A $10 nonrefundable application fee.

GED students must meet the basic admissions requirements.

Transfer students must have a 2.0 GPA, 12 semester hours, or 18 quarter hours, and have good standing at the institution they are leaving.

International students must obtain admission three months before planned registration. Also required are the $10.00 registration fee; certified transcripts; a letter of recommendation from the head of the previous school; affidavit of support; admission deposit of two semesters of room, board, and tuition (plus summer tuition); a 12-month health insurance deposit; and passing score on TOEFL examination for non-native English language students.

Conditional acceptance is available for applicants not meeting the entrance requirements. Successful completion of two semesters permits transition to regular student status.

Early admission is available for academically gifted students in their junior or senior year in high school.

Admission Application Deadline

Rolling admissions; should submit application two weeks before start of semester of enrollment; applicant is informed as soon as admission decision is made.

Admission Contact

James O. Heyward, Director of Admissions, Alabama A&M University, PO Box 908, Normal, AL 35762; (205) 851-5245 or 800-553-0816.

GRADUATION REQUIREMENTS

Completion of the school's curriculum with a minimum 2.00 GPA. Candidate must earn half or more of the credits toward his/her major at Alabama A&M University. No more than 25 semester hours of work from other institutions will apply. Last two semesters of classes must be taken from Alabama A&M. Some courses of study may require completion of the National Teacher Examination or the Graduate Record Examination during the senior year. Attendance at commencement exercises is mandatory.

Grading System

A-F; W=Withdraw, WP= Withdraw while passing, WF=Withdraw while failing, I=Incomplete, P=Passing, Au=Audit.

STUDENT BODY PROFILE

Total enrollment (male/female): 2,400/2,815

From in-state: 3,820

Full-time undergraduates (male/female): 1,680/1,973

Part-time undergraduates (male/female): 139/164

Graduate students (male/female): 579/680

Ethnic/Racial Makeup

African American, 4,108; Hispanic, 11; Native American, 1; Other/Unclassified, 45

Class of 1995 Profile

Number of applicants: 3,380

Number accepted: 2,380

Number enrolled: 1,036

Median SAT score: 340 Verbal, 350 Math

Median ACT score: 16.3

Average high school GPA: 2.41

Transfer applicants: 620

Transfers accepted: 410

Transfers enrolled: 138

FACULTY PROFILE

Number of faculty: 357

Student-teacher ratio: 19:1

Full-time faculty: 281

Part-time faculty: 76

Tenured faculty: 187

Faculty with doctorates or other terminal degrees: 60%

SCHOOL CALENDAR

1991–92: August–May

Commencement and conferring of degrees: May

One summer session.

DEGREES OFFERED AND NUMBER CONFERRED 1991–1992:

Bachelor of Arts

English: 8

French: n/a

History: 3

Music: n/a

Political Science: n/a

Psychology: 1

Social Work: 15

Sociology: 5

Bachelor of Science

Accounting: 19

Agribusiness: n/a

Agribusiness Education: n/a
Agribusiness Management: n/a
Agricultural Economics: n/a
Animal Science: n/a
Art Education: n/a
Botany: n/a
Business Administration: n/a
Chemistry: n/a
Chemistry Honors: n/a
Child Develpment Associate: n/a
Civil Engineering: n/a
Civil Engineering Technology: n/a
Commercial and Advertising Art: n/a
Community and Extension: n/a
Computer Science: 72
Dietetics: n/a
Early Childhood Education: 26
Economics: n/a
Education: n/a
Electrical Engineering Technology: n/a
Elementary Education: 71
Environmental Science: n/a
Family Resource Management: n/a
Fashion Design: n/a
Fashion Merchandising: n/a
Finance: n/a
Food Science and Technology: n/a
Forest Operations Management: n/a
Home Economics Education: n/a
Horticulture: n/a
Hospitality Food Systems: n/a
Industrial Arts Education: n/a
Instrumental Music: n/a
Interior Design: n/a
Learning Disabilities: n/a
Logistics: n/a
Management: n/a
Marketing: n/a
Mathematics: 8
Mechanical Drafting and Design
   Technology: n/a

Mechanical Engineering Technology: n/a
Medical Technology: n/a
Mental Retardation: n/a
Middle School Education: n/a
Music Education: n/a
Office Systems Management: n/a
Physical Education: 8
Physics: n/a
Printing Production Management: n/a
Secondary Education: n/a
Soil Science: n/a
Special Education: 34
Speech Pathology: 18
Technical Studies: n/a
Telecommunications: 20
Trade and Industrial Education: n/a
Urban Planning: n/a
Zoology: n/a

Pre-professional
Nursing: n/a
Veterinary Medicine: n/a

Master's Degree
Agricultural Business: n/a
Agriculture Education: n/a
Animal Industries: n/a
Art Education: n/a
Business Administration: n/a
Business Education: n/a
Community Planning: n/a
Computer Science: n/a
Early Childhood Education: n/a
Economics: n/a
Education: n/a
Elementary Education: n/a
Home Economics Education: n/a
Industrial Technology: n/a
Sociology: n/a
Soil Science: n/a

Special Education: n/a

Speech Pathology: n/a

Speech Pathology Education: n/a

Urban Studies: n/a

Doctorate
Physics: n/a

Plant and Soil Science: n/a

SPECIAL PROGRAMS

One-week college orientation is provided for entering students at no cost; parents may attend.

Cooperative programs are offered in Medical Technology, Pre-Nursing, Pre-Veterinary Medicine.

Pre-professional programs are offered in Medicine, Dentistry, and Law.

Dual degree, cooperative, and reciprocal programs with other institutions are available in various fields of study. Cooperating schools include Athens State College, Georgia Institute of Technology, John C. Calhoun State Community College, Oakwood College, Tuskegee University, University of Alabama, and University of Tennessee.

Cross-registration is available with Athens State College and the University of Alabama in Huntsville.

Honors program provides encouragement to students through the President's Cup Award for undergraduate students maintaining a 4.00 GPA for two consecutive 12-hour semesters. The President's Award, Dean's List, Honor Roll, and Freshman Honor Roll are among other ways students are recognized for academic achievement.

Cooperative Education Program allows students to alternate six months of full-time study with six months of full-time career related work. Available to undergraduate and graduate students.

Students participating in internships are given full-time student status with six semester hours of course work.

Continuing education and weekend college programs offer students credit and non-credit courses on and off campus; programs meet the needs of working adults needing flexible scheduling.

Mandatory ROTC is required for male students for the first two semesters of the freshman year. Qualifying students may go on to advanced training for a commission as a second lieutenant in the U.S. Armed Forces. Female students are encouraged to enroll in the program. Exemptions are made for part-time students, former members of the U.S. Armed forces, and by permission of a physician.

ROTC Advanced Skills and Training Program helps cadets improve skills in mathematics, written and spoken English, reading, and cognitive skills.

Advanced Placement (AP) grants college credit for postsecondary level work completed in high school. Students who score 3 on the AP test will receive credit.

ATHLETIC PROGRAMS

Alabama A&M is a member of the National Collegiate Athletic Association (NCAA), National Athletic Intercollegiate Association (NAIA), and Southern Intercollegiate Athletic Conference (SIAC).

Intercollegiate sports: men's basketball, cross-country, football, soccer, swimming, and track & field; women's basketball, cross-country, swimming and diving, tennis, track & field, and volleyball.

Intramural sports: basketball, tennis, track & field, and volley ball.

Athletic Contact
Vann Pettaway, Alabama A&M University, Normal, AL 35762; (205) 851-5360.

LIBRARY HOLDINGS

The library houses 521,749 bound volumes, 115,145 microform titles, 1,659 periodical subscriptions, and 4,542 audiovisuals. Computers and typewriters are available for student use. Library has an online catalog and provides DIALOG searching for a fee for students, faculty, and staff.

STUDENT LIFE
Special Regulations
Class attendance required. Boarding freshmen cannot have cars on campus. All boarding students must purchase a meal card. Mandatory health protection plan is necessary for all full-time undergraduate students. Mandatory ROTC enrollment is required during first two semesters of freshman year.

Campus Services
Health center, personal/psychological counseling, career planning and placement, career awareness laboratory, writing laboratory, reading laboratory, mathematics laboratory, special education center, and testing services for LSAT, NTE, ACT, CLEP, NSA, DOT, and TOEFL.

Campus Activities
Group activities include concert, theater, band, and choir. Students can get involved in the student-run newspaper or the yearbook. The campus has a student-run radio station.

Leadership opportunities can be found in the more than 21 departmental organizations including the Malcolm X Historical Society. Greek-letter societies include Alpha Kappa Alpha, Delta Sigma Theta, Sigma Gamma Rho, and Zeta Phi Beta sororities, as well as Alpha Phi Alpha, Kappa Alpha Psi, Omega Psi Phi Fraternity, and Phi Beta Sigma fraternities. Honor societies include Alpha Kappa Mu, Beta Kappa Chi National Scientific Honor Society, and Kappa Delta Pi Educational Honor Society. Social and service organizations are governed by the Inter-Club Council and the La Congo Council.

Normal is a suburb located two miles outside of Huntsville, Alabama, which is a city of 170,000 people, located 100 miles north of Birmingham. Huntsville, the home of the U.S. Space and Rocket Center and the U.S. Space Camp, is served by major airlines and bus companies. Social and cultural activities and entertainment are easily accessible to Alabama A&M students on campus and in the nearby city.

Housing Availability
2,000 housing spaces; freshman housing guaranteed; 47% of the students choose to live on campus.

Handicapped Services
Wheelchair accessibility and services for the visually impaired.

NOTABLE ALUMNI
John H. Brown, 1946–Professor and dentist; founder and director, Meharry Medical College Hospital of Dentistry

Dr. William Cox, 1964–President, Ed Cox, Matthews & Associates

John Stallworth, 1974 and 1988–President, Madison Research Corporation; former professional football player

Carter D. Womack, 1973–Executive vice president, *The Black Collegian*

ALABAMA STATE UNIVERSITY

HISTORY

Alabama State University is a four-year, state-supported, coed, liberal arts university found in 1866 as Lincoln Normal School, a private school for blacks located in Marion, Alabama. In 1874, the state reorganized Lincoln to establish the State Normal School and University for the Education of the Colored Teachers and Students. Because of racial tensions in Marion, the school was moved to Montgomery in 1887 and changed its name to Alabama Colored Peoples University. In 1889, the name was changed to State Normal School for Colored Students. In 1920, the first instruction at postsecondary level was offered and the institution became a junior college.

The first bachelor's degree was awarded in 1931, the first master's degree, in 1943. Between 1921 and 1954, the institution was reorganized as a four-year institution and changed its name three times to: State Teachers College in 1929; to Alabama State College for Negroes in 1949; and to Alabama State College in 1954.

In 1954, the college was caught up in the famous Montgomery Bus Boycott and the "direct action" campaigns of the Civil Rights Movement. Overcoming counteraction by state authorities and others, the college was granted "university status" in 1969 and adopted its present name.

It was largely through the efforts of William Burns Paterson, who became president in 1878, that the institution became the first state-supported institution for the training of black teachers in the United States. During his administration the school graduated its first six students. Regarded as the founder, Paterson led the university for over 37 years through many "unsurmountable odds" that threatened to close the school.

As a state institution, the school's mission is to provide quality programs to any student who desires to pursue higher education for personal, occupational, or professional growth regardless of socioeconomic status, or racial, ethnic, or cultural background.

The campus occupies 138 acres in the historical Centennial Hill area of Montgomery, Alabama. Across the street sits the beautiful Municipal Oak Park, one of the few

915 S. Jackson St.
Montgomery, AL
36101-0271
Phone: (205) 293-4100
Toll-free in-state:
800 354-8865
Toll-free out-state:
800-253-5037 or
800-253-5038
Fax: (205) 269-5879

Total Enrollment:
5,490

Level of Selectivity:
Noncompetitive;
slightly competitive
for teacher education

space transit planetariums in the nation. Two new facilities are the Tullibody Fine Arts Complex and the Music Hall.

ACCREDITATION

Alabama State University is accredited by the Southern Association of Colleges and Schools (SACS) to award the Associate of Science, Bachelor of Arts, Bachelor of Science, Master's of Education, and Specialist in Education degrees.

Other Accreditation

Alabama State Department of Education

National Association of Schools of Music Education and Certification

National Association of State Directors of Teacher Education and Certification

National Council for Accreditation of Teacher Education

COSTS PER YEAR

1993–94 Tuition: $1,608 (in-state); $3,216 (out-state)

Room and board: $1,250 (room); $850 (board)

Special fees: $125

Books: $500

Estimated total cost: $4,333 (in-state); $5,941 (out-state)

FINANCIAL AID
1991–92 Institutional Funding

Number of scholarships and grants: 623

Total amount of scholarships and grants: $1,216,925

Range of scholarships and grants: $600 to $2,700

1991–92 Federal and State Funding

Number of scholarships and grants: 3,243

Total amount of scholarships and grants: $5,151,667

Range of scholarships and grants: $600 to $2,400

Number of loans: 2,385

Total amount of loans: $4,873,036

Range of loans: $200 to $2,625

Number of work-study: 956

Total amount of work-study: $1,350,036

Range of work-study: $300 to $2,400

Financial Aid Specific to the School

80% of the student body received financial aid during 1991–92.

Alabama State provides numerous scholarships to high school and junior college graduates with financial need who have demonstrated high academic achievement and personal ambition.

Athletic scholarships are awarded in football and basketball.

LEEP (Law Enforcement Education Program) provides financial assistance for those who plan a career in law enforcement.

Cooperative Education Program alternates classroom study with related paid work experience. The program provides academic credit and full-time status during co-op placement.

Thurgood Marshall Black Education Fund provides a four-year scholarship at this public black college. Qualifying student must have a high school GPA of 3.0 or better, and a SAT score of 1,000 or ACT score of twenty-four or more. Students must be recommended by high school counselor as exceptional or exemplary in the creative or performing arts. Scholarship pays tuition, fees, room, and board, not to exceed $6,000 annually.

Army and cooperative Air Force ROTC programs offer two- and four-year scholarships that pay tuition, fees, books, and other expenses, and provide a monthly stipend of $100.

Alabama Student Assistance Program is available to students who are residents of Alabama and who demonstrate financial need.

Financial Aid Deadline
June 1

Financial Aid Contact
Mr. Billy Brooks, Director, Office of Student Financial Aid, Paterson Hall, Room 103, Alabama State University, Montgomery, AL 36101-0271; (205) 293-4324.

ADMISSION REQUIREMENTS
Open admissions except for Teacher Education. SAT or ACT required for counseling/placement except for Teacher Education.

Entrance Requirements
Graduation from high school with a minimum number of units to include: 3 English, 3 mathematics, 3 natural sciences, 3 social studies, and 8 foreign language. Proof of a recent physical is needed.

GED students must meet basic admission requirements.

International students must take the TOEFL examination.

Transfer students must submit college transcript, qualify for readmission at previous college or university attended, and have a 2.0 GPA.

Early admission allows academically gifted high school students the opportunity to enroll in college for credit before completing high school.

Admission Application Deadline
Rolling admission provides no specific date for notification of admission so applicant is informed as soon as admission decision is made.

Admission Contact
Debbie Moore, Office of Enrollment Management, Kilby Hall, University Boulevard, Alabama State University, Montgomery, AL 36101-0271; (205) 293-4291 or 800-354-8865 (in-state); 800-253-5037 or 800-253-5038 (out-state).

GRADUATION REQUIREMENTS
A minimum of 68 credit hours and completion of the core requirements to include a computer course are needed for an associate's degree. A minimum of 128 credit hours and completion of the core requirement to include 6 hours of mathematics, 8 hours of science, and a computer course are needed for all bachelor's degrees.

Grading System
A–F; I=Incomplete; W=Withdrawal; P=In progress; AU=Audit.

STUDENT BODY PROFILE
Total enrollment (male/female): 2,306/3,184

From in-state: 3,690

Other regions: 24 states, 6 foreign countries

Full-time undergraduates (male/female): 1,973/2,724

Part-time undergraduates (male/female): 177/243

Graduate students (male/female): 157/216

Ethnic/Racial Makeup
African American, 5,382; Hispanic, 11; Native American, 1; Caucasian, 66; International, 30.

Class of 1995 Profile
Number of applicants: 5,075

Number accepted: 3,825

Number enrolled: 1,512

Median SAT score: 310V; 340M

Median ACT score: 16 (Enhanced)

Average high school GPA: 2.49

Transfer applicants: 620

Transfers accepted: 321

Transfers enrolled: 219

FACULTY PROFILE
Number of faculty: 300

Student-teacher ratio: 21:1

Full-time faculty: 210

Part-time faculty: 90

Tenured faculty: 92

Faculty with doctorates or other terminal degrees: 62%

SCHOOL CALENDAR

1992–93: August 16–May 13 (semester hours)

Commencement and conferring of degrees: May 15

One summer session.

DEGREES OFFERED AND NUMBER CONFERRED 1991–92:

Associate's Degrees

Business Management and Administrative Services: 1

Computer Science: 1

Child Development: 2

Bachelor of Arts

Art: 3

English: n/a

History and Government/History Education: 1

Journalism: 3

Language Arts: 2

Marine Biology: n/a

Political Science: 10

Radio and TV Broadcasting: 9

Sociology: 5

Spanish: 1

Speech Communication: n/a

Theater: n/a

Bachelor of Science

Accounting: 24

Biology Education: 15

Business Education: 4

Business Management and Administrative Services: 12

Business Marketing: 9

Chemistry/Chemistry Education: 7

Child Development: 2

Computer Information Science: 4

Computer Science: 16

Criminal Justice: 21

Early Childhood Education: n/a

Economics: n/a

Elementary Education: 7

Engineering (dual degree): n/a

English Education: n/a

Finance: 8

Human Services: n/a

Laboratory Technology: n/a

Marketing: n/a

Mathematics: 13

Mathematics Education: 2

Mathematics/Engineering (dual degree): 1

Music/Music Education: 4

Office Supervision and Management: 11

Parks and Recreation: 7

Physical Education Teaching and Coaching: 1

Physics: 1

Psychology Education: 10

Public Relations: 7

Reading Education: 1

Recreation: n/a

Science Teacher Education: 1

Secondary Education: n/a

Social Science Education: 6

Social Work: n/a

Special Education: 3

Traffic Education: n/a

Master's of Education

Biology: n/a

Counseling: n/a

Early Childhood Education: n/a

Educational Administration: n/a

English: n/a

Instructional Media: n/a

Mathematics: n/a

Music: n/a

Physical Education: n/a

Reading: n/a

Science: n/a

Social Science: n/a

Special Education: n/a

Specialist in Education

Counseling: n/a

Educational Administration: n/a

Elementary Education: n/a

English: n/a

SPECIAL PROGRAMS

Accelerated Study Program allows students to complete their undergraduate degree in a shorter period of time than the traditional period of four years.

Advanced Placement (AP) grants college credit for postsecondary work completed in high school. Students scoring three to five points on the AP test will receive credit by examination for each course.

College Level Examination Program (CLEP) determines the academic relevance of nontraditional educational experiences, such as the military, on-the-job training, or other life experiences, through a series of tests and may grant students college credit for these experiences.

College orientation session is offered for three days for $50 prior to the beginning of classes to acquaint students to the college and to prepare them for college life.

Cooperative Education Program allows students to alternate classroom study with related paid work experience. The program provides academic credit and full-time status during co-op placement.

The honors program offers academically talented students a challenging program of study that includes special classes, seminars, colloquia, cultural activities, and special recognition to motivate participants.

Internships and The Leadership Training Program provide training or graduate assistance pursuing a degree in counseling.

Off-campus study allows students to take courses at other institutions for credit through the National Student Exchange program.

The part-time degree program allows students to earn an undergraduate degree while attending part time.

Remedial courses are offered to entering students to bring them up to admission standards and to help them adjust for success in college.

ROTC provides training in military science for commission as a second lieutenant in the U. S. Army and Air force. Two- and four-year scholarships are available.

Student Retention Program and the Learning Assistance Program provide developmental courses, counseling, and cultural activities to students who need aid to succeed in college.

Study Abroad Program allows students to go to a foreign country for a specified period of time for part of their college education.

Three/two dual engineering degree program in cooperation with Auburn University and Tuskegee University allows students to get two degrees—one in liberal arts from home school and one in engineering from cooperating school—by completing three years at matriculated school and two years at cooperating school.

ATHLETIC PROGRAMS

Alabama State is a member of the National Collegiate Athletic Association (NCAA), all Division I teams, except men's football (Division I-AA); and the Southern Athletic Conference. Intercollegiate sports: men's football, basketball, cross-country, golf, tennis, and track; women's basketball, cross-country, tennis, track, and volleyball.

Intramural sports: basketball, field hockey, swimming, track, and volleyball.

Athletic Contact

Dr. Tommy Frederick, Athletic Department, Alabama State University, Lockhart Gymnasium, Montgomery, AL 36195-0301; (205) 293-4442.

LIBRARY HOLDINGS

The Levi Watkins Learning Center houses the library which holds 220,000 bound volumes, 755 periodical subscriptions, 10,500 microforms, 5,000 audiovisual materials, and 100 computers available in computer center. Special collections include the Ollie L. Brown Afro-American Heritage Collection and the E. D. Nixon Archival Collection (Montgomery's most prominent black leader of the 1950s).

STUDENT LIFE
Campus Regulations

Class attendance required; $120 to register car; all resident halls are nonsmoking.

Campus Services

Health clinic, personal and psychological counseling, career planning and placement, day care, student orientation, consultation and outreach, testing and psychological services, and religious activities.

Campus Activities

Social and cultural activities include theater, band, chorale, orchestra, musical concerts, and a speakers series, featuring noted artists and professional groups. Students may get involved in the student-run newspaper and yearbook. Communication majors or volunteers may work in the student radio station, WVAS, 90.7 FM.

Leadership opportunities are found in the Student Government Association (SGA) or the various other interest clubs and organizations. Greek-letter fraternities include Alpha Phi Alpha, Kappa Alpha Psi, Omega Psi Phi, Phi Beta Sigma, and Alpha Phi Omega; sororities include Alpha Kappa Alpha, Delta Sigma Theta, Sigma Gamma Rho, and Zeta Phi Beta. Honor societies are also represented on campus.

Located in the heart of Montgomery on South Jackson Street, the campus is within walking distance of the business district, the Municipal Civic Center, museums, art galleries, theaters, medical centers, the state archives, and historical sites. Montgomery has historical roots in the Civil Rights movement and is the home of the Civil Rights Memorial. The houses, especially those on South Jackson, were built by some of America's most prominent African Americans. Martin Luther King, Jr., lived in the pastorium of the Dexter Avenue Baptist Church, at 309 South Jackson, during his time in Montgomery. It was here that he saw empty buses running along Jackson Street and realized the boycott was a success. The campus adjoins interstate highway 85 and is about two miles from the Montgomery interchange of interstate highways 65 and 85. It is not far from other metropolitan cities such as Birmingham, Alabama, and Atlanta, Georgia.

Housing Availability

2,005 housing spaces are available on a first-come-first-served basis. The school has eight dormitories for females and five for males; McGinty and Finley (East/West) are available for students with at least a 3.0 GPA.

Handicapped Services

Services include wheelchair accessibility and services for the visually impaired. Services to the physically challenged arc coordinated through the Comprehensive Counseling Center.

NOTABLE ALUMNI

Dr. Wiley Bolden, 1939–Professor emeritus, Georgia State University

Yvonne Kennedy, Ph.D., 1964–President, Bishop Junior College; 1991–92 national president, Delta Sigma Theta sorority

William Peterson, 1935–Judge, Circuit Court, Cook County, Chicago, Illinois

Lynette Taylor, 1936–President, Taylor Enterprises

Charles H. Wright, 1939–Retired obstetrician, Detroit, Michigan

BISHOP STATE COMMUNITY COLLEGE

351 N. Broad St.
Mobile, AL 36603-
5898
Phone: (205) 690-6800
or 6801 (Main
Campus)
Toll-free in-state:
800-523-7235
(Mobile/Washington
Counties)
Fax: (205) 438-5403

Total Enrollment:
2,144

Level of Selectivity:
Noncompetitive

Motto:
A Commitment to a
Program of Excellence

HISTORY

Bishop State Community College is a two-year, state-supported, comprehensive, coed college founded in 1927. Bishop State began as a branch of Alabama State University, called the Alabama State College Branch (Mobile Center). For several years it only provided extension courses for in-service teachers during the summer months. In September of 1938, the college was established as an all-year, two-year college.

The college became a state junior college in 1965 and was officially named Mobile State Junior College. This move gave the institution its first independent legal status. The school was renamed S. D. Bishop State Junior College in 1971 to honor Dr. S. D. Bishop, the college's first president. To more accurately reflect the growth and vocational offerings, the school became Bishop State Community College in 1985. As part of the Alabama College System, the state-supported network of two-year community, junior, and technical colleges, Bishop serves to provide high quality educational opportunities to all residents of Alabama at an affordable cost.

The main campus consists of six modern buildings situated on nine acres. The two other campuses include Carver Campus, 414 Stanton St., Mobile, AL 36617; (205) 473-8692; and Southwest Campus, 925 Dauphin Isle Parkway, Mobile, AL 36605; (205) 479-0003.

ACCREDITATION

Bishop State Community College is accredited by the Southern Association of Colleges and Schools (SACS) to award the Associate of Arts, Associate of Science, and Associate in Applied Science degrees, and provide certificates at the community college level.

Other Accreditation

Alabama Board of Nursing

American Board of Funeral Service Education, Inc.

National League for Nursing

COSTS PER YEAR

1992–93 Tuition: $1,105 (in-state); $1,855 (out-state)

Room and board: none

Special fees: $125

Books: $500

Estimated total cost: $1,730 (in-state); $2,480 (out-state)

FINANCIAL AID

1991–92 Institutional Funding

Number of scholarships and grants: 1,222

Total amount of scholarships and grants: $73,693

Range of scholarships and grants: $200–$2,400

1991–92 Federal and State Funding

Total amount of scholarships and grants: $1,377,171

Financial Aid Specific to the School

57% of the student body received financial aid during 1991–92.

Leadership Scholarships are awarded to selected incoming students with leadership potential and past participation in certain student activities.

Performing Arts Scholarships are available to students in band, choir, painting, drawing, creative writing, photography, and dramatics.

Presidential and Academic Scholarships are awarded to incoming freshmen for outstanding academic achievement.

Endowed Scholarships are awarded to students selected by members of organizations and by private donors.

Athletic Scholarships are awarded in baseball, basketball, and cheerleading.

Cooperative Education Program alternates classroom study with related paid work experience. The program provides academic credit and full-time status during co-op placement.

Army, Air Force, or Navy ROTC programs offer two- and four-year scholarships that pay tuition, fees, books, and other expenses, and provide a monthly stipend of $100.

Alabama Student Assistance Program provides grants to students who are residents of Alabama and who demonstrate financial need.

Financial Aid Deadline

August 20 (priority)

Financial Aid Contact

John L. Keith, Director of Financial Aid, Bishop State Community College, 351 North Broad St., Mobile, AL 36603-5898; (205) 690-6458 or 6459.

ADMISSION REQUIREMENTS

Open admission

Entrance Requirements

Graduation from high school, official high school transcript, proof of recent physical, and proof of immunization against measles; men 18 to 26 must provide proof of registration with selective service.

GED students must meet basic admission requirements.

International students must submit official transcripts in English; students from non-English-speaking countries must pass the TOEFL examination with a minimum score of 400; international students must provide proof of ability to pay all college costs.

Transfer students must submit official transcript for all previous college work; must qualify for readmission at previous college or university attended.

Early admission allows academically gifted high school students the opportunity to enroll for college credits before completing high school. Student must have recommendation from high school counselor or principal.

Admission Application Deadline

Rolling admission provides no specific date for notification of admission so applicant is informed as soon as admission decision is made.

Admission Contact

Delayne Banks, Coordinator of Admissions and Records, Bishop State Community College, 351 North Broad St., Mobile, AL 36603-5898; (205) 690-6800 or 6801; or 800-523-7235.

GRADUATION REQUIREMENTS

Minimum of 96 quarter hours and completion of core requirements to include the following: 10 English, 15 science and mathematics, 10 social sciences, and 3 physical education.

Grading System

A–F; AU=Audit; FA=Failure for lack of attendance; I=Incomplete; IP=In Progress; W=Withdrawal (Official); WF=Failing at the time of withdrawal.

STUDENT BODY PROFILE

Total enrollment (male/female): 708/1,436

From in-state: 2,080

Full-time undergraduates (male/female): 269/546

Part-time undergraduates (male/female): 425/904

Ethnic/Racial Makeup

African American, 1,244; Hispanic, 21; Asian, 21; Native American, 21; Caucasian, 816; International, 21.

Class of 1995 Profile

Number of applicants: 1,091

Number accepted: 971

Number enrolled: 903

FACULTY PROFILE

Number of faculty: 91

Student-teacher ratio: 15:1

Full-time faculty: 51

Part-time faculty: 40

Ethnic/Racial Makeup

African American, 30; Asian, 2; Other/unclassified, 59.

SCHOOL CALENDAR

1992–93: August–June (quarter hours)

Commencement and conferring of degrees: June

One summer quarter.

DEGREES OFFERED 1991–92:
Associate of Arts

Art

Economics

English

History

Liberal Arts

Political Science

Psychology

Social Science

Sociology

Associate of Science

Accounting

Biology

Business

Business Management

Chemistry

Child Care

Computer Science

Criminal Justice

Education

English

Mathematics

Physical Education

Physics

Political Science

Pre-Dentistry

Pre-Law

Pre-Professional Medicine

Respiratory Therapy

Science

Sociology

Speech

Teacher Aide

Associate of Applied Science

Accounting

Biomedical Equipment Technology

Chemical Technology

Computer Information Systems

Criminal Justice

Data Processing

Deaf Interpreter

Dietetic Technician

Early Childhood Education

Emergency Medical Technology

Fire Services

Funeral Service

Library Technical Assistant

Medical Assistant

Medical Records Technician

Medical Technology

Nursing

Occupational Therapist

Office Management

Physical Therapist

Radiographer

Respiratory Therapy

Waste Water Management

SPECIAL PROGRAMS

Accelerated High School Program grants college credit for postsecondary work completed in high school.

Adult Education Program is available for nontraditional students returning to school or working full time.

Associate in Applied Technology degree can be earned in Cooperation with Alabama Aviation Technical College, Carver State Technical College, and Southwest State Technical College.

College Level Examination Program (CLEP) determines the academic relevance of nontraditional educational experiences, such as the military, on-the-job training, or other life experiences, through a series of tests and may grant students college credit for these experiences.

College orientation is offered at no cost to entering students for one week prior to the beginning of classes to acquaint students with the college and to prepare them for college life.

Cooperative Education Program alternates classroom study with related paid work experience. The program provides academic credit and full-time status during co-op placement.

Extended day and community service programs provide educational programming in the evening.

Part-time degree programs allow students to earn an undergraduate degree while attending part time.

Remedial courses are offered to entering students to bring them up to admission standards and to help them adjust for success in college.

ROTC provides training in military science for commission as a second lieutenant in the U. S. Air Force.

Student Support Services provide developmental courses, counseling, and cultural activities to students who need aid to succeed in college.

Transfer program provides transfer courses and sequences in mathematics and sciences, social sciences, humanities, and physical education for students planning to transfer to a four-year institution.

Vocational/Career Program is designed to train students in skills that will enable them to enter the job market.

ATHLETIC PROGRAMS

Bishop State is a member of the National Junior College Athletic Association (NJCAA)

Intercollegiate sports: men's basketball and women's basketball.

Intramural sports: baseball.

Athletic Contact

Athletic Department, Bishop State College, 351 Broad St., Mobile, AL 36603; (205) 690-6436 or (215) 690-6447.

LIBRARY HOLDINGS

The library has 45,000 bound volumes, 2,900 microforms, 218 periodical subscriptions, 2,000 audiovisuals, and 75 computers for student use.

STUDENT LIFE
Campus Regulations

Class attendance required; cars must be registered; students must attend chapel.

Campus Services

Health care, counseling, career planning and placement, child care, community service courses, remedial instruction, retention services, and chapel services.

Campus Activities

Social and cultural activities include theater, chorale, concerts, band, and dance. The College Bowl, an academic quiz contest, is a highlight each year. Students may work on the *Newsline* (student-run newspaper), the *Sword* (yearbook), or *Around Campus* which publishes activities, important events, and happenings concerning the campus community.

Leadership opportunities are found in the Student Government Association, Baptist Student Union, and other student clubs and organizations.

Bishop State is located in downtown Mobile which provides students with access to shopping and dining. Mobile is Alabama's oldest city and only seaport and has a population of approximately 205,000. More than one-third of the population is African American. Points of interest include Bellingrath Gardens and Homes, Mobile's historic district, Fort Gaines, and the U.S.S. Alabama Battleship Park. Annual events include the Senior Bowl Game and Mardi Gras Day.

Handicapped Services

Designated parking spaces have been marked for physically challenged students.

NOTABLE ALUMNI

Dr. Yvonne Kennedy, 1964–President, Bishop State Community College

CONCORDIA COLLEGE

HISTORY

Concordia College is a private, two-year, coed college influenced by the presence of Lutheran missionaries in Alabama in 1922. Four females were part of the first class to graduate in 1926. The name of the institution was changed in 1980 from Alabama Lutheran Academy and College to Concordia College.

In response to the needs of church, community and state, Concordia's mission is to "provide an opportunity for individuals to obtain knowledge through Christian-oriented educational programs and services in an environment designed to meet their spiritual, academic, social, and physical needs." This mission was shaped by the inspiration of the Lutheran Church Missouri Synod (LCMS), to provide an educational curriculum that helps students grow in Christian faith.

The campus includes 9 buildings, all recently built or renovated. Still standing are buildings that were dedicated by the director of missions C. F. Drewes in 1925.

ACCREDITATION

Concordia College is accredited by the Southern Association of Colleges and Schools to award the Associate of Arts degree.

Other Accreditation

State Department of Education

COSTS PER YEAR

1992-93 Tuition: $3,156

Room and board: $1,100 (room); $1,600 (board)

Special fees: $256

Books: $250

Estimated total cost: $6,362

1804 Green St.
Selma, AL 36701
Phone: (205) 874-5700
Fax: (205) 875-5755

Total Enrollment:
383

Level of Selectivity:
Noncompetitive

FINANCIAL AID

1991–92 Institutional Funding

Number of scholarships and grants: 232

Range of scholarships and grants: $600 (average)

1991–92 Federal and State Funding

Number of scholarships and grants: $140

Range of scholarships and grants: $800 (average)

Financial Aid Specific to the School

During the 1991–92 school year, 97% of the student body received financial aid.

Academic scholarships are available to freshmen with a cumulative high school average of 3.0 or higher. Awards range from $500 to $1,600 per academic year.

Activities scholarships are available through various departments to qualified students. Awards range from $200 to $1,000 per year. These scholarships assist students involved with band, basketball, or choir.

The Board of Regents awards scholarships ranging from $200 to $500, based upon academic achievement, character, and need.

The Faculty Scholarship is awarded to students based on achievement, character, and need. Awards range from $200 to $500.

There are approximately 10 alumni or endowed scholarships available based on academic achievement and need. Most are available to active members of the Lutheran Church.

The Ellwanger Memorial Endowment Scholarship Fund provides scholarships for minority students who attend Concordia College and are preparing for full-time church work. This fund was established by the Ellwanger family in memory of their parents, Dr. Walter H. Ellwanger (past president) and Mrs. Jesse Ellwanger (instructor).

The Lutheran Brotherhood Scholarship is for Lutheran graduates accepted to Concordia. The award is usually $500.

Full or partial tuition waivers are available for employees and their children. College work-study is also available.

The Alabama Student Assistance Program and Alabama Student Grant program are available to residents of Alabama attending schools in the state. The grant program usually awards up to $600.

Southern District Aid provides financial assistance to students preparing for the professional ministries of the Lutheran Church-Missouri Synod.

The Ethnic Minority Scholarship is available for students who are a racial minority in a LCMS congregation attending a LCMS college or seminary.

The Aid Association for Lutherans allocates money for scholarships.

Financial Aid Deadline

August 15

Financial Aid Contact

Director of Financial Aid, Concordia College, 1804 Green St., Selma, AL 36701; (205) 874-5700

ADMISSION REQUIREMENTS

ACT required; open admissions.

Entrance Requirements

High school transcript with a minimum 2.0 GPA, and completion of the following units: 4 English, 2 mathematics, 1 science, and 3 social sciences. Letters of recommendation and an interview required for some students. A $10 application fee is required.

GED students must meet basic admission requirements.

Transfer students must submit previous college transcripts. If cumulative GPA is not satisfactory, transfers may exclude a maximum of nine semester hours or 12 quarter hours of lowest grades to bring GPA up. Transfers must take excluded courses over at Concordia.

International students must meet requirements for regular admission. Must pay tuition, fees, room, and board in advance, and must be able to read, write, and speak English.

Admission Application Deadline
September 2

Admission Contact
Dr. McNair Ramsey, Dean of Student Services, Concordia College, Selma, AL 36701; (205)874-5736; Fax: (205) 875-5755.

GRADUATION REQUIREMENTS
A minimum of 64 credit hours and completion of the core program to include 6 hours of mathematics, 8 hours of science, 1 hour of computer science (business administration, elementary education majors); 16 of the last 24 credit hours must be earned at Concordia.

Grading System
A-F; F/AB=Failure for Excessive Absences; W=Withdrawn; WP=Withdrawn Passing; W/F=Withdrawn Failing; I=Incomplete; AUD=Audit; P=Pass; N=No Grade Submitted

STUDENT BODY PROFILE
Total enrollment (male/female): 57/326

From in-state: 90%

Other regions: 7 states; 2 foreign countries

Full-time undergraduate (male/female): 59/210

Part-time undergraduate (male/female): 25/89

Ethnic/Racial Makeup
African-American, 364; Caucasian, 15; International, 4.

Class of 1995 Profile
Number of applicants: 470

Number accepted: 470

Number enrolled: 202

FACULTY PROFILE
Number of faculty: 32

Student-faculty ratio: 28:1

Full-time faculty: 26

Part-time faculty: 6

Faculty with doctorates or other terminal degrees: 15%

SCHOOL CALENDAR
1992–93: August 31–April 30 (semesters)

Commencement and conferring of degrees: May

One summer session.

DEGREES OFFERED 1991–92:
Associate of Arts (A. A.)
Business Administration

Business Education

Elementary Education

Liberal Arts/General Studies

Graduates that later obtain higher degrees:
100%

SPECIAL PROGRAMS
A two-day orientation session is offered at no cost to entering students; parents may attend.

Academic remediation is provided for entering students to help bring them to admission standards.

Part-time degree programs and adult continuing education programs are offered during the day and in the evenings.

Career counseling assists students in assessing skills and interests for specific careers.

Student support services provides developmental courses, counseling, and cultural activities to students who need aid to succeed in college.

ATHLETIC PROGRAMS
Concordia College is a member of the Alabama Junior College Conference and the National Junior College Athletic Association.

Intercollegiate sports: men's basketball and women's basketball.

Intramural: basketball, softball, table tennis, and volleyball.

LIBRARY HOLDINGS

The library houses 41,230 bound volumes, 12 microforms, 106 periodical subscriptions, 1,300 audiovisuals, and 40 computer terminals for students use.

STUDENT LIFE

Campus Services

Health services, personal/psychological counseling, career placement, counseling, and tutoring.

Campus Activities

Social and cultural activities include theater/drama and the choral group for singing. Students can get involved in the student-run newspaper, *The Hornet Tribune*.

Leadership opportunities can be found in such groups as the Student Government Association (SGA); Residence Hall Student Services, The Gentlemen's Care Group; Phi Theta Kappa; and the Ambassadors' Club.

The 22-acre campus is located in the small town of Selma, Alabama, the scene of the 1965 Selma to Montgomery march for voters' rights. The city of Selma is within an hour of Montgomery and less than two hours from Birmingham. The cities of Selma, Montgomery and Birmingham are historic landmarks of the civil rights movement led by Dr. Martin Luther King, Jr. Served by bus, rail and air, these cities provide both a rich cultural history and a variety of social activities.

Housing Availability

355 housing spaces available.

Handicapped Services

Wheelchair accessibility.

NOTABLE ALUMNI

Dr. Julius Jenkins–President, Concordia College

J. F. DRAKE STATE
TECHNICAL COLLEGE

HISTORY

J. F. Drake State Technical College is a two-year, state-supported, coed, vocational-technical college founded in 1961 as Huntsville State Vocational Technical School. In 1962, the institution was established on a 30-acre plot donated by Alabama A&M University. In 1966, the school was renamed in honor of Dr. Joseph Fanning Drake, president of Alabama A&M for 35 years. Upon receiving technical college status in 1973, the school was authorized by the State Board of Education to offer the Associate in Applied Technology Degree (AATD) and thus changed its name to J. F. Drake State Technical College.

Drake's mission is to provide vocational-technical education through academic and occupational training—from basic education through two-year technical programs. Students develop marketable skills in vocational-technical areas at J. F. Drake, one of a network of 40 postsecondary institutions of its kind in the state of Alabama.

The 30-acre campus houses 8 buildings in the north central part of Alabama.

ACCREDITATION

J. F. Drake is accredited by the Southern Association of Colleges and Schools to award the Associate in Applied Technology degree. Diplomas and certificates also are awarded.

Other Accreditation

Alabama State Department of Postsecondary Education

COSTS PER YEAR

1992–93 Tuition: $1,200 (in-state); $2,100 (out-state)

Room and board: none

Special fees: $125

3421 Meridan St. N
Huntsville, AL 35811
Phone: (205) 539-8161
Fax: (205) 539-6439

Total Enrollment:
979

Level of Selectivity:
Noncompetitive

Books: $500

Estimated total cost: $1,825 (in-state); $2,725 (out-state)

FINANCIAL AID
Financial Aid Specific to the School

85% of the student body received financial aid during 1991–92.

Police Officers' and Fire Fighters' Survivors Educational scholarships provide tuition assistance and aid with other academic costs for an undergraduate student who is the dependent child or unmarried widow(er) of a law enforcement officer or fire fighter who died in the line of duty. Contact financial aid office for more information.

Job Training Partnership Act (JTPA) program assists dislocated workers or disadvantaged persons with tuition, fees, supplies, tools, and need-based pay of $2.00 an hour for each hour in attendance.

Part-time or temporary employment is available in the various departments. Students should ask their instructor for assistance.

Cooperative Education Program combines classroom study with related paid work experience. The program provides academic credit and full-time status during co-op placement.

Alabama National Guard Educational Assistance Program provides financial assistance to Alabama National Guard members who are residents of the state. Additional information and applications are available from the commander of each national guard unit.

Alabama Student Assistance Program provides assistance to students who are residents of the state and demonstrate financial need.

Trade Readjustment Act (TRA) assists individuals who become unemployed as a result of increased imports and who cannot locate suitable employment without additional training. Candidate must be certified by the Alabama State Employment Agency.

Vocational Rehabilitation program provides grant-in-aid covering fees, books, and supplies for persons with physical disabilities. For more information write to Alabama Vocational Rehabilitation Services, 407 Governors Dr. SW, Huntsville, AL 35801 or to Director of Vocational Rehabilitation, Room 416, State Office Building, Montgomery, AL 36104.

Financial Aid Deadline
Continuous

Financial Aid Contact

Director of Financial Aid, J. F. Drake Technical College, 3421 Meridan St., North, Huntsville, AL 35811; (205) 539-8161.

ADMISSION REQUIREMENTS
Open admission

Entrance Requirements

Graduation from an accredited high school, official high school transcript, proof of immunization against measles, and proof of physical by medical physician; Licensed Practical Nurse (LPN) must past LPN entrance test and interview; JTPA students must submit training authorization form. A $5 application fee is required.

GED students must meet basic admission standards.

Transfer students must submit official transcripts from all previous colleges attended and have a 2.0 GPA (less than 2.0 will be admitted on academic probation). "C" or better course grades are transferable.

Admission Application Deadline

Rolling admission provides no specific date for notification of admission so applicant is informed as soon as admission decision is made.

Admission Contact

Mrs. Mary Malone, Director of Admissions, J. F. Drake State Technical College, Huntsville, AL 35811; (205) 539-8161, Ext. 110.

GRADUATION REQUIREMENTS

A minimum of 61 to 111 hours, depending on program; completion of core requirements to include the following quarter hours: 10 English, 25 mathematics, 5 science, 10 social science, 5 computer science, and 15 vocational-technical.

Grading System

A–F; I=Incomplete, W=Withdrawal; WP=Withdraw Passing; WF=Withdraw Failing; AU=Audit; S=Satisfactory, no credit; U=Unsatisfactory, no credit; IP=In Progress, no credit.

STUDENT BODY PROFILE

Total enrollment (male/female): 734/245

From in-state: 881

Full-time undergraduates (male/female): 439/246

Part-time undergraduates (male/female): 220/74

Ethnic/Racial Makeup

African American, 441; Others/unclassified, 538.

Class of 1995 Profile

Number of applicants: 234

Number accepted: 229

Number enrolled: 200

SCHOOL CALENDAR

1992–93: August–July (quarter hours)

Commencement and conferring of degrees: May

One summer quarter session.

DEGREES OFFERED 1991–92:

Accounting Technology

Air Conditioning and Refrigeration

Automotive Mechanics

Barbering

Carpentry

Computer Information Systems

Cosmetology

Drafting and Design Technology

Graphics and Printing Communications

Industrial Electronics Technology

Machine Tool Technology

Office Management

Practical Nursing

Secretarial and Clerical Technology

Small Engine Repair

Welding

SPECIAL PROGRAMS

Cooperative Education Program combines classroom study with related work experience. The program provides academic credit and full-time status during co-op placement. Student must be able to complete two work periods, and have a "C" average. Contact career development center at college for more information.

Cooperative Study Abroad Program allows students to go to a foreign country for a specified period of time for part of their college education.

Remedial courses are offered to entering students to bring them up to admission standards and to help them adjust for success in college.

LIBRARY HOLDINGS

Computers are available for student use in various locations.

STUDENT LIFE
Special Regulations

Eight mandatory academic counseling sessions

Campus Services

Career counseling and placement and tutorial services.

Campus Activities

Leadership opportunities are found in such organizations as the Vocational Industrial Clubs of America. The National Vocational Technical Honor Society is represented on campus to promote the occupational, vocational, and technical programs. Interested students may become involved with *The Orbit* (student-run newspaper).

Drake Tech is located in northeastern Huntsville, home of the NASA Marshall Space Flight Center, The U.S. Army Missile Command, Strategic Defense Command, The Redstone Arsenal, and a host of high technology industrial centers. The area is one of the fastest growing engineering and technology centers in the South. Huntsville offers students access to museums, shopping, and fine restaurants.

LAWSON STATE
COMMUNITY COLLEGE

HISTORY

Lawson State Community College is a two-year, state-supported, coed college formed in 1975 by the merging of two separate state-supported institutions: Wenonah State Technical Institute, established in 1949, and Lawson State Junior College, established in 1963. Dr. T. A. Lawson was director of the Wenonah State Technical Institute and later assumed the responsibilities as first president of Lawson State Junior College in 1963.

When Wenonah and Lawson became one institution, Lawson State Community College became the only public, two-year, coed community college in central Alabama serving the needs of black students. The school's mission is to provide educational programs and services that are comprehensive, flexible, accessible, and community related. Together, with the Wenonah High School and Wenonah Elementary School, Lawson State Community College helps to form an educational complex for high academic achievement. It is also part of the Alabama College System.

The suburban campus consists of twelve buildings on 98 acres with the academic part of the campus on the northern side of Wilson Road and the technical part on the southern side of Wilson Road. Facilities include a Learning Resource Center, which houses the library, and the Shop Building No. 2 for classes in plumbing, carpentry, cabinet making, and masonry.

ACCREDITATION

Lawson State is accredited by the Southern Association of Colleges and Schools (SACS) to award the Associate of Arts, Associate of Science, and Associate of Applied Science degrees.

Other Accreditation

Alabama State Department

National League for Nursing

3060 Wilson Rd.
Birmingham, AL
35221
Phone: (205) 925-2515
Fax: (205) 929-6316

Total Enrollment:
1,738

Level of Selectivity:
Noncompetitive

COSTS PER YEAR

1992–93 Tuition: $850 (in-state); $1,600 (out-state)

Room and board: none

Special fees: $200

Books: $500

Estimated total cost: $1,550 (in-state); $2,300 (out-state)

FINANCIAL AID

1991–92 Institutional Funding

Number of scholarships and grants: 300

Total amount of scholarships and grants: $35,000

1991–92 Federal and State Funding

Total amount of scholarships and grants: $1,439,025

Financial Aid Specific to the School

86% of the student body received financial aid du8ring 1991–92.

Athletic scholarships are awarded based on criteria established by the scholarship committee and on athletic abilities.

Performance grants are awarded based on criteria established by the scholarship committee and on involvement in the performing arts.

Scholars Bowl Team may award an individual scholarship to students based on merit and talent.

Senior Adult Scholarship Program is a free tuition program for senior citizens sixty years of age and older.

Veterans Administration Educational Assistant Program is available for veterans or survivors and dependents of veterans.

Alabama GI Dependents Scholarship Program offers financial assistance to eligible dependents of disabled veterans who were permanent residents of Alabama prior to entry into military service. Maximum education benefits include tuition, textbooks, and lab fees for four years.

Financial Aid Deadline

April 15

Financial Aid Contact

Sheryl Threate, Coordinator of Financial Aid, Lawson State Community College, 3060 Wilson Rd., Birmingham, AL 35221; (205) 925-2515

ADMISSION REQUIREMENTS

Open admission.

Entrance Requirements

Graduation from an accredited high school and completion of the following Carnegie units: 4 English, 1 mathematics, 1 science, 3 social sciences, and 7 electives.

GED students must meet basic admission requirements.

International students must submit translated copy of all high school transcripts, pass the TOEFL examination with a score of 450 or better, and provide proof of ability to pay all college costs.

Transfer students must submit official transcript of all previous college work, have a 2.0 GPA, and qualify for readmission at previous college or university attended.

Early admission allows academically gifted high school students the opportunity to enroll in college full time before completing high school.

Admission Application Deadline

Open admission except for nursing and medical technology programs.

Admission Contact

Mrs. Myra Davis, Coordinator of Admissions/Records, Lawson State Community College, 3060 Wilson Rd. SW, Birmingham, AL 35221; (205) 925-2515, ext. 309 or Fax: (205) 929-6316.

GRADUATION REQUIREMENTS

A minimum of 96 quarter credits and completion of the core requirements to include 10 quarter hours of mathematics, 10 quarter hours of science, and 3 quarter hours of physical education. 1 computer course is required for business majors; all students must complete at least 24 quarter hours and last year at Lawson State.

Grading System

A–F; FA=Failure for lack of attendance; I=Incomplete; AU=Audit; W=Withdraw; WP=Withdraw Passing; WF=Withdraw Failure; S=Satisfactory; U=Unsatisfactory.

STUDENT BODY PROFILE

Total enrollment (male/female): 574/1,164

From in-state: 1,721

Full-time undergraduates (male/female): 448/908

Part-time undergraduates (male/female): 126/256

Ethnic/Racial Makeup

African American, 1,721; International, 17.

Class of 1995 Profile

Number of applicants: 800

Number accepted: 800

Number enrolled: 792

FACULTY PROFILE

Number of faculty: 80

Student-teacher ratio: 20:1

Full-time faculty: 38

Part-time faculty: 42

Faculty with doctorates or other terminal degrees: 8%

SCHOOL CALENDAR

1992–93: August–June (quarter hours)

Commencement and conferring of degrees: June

One summer session.

DEGREES OFFERED 1991–92:

Associate of Arts

English

General Studies

Health, Physical Education and Recreation

History

Mathematics

Political Science

Pre-Law

Psychology

Sociology

Associate of Science

Business Administration

Business Education

Engineering

Mathematics

Music Education

Pre-dentistry

Pre-medical

Pre-Pharmacy

Science

Teacher Education

Associate of Applied Science

Accounting

Biomedical Equipment Technology

Computer Information System

Criminal Justice

Dietetic Technician

Drafting and Design Technology

Electrical Technology

Electroencephalographic Technician

Electronics

Electronics Engineering

Electronic Engineering Technology

Emergency Medical Technician

Health Data Processing Technician

Legal Secretary

Maintenance Mechanic Technology

Management and Supervision Technology

Medical Assistant

Medical Record Technician

Medical Secretary

Multiple Competency Clinical Technician

Nursing

Occupational Therapy Assistant

Optometric Technician

Physical Therapist Assistant

Radiological Technologist

Recreational Leadership

Respiratory Therapist

Secretarial Science

Social Worker Technician

College Certificates

Auto Body Technology

Barbering

Cabinet Making and Carpentry

Clerical Technology

Commercial Foods Preparation

Commercial Sewing

Cosmetology

Drafting and Design Technology

Electrical Technology

Electronics Technology

Masonry

Micro-Computer Operation and Child
Development

Plumbing and Pipe Fitting

Maintenance Mechanic

Graduates That Later Obtain Higher Degrees:
2%

SPECIAL PROGRAMS

Accelerated High School Program for high school juniors and seniors grants college credit for postsecondary work completed in high school.

Adult and Continuing Education Program is available for nontraditional students returning to school or working full time.

College orientation is offered to entering students at no cost prior to the beginning of classes to acquaint students with the college and to prepare them for college life.

Evening classes are offered to students who wish to complete a two-year program in a professional area, or to students who wish to increase proficiencies and broaden their educational and cultural background.

Honors program offers academically talented students a challenging program of study that includes special classes, seminars, colloquia, cultural activities, and special recognition to motivate participants.

Part-time degree program allows students to earn an undergraduate degree while attending part time.

Remedial courses are offered to entering students to bring them up to admission standards and to help them adjust for success in college.

ROTC provides training in military science for commission as a second lieutenant in the U. S. Air Force. Two- and four-year scholarships are available.

Student Support Services provide developmental courses, counseling, and cultural activities to students who need aid to succeed in college.

Study abroad program in cooperation with other countries allows students to study abroad for part of their degree program.

The Upward Bound program generates academic skills and motivation necessary for success in education beyond high school for at-risk students.

ATHLETIC PROGRAMS

Lawson State is a member of the National Junior College Athletic Association (NJCAA).

Intercollegiate sports: men's basketball; women's basketball. Intramural sports: swimming and diving, tennis, track & field, and volleyball.

Athletic contact:

Mr. Eldridge O. Turner, Chairperson, Department of Physical Education, Lawson State College, 3060 Wilson Rd., Birmingham, AL; (205) 925-2515, Ext. 265.

LIBRARY HOLDINGS

The Learning Resource Center houses 30,000 bound volumes, 160 periodical subscriptions, 12,599 microforms, 1,300 audiovisuals, and 75 computers for student use. A special collection on black history is archived in the Dr. Martin Luther King, Jr. Memorial Collection.

STUDENT LIFE
Campus Regulations

Class attendance required.

Campus Services

Health care, career counseling and placement, student employment, remedial instruction, testing for ACT, and tutoring.

Campus Activities

Social and cultural activities include theater, chorale, and dance. Annual activi-

ties include quarterly convocations, a Christmas musical, Afro-American History Month, Career Fair, Blue and Gold Week, Martin Luther King Celebration, Homecoming, Art Exhibition, and a President's Reception. The Scholar's Bowl Team competes in intercollegiate competition with other Alabama junior colleges.

Students may get involved in the student-run publications or the college television station.

Leadership opportunities are found in the Student Government Association (SGA) and other campus organizations.

Located in the southwest section of Birmingham, Alabama, Lawson State Community College serves students from the entire area of Jefferson and Northern Shelby Counties. The campus is readily accessible to interstates I-59 and I-65, and U.S. Highway 11. Birmingham supports a symphony orchestra, ballet companies, and theater groups. There are public parks for recreational and outdoor activities. Birmingham is the largest city in the state of Alabama and more than half the population is African American.

Handicapped Services

Wheelchair accessibility, counseling, special assistance, and special facilities for the physically challenged.

LOMAX-HANNON JUNIOR COLLEGE

PO Box 779
Greenville, AL 36037
Phone: (205) 382-2115

Total Enrollment:
60

Level of Selectivity:
Noncompetitive

HISTORY

Lomax-Hannon Junior College is a two-year, church-affiliated, coed institution conceived in 1889 during the annual conference at Mt. Zion A.M.E. Zion Church in Montgomery, Alabama. It wasn't until 1893 that the college was established. The purpose of the school was to provide black girls and boys with a high school and junior college education. For a long time this was the only high school in Butler County. In 1968, due to the efforts of Bishop G. Dunston, the college became a quality institution of higher education. The School of Religion was added in the first half of the 20th century, while the high school department was terminated in 1975.

The college's mission is to provide a quality two-year liberal arts program in a humane and Christian environment. It strives to give students an opportunity to become self-motivated, to pursue their own interests, and fulfill their individual needs.

The campus is situated on 20 acres, with seven buildings constructed primarily after 1956. The historic Zion Hall (originally known as the A.M.E. Zion Theological Institute), the oldest building on campus, is listed in the Alabama Register of Landmarks and Heritage. Plans are under way for the restoration and preservation of this unoccupied building. A senior citizen adult day care program is housed in the J. W. Alstork Memorial Building. This privately supported junior college is run by the African Methodist Episcopal Zion Church.

ACCREDITATION

Lomax-Hannon is accredited by the Alabama State Department of Education to award the Associate of Arts and Associate of Science degrees.

COSTS PER YEAR

1992–93 Tuition: $1,965

Room and board: $1,484

Special fees: $125

Books: $400

Estimated total cost: $3,974

FINANCIAL AID
Financial Aid Specific to the School
93% of the student body received financial aid during 1991–92.

Charles Mifflin Smith Memorial Scholarship award is given to a freshman who excels in English and plans to complete the second year at Lomax-Hannon.

Lomax-Hannon awards scholarships or tuition waivers to students demonstrating financial need, talent, or both.

Edna Thomas Scholarship awards $500 to a graduating sophomore with a GPA of 3.0 or above planning to pursue a career in business administration.

The Tuition Financing Plan makes loans available to parents at a low interest rate. The loans must be repaid in monthly installments. Contact Fund for Educational Institution, Manchester, NH 03105, or the Tuition Plan of NH, Inc., 18 School Street, Concord, NH 13301.

Vocational Rehabilitation provides grants to cover fees, books, supplies, and other educational expenses to students with physical disabilities.

Veterans Administration benefits are available to veterans and children of disabled veterans.

Alabama State Student Assistance program is available for students who have lived in Alabama for twelve consecutive months prior to the academic year.

Financial Aid Deadline
March 1 (fall); December 1 (spring).
  Continuing students: April 1 (fall);
  December 1 (spring).

Financial Aid Contact
Director of Financial Aid, Lomax-Hannon Junior College, Greenville, AL 36037; (205) 382-2115.

ADMISSION REQUIREMENTS
Open admissions; SAT or ACT required.

Entrance Requirements
Graduation from an accredited high school; submit official high school transcript and proof of a recent physical. A $10 nonrefundable application fee is required.

Graduates of non-accredited high schools are admitted on a conditional basis for the first semester; they must present official certificates indicating successful completion of a four year course of study at the secondary level, based on 16 carnegie units.

GED students must meet basic admission requirements.

Transfer students are required to submit an official transcript of all college work; must have a grade of "C" or better from former institution; less than 2.0 GPA admitted on probation; academic suspension from other postsecondary institutions may be considered upon appeal to the College Admissions Committee; permanent academic suspension students may appeal to the College Admissions Committee after twelve months.

International students must take the TOEFL examination, provide proof of ability to pay all college costs, submit their transcripts, and have them cleared as satisfactory by the Office of Admissions.

Admission Application Deadline
April 30

Admission Contact
Theodora Crenshaw, Director of Admissions, Lomax-Hannon Junior College, PO Box 779, Greenville, AL 36037; (205) 382-2115.

GRADUATION REQUIREMENTS
A minimum of 60 semester hours and completion of core requirements to include 3 English, 6 mathematics, 12 science, and 6 social science; 2.0 GPA; and completion of

at least 30 hours at Lomax-Hannon Junior College.

Grading System

A–F. I=Incomplete, W=Withdrawal, Audit.

SCHOOL CALENDAR

1992–93: August 22–May 3 (semesters)

Commencement and conferring of degrees: May

DEGREES OFFERED 1991–92:
Associate of Arts (A.A.)

Administrative Assistant

Administrative Secretary

Liberal Arts

Associate of Science (A.S.)

Accounting

SPECIAL PROGRAMS

College Level Examination Program (CLEP) determines, through a series of tests, the academic relevance of nontraditional educational experiences, such as the military, on-the-job training, or other life experiences. Those who obtain a minimum "C" score may be granted college credit for these experiences.

College orientation is offered, at no cost, for two to three days prior to the beginning of classes to acquaint new students with the college and to prepare them for college life.

The Developmental Skills Program helps students develop basic skills in verbal and quantitative areas. Students are selected based on high school transcripts and test scores.

Evening programs are available for people unable to attend classes during the day, but who wish to complete a two-year career program. The program is an extension of the day program.

Summer session is offered for courses in high demand.

A transfer program is offered for students who continue their education in senior colleges or universities for additional training.

Veterans Training allows eligible veterans to enroll in and pursue degree programs. Veterans Administration must approve application for programs before educational assistance is authorized.

ATHLETIC PROGRAMS

Lomax-Hannon is a member of the National Junior College Athletic Association (NJCAA)

LIBRARY HOLDINGS

The library holds 850 bound volumes.

STUDENT LIFE
Campus Services

Personal counseling (individual and group), remediation, and tutoring.

Campus Activities

Located in the city of Greenville, Alabama, Lomax-Hannon is within walking distance from the downtown, where students have access to theaters and shopping. For further travel, bus and rail services are available. Montgomery, the state capital, is 40 miles to the north. Montgomery offers students the Museum of Fine Arts, the State archives, and the History Museum. Mobile is 100 miles to the southeast. Mobile's Mardi Gras, though smaller than that of New Orleans, is supposedly the original American pre-Lenten carnival. Birmingham is 100 miles to the north. Points of interest include the Alabama Sports Hall of Fame Museum, Birmingham Botanical Gardens, Sloss Furnaces National Historical Landmark, and Birmingham Museum of Art. The famous Pensacola beach of Florida is 100 miles to the south. The campus is in a quiet neighborhood, yet close to larger cities for social and cultural activities.

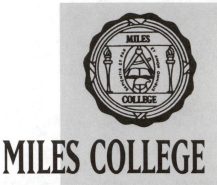

MILES COLLEGE

HISTORY

Miles College is a four-year, private, coed, liberal arts institution founded as Miles Memorial College in 1905 by the Colored Methodist Episcopal Church, which is now called the Christian Methodist Episcopal Church (CME Church). The Alabama and the North Alabama conferences each established educational institutions—one in Thomasville in 1898 and the other at Booker City in 1902. The high school operated at Booker City by the North Alabama conference is considered to be the roots of Miles College.

The reorganization of the school began in 1907, when it became a college and moved to its present site. In 1908, the school was chartered under the laws of the State of Alabama as Miles Memorial College in honor of Bishop William H. Miles, a former slave and ex-minister in the postwar missions of the African Methodist denominations. The first baccalaureate degree was awarded in 1911, the same year the Board of Trustees changed the name to Miles

PO Box 3800
Birmingham, AL
35208
Phone: (205) 923-2771
Toll-free in-state:
800-445-0708
Fax: (205) 923-9292

Total Enrollment:
751

Level of Selectivity:
Noncompetitive

Motto:
Sapienta et pax et amor ominibus
(Knowledge and peace and love for all)

College. Miles College was the only four-year college open to black students for the first half of the twentieth century.

Miles' original mission to provide quality education for the academically disadvantaged and to provide community service, continues today. In keeping with the religious origin and liberal arts tradition, the college assists students in acquiring respect for religious creeds in general, and for the Christian ethnic in particular. The school urges students to fulfill their human and intellectual potentials, and to develop the skills in communication and scholarship necessary for productive lives in American mainstream society.

Comprising 21 buildings, Miles College rests on 35 acres, about six miles west of downtown Birmingham.

ACCREDITATION

Miles College is accredited by the Southern Association of Colleges and Schools (SACS) to award the Bachelor of Arts and Bachelor of Science degrees.

Other Accreditation

Alabama State Department of Education

COSTS PER YEAR

1992–93 Tuition: $3,800

Room and board: $900 (room); $1,400 (board)

Special fees: $650

Books: $400

Estimated total cost: $7,150

FINANCIAL AID
1991–92 Institutional Funding

Number of scholarships and grants: 638

Total amount of scholarships and grants: $272,327

Range of scholarships and grants: $500–$3,800

1991–92 Federal and State Funding

Number of scholarships and grants: 535

Total amount of scholarships and grants: $1,530,433

Range of scholarships and grants: $1,000–$2,500

Number of work-study: 263

Total amount of work-study: $334,346

Financial Aid Specific to the School

85% of the student body received financial aid during 1991–92.

Dean's Scholarship-A is awarded to qualified students with a 3.3 GPA, and Dean's Scholarship-B is awarded to qualified student with at least a 3.0 GPA.

Endowment and Friends of the College have several scholarships available to qualified students based on merit, need, and interests.

The Bishop Scholarship recipients must have a high school GPA of 3.5 to 3.75 and an SAT score of 999 or ACT score of 21.2.

The President's Scholarships are awarded to students who rank in the upper 5% of their class with a GPA of 3.75 to 4.0 and an SAT score of 1100 or ACT composite of 23.

Athletic Grant-in-Aid is offered to students accepted and eligible to participate in the intercollegiate athletic program.

The G. A. Brown Scholarship of $1,000 is offered to an entering freshman student with a GPA of 3.0 majoring in biology, mathematics, or chemistry.

Performance scholarship in band is awarded to an outstanding student who desires to participate in the Miles College Band. An audition is required.

Special Loan Funds assist students who experience unforeseen expenses.

Installment plan allows student to pay college costs in agreed upon installments for a small fee.

Institutional Work-Study Program (IWSP) is available to students not qualifying for college work-study to work in departments of the college.

United Negro College Fund (UNCF) scholarships are awarded to a limited number of students at this school who demonstrate financial need. Some scholarships may be based on location and merit. UNCF scholarships range from $500 to $7,500.

Army and Air Force ROTC offer two- and three-year scholarships that pay tuition, fees, books, and other expenses, and provide a monthly stipend of $100.

Financial Aid Deadline
March 15

Financial Aid Contact
Mrs. Betty B. Edwards, Director of Financial Aid, Miles College, PO Box 3800, Birmingham, AL 35208-0937; (205) 923-2771, ext. 225.

ADMISSION REQUIREMENTS
Open admission. SAT or ACT required for counseling or placement.

Entrance Requirements
Graduation from high school with a minimum of 15 units to include 3 English, 1 history, 3 mathematics, 3 natural science, 3 social science, 2 foreign language, and electives (not more than 2 units); official high school transcript; three letters of character recommendations (one from counselor or teacher); completed medical form by physician; proof of immunization against vaccine-preventable disease. A $25 nonrefundable application fee required.

GED students must submit official copy of GED certificate and meet basic admission requirements.

International students must take the TOEFL examination and provide proof of ability to pay all college costs.

Transfer students must submit transcript of all previous college work, have a minimum 2.0 GPA, qualify for readmission at previous college or university attended, and submit standardized test scores.

Admission Application Deadline
Rolling admission provides no specific date for notification of admission so applicant is informed as soon as admission decision is made; July 1 (fall priority); November 15 (spring priority); April 15 (summer priority).

Admission Contact
Mrs. Gloria Beverly, Director of Recruitment and Admissions, Miles College, PO Box 3800, Birmingham, AL 35208-093; (205) 923-2771, ext. 225 or 226; toll-free: 800-445-0708; fax: (205) 923-9292.

GRADUATION REQUIREMENTS
A minimum of 124 semester hours for bachelor's degree to include the following hours: six mathematics, six science, and a computer course for all students; students must complete 30 hours in residence.

Grading System
A-F; NC=Audit; I=Incomplete; WP= Withdrew Passing; and WF=Withdrew Failing.

STUDENT BODY PROFILE
Total enrollment (male/female): 360/391

From in-state: 588

Other regions: 21 states

Full-time undergraduates (male/female): 300/313

Part-time undergraduates (male/female): 64/74

Ethnic/Racial Makeup
African American, 749; Caucasian, 2.

Class of 1995 Profile
Number of applicants: 281

Number accepted: 281

Number enrolled: 161

FACULTY PROFILE

Number of faculty: 55

Student-teacher ratio: 18:1

Full-time faculty: 41

Part-time faculty: 14

Tenured faculty: 1

Faculty with doctorates or other terminal degrees: 42%

SCHOOL CALENDAR

1992–93: (semester hours)

Commencement and conferring of degrees: May

One summer session.

DEGREES OFFERED AND NUMBER CONFERRED 1991–92:
Bachelor of Arts

English: n/a

English Literature: 5

History and Government: n/a

Music: 1

Political Science: 4

Social Sciences: 10

Bachelor of Science

Accounting: n/a

Biology Education: 2

Business: 32

Business Administration: n/a

Chemistry/Chemistry Education: 3

Communications: 4

Elementary Education: 11

English Education: n/a

History Education: n/a

Language Arts Education: n/a

Mathematics Education: 2

SPECIAL PROGRAMS

Accelerated Study Program allows students to complete their undergraduate degree in a shorter period of time than the traditional period of four years.

Adult or Continuing Education Program is available for nontraditional students returning to school or working full time.

College Level Examination Program (CLEP) determines the academic relevance of nontraditional educational experiences, such as the military, on-the-job training or other life experiences, through a series of tests and may grant students college credit for these experiences.

College orientation is offered at no cost to entering students and their parents prior to the beginning of classes to acquaint students with the college and to prepare them for college life.

Cooperative Education Program combines classroom study with related paid work experience. The program provides academic credit and full-time status during co-op placement.

Cooperative Program allows students to take college credit toward their degree programs in engineering, physics, and veterinary medicine at eight predominantly black colleges in Alabama.

Cross registration allows students from Miles to take courses at the University of Alabama for credit toward a degree program.

Honors program offers academically talented students a challenging program of study that includes special classes, seminars, colloquia, cultural activities, and special recognition to motivate participants.

Off-campus study allows students to take courses at the University of Alabama in Birmingham and at Birmingham-Southern for credit.

Part-time degree programs allow students to earn an undergraduate degree while attending part time.

ROTC provides training in military science for commission as a second lieutenant in the U. S. Army or Air Force. Two-, three–, and four-year scholarships are available.

Student Support Services provide developmental courses, counseling, and cultural activities to students who need aid to succeed in college.

Three/two degree program in engineering allows students to get two degrees—one in liberal arts from home school and one in engineering from Tuskegee—by completing three years at matriculated school and two years at cooperating school.

Three/two degree program in veterinary medicine allows students to get two degrees—one in liberal arts from home school and one in veterinary medicine from Tuskegee—by completing three years at matriculated school and two years at cooperating school.

ATHLETIC PROGRAMS

Miles College is a member of the National Collegiate Athletic Association (NCAA), all Division II; and the Southern Intercollegiate Athletic Conference (SIAC).

Intercollegiate sports: men's basketball, cross-country, football, track & field; women's basketball.

Intramural sports: basketball, cross-country, gymnastics, soccer, swimming and diving, tennis, track & field, volleyball, and weight lifting.

Athletic Contact

Dr. Carolyn Ray, Miles College, Birmingham, AL 35208; (205) 923-2771, ext. 243.

LIBRARY HOLDINGS

The library holds 180,000 bound volumes, 850 microforms, and 250 periodical subscriptions.

STUDENT LIFE
Campus Regulations

Class and church attendance are required; must maintain a 2.5 GPA to join social organizations; on-campus residents must purchase meal plan.

Campus Services

Health, personal and psychological counseling, tutoring, and student support.

Campus Activities

Social activities include theater, the College Concert Choir, concerts, band, and dances. Students may work on *Columns* (student newspaper) or the *Milean* (yearbook).

Leadership opportunities are found in the Student Government Association, the pre-alumni counsel, the student library action committee, or the various other departmental, social, and service organizations. Greek-letter fraternities include Alpha Phi Alpha, Omega Psi Phi, Kappa Alpha Psi, and Phi Beta Sigma; sororities include Alpha Kappa Alpha, Delta Sigma Theta, Sigma Gamma Rho, and Zeta Phi Beta. Honor societies include Alpha Kappa Mu.

Miles College is located six miles west of downtown Birmingham, Alabama, the state's largest city, with a metropolitan population of over 900,000. Miles College is an integral part of the community. Public bus transportation allows students to travel to and from the campus. The city is served by major airlines and passenger rail. Birmingham supports a symphony orchestra, ballet companies, theater groups, and public parks for fun and relaxation.

Housing Availability

370 housing spaces available.

NOTABLE ALUMNI

Richard Arrington, Jr., 1955–Mayor, Birmingham, Alabama

Joseph Black, 1982–Former vice president, Special Markets, Greyhound

Fred Horn, 1950–U.S. senator

Andrew Sneed, Jr.–Special Program coordinator, Alabama State University

Perry W. Ward–President, Lawson State Community College

Luther Steward Williams, 1961–Associate directorate, National Science Foundation

OAKWOOD COLLEGE

Oakwood Rd.
Huntsville, AL 35896
Phone: (205) 726-7000
Toll-free in-state:
800-544-4183
Toll-free out-state:
800-824-5312
Fax: (205) 726-7409

Total Enrollment:
1,334

Level of Selectivity:
Noncompetitive

Motto:
Today's College for
Tomorrow's Leaders

HISTORY

Oakwood College is a four-year, coed, liberal arts college affiliated with the Seventh-day Adventist Church. Oakwood was founded 1896 as the Oakwood Industrial School. In 1904, the name was changed to Oakwood Manual Training School, and it was chartered to grant degrees in 1907. In 1917, the school offered its first instruction at the post-secondary level, and in that same year it changed its name to Oakwood Junior College. In 1944, the present name Oakwood College was adopted. The first bachelor's degrees were awarded in 1945.

Oakwood College has been a member of the United Negro College Fund since 1964. As a Seventh-day Adventist college, Oakwood's mission is "Christ-centered, and designed to integrate faith and learning, as well as prepare students for the job of service in this world."

The 23-building campus occupies 1,185 acres in Huntsville, Alabama. The main campus is on 105 acres, with another 500 acres under cultivation. The campus continues to grow in both programs and facilities. The J. L. Moran building, constructed in 1939, stands with more recently erected buildings such as the Trula E. Wade Residence Hall, constructed in 1991.

ACCREDITATION

Oakwood College is accredited by the Southern Association of Colleges and Schools to award the Bachelor of Arts, Bachelor of Science, Associate of Arts, and Associate of Science degrees.

Other Accreditation

American Dietetic Asociation

National Council for the Accreditation of Teacher Education Council on Social Work Education.

COSTS PER YEAR

1992–93 Tuition: $6,216

Room and board: $1,764 (room); $2,160 (board)

Special fees: $200

Books: $600

Estimated total cost: $10,940

FINANCIAL AID
1991–92 Institutional Funding

Number of scholarships and grants: 210

Total amount of scholarships and grants: $366,934

1991–92 Federal and State Funding

Number of scholarships and grants: 893

Total amount of scholarships and grants: $1,283,100

Number of loans: 674

Total amount of loans: $2,352,934

Number of work-study: 115

Total amount of work-study: $171,150

Financial Aid Specific to the School

72% of the student body received financial aid during 1991–92.

Academic scholarships are available to entering students including transfer students with a 3.0 or better GPA. Also available are scholarships for valedictorians, salutatorians, or class presidents. Academic scholarships are automatically awarded by the Admissions and Records Office.

The Cooperative Program number two is an off-campus employment program with local businesses or professional organizations. Qualifying students must get approval from the office of financial aid.

Performance scholarships are available for Oakwood College class presidents, yearbook editor, and school paper editor.

Three endowed scholarships are available: the Student Missionary, Worthy Student, and Lettie C. Pate awards. These scholarships are available through the Financial Aid Office.

United Negro College Fund (UNCF) scholarships are available to a limited number of entering students scoring high on ACT or ETS exams or having a high school GPA of 3.0. Students must maintain a cumulative GPA of 3.0 in college to renew scholarships.

The Work Education Program (WEP) is designed to develop student work skills and provide financial assistance for educational cost.

Financial Aid Deadline

April 15 (fall & spring)

Financial Aid Contact

Director of Financial Aid, Oakwood College, Huntsville, AL 35896; (205) 726-7208 in Alabama, 800-824-5321 toll free out-state.

ADMISSION REQUIREMENTS

SAT or ACT required

Entrance Requirements

Official high school transcripts with a minimum 2.0 GPA, including a minimum of 11 units: 4 English, 2 mathematics, 2 science, 2 social studies, 1 typing; two character references from a principal, counselor, teacher, or pastor, A $10 nonrefundable application fee is required.

GED students with certificates are accepted. Must meet regular admission standards.

Transfer students must submit previous college transcripts and a statement of honorable dismissal. A maximum of 96 quarter hours may be accepted from a junior college. Only work completed with a 2.0 or above will be transferred from another college. The ACT or SAT requirement will be waived if applicant has completed one quarter or semester each of college level English and mathematics with a grade of "C" or above.

International students must meet requirements for regular admission and students form non-English-speaking countries must have a minimum TOEFL examination score of 500.

Early admission allows qualified students to enter college full time before completing high school.

Admission Application Deadline

Rolling admission provides no specific date for notification of admission so applicant is informed as soon as admission decision is made; early decision provides notification of acceptance early in applicant's twelfth year of high school.

Admission Contact

Director of Admissions and Records, Oakwood College, Huntsville, AL 35896; 800-824-5312 toll free out-state, 800-544-4183 toll free in-state.

GRADUATION REQUIREMENTS

Bachelor's degree candidates must satisfactorily complete a minimum of 192 quarter hours to include the general education requirements with a cumulative GPA of 2.0 or better. Students must complete all required remedial courses, remove all admission deficiencies, and take an exit examination.

Associate's degree candidates must satisfactorily complete 96 quarter hours to in-

Eva B. Dykes Library, Oakwood College

clude the general education requirements. Students must complete all required remedial courses, remove any admission deficiencies, and take an exit examination; a minimum of 24 quarter hours must be taken at Oakwood College.

Grading System

A-F; FA=Failure due to Absences; AU=Audit; DG=Deferred grade; I=Incomplete; NC=Non-credit; P/U=Pass/Unsatisfactory; W=Withdrew

STUDENT BODY PROFILE

Total enrollment (male/female): 627/707

From in-state: 239

Full-time undergraduates (male/female): 575/649

Part-time undergraduates (male/female): 52/58

Ethnic/Racial Makeup

African American, 1,153; Hispanic, 2; Native American, 1; Caucasian, 3; International, 154; Other/unclassified, 24.

Class of 1995 Profile
Number of applicants: 908

Number accepted: 577

Number enrolled: 352

Median SAT score: 379V; 371M

Median ACT score: 16

Average high school GPA: 2.81

Transfer applicants: 77

Transfers accepted: 77

Transfers enrolled: 67

FACULTY PROFILE
Number of faculty: 120

Student-teacher ratio: 12:1

Full-time faculty: 76

Part-time faculty: 46

Tenured faculty: 33

Faculty with doctorates or other terminal degrees: 66%

SCHOOL CALENDAR
1992–93: September–May (quarters)

Commencement and conferring of degrees: May

One six-week summer session.

DEGREES OFFERED AND NUMBER CONFERRED 1991–92:
Bachelor of Arts
Arts: 1

Biology: 24

Chemistry: 1

Communications: n/a

English: 1

History: 9

Music: 2

Physical Education: n/a

Psychology: 4

Religion: n/a

Social Work: 16

Theology: 21

Bachelor of Science
Accounting: 12

Biochemistry: 5

Biology: n/a

Business Education: 1

Business Management: 5

Chemistry: n/a

Chemistry Education: n/a

Computer Science: 6

Early Childhood Education: 1

Economics: 2

Elementary Education: 8

English Education: n/a

Food and Nutrition: 2

General Studies: 1

History Education: n/a

Home Economics Education: n/a

Human Development and Family Studies: 5

Language Arts Education: 1

Mathematics: 1

Mathematics Education: n/a

Medical Technology: 2

Music Education: n/a

Natural Science: 3

Nursing: 15

Office Systems Management: n/a

Philosophy: 3

Physical Education: n/a

Psychology: n/a

Religious Education: 1

Social Science Education: n/a

SPECIAL PROGRAMS
The Advanced Placement Program (AP) allows high school students to take various courses for college credit during their junior or senior year in high school. Credits toward graduation are granted to entering

freshmen who have passed one or more AP examinations with a score of 3, 4, or 5.

Adventist College Abroad (ACA) consortium provides opportunities to qualified undergraduate students for study in other countries with credit applied to requirements for their degree programs at their home colleges.

The College Level Examination Program (CLEP) grants college credit for non-traditional educational experiences such as the military, work, or other life experience by taking the CLEP exam administered by the College Entrance Examination Board.

Cooperative Program number one allows students to request permission to attend a class offered at one the cooperating institutions, including Alabama A&M University, Athens State College, John C. Calhoun State Community College, The University of Alabama in Huntsville, and Oakwood College.

Cooperative Program number two allows students to work at off-campus business or professional establishments.

The dual degree offers a Bachelor of Science degree in Natural Science from Oakwood and a medical, dental, or optometry degree from a profession school, upon completion of three years in an accredited undergraduate program, of which at least the last year was at Oakwood. Upon successful completion of the first year of medical, dental, or optometry program, student receives a B.S. in natural science; upon successful completion of program at respective professional school, student receives a professional degree.

The Freshman Studies Program is a composite of diagnostic, instructional, and supportive services to first-year students. Components of the program include college orientation, diagnostic assessment (administered to all new freshmen who have not taken the ACT or SAT during freshman orientation week), academic advisement, and program planning.

Home Study International credits, from the Extension Division of the Associated Colleges of Seventh-day Adventists, are accepted by Oakwood College.

A research and independent study course is available in certain departments to provide qualified students an opportunity to work on problems or topics of special interest, to engage in research projects, and to do scholarly study as advanced work.

Student Missionary Program allows several Oakwood students to go to foreign lands and serve as missionaries.

ATHLETIC PROGRAMS

Intramural sports: basketball, flagball, softball, and swimming.

LIBRARY HOLDINGS

The Eva B. Dykes Library holds over 109,317 volumes. Special collections include black studies materials and materials related to Seventh-day Adventist black history, which are housed in a special museum exhibit room.

STUDENT LIFE
Special Regulations

All registered students (on and off campus) are required to attend chapel; freshmen are not permitted to bring automobiles to the college or operate automobiles owned by other individuals; all unmarried students are required to live in one of the college residence halls and to board in the college cafeteria unless they live with parents or with other close relatives in the area; students must maintain a 2.0 for membership in extracurricular activities and a 2.5 to hold office.

Campus Services

Health, career planning and placement, academic support, peer-tutoring, religious services (including chapel), Sabbath School, student literature evangelism program, residence hall worship hours, and many prayer bands.

Campus Activities

Social and group activities include religious convocations conducted by distinguished guest speakers. The arts and lecture series brings lecturers and artists to campus. Students can join the yearbook staff or the student-run newspaper staff. Communication majors can work at the student-run radio station, WOCG.

Leadership opportunities are found in such groups as the United Student Movement (USM), Adventist Youth Society (ATS), Ministerial Forum, residence clubs, or various department clubs in science, pre-law, business, education, social work, music, home economics or nursing.

Oakwood College is located in Huntsville, Alabama, in the north central part of the state, with a population of approximately 160,000. The campus is 5 miles northwest of downtown. Major bus lines and airlines service the city, as well as local taxi service. The city of Huntsville is home to one of the major space research and development centers in the world. Many department stores are available to students in the Madison Square Mall. Constitution Hall Village offers a glimpse of southern life in the early 1800s. The Madison County Nature Trail provides a sanctuary of wildlife, and several museums and theaters provide a wealth of culture and entertainment.

Housing Availability

1,142 housing spaces; 534 freshman spaces.

NOTABLE ALUMNI

Dr. Thelma D. Anderson–Chairperson, Albany State College Business Department

Ina M. Boon–Former director, NAACP Region IV, St. Louis, MO

Clifton Davis (theology degree from Oakwood College)–Star of TV's "AMEN"

Lloyd B. Mallory–Concert director, Lincoln University (PA)

Witley A. Phipps–Pastor, Capitol Hill S.D.A. Church, Washington, D.C.

Dr. Benjamin F. Reaves, 1955–President, Oakwood College

SELMA UNIVERSITY

1501 Lapsley St.
Selma, AL 36701
Phone: (205) 872-2533
Fax: (205) 872-7746

Total Enrollment:
287

Level of Selectivity:
Noncompetitive

HISTORY

Selma University (SU) is a four-year, private, coed, liberal arts institution affiliated with the Alabama State Missionary Baptist Convention. It was founded in 1878 as the Alabama Baptist Normal and Theological School to train blacks to become ministers and teachers. Later that year, the school purchased the old Selma Fair Grounds and moved into the exposition buildings.

Selma University was incorporated in 1881 under its second president who was born a slave. In 1884, under its third president, the first class of 11 men and women graduated. The institution was officially named Selma University in 1908, enabling it to confer degrees and grant diplomas. The university included an elementary school, high school, college, and theological school until 1956 when the pre-college programs were discontinued.

Owned and supported by the Alabama State Missionary Baptist Convention, Inc., SU continues to provide higher education to the black constituency in the state of Alabama, to the Selma community, and to the "Black Belt" region of the state. SU is dedicated to preparing students for useful and responsible living and for Christian leadership.

The 35-acre, 12-building campus includes the Jemison-Owen Auditorium-Gymnasium, the Stone-Robinson Library, and the New Dinkins Memorial Chapel, rebuilt in 1920 after a fire destroyed the previous chapel. Most campus facilities were built before 1980.

ACCREDITATION

Selma University is accredited by the Southern Association of Colleges and Schools (SACS) to award the Associate of Arts, Associate of Science, Bachelor of Arts in Religion, and the Bachelor of Science degrees.

Other Accreditation

State of Alabama Department of Education

COSTS PER YEAR

1992–93 Tuition: $3,440

Room and board: $2,200

Special fees: $125

Books: $500

Estimated total cost: $6,265

FINANCIAL AID

1991–92 Institutional Funding

Total amount of scholarships and grants: $90,209

1991–92 Federal and State Funding

Total amount of scholarships and grants: $1,309,765

Financial Aid Specific to the School

95% of the student body received financial aid during 1991–92.

Athletic scholarships are awarded to students participating in intercollegiate basketball and baseball.

E. W. Lindsey and W. J. Bonner Scholarship is awarded to one or two students from Pickens County. Athletes are not eligible to receive this scholarship.

Performance Scholarships in music are awarded to talented students participating in choir, band, dance, or drama.

Minority Biomedical Research Support Program in the Natural Sciences provides qualified students a salary of $4,200 per year and $700 for travel allowance. Students must maintain a "B" average in all science and mathematics courses.

College work-aid is available to students not qualifying for college work-study to work in departments of the college.

Army ROTC offers two- and three-year scholarships that pay tuition, fees, books, and other expenses, and provides a monthly stipend of $100.

Religion Scholarships are awarded to any licensed minister, regardless of denomination.

Association Scholarships are sponsored by many associations affiliated with the Alabama Baptist State Convention. Scholarships range from $50 to $200.

The Charles A. Tunstall Scholarship is awarded to a minister in the Division of Religion who is in need of financial assistance.

The Frank Milton Smith Memorial Scholarship is given to a minister or ministers in the Division of Religion.

Greater Saint Mark Baptist Church Scholarship is given annually to a student or students in the area of Christian Education or Religion.

Financial Aid Deadline

April 15

Financial Aid Contact

Director of Financial Aid, Selma University, 1501 Lapsley St., Selma, AL 36701; (205) 872-2533.

ADMISSION REQUIREMENTS

Open admission

Entrance Requirements

Graduation from an accredited high school and completion of the following units: 3 English, 1 mathematics, 2 science, and 3 social science; submit official high school transcript; submit letters of recommendation; and have a physical examination.

GED students must meet basic admission requirements.

International students must take the TOEFL examination and provide proof of ability to pay all college costs.

Transfer students must submit high school and college transcripts, provide recommendations, and qualify for readmission at previous college or university attended.

Admission Application Deadline

August 26; rolling admission provides no specific date for notification of admission so applicant is informed as soon as admission decision is made.

Admission Contact

Raymond C. Brown, Director of Admissions, Selma University, Selma, AL 36701; (205) 872-2533, ext. 29.

GRADUATION REQUIREMENTS

A minimum of 66 semester hours and completion of the core requirements for an associate's degree; a minimum of 126 semester hours and completion of 6 hours of mathematics, 6 hours of science, and 1 computer course for certain majors for a bachelor's degree.

Grading System

A-F; FA=Failure for excessive absence; I=Incomplete; AU=Audit; WP=Withdrawal Passing; WF=Withdrawal Failing; P=Pass; F=Fail; NC=Non-Credit.

STUDENT BODY PROFILE

Total enrollment (male/female): 158/129

From in-state: 273

Full-time undergraduates (male/female): 133/111

Part-time undergraduates (male/female): 22/19

Ethnic/Racial Makeup

African American, 273; Other/unclassified, 14.

Class of 1995 Profile

Number of applicants: 200

Number accepted: 200

Number enrolled: 124

Transfers enrolled: 12

FACULTY PROFILE

Number of faculty: 27

Student-teacher ratio: 11:1

Full-time faculty: 19

Part-time faculty: 8

SCHOOL CALENDAR

1992–93: August–May (semester hours)

Commencement and conferring of degrees: May

One summer session.

DEGREES OFFERED 1991–92:

Associate of Arts

English

History

Liberal Arts/General Education

Music

Associate of Science

Computer Science

Mathematics and Physics

Physical Education

Political Science

Sociology

Associate of Applied Science

Data Processing
Secretarial Science

Bachelor of Arts

Religion

Bachelor of Science

Biology

Business Administration and Management

Information Systems

Certificate

Bible and Theology

SPECIAL PROGRAMS

College orientation is offered at no cost to entering students prior to the beginning of classes to acquaint students with the college and to prepare them for college life.

English as a Second Language is a program that offers courses in English for students whose native language is not English.

Honors Program offers academically talented students a challenging program of study that includes special classes, seminars, colloquia, cultural activities, and special recognition to motivate participants.

Individualized Majors allow students to create their own major program(s) of study.

Part-time degree program allows students to earn an undergraduate degree while attending part time.

Remedial courses are offered to entering students to bring them up to admission standards and to help them adjust for success in college.

ROTC provides training in military science for commission as a second lieutenant in the U.S. Army. Two- and four-year scholarships are available.

Student Support Services provide developmental courses, counseling, and cultural activities to students who need aid to succeed in college.

Upward Bound provides academic counseling and cultural enrichment programs to high school students in grades 10, 11, and 12 who are disadvantaged and are in pursuit of college education. Some credit courses may be offered.

ATHLETIC PROGRAMS

Selma University is a member of the National Junior College Athletic Association (NJCAA).

Intercollegiate sports: men's baseball, basketball, and track; women's basketball.

Intramural sports: basketball, softball, and volleyball.

Athletic Contact

Homer Davis, Jr., Director of Athletics, Selma University, 1501 Lapsley St., Selma, AL 36701; (205) 872-9745.

LIBRARY HOLDINGS

The Stone-Robinson Library holds 45,000 bound volumes, 30 periodical subscriptions, 275 audiovisuals; 25 computers for student use in the computer center.

STUDENT LIFE
Campus Regulations

Cars must be registered; class attendance and chapel mandatory; students must live on campus and purchase meal cards unless they commute from home; all freshmen required to take Freshman Experience for one credit.

Campus Services

Health, personal counseling, remediation, and tutoring.

Campus Activities

Social and cultural activities include musical concerts and a Lyceum Series. Annual activities include Founder's Day, Religious Emphasis Week, Freshman-Sophomore Ball, Greek and Club Shows, Class Talent Shows, and the Coronation Ball. The campus quarterly publication is the *Selma University Chronicle*.

Leadership opportunities are found in the Student Government Association (SGA). Greek-letter societies include one national fraternity and one national sorority. Phi Theta Kappa national honor society and one local honor society are represented on campus.

Located in Selma, Alabama, the campus is within walking distance to the nearby shopping center and only 45 miles west of Montgomery, the state capital. In 1965, the famous march for civil rights for blacks on the Pettus Bridge led by Martin Luther King, Jr. originated in the Brown Chapel Church in Selma, Alabama.

Housing Availability

200 housing spaces; first-come, first-served basis.

NOTABLE ALUMNI

Alvin A. Cleveland, Sr.–Religion professor, Selma University

Burnest Webster Dawson–President, Selma University

STILLMAN COLLEGE

WELCOME TO
STILLMAN COLLEGE
FOUNDED 1876

3600 Stillman Blvd.
Tuscaloosa, AL 35403
Phone: (205) 349-4240
Toll-free in-state:
800-523-6331
Toll-free out-state:
800-841-5722
Fax: (205) 758-0821

Total Enrollment:
822

Level of Selectivity:
Noncompetitive

Motto:
We Can Do It
Better Together

HISTORY

Stillman College is a four-year, coeducational, private college affiliated with the Presbyterian Church. Stillman began in 1876 as Tuscaloosa Institute, a school for the theological training of African American ministers. In 1898, the school's name changed to Stillman Institute, and in 1948, it changed to Stillman College.

The educational focus of Stillman grew well beyond theology as other academic programs were added. In 1899, the general assembly approved the enrollment of women. In 1948, the school became a four-year, liberal arts institution, and it awarded its first bachelor's degrees in 1951.

"Proud of its history and its relationship to the Presbyterian Church, Stillman aims to utilize the best of its heritage as it moves into the future by providing an environment that is both Christian and intellectual." The college's enrollment is small enough to permit personalized and individualized attention to students while providing a vast educational experience.

Stillman College's 15-building campus spreads over 100 picturesque acres within the city of Tuscaloosa, Alabama. Though Italian Renaissance architecture is predominant, most building interiors are completely renovated.

Stillman is committed to increasing the number of freshmen who complete their bachelor's degrees within 5 years. The school recently received funding for two programs: Bell South Foundation provided $70,000 to enhance the freshman experience, and the United Negro College Fund and Lilly Endowment gave money to track students from recruitment to graduation, with a focus on retention. The college became a United Negro College Fund (UNCF) member school in 1963.

ACCREDITATION

Stillman College is accredited by the Southern Association of Colleges and Schools to award the Bachelor of Arts and Bachelor of Science degrees.

Other Accreditation

American Council on Education

Alabama State Department of Education

COSTS PER YEAR

1992–93 Tuition: $4,460

Room and board: $1,071 (room); $1,683 (board)

Special fees: $50

Books: $800

Estimated total cost: $8,064

FINANCIAL AID
1991–92 Institutional Funding

Number of scholarships and grants: 250

Total amount of scholarships and grants: $695,000

Range of scholarships and grants: $600–$2,780

1991–92 Federal and State Funding

Number of scholarships and grants: 1,520

Total amount of scholarships and grants: $1,495,656

Range of scholarships and grants: $600–$1,800

Number of loans: 460

Total amount of loans: $920,000

Range of loans: $750–$2,188

Number of work-study: 250

Total amount of work-study: $181,970

Range of work-study: $728 average

Financial Aid Specific to the School

92% of the student body received financial aid during 1991–92.

The Academic Management Services Budget Payment Plan allows payment of college cost in ten monthly payments. This plan includes life benefit coverage, and it costs $45.00.

The Alabama Student Grant Program (ASGP) is available to residents of the state attending independent, non-profit institutions.

The Army ROTC scholarships offers two-, three-, and four-year scholarships that pay tuition, books, and other expenses, and provide a monthly stipend of $100.

The Bellingrath Scholarship is awarded to students of exceptional academic talent. The scholarship covers tuition, room and board, books, and personal expenses.

The Cordell and Marie Wynn scholarships are awarded to students based on leadership service, character, and academic success.

The Eckerd award is based on academic achievement.

Full or partial tuition waivers are available for Stillman College employees and their children.

The installment plan permits payment of tuition and board in 8 installments or as agreed, with a percentage rate of 15% on unpaid balance.

The Performing Arts scholarships are awarded to students who are exceptional in vocal or instrumental music and participate in the choir or band.

United Negro College Fund (UNCF) scholarships are available to entering students who score high on ACT or ETS exams or students with a high school GPA of 3.0 or better. Students must maintain a cumulative GPA of 3.0 in college to renew scholarships.

Financial Aid Deadline

March 1 (priority); June 15 (fall); December 1 (spring)

Financial Aid Contact

Dr. Richard Cosby, Director of Financial Aid, Stillman College, PO Box 1430, Tuscaloosa, AL 35403; (205) 349-4240, ext. 231.

ADMISSION REQUIREMENTS

Open admission; SAT or ACT must be on file.

Entrance Requirements

A high school diploma with at least 15 units: 4 English, 1 mathematics, 1 science, 1 history, and 8 electives. Must have a "C" average in the courses noted above. A nonrefundable fee of $10.00 must be submitted with application.

GED students must have a minimum passing score of 40 for each area and an overall score of 45.

Transfer students must have a "C" average or better for unconditional admission. Two-year institution transfers with programs complimentary to Stillman are accepted with advanced standing.

International students must meet regular admission requirements. Students must submit proof of adequate funds to cover all college costs and must pass the TOEFL exam with a minimum score of 500. Foreign students from English-speaking countries are exempt from the TOEFL exam.

Stillman College Campus

Conditional admission students must have a GPA of at least 1.60 and the 15 units needed for regular admission.

Admission Application Deadline

August 15 (fall); December 15 (spring); April 15 (summer). Rolling admission provides no specific date for notification of admission so applicant is informed as soon as admission decision is made; early admission allows qualified students to enter college full time before completing high school.

Admission Contact

Office of Admissions, Stillman College, PO Box 1430, Tuscaloosa, AL 35403; (205) 349-4250, fax: (205) 758-0821.

GRADUATION REQUIREMENTS

Student must complete at least 124 semester hours to include 58 hours of core or general education requirements. Must have a 2.0 in major area or 2.5 for a teaching certificate. Students must pass tests in English, reading, and mathematics by sophomore year.

Grading System

A-F; I=Incomplete; WD=Withdrawal without credit; WP=Withdrawal while passing; WF=Withdrawal while failing.

STUDENT BODY PROFILE

Total enrollment (male/female): 256/566

From in-state: 572

Other regions: 28 states, 2 foreign countries

Full-time undergraduates (male/female): 252/557

Part-time undergraduates (male/female): 4/9

Ethnic/Racial Makeup

African American, 812; International, 10.

Class of 1995 Profile

Number of applicants: 956

Number accepted: 667

Number enrolled: 240

Transfer applicants: 143

Transfers accepted: 84

Transfers enrolled: 54

FACULTY PROFILE

Number of faculty: 62

Student-teacher ratio: 15:1

Full-time faculty (male/female): 28/26

Part-time faculty (male/female): 4/4

Tenured faculty (male/female): 20

Faculty with doctorates or other terminal degrees: 44%

SCHOOL CALENDAR

1992–93: August 20–May 7 (semesters)

Commencement and conferring of degrees: May

One summer session.

DEGREES OFFERED 1991–92:
Bachelor of Arts

Communications

English

History and Government/History Education

International Studies

Music/Music Education

Philosophy/Religion

Sociology

Bachelor of Science

Biology

Business

Chemistry

Elementary Education

Health, Physical Education and Recreation

Mathematics

Physics

Psychology Education

Recreation Education

Social Work

Pre-Professional Programs

Engineering

Law

Medicine

Ministry

SPECIAL PROGRAMS

All entering students must attend a mandatory, four-day college orientation at no cost; parents may attend.

The General Education Improvement Program provides academic remediation to high-risk students to help them develop skills necessary to succeed in college.

The honors program provides academically talented students an opportunity to participate in more creative and independent studies. To qualify, entering students must have a score of 20 or 800 respectively on the ACT or SAT, or a high school average of "B." Continuing students and transfers must maintain a cumulative GPA of 3.0 or better.

A cooperative student exchange program is offered with Alma College in Michigan and Marietta College in Ohio.

The Cooperative Education Program provides the student the opportunity to combine formal education with paid work experience. Student must have completed 32 hours at Stillman with a GPA of 2.30 or better.

The Cooperative Army and Air Force ROTC with the University of Alabama provides training in military science for commission as second lieutenant in the U.S. Armed Forces. The program is open to all full-time students and offers two- and three-year scholarships.

A cooperative three/two dual degree in engineering, nursing, or social work is offered in conjunction with the University of Alabama. Students take 3 years of course work at Stillman and 2 years at the University of Alabama. Upon completion of the program, the student will be awarded a bachelor's degree from each institution.

A cooperative three/three dual degree program in law with St. John's University is also offered. Students complete 3 years at Stillman and 3 years at St. John's. Upon completion of the first year at St. John's, students receive a liberal arts degree from Stillman; upon completion of program, students receive a Doctor of Jurisprudence degree.

The College Level Examination Program (CLEP) grants college credit for scores received on the CLEP general examination for nontraditional educational experiences such as the military, work, or other life experiences. The college will award a maximum of 30 semester hours through CLEP.

The Advanced Placement (AP) program allows qualifying high school students to take various college courses for credit during their junior and senior years.

The junior study abroad program allows students to substitute the junior year course work for study abroad in an approved international studies program.

A cooperative pre-med program with MeHarry Medical College is available for students.

An alcohol and drug prevention program is sponsored through the student development center.

ATHLETIC PROGRAMS

Stillman College is a member of the National Collegiate Athletic Association (NCAA), Division III.

Intercollegiate Sports: men's basketball, cross-country, and tennis; women's basketball and tennis.

Intramural sports: bowling, softball, and volleyball.

LIBRARY HOLDINGS

The William H. Sheppard Library houses 91,000 volumes, 1,200 microforms, 900 audiovisual materials, and 365 periodical subscriptions. Special collections include the Birthright Furniture Collection, the Martha L. O'Rourke Afro-American Collection, and a microfilm collection from the Schomburg Collection of Negro Life and History from the New York Public Library.

STUDENT LIFE
Special Regulations

Students must attend a four-day orientation. All cars must be registered; unlicensed drivers are not permitted to operate a vehicle on campus. Documentation of two measle immunizations is required.

Campus Services

Health center, personal and psychological counseling, career planning and placement, and religious services, including chapel.

Campus Activities

Group and cultural activities include theater, band, concerts, chorale, and a lecture series. Students can get involved in the student-run newspaper *(The Tiger's Paw)* or the yearbook *(The Stillmanite)*.

Leadership opportunities can be found in the Student Government Association, the Christian Student Association, or numerous college-wide committees. Greek-letter societies include Alpha Kappa Alpha, Delta Sigma Theta, Sigma Gamma Rho, and Zeta Phi Beta sororities; and Alpha Phi Alpha, Kappa Alpha Psi, Omega Psi Phi, and Phi Beta Sigma fraternities. Honor societies represented include Gamma Iota Sigma and Alpha Kappa Mu.

Stillman College is located in the suburbs of Tuscaloosa, Alabama, a small town of approximately 76,000 people. The city is served by major bus, rail, and air lines. The campus is within walking distance of downtown and approximately 45 minutes from Birmingham, the largest city in Alabama. Birmingham offers a rich history of the civil rights movement. Auto racing, thoroughbred racing, museums, theaters, and concerts are part of Birmingham, as well as the Iron Bowl and the All American Bowl, two intercollegiate college football events.

Housing Availability

622 housing spaces available; freshman housing guaranteed.

TALLADEGA COLLEGE

627 W. Battle St.
Talladega, AL 35160
Phone: (205) 362-0206
Toll-free in-state:
800-762-2468
Toll-free out-state:
800-633-2440
Fax: (205) 362-2268

Total Enrollment:
615

Level of Selectivity:
Slightly competitive

Motto:
An Education of
Distinction

HISTORY

Talladega College (TC) is a four-year, private, coed, liberal arts institution affiliated with the United Church of Christ. It was founded in 1867 by former slaves William Savery, Thomas Tarrant, and other freedmen from across the state who upheld "the education of our children and youth as vital to the preservation of our liberties, and true religion as the foundation of all real virtue." It was the first college opened to blacks in the State of Alabama.

The college began in a one-room school house and later moved to Swayne Hall, formerly the Talladega Baptist Male High School, built by slaves as a primary school for white males. It was incorporated in 1869 and chartered in 1889. The first instruction at the postsecondary level was in 1890 and the first baccalaureate degree was awarded in 1895. Talladega College was, until 1916, the only institution in Alabama conferring college degrees without regard to race.

Talladega College's mission is to foster leadership and instill in its graduates the values of morality, intellectual excellence, and hard work.

The 17-building campus is situated on 50 acres surrounded by 80 acres of gently rolling woodlands. Swayne Hall, the president's home, and Savery Library are all historic landmarks. The Savery Library has the Amistad Mural printed on the wall that depicts the successful quest for freedom by captured Africans aboard the slave ship *Amistad*. This historically black college is a United Negro College Fund member school.

ACCREDITATION

Talladega College is accredited by the Southern Association of Colleges and Schools (SACS) to award the Bachelor of Arts and Bachelor of Science degrees.

Other Accreditation

Council on Social Work Education

COSTS PER YEAR

1993–94 Tuition: $4,373

Room and board: $2,364

Special fees: $207

Books: $500

Estimated total cost: $7,444

FINANCIAL AID

1990–90 Institutional Funding

Number of scholarships and grants: 218

Total amount of scholarships and grants: $455,238

Range of scholarships and grants: $200–$6,817

1990–91 Federal and State Funding

Number of scholarships and grants: 690

Total amount of scholarships and grants: $1,468,426

Number of loans: 328

Total amount of loan: $463,790

Number of work-study: 325

Total amount of work-study: $197,526

Financial Aid Specific to the School

92% of the student body received financial aid during 1991–92.

Dean's I Scholarship provides $2,000 and is renewable for three years with the maintenance of 3.15 GPA. Students must rank in the upper 15% of their class, with a GPA of 3.3 to 3.49, SAT of 870, or ACT of 20.

Dean's II Scholarship provides $1,000 and is renewable for three years with the maintenance of 3.0 GPA, SAT of 780, or ACT of 18.

Presidential I Scholarship provides tuition, fees, room, and board for residential students up to $6,817. Qualifying students must rank in the upper 5% of their class, have a high school GPA of 3.75 or better, and a SAT score of 1100 or ACT Composite of 26. This scholarship is renewable for three years with the maintenance of 3.50 GPA.

Presidential II Scholarship provides tuition and fees up to $3,000 and is renewable for three years with the maintenance of a 3.3 to 3.74 GPA. Qualifying students must rank in the upper 10% of their class, have a high school GPA of 3.5 or better, and a SAT score of 1000 or ACT score of 23.

Athletic scholarships are awarded to talented students participating in intercollegiate sports.

College work-aid is available to students not qualifying for college work-study to work in departments of the college.

Deferred payment plan allows students to pay college costs in two or three installments during the semester.

United Negro College Fund (UNCF) scholarships are awarded to a limited number of students at this school who demonstrate financial need. Some scholarships may be based on location and merit. UNCF scholarships range from $500 to $7,500.

Army ROTC offers two- and three-year scholarships that pay tuition, fees, books, and other expenses, and provide a monthly stipend of $100.

Financial Aid Deadline
May 15 (priority)

Financial Aid Contact
Johnny Byrd, Director, Student Financial Aid, Talladega College, W. Battle St., Talladega, AL 35160; (205) 362-2752.

ADMISSION REQUIREMENTS
SAT or ACT required

Entrance Requirements
Graduation from an accredited high school and completion of the following 16 carnegie units: 4 English, 4 mathematics, 4 science, and 4 history; minimum 2.0 GPA; rank in the upper half of graduating class; some foreign language recommended; and proof of a recent physical. A $10 nonrefundable application required.

GED students must meet basic admission requirements.

International students must pass the TOEFL examination with a score of 500 or more, provide proof of ability to pay all college costs, and provide proof of a recent physical.

Transfer students must submit high school and college transcripts; qualify for readmission at previous college or university attended; have a minimum 2.0 GPA; need recommendation from previous college; transfer a maximum of 69 credits.

Early admission allows academically gifted high school students the opportunity to enroll in college for credit before completing high school.

Admission Application Deadline
Rolling admission provides no specific date for notification of admission so applicant is informed as soon as admission decision is made.

Admission Contact
Mr. Monroe Thornton, Office of Admissions, Talladega College, Talladega, AL 35160; (205) 362-0206, ext. 253 or toll-free 800-633-2440 (out-state); 800-762-2468 (in-state) Fax: (205) 362-2268.

GRADUATION REQUIREMENTS
A minimum of 126 credit hours and completion of the core requirements to include the following hours: 12 mathematics; 8 science, and 1 computer course for business, economics, public administration, math, and science majors.

Grading System
A-F; W=Withdraw; I=Incomplete.

STUDENT BODY PROFILE
Total enrollment (male/female): 203/412

From in-state: 400

Other regions: 24 states

Full-time undergraduates (male/female): 189/383

Part-time undergraduates (male/female): 14/29

Ethnic/Racial Makeup
African American, 597; Hispanic, 6; Other/unclassified, 12.

Class of 1995 Profile
Number of applicants: 948

Number accepted: 512

Number enrolled: 316

Median SAT score: 350V; 325M

Median ACT score: 16

FACULTY PROFILE

Number of faculty: 60

Student-teacher ratio: 13:1

Full-time faculty: 44

Part-time faculty: 16

Faculty with doctorates or other terminal
degrees: 69%

SCHOOL CALENDAR

1992–93: August–May (semester hours)

Commencement and conferring of degrees:
May

One summer session.

DEGREES OFFERED 1991–92:
Bachelor of Arts

Biology

Business Administration

Chemistry

Computer Science

English

English/Communications

History

Mathematics

Music Education

Music Performance (voice and piano)

Psychology

Physics

Public Administration

Rehabilitation (Deaf and Blind)

Social Work

Sociology

SPECIAL PROGRAMS

Accelerated Study Program allows students to complete their undergraduate degree in a shorter period of time than the traditional four years.

Adult or Continuing Education Program is available for nontraditional students returning to school or working full time.

Advanced Placement (AP) grants college credit for postsecondary work completed in high school.

College orientation is offered at no cost to entering students for two days prior to the beginning of classes to acquaint students with the college and to prepare them for college life.

Cooperative Education Program alternates and combines classroom study with related paid work experience. The program provides academic credit and full-time status during co-op placement.

Cooperative Program allows students to take college credit toward their degree programs in English, physics, and veterinary medicine at Tuskegee University.

Cooperative Programs are available in allied health with Tuskegee University and Georgia State University and in biomedical science with Meharry Medical College.

Honors program offers academically talented students a challenging program of study that includes special classes, seminars, colloquia, cultural activities, and special recognition to motivate participants.

Individualized majors allow students to create their own major program(s) of study.

Internships in various disciplines allow students to apply theory to on-the-job training in industry and business.

The MARC (Minority Access to Research Centers) Honors Undergraduate Research Training Program (MHURT) is designed to foster research in basic medical, biological, preclinical, and related natural and behavioral sciences. MARC trainees have spent research summers at Purdue, University of California at Berkeley, Sloan Kettering, University of Florida, Atlanta University, University of Alabama in Birmingham, University of Rochester, and M.I.T.

Minority Biomedical Research Support (MBRS) Program provides faculty and students the opportunity to engage in year-round biomedical research. Students who are selected work on a research project as assistants to MBRS investigators receive a salary, and sometimes, receive course credits for their efforts.

Off-campus study allows students to take courses for credit at any of seven member schools of the Alabama Center for Higher Education.

Part-time degree program allows students to earn an undergraduate degree while attending classes part time.

Remedial courses are offered to entering students to bring them up to admission standards and to help them adjust for success in college.

ROTC provides training in military science for commission as a second lieutenant in the U.S. Army.

Student Support Services provide developmental courses, counseling, and cultural activities to students who need aid to succeed in college.

Study Abroad Program allows students to go to a foreign country for a specified period of time for part of their college education.

Three/two degree program in engineering with Tuskegee University, Georgia Institute of Technology, or Auburn University allows students to earn two degrees—one in liberal arts from home school and one in engineering from cooperating school—by completing three years at matriculated school and two years at cooperating school.

Three/two degree program in law with St. John's University School of Law allows students to earn two degrees—one in liberal arts from home school and one in law from cooperating school—by completing three years at matriculated school and two years at cooperating school.

Three/two degree program in nursing with Jacksonville State University allows students to get two degrees—one in liberal arts from home school and one in nursing from cooperating school—by completing three years at matriculated school and two years at cooperating school.

Three/two degree program in pharmacy with Florida Agricultural and Mechanical University allows students to get two degrees—one in liberal arts from home school and one in pharmacy from cooperating school—by completing three years at matriculated school and two years at cooperating school.

Three/two degree program in veterinary medicine with Tuskegee University and Samford University allows students to get two degrees—one in liberal arts from home school and one in Veterinary Medicine from cooperating school—by completing three years at matriculated school and two years at cooperating school.

ATHLETIC PROGRAMS

Talladega College is a member of the National Association of Intercollegiate Athletics (NAIA).

Intercollegiate sports: men's basketball; women's basketball. Intramural sports: basketball, football, tennis, and volleyball.

Athletic Contact

Mr. Wylie Tucker, Talladega College, 627 W. Battle St., Talladega, AL 35160; (205) 362-0206, ext. 269.

LIBRARY HOLDINGS

The Savery Library holds 86,943 bound volumes, 1,725 microforms, 477 periodical subscriptions, 14,250 audiovisuals; 50 computers for student use in computer center. Special collections include the Schomburg Collection and The Black Studies Collection.

STUDENT LIFE
Campus Regulations

Car permitted without restrictions; quiet hours.

Campus Services

Health center, personal and psychological counseling, and remedial instruction in reading, writing, and math.

Campus Activities

Social and cultural activities include theater group, chorale, dance, concerts, films, lectures, recitals, and art shows. Numerous workshops, forums, and lectures expose students to a variety of outstanding artists; scientists; and political, business, and civic leaders throughout the year. Students may work on the *Talladega Student Star* (student-run newspaper) or the *Amistad* (yearbook).

Leadership opportunities are found in the Student Government Association or the more than 20 other clubs, such as the Wilderness Club or the Pre-law Society. Greek-letter fraternities include Alpha Phi Alpha, Kappa Alpha Psi, Omega Psi Phi, and Phi Beta Sigma; sororities include Alpha Kappa Alpha, Delta Sigma Theta, Sigma Gamma Rho, and Zeta Phi Beta. Honor societies are also represented on campus.

Located in the city of Talladega, the campus is situated between Atlanta (75 miles east) and Birmingham (40 miles west), and 25 miles south of the city of Anniston. These cities offer many cultural and entertainment activities. Talladega, with a population of 19,800, offers shopping, restaurants, and theaters, as well as hunting, hiking, and fishing. The city is accessible by bus and private car. The airport and passenger rail services are 20 miles from campus. The highest point in Alabama, Cheaha Mountain, is 17 miles north in Talladega National Forest. The city is home to the Alabama School for the Blind and Alabama School for the Deaf.

Housing Availability

530 housing spaces; four dormitories; freshman-only housing available.

NOTABLE ALUMNI

Oscar William Adams, Jr.–State Supreme Court justice

Aaron Brown–President emeritus, Albany State

Jewel Plummer Cobb–Former president, California State University, Fullerton

Ruth Simm Hamilton–Professor; Michigan State University trustee

Dr. William R. Harvey–President, Hampton University

Alberta Helyn Johnson–First African American woman elected to public office in Wyoming

Margaret B. Wilson, Esq.–Assistant attorney general, Missouri; civil rights leader

Dr. Geraldine Pittman Woods–Health education consultant

TRENHOLM STATE TECHNICAL COLLEGE

1225 Air Base Blvd.
Montgomery, AL
36108
Phone: (205) 832-9000
Fax: (205) 832-9777

Total Enrollment:
704

Level of Selectivity:
Noncompetitive

HISTORY

Trenholm State Technical College is a two-year, state-supported, coed, technical college founded in 1965. Trenholm State's mission is to provide education that will prepare students for meaningful employment, leadership, and citizenship.

ACCREDITATION

Trenholm State Technical College is accredited by the Southern Association of Colleges and Schools to award the Associate of Science and Associate of Applied Science degrees.

Other Accreditation

American Dental Association

American Medical Association

Commission on Occupational Education Institutions

National League for Nursing

COSTS PER YEAR

1992–93 Tuition: $ 1,404 (in-state); $ 1,962 (out-state)

Room and board: None

Special fees: $125

Books: $500

Estimated total cost: $2,029 (in-state); $2,587 (out-state)

FINANCIAL AID
Financial Aid Specific to the School

85% of the student body received financial aid during 1991–92.

Alabama Student Assistant Grants are awarded for up to $2,500 to residents of the state who demonstrate financial need.

Cooperative Education Program combines classroom study with related paid work experience. The program provides academic credit and full-time status during co-op placement.

Deferred payment plan allows students to pay college costs in two or three installments during the semester.

Full or partial tuition waivers are available to senior citizens on a space available basis.

Low-interest, long-term loans are available for students attending Trenholm who demonstrate financial need.

Financial Aid Deadline
March 15

Financial Aid Contact
Director of Financial Aid, Trenholm State Technical College, 1225 Air Base Blvd., Montgomery, AL 36108; (205) 832-9000.

ADMISSION REQUIREMENTS
Open admission. ASSET test used for placement.

Entrance Requirements
Graduation from an accredited high school with a minimum "C" average; official high school transcript; and interviews for Dental Assistant and Practical Nursing programs. A $10 application fee is required (may be waived for student demonstrating financial need).

GED students must meet basic admission requirements.

Transfer students must submit high school and college transcripts and qualify for readmission at previous college or university.

Admission Application Deadline
Rolling admission provides no specific date for notification of admission so applicant is informed as soon as admission decision is made.

Admission Contact
Jean Taylor, Director, Financial Aid/Public Relations/Admissions, Trenholm State Technical College, 1225 Air Base Blvd., Montgomery, AL 36108; (205) 832-9000, ext. 735; Fax: (205) 832-9777.

GRADUATION REQUIREMENTS
A minimum of 73 credit hours and completion of the core requirements to include 3 hours of mathematics and 1 computer course for accounting, stenography, and industrial electricity majors.

Grading System
A-F; I=Incomplete, W=Withdraw, U=Unsatisfactory, P=Pass, AU=Audit

STUDENT BODY PROFILE
Total enrollment (male/female): 359/345

From in-state: 697

Full-time undergraduates (male/female): 194/186

Part-time undergraduates (male/female): 165/159

Ethnic/Racial Makeup
African American, 542; Other/unclassified, 171.

Class of 1995 Profile
Number of applicants: 600

Number accepted: 456

Number enrolled: 159

FACULTY PROFILE
Number of faculty: 48

Student-teacher ratio: 16:1

Full-time faculty: 37

Part-time faculty: 11

Faculty with doctorates or other terminal degrees: 30%

SCHOOL CALENDAR

1992–93: August–May (quarters hours)

Commencement and conferring of degrees: May

DEGREES OFFERED 1991–92:
Associate of Applied Science

Auto Body Repair

Computer Information Systems

Electrical and Electronics Technologies

Associate of Science

Accounting

Dental Assistant

Food Services Technology

Legal Secretary

Medical Records Administration

Medical Secretary

Office Management

Practical Nursing

Secretarial Studies

Graduates that later obtain higher degrees:

30%

SPECIAL PROGRAMS

Adult or Continuing Education Program is available for nontraditional students returning to school or working full time.

Cooperative Education Program combines classroom study with related paid work experience. The program provides academic credit and full-time status during co-op placement.

Internships in various disciplines allow students to apply theory to on-the-job training in industry, business, hospitals, and clinics.

Part-time degree programs allow students to earn an undergraduate degree while attending part time.

Remedial courses are offered to entering students to bring them up to admission standards and to help them adjust for success in college.

Student Support Services provide developmental courses, counseling, and cultural activities to students who need aid to succeed in college.

ATHLETIC PROGRAMS

Intramural sports: basketball and softball.

LIBRARY HOLDINGS

The library holds 440 bound volumes, 30 periodical subscriptions, and 255 audiovisuals. Computers are available for student use.

STUDENT LIFE
Campus Regulations

Class attendance required.

Campus Services

Health, personal counseling, career planning and placement, and remediation.

Campus Activities

Trenholm is located in Montgomery, the capital city of Alabama, population approximately 300,000. The college is 100 miles south of Birmingham in the central part of the state. Historical points of interest include City Hall, where Rosa Parks was tried for refusing to give up her bus seat; Miss White's School, officially named the Montgomery Industrial School for Negro Girls, where leaders of Montgomery's black community were educated; and Dexter Parsonage where the Rev. Martin Luther King, Jr. lived while pastor of what is now the Dexter Avenue King Memorial Baptist Church. The city offers historical experiences related to the civil rights movement. Students also enjoy shopping, dining, churches, museums, and other recreational and spiritual activities.

Housing Availability

None

TUSKEGEE UNIVERSITY

HISTORY

Tuskegee University (TU) is a four-year, private, state-related, coed, liberal arts institution. It was founded in 1881 as Tuskegee Normal and Industrial Institute to educate rural black youth in Alabama. A former slave, Lewis Adams, and a former slave owner, George W. Campbell, negotiated a political deal that engineered the passage of legislation that appropriated $2,000 annually for teachers' salaries for a school to educate black youth in Macon and surrounding counties. They wrote to Hampton Institute for a teacher recommendation and the principal sent 26-year-old Booker T. Washington.

Later in 1881, Booker T. Washington opened TU, serving as its first principal. It humbly began with 30 men and women, primarily from Macon County, in a one-room shanty. The next year Washington purchased a 100-acre abandoned plantation, which became the nucleus of Tuskegee's present campus. Dr. Washington died at Tuskegee on November 14, 1915, and is buried on the campus.

Tuskegee, AL 36088
Phone: (205) 727-8500
Fax: (205) 727-5276

Total Enrollment:
3,598

Level of Selectivity:
Slightly competitive

Motto:
Peace through
Education

The first class graduated from the Tuskegee Normal School in 1885. Incorporated in 1893, the first instruction of post-secondary level was offered in 1923. The first baccalaureate degree was awarded in 1925. In 1937, the school's name changed to Tuskegee Institute, and the present name was adopted in 1967 when the school achieved university status.

Tuskegee University is a privately controlled yet state-related, professional, scientific, and technical institution with four-year and graduate degree programs. TU boasts a long list of notable alumni and leaders. George Washington Carver, its most notable alumni, is know for his research on the use of peanuts and sweet potatoes. Others include Lionel Richie, renowned singer, song-writer, and winner of five Grammy Awards and General Daniel "Chappie" James, first black Four-Star General in the Armed Forces.

TU was the first black college to be designated as a Registered National Landmark and has the distinction of being the only existent college designated a National Historic Site and District by Congress. It was the first site for the training of black military pilots and has had more graduates become flag officers than any other institution. Tuskegee also established the first nursing degree program in Alabama. The founder of the United Negro College Fund (UNCF) was Dr. Frederick D. Patterson, third president of Tuskegee University. Tuskegee is unique in that it is the only historical black institution that enjoys private control and state land grant status.

ACCREDITATION

Tuskegee University is accredited by the Southern Association of Colleges and Schools to award the Bachelor of Arts, Bachelor of Science, Master's, and Doctorate of Veterinary Medicine degrees.

Other Accreditation

Accreditation Board of Engineering and Technology, Inc.

American Chemical Society

American Dietetic Association

American Medical Association

American Veterinary Medical Association

Committee on Allied Health Education and Accreditation

Council on Social Work Education

National Architectural Accrediting Board

National League for Nursing

COSTS PER YEAR

1993–94 Tuition: $6,535

Room and board: $3,270

Special fees: $300

Books: $ 550

Estimated total cost: $ 10,655

FINANCIAL AID
1991–92 Institutional Funding

Number of scholarships and grants: 250

Total amount of scholarships and grants: $812,587

Range of scholarships and grants: $200–$1,187

1991–92 Federal and State Funding

Number of scholarships and grants: 2,565

Total amount of scholarships and grants: $4,401,619

Range of scholarships and grants: $5,749 average

Number of loans: 4,134

Total amount of loans: $12,098,506

Range of loans: $3,000–$3,500

Number of work-study: 768

Total amount of work-study: $1,173,141

Range of work-study: $1,000–$1,500

Financial Aid Specific to the School

92% of the student body received financial aid during 1991–92.

Athletic scholarships are available to students who participate in intercollegiate sports.

Distinguished Scholarships range from $500 to full tuition for prospective freshmen with high academic performance and leadership abilities. Awards are renewable for students who maintain a 3.0 GPA.

Health Education Assistant Loans are available to students in Veterinary Medicine who demonstrate financial need. Students must work in area of need upon completion of program.

Health Profession Student Loans are awarded up to $2,500 for qualifying students in Veterinary Medicine who demonstrate financial need.

Merit-based scholarships are awarded to students based on academic performance and departmental recommendations.

Performance grants in music are available to students participating in choir and band.

Nursing Student Loans are available to students enrolled in the School of Nursing who demonstrate financial need.

Presidential Citation Scholarships provide full tuition to National Merit Scholarship Finalists and Semifinalists. Scholarships are renewable for an additional three years of undergraduate study provided the recipient maintains at least a 2.75 GPA.

Deferred payment plan allows students to pay college costs in two or three installments during the semester.

Cooperative Education Program alternates classroom study with related paid work experience. The program provides academic credit and full-time status during co-op placement.

United Negro College Fund (UNCF) scholarships are awarded to a limited number of students at this school who demonstrate financial need. Some scholarships may be based on location and merit. UNCF scholarships range from $500 to $7,500.

Thurgood Marshall Black Education Fund provides a four-year scholarship at this public black college. Qualifying students must have a high school GPA of 3.0 or better and a SAT score of 1000 or ACT score of 24 or more. Students must be recommended by high school counselor as exceptional or exemplary in the creative or performing arts. Scholarship pays tuition, fees, room, and board, not to exceed $6,000 annually.

Army or Air Force ROTC offer two- and four-year scholarships that pay tuition, fees, books, and other expenses, and provide a monthly stipend of $100.

Alabama Student Assistant Grant awards up to $2,500 to residents of Alabama who demonstrate financial need.

Macon County Scholarships are available for Macon County residents who demonstrate exceptional financial need.

Financial Aid Deadline
March 31 (priority)

Financial Aid Contact
Barbara Bradley, Director of Financial Aid, Tuskegee University, Tuskegee, AL 36088; (205) 727-8201.

ADMISSION REQUIREMENTS
SAT (900) or ACT (18) required

Entrance Requirements
Graduation from an accredited high school and completion of the following 15 units: 3 English, 3 mathematics, 2 science, 3 social science, and 4 academic electives; official high school transcript with minimum "C" average. A $25 application fee is required.

GED students must meet basic admission requirements and have a score of at least 45 for non-high school graduates.

International students must take the TOEFL examination and provide proof of ability to pay all college costs.

Transfer students must qualify for readmission at previous college or university attended.

Early admission allows academically gifted high school students the opportunity to enroll in college full time before completing high school.

Early decision admits high school students in their junior or senior year to the college of their first choice. Financial aid is determined at time of early decision.

Admission Application Deadline

Rolling admission provides no specific date for notification of admission so applicant is informed as soon as admission decision is made; April 15 (fall); November 1 (spring).

Admission Contact

Ann Ware, Director of Admissions, Carnegie Hall, Tuskegee University, Tuskegee, AL 36088; (205) 727-8500.

GRADUATION REQUIREMENTS

A minimum of 124 credit hours and completion of the core requirements to include 3 credit hours of math and a computer course for business and engineering majors.

Grading System

A-E; P=Pass; F=Fail; S=Satisfactory; U=Unsatisfactory; W=Withdrawal; I=Incomplete; Y=Unauthorized Withdrawal; WP=Withdrawal Pass; WF=Withdrawal Fail; NG=No Grade.

STUDENT BODY PROFILE

Total enrollment (male/female): 1,727/1,871

From in-state: 754

Other regions: 43 states, 34 foreign countries

Full-time undergraduates (male/female): 1,462/1,584

Part-time undergraduates (male/female): 70/75

Graduate students (male/female): 195/212

Ethnic/Racial Makeup

African American, 3,210; Hispanic, 94; Caucasian, 112; International, 182.

Class of 1995 Profile

Number of applicants: 3,591

Number accepted: 2,558

Number enrolled: 850

Median SAT score: 820

Median ACT score: 19

Average high school GPA: 2.70

Transfer applicants: 278

Transfers accepted: 199

Transfers enrolled: 66

FACULTY PROFILE

Number of faculty: 307

Student-teacher ratio: 13:1

Full-time faculty (male/female): 247/50

Part-time faculty (male/female): 8/2

Tenured faculty: 135

Faculty with doctorates or other terminal degrees: 69%

Ethnic/Racial Makeup

African American, 149; Hispanic, 7; Asian, 106; Other/unclassified, 45.

SCHOOL CALENDAR

1992–93: September–May (semester hours)

Commencement and conferring of degrees: May and August

One summer session.

DEGREES OFFERED AND NUMBER CONFERRED 1991–92:
Bachelor of Arts

Architecture: n/a

English: n/a

Bachelor of Science

Accounting: 17

Aerospace Science Engineering: n/a

Agribusiness Education: n/a

Agribusiness Science: 38
Agronomy and Soils: n/a
Animal and Poultry Sciences: n/a
Biology: n/a
Biology Education: n/a
Business Administration: 62
Chemical Engineering: n/a
Chemistry: 4
Clothing and Related Arts: n/a
Computer Science: 5
Construction Science and Management: n/a
Dietetics: n/a
Early Childhood Education: 2
Economics: n/a
Electrical Engineering: n/a
Elementary Education: 6
Engineering: 108
English: 8
Extension and Technical Education: n/a
Finance: n/a
Food and Nutritional Science: n/a
General Science Education: n/a
Health Professions: 40
History: 24
Home Economics Education: n/a
Hospitality Management: n/a
Industrial Arts Education: n/a
Language Arts Education: n/a
Management Science: n/a
Marketing: n/a
Mathematics: n/a
Mathematics Education: 14
Mechanical Engineering: n/a
Medical Technology: n/a
Mental Retardation: n/a
Nursing: n/a
Occupational Therapy: n/a
Physical Education: n/a
Physical/Natural Science: 52
Physics: n/a
Plant and Soil Sciences: n/a
Political Science: n/a
Psychology: 22

Social Work: 13
Sociology: 9
Special Education: 1
Veterinary Medicine: 50

Master of Education
Agribusiness Education: n/a
Biology: n/a
Counseling and Student Development: n/a
Early Childhood Education: n/a
Educational Administration: n/a
Educational and Technical Education: n/a
Elementary Education: n/a
General Science Education: n/a
Home Economics Education: n/a
Personnel Administration: n/a
School Counseling: n/a
Science in Supervision: n/a

Master of Science
Agribusiness Education: n/a
Agricultural Science: 8
Animal and Poultry Science: n/a
Biology: n/a
Chemistry: n/a
Counseling and Student Development: n/a
Early Childhood Education: n/a
Education and Technical Education: n/a
Educational Administration: n/a
Electrical Engineering: n/a
Elementary Education: n/a
Engineering: 16
Environmental Sciences: n/a
Food and Nutritional Sciences: n/a
General Science Education: n/a
Health Professions: 5
Home Economics Education: n/a
Mechanical Engineering: n/a
Personnel Administration: n/a
Physical/Natural science: 2
Plant and Soil Sciences: n/a
School Counseling: n/a
Science in Supervision: n/a
Veterinary Science: n/a

Doctorate
Veterinary Medicine: n/a

Graduates that later obtain higher degrees:
75%

SPECIAL PROGRAMS

Freshman Accelerated Start-up and Training for Retention in the Engineering Curricula (FASTREC) program allows students to earn 7 semester credit hours towards their bachelor's degree in engineering.

Adult or Continuing Education Program is available for nontraditional students returning to school or working full time.

Advanced Placement (AP) grants college credit for postsecondary work completed in high school. Students scoring 3 to 5 on the AP test will receive credit by examination for each course and advanced placement.

College Level Examination Program (CLEP) determines the academic relevance of nontraditional educational experiences such as the military, on-the-job training, or other life experiences, through a series of tests and may grant students college credit for these experiences.

College orientation is offered to entering students for ten days at no cost prior to the beginning of classes to acquaint students with the college and to prepare them for college life.

Cooperative Education Program alternates classroom study with related paid work experience. The program provides academic credit and full-time status during co-op placement.

Cooperative Program allows students to take college credit toward their degree programs at North Carolina State University at Raleigh, University of Michigan, Virginia Polytechnic Institute and State University, Bethune-Cookman College, College of the Virgin Islands, Stillman College, and Rust College.

English as a Second Language is a program that offers courses in English for students whose native language is not English.

Honors program offers academically talented students a challenging program of study that includes special classes, seminars, colloquia, cultural activities, and special recognition to motivate participants.

Minority Introduction to Engineering (MITE) exposes students who have completed the eleventh grade to various aspects of engineering.

Off-campus study allows students to take courses for credit at the Alabama Center for Higher Education.

Part-time degree programs allow students to earn an undergraduate degree while attending part time during the day.

Pre-College Summer Programs and Pre-Freshman Enrichment I and II provide high school students who have completed the ninth and tenth grade an opportunity to participate in mathematics, chemistry I and II, physics I and II, and engineering graphics instruction.

Remedial courses are offered to entering students to bring them up to admission standards and to help them adjust for success in college.

Research Apprenticeship for Disadvantaged High Schoolers (RADHS) is for students who have completed the eleventh grade. It is designed to provide high school juniors/rising seniors the opportunity for "hands on" laboratory experience under the supervision of research faculty. Students are provided with a stipend of $1,000 for the duration of the program.

ROTC provides training in military science for commission as a second lieutenant in the U. S. Army and Air Force. Two- and four-year scholarships are available.

Student Support Services provide developmental courses, counseling, and cultural activities to students who need aid to succeed in college.

Study Abroad Program allows students to study in a foreign country for part of their college education.

Three/two dual degree program in engineering allows students to get two degrees—one in liberal arts from home school and one in engineering form Auburn University,

Iowa State University of Science and Technology, University of Michigan, or Idaho State University—by completing three years at matriculated school and two years at cooperating school.

Three/two dual degree program in forestry allows students to get two degrees—one in liberal arts from home school and one in forestry from Auburn University, Iowa State University of Science and Technology, University of Michigan, or Idaho State University—by completing three years at matriculated school and two years at cooperating school.

ATHLETIC PROGRAMS

Tuskegee University is a member of the National Collegiate Athletic Association (NCAA), all Division II, and the Southern Intercollegiate Athletic Association.

Intercollegiate sports: men's basketball, cross-country, football, riflery, soccer, tennis, and track & field; women's basketball, cross-country, riflery, tennis, track & field, and volleyball.

Intramural: badminton, basketball, football, gymnastics, riflery, soccer, swimming and diving, tennis, track & field, and volleyball.

Athletic Contact

James Martin, Athletic Director, Tuskegee University, Tuskegee, AL 36088; (205) 727-8848 or 8344.

LIBRARY HOLDINGS

The Hollis Burke Frissel Library and special department libraries hold 283,000 volumes, 1,150 periodicals, 28 foreign and domestic newspapers, 110,201 microforms, 2,300 audiovisual materials, and 15,000 select government documents. Special collections include the Booker T. Washington Collection and Archives, consisting of manuscripts, books, rare books, photographs, and other artifacts by and about Africa and

African Americans. It contains more than 100,000 items and constitutes one of the few very strong collections of its kind in existence. Other important collections include the General Chappie James Collection and the Margaret Washington Collection.

STUDENT LIFE
Campus Regulations

Class attendance required; cars must be registered; students required to live on campus through sophomore year; each student required to take one semester of general orientation during freshman year. Alcohol is prohibited; curfews, quiet hours, and dorm visitation enforced.

Campus Services

Health care, personal and psychological counseling, career planning and placement, student employment, daycare, remedial instruction in reading and writing, chapel, and religious activities.

Campus Activities

Social and cultural activities include theater, chorale, debate team, jazz ensemble, marching bands, films, concerts, and lecture series. Students may work on student publications, such as the *Campus Digest, Business Gazette, Engineer's Voice, Architecture Newsletter,* the student yearbook, or the monthly student newspaper, the *Surrounding Community.*

Spring is highlighted by the Tuskegee Relays, a well-known annual track & field meet. Greek-letter fraternities and sororities provide much of the social life of the campus. Renowned speakers frequent the campus.

Leadership opportunities are found in the Student Government Association (SGA) or other numerous student-run organizations. Greek-letter fraternities include Alpha Phi Alpha, Kappa Alpha Psi, Omega Psi Phi, and Phi Beta Sigma; sororities include Alpha Kappa Alpha, Delta Sigma Theta, Sigma Gamma Rho, and Zeta Phi Beta. There are also 12 non-Greek organizations.

Honor societies include Alpha Delta Mu (Social Work), Alpha Kappa Delta (Sociology), Alpha Kappa Mu (All Disciplines), Beta Kappa Chi (Natural Sciences), Delta Mu Delta (Business Administration), Eta Kappa Nu (Electrical Engineering), Kappa Delta Pi (Education), Kappa Omicron Phi (Home Economics), Lambda Iota Tau (Literature), Pi Tau Sigma (Mechanical Engineering), Pi Mu Epsilon (Mathematics), Pi Sigma Phi (Music), Phi Delta Kappa (Education), Phi Zeta (Veterinary Medicine), and Sigma Xi (Research Sciences).

Tuskegee University is located in the town of Tuskegee, about 40 miles east of Montgomery, 75 miles south of Birmingham, and 135 miles northeast of Atlanta. The campus is easily accessible by bus and car from Interstate 85 and U.S. Highways 80 and 29. Most students fly into either Montgomery or Atlanta and use automobile transportation to the campus. The climate is considered moderate with very high temperatures in the summer. The campus has several special features, including the George Washington Carver Museum, which preserves the tools and handiwork of the distinguished scientist who taught at Tuskegee, and the George Washington Carver Research Foundation, a center for a variety of research sponsored by government agencies and private industry. Churches of all major denominations, a library, and a museum contribute to the cultural atmosphere of the town.

Housing Availability

1,935 housing spaces; freshman housing given priority; married student housing available.

Handicapped Services

Wheelchair accessibility.

NOTABLE ALUMNI

Robert Benham, 1967–State Supreme Court justice, Georgia

Billy C. Black, 1960–President, Albany State

James Edward Cheek–Former president, Howard University

William L. Dawson, 1955–Musician/composer/conductor; member, Alabama Music Hall of Fame

Melvin Isadore Douglass, 1973–Educator and clergyman

Ralph Waldo Ellison–Novelist

Vera King Farris, 1959–President, Stockton State College

Daniel "Chappie" James, 1942–First black four-star general in the Armed Forces

Herman Delano James, 1965–President, Glassboro State College

Lionel Brockman Richie, Jr.–Singer/songwriter/producer; Grammy Award winner

Keenan Ivory Wayans–TV actor/producer

Elizabeth E. Wright–Founder, Voorhees College

Arkansas

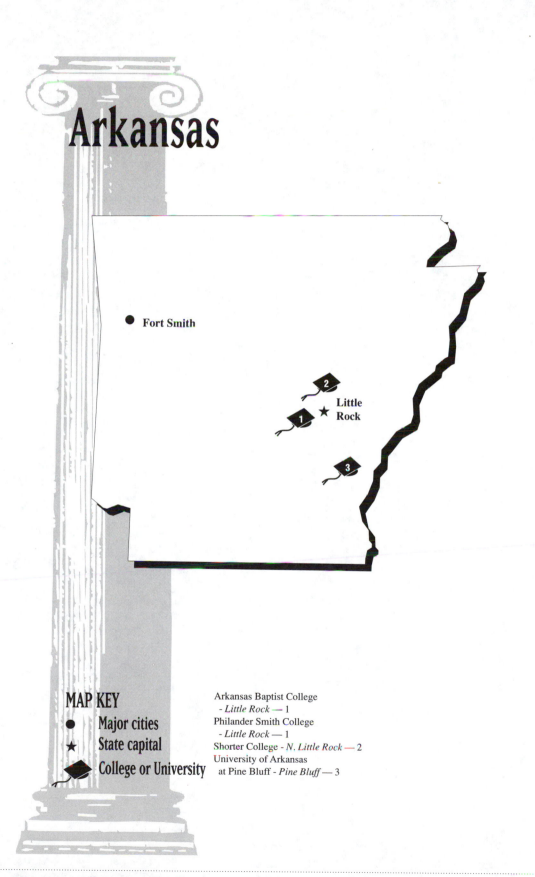

● Fort Smith

2

1 ★ Little
Rock

3

MAP KEY
● Major cities
★ State capital
College or University

Arkansas Baptist College
- *Little Rock* — 1
Philander Smith College
- *Little Rock* — 1
Shorter College - *N. Little Rock* — 2
University of Arkansas
at Pine Bluff - *Pine Bluff* — 3

ARKANSAS BAPTIST COLLEGE

1600 Bishop St.
Little Rock, AR 72202
Phone: (501) 374-7856

Total Enrollment:
291

Level of Selectivity:
Noncompetitive

HISTORY

Arkansas Baptist College (ABC) is a four-year, private, coed, liberal arts college affiliated with the Arkansas Baptist Consolidated Convention. Founded in 1884 as the Minister's Institute, the name changed to the Baptist Institute before becoming Arkansas Baptist college in 1885.

As a church-affiliated institution, Arkansas Baptist provides a liberal arts program in a Christian-centered environment. ABC programs are designed to develop the academic, social, and spiritual potential of each of its students. Arkansas Baptist forms part of a cooperative center with Philander Smith and Shorter College in sharing resources and programs.

ACCREDITATION

Arkansas Baptist College is accredited by the North Central Association of Colleges and Schools to award the Bachelor of Arts and Bachelor of Science degrees.

COSTS PER YEAR

1992–93 Tuition: $1,670

Room and board: $2,420

Special fees: $125

Books: $500

Estimated total cost: $4,715

FINANCIAL AID

Financial Aid Specific to the School

50% of the student body received financial aid during 1991–92.

Academic scholarships are awarded by Arkansas Baptist based on achievement, standardized test scores, and extracurricular activities.

Arkansas State Scholarship Program is available to full-time freshmen, sophomores, and juniors on a need basis.

Eligible students must be U.S. citizens or permanent residents; residents of the state of Arkansas; complete the Pell application for student aid, the AAFSSA or the ACT Need Analysis Services Packet; meet qualification of academic achievement established by the Department of Higher Education; not owe repayment at any institution or be in default of any federal or state loan program.

Arkansas State Grant is awarded to entering students with a 2.5 GPA who are residents of the state.

Athletic Scholarships are available to students participating in intercollegiate sports.

Governor's Scholarships are available to students with a 3.0 or better GPA.

Financial Aid Deadline
March 15 (priority); May 1

Financial Aid Contact
Evelyn Thomas, Director of Financial Aid, Arkansas Baptist College, 1600 Bishop St., Little Rock, AR 72202; (501) 374-7856.

ADMISSION REQUIREMENTS
SAT or ACT required

Entrance Requirements
Graduation from an accredited high school and completion of the following 18 units: 4 English, 3 mathematics, 2 science, 3 social science, and 6 electives; some foreign language recommended; submit official high school transcript; minimum 2.0 GPA.

GED students must meet basic admission requirements.

Transfer students must submit official transcript of all college work; minimum 2.0 GPA.

International students must submit official certificate of completion of high school; take TOEFL examination; provide proof of ability to pay all college costs.

Early admission allows academically gifted high school students the opportunity to enroll in college full time before completing high school.

Admission Application Deadline
Rolling admission provides no specific date for notification of admission so applicant is informed as soon as admission decision is made.

Admission Contact
Annie Hightower, Registrar, Arkansas Baptist College, 1600 Bishop St., Little Rock, AR 72202; (501) 574-7856, Ext. 19.

GRADUATION REQUIREMENTS
A minimum of 124 credit hours and completion of core requirements to include 9 hours of religion; minimum 2.0 GPA; 30 hours in residence.

Grading System
A-F; I=Incomplete; W=Withdrew

STUDENT BODY PROFILE
Total enrollment (male/female): 145/146

From in-state: 218

Full-time undergraduates (male/female): 123/123

Part-time undergraduates (male/female): 22/23

Ethnic/Racial Makeup
African American, 288; Other/unclassified, 3.

Class of 1995 Profile
Number of applicants: 97

Number accepted: 97

Number enrolled: 97

Transfers enrolled: 29

FACULTY PROFILE
Number of faculty: 23

Student-teacher ratio: 14:1

Full-time faculty: 12

Part-time faculty: 11

SCHOOL CALENDAR

1992–93: August–May (semester hours)

Commencement and conferring of degrees: May

One summer session.

DEGREES OFFERED 1991–92:

Business Administration

Computer Science

Elementary Education

Liberal Arts/General Studies

Religious Studies

Secondary Education

Social Work

SPECIAL PROGRAMS

Accelerated Study Program allows students to complete their undergraduate degree in a shorter period of time than the traditional four years.

Adult or Continuing Education Program is available for nontraditional students returning to school or working full time.

Part-time degree program allows students to earn an undergraduate degree part time.

Remedial courses are offered to entering students to bring them up to admissions standards and to help them adjust for success in college.

ATHLETIC PROGRAMS

Arkansas Baptist College is a member of the National Association of Intercollegiate Athletics.

Intercollegiate sports: men's basketball; women's basketball, softball, and volleyball

Athletic Contact

Bobby Carye, Director of Athletics, Arkansas Baptist College, 1600 Bishop St., Little Rock, AR 72202; (501) 373-6886.

LIBRARY HOLDINGS

The library houses 23,550 bound volumes; 25 computers available for student use in computer center.

STUDENT LIFE

Campus Services

Health services, career planning and placement; student employment services; day-care for preschoolers; remedial instruction.

Campus Activities

Social and cultural activities include chorale and religious activities.

Arkansas Baptist is located in Little Rock, the capital of Arkansas, population 395,000. The city is served by mass bus and passenger rail service. The airport is eight miles away. Little Rock is one of the fastest-growing cities in the United States, offering students access to fine dining, shopping, concerts, and plays.

Housing Availability

90 housing spaces.

PHILANDER SMITH COLLEGE

HISTORY

Philander Smith College (PSC) is a four-year, private, liberal arts institution affiliated with the United Methodist Church (UMC). It was founded in 1877 as Walden Seminary to provide educational opportunities for freedmen west of the Mississippi River. In 1882, Adeline Smith, the widow of Philander Smith, donated $10,500 to Walden Seminary. As a gesture of gratitude, the seminary was renamed Philander Smith College. The following year, 1883, the college was chartered as a four-year institution and conferred its first bachelor's degree in 1888.

Over the succeeding 60 years, the academic programs were expanded and strengthened. In 1949, Philander Smith College was fully accredited by the North Central Association of Colleges and Schools. By 1983, approval for accreditation was received from the Arkansas State Department of Education.

Today, Philander Smith College continues its rich Christian heritage. Through ties to the United Methodist

812 W. 13th St.
Little Rock, AR 72202
Phone: (501) 375-9845
Toll-free:
800-446-6772

Total Enrollment:
640

Level of Selectivity:
Noncompetitive

Motto:
Ye Shall Know the
Truth and the Truth
Shall Make You Free

Church, the college strives to instill the desire to serve. Philander Smith College is proud to have earned the designation as the "College of Service and Distinction."

The 20-acre campus houses 20 buildings including the Wesley Chapel and Parsonage of the UMC. Recently, an outdoor sports field and paved track were completed.

ACCREDITATION

Philander Smith College is accredited by the North Central Association of Colleges and Schools (NCACS) to award the Bachelor of Arts and Bachelor of Science degrees.

Other Accreditation

Arkansas State Department of Education

University Senate of the United Methodist Church

COSTS PER YEAR

1991–92 Tuition: $2,620

Room and board: $2,415

Special fees: $125

Books: $500

Estimated total cost: $5,660

FINANCIAL AID

Financial Aid Specific to the School

85% of the student body received financial aid during 1991–92.

Athletic scholarships are available for talented students participating in intercollegiate sports.

Endowed scholarships, grants, and assistantships from friends and alumni associations and corporations number 65 and are based on merit, need, and interest.

Performance scholarships are available for talented students participating in music and drama activities.

Rockefeller scholarships are available to students who have a 2.75 or better GPA.

William and Lois Wilson Adams Endowment Fund awards are available to students with a record of academic success who are willing to uphold the values of the college.

Cooperative Education Program alternates classroom study with related paid work experience in all majors. The program provides academic credit and full-time status during co-op placement.

Army ROTC, in cooperation with the University of Arkansas at Little Rock, offers two-, three-, and four-year scholarships that pay tuition, fees, books, and other expenses, and provide a monthly stipend of $100.

Arkansas Rural Endowment Fund is a long-term loan guaranteed by SLGF with a maximum amount of $2,500 to be repaid at 9% interest.

Arkansas State Scholarship Program is awarded to full-time freshmen, sophomores, and juniors on a need basis. Eligible students must be U.S. citizens or permanent residents; be residents of the State of Arkansas; have completed the Pell application for student aid, the AAFSSA, or the ACT Need Analysis Services packet; meet qualification of academic achievement established by the Department of Higher Education; not owe repayment at any institution for the Pell Grant, SEOG, or SSIG; and not be in default of any federal or state loan program.

Arkansas State Grant is awarded to entering students with a 2.5 GPA who are residents of the state.

Governor's scholarships are available to students with a 3.0 or better GPA.

United Methodist Church Scholarships and Loans are awarded to members of the United Methodist Church who are citizens of the United States and who maintain a "C" average in an accredited program.

United Negro College Fund (UNCF) scholarships are awarded to a limited number of students at this school who demonstrate financial need. Some scholarships may be based on location and merit. UNCF scholarships range from $500 to $7,500.

Financial Aid Deadline
June 30 (fall); November 15 (spring)

Financial Aid Contact
Betty Goodwin, Director of Financial Aid, Philander Smith College, 812 W. 13th St., Little Rock, AR 72202; (501) 370-5350.

ADMISSION REQUIREMENTS
ACT preferred (students may take the ACT after enrolling) or SAT.

Entrance Requirements
Graduation from an accredited high school and completion of the following 16 units: 3 English, 2 mathematics, 2 from two of the following: foreign language, science, or social science; and 7 electives (no more than 4 vocational or commercial subjects). Submit official high school transcript and have at least a "C" average (students with less than a "C" average may be admitted on one-semester probation status). A $5 non-refundable fee is required.

GED students must meet basic admission requirements.

Transfer students must submit official transcripts from high school and all previous colleges attended; have a 2.0 cumulative GPA; be in "good standing" at the last institution attended; and transfer a maximum of 62 hours from regionally accredited junior college. All passing grades are accepted from accredited four-year institutions. Transfer students from an unaccredited college must submit results of CLEP General Exams.

International Students must submit official certificates of all secondary and college work and copies of results on all national examinations (G.C.E., etc); students from non-English-speaking countries must submit the Test of English as a Foreign Language (TOEFL). To evaluate post-secondary course-work, it is sometimes necessary for the college to use a professional evaluation service at the applicant's expense (80–100 U.S. dollars). The college will notify the applicant if this service is required. The applicant is required to submit a Financial Certification Form verifying that $12,820 is available annually and have a F-1 Visa or Exchange Visitor Visa to enter United States for the purpose of study.

Early admission allows academically gifted high school students the opportunity to enroll in college for credit before completing high school.

Admission Application Deadline
August 15 (fall); December 15 (spring); May 30 (summer I); June 15 (summer II); rolling admission provides no specific date for notification so applicant is informed as soon as admission decision is made.

Admission Contact
Anne Williams, Director of Admissions, Philander Smith College, 812 W. 13th St., Little Rock AR 72202; (501) 370-5217.

GRADUATION REQUIREMENTS
Have a minimum of 124 credit hours and complete core requirements; have a 2.0 GPA (2.50 GPA for Teacher Education); complete 22 of last 32 semester hours at Philander Smith College; pass an English Proficiency Test in usage, speech, and writing; take the Graduate Record Examination or the National Teachers Examination; apply for graduation; be approved by faculty on the basis of academic record and personal character.

Grading System
A-F; I=Incomplete; Aud=Audit (no credit); NR=No grade/no record; WP=Withdrew Passing; WF=Withdrew Failing;

STUDENT BODY PROFILE
Total enrollment (male/female): 310/330

From in-state: 480

Other regions: 8 states and 3 foreign countries

Full-time undergraduates (male/female): 240/250

Part-time undergraduates (male/female):
  60/65

Graduate students (male/female): 10/15

FACULTY PROFILE

Number of faculty: 68

Student-teacher ratio: 16:1

SCHOOL CALENDAR

1992–93: August 24–May 14 (semester
  hours)

Commencement and conferring of degrees:
  May 15

Two summer sessions.

DEGREES OFFERED 1991–92:

Art/Studio

Biology Education

Business Administration

Business Education

Chemistry

Economics

Elementary Education

English/Education

English/Mass Communication (cooperative
  program with other institutions)

Health, Physical Education, and Recreation

Home Economics

Mathematics/Education

Medical Technology (cooperative program)

Music

Philosophy and Religion

Physical Education

Political Science

Psychology

Secretarial Science

Science Education

Social Work

Sociology

Special Education

Physics

Pre-Professional Programs

Dentistry

Engineering

Law

Medicine

Ministry

Nursing

Pharmacy

SPECIAL PROGRAMS

Adult/Continuing Education Programs are available for nontraditional students returning to school or working full time.

Advanced Placement (AP) grants college credit for postsecondary work completed in high school. Students scoring 3 on the AP test will receive credit by examination for each course and advanced placement.

Black Executive Exchange Program (BEEP) is sponsored by the National Urban League and various local corporations; BEEP provides opportunities for black college students to interact with black executives in actual industry settings.

College Level Examination Program (CLEP) determines the academic relevance of nontraditional educational experiences such as the military, on-the-job training, or other life experiences, through a series of tests and may grant students college credit for these experiences.

Cooperative Education program combines classroom study with related paid work experience. The program provides academic credit and full-time status during co-op placement.

English as a Second Language Program offers courses in English for students whose native language is not English.

Honors program offers academically talented students a challenging program of study that includes special classes, seminars, colloquia, cultural activities, and special recognition to motivate participants.

Internships in various disciplines offer students the opportunity to apply theory to on-the-job training in business, industry, hospitals, and clinics.

A joint B.S. degree program in medical technology with Arkansas Baptist Medical Center's School of Medical Technology is offered.

Part-time (day and evening) degree programs allow students to earn undergraduate and graduate degrees on a part-time basis.

Remedial courses are offered to entering students to bring them up to admission standards and to help them adjust for success in college.

ROTC in cooperation with the University of Arkansas at Little Rock provides training in military science for commission as a second lieutenant in the U.S. Army. Two-, three-, and four-year scholarships are available.

Three/two dual degree program in engineering in cooperation with Tuskegee University allows students to get a liberal arts degree from home school and an engineering degree from cooperating school by completing three years at Philander and two years at Tuskegee.

Upward Bound provides academic counseling and cultural enrichment programs to high school students in grades 10, 11, and 12 who are disadvantaged and in pursuit of a college education. Some credit courses are offered.

ATHLETIC PROGRAMS

Philander Smith College is a member of the Interregional Athletic Conference (IRAC) and the National Association of Intercollegiate Athletics (NAIA).

Intercollegiate sports: men's baseball, basketball, track & field, and soccer; women's basketball, track & field, and volleyball.

Intramural sports: basketball, tennis, and volleyball.

Athletic Contact

Matthew Summerville, Consultant for Athletics, Philander Smith College, Little Rock, AR 72202; (501) 370-5370.

LIBRARY HOLDINGS

M. L. Harris Library contains 85,000 volumes, 2,411 microforms, 4,855 audiovisuals, and 365 periodical subscriptions. Special collections include a Juvenile Collection.

STUDENT LIFE

Special Regulations

Freshmen required to live on campus unless they are residents of the Greater Little Rock area or were given special permission to reside elsewhere; assemblies required; dorm visitation from 12PM to 10:30 PM; curfew and quiet hours enforced; alcohol not permitted on campus.

Campus Services

Health, career counseling and placement, student employment, tutoring, remediation, chapel, and religious activities.

Campus Activities

Social and cultural activities include theater, lyceums, chorale, and band. The Little Theater Guild features two to three full length productions each year. Students may get involved in the *Panther* (student-run newspaper) or the *Philanderian* (yearbook). Communication majors or volunteers can work at KPSC, the college radio station.

Mandatory cultural and educational assemblies are held every Thursday. Vesper programs take place monthly. Annual programs scheduled include Dr. M. L. King Birthday Celebration; Black History Month activities that includes renowned speakers; and the Founder's Day Celebration.

Leadership opportunities are found in the Student Government Association (SGA) or in the various departmental clubs, such as biology, business, language, and home economics. Students interested in acting or writing can join the Art Guild or Writers Club.

Greek-letter fraternities include Alpha Phi Alpha, Kappa Alpha Psi, Omega Psi Phi, and Phi Beta Kappa; sororities include Alpha Kappa Alpha, Delta Sigma Theta, Sigma Gamma Rho, and Zeta Phi Beta. Honor societies include Alpha Kappa Mu and Beta Kappa Chi, which represent the highest distinction in the field of pure science in black colleges and universities.

PSC is located in Little Rock, the capital of Arkansas with a population of 395,000. The city is served by a mass bus system. Passenger rail is 2.5 miles away and the airport is 8 miles away. Located in one of the fastest-growing cities in the United States, students have access to fine dining, shopping, concerts, and plays.

Housing Availability

220 housing spaces available.

NOTABLE ALUMNI

Hubert (Geese) Ausbie–Former Harlem Globetrotter

Alvertis (Al) Bell–Executive, Barry Gordy Record Co.

Jocelyn Elders, 1952–Surgeon General of the United States

Dr. Eddie Reed, MD–Cancer researcher

Lottie Shackleford, 1979–First woman mayor, largest city in Arkansas

Ozell Sutton, 1950–Past national president, Alpha Phi Alpha Fraternity, Inc.

Myer L. Titus–President, Philander Smith College

SHORTER COLLEGE

604 Locust St.
North Little Rock, AR
72214
Phone: (501) 374-6305

Total Enrollment:
120

Level of Selectivity:
Noncompetitive

HISTORY

Shorter College (SC) is a two-year, private, coed, liberal arts college affiliated with the African Methodist Episcopal (AME) Church. SC was founded in 1886 as a four-year institution under the name Bethel University. In 1903 the name changed to Shorter College. It became a two-year college in 1955.

SC is part of a cooperative center with nearby Arkansas Baptist and Philander Smith Colleges. The purpose of the cooperative center is to provide students with combined resources and programs. SC is an open-admission school that believes everyone should have an opportunity to pursue higher education and to develop to his/her full potential. To this end, Shorter provides a liberal arts education leading to career degrees or liberal arts transfer degrees.

ACCREDITATION

Shorter College is accredited by the North Central Association of Colleges and Schools to award the Bachelor of Arts and Bachelor of Science degrees.

COSTS PER YEAR

1992–93 Tuition: $1,606

Room and board: $1,000 (room); $1,100 (board)

Special fees: $125

Books: $250

Estimated total cost: $4,081

FINANCIAL AID

Financial Aid Specific to the School

85% of the student body received financial aid during 1991–92.

Arkansas State Grant is awarded to entering students with a 2.5 GPA who are residents of the state.

Arkansas State Scholarship Program is awarded to full-time freshmen, sophomores and juniors on a need basis. Eligible students must be U.S. citizens or permanent residents; residents of Arkansas; complete the Pell application for student aid, the AAF-SSA, or the ACT Need Analysis Services packet; meet qualifications of academic achievement established by the Department of Higher Education; not owe repayment at any institution or be in default of any federal or state loan program.

Athletic scholarships are available for students participating in intercollegiate sports.

Cooperative Education Program combines classroom study with related paid work experience. The program provides academic credit and full-time status during co-op placement.

Governor's scholarships are available to students with a 3.0 GPA or better.

Performance scholarships are available for music students.

President's scholarships are available for academically talented students.

Financial Aid Deadline

April 15 (priority)

Financial Aid Contact

Randall H. Day, Director of Financial Aid, Shorter College, 604 Locust St., North Little Rock, AR 72114

ADMISSION REQUIREMENTS

Open admission. SAT or ACT required for placement and counseling.

Entrance Requirements

Graduation from an accredited high school and completion of the following 15 units: 3 English, 1 mathematics, 2 science, 1 social science, and 9 electives; submit official high school transcript; interview recommended. A $35 nonrefundable application fee required.

GED students must meet basic admission requirements.

Transfer students must submit official transcript of all college work, minimum 2.0 GPA.

International students must submit official certificate of high school completion, take TOEFL examination, and provide proof of ability to pay all college costs.

Early admission allows academically gifted high school students the opportunity to enroll in college before completing high school.

Admission Application Deadline

Rolling admission provides no specific date for notification of admission so applicant is informed as soon as admission decision is made.

Admission Contact

Delores Voliber, Director of Admission, 604 Locust St., Shorter College, North Little Rock, AR 72114; (501) 374-6305.

GRADUATION REQUIREMENTS

A minimum of 64 credit hours and completion of core requirements to include 6 English, 3 science, 3 social science.

Grading System

A–F; I=Incomplete; W=Withdraw;

STUDENT BODY PROFILE

Total enrollment (male/female): 468/588

From in-state: 102

Other regions: 5 states, 2 foreign countries

Full-time undergraduates (male/female): 40/38

Part-time undergraduates (male/female): 21/21

Ethnic/Racial Makeup

African American, 108; International, 12.

Class of 1995 Profile

Number of applicants: 107

Number accepted: 96

Number enrolled: 51

Transfers enrolled: 28

FACULTY PROFILE

Number of faculty: 24

Student-teacher ratio: 5:1

Full-time faculty: 20

Part-time faculty: 14

SCHOOL CALENDAR

1992–93: August–May

Commencement & conferring of degrees:
  May

One summer session.

DEGREES OFFERED 1991–92:

Allied Health

Business Management

Computer Science

Education

Fire Science

Liberal Arts (transfer)

Medical Technology

Office Management

Science

Secretarial

Social Science

Social Work

Graduates that go on to higher degrees upon graduation: 40%

SPECIAL PROGRAMS

Adult or Continuing Education Program is available for nontraditional students returning to school or working full time.

Advanced Placement (AP) grants college credit for postsecondary work completed in high school. Students scoring 3 to 5 on the AP test will receive credit by examination for each course and advanced placement.

College orientation is offered for $25 to entering students for two days prior to the beginning of classes to acquaint students with the college and to prepare them for college life.

Cooperative Education Program combines classroom study with related paid work experience. The program provides academic credit and full-time status during co-op placement.

Cross-registration with cooperative center members, including Arkansas Baptist and Philander Smith Colleges, allows students to take courses not offered at Shorter.

Internships in various disciplines allow students to apply theory to on-the-job training in industry and business.

Part-time degree program allows students to earn an undergraduate degree part time.

Remedial courses are offered to entering students to bring them up to admission standards and to help them adjust for success in college.

ATHLETIC PROGRAMS

Shorter College is a member of the National Junior College Athletic Association (NJCAA).

Intercollegiate sports: Men's basketball.

LIBRARY HOLDINGS

The library houses 11,746 bound volumes.

STUDENT LIFE

Special Regulations

Mandatory chapel attendance; dress code.

Campus Services

Health center, personal and psychological counseling, student employment services, remedial instruction, legal services, chapel and religious activities.

Campus Activities

Social and cultural activities include theater and chorale.

Leadership opportunities can be found in the Student Government Association (SGA) or the various other organizations including the Campus Ministry and computer science, business, and dramatics clubs. Local fraternities and sororities include Alpha Phi Delta and Beta Theta.

Shorter College is located in Little Rock, the capital of Arkansas, population 395,000. The city is served by mass bus and passenger rail. The airport is eight miles away. Students have access to fine dining, shopping, concerts, and plays.

Housing Availability

50 housing spaces

Handicapped Services

Wheelchair accessibility.

UNIVERSITY OF ARKANSAS
AT PINE BLUFF

N. Cedar St.
Pine Bluff, AR 71601
Phone: (501) 543-8000
Toll-free:
800-264-6585
Fax: (501) 534-2021

Total Enrollment:
3,709

Level of Selectivity:
Slightly competitive

Motto:
Quality Education with
a Personal Touch

HISTORY

The University of Arkansas at Pine Bluff (UAPB) is a four-year, private, coed, liberal arts institution founded in 1875 as the Branch Normal College. The first classes were taught to 7 students in a rented frame building in Pine Bluff.

In 1882, the state erected a two-story brick building on a 50-acre lot in suburban Pine Bluff. Between 1881 and 1894 ten Bachelor of Arts degrees were awarded. From 1894–1929 Branch Normal College operated as a junior college.

In 1927 several significant changes took place: first, the governor appointed an independent board of trustees; second, the state legislature appropriated $275,000 to begin building a new campus just outside of the city. Finally, funds from the General Education Board and the Rosenwald Fund, totalling $216,000, were donated to aid the project.

By 1929, the school became known as Arkansas Agricultural, Mechanical and Normal College. In 1933, Arkansas AM&N was certified to grant baccalaureate degrees. Between 1935 and 1940 two aggressive building programs resulted in the campus doubling in size by the late 1960s. Additions included academic and administrative buildings, student service facilities, additional living quarters for faculty and students, and an expansion in services and research facilities of the 220-acre College Farm and Agri-Lab. On July 1, 1972, Arkansas AM&N merged into the University of Arkansas System and was renamed University of Arkansas at Pine Bluff.

As a land grant institution, UAPB is committed to providing quality educational programs in the agricultural sciences as well as the arts and sciences. UAPB works to recruit students who are from a variety of cultures and backgrounds.

ACCREDITATION

University of Arkansas at Pine Bluff is accredited by the North Central Association of Colleges and Schools to award the Bachelor of Arts, Bachelor of Science degrees, and Master's degrees.

Other Accreditation

American Home Economics Association

International Association of Counseling Services

National Association for the Accreditation of Teacher Education

National Association for Schools of Music

National League for Nursing

COSTS PER YEAR

1992–93 Tuition: $1,320 (in state); $3,140 (out-state)

Room and board: $1,940

Special fees: $125

Books: $500

Estimated total cost: $3,885 (in-state); $5,705 (out-state)

FINANCIAL AID

1991–92 Institutional Funding

Number of scholarships and grants: 429

Total amount of scholarships & grants: $357,299

Range of scholarships & grants: $50–$2,500

1991–92 Federal and State Funding

Number of scholarships and grants: 2,587

Total amount of scholarships and grants: $4,441,280

Range of scholarships and grants: $100–$2,400

Number of loans: 1,389

Total amount of loans: $3,609,305

Range of loans: $500–$4,000

Number of work-study: 1,100

Total amount of work-study: $700,000

Range of work-study: $250–$1,200

Financial Aid Specific to the School

86% of the student body received financial aid during 1991–92.

Academic Challenge Scholarship Program is available to high school graduates who enroll as first-time students at the university; have completed the recommended precollegiate core curriculum; and meet criteria established by the Arkansas Department of Higher Education.

Academic scholarships are awarded to students who are residents of Arkansas and have scored 21 or better on the ACT or rank in the top 10% of the class. The scholarships are for tuition only and are available for a maximum of 8 semesters.

AP & L Matching Fund Grants of $200 are awarded by Arkansas Power and Light to students in the marching band.

AP & L Scholarships of $500 are awarded by Arkansas Power and Light to accounting students who have achieved academic excellence and demonstrate qualities of leadership and professional promise.

AP & L Student Investment Scholarships of $1,500 are awarded by Arkansas Power and Light to third- and fourth-year students in teacher education who have a GPA of 2.50, are majoring in mathematics, and are committed to teaching in Arkansas for at least three years.

Army ROTC scholarships are available for selected high school seniors who desire to pursue a military career. Scholarships pay for tuition, laboratory fees, books, and other expenses, as well as provide a monthly stipend of $100. Three-, two-, and one-year scholarships are awarded on a competitive basis to freshmen, sophomores, and juniors. Contact chair of Military Science Department.

Athletic scholarships are available for students participating in intercollegiate sports.

Chancellor's scholarships offer up to $4,500 annually for tuition, books, and fees to entering freshmen with at least a 3.5 GPA and at least a 1000 composite SAT score or 24 ACT score. Awards are made on a competitive basis. Students must maintain a 3.2 GPA to renew scholarship each year. Students must also reside on campus freshman and sophomore years. For more information contact (501) 541-6583.

Cooperative Education Program alternates and combines classroom study with related paid work experience. The program provides academic credit and full-time status during co-op placement.

Emergency Secondary Education Loan Programs provide loans for full-time students who are residents of the state, U.S. citizens, or permanent residents with a 2.5 GPA who plan to teach in approved shortage areas of Arkansas secondary schools for at least 5 years. Repayment of loan can be made by teaching 5 years in Arkansas after certification.

Endowed, corporate, and friends scholarships total over 90.

Governor's Scholarship Program provides $2,000 merit grants per year to 100 of Arkansas' academically superior high school graduates. The scholarship is for undergraduate studies and is renewable for four years provided the student maintains a cumulative college GPA of 3.0 on the 4.0 scale.

Job Training Partnership Act is an educational program that assists youth and unskilled adults to enter the job market by paying for tuition, books, and other expenses to complete classroom work.

Minority Presence Scholarship Grant Program awards tuition to academically strong minority students who enter UAPB. Applicants must be residents of Arkansas, have received their high school or GED in the state of Arkansas, must have an ACT score of 21, and graduated in the top 10% of their class. Transfer students must meet same criteria.

Other Race Scholarships, totalling $50,000, are awarded to nontraditional minorities.

Paul Douglass Teacher Scholarship Program provides scholarships/loans to outstanding undergraduates interested in teaching pre-school, elementary, or secondary school as a career. Grants range up to $5,000 per academic year and are based on academic performance. Recipients are obligated to teach in any state for 2 years for every year of scholarship assistance.

State Scholarships are available to residents of Arkansas enrolled as full-time students and who demonstrate financial need based on the CSX Arkansas Application for Federal and State Aid.

Thurgood Marshall Black Education Fund provides a four-year scholarship at this public black college. Qualifying students must have a high school GPA of 3.0 or better and an SAT score of 1000 or ACT score of 24 or more. Students must be recommended by high school counselor as exceptional or exemplary in the creative or performing arts. Scholarship pays tuition, fees, room, and board not to exceed $6,000 annually.

Tuition waiver for senior citizens age 60 and over on a space available basis.

Financial Aid Deadline
April 15 (fall); November 15 (spring)

Financial Aid Contact
Ray Watley, Director of Financial Aid, University of Arkansas at Pine Bluff, N. Cedar St., Pine Bluff, AR 71601; (501) 543-8301.

ADMISSION REQUIREMENTS
SAT accepted; ACT (19) preferred

Entrance Requirements
Graduation from an accredited high school and completion of the following 15 units: 4 English, 2 mathematics, 2 natural science, 3 social sciences, 2 foreign language, and 2 electives; submit official high school transcript; minimum "C" average; a composite ACT score of 19; proof of immunization.

GED students must meet basic admission requirements.

Transfer students with more than 30 hours must submit official transcripts from all previous colleges attended; students with less than 30 hours must also submit ACT or SAT scores; applicants with less than a "C" average may be admitted on a probationary basis. All students are required to submit an immunization record. Students may transfer up to 68 credits from a junior or community college.

International Students must submit certified copies of all previous academic records, with English translation of these documents; pass TOEFL examination with a minimum score of 500; provide proof of ability to pay all college cost.

Early admission allows academically gifted high school students the opportunity to enroll in college for credit before completing high school.

Admission Application Deadline
August 1

Admission Contact
Kwurly M. Floyd, Director of Admissions, University of Arkansas at Pine Bluff, N. Cedar St., Pine Bluff, AR 71601; (501) 543-8493; toll-free 800-264-6586.

GRADUATION REQUIREMENTS
A minimum of 62 semester hours for an associate's degree and a minimum of 124 semester hours for a bachelor's degree; completion of core requirements to include 6 English, 11 science, 9 social sciences, 6 humanities, 5 physical education, and 5 physical education; satisfy English proficiency by junior year; complete comprehensive exam in major field; 2.0 GPA.

Grading System
A-F; I=Incomplete; Aud=Audit (no credit); NR=No grade/no record; W=Withdrawal; R=Repeated (no credit)

STUDENT BODY PROFILE
Total enrollment: 3,709

From in-state: 3,253

From other regions: 28 states, 4 foreign countries

Full-time undergraduates (male/female): 1,118/1,730

Part-time undergraduates (male/female): 362/446

Graduate students (male/female): 11/42

Ethnic/Racial Makeup
African American, 3,004; Hispanic, 7; Native American, 6; Caucasian, 681; International, 11.

Class of 1995 Profile

Number of applicants: 1,454

Number accepted: 1,099

Number enrolled: 718

Median ACT score: 16.11

Transfer applicants: 514

Transfers accepted: 425

Transfers enrolled: 214

FACULTY PROFILE

Number of faculty: 196

Student-teacher ratio: 19:1

Full-time faculty (male/female): 91/69

Part-time faculty (male/female): 21/15

Faculty with doctorates or other terminal
  degrees: 60%

Ethnic/Racial Makeup

African American, 145; Other/unclassi-
fied, 51.

SCHOOL CALENDAR

1993–94: August 16–May 13 (semester
  hours)

Commencement and conferring of degrees:
  May 14

Two summer semesters.

DEGREES OFFERED & NUMBER CONFERRED 1991–92:

Bachelor of Arts

Gerontology: 5

History and Government/History
  Education: n/a

Journalism: n/a

Political Science: 12

Social Work: 15

Sociology: 4

Bachelor of Science

Accounting: 28

AgriBusiness: 3

Agricultural Economics: n/a

Agricultural Education: n/a

Agronomy: 2

Animal Science: 1

Art Education: 3

Biology Education: 3

Business Administration: 42

Business Education: 9

Chemistry/Chemistry Education: 3

Child and Family Development: 3

Community Recreation: 4

Computer Science: 13

Criminal Justice: n/a

Dietetics: n/a

Early Childhood Education: 1

Economics: 6

Elementary Education: n/a

English/English Education: 1

Fashion Merchandising: 6

Finance: n/a

Fisheries, Biology: n/a

French/French Education: n/a

Home Economics Education: 1

Hospitality and Food Service Management:
  4

Industrial Technology: 11

Mathematics Education: 2

Music/Music Education: 6

Nursing: 17

Parks and Community Recreation: n/a

Philosophy and Religion: n/a

Physical Education: n/a

Physics: 1

Pre-Engineering: n/a

Psychology Education: 17

Recreation Education: 6

Restaurant Management: n/a

Social Science: 2

Special Education: 4

Speech and Drama: 19

Theater Arts: n/a

Trade and Industrial Education: n/a

SPECIAL PROGRAMS

Adult/Continuing Education Programs are available for nontraditional students returning to school or working full time.

College Level Examination Program (CLEP) determines the academic relevance of nontraditional educational experiences such as the military, on-the-job training, or other life experiences through a series of tests, and may grant students college credit for these experiences.

College orientation is mandatory for entering students for two days at no cost prior to the beginning of classes to acquaint students with the college and to prepare them for college life.

Cooperative Education Program alternates and combines classroom study with related paid work experience. The program provides academic credit and full time status during co-op placement.

English as a Second Language Program offers courses in English for students whose native language is not English.

Honors Program offers academically talented students a challenging program of study that includes special classes, seminars, colloquia, cultural activities, and special recognition to motivate participants.

Internships in various disciplines offer students the opportunity to apply theory and training in actual settings such as business/industry and hospitals/clinics.

Nursing and Social Work majors have arrangements with six members of the Cooperative Education Program for off-campus study.

Part-time (day and evening) Degree Programs allow students to earn undergraduate and graduate degrees on a part-time basis.

Remedial courses are offered to entering students to bring them up to admission standards and to help them adjust for success in college.

ROTC provides training in military science for commission as a second lieutenant in the U.S. Army. One-, two-, and three-year scholarships are available.

Study Abroad Program allows students to take courses at foreign colleges, institutes, and universities.

Three/two dual degree program in engineering allows students to get two degrees—one in liberal arts from home school and one in engineering from University of Arkansas at Fayetteville—by completing three years at matriculated school and two years at cooperating school.

ATHLETIC PROGRAMS

University of Arkansas at Pine Bluff is a member of the National Collegiate Athletic Association (NCAA) and the National Association of Intercollegiate Athletics (NAIA).

Intercollegiate sports: men's basketball, cross-country, football, golf, tennis, and track & field; women's basketball, cross-country, golf, tennis, track & field, and volleyball

Intramural sports: basketball, flag football, handball, racquetball, softball, tennis, and volleyball.

Athletic Contact

Archie Cooley, Athletics Director, University of Arkansas at Pine Bluff, N. Cedar St., Pine Bluff, AR 71601; (501) 541-6585.

LIBRARY HOLDINGS

The Watson Memorial Library houses 208,00 bound volumes, 147,075 microforms, 810 periodical subscriptions, 1,150 audiovisuals, and several computers for student use. Special collections include the John M. Ross, Knox Nelson, and J. B. Watson Collections.

STUDENT LIFE

Special Regulations

Mandatory two-day college orientation session for freshmen and transfers; cars must be registered.

Campus Services

Health center; personal and psychological counseling; career counseling and placement; student employment services; remediation; tutoring; post office; testing service for ACT, CLEP, GRE, NTE, and GMAT; religious activities.

Campus Activities

Social and cultural activities include theater, band, and chorale. Annual events include the candlelight march, concert, and other programs commemorating Dr. Martin Luther King, Jr. during the month of January. Spring Emphasis Week, Women's Day Convocation, and Black History Month are celebrated each year. Students may get involved in the *Arkansawyer* (student-run newspaper) or the *Lion,* an annual student publication supervised by a faculty advisor.

The Lyceum Program provides concerts, art exhibits, lecturers, and dramatic presentations. The Student Union Governing Board works to create and improve the university's social, cultural, and recreational atmosphere and serves as an advisory board to the Director of the student union.

Leadership opportunities can be found in the Student Government Association or the various other clubs and organizations on campus. Greek-letter fraternities include Alpha Phi Alpha, Kappa Alpha Psi, Omega Psi Phi, and Phi Beta Kappa; sororities include Alpha Kappa Alpha, Delta Sigma Theta, Sigma Gamma Rho, and Zeta Phi Beta. Honorary societies are also represented on campus.

The city of Pine Bluff is located on the Arkansas River that provides an exciting variety of water recreation including boating, fishing, swimming, and camping. The Southeast Arts and Sciences Center and the Convention Center are home to the area's cultural and pop entertainment. Pine Bluff is located 45 miles southeast of Little Rock and 150 miles southwest of Memphis, Tennessee.

Housing Availability

1,000 housing spaces, including a new student dorm and newly remodeled dormitories.

Handicapped Services

Wheelchair accessibility

NOTABLE ALUMNI

Janese M. Bland, 1980–Editor and columnist, *Hollywood Gazette*

Willie Miles Burns, 1939–Vice president, Johnson Publishing Co.

L. C. Greenwood, 1969–Former professional athlete, Pittsburgh Steelers; construction executive

Dr. Dorothy Littlejohn Magett, 1953–Deputy Superintendent of Public Instruction, State of Illinois

Rev. Florida Morehead, 1969–Executive director, National Society of Black Engineers

Thomas L . Stevens, 1954–President, Los Angeles Trade and Technical College, Los Angeles, California

California

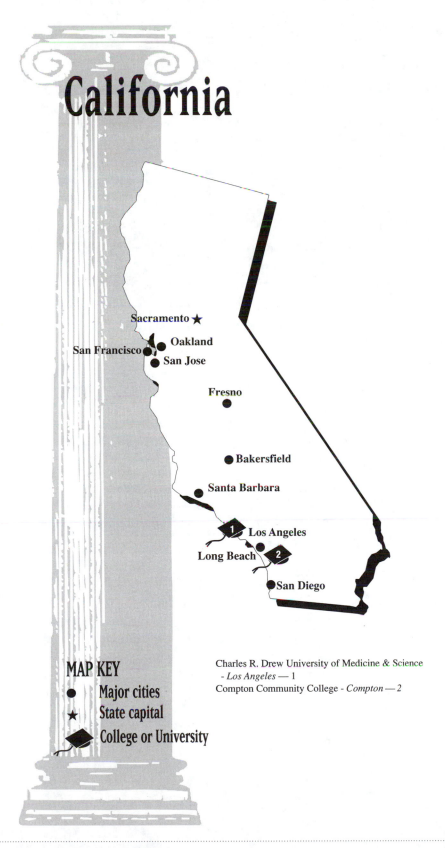

Sacramento ★

Oakland

San Francisco

San Jose

Fresno

Bakersfield

Santa Barbara

1 Los Angeles

Long Beach 2

San Diego

MAP KEY

● Major cities

★ State capital

◆ College or University

Charles R. Drew University of Medicine & Science
- *Los Angeles* — 1
Compton Community College - *Compton* — 2

CHARLES R. DREW UNIVERSITY OF MEDICINE AND SCIENCE

1621 E. 120th St.
Los Angeles, CA
90059
Phone: (213) 563-4960
Fax: (213) 563-4988

Total Enrollment:
140

Level of Selectivity:
Competitive

Motto:
Care with competence
and compassion

HISTORY

Charles R. Drew University of Medicine and Science is a private four-year professional medical school. Recommended by the McCone Commission after the civil disturbance in Watts in 1965, The Charles R. Drew post Graduate School of Medicine (CRDPSOM) was chartered in 1966 as a private non-profit corporation. In 1969, it opened its doors as the educational component of the King/Drew Medical Center, allied in its vision and purpose with the Martin Luther King, Jr. General Hospital where students receive clinical experience. The institution's official name was changed to the Charles R. Drew University of Medicine and Science to reflect an expanded academic role and identity in 1987.

The school pursues a mission that embraces the needs and problems of society's most disadvantaged and neglected communities. It is a global perspective... one that finds commonality in the plight of the urban ghetto of Los Angeles, the rural villages of Africa, and the peasant farmlands of Asia.

The Drew mission finds inspiration in the life and work of the man for whom the university is named, Dr. Charles R. Drew, a distinguished surgeon who gave courage and offered talent to the care of others, and left behind a legacy of medical discovery. His research and application theories regarding blood and its preservation are among the most significant developments in contemporary medicine, yet Dr. Drew died as a result of being denied blood plasma because he was a black man.

One of only four black medical schools in the nation, Charles R. Drew University interprets its mission in a unique approach of academic models and community programs that address the medical, educational, social, and economic needs of underserved populations. The Drew/UCLA Medical Education Program offers a curriculum and clinical programs for graduate and post-graduate studies in medicine.

ACCREDITATION

American Medical Association (joint program through UCLA)

COSTS PER YEAR

1992–93 Tuition: $3,833 (in-state); $11,532 (out-state)

Room and board: $7,380

Special fees: $2,386

Books: $2,140

Estimated total cost: $15,739 (in-state); $23,438 (out-state)

FINANCIAL AID

Financial Aid Specific to the School

85% of the student body received financial aid during 1991–92.

Financial Aid Contact

Mr. Kelvin Kelly, Associate Controller, Charles R. Drew University, 1621 E. 120th St., Los Angeles, CA 90059; (213)563-4960.

ADMISSION REQUIREMENTS

MCAT required

Entrance Requirements

Medical College Admission Test (MCAT) scores must be submitted by May 28 (MCAT exam should be completed no more than four years prior to matriculation). Other requirements include: one year of college mathematics, to include at least one course in calculus; one year of college physics, with laboratory; two years of college biology, with laboratory; two years of college chemistry, with laboratory and including at least one course in organic chemistry or quantitative analysis; at least one year of organic chemistry; one year of college English; and one year of a foreign language, preferably Spanish (exempt if proficiency exam passed). Courses recommended under the requirement for biology are cell biology, genetics, embryology, physiology, histology, and anatomy. Courses under the requirement for English may include composition, literature, or other courses emphasizing reading comprehension. Three letters of recommendation or composite report from a pre-professional advisory committee of the student's college or university are needed by January 29. Interview by two members of the Admissions Committee by May 28. Premedical requirements must be met by all students. Application for admission should be sent to the American Medical College Admission Service (AMCAS), Association of American Medical College, 2450 N. Street, N.W., Washington, DC 20037 by November 15th of the year preceding anticipated entry. A $30 application fee is required.

Transfer students may be admitted with advanced standing into the third year only of the Drew/UCLA Medical Education Program. Minimum requirements for all transfer applicants to the third year shall include the following: successful completion of the first two years of pre-clinical or basic science course requirements at any fully accredited United States or Canadian medical school and satisfactory or passing performance on the National Board of Medical Examiners/ United States Medical License Examination Part 1.

Application for transfer into the third year from foreign or United States citizens who have completed the first two years of pre-clinical or basic science course requirements at foreign, non-Canadian, or unaccredited medical schools will not be accepted.

Admission Application Deadline

November 15 of the year preceding anticipated entry.

Admission Contact

Roland Betts, Charles R. Drew University of Medicine and Science, Office of Student Medical Affairs, 1621 East 120th St., Los Angeles, CA 90059; (213) 563-4960.

GRADUATION REQUIREMENTS

Completion of two basic science years at the Westwood campus of the UCLA School of Medicine to include the following for the first year fall semester: 5 behavioral sciences, 2 biomathematics, 1 doctoring, 8 gross anatomy, 4 interactive teaching (I & II), medical ethics, and 5 microscopic anatomy; first year spring: 6 basic neurology, 5 biological chemistry, 4 biological chemistry lab, 8 physiology, and doctoring; second year fall: 2 epidemiology, 8 general pathology, 5 general pharmacology, 2 interactive teaching, 8 microbiology and immunology, and no clinical correlates; second year spring: 12 pathophysiology of disease, 12 clinical fundamentals, 1 clinical pharmacology, 3 psychopathy, and 2 genetics.

Completion of junior-senior clinical continuum at King/Drew Medical Center of 58-week clerkship must include the following weeks: two anesthesiology, fourteen medicine (I and II), eight obstetrics-gynecology, two otorhinolaryngology, eight pediatrics, two primary core, two primary care selective, six psychiatry, two radiology, and twelve surgery (I and II). Also needed are 21 months (one-half day/week) of primary care continuum and 20 weeks of electives, of which eight weeks must be sub-internships selected from UCLA handbook and four weeks must be at the 400 level; the remaining twelve weeks may be taken at any site by approval of the Dean of Student Affairs.

Completion of a one-week prologue to medicine course is conducted at UCLA.

Grading System

A–F, I=Incomplete; Plus and minus suffixes to letter grades may be submitted

STUDENT BODY PROFILE

Total enrollment: 140

Ethnic/Racial Makeup

African American, 70; Hispanic, 42; Other/unclassified, 28.

SCHOOL CALENDAR

1992–93: (semesters)

Commencement and conferring of degrees: May

One summer session for seniors.

DEGREES OFFERED 1991–92

M.D. degree

SPECIAL PROGRAMS

The Allied Health Program requires the completion of a minimum of 40 to 100 hours in community service, depending on program. The field placement is an independent study and must be based on one of the six general education themes, a clinical topic, or a research interest. The study must be approved by the Allied Health faculty member supervising the project.

Charles R. Drew University Medical Magnet High School focuses on nurturing and encouraging underserved students to practice medicine. The curriculum and training exposes ninth and twelfth grade students to careers in the health care and scientific professions. The program gives each student the academic foundation necessary to successfully qualify and compete in college. High school electives are devoted to work assignments in hospitals, community health agencies, or in doctors' offices; some students are assigned to research laboratories of Drew University for one-on-one research assignments. Students are also required to develop a science project and encouraged to enter the Los Angeles County Science Fair and other local competitions. The teacher/student ratio is 1/20; the maximum enrollment is 203. For acceptance, students must complete the "Choices Brochure" issued by the California School District.

Drew MCAT Preparation Program is an intensive summer MCAT prep program. This seven-week program prepares students for the "new" MCAT, with coursework in scientific reading, critical thinking, science problems, writing, verbal reasoning, and physical and biological sciences. The application deadline date is March 31. Contact Office of Pre-Med Programs; (213) 563-4926.

Drew/UCLA Medical Education Program is especially designed to attract those students who have an interest in addressing the concerns of underserved populations, and who are prepared to do so with competence and compassion. Graduate medical students accepted into this program will benefit from the best efforts of both Drew and UCLA in a combined curriculum. The first and second years for all students will be spent chiefly at the Westwood campus of UCLA. All students who seek admission to the first year of the Drew/UCLA Medical Education Program are required to initiate their application through the American Medical College Admission Service (AMCAS).

Also offered are the Pre-Matriculant Reinforcement in Medical Education (PRIME) Program at Drew University and the Prologue at UCLA. Prior to the beginning of classes in the first year, students are required to attend the three-week PRIME Program conducted at Drew University. The purpose of the PRIME Program is to orient students to the King/Drew Medical Center and the surrounding community and to introduce students to the academic rigors of medical school, stressing learning skills. Prior to the final two-year clinical program at King/Drew Medical Center, students take a one week prologue or introduction to medicine course at UCLA.

Five Research Institutes, sponsored by Drew University, conduct collaborative research initiated by individual investigators. University research programs include the Biobehavioral Institute, which focuses on the relationship between behavior, culture, and biology in health and disease; the Neurological Sciences Institute, which conducts research on neurological problems and disorders; the International Health Institute, which extends the Drew mission of research and training to some sixteen countries in Africa, Asia, and South and Central America in collaboration with other international health organizations; the Research Training Institute, which sponsors the Minority Biomedical Research (MBRS) Program, the Minority Access to Research Centers (MARC) Program, and the Minority High School Research Apprentice (MHSSRA) Program to encourage faculty research and the entry of minority students into biomedical research; and the Community and Preventive Medicine Institute, which develops strategies for the prevention of illness and health promotion.

STUDENT LIFE
Special regulations
Students are bound by the conduct of the Medical Code of Ethics. An automobile is required for transportation to affiliated hospitals in second, third, and fourth years.

Handicapped services
Wheelchair accessibility.

NOTABLE ALUMNI
Adelaide Willis, M.D.–Drew faculty

Artis Woodward, M.D.–President, Drew Alumni Association

COMPTON COMMUNITY COLLEGE

1111 Last Artesia Blvd.
Compton, CA 90221-5393
Phone: (310) 637-2660

Total Enrollment:
5,700

Level of Selectivity:
Noncompetitive

Motto:
Vincit Omnia Veritas
(Truth Conquers All)

HISTORY

Compton Community College (CCC) is a state-supported, two-year, coed college founded in 1927. As a department of Compton-Union High School, it is one of the few four-year junior colleges in the nation that combines the eleventh and twelfth grades of high school with the first and second year of college. In 1963, it moved to its present location.

Compton's mission is to help each student acquire the knowledge, skills, and attitudes essential to a productive life and personal well-being. The college offers students community service and cultural programs, technical and vocational programs, programs with business and industry, excellence in instruction, professional growth of faculty and staff, and more. Compton is a member of the American Council on Education.

ACCREDITATION

Compton Community College is accredited by the Western Association of Schools and Colleges to award the Bachelor of Arts and Bachelor's degrees. Certificates are also awarded.

COSTS PER YEAR

1991–92 Tuition: $120 (in-state); $3,180 (out-state)

Special fees: $125

Books: $400

Estimated total cost: $645 (in-state); $3,705 (out-state)

FINANCIAL AID
Financial Aid Specific to the School

80% of the student body received financial during 1991–92.

Athletic scholarships are available to students participating in intercollegiate sports.

Other scholarships are awarded on the basis of academic achievement and financial need.

Emergency non-interest loans of $50 are available for a short period for unexpected expenses.

The Cooperative Education Program combines classroom study with related paid work experience. The program provides academic credit and full-time status during co-op placement.

California Students Aid Commission administers the Cal A, B, and C Grants to students who are U.S. citizens and California residents and who demonstrate financial need.

The state-funded Board of Governors Grant (BOGG) helps to low-income California residents who pay the enrollment fee.

Financial Aid Deadline
May 15

Financial Aid Contact
Director of Financial Aid, Compton Community College, 111 Last Artesia Blvd., Compton, CA 90221; (310) 637-2660.

ADMISSION REQUIREMENTS
Open admission.

Entrance Requirements
Students under eighteen must have graduated from high school and must pass the California High School Proficiency Test or receive approval from high school counselor. Any person over eighteen years of age who is a legal resident of California is eligible to attend Compton.

GED students must meet basic admission requirements.

Transfer students are required to submit high school and college transcripts.

International Students must submit a complete official transcript of all high school and college work translated in English, take the TOEFL examination, and provide proof of ability to pay all college costs.

Early admissions allows academically gifted high school students the opportunity to enroll in college before completing high school.

Admission Application Deadline
Rolling admission provides no specific date for notification of admission so applicant is informed as soon as admission decision is made.

Admissions Contact
Dr. Essie French-Preston, Associate Dean of Enrollment Services, Compton Community College, Compton, CA 90221; (310) 637-2660, ext. 400.

GRADUATION REQUIREMENTS
A minimum of 60 units and completion of the core requirements to include the following units: 9 humanities, 6 English, 6 science (one lab), 3 mathematics, 3 literature and philosophy, and 3 foreign language. A 2.0 or "C" average is needed.

Grading System
A–F; CR=Satisfactory; NC=Non-satisfactory; IP=In Progress (course extends beyond semester); RD=Report Delayed; W=Withdrawal.

STUDENT BODY PROFILE
Total enrollment (male/female):
  2,166/3,534

From in-state: 5,073

Full-time undergraduates (male/female):
  866/1,414

Part-time undergraduates (male/female):
  1,300/2,120

Ethnic/Racial Makeup
African American, 3,420; Hispanic, 1,482; Asian, 114; Native American, 57; International, 114.

Class of 1995 Profile

Number of applicants: 1,383

Number accepted: 100%

FACULTY PROFILE

Number of faculty: 348

Student-teacher ratio: 24:1

Full-time faculty: 101

Part-time faculty: 247

Faculty with doctorates or other terminal
degrees: 20%

SCHOOL CALENDAR

1991–92: September 3–June 18 (semesters)

Commencement and conferring of degrees:
June 19

One summer session.

DEGREES OFFERED 1991–92:
Associate of Arts

Accounting

Allied Health

Art

Automotive Technology

Biology

Business Administration/Management

Chemistry

Child Care

Computer Technologies

Criminal Justice

Data Processing

Drafting

Economics

Engineering Technology

English

Family and Consumer Economics

Food Science

French

Geography

German

Graphic Communications

History

Liberal Arts

Law Enforcement

Machine/Tool Technology

Marketing

Mathematics

Mechanical Engineering

Medical Assistance

Music

Nursing

Nutrition

Office Management

Paralegal

Philosophy

Photography BA

Physical Education BA

Physical Sciences

Physics

Practical Nursing

Psychology

Recreational services

Respiratory Therapy

Science Technologies

Secretarial

Spanish

Speech

Theater Arts

Welding

Associate Degree (Occupational)

Accounting

Art

Auto Collision Repair

Business

Business Management

Child Development

Clothing and Textiles

Computer Information Systems

Construction

Criminal Justice

Drafting Technology

Economics

Electronics

Emergency Medical Technology

Engineering

Fire Sciences

Graphic Communication

Machine Technology

Management

Marketing

Nursing

Photography

Radiologic Technology

Recreation and Leisure

Secretarial

Welding Technology

Word Processing

Certificates

Accounting

Art

Auto Collision Repair

Automotive Repair

Automotive Technology

Bilingual/Bicultural

Business Management and Administration

Child Development

Computer Aided Design

Computer Numerical Control

Computer Programming

Construction

Cosmetology

Criminal Justice

Electronic Technician

Emergency Medical Technology

General Office

Graphic Communication

Machine Technology

Management

Mechanical Engineering

Paramedic Program

Photography

Recreation and Leisure

Telecommunications

Vocational Nursing

Welding

Word Processing

Percent of graduates that later obtain higher degrees:

30%.

SPECIAL PROGRAMS

Accelerated Study Program allows students to complete their undergraduate degree in a shorter period of time than the traditional period of four years.

Adult or Continuing Education Program is available for nontraditional students returning to school or working full time.

English as a Second Language is a program that offers courses in English for students whose native language is not English.

Extended Opportunity Programs and Services (EOP & S) is a program designed to recruit and increase success rate of ethnic minorities and/or economically disadvantaged groups. The program seeks to equalize educational opportunities and make education a reality for students who have traditionally been excluded.

An honors program offers academically talented students a challenging program of study that includes special classes, seminars, colloquia, cultural activities, and special recognition to motivate participants.

Part-time degree programs allow students to earn an undergraduate degree while attending school part time.

Remedial courses are offered to entering students to bring them up to admission standards.

Special programs and services are available for the learning disabled, visually impaired, hearing impaired, and speech disabled.

The Study Abroad Program allows students to go to a foreign country (Spain or Jamaica) for a specified period of time for part of their college education.

ATHLETIC PROGRAMS

Compton Community College is a member of the Southern California Conferences, Western State Conference (football), and the South Coast Conference (women's basketball).

Intercollegiate sports: men's baseball, basketball, football, cross-country, soccer, and track; women's baseball, basketball, cross-country, soccer, and track.

Intramural sports: baseball, basketball, football, tennis, track, and soccer.

LIBRARY HOLDINGS

The library hold 41,985 bound volumes, 400 periodical subscriptions, 6,000 microform titles, 1,862 audiovisuals, four computers for student use, and one electric typewriter.

STUDENT LIFE

Campus Services

Health clinic, personal and psychological counseling, career counseling and placement, and student employment services.

Campus Activities

Social and cultural activities include theater, band, concerts, chorale, dance, a lecture series, films, art exhibits, and a music conservatory. Students may get involved in writing or photography for the *Tartar Shield,* a weekly newspaper or the *News of Compton Community College,* an information report published by the college every six months.

Leadership opportunities are found in the Student Government Association. Special interest clubs are African-American Student Union, Christian Club, International Student Organization, Latino-American Student Club, Disabled Student Association, and California Nurses Student Association. Alpha Gamma Sigma (Tau Chapter) honor society is represented on campus. The greek-letter society Phi Beta Lambda (Future Business Leaders of America) is also represented.

Located in the city of Compton, Compton Community College students have access to a variety of entertainment both on campus and in the surrounding cities. Los Angeles is an half hour away and Pasadena is 30 miles to the north. Within fifteen miles from the campus are the famous Redondo Beach and Long Beach. Hollywood, where Universal Studios and Warner Bros. Studios are located, is within a 30-minute drive. Disneyland in Anaheim, California, is 45 minutes to one hour from the campus. San Diego is approximately 120 miles from Los Angeles, and Death Valley National Monument is 350 miles away.

Delaware

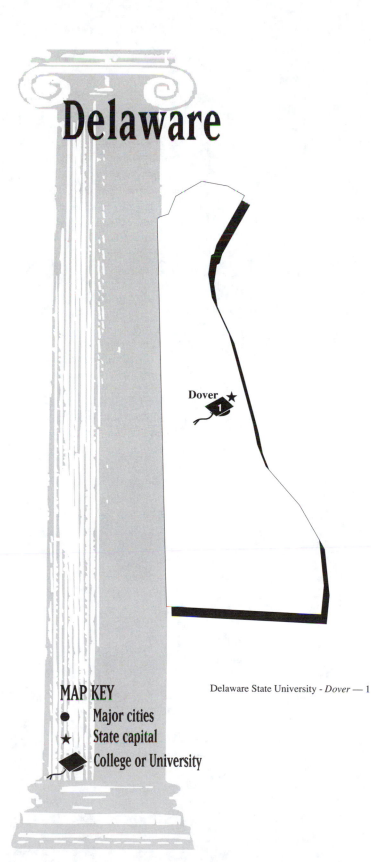

Dover

Delaware State University - *Dover* — 1

MAP KEY
- ● Major cities
- ★ State capital
- 🎓 College or University

DELAWARE STATE UNIVERSITY

Dover, DE 19901
Phone: (302) 739-4917

Total Enrollment:
2,882

Level of Selectivity:
Moderately
competitive

Motto:
A Past to Honor: A
Future to Insure

HISTORY

Delaware State University (DSU) is a four-year, state-supported, coed, liberal arts college founded in 1891 as The State College for Colored Students. It was established as a result of the 58th General Assembly of the State of Delaware passing legislation establishing a college for the education of colored students in agriculture and the mechanical arts. This law was built on provisions of the Morrill Acts of 1862 and 1890, which provided for land grant colleges.

DSU serves as the land grant institution for the state, providing higher education for the academically challenged and the academically gifted. Delaware State is committed foremost to academic excellence and intellectual competence. It strives to provide and maintain a corps of scholars, lecturers, and educators dedicated to the enlightenment of mankind. The college is now a comprehensive institution, including agricultural, technical, liberal arts, fine arts, business, engineering studies, teacher education, and professional training.

From a one-plant facility in 1891, DSU is now a 400-acre campus with thirteen modern buildings including a science center, a library/learning resource center, an ETV building, and an agricultural center.

ACCREDITATION

Delaware State University is a member of the Middle States Association of Colleges and Secondary Schools (MSACS) to award the Bachelor of Arts, Bachelor of Science, and Master's degrees.

Other Accreditation

Accreditation Board for Engineering and Technology

Accrediting Council on Education in Journalism and Mass Communication

American Assembly of Collegiate Schools of Business

American Chemical Society

American Council on Pharmaceutical Education

American Physical Therapy Association

Council of Social Work Education

Delaware State Board of Education

National Architectural Accrediting Board

National Council for Accreditation of Teacher Education

National League of Nursing

COSTS PER YEAR

1992–93 Tuition: $1,701 (in-state); $4,561 (out-state)

Room and board: $1,860 (room); $1,350 (board)

Special fees: $185

Books: $600

Estimated total cost: $5,696 (in-state); $8,556 (out-state)

FINANCIAL AID

1991–92 Institutional Funding

Number of scholarships and grants: 1,185

Total amount of scholarships and grants: $1,528,540

Range of scholarships and grants: $500–$1,500

1991–92 Federal and State Funding

Number of scholarships and grants: 1,315

Total amount of scholarships and grants: $1,637,773

Range of scholarships and grants: $770–$1,700

Number of loans: 577

Total amount of loans: $1,555,584

Range of loans: $500–$2,500

Number of work-study: 1,005

Total amount of work-study: $175,739

Range of work-study: $400–$1,200

Financial Aid Specific to the School

60% of the student body received financial aid during 1991–92.

Departmental Scholarships are awarded to eighteen juniors or seniors who have studied at least one full year at DSU with a minimum 3.25 GPA, shown excellence in a major field, intend to pursue graduate school, and have performed an approved supervised project in the major. Scholarships are $500 a year. Students should apply to their department the spring prior to the award.

Athletic scholarships may pay up to 100% of expenses for students participating in varsity football, basketball, wrestling, or track. For more information contact the coach of a particular sport.

Endowed scholarships number approximately 20.

Music scholarships are awarded to students with exceptional musical abilities who participate in the college band, choir, or other musical groups. Apply to the music department the spring prior to the semester of award.

Thurgood Marshall Black Education Fund provides a four-year scholarship at this public black college. Qualifying students must have a high school GPA of 3.0 or better and a SAT score of 1000 or ACT score of 24 or more. Students must be recommended by high school counselor as exceptional or exemplary in the creative or performing arts. Scholarship pays tuition, fees, room, and board, not to exceed $6,000 annually.

Army and Air Force ROTC offer two-, three-, and four-year scholarships that pay tuition, fees, books, and other expenses, and provide a monthly stipend of $100.

Christa McAuliffe Teacher Scholarship Loan Program is a state funded program to encourage residents of Delaware to pursue a teaching career in public elementary or secondary education. Freshmen must be in the upper half of the high school graduating class and have a SAT score of 1050 or ACT score of 25. The loan may be renewed for up to four years provided the student maintains a GPA of at least 2.75. Repayment is made by either teaching in Delaware Public Schools or paying by cash over a period of five years at 9% interest. Contact the Delaware Postsecondary Commission; (302) 571-3240.

Delaware Post Secondary Scholarships are awarded to state residents attending colleges and universities within the state and who demonstrate financial need. Maximum award amount is $1,000. Contact the Delaware Postsecondary Commission, Carvel State Office Bldg., 820 French St., Wilmington, DE 19801; (302) 571-3240.

Delaware Nursing Incentive Scholarship Program awards funds on a merit basis to encourage nursing careers at state-operated hospitals. Contact should be made by May 31st to the Delaware Postsecondary Education Commission, Carvel State Office Bldg., 820 French St., Wilmington, DE 19801; (302) 571-3240.

Delaware State Grant program is available to all residents of the state who are enrolled full time and demonstrate financial need.

Delaware State Incentive Grant is awarded to forty students who are state residents with a minimum 3.50 GPA and who have completed 30 semester hours. The amount of the grant is $1,250.

Delaware State Scholarships are awarded to entering students with a 3.0 or better GPA and who rank in the top 25% of their class. SAT, ACT, or CEEB scores must be submitted. The application for admission serves as initial application for these scholarships.

Paul Douglass Teacher Scholarship program provides grants to outstanding undergraduates interested in teaching pre-school, elementary, or secondary school as a career. Grants range up to $5,000 per academic year. Qualifying students must have graduated in the top 10% of their class. Recipients are obligated to teach in any state for two years for every year of scholarship assistance.

Financial Aid Deadline

June 1

Financial Aid Contact

Leo Lecompte, Director of Student Financial Aid, Delaware State University, Dover, DE 19901; (302) 736-4908

ADMISSION REQUIREMENTS

SAT or ACT required.

Entrance Requirements

Graduation from an accredited high school and completion of the college prep curriculum with the following 15 units: 4 English, 2 mathematics, 2 science (1 laboratory), 2 social studies/history, and 5 electives; must have "C" average; recommendations from school counselor and school administrator are needed. A $10 application fee is required.

GED students must meet basic admission standards.

Transfer students must submit official transcripts of all previous college work, have a cumulative GPA of 2.0, be in good standing at the last institution attended, and take last 30 hours at DSU. Transfers must meet the predictive average requirement and SAT requirement for freshman students.

International Students must submit official transcripts of all secondary and college work and submit results on all national examinations, such as GCE. Students from non-English-speaking countries must pass the TOEFL examination and prove ability to pay all college costs.

Admission Application Deadline
June 1 (fall); December 1 (spring)

Admission Contact
Jethro C. Williams, Director of Admissions, Office of Admissions, Delaware State University, Dover, DE 19901; (302) 736-4917.

GRADUATION REQUIREMENTS
A minimum of 121 semester hours and completion of the core requirements to include the following hours: 6 mathematics, 6 natural science, 7 social science, 11 basic intellectual skills, and 12 humanities; minimum 2.0 GPA; "C" average or better in all major courses; and last 30 hours completed at DSU.

Grading System
A–F; I=Incomplete; AU=Audit (no credit); NR=No grade/no record; W=Withdrawal; S=Satisfactory; U=Unsatisfactory; P=Passing;

STUDENT BODY PROFILE
Total enrollment (male/female): 1,232/1,650

From in-state: 1,844

Other regions: 26 states and 7 foreign countries

Full-time undergraduates (male/female): 962/1,161

Part-time undergraduates (male/female): 196/305

Graduate students (male/female): 74/184

Ethnic/Racial Makeup
African American, 1,760; Hispanic, 51; Asian, 16; Native American, 11; Caucasian, 1,003; International, 41.

Class of 1995 Profile
Number of applicants: 1,865

Number accepted: 1,212

Number enrolled: 485

Average high school GPA: 2.49

FACULTY PROFILE
Number of faculty: 157

Student-teacher ratio: 15:1

Full-time faculty (male/female): 62/38

Part-time faculty: 57

Faculty with doctorates or other terminal degrees: 57%

SCHOOL CALENDAR
1992–93: August 26–May 7 (semester hours)

Commencement and conferring of degrees: May 8

One summer session.

DEGREES OFFERED 1991–92:
Bachelor of Arts
Communications

Criminal Justice

Drama

Fine Arts

French

Journalism

Parks and Recreation

Political Science

Psychology

Secretarial Programs

Sociology

Social Work

Spanish

Theater

Bachelor of Science
Accounting

Aerospace Aeronautical Engineering

Agribusiness

Agricultural Sciences

Airline Piloting/Aviation

Art/Art Education

Biology

Business Administration/Management

Chemistry

Computer/Information Sciences

Early Childhood Education

Education

Electrical Engineering

Elementary Education

Engineering

Health, Physical Education, and Recreation

History

Horticultural Sciences

Hotel/Restaurant Management

Junior High Education

Marketing Management

Mathematics

Music Education

Natural Resources

Nursing

Physical Education

Physics

Protective Services

Soil and Water Sciences

Special Education

Trade Technical Education

Vegetation Management

Wildlife Management

Bachelor of Technology

Agri-Business Technology

Agricultural Engineering Design

Agricultural Engineering Technology

Business Administration Technology

Business Technology

Chemical Laboratory Technology

Civil Engineering Technology

Criminal Justice Technology

Data Processing Technology

Dental Hygiene Technology

Electronics/Electrical Engineering Technology

Engineering Drafting Technology

Engineering Technology

Environmental Engineering Technology

Executive Secretary Technology

Fire Protection Technology

Food Service Technology

Hotel/Motel Restaurant Management Technology

Human Services Technology

Industrial Engineering Technology

Journalism Technology

Library Science Technology

Manufacturing Engineering Technology

Mechanical Engineering Technology

Medical Laboratory Technology

Natural Resources Technology

Science Education Technology

Pre-Professional

Engineering

Veterinary Medicine

SPECIAL PROGRAMS

Accelerated Study Program allows students to complete their undergraduate degree in a shorter period of time than the traditional period of four years.

Adult/Continuing Education Programs are available for nontraditional students returning to school or working full time.

Advanced Placement (AP) grants college credit for postsecondary work completed in high school. Students scoring three on the AP test will receive credit by examination for each course.

College Level Examination Program (CLEP) determines the academic relevance of nontraditional educational experiences such as the military, on-the-job training, or other life experiences, through a series of tests and may grant students college credit for these experiences.

College orientation is offered for $35 to entering students for four days prior to the beginning of classes to acquaint students with the college and to prepare them for college life; parents may attend.

Cooperative Education Program combines classroom study with related paid work experience. The program provides academic credit and full-time status during co-op placement.

English as a Second Language Program offers courses in English for students whose native language is not English.

Honors program offers academically talented students a challenging program of study that includes special classes, seminars, colloquia, cultural activities, and special recognition to motivate participants.

Individualized majors allow students to create their own major program(s) of study.

Internships in various disciplines offer students the opportunity to apply theory and training in actual settings, such as business and industry or hospitals and clinics.

Part-time (day and evening) degree programs allow students to earn undergraduate and graduate degrees on a part-time basis.

Remedial courses are offered to entering students to bring them up to admission standards and to help them adjust for success in college.

ROTC provides training in military science for commission as a second lieutenant in the U.S. Army or Air Force. Two- and four-year scholarships are available.

Student Exchange Program allows students to attend cooperating school for a specified period for credit toward degree program at home school.

Three/two degree program in engineering in cooperation with the University of Delaware allows students to get two degrees—one in liberal arts from the home school and one in engineering from the cooperating school—by completing three years at matriculated school and two years at cooperating school.

ATHLETIC PROGRAMS

Delaware State University is affiliated with the National Collegiate Athletic Association (NCAA), Division I, and the Mid-Eastern Athletic Conference.

Intercollegiate sports: men's baseball, basketball, football, cross-country, track & field, tennis, and wrestling; women's basketball, cross-country, track & field, tennis, and volleyball.

Intramural sports: Basketball, bowling, softball, table tennis, tennis, track & field, and volleyball.

Athletic Contact

John Martin, Director of Athletics, Delaware State University, Dover, DE 19901; (302) 736-4928

LIBRARY HOLDINGS

The William C. Jason Library holds 208,776 bound volumes, 319,786 microforms, 1,055 periodical subscriptions, and 230,000 government documents. Special collections include the Delaware Collection and the Black American Collection.

STUDENT LIFE

Special Regulations

Alcohol is not permitted on campus; automobiles must be registered at a cost of $1.00. Dorm visiting hours are Sunday through Thursday, 4–11 pm and Friday through Saturday, 8 pm–2 am.

Campus Services

Student health, personal and psychological counseling, career placement, student support, and tutoring services; and religious activities.

Campus Activities

Social and cultural activities include theater, chorale, band, dance, modeling, and karate. Annual activities include religious emphasis week and art exhibitions of student and faculty work. Students may work on the *Hornet* (student-run newspaper) or the *Statesman* (yearbook). Communication majors may work in the student-run radio station, WDSC.

Leadership opportunities are found in such groups as the Student Government Association (SGA) or the more than 30 department clubs and interest groups, such as the Men's Council or Women's Senate (two self-governing bodies within residence halls). Greek letter fraternities include Alpha Phi Alpha, Omega Psi Phi, Kappa Alpha Psi, and Phi Beta Sigma; sororities include Alpha Kappa Alpha, Delta Sigma Theta, Zeta Phi Beta, and Sigma Gamma Rho. Honor societies include Alpha Chi, Alpha Kappa Mu, Delta Mu Delta, Epsilon Delta Epsilon, Kappa Delta Pi, Phi Alpha Theta, Psi Chi, and Pinnacle. Professional societies include Phi Beta Lambda, Inc., Pre-Medical Society, and Student National Education Association. Social and service organizations include Alpha Phi Omega, Kappa Kappa Psi, and Groove Phi Groove.

Delaware State University is located in the state capital, Dover, population approximately 22,500. Dover offers shopping, fine dining, and museums. Points of interest include the home of John Dickinson, signer of the Declaration of Independence and the Constitution of the United States. The city is close to several resort areas, including Rehoboth Beach in Delaware, Ocean City in Maryland, or Cape May in New Jersey. All major mass transit systems—air, bus, and rail—are available.

Housing Availability
1,002 housing spaces.

Handicapped Services
Services include wheelchair accessibility, elevators, special parking, and specially equipped restrooms. The campus is in the process of lowering telephones and drinking fountains.

Florida

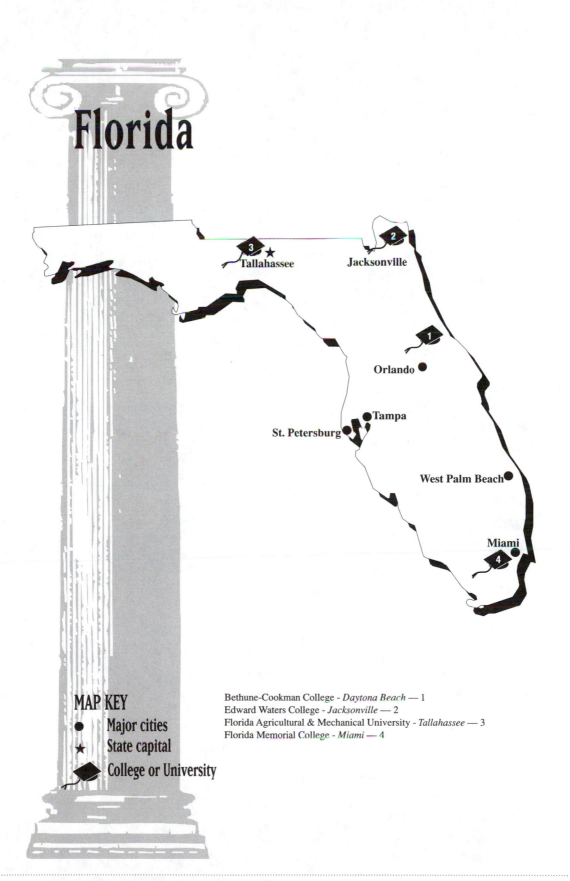

MAP KEY

● Major cities

★ State capital

◆ College or University

Bethune-Cookman College - *Daytona Beach* — 1
Edward Waters College - *Jacksonville* — 2
Florida Agricultural & Mechanical University - *Tallahassee* — 3
Florida Memorial College - *Miami* — 4

BETHUNE-COOKMAN COLLEGE

640 Second Ave.
Daytona Beach, FL
32115
Phone: (904) 255-1401
Toll-free:
800-448-0228
Fax: (904) 257-5338

Total Enrollment:
2,301

Level of Selectivity:
Slightly competitive

Motto:
Enter To Learn,
Depart To Serve

HISTORY

Founded in 1904, Bethune-Cookman College is a four-year, private, coed college affiliated with the United Methodist Church. It is the architectural offspring of the union between Cookman-Collegiate Institute, founded in 1872 by Reverend D.S.S. Darnell, and Daytona Normal and Industrial Institute for Girls, founded in 1904 by Dr. Mary McLeod Bethune. This historic merger took place in 1923.

From 1923 to 1932, the school served as a rudimentary training center for students. In 1932, it functioned as a high school and junior college. Bethune-Cookman became a four-year college in 1942, awarding its first Bachelor of Science degree in 1943.

Bethune-Cookman's mission is to serve the educational, cultural, and social needs of its students in the Christian tradition. The current president, Dr. Oswald P. Bronson, Sr. says "Excellence in academic study as a religious endeavor is given top priority at Bethune-Cookman." This excellence results from such emphases as small classes, low student-to-teacher ratios, research efforts, broad-based curriculum offerings, and dynamic teachers.

The home of Dr. McLeod on this campus was declared a national historic landmark by the National Park Service of the U.S. Department of the Interior in 1975. The thousands who tour the foundation are reminded of the spirit of Bethune, the founder and first president of Bethune-Cookman College.

ACCREDITATION

Bethune-Cookman College is accredited by the Southern Association of Colleges and Schools to award the Bachelor of Arts and Bachelor of Science degrees.

Other Accreditation

American Medical Association Committee on Allied Health Education

Florida State Board of Nursing

Florida State Department of Education for Specified Programs

National Council for Accreditation of Teacher Education

University Senate of the United Methodist Church

COSTS PER YEAR

1992–93 Tuition: $4,965

Room and board: $1,755 (room), $1,488 (board)

Special fees: $437

Books: $500

Estimated total cost: $9,145

FINANCIAL AID

1991–92 Institutional Funding:

Number of scholarships and grants: 576

Total amount of scholarships and grants: $1,659,421

Range of scholarships and grants: $100–$8,000

1991–92 Federal and State Funding:

Number of scholarships and grants: 1,598

Total amount of scholarships and grants: $6,471,352

Range of scholarships and grants: $100–$4,000

Number of loans: 1,493

Total amount of loans: $5,143,929

Range of loans: $100–$4,000

Number of work-study: 525

Total amount of work-study: $846,570

Range of work-study: $1,000–$1,600

Financial Aid Specific to the School

During the 1991–92 school year, 97% of the student body received financial aid.

Cooperative education programs in all majors allow students to get paid work experience.

College Work Aid program is available for students who do not qualify for college work-study. Students are hired by department majors.

Tuition waivers are available for employees and their children. College work-study is also available.

The Army and Air Force ROTC programs offer two- and three-year scholarships. ROTC scholarships pay for tuition, fees, books, and other expenses, and provide a monthly stipend of $100.

Florida Student Assistant Grant Program (FSAG) assists students who demonstrate high financial need. Applicant must be a resident of Florida for at least two years. Priority deadline is April 15. Grants average $200 to $1,300 per year.

Florida Tuition Voucher Fund (FTVF) is available for students who meet the Florida residency requirements of at least two years at the beginning of the school year. Awards average $1,150 per year depending on state funds.

Florida residents may be eligible for $200–$1,300 each academic year through the Florida Student Association.

Florida "Chappie" James' Most Promising Teachers Scholarship Loan Program is available for high school seniors who plan to have a career as a public school teacher in Florida.

United Negro College Fund (UNCF) scholarships are awarded to a limited number of students at this school who demonstrate financial need. Some scholarships are be based on location and merit. UNCF scholarships range from $500 to $7500.

Financial Aid Deadline
March 1 (priority date)

Financial Aid Contact
Mr. Joseph Coleman, Director of Financial Aid, Bethune-Cookman College, Daytona Beach, FL 32115; (904) 255-1402.

ADMISSION REQUIREMENTS
SAT or ACT is highly recommended or must be taken in freshman year.

Entrance Requirements
A high school diploma with 24 units: 4 English, 3 mathematics, 3 science, 1 American history, 1 world history, 1/2 American government, 1/2 economics, 1/2 vocational education, 1/2 performing arts, 1/2 management skills, and 1/2 physical education, 9 electives; two letters of recommendation; a mandatory pre-entrance medical record; as well as a written essay, and an interview with college officials. A nonrefundable $25 application fee is due by July 30.

GED students must meet the basic admission requirements.

Transfer students must have a minimum GPA of 2.0, must complete one full year of residency and 30 semester hours at the college, and must submit two letters of recommendation, as well as a written essay.

International students must pass the TOEFL examination. Students whose native language is English and have studied in this country for at least one year are required to take the SAT or ACT.

Admission Application Deadline
July 30 (fall); December 1 (spring); early admission allows qualified students to enter college full time before completing high school.

Admission Contact
Ms. Gloria Bartley, Coordinator of Admissions and Recruitment, Bethune-Cookman College, 640 Second Ave., Daytona Beach, FL 32115; (904) 255-1402, ext. 333 or 800-448-0228.

GRADUATION REQUIREMENTS
Minimum of 124 credit hours with 6 hours in a foreign language, 6 hours in mathematics, 6 hours in science, 1 hour in computer science, and a 2.0 cumulative GPA in a major field of study. Must pass all sections of the College Level Academic Skills Test (CLAST), complete the mandatory orientation week program for freshmen or new students, complete a senior seminar, write a senior research paper, and pass a senior exit examination. The last semester of the senior year must be completed on the campus, and one full year of study must have been obtained at Bethune-Cookman College.

Grading System
A-F; I=Incomplete; AU=Audit; NG=No grade; S=Pass for pre-college courses.

STUDENT BODY PROFILE
Total enrollment (male/female): 921/1,380

From in-state: 1,933

Other regions: 30 states; 7 foreign countries

Full-time undergraduates (male/female): 995/1,343

Part-time undergraduates (male/female): 25/38

Ethnic/Racial Makeup

African American, 2,232; Hispanic, 23; Caucasian, 23; International, 23.

Class of 1995 Profile

Number of applicants: 1,736

Number accepted: 1,427

Number enrolled: 603

Median SAT score: 373V; 383M

Median ACT score: 16

Average high school GPA: 2.45

Transfer applicants: 200

Transfers accepted: 155

Transfers enrolled: 69

FACULTY PROFILE

Number of faculty: 200

Student-teacher ratio: 16:1

Full-time faculty: 123

Part-time faculty: 77

Tenured faculty: 14

Faculty with doctorates or other terminal degrees: 46%

SCHOOL CALENDAR:

1992-93: August 23–April 29 (semesters)

Commencement and conferring of degrees: May

One summer session.

DEGREES OFFERED AND NUMBER CONFERRED 1991–92:

Bachelor of Arts

English/English Education: 4

Music/Music Education: 1

Political Science: 8

Sociology: 9

History/History Education: 2

Mass Communications Education: 17

Bachelor of Science

Accounting: 23

Biology: 3

Business Administration: 43

Business Education: 1

Computer Information Systems: 6

Computer Science: 6

Criminal Justice: 34

Early Childhood Education: 7

Elementary Education: 26

Hospitality Management: 7

Management: 13

Marketing: 6

Medical Technology: 5

Nursing: 7

Physical Education: 1

Psychology: 20

SPECIAL PROGRAMS

Mandatory free college orientation week for all freshmen and new students to acquaint them with the facilities, faculty, and history; parents may attend.

The National Youth Sports Programs provide educational and cultural opportunities as well as a sports program and health services to approximately 400 youth in the community.

The Cooperative Education Program in all divisions integrates student education with generally paid work experience. Students must have a 2.0 GPA to apply.

A three/two dual degree program in engineering is offered in conjunction with the University of Florida, Florida Atlantic University, Florida A&M University, and Tuskegee. The program allows students to receive a liberal arts degree from their home school and an engineering degree from the cooperating school by completing three years at the matriculated school and two years at the cooperating school.

The Air Force and Army ROTC, in co-operation with Embry-Riddle Aeronautical University, offers courses in military science for a commission officer as a second lieutenant in the U.S. Armed Forces. Two- and three-year scholarships are offered with this program.

The Office of Student Retention provides academic assistance to all students.

Early admission for students who score in the top 15% on statewide or national tests may seek admission after their junior year.

The Employable Training Program assists in employment training for high school dropouts in the community.

The Reach Program is a full-day child care center for ages 4-14 that serves as a teacher-training program.

The Weekend Continuing Education Program is held on 8 sites throughout Florida and serves the needs of students who have completed general studies and are moving into upper division courses.

ATHLETIC PROGRAMS

Bethune-Cookman is a member of the National Collegiate Athletic Association (NCAA), Div. I; Div IA for football.

Intercollegiate sports: men's baseball, basketball, cross-country football, tennis, and track & field; women's basketball, cross-country, tennis, track & field, and volleyball.

Intramural sports: basketball, football, racquetball, table tennis, and volleyball.

Athletic Contact

Mr. Lloyd Johnson, Bethune-Cookman College, 640 Second Ave., Daytona Beach, FL 32115; (904) 255-1401, ext. 316.

LIBRARY HOLDINGS

The library houses 141,000 volumes, 35,000 microforms, 1,100 recordings, 1,000 audiovisuals, 800 periodical subscriptions, 135 computers for student use, a special African American Collection, and a Methodist Church collection. Several CD-ROM databases are available.

STUDENT LIFE

Special Regulations

Must attend college orientation program, and reside at least one year on campus. The student must also maintain a 2.8 GPA to join a service/social organization.

Campus Services

Health center, psychological counseling, late night transport, remedial instruction, career planning and placement services, and religious services, including chapel.

Campus Activities

Social activities include theater, concerts, dances, and chorale. Students may work on the Bethune-Cookman yearbook (the *B-Cean*) or the school's student newspaper *The Wildcat*.

Leadership opportunities can be found in the Student Government Association or numerous other student-run organizations. The Reach Program gives students an opportunity to provide service to the surrounding community.

Greek-letter societies include Alpha Kappa Alpha, Delta Sigma Theta, Sigma Gamma Rho, and Zeta Phi Beta sororities, as well as Alpha Phi Alpha, Kappa Alpha Psi, Omega Psi Phi, and Phi Beta Sigma fraternities. Honor societies include Alpha Chi, Alpha Kappa Mu, Alpha Mu Gamma, Beta Kappa Chi, Honors in Teacher Education Certification (HITEC teacher/ed), Kappa Delta Pi, Minority Access to Research Careers (March-Science), Phi Beta Lambda Business, and Psi Chi National. Two social/service organizations are also represented on campus.

The 32-building campus offers easy access to business centers, theaters, museums, recreational facilities, and churches. Because Bethune-Cookman is located in a resort area, its faculty and students are within easy reach of the Atlantic Ocean, home of some of the world's most famous beaches. Walt Disney World, EPCOT, and the Kennedy Space Center are within hours of the campus. Public transportation provides easy access to Orlando, only 60 miles away, as well as Miami and Tallahassee, each about 200 miles away. Bethune-Cookman's students have access to a variety of entertainment, social, and cultural activities on the campus, and recreational activities in the surrounding cities.

Housing Availability

1,540 housing spaces; 565 freshman spaces. Secured housing is available by paying a $700 deposit. The regular $100 deposit provides housing on a first come, first served basis.

Handicapped Services

Wheelchair accessibility.

NOTABLE ALUMNI

Oswald P. Bronson, Sr., 1950–President, Bethune-Cookman College

Charles Fletcher, 1968–Finance planner, IBM

Herbert Helmsley, 1955–Founder, Bethune Medical Center

William F. Kornegay, 1954–General Motors

Astrid Mack, 1960–Associate professor, University of Miami's School of Medicine

Sadye Martin–Mayor, Plant City, Florida

Alfred S. Smith–Assistant vice president, Alabama State University

EDWARD WATERS COLLEGE

1658 Kings Rd.
Jacksonville, FL
32209
Phone: (904) 355-3030
Fax: (904) 366-2544

Total Enrollment:
634

Level of Selectivity:
Noncompetitive

Motto:
Excellence With
Courage

HISTORY

Edward Waters College (EWC) is a four-year, liberal arts, coed college affiliated with the African Methodist Episcopal (AME) Church. It was founded in 1866 as Brown Theological Institution for the training of African American clergy in the AME Church. In 1870, the name changed to Brown Theological Institute, which was chartered in 1872. Two years later the name changed to Brown University.

From 1874 to 1883, the school witnessed financial difficulty, had a series of name changes, and moved to a new location. In 1883, the school reopened as East Florida Conference High School in Jacksonville. To more accurately reflect program changes, the name was changed to Edward Waters College in 1892.

Edward Waters College has a history of survival despite hardships. In 1904, the school was hit by a disastrous fire that destroyed most of Jacksonville. After several years in rented quarters, the school acquired the site that it now occupies. The 21-acre campus is situated on both sides of Kings Road in the eastern section of Jacksonville. The campus facilities are a mixture of historic and modern buildings.

"The college holds dual distinction as Florida's oldest independent institution of higher learning and the first institution established for the education of African Americans in the state." President Robert Mitchell says, "Our ultimate goal is to return the college to its rightful place in the collegiate realm and as a center of African American culture on the first coast of Florida." The college became the 43rd member of the United Negro College Fund (UNCF) in 1985.

ACCREDITATION

Edward Waters College is accredited by the Southern Association of Colleges and Schools to award the Bachelor of Arts and Bachelor of Science degrees.

Other Accreditation

State Board of Independent Colleges and Schools

COSTS PER YEAR

1992–93 Tuition: $3,466

Room and board: $1,600 (room); $1,800 (board)

Special fees: $100

Books: $500

Estimated total cost: $7,466

FINANCIAL AID

Financial Aid Specific to the School

98% of students received financial aid during 1991–92.

Athletic scholarships are awarded to students participating in intercollegiate sports.

The Williams Foundation Scholarship provides two full four-year scholarships covering tuition, fees, books, room, and board to entering freshmen with a "B" average or above. Students must maintain a "B" average to renew scholarships.

Bessie M. Gibson Scholarships are awarded to students demonstrating financial need and majoring in English, reading, or music. Awards are limited to $600 per year.

Henry Eddie Daniels Scholarship loans provide up to $500 per year to students with good academic standing majoring in religion/philosophy.

Performance Awards are made when available to students participating in choir, or student government. Students must demonstrate financial need.

The Cooperative Education Program combines classroom study with practical work experience in two majors.

Tuition waiver is available to full-time employees of Edward Waters with six months continuous employment. Enrollment is limited to six hours of classes per semester.

United Negro College Fund Scholarships are awarded to a limited number of entering students scoring high on the ACT or ETS exams, or students with a high school GPA of 3.0 or better. To renew awards students must maintain a cumulative GPA of 3.0.

The deferred payment plan allows students to pay for college cost in three installments during the semester. The second and third installments for fall are due in October and November; the second and third installments for spring are due in February and April.

Florida Student Assistance Grants (FSAG) are awarded to students based on financial need. Students or their parents must have been a resident of Florida for at least two years. Student must earn 24 semester hours with a GPA of 2.0 or higher for the year a grant is received. Grants range from $200 to $1,200 per year.

Florida Tuition Vouchers (FTV) are awarded to two Florida residents who attend an approved private college and meet the requirements for FSAG listed above.

Financial Aid Deadline

April 1 (priority). Continuous notification.

Financial Aid Contact

Mr. Lorenzo Woodward, Director of Financial Aid, Edward Waters College, Jacksonville, FL 32209; (904) 355-3030, ext. 214.

ADMISSION REQUIREMENTS

Open admissions. SAT or ACT (recommended ACT score of 18 or SAT score of 840 for teacher education program). CEEB CAT required.

Entrance Requirements

A high school transcript with the following units recommended: four English, two mathematics, two social sciences, two natural sciences, five electives. Students interested in teacher education must pass the Enhanced ACT with a score of at least nineteen or the SAT with a score of at least 840. A complete physical is required. A $15 nonrefundable application fee is required.

GED students must meet basic admission requirements.

Transfer students must present an official college transcript and show evidence of being in good financial standing at their previous school.

International students must submit official transcripts from all schools attended and must prove evidence of ability to pay all college cost. TOEFL exam required for students from non-English-speaking countries.

Admission Application Deadline

July (fall); December (spring). Rolling admission provides no specific date for notification of admission so applicant is informed as soon as admission decision is made. Advanced Placement. Continuous notification.

Admission Contact

Mrs. Mercedes Cullins, Acting Registrar, Edward Waters College, 1658 Kings Rd., Jacksonville, FL 32209; (904) 366-2528.

GRADUATION REQUIREMENTS

A minimum of 120 semester hours including the core requirements; one computer science (business majors); students must pass the College Level Academic Skills Test (CLAST) before their junior year.

Grading System

A-F; I=Incomplete; W=Withdraw

STUDENT BODY PROFILE

Total Enrollment (male/female): 402/232

From in-state: 507

Other regions: 15 states; 8 foreign countries

Full-time undergraduates: (male/female): 187/346

Part-time undergraduates (male/female): 35/66

Ethnic/Racial Makeup

African American, 628; Other/unclassified, 6

FACULTY PROFILE

Number of faculty: 49

Student-teacher ratio: 12:1

Full-time faculty: 33

Part-time faculty: 16

Faculty with doctorates or other terminal degrees: 10%

SCHOOL CALENDAR

1991–92: September 2–May 8 (semesters)

Commencement and conferring of degrees: May 9

One summer session.

DEGREES OFFERED 1991–92:

Bachelor of Arts
English

History

Mass Communications

Organizational Management

Religion

Sociology

Bachelor of Science
Accounting

Biology

Business Administration

Chemistry

Computer Science

Criminal Justice

Early Childhood Education

Elementary Education

Mathematics

Organizational Management

Physical Education

Psychology

Public Administration

Secondary Education

Social Science

Pre-Professional Programs
Airway Science

SPECIAL PROGRAMS

The remediation program provides remedial courses for entering freshmen to bring them to admission standards and help them succeed in college.

The Cooperative Education Program gives students the opportunity to gain practical paid work experience while completing their degree program.

The Cooperative Study Abroad Program allows students to take courses abroad towards a degree program.

Advanced Placement (AP) allows high school students to receive credit for college courses taken during their senior year in high school, through scores received on the College Board AP tests.

Cross registration with Jacksonville University and the University of North Florida enables students to take courses at cooperating schools to meet requirements toward their majors.

The cooperative three/two dual degree in Engineering is offered with the University of Miami. Student completes three years at Edward Waters and two years at the University Miami. Upon completion of fourth year, student receives a Bachelor's degree; upon completion of fifth year, student receives an Engineering degree.

The Cooperative Army ROTC with the University of North Florida and the Navy ROTC with Jacksonville University provide training in military science for commission as a second lieutenant in the U.S. Armed Forces. Two- and three-year scholarships are available.

The individualized majors program allows students to create their own major programs of study.

Upward Bound provides academic counseling and cultural enrichment programs to high school students in their senior year who are disadvantaged and are in pursuit of a college education; some course credit may be offered.

ATHLETIC PROGRAMS

Edward Waters is a member of the National Association of Intercollegiate Athletics (NAIA) and the Eastern Intercollegiate Athletic Conference (EIAC).

Intercollegiate sports: men's basketball, track & field, softball, baseball, and cross-country; women's basketball, track & field, softball, baseball, and cross-country.

Intramural sports: basketball, tennis, softball, volleyball.

LIBRARY HOLDINGS

The Centennial Library holds 132,000 volumes, 231 periodical subscriptions, 175 audiovisuals, 499 microforms, and 125 computers for student use. Special collections include an African American Print Collection and a permanent exhibit of African Art and ethnographic objects.

STUDENT LIFE

Campus Services
Health, counseling, career counseling, remedial assistance, and religious services.

Campus Activities
Social and group activities include dance, theater, and chorale. Other groups include the debating team and the cheerleading squad. Students can join the newspaper or yearbook staff, or get involved in the student-run radio station.

Leadership opportunities can be found in student groups, such as the Student Government Association, the science club, the student ministerial group or the international club. Greek-letter societies and honor societies are also represented.

Edward Waters College makes a concerted effort to develop and maintain an environment in which living and learning are interrelated and enjoyable. There are numerous opportunities for social interaction on campus.

The campus is situated on 23 acres in the city of Jacksonville, Florida, the third largest city in Florida with a population of approximately 500,000. Jacksonville is less than 20 miles from Georgia's state line, located on the mouth of St. Johns River. The campus is served by a mass transit bus system. The city's airport is about fifteen miles from Edward Waters College. Jacksonville's symphony orchestra attracts many distinguished artists, and several museums provide cultural exhibits. Florida's tropical weather offers many opportunities for outdoor recreational activities.

Housing Availability

275 housing spaces. Available on a first come, first serve basis.

NOTABLE ALUMNI

Dr. Lawrence Callahan–Founder and manager of five interdenominational churches in Florida and the Bahamas

Dr. Frederick Harper–Publisher and faculty member, Howard University

William Roberts–Attorney-at-Law, Jacksonville

Jim Robinson–President, Robinson's Marketing Co.

FLORIDA AGRICULTURAL AND MECHANICAL UNIVERSITY

1500 Wahnish Way
Tallahassee, FL 32307
Phone: (904)599-3796
Fax: (904) 561-2428

Total Enrollment:
9,200

Level of Selectivity:
Moderately
competitive

Motto:
Excellence With
Caring

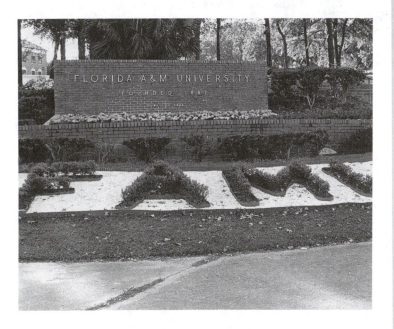

HISTORY

Florida A&M University (FAMU) is a four-year, state-supported, coed, liberal arts institution, founded in 1887 as the State Normal College for Colored Students. In 1890, the school became a land grant institution. In 1891, the college was moved from Copeland Street to its present location and became the State Normal and Industrial College for Colored Students.

In 1905, postsecondary level instruction was first offered. Four years later, the name was changed to Florida Agricultural and Mechanical College. It wasn't until 1910 that the first baccalaureate degree was awarded. When the school became a university in 1953 the present name was adopted. In 1984, the university was granted authority to offer its first Doctor of Philosophy degree. Five years later, the first Ph.D. in Pharmacology was awarded.

The school opened with 2 instructors and 15 students. Presently, it employs more than 460 full-time faculty and enrolls more than 9,000 students. The university was ranked fourth in the nation in enrolling National Achievement finalists. One of nine universities in the State University System of Florida, FAMU places great emphasis on instruction, research, and service to promote academic excellence and to improve the quality of life for those it serves. As a land grant school, the institution is mandated to give high priority to continuing education and public service.

Located on 419 acres, the 109-building campus is a blend of modern and traditional buildings. The Black Archives Research Center and Museum has become a tourist attraction. The most recent buildings include the President's home and the College of Engineering. Plans are underway for a new research facility in arts and for a science classroom building.

ACCREDITATION

Florida A&M University is accredited by the Southern Association of Colleges and Schools (SACS) to award the Associate of Arts, Bachelor of Arts, Bachelor of Science, and Master's degrees, and to award the Ph.D. (Pharmacy).

Other Accreditation

Accreditation Board of Engineering and Technology

Accrediting Council on Education in Journalism and Mass Communication

American Assembly of Collegiate Schools of Business

American Association of Colleges of Nursing

American Association of Colleges of Pharmacy

American Association of Colleges for Teacher Education

American Association of Higher Education

American Council on Pharmaceutical Education

American Physical Therapy Association

Council on Social Work Education

National Architectural Accrediting Board

National Council for Accreditation of Teacher Education

National League for Nursing

COSTS PER YEAR

1992–93 Tuition: $1,509 (in-state); $5,650 (out-state)

Room and board: $1,562 (room); $1,178 (board)

Special fees: $125

Books: $500

Estimated total cost: $4,874 (in-state); $9,015 (out-state)

FINANCIAL AID

1990–91 Institutional Funding

Number of scholarships and grants: 1,302

Total amount of scholarships and grants: $73,718

Range of scholarships and grants: $50–$8,250

1991–92 Federal and State Funding

Number of scholarships and grants: 3,654

Total amount of scholarships and grants: $26,871

Range of scholarships and grants: $150–$6,420

Number of loans: 2,646

Total amount of loans: $71,612

Range of loans: $100–$6,039

Number of work-study: 450

Total amount of work-study: $70,499

Range of work-study: $250–$1,591

Financial Aid Specific to the School

100% of the student body received financial aid during 1991–92.

Academic Achievement Awards include alumni scholarships, School of Business and Industry Awards, Greyhound Corporation Awards, Selby Foundation Grants, General Foods Corporation Awards, and U.S. Sugar Corporation Scholarships. These awards range from $100 to $1,000 to assist non-need freshmen with their financial obligations.

Athletic scholarships are awarded to students who participate in intercollegiate sports.

Creative Arts/Performance Awards are available to students in journalism, choir, theater, and visual arts.

Critical Teacher Shortage Trust Fund assists upper division students preparing to become teachers with up to $2,000.

Presidential Scholar Awards allow students to receive $1,000 per academic year for maintenance of academic excellence. Florida high school students and transfer students may qualify.

Trust funds and other sources of monies are available to students in teacher education to defray their costs.

Deferred payment plan allows a family to pay tuition in installments.

Tuition waivers are available for FAMU full- or part-time employees and their children. Waivers are also available for senior citizens.

Cooperative Education Program alternates classroom study with related paid work experience. The program provides academic credit and full-time status during co-op placement.

Thurgood Marshall Black Education Fund provides a four-year scholarship at this public black college. Qualifying student must have a high school GPA of 3.0 or better and a SAT score of 1,000 or ACT score of 24 or more. Students must be recommended by high school counselor as exceptional or exemplary in the creative or performing arts. Scholarship pays tuition, fees, room, and board, not to exceed $6,000 annually.

Army and Navy ROTC, and Air Force ROTC in cooperation with Florida State University, offer two- and four-year scholarships that pay tuition, fees, books, and other expenses, and provide a monthly stipend of $100.

Florida Teacher Scholarship-Loan Program allows Florida juniors and seniors aspiring to become teachers $4,000 per academic year. Students are obligated to teach in a Florida public school to repay loan.

Florida Teacher Tuition Reimbursement Program provides up to $78 per credit hour to be reimbursed to certified teachers seeking further certification in designated areas.

Financial Aid Deadline
April 1

Financial Aid Contact
Mr. Alton W. Royal, Director of Financial Aid, Florida Agricultural and Mechanical University, PO Box 312, Tallahassee, FL 32307; (904) 579-3730.

ADMISSION REQUIREMENTS
SAT (800) or ACT (17) required; SAT (900); ACT (19) for Engineering degree.

Entrance Requirements
Graduation from an accredited high school with the following 19 units: 4 English, 3 mathematics, 3 science, 3 social science, 2 foreign language, and 4 electives; submit official high school transcript with minimum 2.5 GPA; applicants with at least 3.0 GPA admitted regardless of SAT/ACT results; students with low SAT/ACT scores, but gifted with other talents, may be eligible for admission; proof of immunization for rubella and rubella required for admission. State residents given preference. A $20 non-refundable application fee is required.

GED students must meet basic admission requirements.

Students transferring 60 hours must have 2.5 GPA and have passing CLAST (College Level Academic Test) scores; for less than 60 transfer hours, student must submit official high school and college transcripts and meet same requirements as new freshmen.

International students must submit official transcripts of all high school and college work; must provide proof of ability to pay all college costs; those from non-English-speaking countries must have minimum 500 TOEFL examination score.

Early admission is granted to high school juniors with high SAT or ACT scores and "B" or better averages. Students are admitted upon recommendation from high school administrator.

Admission Application Deadline

July 1; rolling admission provides no specific date for notification of admission so applicant is informed as soon as admission decision is made.

Admission Contact

Mrs. Barbara Cox, Deputy Registrar for Admissions, Florida A&M University, Tallahassee, FL 32307; (904) 599-3796.

GRADUATION REQUIREMENTS

A 120-credit-hour minimum and completion of the core requirements to include the following hours: 6 mathematics, 8 science, and 1 computer course for business, engineering, graphic arts, journalism, math, and technology majors; minimum 2.0 GPA; and last year in residence. A minimum of 60 hours for Associate's degree.

Grading System

A–F; S=Satisfactory; U=Unsatisfactory; W=Withdraw; N=No reported grade; I=Incomplete; DP=Dissertation Pending; X=Audit; P=Pass; TP= Thesis Pending.

STUDENT BODY PROFILE

Total enrollment (male/female): 4,048/5,152

From in-state: 5,785

Other regions: 46 states; 6 countries

Full-time undergraduates (male/female): 3,182/4,243

Part-time undergraduates (male/female): 621/679

Graduate students (male/female): 206/269

Ethnic/Racial Makeup

African American, 8,045; Hispanic, 155; Asian, 73; Caucasian, 807; International, 120.

Class of 1995 Profile

Number of applicants: 4,476

Number accepted: 2,730

Number enrolled: 2,238

Median ACT score: 17

Average high school GPA: 2.50

FACULTY PROFILE

Number of faculty: 670

Student-teacher ratio: 24:1

Full-time faculty: 468

Part-time faculty: 202

Tenured faculty: 164

Faculty with doctorates or other terminal degrees: 60%

SCHOOL CALENDAR

1993–94: August 22–May 29 (semester)

Commencement and conferring of degrees: May 30

Two summer sessions.

DEGREES OFFERED 1991–92:

Bachelor of Arts

Criminal Justice

Dramatic Arts/Theater

English

Fine Arts

Foreign Language

History

International Relations

Journalism

Magazine Production

Medical Record Administration

Music

Philosophy
Philosophy and Religion
Photography
Political Science
Psychology
Public Administration
Public Relations
Religious Studies
Social Work
Sociology
Theater

Bachelor of Science

Accounting
Afro-American Studies
Agricultural Business
Agricultural Science
Animal Science
Architectural Technology
Architecture
Art Education
Banking and Finance
Biology
Business Economics
Business Education
Business Management
Chemical Engineering
Chemistry
Civil Engineering
Civil Engineering Technology
Computer and Information Systems
Construction Engineering Technology
Economics
Electrical Engineering
Electronic Engineering Technology
Elementary Education
English Education
Entomology
Graphic Arts Technology
Health Care Administration
Industrial Arts Education

Industrial Engineering
Landscape Design and Management
Marketing and Purchase
Mathematics
Mathematics Education
Mechanical Engineering
Music Education
Nursing
Occupational Therapy
Office Administration
Pharmacy
Physical Education
Physical Therapy
Physics
Recreation
Respiratory Therapy
Science Education
Secondary Education
Social Studies Education
Vocational-Industrial Education

Doctorate

Chemical Engineering
Medical Chemistry

Master's of Business Administration

Accounting
Finance
Management Information Systems
Marketing

Master's of Education

Adult Education
Agricultural and Extension
Business Education
Early Childhood Education
Elementary Education
Guidance and Counseling
Health, Physical Education, and Recreation
Industrial Education
Intermediate Education
Secondary Education

Master's of Science

Architecture

Chemical Engineering

Civil Engineering

Community Psychology

Electrical Engineering

Mechanical Engineering

Medical Chemistry

Pharmacy/Toxicology

School Psychology

Pre-Professional

Architectural Studies

Dentistry

Law

Medicine

Veterinary Medicine

SPECIAL PROGRAMS

Accelerated Degree Program gives opportunity for undergraduates to earn a degree in a shorter period of time than the traditional four years.

Adult/Continuing Education Program is available for nontraditional students returning to school or working part time.

Advanced Placement (AP) allows high school students to get college credit for high scores on the College Board AP tests.

College orientation is offered to entering students for four days at no cost prior to the beginning of classes to acquaint students with the college and to prepare them for college life.

Cooperative Education Program alternates formal academic study with practical work experience in 12 majors. The program provides academic credit and full-time status during co-op placement.

Cooperative Study Abroad enables some students to go to Africa, Colombia, San Salvador, England, Puerto Rico, Australia, and Switzerland for part of their college education and degree requirements.

Joint College Engineering Program with Florida State University (FSU) allows students to earn an engineering degree at FAMU while having access to courses at FSU.

Honors Program offers academically talented enrollees a challenging program that enables them to accelerate completion of their basic requirements, enroll in reduced classes, develop leadership skills, have honors courses identified on transcript, and be recognized at annual convocation.

Intern program gives students an opportunity to work in the community as part of core program during summer and mid-winter.

Off-campus study allows students to take courses at Florida State University for credit and study architecture in business and government while attending Washington D.C.'s School of Architecture. Pharmacy and medical students study at four hospitals in Miami, Florida, and at the University of Miami's Medical School.

Part-time degree program allows students to earn an undergraduate degree while attending part time in the daytime or evenings, or during the summer sessions.

PIM (Program in Medical Science) in cooperation with Florida State University (FSU) provides a special route to medical school for students at FAMU and FSU before entering medical school.

Remedial courses are offered to entering students to bring them up to admission standards and to help them adjust for success in college.

ROTC provides military science training for commission as second lieutenant in the Army or Navy. Air Force ROTC is a cooperative effort with Florida State University.

ATHLETIC PROGRAMS

Florida A&M University is a member of the National Collegiate Athletic Association (NCAA), all Division I, except men's football which is Division I-AA; and the Mid-Eastern Athletic Conference (MEAC).

Intercollegiate sports: men's baseball, basketball, cross-country running, golf, swimming and diving, tennis, and track & field; women's basketball, cross-country, golf, softball, tennis, track & field, and volleyball.

Intramural sports: basketball, cross-country, football, tennis, and volleyball.

Athletic Contact

Dr. Walter Reed, Florida A&M University, 1500 Wahnish Way, Tallahassee, FL 32307; (904) 599-3868.

LIBRARY HOLDINGS

The Samuel H. Coleman Library holds 485,985 bound volumes, 82,000 microfilms, 3,300 periodicals, 62,610 audiovisuals, and 100 computer terminals. The Florida Black Archives Research Center and Museum houses the state's special collection of materials on the history of African Americans.

STUDENT LIFE

Special Regulations

Class attendance compulsory for all students.

Campus Services

Health center, personal and psychological counseling, career placement counseling, women's center, on-campus shuttle, intercampus shuttle with Florida State University, late night escort, remedial instruction, and religious activities.

Campus Activities

Social and cultural activities include theater, chorale, band, art exhibits, concerts, and lecture series. The gospel choir released an album in 1985. FAMU's "Marching 100 Band" is world renowned. Students may get involved in the student-run newspaper or radio station, WUMF-FM.

Leadership opportunities are found in the Student Government Association or the

more than 100 student organizations including the literary guild, fashion/modeling club, religious groups, departmental clubs, and interest groups. FAMU has the largest women's athletic program of any historically black institution in the United States. The school has a fully equipped television studio and photography lab.

Greek-letter fraternities include Alpha Phi Alpha, Kappa Alpha Psi, Omega Psi Phi, and Phi Beta Sigma; sororities include Alpha Kappa Alpha, Delta Sigma Theta, Sigma Gamma Rho, and Zeta Phi Beta. Honor societies are represented on campus, including Sigma Xi.

Located in Tallahassee, Florida Agricultural and Mechanical University is a mere 22 miles from the Gulf of Mexico, overlooking numerous lakes, with beautiful public parks nearby. Eight blocks from the bustling Capitol Complex, FAMU can be reached by bus, shuttle, and automobile. Shuttles transport students to and from malls, offices, and recreational areas in close proximity.

Housing Availability

Nine permanent residence halls. All freshmen and students with less than 12 semester hours whose homes are farther than 35 miles from campus must reside in university dorms. Freshmen are given priority. Freshman-only dorms available.

Housing available for married students. Off-campus housing permitted.

Handicapped Services

Course substitution may be made by University Admission Committee if enrollee is hearing impaired, visually impaired, dyslexic, or learning disabled (LD).

NOTABLE ALUMNI

Nat "Cannonball" Adderly, 1951–Jazz musician

Althea Gibson, 1953–Professional tennis player

Joseph W. Hatchett, 1954–U.S. Circuit judge, 5th Circuit, Tallahassee, Florida

Frederick S. Humphries, 1957–Florida
A&M University's 8th president

Rev. Cecil Murray–Senior minister, First
AME Church, Los Angeles, California

FLORIDA MEMORIAL COLLEGE

HISTORY

Florida Memorial College is a four-year, private, coed, liberal arts college affiliated with the Baptist Church. Its origins are with Florida Baptist Institute, founded in 1879, and Florida Baptist Academy, founded in 1892. The two institutions merged in 1941 to form Florida Normal and Industrial Memorial Institute. The school became a four-year college and awarded its first bachelor's degree in 1949.

In 1950, this college was renamed Florida Normal and Industrial Memorial College. The present name, Florida Memorial College, was acquired in 1963. Originally located in St. Augustine, Florida, the facility was moved in 1968 to its present location.

As the college continues to grow, it holds to the belief that education contributes to the quality of a person's life. The definitive mission of Florida Memorial College is to inculcate in students a desire for life-long learning and to encourage in them a commitment to leadership through service that will enhance their lives and the lives of others. It

15800 NW 42nd Ave.
Miami, FL 33054
Phone: (305) 625-4141
Toll-free out-state:
800-822-1362

Total Enrollment:
2,172

Level of Selectivity:
Slightly competitive

Motto:
Leadership, Character,
Service

is dedicated to free exchange of ideas, pursuit of knowledge, and the transmission of black history and heritage.

The campus consists of a cluster of modern air-conditioned buildings, none of which is more than a three-minute walk from the farthest point on campus. Florida Memorial also offers courses at four off-campus centers, including: Hialeh Center in Hialeh, FL; Charles R. Drew Center in Miami, FL; and Richmond Heights Center in Richmond Heights, FL. The William Lehman Aviation Center is a $7.4 million, three-story, state-of-the-art complex that contains modern spacious classrooms, laboratories, and simulation trainers for airway sciences. This traditionally black college is a United Negro College Fund member school.

ACCREDITATION

Florida Memorial College is accredited by the Southern Association of Colleges and Schools (SACS) to award the Bachelor of Arts and Bachelor of Science degrees.

COSTS PER YEAR

1992–93 Tuition: $3,800

Room and board: $1,400 (room); $1,400 (board)

Special fees: $800

Books: $500

Estimated total cost: $7,900

FINANCIAL AID

Financial Aid Specific to the School

95% of the student body received financial aid during 1991–92.

Florida Memorial College gives scholastic awards to first-time enrollees who have a 3.0 GPA and meet other criteria.

Athletic scholarships are available to students who participate competitively in basketball, baseball, track, and volleyball.

Honors program awards scholarships and institutional grants-in-aid to students who have a 3.0 or better GPA and are enrolled in the honors program. Contact Director of Honors Program at the college for more information.

Performance or cultural scholarships are awarded to students who demonstrate outstanding musical and/or artistic ability.

The President's Discretionary Scholarship is awarded on a non-renewable basis to a full-time student selected by the president based on academic achievement, talent, or community service.

Sutton-Grant Scholarship is awarded to a student who has been at the college for at least one semester, has a 3.0 GPA or better, and is not a part of the honors program.

International students with a 3.0 GPA or better may be eligible for a Sarah Hoo International scholarship.

Joe Addison Physical Education Incentive Scholarship is awarded to upperclassmen majoring in physical education with a minimum 2.5 GPA.

Karol Adamieckl Incentive Scholarships are given to Polish exchange students attending this college.

Deferred payment plan enables students whose loans or grants have not come through, to defer a portion of the basic tuition, fees, room, and board until loans are received. A fee of $50 is charged to initiate such a plan. All loans/grants must be signed over to the students' accounts.

A 10-month installment plan provides students an opportunity to pay college costs in agreed upon installments.

United Negro College Fund (UNCF) scholarships are awarded to a limited number of students at this school who demonstrate financial need. Some scholarships may be based on location and merit. UNCF scholarships range from $500 to $7,500.

Army and cooperative Air Force ROTC with the University of Miami offer two- and four-year scholarships that pay tuition, fees, books, and other expenses, and provide a monthly stipend of $100.

Veterans Administration educational benefits are available for students working toward teacher certification.

Florida Tuition Voucher program provides assistance for residents of Florida who demonstrate financial need.

Florida Student Assistance Grant provides one-year awards that may range from $200–$1,300 to Florida residents who demonstrate financial need and who attend Florida post-secondary institutions.

Financial Aid Deadline
April 1 (priority); March 1 (reapplication)

Financial Aid Contact
Mr. Walter G. Alexander, Director of Financial Aid, Florida Memorial College, 15800 NW 42nd Ave., Miami, FL 33054; (305) 625-4141.

ADMISSION REQUIREMENTS
SAT or ACT required, used for advisement/placement; SAT (840) or ACT (17) required for education majors.

Entrance Requirements
Graduated from an accredited high school with the following units: 4 English, 1 science, and 4 social science; a minimum 2.0 grade GPA, medical history form completed by a certified physician; a letter of recommendation from principal, counselor, or teacher; and a personal essay. A $15 nonrefundable application fee is required.

Conditional or probationary admission is available on an individual basis for students graduating from non-accredited high schools or students who don't meet specific academic requirements.

GED students must meet basic requirements and pass the GED test.

Transfer students must submit official transcripts from all colleges attended and meet basic admission requirements, including medical exam. If transferring less than 30 hours students must submit high school transcript, letter of recommendation, and personal essay. Transfers from Florida community or junior college with an Associate of Arts degree will be accepted as juniors; transfers from out of state community and/or junior colleges will be considered for junior standing upon recommendation of the Office of Academic Affairs.

International students must meet basic admission requirements, pass the TOEFL examination, or enroll in ESL course if score. Students must provide affidavit of support by student sponsor, provide proof of ability to pay all college cost, and provide notarized English translations of all documents submitted in language other than English.

Admission Application Deadline
December 1 (spring). Early Admission allows academically gifted students with the acceptable criteria to enroll for college credits before completing high school. Rolling admission provides no specific date for notification of admission so applicant is informed as soon as admission decision is made.

Admission Contact
Mrs. Peggy Kelley, Director of Admissions and International Student Advisor, Florida Memorial College, 15800 NW 42nd Ave., Miami, FL 33054; (305) 625-4141, Ext. 255; toll-free 800-222-1362 (in-state); 800-822-1362 (out-state).

GRADUATION REQUIREMENTS
A minimum of 124 hours and completion of core requirements to include: 9 hours of English, 6 hours of math, 6 hours of science, 6 hours of foreign language, and 1 computer course; a GPA of 2.0 or higher; last 30 hours and/or last year must be in residence at Florida Memorial College.

Grading System
A–F; I=Incomplete, AU=Audit; P=Pass; W=Official withdrawal from college; WD=Withdrawal from specific course; WP=Withdrawal passing.

STUDENT BODY PROFILE

Total enrollment (male/female): 977/1,195

From in-state: 1,480

Other regions: 15 states, 10 foreign countries

Full-time undergraduates (male/female): 782/956

Part-time undergraduates (male/female): 200/234

Ethnic/Racial Makeup

African American, 1,700; Hispanic, 434, International, 38.

Class of 1995 Profile

Number of applicants: 875

Number accepted: 831

Number enrolled: 632

Average high school GPA: 2.50

FACULTY PROFILE

Number of faculty: 83

Student-teacher ratio: 17:1

Full-time faculty: 12

Part-time faculty: 71

Faculty with doctorates or other terminal degrees: 60%

SCHOOL CALENDAR

1992–93: August 19–May 7 (semester hours)

Commencement and conferring of degrees: May 9

One summer session.

DEGREES OFFERED 1991–92:

English and Modern Foreign Languages

Political Science

Psychology

Religion and Philosophy

Sociology

Bachelor of Science

Accounting

Air Traffic Controller

Airway Computer Science

Aviation Flight Maintenance

Aviation Management

Biology

Business Administration

Business Data Processing

Computer Science

Criminal Justice

Elementary Education

Mathematics

Medical Technology

Physical Education

Pre-Professional Engineering

Public Administration

Transportation Management

Urban Studies

SPECIAL PROGRAMS

Advanced Placement (AP) grants college credit for postsecondary work completed in high school. Students passing the AP test will receive credit by examination for each course.

College Level Examination Program (CLEP) determines the academic relevance of nontraditional educational experiences, such as the military, on-the-job training, or other life experiences, through a series of tests and may grant students college credit for these experiences.

College orientation is offered at no cost to entering students for one week at the beginning of classes to acquaint students with the college and to prepare them for college life. Parents may be included.

Cooperative Education Program combines classroom study with related paid work experience. The program provides academic credit and full-time status during co-op placement.

Continuing Education (CE) program offers a non-degree program for Protestant clergy and laymen and a career development program for Haitian adults.

Credit by examination may be taken for work experience. Student must submit a statement from work supervisor to the division chairperson suggesting work experience comparable to course description or submit a transcript from unaccredited institution where student has taken similar course with "C" or better grade. If students pass exam, a grade of "P" will be assigned; however, if students fail exam, a grade of "F" will be assigned. Fee for exam is $15 a credit hour.

Honors program offers academically talented students a challenging program of study that includes special classes, seminars, colloquia, cultural activities, and special recognition to motivate participants. Lower division students must maintain a 3.0 GPA while upper level students must maintain a 3.5 GPA.

Internship Preparation Seminar must be taken by any student seeking an internship during the college course work.

Off-campus study is available at four off-campus centers located within a thirty-mile radius of the main campus. The four centers are Hialeah, Charles R. Drew, Kinloch Park, and Richmond Heights.

Part-time degree programs allow students to earn an undergraduate degree while attending part time during the evening.

Remedial courses are offered to entering students to bring them up to admission standards and to help them adjust for success in college.

ROTC provides training in military science for commission as a second lieutenant in the U.S. Army and Air Force. Two- and four-year scholarships are available.

Weekend and evening classes are offered both on and off campus.

ATHLETIC PROGRAMS

Florida Memorial is a member of the National Association of Intercollegiate Athletics (NAIA).

Intercollegiate sports: men's baseball, basketball, cross-country, and indoor/outdoor track & field; women's basketball, cross-country, indoor/outdoor track & field, and volleyball.

Intramural sports: basketball, golf, soccer, swimming and diving, and tennis.

LIBRARY HOLDINGS

The College Library has over 90,000 bound volumes, 405 periodical subscriptions, 7,613 microforms, and 450 audiovisuals.

STUDENT LIFE

Special regulations:

Cars are permitted with a $10 parking decal; quiet hours and curfews enforced; out-of-town students are expected to live on the campus unless permission is granted; weekly chapel attendance required; senior year residency required.

Campus Services

Health center, career planning and placement, testing service for the College Level Academic Skills Test (CLAST).

Campus Activities

Social and cultural activities include theater, band, chorale, lectures, displays, exhibits, dances, and movies. The J.C. Sams Activity center is a meeting place on the shore of the campus lake with game rooms, entertainment facilities, and conference rooms. Students may work on the Lion's Den (student published newspaper).

Leadership opportunities are found in the Student Government Association (SGA) or the various other organizations, such as the drama clubs, theater groups, eating clubs, Bahaman Student Association, or the International Student Association.

The Christian Student Union is a favorite of Florida Memorial College students. Greek-letter fraternities include Alpha Phi Alpha, Kappa Alpha Psi, Omega Psi Phi, and Phi Beta Sigma; sororities include Alpha Kappa Alpha, Delta Sigma Theta, Sigma Gamma Rho, and Zeta Phi Beta. Honor societies are represented on campus.

Florida Memorial is located in the metropolitan city of Miami, population 1,850,000. The campus and the community are linked by the Miami Metro rapid rail system. The city of Miami is further serviced by bus and air transportation. Points of interest include Metro-Dade Cultural Center, the Metro Zoo, Parrot Jungle, and Vizcaya, a 10-acre Italian Renaissance-style villa. Horseback riding, horse racing, and Miami's famous beaches are a few favorite entertainment activities. The Palmetto Expressway and the Turnpike give easy access to the shopping, fine dining, cultural activities, and the four off-campus centers.

Housing Availability

1,520 housing spaces; four modern air-conditioned residence halls are available for men and women; freshmen are guaranteed housing; freshman-only housing; off-campus living is permitted.

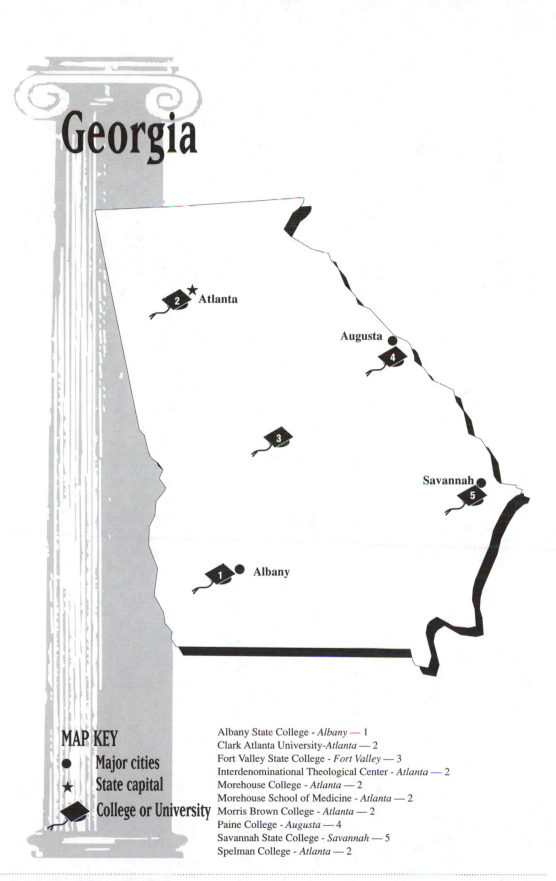

Georgia

Atlanta

Augusta

Savannah

Albany

MAP KEY

● Major cities

★ State capital

◆ College or University

Albany State College - *Albany* — 1
Clark Atlanta University-*Atlanta* — 2
Fort Valley State College - *Fort Valley* — 3
Interdenominational Theological Center - *Atlanta* — 2
Morehouse College - *Atlanta* — 2
Morehouse School of Medicine - *Atlanta* — 2
Morris Brown College - *Atlanta* — 2
Paine College - *Augusta* — 4
Savannah State College - *Savannah* — 5
Spelman College - *Atlanta* — 2

ALBANY STATE COLLEGE

504 College Dr.
Albany, GA 31705-2797
Phone: (912) 430-4600
Toll-free in-state:
800-822-7267
Fax: (912) 430-3936

Total Enrollment:
3,106

Level of Selectivity:
Slightly competitive

Motto:
College Education on
a Personal Level

HISTORY

Albany State College is a four-year state-supported, coed, liberal arts college that was founded in 1903 as Albany Bible and Manual Training Institute. The mission was to train black teachers how to teach basic skills and to train black students in the trades and industries, with special emphasis on domestic science and art. The school was initially supported by religious and private organizations.

In 1917 when the school became a two-year, state-supported institution, the name changed to Georgia Normal and Agricultural College. In 1932, the institution became part of the University System of Georgia, and in 1943, the college was granted four-year status, assuming its present name Albany State College.

As the college continued to grow, the mission changed to meet present-day educational needs. Teaching, research, and community service were adopted into the mission of the college. A graduate program was established in 1972 through other colleges. In 1981, the college began to offer a graduate program that was solely delivered by the faculty and staff of Albany State.

An aggressive ten million dollar expansion included a new criminal justice building, a modern student union, and a library earmarked for completion by 1994. The 128-acre campus has both traditional and modern buildings.

ACCREDITATION

Albany State College is accredited by the Southern Association of Colleges and Schools to award the Associate's, Bachelor of Arts, Bachelor of Science, and Master's degrees.

Other Accreditation

Georgia Department of Education

National Council for Accreditation of Teacher Education

National League for Nursing

COSTS PER YEAR

1992–93 Tuition: $1,731 (in-state); $4,023 (out-state)

Room and board: $1,224 (room); $1,350 (board)

Special fees: $390

Books: $675

Estimated total cost: $4,020 (in-state); $7,662 (out-state)

FINANCIAL AID

1991–92 Institutional Funding

Number of scholarships and grants: 690

Total amount of scholarships and grants: $693,835

Range of scholarships and grants: $100–4,500

1991–92 Federal and State Funding

Number of scholarships and grants: 2,247

Total amount of scholarships and grants: $3,174,479

Range of scholarships and grants: $250–2,400

Number of loans: 1,145

Total amount of loans: $2,223,572

Range of loans: $200–4,000

Number of work-study: 688

Total amount of work-study: $736,655

Range of work-study: $800–7,500

Financial Aid Specific to the School

82% of the student population received financial aid during 1991–92.

Albany State College Foundation awards a limited number of scholarships to students with a minimum SAT score of 900 and a high school GPA of 3.0 or better.

Allied Health Sciences Scholarships award $1,000 toward tuition and other fees to students who enroll in the Allied Health Sciences programs.

Athletic Scholarships are available through the Director of Intercollegiate Athletics.

Presidential Scholarships, based on academic achievement, are awarded to 10 students each academic year in the amount of $4,500.

Regents' Scholarships are available to Georgia residents who rank in the top 25% of their high school class and demonstrate financial need. The maximum award is $750 per academic year.

Music Scholarships are available through the chairperson of the Department of Fine Arts.

Social work scholarships of $1,000 are available to students enrolling in social work.

A Criminal Justice Scholarship of $1,000 is available to students enrolling in the Criminal Justice program.

Transfer (Desegregation) Scholarships are available to students enrolling from transfer programs at Darton College. Students must be in good standing and pursuing their first baccalaureate degree. The scholarship is $1,000 yearly.

The Cooperative Education Program alternates academic study with related paid work experience. The program provides academic credit and full-time status during co-op placement.

The Thurgood Marshall Black Education Fund provides a four-year scholarship at this public black college. Qualifying student must have a high school GPA of 3.0 or better, and a 1,000 or better SAT score or a 24 or better ACT score. Students must be recommended by high school counselor as exceptional or exemplary in the creative or performing arts. Scholarship pays tuition, fees, room, and board, not to exceed $6,000 annually.

Army ROTC offers two- and four-year scholarships that pay tuition, fees, books, and other expenses, and provide a monthly stipend of $100 for advanced training.

Georgia Incentive Scholarships, based on financial need, are available to legal residents of Georgia; they do not cover total cost of attendance.

The James H. Porter Academic Scholarship is available to a full-time undergraduate who resides in Georgia. Applicant must have an SAT composite score of 1,000 or better, a 3.0 GPA, and meet additional criteria required by the Board of Regents.

Financial Aid Deadline

April 15 (fall); February 15 (spring)

Financial Aid Contact

Ms. Kathleen J. Caldwell, Director of Admissions and Financial Aid, Albany State College, Albany, GA 31705; (912) 430-4650

ADMISSION REQUIREMENT

SAT or ACT required.

Entrance Requirements

High school diploma with a minimum of 15 units: 4 English, 3 mathematics, 3 science, 3 social science, and 2 foreign language. Each applicant must submit a social security number; a personal interview, achievement, aptitude, and psychological tests may be required as deemed necessary. A nonrefundable $10 application fee is required.

GED students must meet the basic admission requirements.

Transfer students may be required to submit high school transcripts and ACT or SAT scores; evidence of all courses completed at other institutions must be submitted; a maximum of 135 academic quarter hours with a minimum grade "C" from an accredited senior college may be applied to the program in which the student plans to enroll.

International students must meet regular admissions requirements, pass the Test of English as a Foreign Language (TOEFL), and show evidence of financial support.

Early admission allows qualified students to enter college full time before completing high school.

Admission Application Deadline

September 1 (fall); December 1 (winter); March 1 (spring); May 15 (summer)

Admission Contact

Director of Admissions and Financial Aid, Albany State College, 504 College Dr., Albany, GA 31705-2797; (912) 430-4646; 800-822-7265 (in-state). Fax: (912) 430-3936.

GRADUATION REQUIREMENTS

A minimum of 186 quarter hours including the core requirements of 10 hours of mathematics; 10 hours of science; 1 computer course for math and business majors; 3 hours of music appreciation; 5 hours fundamental speech; 6 hours of health and physical education; and 3 hours of activity courses. Exemption to activity-type courses allowed in specific circumstances. Must have a 2.0 GPA; must satisfactorily pass the Regents' Test or its equivalent for foreign and handicapped students; must complete a political science course in American government (PSC 201); must complete a year in residence with a minimum of 45 quarter hours; and must take an exit examination or major area examination.

Grading System

A-F; I=Incomplete; W=Withdrawal; S=Satisfactory; U=Unsatisfactory; V=Audit;

K=credit by examination program (CLEP or AP)

STUDENT BODY PROFILE
Total enrollment (male/female): 2,050/1,056

From in-state: 2,902

Other regions: 5 states

Full-time undergraduates (male/female): 1,472/759

Part-time undergraduates (male/female): 356/183

Graduate students (male/female): 222/114

Ethnic/Racial Makeup
African American, 2,632; Hispanic, 14; Native American, 6; Caucasian, 454.

Class of 1995 Profile
Number of applicants: 1,649

Number accepted: 1,260

Number enrolled: 673

Median SAT score: 375M; 350V

Transfer applicants: 439

Transfers accepted: 203

Transfers enrolled: 157

FACULTY PROFILE
Number of faculty: 150

Student-teacher ratio: 16:1

Full-time faculty: 135

Part-time faculty: 15

Faculty with doctorates or other terminal degrees: 70%

SCHOOL CALENDAR:
1992–93: September 1–June 12 (quarter hours)

Commencement and conferring of degrees: June 6

One summer session.

DEGREES OFFERED AND NUMBER CONFERRED 1991–92:

Associate of Arts
Forensic Science: n/a

Security Management: n/a

Bachelor of Arts
Art: 1

Biology: n/a

Chemistry: n/a

Computer Science: 12

Criminal Justice: 32

English: n/a

French: n/a

History and Government: n/a

Mathematics: n/a

Music: n/a

Political Science: n/a

Sociology: 10

Spanish: n/a

Speech: 2

Theater: n/a

Bachelor of Science
Accounting: 21

Administrative Systems: 3

Allied Health Sciences: 23

Biology Education: 14

Chemistry Education: n/a

Early Childhood Education: 14

English Education: n/a

Forensic Sciences: n/a

Health and Physical Education: 3

History Education: n/a

Management: 32

Marketing: 6

Mathematics Education: 6

Middle Grades Education: 5

Music Education: n/a

Nursing: 29

Office Administration: n/a

Psychology Education: 5

Secondary Education: 3

Secretarial Science: 3

Science: n/a

Social Work: 7

Special Education: 2

Specialist in Education Leadership

Pre-Professional Degree

Dentistry: n/a

Medicine: n/a

Pharmacy: n/a

Graduates that later obtain higher degrees:

10%

SPECIAL PROGRAMS

Academic remediation provides remedial courses for entering students to bring them up to admissions standards.

Adult continuing education is available for nontraditional students returning to school or working full time.

The Advanced Placement (AP) Program grants college credit for postsecondary work completed in high school. Student scoring 5 or more on the AP tests will receive 5 quarter hours credit for each course and advanced placement.

Army ROTC, in cooperation with Fort Valley State College, provides training in military science for a commission as a second lieutenant in the U.S. armed forces. Two- and four-year scholarships are available.

The College Level Examination Program (CLEP) determines the academic relevance of nontraditional educational experiences such as the military, on-the-job-training, or other life experiences through a series of tests and may grant students college credit for these experiences.

College orientation is offered for two days prior to the beginning of classes for $40.00 to acquaint students with the college and to prepare them for college life; parents may attend.

The Cooperative Education Program alternates classroom study with related paid work experience in eleven majors.

The Cooperative Study Abroad Program allows students to go to a foreign country for part of their college education.

Full or partial tuition waivers are available for senior citizens when class space is available.

Graduate courses are open to undergraduates for credit.

Honors programs offer academically talented students a challenging program of study that includes special classes, seminars, cultural activities, and recognition to motivate participants.

The Joint Enrollment Program allows students to enroll for college credit while attending local high school.

Off-campus study is available at Abraham Baldwin Agricultural College, Bainbridge College, and Waycross College.

Part-time degree programs allow students to earn an undergraduate degree part time (daytime, evenings, weekends, or summer).

Pre-professional programs are available in medicine, medical technology, pharmacy, and law.

The three/two degree program gives students the opportunity to get two degrees—one in liberal arts from the home school and one in engineering from Georgia Institute of Technology. Students must complete three years at the matriculated school and two years at the cooperating school.

ATHLETIC PROGRAMS

Albany State is a member of the Southern Intercollegiate Athletic Conference (SIAC) and the National Association of Intercollegiate Athletics (NAIA).

Intercollegiate sports: men's baseball, basketball, cross-country, tennis, and track & field; women's basketball, cross-country, tennis, and track & field.

Intramural sports: baseball, basketball, softball, swimming and volleyball.

LIBRARY HOLDINGS

The library is fully automated and has 180,000 volumes, 470,000 microforms, 600 periodical subscriptions, 500 audiovisuals, and 65 computers for student use located in various areas on campus. CD-ROM and on-line searching is available to students. Special collections include the William Reese Medical collection, the black literature collection, and books by Dr. Joseph Winthrop Holley.

STUDENT LIFE

Special Regulations

Class attendance is compulsory; cars must be registered; curfews are enforced. Students from outside the Albany area are expected to live on campus.

Campus Services

Health center; personal and psychological counseling; late night transport; remedial instruction; career planning and placement; testing for GMAT, LSAT, SAT, and CLEP; and nondenominational religious activities.

Campus Activities

Social and cultural activities include theater, chorale, dances, band, and a speaker series. During the annual Co-Etiquette Week, the office of student activities sponsors a fashion show, art exhibit, lecturers, and nationally-renowned speakers. The week culminates in the crowning of Mr. Esquire and Miss Charm. Interested students may work on the *Albany State Ram* (yearbook) or the *Student Voice* (student newspaper).

Leadership opportunities are found in the Student Government Association and numerous other student run organizations.

Greek Letter societies include Alpha Phi Alpha, Kappa Alpha Psi, Omega Psi Phi, and Phi Beta Sigma fraternities; and Alpha Kappa Alpha, Delta Sigma Theta, Sigma Gamma Rho, and Zeta Phi Beta sororities. National Honor Societies represented on campus include Alpha Kappa Mu, Sigma Rho Sigma , Phi Alpha Theta, Phi Beta Lambda, Kappa Delta Pi, and Alpha Phi Sigma. The college participates in the selection of Who's Who Among Students in American Universities and Colleges. The Veteran's Fraternity, Alpha Sigma Mu, is open to all veterans.

Albany State College is located 32 miles south of Plains, Georgia, home of former President Carter, and 145 miles from the metropolitan city of Atlanta. Albany is a progressive city of more than 100,000 people; it offers education, recreation, health services, commerce, and industry.

Housing Availability

892 housing spaces. Freshman housing guaranteed.

Handicapped Services

Wheelchair accessibility.

NOTABLE ALUMNI

Alice Coachman Davis–First black Olympic gold medalist, women's track and field

Evelyn A. Hodge–Reading supervisor, Alabama State College

William A. Hopkins, 1968–Director of small business affairs, Georgia

William A. Johnson–Vice president of Fiscal Affairs, Albany State College

CLARK ATLANTA UNIVERSITY

James P. Brawley Dr.
at Fair St., SW
Atlanta, GA 30314
Phone: (404) 880-8000
Toll-free in-state:
800-688-7228 or 3228
Fax: (404) 880-8222

Total Enrollment:
3,507

Level of Selectivity:
Slightly competitive

Motto:
I'll Find A Way Or
Make One
(Atlanta University);
Culture For Service
(Clark College)

HISTORY

Clark Atlanta University (CAU) is a four-year, private, comprehensive, coed liberal arts university, established in 1988 as a result of a merger between Atlanta University founded in 1865 and Clark College found in 1869.

Atlanta University was founded by the American Missionary Association in 1865, with later assistance from the Freedmen's Bureau. In 1930, undergraduate courses were discontinued and Atlanta University became a graduate and professional school. Atlanta University, before consolidation, was the nation's oldest graduate institution serving a predominantly African American student body.

Clark College was found in 1869 as Clark University by the Freedmen's Aid Society of the Methodist Episcopal Church, which later became the United Methodist Church. Its purpose was to provide blacks in the south with a formal education. The institution was chartered by the state of Georgia in 1877. The first bachelor's degree was awarded in 1883. In 1940, the name was changed to Clark College.

Clark Atlanta University combines the rich history between two historically black schools to offer the foundation necessary to acquire the knowledge, skills, and confidence essential for modern society. It exists today as the only totally private, urban, historically black university in the country. Its comprehensive academic programs culminate in the bachelor's, master's, and doctoral degrees in many fields.

Situated on sixty-two acres, the 30-building campus includes a $45 million dollar state-of-the-art research center and the Catherine Hughes Art Gallery, which houses one of the largest African American art collections in the world. This traditionally black university is a UNCF member school and part of the Atlanta University Center, cluster of six predominately black colleges and universities.

ACCREDITATION

Clark Atlanta is accredited by the Southern Association of Colleges and Schools to award the Bachelor of Arts, Bachelor of Science, Master's, and Doctorate degrees.

Other Accreditation

American Dietetic Association

American Library Association

Council on Social Work Education

National Council for Accreditation of
  Teacher Education

COSTS PER YEAR

1992–93 Tuition: $6,300

Room and board: $1,876 (room); $1,876
  (board)

Special fees: $800

Books: $400

Estimated total cost: $11,252

FINANCIAL AID

1991–92 Federal and State Funding

Range of scholarships and grants:
  $200–$2,000

Financial Aid Specific to the School

85% of the student body received financial aid during 1991–92.

Aetna Life and Casualty Foundation Scholarship is for students who do not qualify for the federal and state loan program. CAU receives $4,000 annually from Aetna to make awards on a competitive basis.

Athletic scholarships are available for students who participate in intercollegiate sports.

CAU has approximately 30 alumni or endowed scholarships, grants, or loan programs based on merit, need, special interest, or geographic location.

Mathematic scholarships are awarded through the Joseph J. Dennis Endowed Scholarship. Scholarships start at $100 and are awarded annually to juniors and seniors with a 3.25 GPA in math or computer science and an overall GPA of 3.0.

Performance scholarships are available for students in music, including band, jazz orchestra, and choir.

Undergraduate Minority Access To Research Careers (UMARC) is awarded to sophomore students with at least a 3.0 GPA, majoring in biology, chemistry, physics, mathematics, or psychology, and interested in biomedical research. Qualified students receive a $5,000 stipend, tuition, fees, and funds for travel to scientific meetings. Inquiries should be addressed to UMARC's program director, Clark Atlanta University.

Pickett and Hatcher Education Loan Fund may be awarded to students who demonstrate good character, citizenship, health, moral responsibility, attitude, and scholastic achievement. Student must attend full time during period of loan, have a 2.0 or better GPA, and make loan request by July 1 for fall semester. The maximum amount a student can borrow is $1,200.

Foreign Student Grants are available to students who will complete their sophomore year by the beginning date of the grant and have some proficiency in language of host country. Grants range from $100 to $1,000.

Assistantships provide stipends and experience year round in various departments. Assistantships are selected by the department chairperson.

Cooperative Education Program alternates classroom study with related paid work experience in all majors. The program provides academic credit and full-time status during co-op placement.

Deferred payment plan allows students to pay college costs in two or three installments during the semester.

Tuition waivers are available to part-time or full-time employees and their children.

United Negro College Fund (UNCF) scholarships are awarded to a limited number of students at this school who demonstrate financial need. Some scholarships may be based on geographic location and merit. UNCF scholarships range from $500 to $7,500. The Benjamin E. Mays UNCF scholarship is awarded to the junior student who exemplifies dedication to excellence as demonstrated by Dr. Mays. Inquires should be address to CAU's scholarship and awards committee.

Army ROTC and cooperative Air Force or Navy ROTC, with Georgia Institute of Technology, offer two- and four-year scholarships that pay tuition, fees, books, and other expenses, and provide a monthly stipend of $100.

Georgia Private College Tuition Equalization Grant is awarded to Georgia residents who attend private schools and demonstrate financial need. The 1990–91 awards averaged $921. Awards are contingent on availability of funds.

Georgia Student Incentive Grant (SIG) is awarded to Georgia residents who demonstrate financial need. SIG ranges from $600 to $2,000.

Financial Aid Deadline
April 30

Financial Aid Contact
Mrs. Sheila Brown, Director of Financial Aid, Clark Atlanta University, Atlanta, GA, 30314; (404) 880-8069 or 800-688-8243

ADMISSION REQUIREMENTS
SAT (430M; 420V) or ACT required

Entrance Requirements
Entering students must have graduated from an accredited high school and submitted an official high school transcript including completion of the following units: 4 English, 2 math, 2 social science, 2 science, 1 foreign language; two letters of recommendation, a personal statement, and participated in an interview. A nonrefundable $20 application fee is required.

GED students must meet basic admissions requirements.

Transfer students must have a minimum of 2.0 GPA, three recommendations, an interview, and college transcripts from all previous colleges attended.

International students must meet basic admission requirements and take the TOEFL examination.

Early admission allows academically gifted high school students the opportunity to enroll in college full time before completing high school.

Admission Application Deadline
Rolling admission provides no specific date for notification of admission so applicant is informed as soon as admission decision is made; March 1 (priority fall); November 1 (priority spring)

Admission Contact
Ms. Peggy Wade, Associate Director of Admissions, Clark Atlanta University, James P. Brawley Dr. at Fair Street, SW, Atlanta, GA 30314-4389; (404) 880-8017, or 800-688-3228 or 7228.

GRADUATION REQUIREMENTS
A minimum of 122 credits and completion of core requirements to include: 3 hours of math, 3 hours of science, and 1 computer course.

Grading System
A–F, W=Withdrawal, I=Incomplete

STUDENT BODY PROFILE
Total enrollment (male/female):
 1,209/2,691

From in-state: 1,599

Other regions: 43 states; 48 foreign countries

Full-time undergraduates (male/female):
 855/1,904

Part-time undergraduates (male/female):
 44/97

Graduate students (male/female): 310/690

Ethnic/Racial Makeup
African American, 3,705: International, 117; Other/unclassified, 78.

Class of 1995 Profile
Number of applicants: 4,502

Number accepted: 2,476

Number enrolled: 867

FACULTY PROFILE

Number of faculty: 200

Student-teacher ratio: 19:1

SCHOOL CALENDAR

1992–93: August 28–May 15 (semester hours)

Commencement and conferring of degrees: May 24

One summer session.

DEGREES OFFERED 1991–92:

Bachelor of Arts

Accounting

Art/Art Education

Business Administration/Business Education

Early Childhood Education

Economics

Elementary/Middle Grades Education

English/English Education

Fashion Design

Fashion Merchandising

French/French Education

General Science Education

German

History/History Education

Mass Media Arts

Mathematics

Medical Illustration

Music/Music Education

Office Administration

Philosophy

Physical Education

Political Science/Political Science Education

Psychology

Religion

Sociology

Spanish/Spanish Education

Speech Communication

Theater Arts

Bachelor of Science

Allied Health (dual degree)

Biology

Chemistry

Child Development

Community Health Education

Computer Science

Engineering (dual degree)

Hotel Management

Mathematics

Medical Records Administration

Medical Technology

Nutrition

Physics

Social Work

Master's Degree and Ph.D.

African Studies

Biology

Business Administration

Computer Science

Counseling and Human Development

Criminal Justice Administration

Economics

Education

English

Exceptional Student Education

Foreign Languages

Humanities

History

International Affairs

Library and Information Studies

Mathematics

Public Administration

Physics

Political Science

Public Administration

Social Work

Sociology

Pre-Professional

Dentistry

Engineering

Law

Medicine

Pharmacy

Seminary Studies

SPECIAL PROGRAMS

Accelerated Study Program allows students to complete their undergraduate degree in a shorter period of time than the traditional period of four years.

Advanced Placement (AP) grants college credit for postsecondary work completed in high school. Students scoring three on the AP test will receive credit by examination for each course and advanced placement.

College orientation is offered to entering students at a cost of $75 prior to the beginning of classes to acquaint students to the college and prepare them for college life; parents may be included.

Continuing Education program allows adults to continue or resume their educational interest on a full- or part-time basis in a variety of credit and non-credit areas. These activities include short courses, seminars, conferences, and workshops.

Cooperative Education Program combines classroom study with related paid work experience. The program provides academic credit and full-time status during co-op placement.

High-tech classrooms and a variety of software programs facilitate computer-assisted instruction.

The honors program offers academically talented students a challenging program of study that includes special classes, seminars, colloquia, cultural activities, and special recognition to motivate participants.

Joint Enrollment Program (JEP) allows eligible juniors or seniors to enroll at a participating college to fulfill some of the requirements to graduate from high school, while receiving credits toward a degree.

Part-time degree programs allow students to earn an undergraduate degree while attending part time.

Pre-Professional programs available in dentistry, law, medicine, pharmacy, and seminary studies. Students follow the science and math sequence as undergraduates in preparation for professional school.

Remedial courses are offered to entering students to bring them up to admission standards and to help them adjust for success in college.

ROTC provides training in military science for commission as a second lieutenant in the U.S. Armed Forces. Two- and four-year scholarships are available in the Army, Navy, and Air Force ROTC.

Study Abroad Program in Spain, France, Germany, and Kenya allows students to go to a foreign country for a specified period of time for part of their college education.

Three/two dual degree program in engineering allows students to get two degrees, one in liberal arts from home school and one in engineering from Georgia Institute of Technology, by completing three years at matriculated school and two years at cooperating school.

ATHLETIC PROGRAMS

CAU is a member of the National Collegiate Athletic Association (NCAA), Division II; and a charter member of the Southern Intercollegiate Athletic Conference (SIAC).

Intercollegiate sports: men's basketball, football, tennis, and track & field; women's basketball, tennis, track & field, and volleyball.

Intramural sports: basketball, track & field, and volleyball.

Five SIAC divisional championships in the past eight years attest to the strength of the university's athletic program.

LIBRARY HOLDINGS

The cooperative Robert W. Woodruff Library holds 374,292 bound volumes,

247,167 microforms, 47,115 bound periodicals, 1,372 periodical subscriptions, 2800 audiovisuals, 115,822 government documents, 13,916 theses and dissertations, and 200 computers in the computer center for student use. Special collections include Carnegie Art Reference Set, the Henry P. Slaughter and Countee Cullen Memorial Collection of graphic and performing arts, the Southern Regional Council papers on race relations and socioeconomic conditions in the Southeast (1994–1968), First World Publication, and many others.

STUDENT LIFE

Campus Services

Health clinic, personal and psychological counseling, career counseling and placement, late night escort service.

Campus Activities

Social activities include theater, concerts, chorale, dances, and bands. The university's Spring Arts Festival is an annual event attracting musicians, artists, writers, actors, dancers, and lecturers from throughout the nation. Other activities include a lecture series. Students may get involved in the student publications or the student-run jazz radio station, WCLK-FM. CAU-TV is a university cable station and Atlanta's first and only educational access television station.

Leadership opportunities are found in the Student Government Association (SGA) and the more than 50 other groups. Greek-letter fraternities include Alpha Phi Alpha, Kappa Alpha Psi, Omega Psi Phi, and Phi Beta Sigma; sororities include Alpha Kappa Alpha, Delta Sigma Theta, Sigma Gamma Rho, and Zeta Phi Beta. Honor societies include Alpha Kappa Mu and nine departmental honor societies.

Many opportunities exist for CAU students to interact with students at other Atlanta University Center institutions, including Spelman College, Morehouse College, Morris Brown College, Interdenominational Theological Center, and Morehouse School of Medicine.

Clark Atlanta is located in the metropolitan city of Atlanta, the capital of Georgia, with a population of over two million. The city is served by mass air, rail, and bus. Local transportation on the MARTA provides easy access to downtown, the airport, or virtually anywhere in the metro area.

The campus is located one mile west of downtown, close to Underground Atlanta, with its quaint shops. Students have access to fine dining, world-class shopping, art galleries, museums, and the Atlanta Symphony or Ballet. The Atlanta Hawks, Braves, and Falcons offer major league sports. Major recording artists frequent the city. Points of interest include the Martin Luther King, Jr. Center for Non-violent Change, The Jimmy Carter Presidential Library, Stone Mountain Park, and Six Flags Over Georgia Amusement Park. Other activities include boating, fishing, and golfing. The World Congress Center hosts many national conferences. The city of Atlanta is an international center for business, banking, and social change, offering students many professional opportunities.

Housing Availability

1,039 housing spaces within eight dormitories; freshman housing guaranteed; advanced payment required to guarantee housing.

NOTABLE ALUMNI

Marva Collins, 1957–Founder and director, Westside Preparatory School, Chicago

FORT VALLEY STATE COLLEGE

805 State College Dr.
Fort Valley, GA 31030
Phone: (912) 825-6307
Toll-free in-state:
800-248-7343

Total Enrollment:
2,368

Level of Selectivity:
Slightly competitive

HISTORY

Ford Valley State College (FVSC) is a four-year, state-supported, liberal arts, coed college founded in 1895. Fort Valley State is the result of the 1939 merger between Fort Valley High and Industrial School and the State Teachers and Agricultural College.

The Fort Valley High and Industrial School was established in 1895, by leading white and negro citizens for the education of blacks in the south. Through private donations the school continued to grow. Students helped to construct several of the buildings between 1926 and 1937. An affiliation with the American Church Institute was discontinued in 1939 when the state took control of the school.

The State Teachers and Agricultural College was established in 1902 with the enrollment of seven young people. In 1916, the school became a senior high school. By an act of the Georgia legislature in 1922, the school was named the Agriculture and Mechanical School. The school was renamed State Teachers and Agricultural College in 1931.

The 1939 consolidation of Fort Valley and State Teachers and Agricultural College was made possible initially by a grant from the Julius Rosenwald Fund. Two years later, the first bachelor's degree was awarded in 1941. The school became part of the University System of Georgia, a consortium of 34 public colleges and universities, and it also became one of two land grant institutions in the state of Georgia. As a land grant school, this traditionally black college continues its mission to provide educational opportunities for all segments of the population.

Fort Valley is located on 650 acres, with approximately 56 buildings. The campus architecture is a blend of stately white buildings constructed by students in the early 1900s and ultramodern buildings of succeeding decades.

ACCREDITATION

Fort Valley State College is accredited by the Southern Association of Colleges and Schools to award the Associate of Science, Bachelor of Arts, and Bachelor of Science degrees.

Other Accreditation

Accreditation Board of Engineering and
   Technology

Accrediting Commission for Independent
   Colleges and Schools

American Home Economics Association

American Veterinary Medical Association

Council on Rehabilitation Education

National Council for Accreditation of
   Teacher Education

COSTS PER YEAR

1992–93 Tuition: $1,593 (in-state); $4,071
   (out-state)

Room and board: $1,050 (room); $1,260
   (board)

Special fees: $354

Books: $400

Estimated total cost: $4,657 (in-state);
   $7,135 (out-state)

FINANCIAL AID

Financial Aid Specific to the School

93% of the student body received financial aid during 1991–92.

Fort Valley awards a limited number of scholarships to entering freshmen who demonstrate high scholarship and financial need.

Emergency short-term loans are available through the college. Most loans are limited to $50 and must be repaid within 30 days.

Athletic scholarships are available to students participating in intercollegiate sports.

The Pickett and Hatcher Education Loan is a private loan program available for qualifying full-time students at this school. Contact Pickett & Hatcher Education Fund, PO Box 2128, Columbus, GA 51902.

Performing scholarships in music are available to exceptional students in music and marching band.

Vocational Rehabilitation Educational Benefits make available tuition, fees, books, supplies, and sometimes transportation for residents of Georgia who are determined disabled. Benefits are available for a maximum of twelve quarters.

Thurgood Marshall Black Education Fund provides a four-year scholarship at this public black college. Qualifying students must have a high school GPA of 3.0 or better, and a SAT score of 1,000 or ACT score of 24 or more. Students must be recommended by high school counselor as exceptional or exemplary in the creative or performing arts. Scholarship pays tuition, fees, room, and board, not to exceed $6,000 annually.

Army ROTC offers two-, three- and four-year scholarships that pay tuition, fees, books, and other expenses, and provides a monthly stipend of $100.

Georgia Student Incentive Grant (SIG) is awarded to Georgia residents who demonstrate financial need. SIG grants range from $600 to $2,000.

Financial Aid Deadline
April 1

Financial Aid Contact

Ms. Jeanette K. Huff, Financial Aid Director, Troupe Building, Fort Valley State College, Fort Valley, GA 31030; (912) 825-6351.

ADMISSION REQUIREMENTS

SAT (750) or ACT (16) required

Entrance Requirements

Graduation from an accredited high school and completion of the following units: 4 English; 2 mathematics; 2 science; 3 social science; and 7 electives. Students must also have an official high school transcript and proof of physical examination.

GED students must meet the basic admission requirements.

Transfer students must submit official high school transcript and transcripts from all previous colleges; students must have a 2.0 GPA and two recommendations.

International student criteria is the same as for all incoming students. Students are required to make an advanced payment of approximately $3,150 or the present cost of matriculation and fees for one year, excluding room and board charges or books. Foreign students should not leave their country for enrollment at Fort Valley before this requirement is met.

Early admission allows academically gifted high school students the opportunity to take courses for credit before completing high school.

Admission Application Deadline

September 1 or ten days prior to beginning of each quarter of enrollment.

Admission Contact

Mrs. Delia W. Taylor, Director of Admissions, Troup Building, Fort Valley State College, Fort Valley, GA 31030; (912) 825-6307 or 800-248-7343 (in-state).

GRADUATION REQUIREMENTS

A minimum of 90 quarter hours are required for associate's degrees. A minimum of 180 quarter hours are required for a bachelor's degree, and students must complete the core requirements to include 20 hours of mathematics and science, 20 hours of social studies, 20 hours of humanities, and 1 computer course for math, electronics engineering technology, or criminal justice majors. Students must pass exit competency examination.

Grading System

A–F; W=Withdrawal; I=Incomplete; IP=In Progress

STUDENT BODY PROFILE

Total enrollment: 2,197

From in-state: 1,999

Other regions: 15 states; 5 foreign countries

Full-time undergraduates (male/female): 732/931

Part-time undergraduates (male/female): 100/127

Graduate students (male/female): 135/172

Ethnic/Racial Makeup

African American, 2,021; Hispanic, 22; Asian, 22; Native American, 22; International, 22; Other/unclassified, 88.

Class of 1995 Profile

Number of applicants: 1,535

Number accepted: 1,105

Number enrolled: 475

FACULTY PROFILE

Number of faculty: 154

Student-teacher ratio: 14:1

Full-time faculty: 147

Part-time faculty: 7

Faculty with doctorates or other terminal degrees: 57%

SCHOOL CALENDAR

1992–93: September–June (quarter hours)

Commencement and conferring of degrees: June and August

One summer session.

DEGREES OFFERED 1991–92:

Bachelor of Arts

English

History

Mass Communication

Office Administration

Political Science

Social Welfare

Sociology

Bachelor of Science

Accounting

Agricultural Economics

Agricultural Engineering Technology

Agronomy

Animal Science

Biology

Botany

Business

Business Administration

Business Management

Chemistry

Childcare

Computer Information Systems

Computer Science

Criminal Justice

Dairy Husbandry

Early Childhood Education

Economics

Electronic Engineering Technology

Elementary Education

Food Management

Home Economics

Marketing

Mathematics

Middle Grades Education

Ornamental Horticulture

Physical Education

Physics

Plant Science

Psychology

Veterinary Technology

Zoology

Associate of Science

Agricultural Engineering Technology

Criminal Justice

Electronic Engineering Technology

Office Administration

Ornamental Horticulture

SPECIAL PROGRAMS

Adult or Continuing Education Program is available for nontraditional students returning to school or working full time.

College Level Examination Program (CLEP) determines the academic relevance of nontraditional educational experiences, such as the military, on-the-job training, or other life experiences, through a series of tests and may grant students college credit for these experiences. A maximum of 45 quarter hours of credit by exam may be applied toward graduation requirements.

A one-week college orientation is required for incoming students at no cost prior to the beginning of classes to acquaint students with the college and prepare them for college life.

The Cooperative Education Program alternates classroom study with related paid work experience. The program provides academic credit and full-time status during co-op placement. Students may earn five hours each quarter for a maximum of fifteen co-op hours of credit.

The part-time degree program allows students to earn an undergraduate degree while attending part time.

Remedial courses are offered to entering students to bring them up to admission standards and to help them adjust for success in college.

Robins Residence Center in cooperation with Fort Valley offers courses to qualified military and civilian employees of Robins Air Force Base for associate or bachelor's degrees in electrical engineering technology.

Study Abroad Program allows students to go to a foreign country for a specified period of time for part of their college education. Options are available in West Africa and Europe.

Three/two engineering degree program, in cooperation with Georgia Institute of Technology, allows students to get two degrees: one in liberal arts from the home school and one in engineering from cooperating school. Students must complete three years at Fort Valley and two years at Georgia Institute of Technology.

ATHLETIC PROGRAMS

Member of the National Collegiate Athletic Association (NCAA), Division II; and the Southern Intercollegiate Athletic Conference.

Intercollegiate sports: men's basketball, football, tennis, and track & field; women's basketball, tennis, track & field, and volleyball.

Intramural sports: basketball and soccer.

Athletic Contact

Mr. Douglas Porter, Fort Valley State College, Fort Valley, GA 31030; (912) 825-6208

LIBRARY HOLDINGS

The Henry Alexander Hunt Library holds 190,062 bound volumes, 1,263 periodical subscriptions, 250 audiovisuals, and 100 computers for students use in the library and computer center. A special collection includes black literature and artifacts. A curriculum center located near the library houses the Georgia adopted textbooks.

STUDENT LIFE

Special Regulations

All motor vehicles must be registered with the college; students living in dorms are required to purchase meal tickets; orientation week program is required.

Campus Services

Health center, personal and psychological counseling, career counseling and placement for graduating students, student employment services, and remedial tutoring.

Campus Activities

Social and cultural activities include theater, band, chorale and dance. Students may work on the student-run newspaper and yearbook.

Leadership opportunities are found in the Student Government Association (SGA) or the more than 70 college organizations, such as departmental clubs and special interest groups. Greek letter fraternities include Alpha Phi Alpha, Kappa Alpha Psi, Omega Psi Phi, and Phi Beta Sigma; sororities include Alpha Kappa Alpha, Delta Sigma Theta, Iota Phi Lambda, Sigma Gamma Rho Society, and Zeta Phi Beta. National Honors Societies include Alpha Kappa Mu, Beta Kappa Chi, Alpha Mu Gamma, Phi Alpha Theta, and Phi Alpha.

Fort Valley is located in middle Georgia in the small city of Fort Valley, with a population of approximately 8,200. Known as the peach growing center in Georgia, the Georgia Peach Festival is held annually in Fort Valley. Points of interest include the national headquarters of the American Camellia Society which houses acres of camellias and a museum with over 300 porcelain birds. The city of Macon is approximately 30 miles away and offers shopping, the Harriet Tubman Historical and Cultural Museum, swimming, and the Cherry Blossom Festival. The nearest metropolitan city is Atlanta, which is 100 miles away. The nearest airport is less than 30 miles from the campus.

Housing Availability

1,048 housing spaces; freshman housing given priority.

NOTABLE ALUMNI

Dr. James L. Hill, 1963–Dean, Albany State College

Dr. Cordell Wynn–President, Stillman
  College

INTERDENOMINATIONAL THEOLOGICAL CENTER

671 Beckwith St., SW
Atlanta, GA 30314
Phone: (404) 527-7700

Total Enrollment:
383

Level of Selectivity:
Moderately
competitive

Motto:
Students enter, leaders
graduate

HISTORY

The Interdenominational Theology Center (ITC) is a collection of private graduate schools of theology. It was founded in 1958 through the mutual efforts of four denominations, representing several schools of theology, for the purpose of training African American ministers. The center represents a consortium of several schools of theology, creating a ecumenical cluster. The schools and their denominations, in order of dates of establishment include the following: Morehouse School of Religion, Baptist (1867); Gammon Theological Seminary, United Methodist (1883); Turner Theological Seminary, African Methodist Episcopal (1885); Phillips School of Theology, Christian Methodist Episcopal (1944); Johnson C. Smith Theological Seminary, Presbyterian USA (1867); and Charles H. Mason Theological Seminary, Church of God in Christ (1970).

ITC considers itself an intellectual arm of the church. It has provided more than 35% of all trained black ministers in the world and 50% of all black chaplains in the United States military, including the highest ranking female chaplain. The mission of the school is to serve black religious communities by providing quality theological education that gives students a knowledge base on which to eradicate some of society's problems. This unique consortium of six seminaries is a bible-centered, social action oriented center, proficient in the study of black religion, including churches of Africa and the Caribbean.

The modern nine-building campus is situated on ten acres at the northern edge of Atlanta's historic black college district. Each seminary has its own dean and board of directors. Each provides for its own student financial aid and housing. This traditionally black consortium of schools is a United Negro College Fund member and a member of the Atlanta University Center, a cluster of six predominately black colleges and universities.

ACCREDITATION

ITC is accredited by the Association of Theological Schools to award the Master of Arts and doctorate degrees.

Other Accreditation

Southern Association of Colleges and Schools

COSTS PER YEAR

1992–93 Tuition: $3,250 (constituents); $4,250 (non-constituents)

Room and board: $1,430 (room); $1,450 (board)

Special fees: $165

Books: $400

Estimated total cost: $6,695 (constituents): $7,695 (non-constituents)

FINANCIAL AID

1992–93 Institutional Funding

Total amount of scholarships and grants: $100,000

Financial Aid Specific to the School

85% of the student body received financial aid during 1991–92.

Denominational gifts and grants are available through respective denominations. Applications should be filed with respective dean.

The UNCF scholarship is awarded to a student with a cumulative GPA of 3.5 or above. Student must be recommended by ITC faculty and have been matriculated for one academic year.

The Benjamin E. Mays Fellowship in ministry is awarded to outstanding black North American men and women pursuing a Master of Divinity degree to become an ordained minister. The program is administered by the Fund for Theological Education, Inc., New York, NY.

The National Association of Minister's Wives and Minister's Widows honor awards are given to two students based on academic achievement.

ITC has an additional seven alumni or endowed scholarships or awards.

The United Church of Christ Scholarship Fund is available for United Church of Christ students on approval of the scholarship committee of the south east conference.

Gammon Theological Seminary (United Methodist) has seventeen alumni or endowed scholarships and awards based on merit, interest, and denominational contributions.

Mason Theological Seminary (Church of God in Christ) has approximately six alumni or endowed scholarships and awards based on merit, interest, and denominational contributions.

Morehouse School of Religion (Baptist) has approximately 22 alumni or endowed scholarships and awards based on merit, interest, and denominational contributions.

Phillips School of Theology (Christian Methodist Episcopal) has approximately seven alumni or endowed scholarships and awards based on merit, interest, and denominational contributions.

Johnson C. Smith (Presbyterian USA) has approximately twelve alumni or endowed scholarships and awards based on merit, interest, and denominational contributions.

Turner Theological Seminary (African Methodist Episcopal) has approximately twelve alumni or endowed scholarships and awards based on merit, interest, and denominational contributions.

Financial Aid Deadline
April 1

Financial Aid Contact
Mrs. Elizabeth Littlejohn, Director of Financial Services, ITC, 671 Beckwith St., Atlanta, GA 30314; (404) 527-7724.

ADMISSION REQUIREMENTS
GRE required

Entrance Requirements
Students need a bachelor's degree or its equivalent from an accredited college or university with a minimum 2.0 GPA; an official transcript of all academic records; and endorsement by respective denomination with a certificate by a major denominational official and the Academic Dean or Administrative Dean of either one of the affiliated seminaries, indicating acceptability of the prospective student. Auditors also must have the approval of the Administrative Dean or the respective dean representing the applicant's denomination. A $25 nonrefundable application fee is required.

Transfer students must present a letter of honorable withdrawal and an official transcript from that seminary.

International students must have a bachelor's degree from an accredited school; must be recommended by a respective dean; should apply six months to a year prior to enrollment. A $25 application fee is required.

Admission Application Deadline
Six months prior to expected date of admission.

Admission Contact
The Registrar, Interdenominational Theological Center, 671 Beckwith St., SW, Atlanta, GA 30314; (404) 527-7707.

GRADUATION REQUIREMENTS
Must complete denominational history, policy and doctrine for constituent's denomination; must pass test in English proficiency; must complete requirements within five years from date of registration. A $50 graduation fee is due 30 days before end of last semester.

Grading System
A–F, (instructor may use the scientific approach); I=Incomplete; W=Withdraw; WU=Withdraw Unofficially; NG=Courses continuing beyond a semester and other designated course.

STUDENT BODY PROFILE
Total enrollment: 383

From in-state: 1,915

Other regions: 41 states; 12 foreign countries

Graduate students (male/female): 280/103

Ethnic/Racial Makeup

African American, 344: International, 20; Other/unclassified, 19.

FACULTY PROFILE

Number of faculty: 41

Student-teacher ratio: 13:1

Full-time faculty: 26

Part-time faculty: 15

Faculty with doctorates or other terminal degrees: 75%

SCHOOL CALENDAR

1992–93: August 24–May 6 (semester hours)

Commencement and conferring of degrees: May 8

One summer session.

DEGREES OFFERED 1991–92:

Master of Arts in Christian Education

Master of Arts in Church Music

Master of Divinity

Doctor of Ministry (cooperative)

Doctor of Sacred Theology (cooperative)

SPECIAL PROGRAMS

Black Women in Church and Society is a program of study to foster a better understanding of the changing roles of women in church and society. The program hopes to develop a resource/research center and collect data about black women.

Charles B. Copher Annual Faculty Lecture Series provides opportunity for faculty to present their research findings. The program seeks to keep faculty on the cutting edge of their respective disciplines.

Continuing Education (CE) programs include a three-year CE program for ministers with seminary education to keep them updated; a three-year CE program for minis-

ters who do not qualify for the graduate program, but would like to keep abreast in the field; or a three-year CE program designed to meet the needs of the lay person.

National Issues is a community-based series of open discussions that afford citizens to address issues of major domestic policy with policy makers.

Religious Heritage of the African World promotes the continuation of the interdenominational and interdisciplinary academic church. Through interdisciplinary and cross disciplinary approaches in research, especially in theological education, the black experience is the primary focus.

World Religions is a three-year cycle of elective courses taught by visiting scholars and practitioners to foster an understanding and appreciation of international religious diversity and pluralism.

LIBRARY HOLDINGS

The cooperative Robert E. Woodruff Library holds 374,292 bound volumes 111,000 microforms, 47,115 bound periodicals, 1,372 periodical subscriptions, 2,800 audiovisuals, 115,822 government documents, 13, 916 thesis and dissertations, and 200 computers in the computer center for student use. Special collections include Carnegie Art Reference Set, the Henry P. Slaughter and Countee Cullen Memorial Collection of material on graphic and performing artists, the Southern Regional Council papers on race relations and socioeconomic conditions in the Southeast (1944–1968), the First World Publication, and many others.

STUDENT LIFE

Campus Services

Health, personal and psychological counseling, pastoral counseling, chapel services, and religious activities.

Campus Activities

ITC offers a variety of religious, social, cultural, and recreational activities. Leadership opportunities are found in the Student Christian League which represents the ITC student body and offers a wide variety of seminarian activities. Honor societies include the International Society of Theta Phi Honor Society. Publications include the biannual *Journal of the Interdenominational Theological Center* as well as a series entitled *Black Church Scholars*.

The churches of the city, human service agencies, hospitals, and phenological institutions provide laboratories for students preparing for the Christian ministry.

Many opportunities exist for students to interact with students at other Atlanta University Center institutions including Clark Atlanta University, Spelman College, Morehouse College, Morris-Brown College, and Morehouse School of Medicine.

ITC is located in the metropolitan city of Atlanta, the capital of Georgia, with a population of over two million. The city is served by mass air, rail, and bus systems. Local transportation on the MARTA provides easy access to downtown, the airport, or virtually anywhere in the metro area.

The campus is located one mile west of downtown, close to Underground Atlanta, with its quaint shops. Students have access to fine dining, world-class shopping, art galleries, museums, and the Atlanta Symphony or Ballet. The Atlanta Hawks, Braves, and Falcons offer major league sports. Major recording artists frequent the city. Points of interest include the Martin Luther King, Jr. Center for Non-violent Change, the Jimmy Carter Presidential Library, Stone Mountain Park, and Six Flags over Georgia Amusement Park. Other activities include boating, fishing,

and golfing. The World Congress Center hosts many national conferences. The city of Atlanta is an international center for business, banking, and social change, offering students many professional opportunities.

Housing Availability

Four dormitories, 37 apartments, and 20 efficiency units are available for married students on a first-come-first-served basis.

NOTABLE ALUMNI

Rev. Charles Blake, 1965–Bishop, First Southern California Jurisdiction, Church of God in Christ

Oswald P. Bronson, Ph.D., 1959–President, Bethune-Cookman College; Former ITC president

Tyrone L. Burkette, Ph.D., 1970–President, Barber-Scotia College; former Associate Executive, North Carolina Synod of the Presbyterian Church (USA)

Jacquelyn Grant, Ph.D., 1973–Ordained Elderly, African Methodist Episcopal Church; Associate Minister, Flipper Temple A.M.E. Church

Cornelius L. Henderson, Ph.D., 1969–Superintendent, Atlanta-Emory District of the United Methodist Church North Georgia Conference

Rev. Ezekial Kutjok, 1977–General Secretary, Sundan Council of Churches (three million parishioners)

Rev. Otis Moss, 1959–Pastor, Olivet Institutional Baptist Church, Cleveland, Ohio

MOREHOUSE COLLEGE

830 Westview Dr.
Atlanta, GA 30314
Phone: (404) 215-2632
Toll-free out-state:
800-992-0642
Fax: (410) 319-1013

Total Enrollment:
2,992

Level of Selectivity:
Slightly competitive

Motto:
To Uplift the Human
Race through
Responsible
Citizenship

HISTORY

Morehouse is a private, independent, four year, liberal arts college for men. It was founded in 1867 in Augusta, Georgia as the Augusta Institute; its purpose, to train freed slaves to read and write. The school moved to Atlanta, Georgia in 1879 and expanded its scope to prepare blacks for the ministry. Consequently, it was called Atlanta Baptist Seminary. In 1894 the first college instruction was introduced and in 1897 the first bachelor's degree was granted and the seminary changed to Atlanta Baptist College. In 1913, the name changed to its present name, Morehouse College. The Morehouse School of Medicine was established in 1975 and became independent of the college in 1981.

A cooperative agreement was established in 1929 among Clark Atlanta University, Spelman College, and Morehouse College. The cooperative later expanded to include Morris Brown College, the Interdenominational Theological Center and the Morehouse School of Medicine. The subsequent conglomeration is presently called the Atlanta University Center and allows students to use the facilities of a large university community while attending a smaller liberal arts college.

Although Morehouse expanded its facilities and programs, it holds true to its mission to educate and nurture black male leadership. The nation's only historically all black-male college feels a special responsibility for teaching its students about the history and culture of blacks. This commitment to develop men with disciplined minds who will lead lives of leadership, service, and self-realization is evident in the fact that Morehouse has a legacy of producing black male leaders who are dynamic in their varied professions. President Leroy Keith states, "Morehouse has an illustrious history of excellence in the provision of educational opportunities; our alumni have distinguished themselves in many professions throughout the world." The school can boast of a long list of distinguished leaders such as Dr. Martin Luther King, Jr., Maynard Jackson, Andrew Young, and Edwin Moses to name a few. Notables like Oprah Winfrey and Spike Lee have donated millions of dollars for scholarship endowments.

Dotted with a mixture of old and an increasing number of new buildings, the campus forms part of the Atlanta University Center, the largest private educational complex with a predominantly black enrollment in the world. The Martin Luther King, Jr. International Chapel is a multi-purpose facility named in honor of the college's most distinguished alumnus. This historically Black College is a United Negro College Fund member school and is one of three black institutions with a Phi Beta Kappa Honor Society represented on campus.

ACCREDITATION

Morehouse is accredited by the Southern Association of Colleges and Schools (SACS) to award the Bachelor of Arts and Bachelor of Science degrees.

COSTS PER YEAR

1991–92 Tuition: $6,150

Room and board: $2,850 (room); $2,130 (board)

Special fees: $1,280

Books: $500

Estimated total cost: $12,910

FINANCIAL AID

1991–92 Institutional Funding

Total amount of scholarships and grants: $3,330,441

1991–92 Federal and State Funding

Total amount of loans: $4,500,000

Range of work-study: $1,500–$2,500

Financial Aid Specific to the School

90% of the student body received financial aid during 1991–92.

Army, Navy, and Air Force in cooperation with Georgia Technical Institute offer two- and three-year scholarships that pay tuition, fees, books, and other expenses as well as provide a monthly stipend of $100.

Athletic scholarships are available to students participating in intercollegiate sports.

Performance grants are available to students in music and drama.

The Cooperative Education Program alternates academic study with paid related work experience. The program provides academic credit and full-time status during co-op placement.

The Deferred Payment Plan allows students to pay college costs in two or three installments during the semester.

Oprah Winfrey and Spike Lee Scholarships are available.

Regent Scholarships are available to Georgia Residents who rank in the top 25% of their class. Recipients must work full time in the state of Georgia for one year.

Student Incentive Grants are awarded to full-time Georgia residents only.

UNCF scholarships are available at this school to students who demonstrate financial need. Some awards may also be based on merit and location. Awards range from $500 to $7,500.

Financial Aid Deadline
April 1 (fall & spring)

Financial Aid Contact
Office of Admissions, Morehouse College, 830 Westview Dr., Atlanta, GA 30314; (404) 215-2638

ADMISSION REQUIREMENTS
SAT (preferred); ACT (accepted)

Entrance Requirements
Graduation from an accredited high school; submit an official high school transcript to include the following units: 4 English, 3 math, 2 natural sciences, and 2 social sciences; submit a written essay; must submit proof of a recent physical. An interview may be requested. A $35.00 nonrefundable application fee is required.

GED students must meet the basic admission requirements and take the SAT or ACT exam.

Transfer students must have completed 26 semester/39 quarter hours of college work from an accredited institution with a minimum 2.5 grade point average on a 4.0 scale; a minimum of 60 semester/90 quarter hours must be completed at Morehouse College; a maximum of 60 semester hours is transferable to Morehouse.

International students must take the Test of English as a Foreign Language (TOEFL), unless they are residents of English-speaking countries; must complete the East or West African Examination or have obtained and performed competently on the General Certificate of Education; must take the Scholastic Aptitude Test if enrolling as a freshman; must file an Affidavit of Support that indicates who will take responsibility for expenses while at Morehouse.

Early admission students must have completed at least two years of high school; must have a GPA of 3.0 or better on 4.0

scale; must have a high SAT score; and must be recommended by high school principal and guidance counselor.

Joint enrollment allows students to take freshman-level courses at Morehouse while enrolled in a public high school in the metropolitan Atlanta area. Selection is made on basis of GPA, SAT, recommendation of high school guidance counselor and a personal interview.

Admission Application Deadline
February 15 (fall); October 15 (spring)

Admission Contact
Mr. Sterling H. Hudson, Director of Admissions, Morehouse College, 830 Westview Dr. SW, Atlanta, GA 30314; (404) 215-2632 or 800-992-0642.

GRADUATION REQUIREMENTS
A minimum of 124 semester hours to include the core requirements; 12 semester hours of a foreign language or its equivalent; 6 semester hours of science and math; 1 computer course for accounting, engineering, finance, management, and math majors; completion of both the freshman orientation seminar and weekly assembly is required for graduation; must attend graduation ceremonies.

Grading System
A-F; I=Incomplete; W=Withdrawal; WP=Withdrawal Passing; WF=Withdrawal Failing; P/F=Pass/Fail.

STUDENT BODY PROFILE
Total enrollment: 2,992

From in-state: 536

Other regions: 40 states, D.C., and 15 foreign countries

Full-time undergraduates: 2,787

Part-time undergraduates: 205

Ethnic/Racial Makeup

African Americans, 2,930; International, 62.

Class of 1995 Profile

Number of applicants: 3,390

Number accepted: 1,468

Number enrolled: 751

Median SAT score: 480V; 523M

Median ACT score: 23

Transfer applicants: 418

Transfers accepted: 209

Transfers enrolled: 136

FACULTY PROFILE

Number of faculty: 178

Student-teacher ratio: 17:1

Full-time faculty: 150

Part-time faculty: 28

Faculty with doctorates or other terminal degrees: 74

SCHOOL CALENDAR

1992–93: August–May

Commencement and conferring of degrees: May

One summer session.

DEGREES OFFERED 1991–92:

Bachelor of Arts

Art

Drama

Economics

English

French

German

History

International Studies

Mass Communication

Music

Philosophy

Political Science

Religion

Social Welfare

Sociology

Spanish

Bachelor of Science

Accounting

Actuarial Science

Banking and Finance

Biology

Business Management

Chemistry

Chemistry/Engineering

Computer Science

Computer Science/Engineering

Economics

Education

Health and Physical Education

Insurance

Interdisciplinary Science

Interdisciplinary Science/Engineering

Marketing

Mathematics

Mathematics/Engineering

Physics

Physics/Engineering

Psychology

Urban Studies

Percent of Graduates That Go On to Higher Degrees upon Graduation:

10% enter medical school

7% enter law school

12% enter business school

10% enter arts & sciences

10% unclassified

SPECIAL PROGRAMS

Advanced Placement allows high school students to take various college courses for credit during their junior or senior year. Credit is granted for a score of four or above on the College Board AP test. Some departments grant credit for a score of three. Consult high school guidance counselor for more information.

The College Level Examination Program (CLEP) grants college credit for nontraditional educational experiences such as the military, work or other life experiences by taking the CLEP exam administered by the College Entrance Examination Board. A maximum of 24 semester hours may be granted.

College orientation is offered to entering students before classes begin to orient students to the college and to prepare them for college life.

Cooperative Education Program alternates formal academic study with practical work experience in major.

Cross-registration allows students to take courses not available at their home school at one of the five schools in the Atlanta University Center.

Dual Degree Programs in architecture and engineering

Exchange Student Program is available on campus.

The Ford Foundation and the Dana Foundation are designed to encourage students to teach on a college level.

The Health Professions Program is designed to aid those students entering medical and dental schools.

Honors programs offer academically talented students a challenging program of study that includes special classes, seminars, cultural activities and special recognition to motivate participants.

International Studies Program allows students to go to a foreign country for a specified period of time as part of their college education.

Remedial Program provides remedial courses for entering students to bring them up to admissions standards.

The Ronald McNair/Project SPACE Program encourages science and engineering students to pursue careers in research and college level teaching.

ROTC provides training in military science for commission as a second lieutenant in the U.S. Army, Navy, Air Force.

Three-two dual degree in engineering offered in conjunction with Georgia Tech, Boston University, Auburn University, the University of Michigan, and other institutions.

ATHLETIC PROGRAMS

Morehouse College is a member of the Southern Intercollegiate Athletic Conference (SIAC) and the National Collegiate Athletic Association (NCAA), Division II.

Intercollegiate sports: men's basketball, cross country, football, tennis, track & field (indoor & outdoor), swimming.

Intramural sports: baseball, basketball, bowling, soccer, swimming, table tennis, tennis.

LIBRARY HOLDINGS

Robert W. Woodruff Library houses 560,000 bound volumes, 11,000 microforms, 1,200 periodical subscriptions, 800 audiovisuals and 120 computers for student use.

STUDENT LIFE

Special Regulations

Class attendance is required; registered cars permitted without restriction; must maintain a 2.5 to join social organization; freshmen must attend one-hour weekly orientation seminar; all students must attend one-hour weekly college assembly.

Campus Services

Health center, personal and psychological counseling, remedial programs, student employment services, religious services, chapel services, graduate placement, independent study.

Campus Activities

Social activities include theater (the Morehouse-Spelman Players), concerts, dances, Glee Club, and marching band. Journalism students may work on the monthly publication *(The Maroon Tiger),* or the yearbook *(The Torch).*

Leadership opportunities can be found in the Student Government Association (SGA). The General Assembly, Student Council, and Student Court comprises the basic structure of the SGA. Chapel Assistants, Forensics Team, and Frederick Douglass Tutorial Institute are a few of the many student organizations. National fraternities include Alpha Phi Alpha, Kappa Alpha Psi, Omega Psi Phi, Phi Beta Sigma. Two local fraternities include Alpha Pi Omega, and Iota Phi Theta. Honor societies include Phi Beta Kappa, Beta Kappa Chi, French Honor Society, Alpha Tsu Delta, Alpha Kappa Delta, and Phi Alpha Theta.

Morehouse is located in the dynamic city of Atlanta which is known as the cultural and economic mecca of the South. The college provides for a quality education while the surrounding community provides an array of social and cultural activities. Professional ball games, theaters, concerts, art galleries, fine restaurants and malls are all accessible by the public transit system and can be found all over the metropolitan area. Places of interest include Georgia's Stone Mountain Park, Martin Luther King (MLK), Jr. Center for Nonviolent Social Change, Martin Luther King, Jr. National Historic Site, The Antebellum Plantation, Six Flags Over Georgia, and Carter Presidential Center, Museum and Library. The campus is located one mile west of downtown Atlanta.

Housing Availability

1,250 housing spaces.

Handicapped Services

Include wheelchair accessibility.

NOTABLE ALUMNI

Lerone Bennett, Jr., 1949/1966–Executive editor, *Ebony* magazine; author

Samuel Dubois Cook, 1948–President, Dillard University

Maynard Jackson, 1956–Mayor, Atlanta, Georgia

Robert Johnson, 1948–Publisher, *Jet* magazine

Rev. Dr. Martin Luther King, Jr., 1948–Nobel Prize laureate; civil rights leader

Spike Lee, 1979–Filmmaker

Edwin Moses, 1978–U.S. Olympic champion

Samuel Nabrit, 1925–First black member of Atomic Energy Commission; former Texas Southern University President

Louis Sullivan, MD., 1954–Head of U.S. Health & Human Services Dept.

MOREHOUSE SCHOOL OF MEDICINE

HISTORY

Morehouse School of Medicine (MSM) is a four-year, private, professional medical school. MSM was established in the early 1970s as the School of Medicine at Morehouse College. In 1981, the Medical School became independent. For clinical instruction, MSM is affiliated with Grady Memorial Hospital, Southwest Hospital and Medical Center, Georgia Regional Hospital, West Paces Ferry Hospital, and Tuskegee VA Medical Center.

Originally a two-year educational program in basic medical sciences, the Morehouse School of Medicine is now a four-year medical doctor degree granting institution. The chartered class of twenty-four students entered Morehouse's two-year basic sciences program in 1978. Those students and the subsequent two classes transferred to other medical training schools for two years to receive their M.D. degrees. Morehouse School of Medicine received authorization to begin a four-year, degree granting institution in 1981. That same year, Dr. Louis Sullivan became president. In 1982, MSM was given authorization to development a program to award the Doctor of Medicine degree.

During the summer of 1983, third-year medical students began clinical rotations at Grady Memorial Hospital in cooperation with the Emory University School of Medicine (EUSM). In 1985, the Liaison Committee on Medical Education (LCME) granted MSM full accreditation to award the M.D. degree. The first class of M.D.s trained by Morehouse School of Medicine graduated May 17, 1985. Since 1985, over 200 students have received the M.D. degree from the school, bringing the number of alumni physicians to 289.

In 1990, the school assumed full responsibility for teaching third-year students in family medicine, surgery, and psychiatry. The remaining third-year clerkship (medicine, obstetrics/gynecology, and pediatrics) continued to be taught in cooperation with Emory University School of Medicine. The Morehouse School of Medicine assumed full responsibility for the third-year medicine clerkship in 1991, and for pediatrics and obstetrics/gynecology in 1993. The Graduate Medical Education program of the school was

720 Westview Dr. SW
Atlanta, GA 30310-1495
Phone: (405) 752-1500

Total Enrollment:
140

Level of Selectivity:
Competitive

Motto:
Knowledge, Wisdom, Excellence, Service

initiated in 1981 when the Family Practice Residency program received accreditation from the Accrediting Council for Graduate Medical Education (ACGME).

Morehouse College originally received a federal grant to study the feasibility of developing a two-year program to train students for careers as primary care physicians. These physicians would work in medically under-served areas, among minorities and poor people. The study revealed a severe shortage of black and minority physicians in the United States and particularly in Georgia's rural and inner city areas. Morehouse accepted the challenge and developed a new medical school. According to Morehouse's President James A. Goodman, "Morehouse remains committed to its original mission to practice medicine in the inner cities and rural areas of this country." Morehouse School of Medicine is the newest member of the Atlanta University Center, a consortium of six independent institutions that constitutes the largest predominantly black private educational complex in the world.

MSM's research facilities are modern and well-equipped, including seventy individual and shared-use laboratories.

ACCREDITATION

Morehouse School of Medicine is accredited by the American Medical Association's Liaison Committee on Medical Education to award the Doctor of Medicine (M.D.) degree. The Doctorate degree in Biomedical Sciences is also awarded.

Other Accreditation

Accrediting Council for Graduate Medical Education

Southern Association of Colleges and Schools

COSTS PER YEAR

1992–93 Tuition: $13,500

Room and board: $10,000 (estimated, off-campus)

Special fees: $1,712

Books: $750

Estimated total cost: $25,962

FINANCIAL AID

1991–92 Institutional Funding

Number of scholarships and grants: 91

Total amount of scholarships and grants: $358,407

Range of scholarships and grants: $250–$11,525

1991–92 Federal and State Funding

Number of scholarships and grants: 18

Total amount of scholarships and grants: $100,248

Range of scholarships and grants: $700–$11,662

Number of loans: 133

Total amount of loans: $1,997,436

Range of loans: $530–$20,000

Number of work-study: 29

Total amount of work-study: $33,843

Financial Aid Specific to the School

Endowed, alumni, friends, and corporation scholarships number 55 and are available to students based on varying criteria such as merit, need, or area of interest.

Institutional scholarships are available to students based on academic merit and need.

Short-term, low-interest institutional loans are available to students.

Cooperative Education Program combines classroom study with related paid work experience. The program provides career-related internships or fieldwork.

Financial Aid Deadline

April 15

Financial Aid Contact

Office of Student Fiscal Affairs, Morehouse School of Medicine, 720 Westview Dr. SW, Atlanta, GA 30310; (405) 572-1500.

ADMISSION REQUIREMENTS

MCAT required

Entrance Requirements

Completion of bachelor's degree and completion of one academic year of the following premedical courses: biology with lab; general chemistry with lab; organic chemistry with lab; physics with lab; college level mathematics; and English including composition. Premedical courses should not be taken on a pass/fail basis. Rather, grades must be received. Also, rigorous introductory courses should be taken, and an interview is required. A $40 non-refundable application fee is required.

The Morehouse School of Medicine accepts applications from the American Medical College Application Service (AMCAS) for first-year entering class beginning June 15 of the year prior to enrollment. The deadline for receipt of all required credentials by AMCAS is December 1 of the year prior to enrollment. AMCAS applications received after December will not be forwarded to MSM.

On receipt of the application from AMCAS, the Admissions Office promptly forwards to applicants supplementary materials that must be submitted to complete the application process. At this stage, a nonrefundable application service fee of $40 is charged by the school. Applicants are encouraged to submit materials well in advance of the deadline to allow sufficient time for receipt of all materials requested. Selected applicants are invited for a personal interview. Following the interview, if granted, final decisions are made by the Committee on Admissions. Applicants are notified as soon as a final admission decision has been made.

Early Decision Admission is an option for applicants whose first-choice is the Morehouse School of Medicine; who agree to apply only to the MSM prior to receiving its admission decision; who present an academic program of a minimum of 90 semester hours; who have a superior academic record and correspondingly strong scores on the MCAT; who submit all required credentials to AMCAS by August 1; who, if invited, appear for a personal interview prior to September 1; and who accept a position in the class, if offered one.

Transfer students may be accepted in limited numbers annually as transfers into the second-year class when vacancies exist; must have attended a LCME accredited U.S. or Canadian school of medicine; must be in good academic standing and have full approval of the dean from previous institution; and have a cogent reason for requesting transfer.

Admission Application Deadline

December 1 (priority); six months prior to date of admission; Rolling admission provides no specific date for notification of admission so applicant is informed as soon as admission decision is made.

Admission Contact

Dr. Angela Franklin, Dean of Student Affairs, Morehouse School of Medicine, 720 Westview Dr., SW, Atlanta, GA 30320-1495; (404) 752-1652.

GRADUATION REQUIREMENTS

A minimum of 183 semester hours; completion of two-years' basic medical science requirements; dissertation/thesis for graduate students; third-year clerkships in ambulatory and in-patient care; fourth-year clerkships in ambulatory and rural care; and completion of Parts I and II of the National Board of Medical Examiners.

Grading System

A-F; P=Pass, satisfactory performance; I=Incomplete

STUDENT BODY PROFILE

Total enrollment (male/female): 70/70

From in-state: 98

Graduate students (male/female): 70/70

Ethnic/Racial Makeup

African American, 113; Hispanic, 6; Asian, 5; Native American, 1; Caucasian, 12; International, 2.

Class of 1995 Profile

Number of applicants: 1,820

Number accepted: 38

FACULTY PROFILE

Number of faculty: 100

Student-teacher ratio: 4:1

Full-time faculty (male/female): 52/31

Part-time faculty (male/female): 13/4

Tenured faculty (male/female): 9/4

Faculty with doctorates or other terminal
  degrees: 100%

Ethnic/Racial Makeup

African American, 80; Asian, 7; Other/ unclassified, 13.

SCHOOL CALENDAR

1992–93: (semester hours)

Summer session

DEGREES OFFERED 1991–92:

Biomedical Sciences (Ph.D.)

General Internal Medicine

General Pediatrics (cooperative)

Doctor of Medicine (M.D) Residency Programs

Ambulatory Adult Health

Family Practice

Internal Medicine

Maternal Child Health

Obstetrics and Gynecology (1994)

Pediatrics (cooperative until 1994)

Public Health and Preventive Medicine

Psychiatry

Radiology

Rural Primary Care

Surgery (1993)

Doctoral Degree (Ph.D.)

Biomedical Sciences

SPECIAL PROGRAMS

AIDS Consortium Center is funded by a $3.7 million grant from the National Institute of Allergy and Infectious Diseases. The program is planned and organized by the Association of Minority Health Professions Schools.

Combined M.D./Ph.D. program is offered in cooperation with Emory University School of Medicine.

Continuing Education (CE) offers Grand Rounds, conferences, workshops, and short courses on various subject throughout the year for community physicians and other health professionals. The various programs qualify for the American Medical Association (AMA) category I credit for physicians. Contact Office of Continuing Medical Education; (404) 752-1632.

CORK Institute on Black Alcohol and Other Drug Abuse is a program established through a one million dollar grant from the Joan B. Kroc Foundation.

Health Promotion Resource Center is a partnership program for communities with less than 50,000 residents. The center provides coordinated services through interagency collaboration.

International programs are offered in Senegal between MSM and Tulane University's School of Public Health and Tropical Medicine; two projects are for the institute of Health and Development of Diop University: 1) to supply technical assistance and training for launching Senegal's first public health training program and 2) to conduct the Knowledge, Attitudes, and Practices survey of traditional healers in Fatick (Senegal), focusing on the relationship between traditional healers and modern medicine.

Kellogg Foundation granted MSM six million dollars for the redirection of education for health professions and to increase the number of health care practitioners.

Morehouse-Drew-Meharry Cancer Consortium and the National Black Leadership Initiative on Cancer are both educational awareness programs.

Research Center in Minority Institutions (RCMI) is a grant from the National Institutes of Health which has enabled MSM to develop its research in biomedical sciences into an area of excellence.

Residency Programs in Family Practice for three years, Preventive Medicine for one year, Psychiatry for four years, Public Health and General Preventive Medicine for two years, and Surgery for five years are offered through the Graduate Medical Education Program and accredited by the Accrediting Council on Graduate Medical Education. The program's mission is to educate and train physicians to practice quality primary care, especially in underserved rural and urban communities in Georgia.

Rural Health Grant is a part of the Area Health Education Centers Program. It was established to improve the geographic distribution and supply of primary health care professionals in medically under-served inner city and rural areas.

LIBRARY HOLDINGS

The MSM library holds 25,000 bound volumes, 800 periodical subscriptions, 25 computers for student use, CD-ROM database searching, and on-line bibliographic services. Robert W. Woodruff Library is part of the Clark Atlanta University Center of which Morehouse School of Medicine is a part. This library holds 47,115 bound volumes, 111,000 microforms, 1,372 periodical subscriptions, 2,800 audiovisuals, 247,167 government documents, 13,916 thesis and dissertations, and 200 computers for student use. For special collection see Clark-Atlanta University.

STUDENT LIFE

Special Regulations

Attendance at clinical clerkships and other clinical experiences involving patient care is required; attendance at tests and final examinations is mandatory.

Campus Services

Health, personal and psychological counseling, and career counseling and placement.

Campus Activities

Student activities include grand rounds. Leadership opportunities are found in Student Government Association (SGA) or the various other organizations, such as the Student National Medical Association, Medical Student Section of the American Medical Association, Pre-Alumni Association, and Student American Medical Association. Alpha Omega Alpha Honor Society is represented on campus.

Many opportunities exist for students to interact with students at other Atlanta University Center Institutions including Clark-Atlanta University, Spelman College, Morehouse College, Morris Brown College, Interdenominational Theological Seminary, and Morehouse College.

MSM is located in the metropolitan city of Atlanta, the capital of Georgia, with a population of over two million. The city is served by mass air, rail, and bus transportation. Local transportation on the MARTA provides easy access to downtown, the airport, or virtually anywhere in the metro area.

Students have access to Underground Atlanta's quaint shops, to fine dining, world-class shopping, art galleries, museums, the Atlanta Symphony, or ballet. The Atlanta Hawks, Braves, and Falcons comprise the city's major sports leagues. Points of interest include the Martin Luther King, Jr. Center for Non-violent Change, the Jimmy Carter Presidential Library, Stone Mountain Park, and Six Flags Over Georgia Amusement Park. Other activities include boating, fishing, and golfing. The World Congress Center hosts many national conferences. The city of Atlanta is an international center for business, banking, and social change, offering students many professional opportunities.

Housing Availability

None on campus; off-campus housing available.

NOTABLE ALUMNI

Bess E. Jones–M.D., M.P.H.–Public Health Department, DeKalb County, GA

Patricia Pelham-Harris, M.D.–Family practice physician, Ogletree Family Center, Crawford, GA

Beverly Simons, M.D.,–New Lower Richland Medical Center, Eastover, SC

Louis W. Sullivan, M.D., 1954–Former secretary, U.S. Department of Health and Human Services; president of Morehouse School of Medicine

MORRIS BROWN COLLEGE

643 Martin Luther
King Jr. Dr. NW
Atlanta, GA 30314
Phone: (404) 220-0270
Fax: (404) 659-4315

Total Enrollment:
2,030

Level of Selectivity:
Slightly competitive

Motto:
Academic Excellence
With a Personal Touch

HISTORY

Morris Brown College (MBC) is a four-year, private, coed, liberal arts institution affiliated with the African Methodist Episcopal Church. It was founded in 1881 "for the Christian education of negro boys and girls in Atlanta." Morris Brown opened with two teachers and 107 students in 1885; it is now an institution with 450 faculty and staff and over 2,000 students.

The school operated on the primary, secondary, and normal school levels until 1894, with a regular academic program and courses in tailoring, dressmaking, home economics, nursing education, commerce, and printing. A theological department for the training of ministers was established in 1894. That same year the College Department began, graduating its first students four years later.

Morris Brown College's status was changed to university in 1913, and it was granted the right to establish and operate branch institutions of learning. The heavy burden imposed by the branches on the school's finances made it necessary to discontinue the branches in 1929, when the present name Morris Brown College was restored.

The primary mission of Morris Brown is to provide educational opportunities in a Christian environment that will enable students to become fully functional persons in society. In fulfilling this mission, the college accepts the obligation to place events and points of view in the context of man's long intellectual history and to expose both to the light of man's best thinking.

MBC became the fourth member of the Atlanta University Center, a cluster of six predominantly black colleges and universities, in 1932. It is also a United Negro College Fund member school.

ACCREDITATION

Morris Brown College is accredited by the Commission on Colleges of the Southern Association of Colleges and Schools (SACS) to award the Bachelor of Arts and Bachelor of Science degrees.

COSTS PER YEAR

1992–93 Tuition: $6,212

Room and board: $2,294 (room); $1,852 (board)

Special fees: 440

Books: 500

Estimated total cost: $11,298

FINANCIAL AID

1991–92 Institutional Funding

Number of scholarships and grants: 669

Total amount of scholarships and grants: $2,468,639

1991–92 Federal and State Funding

Number of scholarships and grants: 2,262

Total dollar amount of scholarships and grants: $3,269,874

Number of loans: 2,197

Total dollar amount of loans: $4,653,536

Number of work-study: 274

Total dollar amount of work-study: $267,888

Financial Aid Specific to the School

87% of the student body received financial aid during 1991–92.

Academic scholarships are awarded to high school seniors with a combined SAT score of at least 800 or a composite ACT score of at least 17, and a minimum cumulative grade point average of 3.10. The scholarship covers tuition and is renewable each year the student maintains a 3.0.

Athletic Grants-in-Aid are awarded to male students who excel in basketball and/or football.

New York City Residents Scholarship Program provides financial aid to low-income students who are enrolled full-time in an undergraduate degree-granting program. The maximum amount of the grant is $650 per year. Contact: New York Urban League, 1500 Broadway, 14th Floor, New York, NY 10036.

Nursing student loans are available for full-time and half-time nursing students. The maximum loan is $2,500 per year. The loan is repayable at 6% over a ten-year period following completion of training.

Performance awards are given to students with exceptional talents participating in band or choir. Band awards range up to $1,000 per year; choir awards range up to $2,000 per year.

Presidential scholarships are available to high school seniors with a combined SAT score of 1,100, and a minimum cumulative average of 3.5. The scholarship covers tuition, fees, room, and board, and is renewable each year the student maintains a 3.0.

Sibling tuition waivers allow siblings to pay one full tuition and one half tuition.

Twins tuition waivers allow twins to pay one full tuition while the second tuition is wavered.

Pennsylvania State Grant Program provides financial aid to Pennsylvania residents who are in need of financial aid to attend postsecondary school as full-time students. The amount varies from $100 to $600 at schools located outside Pennsylvania.

Installment plans include Academic Management Services, East Providence, RI 02914; 800-556-6684; or The Tuition Plan, 57 Regional Dr., Concord, NH; 800-343-0911. Both are monthly plans.

Loan plans include ConSern Loans for Education, PO Box 9696, Washington, DC 20016-9696; 800-767-5628 or (202) 331-9350.

Cooperative Education Program alternates and combines classroom study with related paid work experience. The program provides academic credit and full-time status during co-op placement.

Morris Brown work-aid is an employment program designed for students who need funds to help defray educational expenses. Students work on campus for a maximum of twenty hours per week.

United Negro College Fund (UNCF) scholarships are awarded to a limited number of students at this school who demonstrate financial need. Some scholarships maybe based on location and merit. UNCF scholarships range from $500 to $7,500.

Navy and cooperative Army and Air Force ROTC offer two- and four-year scholarships that pay tuition, fee, books and other expenses, and provide a monthly stipend of $100.

Georgia Student Incentive Grants are available to students who demonstrate substantial financial need and who are attending an eligible college in Georgia. The maximum award is $400 per year.

Georgia Tuition Equalization Grants are available to students who are Georgia residents and are attending private colleges in Georgia on a full-time basis. The grant is $925.00 per year.

Financial Aid Deadline
June 30

Financial Aid Contact
Mr. W. H. Fouche, Director of Student Financial Aid, Morris Brown College, Atlanta, Georgia 30314; (404) 220-0133.

ADMISSION REQUIREMENTS
SAT or ACT required

Entrance Requirements
Graduation from an accredited high school; completion of fifteen Carnegie units, twelve in academic subjects, to include 3 English, 3 mathematics, 3 science, and 3 social sciences; letter of recommendation from high school personnel; and completed physical exam form. A $20 nonrefundable application fee is required.

GED students must meet basic admission requirements.

Transfer students must submit official high school and college transcripts as well as SAT or ACT scores; no more than 92 semester hours transferred; only grades of "C" or higher transferred. A letter of recommendation and completed physical examination form are required. A $20.00 application fee is required.

For students transferring from a non-accredited institution, scholastic performance will be monitored for one year at Morris Brown.

International students must take the TOEFL examination.

Admission Application Deadline

Rolling admission provides no specific date for notification of admission so applicant is informed as soon as admission decision is made.

Admission Contact

Office of Admissions, Morris Brown College, 643 Martin Luther King Jr. Dr. NW, Atlanta, GA 30314; (404) 220-0152 or (404) 220-0309.

GRADUATION REQUIREMENTS

A minimum of 124 credit hours and completion of the core requirements to include the following hours: six mathematics, six science, six social science, and six foreign language. Average grade of "C" or more, or a GPA of at least 2.0; pass the English Qualifying Examination; complete at least one year in residence at MBC; and must participate in all commencement exercises.

Grading System

A-F, I-incomplete, and W-withdraw

STUDENT BODY PROFILE

Total enrollment (male/female): 873/1,157

From in-state: 1,000

Other regions: 38 states, 20 foreign countries

Full-time undergraduates (male/female): 777/1,030

Part-time undergraduates (male/female): 96/127

Ethnic/Racial Makeup

African American, 1,893; International, 100; Other/unclassified, 157.

Class of 1995 Profile

Number of applicants: 3,231

Number accepted: 2,295

Number enrolled: 796

Median SAT score: 331V; 363M

Median ACT score: 16

Average high school GPA: 2.50

Transfer applicants: 465

Transfers accepted: 340

Transfers enrolled: 114

FACULTY PROFILE

Number of faculty: 144

Student-teacher ratio: 13:1

Full-time faculty (male/female): 113

Part-time faculty (male/female): 31

Tenured faculty (male/female): 17

Faculty with doctorates or other terminal degrees: 59%

SCHOOL CALENDAR

1991–1993: August 23–May 14 (semester hours)

Commencement and conferring of degrees: May 23

One summer session (eight weeks at Clark Atlanta University).

DEGREES OFFERED AND NUMBER CONFERRED 1991–92:

Bachelor of Arts

English/English Education: 2

French: n/a

History and Government: n/a

Journalism: n/a

Mass Communications: 9

Music: n/a

Philosophy and Religion: n/a

Public Relations: n/a

Radio/TV, Film: n/a

Religion: n/a

Sociology: 3

Spanish: n/a

Theater Arts: n/a

Bachelor of Science

Accounting: 5

Airway Computer Science: n/a

Architecture (cooperative): 1

Art Education: n/a

Biology: n/a

Biology Education: 8

Business Administration: 21

Business Education: n/a

Business Management: n/a

Chemistry: n/a

Chemistry Education: n/a

Computer Science: 6

Criminal Justice: 8

Early Childhood Education: 6

Economics: 2

Elementary Education: n/a

Engineering (dual degree): n/a

Financial Management: n/a

French Education: n/a

History : n/a

Hotel Administration: 8

Information Processing: n/a

Liberal Arts: n/a

Management: 5

Marketing: 11

Mathematics: n/a

Mathematics Education: 1

Media Management: n/a

Music Education: 2

Nursing: 13

Office Administration: 3

Paralegal Studies: 3

Political Science: 7

Physics: n/a

Psychology Education: 1

Recreation Education: 1

Speech Communication: n/a

Therapeutic Recreation: 3

Urban Studies: 1

Pre-Professional

Dentistry: n/a

Medicine: n/a

Pharmacy: n/a

SPECIAL PROGRAMS

Accelerated Study Program allows students to complete their undergraduate degree in a shorter period of time than the traditional period of four years.

Advanced Placement (AP) grants college credit for postsecondary work completed in high school. Students scoring three on the AP test will receive credit by examination for each course and advanced placement.

College Level Examination Program (CLEP) determines the academic relevance of nontraditional educational experiences, such as the military, on-the-job training or other life experiences, through a series of tests and may grant students college credit for these experiences.

College orientation is offered for $100 to entering students for one week prior to the beginning of classes to acquaint students with the college and to prepare them for college life; parents may attend.

Cooperative Education Program alternates and combines classroom study with related paid work experience. The program provides academic credit and full-time status during co-op placement.

English as a Second Language is a program that offers courses in English for students whose native language is not English.

Off-campus study is offered with the other five members of the Atlanta University Center, which include Clark Atlanta University, Spelman College, Morehouse College, Interdenominational Theological Seminar, and Morehouse School of Medicine.

Part-time degree programs and adult education programs are offered to allow adults to earn a degree while attending part time.

Remedial courses are offered to entering students to bring them up to admission standards and to help them adjust for success in college.

ROTC provides training in military science for commission as a second lieutenant in the U.S. Armed Forces. Naval ROTC, cooperative Army, and Air Force ROTC offer two- and four-year scholarships.

Three/two degree program in engineering allows students to get two degrees—one in liberal arts from home school and one in engineering from Georgia Institute of Technology—by completing three years at matriculated school and two years at cooperating school.

ATHLETIC PROGRAMS

Morris Brown College is a member of the Southern Intercollegiate Athletic Conference (SIAC) and the National Collegiate Athletic Association (NCAA).

Intercollegiate sports: men's basketball, football, tennis, and cross-country track.

LIBRARY HOLDINGS

The cooperative Robert E. Woodruff Library holds 374,292 bound volumes, 111,000 microforms, 47,115 bound periodicals, 1,372 periodical subscriptions, 2,800 audiovisuals, 247,167 government documents, 13,916 thesis and dissertations, and 200 computers in the computer center for student use. Special collections include Carnegie Art Reference Set, the Henry P. Slaughter and Countee Cullen Memorial Collection of materials on graphic and performing artists, the Southern Regional Council papers on race relations and socioeconomic conditions in the Southeast (1944–1968), First World Publication, and many others.

STUDENT LIFE

Campus Services

Legal, health clinic, and personal/psychological counseling.

Campus Activities

Social and cultural activities include theater, chorale, jazz ensemble, orchestra, dance and band. Other activities include Black History Quiz Bowl, mock trials, and debate. Students may get involved in the *Wolverine Observer* (student-run newspaper) or the *Brownite* (yearbook).

Special events include the athletic awards program that recognizes student athletes who have distinguished themselves during the year. MBC's choir is internationally recognized, performances including inaugural ceremonies for Jimmy Carter as governor and president; the Macy's Thanksgiving Day Parade; and the 200th anniversary of the U.S. Constitution in Philadelphia.

Leadership opportunities are found in the Student Government Association (SGA) or the more than thirty other organizations, such as the PKs (Preachers Kids), an organization for sons and daughters of ministers in any denomination who do creative outreach such as prison ministry or tutoring to homeless children. Greek letter fraternities include Alpha Phi Alpha, Kappa Alpha Psi, Omega Psi Phi, and Phi Beta Sigma; sororities include Alpha Kappa Alpha, Delta Sigma Theta, Sigma Gamma Rho, and Zeta Phi Beta.

Many opportunities exist for students to interact with students at other Atlanta University Center Institutions, including Clark Atlanta University, Spelman College, Morehouse College, Interdenominational Theological Center, and Morehouse School of Medicine.

Morris Brown is located in the metropolitan city of Atlanta, the capital of Georgia, with a population of over two million. The city is served by mass air, rail, and bus. Local transportation on the MARTA provides easy access to downtown, the airport, or virtually anywhere in the metro area.

The campus is located near downtown, close to Underground Atlanta, with its quaint shops. Students have access to fine dining, world class shopping, art galleries, museums, and the Atlanta symphony or ballet. The Atlanta Hawks, Braves, and Falcons offer major league sports. Points of interest include the Martin Luther King, Jr. Center for Non-violent Change, the Jimmy Carter

Presidential Library, Stone Mountain, and Six Flags Over Georgia Amusement Park. Recreational activities include boating, fishing, and golfing. The World Congress Center hosts many national conferences. The city of Atlanta is an international center for business, banking, and social change, offering students many professional opportunities.

Housing Availability

700 housing spaces available; off-campus living is permitted.

NOTABLE ALUMNI

Dr. Leonard E. Dawson, 1954–Executive vice president of United Negro College Fund, director of special projects

Major General Albert J. Edmonds, 1964–Assistant chief of staff, US Air Force

Beverly J. Harvard, 1972–Deputy chief of police, Atlanta, GA

Virgil Hall Hodges, 1958–Deputy commissioner, NY State Department of Labor

Robert E. James, 1964–Bank president, Savannah, GA

James Alan McPherson, 1965–Writer; Pulitzer Prize recipient

Percy J. Vaughn, Jr., 1957–Dean, College of Business Administration, Alabama State University

PAINE COLLEGE

1235 15th St.
Augusta, GA 30910
Phone: (706) 821-8200
Toll-free in-state:
800-476-7703
Fax: (706) 821-8293

Total Enrollment:
790

Level of Selectivity:
Noncompetitive

HISTORY

Paine College (PC) is a four-year, private, coed, liberal arts college founded in 1882 as Paine Institute. The history of PC began after the Civil War when the Black members of the Methodist Episcopal Church South formed the Colored (now Christian) Methodist Episcopal (CME) Church. Realizing the need to train black ministers and teachers, the CME Church requested the assistance of its mother church. Each church appointed three people, who joined together to create Paine College.

Paine was chartered in 1883 and offered its first instruction at postsecondary level in 1891. The first bachelor's degree was awarded in 1885, and the present name Paine College was adopted in 1903.

PC is an Historically Black College/University (HBCU) and a United Negro College Fund member school. Its mission is to provide a quality liberal arts education, with an emphasis on ethical and spiritual values, social responsibility, and personal development. The school seeks to emphasize and to enhance the black experience as a part of the total education process.

ACCREDITATION

Paine is accredited by the Southern Association of Colleges and Schools (SACS) to award the Bachelor of Arts and Bachelor of Science degrees.

Other Accreditation

National Council for Accreditation of
  Teacher Education

University Senate of the United Methodist
  Church

COSTS PER YEAR

1992–93 Tuition: $5,200

Room and board: $1,085 (room); $1,654
  (board)

Special fees: $268

Books: $500

Estimated total cost: $8,707

FINANCIAL AID

1991–92 Institutional Funding

Number of scholarships and grants: 259

Total amount of scholarships and grants:
  $316,842

Range of scholarships and grants:
  $250–$2,700

1991–92 Federal and State Funding

Number of scholarships and grants: 505

Total amount of scholarships and grants:
  $400,109

Range of scholarships and grants:
  $400–$1,700

Number of loans: 533

Total amount of loans: $739,331

Range of loans: $250–$4,000

Number of work-study: 395

Total amount of work-study: $567,463

Range of work-study: $300–$2,000

Financial Aid Specific to the School

90% of the student body received financial aid in 1991–92.

Comparable Cost Grants allow CRSA high school students in the top 25% of their class to enroll at Paine College at a tuition cost comparable to that of the state college cost.

Students must present proof of admission to a state system college to be eligible. Grants are renewable if student maintains a full course load and satisfactory progress.

CRSA high school students who graduate in the top 20% of their class and are in a pre-college curriculum are eligible for full tuition scholarships. Scholarships are renewable if the student maintains a full course load and a 3.0 GPA.

Alumni Dependent Grant awards dependents of alumni of Paine College $500 per academic year for college costs. Grant is renewable if student maintains a full course load and satisfactory progress.

Athletic-grant-in-aid is available to students who participate in intercollegiate sports. Students must meet minimum requirements of PC and the minimum requirements of NCAA for Division II institutions.

Endowed, friends, and corporation scholarships number approximately 38 and are based on varying criteria of merit, need, and area of interest.

Performance awards are available in music for students who complete at least fifteen hours a semester and maintain a cumulative GPA of 2.5.

Sibling grants allow first student from a household to pay full tuition and second or subsequent students from the same household to pay half tuition.

Full or partial tuition waivers are available to employees and their children. Waivers are renewable if students maintain a full course load and satisfactory progress.

Deferred payment plan allows students to pay college costs in two or three installments during the semester.

Cooperative Education Program alternates classroom study with related paid work experience. The program provides academic credit and full-time status during co-op placement.

United Negro College Fund (UNCF) scholarships are awarded to a limited number of students at this school who demonstrate financial need. Some scholarships may be based on location and merit. UNCF scholarships range from $500 to $7,500.

UNCF Remission Grant is available for the dependent of a president of a UNCF institution. Grant pays full tuition and is renewable based on the dependent's enrollment in college.

Army ROTC, in cooperation with Augusta College, offers two- and four-year scholarships that pay tuition, fees, books, and other expenses, and provide a monthly stipend of $100.

Georgia Student Incentive Grants provide limited assistance to full-time students who are legal residents of the state of Georgia. The financial aid office must receive a copy of the CSS (College Scholarship Service) or ACT prior to June 1 for student to be considered.

Georgia Tuition Equalization Grant provides grants to full-time students who are legal residents of Georgia attending an accredited private institution in the state of Georgia. Contact the financial aid office for more information.

United Methodist/Christian Methodist Episcopal Minister's Grant is available to one student from each denomination for $800 per academic year. Grant is renewable if students maintain a full course loan and satisfactory progress.

United Methodist/Christian Methodist Episcopal Minister's Dependent Grant provides a dependent of a minister of either denomination a grant of $1,000 per academic year toward college cost. Grant is renewable if student maintains a full course load and satisfactory progress.

United Methodist/Christian Methodist Episcopal Minister's Grant provides $800 per academic year for a minister of either denomination toward college cost. The grant is renewable if minister maintains a full course load and satisfactory progress.

Financial Aid Deadline

April 15 (priority); September 1 (fall); April 15 (spring)

Financial Aid Contact

Mr. Johnny C. Nimes, Director of Financial Aid, 1235 15th St., Augusta, GA 30910-2799; (706) 821-8200.

ADMISSION REQUIREMENTS

SAT or ACT required

Entrance Requirements

Graduation from an accredited high school and completion of the following units: 4 English, 2 mathematics, 2 social studies, 1 natural science, 6 electives; a letter of recommendation; and a written autobiographical essay. A $10 nonrefundable application fee required.

GED students must meet the basic admission requirements.

Transfer students must have a minimum GPA of 2.0. They must submit a transcript of all college work and be in good standing with school attended. Two letters of recommendation, an essay, and a medical history record are also needed. A $10 non-refundable application fee is required.

International students must take the TOEFL exam and show evidence of financial support.

Early admission allows academically gifted high school students the opportunity to enroll in college for credit before completing high school. Qualifying students must have a 3.0 or better GPA; score 800 or more on the SAT or 18 on the ACT; and place in the upper 10% of their class.

Admission Application Deadline

August 1 (fall); December 1 (spring); June 1 (summer)

Admission Contact

Miss Phyllis Wyatt-Woodruff, Director of Enrollment Management, Paine College, 1235 15th St., Augusta, GA 30910; (706) 821-8320; toll-free 800-476-7703.

GRADUATION REQUIREMENTS

A minimum of 124 credit hours and completion of the core requirements to include the following hours: six English, six mathematics, six science, eight foreign language, and two physical education; one computer course for business administration and math majors; 2.0 GPA; and weekly chapel attendance.

Grading System

A-F; W=Withdraw without penalty; WF=Withdrew failing; WP=Withdrew passing, no penalty; NC=Non-credit; NG=No grade financial account not cleared; S=Satisfactory; U=Unsatisfactory; I=Incomplete; V=Audit, no credit; K=Credit by examination; CP=Continued program.

STUDENT BODY PROFILE

Total enrollment (male/female): 221/465

From in-state: 530

Other regions: 22 states, 2 foreign countries

Full-time undergraduates (male/female): 188/401

Part-time undergraduates (male/female): 33/64

Ethnic/Racial Makeup

African American, 675; Hispanic, 1; Caucasian, 9; Other/unclassified, 1.

Class of 1995 Profile

Number of applicants: 1,143

Number accepted: 636

Number enrolled: 225

Median SAT score: 310V; 250M

Median ACT score: 16

Average high school GPA: 2.66

Transfer applicants: 111

Transfers accepted: 59

Transfers enrolled: 26

FACULTY PROFILE

Number of faculty: 61

Student-teacher ratio: 12.8:1

Full-time faculty (male/female): 31/23

Part-time faculty (male/female): 5/2

Tenured faculty: 10

Faculty with doctorates or other terminal degrees: 48%

SCHOOL CALENDAR

1993–94: August 13–May 6 (semester hours)

Commencement and conferring of degrees: May 8

One summer session.

DEGREES OFFERED AND NUMBER CONFERRED 1991–92:

Bachelor of Arts

English: 4

History: 1

Mass Communication: 1

Philosophy and Religion: n/a

Psychology: 4

Sociology: 18

Bachelor of Science

Biology: 1

Business Administration: 19

Chemistry: 2

Early Childhood Education: 3

Mathematics: 6

Middle Grades Education: n/a

Music Education: n/a

Pre-Professional

Allied Health: n/a

Dentistry: n/a

Medicine: n/a

Pharmacy: n/a

Nursing: n/a

Veterinary Medicine: n/a

SPECIAL PROGRAMS

Accelerated Study Program allows students to complete their undergraduate degree in a shorter period of time than the traditional period of four years.

Advanced Placement (AP) allows high school students to earn college credits in various subjects for scores of three or more on the College Board AP tests.

College Level Examination Program (CLEP) determines the academic relevance of nontraditional educational experiences, such as the military, on-the-job training, or other life experiences, through a series of tests and may grant students college credit for these experiences.

College orientation is offered to entering students for one week at no cost prior to the beginning of classes to acquaint students with the college and to prepare them for college life; parents may be included.

Cooperative Education Program alternates classroom study with related paid work experience. The program provides academic credit and full-time status during co-op placement.

Cross registration allows students to take courses at Augusta College and Clark College toward graduation requirements at no additional cost.

Honors program offers academically talented students a challenging program of study that includes special classes, seminars, cultural activities, and special recognition to motivate participants.

Pre-professional Sciences Program prepares students for graduate and professional study in pharmacy, dentistry, medicine, and veterinary medicine. This program also offers students early acceptance to the Medical College of Georgia in nursing and eleven allied health fields.

Remedial courses are offered to entering students to bring them up to admission standards and to help them adjust for success in college.

In cooperation with Augusta College, ROTC provides training in military science for commission as a second lieutenant in the U.S. Army. Two- and four-year scholarships are available.

Study Abroad Program allows students to go to the University of Strasbourg in France for a specified period of time for part of their college education.

Three/two degree program in engineering, in cooperation with Georgia Institute of Technology and Florida A&M University, allows students to get two degrees—one in liberal arts from home school and one in engineering from cooperating school—by completing three years at matriculated school and two years at cooperating school.

ATHLETIC PROGRAMS

Paine is a member of the Southern Intercollegiate Athletic Conference (SIAC), which is affiliated with the National Collegiate Athletic Association (NCAA), Division II.

Intercollegiate sports: men's baseball, basketball, cross-country, and track & field; women's basketball, cross-country, softball, track & field, and volleyball.

Intramural sports: basketball, tennis, track & field, and volleyball.

LIBRARY HOLDINGS

The library holds 85,025 bound volumes, 10,024 microforms, 437 periodical subscriptions, 630 audiovisuals, and 150 computers available for student use. Special collections include a African American Collection of print volumes by and about blacks.

STUDENT LIFE

Campus Services

Health clinic, personal and psychological counseling, career counseling and placement, student employment, remediation, tutoring, chapel, and religious activities.

Campus Activities

Social and cultural activities include theater, concerts, band, jazz ensemble, chorale and dance. The Baptist Student Union and Methodist Student Union provide religious activities. Weekly assemblies present enriching speakers and lecturers. The Teacher Education Program has been cited by the state of Georgia as being a model and boasts a 100% placement record. Students may also become involved with the student publications on campus.

Leadership opportunities are found in the Student Government Association (SGA) and the more than forty groups on campus, such as Modern Dance Group and NAACP. Greek-letter fraternities include Alpha Phi Alpha, Kappa Alpha Psi, Omega Psi Phi, and Phi Beta Kappa; sororities include Alpha Kappa Alpha, Delta Sigma Theta, Sigma Gamma Rho, and Zeta Phi Beta. Honor societies include Alpha Kappa Mu.

Located in Augusta, Georgia, Paine College is 150 miles from metropolitan Atlanta, Georgia. It is also close to Columbia, South Carolina. A mass transit system and two airports provide easy access to Atlanta and Columbia from the campus. Two major malls and numerous shopping centers are available to students. The Riverwalk, a new attraction in the city, is a complex of shops, restaurants, and entertainment spots.

Augusta is internationally recognized as the host city for the Master's Golf Tournament. National performers and cultural events take place in the Augusta Richmond County Civic Center and the Bell Auditorium. Public transportation is available to all parts of the city.

Housing Availability

505 housing spaces; six resident halls; freshman only housing available; off-campus living permitted.

NOTABLE ALUMNI

Morgan C. Brown, Ph.D, 1937–Dean, Bridgewater State College (MA)

Daniel A. Collins, 1936–Dentist, San Francisco, CA

Marshall Gilmore, 1957–Bishop, Dayton, OH

Dr Charles G. Gomillion, 1928–Retired educator, Tuskegee Institute

Dr William H. Harris, 1966–University president, Paine College

Nathaniel Linsey, 1949–Bishop, 9th District, Atlanta, GA

Shirley McBay, 1954–Educational leader

Michael Thurmond, 1975–Lawyer; politician; entrepreneur

Woodie White, 1958–Bishop

Frank Yerby, 1937–Author

SAVANNAH STATE COLLEGE

PO Box 20499
Savannah, GA 31404
Phone: (912) 356-2186
Toll-free:
800-788-0478

Total Enrollment:
2,656

Level of Selectivity:
Slightly competitive

Motto:
Lux Et Veritas
(Tradition Pride
Progress)

HISTORY

Savannah State College is a four-year, stated-supported, coed college founded in 1890 as Georgia State Industrial College for Colored Youth. The school awarded its first baccalaureate degree in 1898, but did not become a four-year college until after 1926. The first women students were admitted as boarders in 1921. The school was officially named Savannah State College in January of 1950.

Savannah was established under the 1890 Land Grant Act that required states to provide educational training for black youth.

Savannah State served as the state of Georgia's land grant institution for blacks until 1947. Savannah State's historical mission to train black students, while of continuing importance, has broadened to embrace all individuals regardless of race, ethnicity, culture, or age. The college is committed to making higher education accessible and excellent.

Due to mandated desegregation in 1979, a program exchange occurred between Savannah State's faculty and students in the Division of Education and Armstrong State College's faculty and students in the Division of Business. This exchange resulted in the creation of a new School of Business at Savannah.

The campus comprises 40 buildings located on 165 beautifully landscaped acres that have an architectural blend of the old and the new. The campus is uniquely located on two city limits, Savannah and Thunderbolt.

ACCREDITATION

Savannah State College is accredited by the Southern Association of Colleges and Schools to award the Associate's, Bachelor of Arts, and Bachelor of Science degrees.

Other Accreditation

Accreditation Board of Engineering and Technology

Council on Social Work Education

National Association of Radio and Telecommunication Engineers (NARTE)

Technology Accreditation Commission of the Accreditation Board of Engineering and Technology

COSTS PER YEAR

1992–93 Tuition: $1,341 (in-state); $4,023 (out-state)

Room and Board: $930 (room); $1,275 (board)

Special fees: $229

Books: $600

Estimated total cost: $4,375 (in-state); $7,057 (out-state)

FINANCIAL AID

Financial Aid Specific to the School

85% of the student body received financial aid during 1991–92.

Approximately 31 endowed or alumni scholarships are available to students. These include athletic awards, academic interest/achievement awards, special achievement/activities awards, and special characteristic awards.

Athletic scholarships are available to students participating in intercollegiate sports.

The Cooperative Education Program allows students to gain paid work experience while gaining credits toward degree programs. Qualifying students must be competent in computer language, have satisfactory academic records, and meet the job specifications of the employer.

The Navy ROTC and the cooperative Army ROTC in conjunction with Armstrong State College offer two- and three-year scholarships that pay tuition, fees, books, and other expenses, and provide a monthly stipend.

Performance scholarships are available for students participating in music and drama.

Regent Scholarships are available to Georgia Residents who rank in the top 25% of their class. Recipients must work full time in the State of Georgia for one year.

Student Incentive Grants are awarded to full-time Georgia residents only.

Thurgood Marshall Black Education Fund provides a four-year scholarship at this public black college. Qualifying students must have a high school GPA of 3.0 or better and a SAT score of 100 or ACT score of 24 or more. Students must be recommended by high school counselor as exceptional or exemplary in the creative or performing arts. Scholarship pays tuition, fees, room, and board not to exceed $6,000 annually.

Financial Aid Deadline

August 1 (priority), September 1 (fall).

Financial Aid Contact

Mr. Tommie Mitchell, Director of Financial Aid, Savannah State College, PO Box 20499, Savannah, GA 31404; (912) 356-2253.

ADMISSION REQUIREMENTS

SAT 750 minimum (350V minimum, 350V minimum)

ACT 19 minimum (18E minimum, 15M minimum)

Entrance Requirements

A high school diploma with 15 units: 4 English, 3 science, 3 mathematics, 3 social science, and 2 foreign language. Students graduating from high school after 1988 must enroll in the college preparatory curriculum program. Students must submit a certificate of immunizations for measles, mumps, and rubella unless exempt for physical or religious reasons. A $10 nonrefundable application fee is due with application.

GED students must score 225 or higher; no score below 35 will be accepted in any area; composite or average score must be 45.

Transfer students must have a minimum 2.0 GPA and meet the college preparatory requirements or complete as soon as possible. Must provide high school and college transcripts.

International students must pass the TOEFL, SAT, or ACT exam, and prove financial ability to pay all college costs.

Provisional admission will be considered for students not completing the basic 15 units. Students must satisfy requirements in the first quarter.

Conditional admission can be granted when SAT composite score is less than 750 and any part is less than 350, or if the ACT score is less than 19 with the English less than 16 or the math less than 11. If less than conditional scores, student will not be accepted on condition.

Admission Application Deadline

Twenty days prior to enrollment quarter. Rolling admission provides no specific date for notification of admission so applicant is informed as soon as admission is made. Early admission allows qualified students to enter college full time before completing high school. Continuous notification.

Admissions Contact

Dr. Roy A. Jackson, Director of Admissions, Savannah State College, PO Box 20499 Savannah, GA 31404; (912) 356-2181.

GRADUATION REQUIREMENTS

A minimum of 185 quarter hours including completion of 90 quarter hours of the core curriculum in humanities, the sciences and social sciences; a cumulative GPA of 2.0; completion of PSC 200 or HIS 202 or 203; passing score on the University of Georgia Language Skills Examination; at least year of residence at Savannah State to include senior year.

Grading System

A-F; pass/fail; WF=withdraw, failing; P=pass; V=audit

STUDENT BODY PROFILE

Total enrollment (male/female):
  1,142/1,514

From in-state: 2,125

Other regions: 28 states; 22 foreign countries

Full-time undergraduates (male/female):
  932/1,235

Part-time undergraduates (male/female):
  165/218

Graduate students (male/female): 46/60

Ethnic/Racial Makeup

African American, 2,284; Hispanic, 27; Asian American, 53; International, 27; Other/unclassified, 265.

Class of 1995 Profile

Number of applicants: 2,021

Number accepted: 1,778

Number enrolled: 693

Median SAT score: 355V; 420M

Median ACT score: 12

FACULTY PROFILE

Number of faculty: 149

Student-faculty ratio: 22:1

Full-time faculty: 129

Part-time faculty: 20

Faculty with doctorates or other terminal degrees: 60%

SCHOOL CALENDAR

1992–93: September 16–June 10 (quarter sessions)

Commencement and conferring of degrees: June 3, 1993

Three summer sessions.

DEGREES OFFERED 1991–92:

Bachelor of Arts

English Language and Literature

History

Mass Communications

Medical Technology

Bachelor of Science

Accounting

Biology

Chemical Engineering

Chemistry

Civil Engineering Technology

Computer Science Technology

Criminal Justice

Electronics Engineering Technology

Environmental Studies

Information Systems

Management and Marketing

Marine Biology

Mathematics

Medical Technology

Physics

Political Science

Social Work

Sociology

Associate of Science

Chemical Engineering Technology

Computer Engineering Technology

Marine Science Technology

Master's Degree

Public Administration

SPECIAL PROGRAMS

The Advanced Placement Program allows high school students to take various college courses for credit during their junior or senior year in high school.

The Army and Navy ROTC prepares students to become commissioned officers in the U.S. armed forces. Two- and three-year scholarships are awarded.

The College Level Examination Program (CLEP) determines the academic relevance of nontraditional educational experiences such as the military, on-the-job training, or other life experiences through a series of tests and may grant college credit for these experiences.

College orientation is offered at no cost for one week prior to the beginning of classes to orient students to the college and prepare them for college life; parents may attend.

The Cooperative Education Program allows students to alternate formal academic study with practical paid work experience in student's major. Students must be competent in the language of computers and meet job specifications.

The Department of Developmental Studies accepts students who do not meet the 15 units required for regular admission. Students must take the College Placement Examination (CPE) as well as Developmental Studies courses 097 or 098.

The Joint High School/College Enrollment Program allows senior high school students to pursue college credit. Students must have a minimum 3.0 high school GPA, 900 minimum SAT score or ACT equivalent, recommendation from counselor or principal, and written parental or guardian consent if under 18.

The marine biology program trains students in ocean geography, seawater, marine biology and marine environments. Completing the program enables students to work as entry-level scientists.

The Minority Access to Research Careers program is a honors program that prepares students for research careers in science.

Pre-professional programs include study in medicine, science, and engineering. Faculty advisors provide consultation to help students work on personal growth and develop study plans to help them succeed in graduate/professional schools.

Remedial courses are offered to entering students to bring them up to admission standards and to help them adjust for success in college.

Special Learning Incentives is a honors program available to talented students. Students participate in special research, independent studies, and enhancement programs. Many of these students are supported by a scholarship of up to $5,000 annually.

Study abroad is available through the International Intercultural Studies Program (IISP). Summer study abroad programs are available in Western Europe, the Soviet Union, Israel, Canada, and Mexico. Undergraduates must have a 2.5 GPA and graduate students must have a 3.0 GPA to qualify.

A three/two dual engineering degree with Georgia Institute of Technology is available. Student attends Savannah State for three years and Georgia Institute for two years receiving a bachelor's degree from Savannah State and an engineering degree from Georgia Institute.

ATHLETIC PROGRAMS

Savannah State is a member of the Southern Intercollegiate Athletic Conference (SIAC) and the National Collegiate Athletic Association (NCAA), Division II.

Intercollegiate sports: men's basketball, cross country running, football, and track & field; women's basketball and track & field.

Intramural sports: basketball, bowling, cross country running, football, tennis, and track & field.

LIBRARY HOLDINGS

The Asa Gordon Library holds 164,810 volumes, 700 periodical subscriptions, 24,263 bound periodicals, 416,050 microforms, 20 newspapers, a vast array of audiovisual materials, and a special collection by and about African Americans.

STUDENT LIFE

Special Regulations

Students must live on campus unless they are commuters who live at home.

Campus Services

Health center, personal and psychological counseling, and career counseling and placement services. The college testing program serves as a national testing center for the GMAT, LSAT, GRE, SAT, NTE, CLEP, and MAT.

Campus Activities

Many activities for cultural enrichment compliment formal education on campus. Assemblies, motion pictures, lecturers, art exhibitions, and drama are some of the activities provided. Students interested in music can become members of the concert choir, band, or Wesleyan choir. Students can take part in the publication of the student newspaper (*Tiger Boar*) or the college yearbook (*The Tiger*). The college radio station (WHCJ-FM) serves as a training unit for the Mass Communication Program and accepts student volunteers.

Leadership opportunities can be sought in the more than 50 student organizations representing athletics, service clubs, honors, media publications, and interest groups, as well as the Student Government Association (SGA). Greek-letter fraternities include Alpha Phi Alpha, Kappa Alpha Psi, Phi Beta Sigma, and

Omega Psi Phi; sororities include Alpha Kappa Alpha, Delta Sigma Theta, Sigma Gamma Rho, and Zeta Phi Beta. Honor societies include Alpha Kappa Mu, Beta Beta Beta, Beta Kappa Chi, Kappa Delta Pi, Phi Beta Lambda, Phi Mu Delta, Pi Gamma Mu, Sigma Delta Chi, Sigma Tau Delta, Tau Alpha Pi, and Biomedical Society.

Savannah State College is located in the coastal city of Savannah, Georgia, with a population of 137,600. Historic Savannah offers many cultural and recreational activities for students. Students have easy access to a resort area known as Tybee Island. Savannah's public transportation allows easy access to Atlanta, Georgia, 250 miles to the northwest, and Charleston, South Carolina, 150 miles to the northeast. Students are within hours of Florida and its beaches.

Housing Availability
1,020 housing spaces.

Handicapped Services
Students who have visual, auditory, or motor handicaps may arrange for local certification of competency with Regents.

NOTABLE ALUMNI
Donnie Cochran, 1976–Lieutenant commander, Blue Angels Pilot

Mayme S. Jefferies–Director of assessment, Edward Waters College

Helen M. Mayes, 1938–Director emeritus, Albany State College

Mary Dawson Walters–First black to head an Ohio State Library Department

SPELMAN COLLEGE

350 Spelman Lane, SW
Atlanta, GA 30314
Phone: (404) 681-3643
Toll-free:
800-982-2411
Fax: (404) 223-1476

Total Enrollment:
1,906

Level of Selectivity:
Competitive

Motto:
Our Whole School
for Christ

HISTORY

Spelman College (SC) is a four-year, private, female liberal arts institution founded in 1881 as Atlanta Baptist Female Academy by two women commissioned by the Baptist church to provide educational opportunities for newly freed black women. Spelman began in a damp church basement with eleven pupils, mostly women, determined to learn to read the bible and write well enough to send letters to their families in the North. The academy first offered postsecondary education in 1897. It adopted its present name in 1924.

Two years after its founding, the former barracks and drill grounds used for federal troops after the Civil War was purchased for the school for $15,000. To pay the enormous debt, the black community raised $4,000, the Negro Baptists of Georgia raised $3,000, and individuals donated $1,300 which left an outstanding balance of $6,700. John D. Rockefeller was so impressed with the school when he visited that before he left he paid the outstanding balance which resulted in a name change to Spelman Seminary in honor of Rockefeller's mother-in-law, Harvey Spelman. Several years later Rockefeller donated $40,000 toward the building of Rockefeller Hall, named in his honor.

Spelman continues to be blessed with friends dedicated to its mission to provide high quality educational opportunities to black women. Recently, Spelman was the recipient of a $20 million gift from entertainer Bill Cosby and his wife Camille to build the Camille Olivia Hanks Cosby Academic Center scheduled to be completed in 1994. The school also receive $37 million from the De-Witt Wallace/Spelman College Fund which was established by the founder of the Reader's Digest Association. The college has gained national recognition as a result of such philanthropic gifts and the fact that it is the basis for the fictional black college in the television show "A Different World."

Despite large-scale development, Spelman has retained its intimate academic atmosphere. In particular, the faculty place special emphasis on the cultural, social, and personal development of each student; sisterhood and individual discovery is encouraged and stressed. Dr. Johnnetta Cole, Spelman's first black woman president, explains that while many presidents would tell students that only one in three students will graduate from their institutions, she tells students that unless three out of three graduate then Spelman's sisterhood has failed. Since Cole became president in 1988, *U.S. News & World Report* ranked the school as the number one liberal arts college in the South.

Spelman's rich history is evident in the diverse architecture of its campus structures. From historic to state-of-the-art, Spelman's 27-building campus is situated on 35 acres. Spelman is an integral part of the Atlanta University Center, a cooperative cluster of six predominately black colleges and universities.

ACCREDITATION

Spelman College is accredited by the Southern Association of Colleges and Schools to award the Bachelor of Arts and Bachelor of Science degrees.

Other Accreditation

National Association of Schools of Music

National Council for the Accreditation of Teacher Education

COSTS PER YEAR

1992–93 Tuition: $6,150

Room and board: $5,000

Special fees: $921

Books: $500

Estimated total cost: $12,571

FINANCIAL AID

1990–91 Institutional Funding

Number of scholarships and grants: 300

Total amount of scholarships and grants: $123,499

Range of scholarships and grants: $500–$2,000

1990–91 Federal and State Funding

Number of scholarships and grants: 1,500

Total amount of scholarships and grants: $2,000,000

Range of scholarships and grants: $794–$2,400

Number of loans: 820

Total amount of loans: $175,000

Range of loans: $450–$4,3000

Number of work-study: 179

Total amount of work-study: $276,929

Range of work-study: $800–$1,600

Financial Aid Specific to the School

85% of the student body received financial aid during 1991–92.

Army, Air Force, or Navy ROTC in cooperation with Georgia Institute of Technology offer two-, three- and four-year scholarships that pay tuition, fees, books, and other expenses, as well as provide a monthly stipend of $100.

Cooperative Education Program alternates and combines classroom study with related paid work experience. The program provides academic credit and full-time status during co-op placement.

Deferred Payment Plan allows students to pay college costs in two or three installments during the semester.

Tuition waivers (full time or part time) available for Spelman employees and their children.

United Negro College Fund (UNCF) scholarships are awarded to a limited number of students at this school who demonstrate financial need. Some scholarships may be based on location and merit. UNCF scholarships range from $500 to $7,500.

Financial Aid Deadline
February 21 (preferred); April 15

Financial Aid Contact
Marvin B. Tanner, Director of Financial Aid, Spelman College, Atlanta, GA 30314; (404) 681-3643, ext. 1471

ADMISSION REQUIREMENTS
SAT or ACT required

Entrance Requirements
Graduation from an accredited high school and completion of the following units: 4 English, 2–3 mathematics (2 algebra and 1 geometry), 2 science (1 lab), 2 history, and 2 foreign language or literature or social science; minimum 2.0 GPA; two recommendations from teacher and counselor; personal essay; evidence of leadership or involvement in area of social concern. A $35 application fee is required.

GED students must meet basic admission requirements.

Transfer students must submit official high school transcript including class rank; submit transcript of all college work; recommendation from last college attended; if student transferring has less than sophomore

Giles Hall, Spelman College

standing SAT or ACT scores must be submitted, "C" or better grades will be transferred; maximum 90 hours transferred from 4 year accredited and 60 hours from 2 year accredited college. Deadline is Feb 1 (fall); November 1 (spring).

International students must meet basic requirements and present school certificate verifying completion of high school; students from non-English-speaking countries must take TOEFL examination; and provide proof of ability to pay all college costs.

Early admission allows academically gifted high school students the opportunity to enroll in college for credit before completing high school.

Admission Application Deadline
February 1 (fall); November 1 (spring)

Admission Contact
Deborah Urquhart, Office of Admission, Spelman College, 350 Spelman Lane SW, Box 277, Atlanta, GA 30314-9811; (404) 681-3643, ext. 2188 or 800-982-2411.

GRADUATION REQUIREMENTS

A minimum of 124 semester hours and completion of core requirements to include 12 natural science, 12 social science, 6 humanities, 6 fine arts; freshman orientation; and last 30 hours in residence.

Grading System

A–F; P=Pass; F=Fail; W=Withdraw

STUDENT BODY PROFILE

Total enrollment: 1,906

From in-state: 403

Other regions: 41 states, 10 foreign countries

Full-time undergraduates: 1,805

Part-time undergraduates: 101

Ethnic/Racial Makeup

African American, 1,869; International, 37.

Class of 1995 Profile

Number of applicants: 3,236

Number accepted: 1,359

Number enrolled: 544

Median SAT score: 468V; 493M

Median ACT score: 22

Average high school GPA: 3.0

Transfers enrolled: 130

FACULTY PROFILE

Number of faculty: 162

Student-teacher ratio: 16:1

Full-time faculty: 114

Part-time faculty: 48

Faculty with doctorates or other terminal degrees: 87%

SCHOOL CALENDAR

1992–93: August 15–May 7 (semester hours)

Commencement and conferring of degrees: May 16

One summer session.

DEGREES OFFERED AND NUMBER CONFERRED 1991–92:

Art: 1

Biochemistry: 3

Biology: 37

Chemistry: 10

Child Development: 17

Computer Science: 9

Drama: 2

Dual Degree: 0

Economics: 43

English: 57

French: 2

General Engineering: 3

Health and Physical Education: 3

History: 5

Human Services: 3

Mathematics: 27

Music: 6

Natural Science: 15

Philosophy: 4

Physics: 4

Political Science: 26

Psychology: 58

Religion: 0

Sociology: 16

Spanish: 6

Pre-Professional

Law: n/a

Medicine: n/a

Graduates that go on to higher degrees upon graduation:

21% enter medical school

29% enter law school

5% enter business school

31% arts & sciences

16% unclassified

SPECIAL PROGRAMS

Accelerated Study Program allows students to complete their undergraduate degree in a shorter period of time than the traditional four years.

Adult or Continuing Education Program is available for nontraditional students returning to school or working full time.

Advanced Placement (AP) grants college credit for postsecondary work completed in high school. Students scoring 3 on the AP test will receive credit by examination for each course and advanced placement.

College Level Examination Program (CLEP) determines the academic relevance of nontraditional educational experiences such as the military, on-the-job training, or other life experiences through a series of test and may grant students college credit for these experiences.

College orientation is offered at no cost to entering students for one week prior to the beginning of classes to acquaint students with the college and to prepare them for college life; parents may attend.

Cooperative Education Program alternates and combines classroom study with related paid work experience. The program provides academic credit and full-time status during co-op placement.

Honors Program offers academically talented students a challenging program of study including special classes, seminars, colloquia, cultural activities, and special recognition to motivate participants.

Individualized majors allow students to create their own major program(s) of study.

Internships in various disciplines allow students to apply theory to on-the-job training in industry, business, and government.

Mentorship program pairs students with leaders in Atlanta's corporate, professional, and civic communities to help strengthen their leadership and management skills and to increase career opportunities.

Nursery school and kindergarten are available for children of students and community residents.

Off-campus study allows students to take courses with members of the Atlanta University Center, a cluster of six black colleges and universities.

Part-time degree program allow students to earn an undergraduate degree part time.

Pre-medical and pre-dental programs offer students the opportunity to complete three years at Spelman and qualify for early admission to medical or dental school. After successful completion of one year of medical or dental school, student is awarded a B.S. from Spelman. Upon completion of program, student receives M.D. or D.D.S.

Remedial courses are offered to entering students to bring them up to admission standards and to help them adjust for success in college.

ROTC provides training in military science for commission as a second lieutenant in the U.S. Air Force, Army, and Navy. Two- and four-year scholarships are available.

Study Abroad Program allows students to go to Brazil, France, Germany, Japan, Senegal, Spain, or Zimbabwe for part of their college education; program is part of the honors program.

Three/two dual degree program in engineering in cooperation with Georgia Institute of Technology, Rochester Institute of Technology, Boston University, Auburn University, and the University of Alabama at Hunstsville allows students to get two degrees—one in liberal arts from home school and one in engineering from cooperating school—by completing three years at matriculated school and two years at cooperating school.

WISE (Women in Science and Engineering) provides opportunities for a limited number of students to pursue a major in science and engineering at Spelman and to engage in research during the summer at NASA centers.

ATHLETIC PROGRAMS

Intercollegiate sports: women's basketball, tennis, track & field, and volleyball.

Intramural sports: softball, swimming, and diving.

Athletic Contact

Ms. Kathleen Richy-Walton, Acting Director of Health, Recreation, and Physical Education; (401) 681-3643, Ext. 7593.

LIBRARY HOLDINGS

The cooperative Robert E. Woodruff Library houses 374,292 bound volumes, 111,000 microforms, 47,115 bound periodicals, 1,372 periodical subscriptions, 2,800 audiovisuals; 200 computers in the computer center for student use. Special collections include the Carnegie Art Reference Set, the Henry P. Slaughter and Countee Cullen Memorial Collection of materials on graphic and performing artists, and the South Regional Council Papers on Race Relations and Socioeconomic Conditions in the Southeast (1044-1968).

STUDENT LIFE

Special Regulations

Cars permitted for juniors and seniors; curfews; quiet hours; dorm visitation 3:30am–11:50pm Sunday, 6:00pm–11:50pm Monday–Friday

Campus Services

Health center, personal and psychological counseling, career planning and placement, student employment services, tutoring, women's center, child care, late-night escort, religious activities.

Campus Activities

Social and cultural activities include theater, band, chorale, art exhibits, a lecture series, and dances. Specific groups include the renowned Spelman Glee Club, Spelman-Morehouse Chorus, and the Spelman-Morehouse Players. Students may work on the *Spotlight* (student-run newspaper), *Reflections* (yearbook), and *Focus* (literary magazine featuring creative writing by Spelman students).

Leadership opportunities can be found in the Student Government Association or the numerous other organizations. Greek-letter sororities include Alpha Kappa Alpha and Delta Sigma Theta. AST (African Sisterhood), a community service organization, was founded at Spelman in 1988.

Many opportunities exist for Spelman students to interact with students at the other Atlanta University Center Institutions: Clark Atlanta University, Morehouse College, Morris-Brown College, Interdenominational Theological Seminary, and Morehouse School of Medicine.

Spelman is located in the metropolitan city of Atlanta, the capital of Georgia, population over 2 million. The city is served by mass air, rail, and bus. Local transportation on the MARTA provides easy access to downtown, the airport, or virtually anywhere in the metro area.

The campus is located one mile west of downtown, close to Underground Atlanta, with its quaint shops. Students have access to fine dining, world-class shopping, art galleries, museums, the Atlanta Symphony or Ballet. Points of interest include the Martin Luther King, Jr. Center for Non-violent Social Change, the Jimmy Carter Presidential Library, Stone Mountain Park, Six Flags over Georgia Amusement Park, and the World Congress Center which hosts many national conferences. The city of Atlanta is an international center for business, banking, and social change, offering students many professional opportunities.

Housing Availability

1,117 housing spaces;, freshman housing guaranteed.

Handicapped Services

Wheelchair accessibility, restrooms, lowered drinking fountains.

NOTABLE ALUMNI

Aurelia Brazeal–U.S. Ambassador to Micronesia

Mattiwilda Dobbs, 1946–Opera diva

Marian Wright Edelman, 1960–Founder, Children's Defense Fund

Marcelite J. Harris–First black woman Air Force Brigadier General

Vernette Honeywood–Artist

Bernice Johnson Reagon–Founder, Black American Culture, National Museum of American History, Smithsonian Institution; 1989 recipient of $275,000 MacArtur fellowship

Esther Rolle–Actress

Alice Walker, 1961, 1963–Writer; Pulitzer Prize recipient

Elynor A. Williams, 1966–Corporate executive, Hanes Group & Sara Lee

Illinois

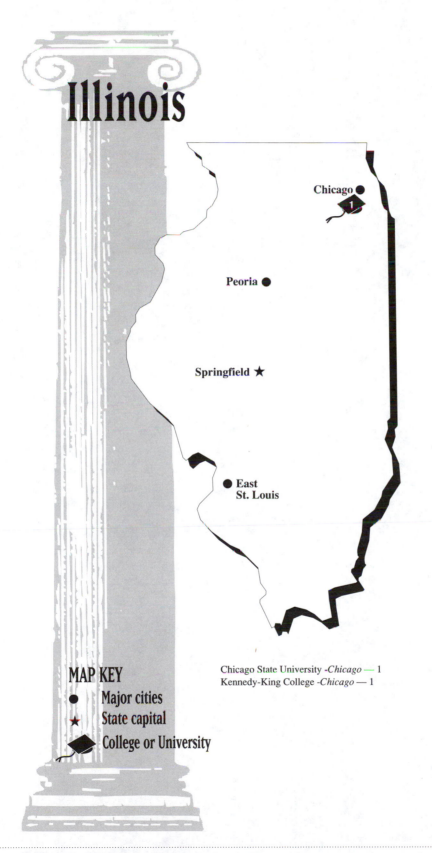

Chicago ●

Peoria ●

Springfield ★

● East
St. Louis

MAP KEY
- ● Major cities
- ★ State capital
- 🎓 College or University

Chicago State University -*Chicago* — 1
Kennedy-King College -*Chicago* — 1

CHICAGO STATE UNIVERSITY

95th St. at King Dr.
Chicago, IL 60628-
1598
Phone: (312) 995-2000

Total Enrollment:
8,648

Level of Selectivity:
Slightly competitive

Motto:
Responsibility

HISTORY

Chicago State University (CSU) is a state-supported, four-year, coed university that was founded in 1867. Chicago State began as an experimental teacher training center under the name of Cook County Normal School. From 1897 to 1972, CSU experienced five name changes. In 1897, it changed to Chicago Normal School; in 1913, to Chicago Normal College; in 1938, to Chicago Teacher's College; in

1965, to Illinois Teachers College; and in 1972, to Chicago State University.

Chicago State takes great pride in its heritage of moving from a normal school to a college and then to a university. The university's triangle logo serves as a reminder of the three transitional stages. As a commuter school, the university is sensitive to the needs of a diverse population. The mission of CSU includes "strengthening undergraduate and graduate education and encouraging minority participation in higher education."

During the 1990s, CSU hopes to graduate at least 75% of its students within seven years and to retain 60% of first-year students. Motivated to provide its students with the highest quality of education, it offers assessment programs, workshops, and training, for both faculty and students.

ACCREDITATION

Chicago State University is accredited by the North Central Association of Colleges and Schools to award the Bachelor of Arts, Bachelor of Science, and Master's degrees.

Other Accreditation

American Dietetics Association

Committee on Allied Health Education and Accreditation

National Council for Accreditation of Teacher Education

National League for Nursing (baccalaureate)

COSTS PER YEAR

1992–93 Tuition: $828 (in-state); $2,484 (out-state)

Room and board: None

Special fees: $200

Books: $500

Estimated total cost: $1,528 (in-state); $3,184 (out-state)

FINANCIAL AID

1991–92 Institutional Funding

Number of scholarships and grants: 599

Total amount of scholarships and grants: $323,934

Range of scholarships and grants: $541 (average)

1991–92 Federal and State Funding

Number of scholarships and grants: 104

Total amount of scholarships and grants: $4,005,072

Range of scholarships and grants: $3,851 (average)

Number of loans: 224

Total amount of loans: $609,915

Range of loans: $2,723 (average)

Number of work-study: 351

Total amount of work-study: $569,772

Range of work-study: $162 (average)

Financial Aid Specific to the School

85% of CSU's student body received financial aid in 1991–92.

Deferred payment plans allow students to pay college costs in two or three installments during the semester for a minimal fee of $10.

Chicago State University Undergraduate Tuition Waiver offers a limited number of tuition waivers to students, senior citizens included, who demonstrate financial need after applying for state and federal financial aid.

Chicago State University Presidential Scholarships are available for a limited number of freshmen students who demonstrate academic excellence and leadership potential in high school.

Chicago State University Talent Scholarships are available for students demonstrating special ability in art, athletics, music, student government, or student publications.

Full athletic scholarships are available along with talent athletic scholarships that pay only tuition.

Equal Opportunity Scholarships are available to females and minorities pursuing programs in educational administration.

Teacher shortage scholarships are available to full-time and part-time students majoring in teaching areas with shortages.

Mathematics or science teacher scholarships are available to students majoring in secondary mathematics or science education.

Special Education Teacher scholarships are available to students majoring in special education.

ROTC offers two- , three- and four-year scholarships that pay tuition, fees, books, and other expenses, and provide a monthly stipend of $100. Work-study is also available.

Illinois Merit Recognition Scholarships offer $500 grants to Illinois students who rank in the top 10% of their senior class.

The Illinois Monetary Award Program (MAP) pays full or part tuition, as well as activity and athletic fees based on student's financial needs.

Illinois Veteran's Grant pays tuition, activity fees, and athletic fees for veterans who have at least one year of active duty in the U.S. Armed Forces.

Police and Fire Personnel Grants are available for spouse and children of any Illinois police or fireman killed in the line of duty.

MIA/POW scholarships are available to spouse and children of any MIA/POW for four calendar years.

Financial Aid Deadline
May 1 (fall and spring)

Financial Aid Contact
Mr. W. Barry McLaughlin, Acting Director of Student Financial Aid, Chicago State University, Chicago, IL 60628; (312) 995-2399.

ADMISSION REQUIREMENTS
SAT or ACT required

Entrance Requirements
Graduation from an accredited high school and completion of the following units: 4 English, 2 mathematics, 2 social studies, and 2 natural sciences. Official high school transcripts required. Two letters of recommendation and an interview may be required. All entering students are required to take the University Exam Program in English, math, and reading.

GED students must meet basic admission requirements and submit an official GED score of at least 225.

Transfer students An official college transcript with a minimum 2.0 GPA is required. Applicants with 30 semester hours or less must meet freshman requirements and take ACT or SAT.

International Students must provide copies of all secondary educational records with translation as necessary, proof of ability to pay all college costs, and a copy of a current Vita. TOEFL scores are required unless 30 semester hours are from an accredited U.S. college or university. International student admission deadlines: June 1 (fall); November 1 (spring); and February 1 (summer).

Admission Application Deadline
August 1 (fall); January 1 (spring); May 1 (summer).

Admission Contact
Ms. Romi Lowe, Director of Admissions, Chicago State University, 95th St. at King Dr., Chicago, IL 60628; (312) 995-2513.

GRADUATION REQUIREMENTS
Minimum of 120 credit hours and completion of the core requirements, with 3 credit hours in math, 12 hours in natural science, and 1 computer course (business & dietetics majors).

Grading System
A-F; I=Incomplete.

STUDENT BODY PROFILE
Total enrollment (male/female): 8684

From in-state: 7,929

Washington Hall, Chicago State University

From other regions: 15 states, 18 foreign countries

Full-time undergraduates (male/female): 2,901/1,303

Part-time undergraduates (male/female): 728/1,619

Graduate students (male/female): 661/1,472

Ethnic/Racial Makeup

African American, 7,208; Hispanic, 305; Native American, 16; Caucasian, 879; International, 261; Other/unclassified, 15.

Class of 1995 Profile

Number of applicants: 2,838

Number accepted: 1,305

Number enrolled: 718

Median ACT score: 16.5

Average high school GPA: 2.39

Transfer applicants: 2,891

Transfers accepted: 1,305

Transfers enrolled: 748

FACULTY PROFILE

Number of faculty: 391

Student-teacher ratio: 30:1

Full-time faculty: 282

Part-time faculty: 109

Tenured faculty: 153

Faculty with doctorates or other terminal degrees: 51.9%

SCHOOL CALENDAR

1991–92: August 26–May 24 (semesters)

Commencement and conferring of degrees: May

Two five-week summer sessions.

DEGREES OFFERED AND NUMBER CONFERRED 1991–92:

Bachelor of Arts

Anthropology: n/a

Art History: n/a

Ceramic Art and Design: n/a

Creative Writing: n/a

English: 10

English Education: n/a

Fashion Merchandising: n/a

Geography: n/a

Graphic Arts: n/a

History: 10

Jazz: n/a

Literature: n/a

Modern Languages: n/a

Music: 4

Painting/Drawing: n/a

Political Science/Government: n/a

Psychology: 26

Sociology: 10

Spanish: n/a

Studio Art: n/a

Studio/craft: n/a

Wind and Percussion Instruments: n/a

Bachelor of Science

Art Education: n/a

Accounting: 59

Bilingual/Bicultural Education: n/a

Biochemistry: n/a

Biology/Biological Sciences: 15

Broadcasting: n/a

Business Administration/Commerce/Management: n/a

Business Education: n/a

Chemistry: 8

Chemistry Education: n/a

Commercial Art: n/a

Computer Information Systems: n/a

Computer Science: n/a

Corrections: n/a

Criminal Justice: n/a

Data Processing: n/a

Dietetics: n/a

Early Childhood Education: 52

Economics: n/a

Education: n/a

Elementary Education: 17

Engineering Studies: n/a

Finance/Banking: n/a

Geography Education: n/a

Health Education: n/a

History Education: n/a

Hotel and Restaurant Management: n/a

Industrial Administration: n/a

Industrial Technology: n/a

Law Enforcement/Police Sciences: n/a

Management: n/a

Marketing/Retailing/Merchandising: n/a

Mathematics: 18

Mathematics Education: n/a

Medical Records Services: n/a

Musical Instrument Technology: n/a

Music Education: n/a

Nursing: n/a

Occupational Safety and Health: n/a

Occupational Therapy: n/a

Physical Education: n/a

Radio and Television Studies: n/a

Radiological Technology: n/a

Recreation and Leisure Services: 3

Retail Management: n/a

Science Education: n/a

Secondary Education: n/a

Spanish Education: n/a

Special Education: 37

Technical Writing: n/a

Master of Arts

Community College Administration: n/a

English : n/a

Educational Administration: n/a

Geography: n/a

History: n/a

Master of Science

Biological Science: n/a

Corrections and Criminal Justice: n/a

Mathematics: n/a

Master's of Science in Education

Bilingual-Bicultural Teaching/Supervision: n/a

Curriculum and Instruction: n/a

Library Science and Communications Media: n/a

Occupational Education: n/a

Physical Education: n/a

School Guidance and Counseling: n/a

Teaching Emotionally Disturbed Children: n/a

Teaching Gifted Children: n/a

Teaching Learning Disabled: n/a

Teaching Moderately Mentally
Handicapped Children: n/a

Teaching Pre-School Handicapped: n/a

Teaching Reading: n/a

Graduates that later obtain higher degrees:
27%

SPECIAL PROGRAMS

The academic remediation program provides remedial courses for entering students to bring them up to admission standards.

The accelerated degree program allows students to earn an undergraduate degree in a shorter period of time than regular degree programs, i.e. three years.

Advanced Placement (AP) provides an opportunity for high school seniors to get college credit for scores in various subjects on the College Board AP tests.

The College Level Examination Program (CLEP) grants college credit for non-traditional educational experiences such as the military, work, or other life experiences through the college entrance exam.

The Cooperative Education Program combines formal academic study with practical work experience in student's major.

FAME/Upward Bound provides academic counseling, academic skills, and cultural enrichment to high school students in grades 10, 11, and 12 who are disadvantaged and are in pursuit of a college education.

The honors program offers academically talented students a challenging program of study that includes special classes, seminars and colloquia, and cultural activities to motivate students.

Cooperative Air Force, Army, and Naval ROTC provides training in military science for commission as a second lieutenant in the U.S. Armed Forces. Two-, three- and four-year scholarships are available.

Study abroad programs are available to students in China, Germany, Nigeria, Liberia, and South Korea. An exchange student program is also available with institutions in the United States.

The adult/continuing education program is available for nontraditional students returning to school or working full time.

Pre-Engineering program guarantees transfer to the engineering program at Illinois Institute of Technology or the University of Illinois. Students follow a mathematics, chemistry, and physics sequence which at Chicago State for three years and then transfer to cooperating school to complete the program.

Pre-Medical Education Program (PEP) Assists students interested in allopathic medicine, osteopathic medicine, chiropractic medicine, dentistry, veterinary medicine, optometry, pharmacy, pediatric medicine, and public health medicine by preparing students to gain admission into health professions.

Undergraduates are allowed to take graduate courses for credit in certain majors.

ATHLETIC PROGRAMS

Chicago State University is a member of the National Collegiate Athletic Association (NCAA), Division I; and the National Association of Intercollegiate Athletics (NAIA).

Intercollegiate sports: men's baseball, basketball, cross-country, golf, soccer, tennis, indoor track & field, and wrestling; women's basketball, cross-country, indoor and outdoor track & field, and volleyball.

Intramural: Badminton, football, gymnastics, softball, swimming, table tennis, tennis, track & field, volleyball, wrestling.

Athletic Contact

Mr. Albert Avant, Athletic Department, Chicago State University, 95th St. at King Dr., Chicago, IL 60628; (312) 995-2995.

LIBRARY HOLDINGS

The Paul and Emily Douglas Library houses 82,540 volumes, 625 microforms,

3,953 audiovisuals, 603 periodical subscriptions, and 25 computers for student use.

STUDENT LIFE

Campus Services

Health center, career planning and placement, tutoring, counseling, women's services, and child care.

Campus Activities

Social or group activities include theater, band, chorale, orchestra, and dance. Students can get involved in the student-run newspaper, *Tempo*; the literary journal, *Menagerie,* and the yearbook, *Emblem.* Communications majors may be interested in the campus radio or television stations. The International Black Writers' Conference is held annually.

Leadership opportunities can be found in the Student Government Association or numerous other student-run organizations. Greek-letter societies include Alpha Kappa Alpha, Delta Sigma Theta, Sigma Gamma Rho, and Zeta Phi Beta sororities, as well as Alpha Phi Alpha, Kappa Alpha Psi, Omega Psi Phi, and Phi Beta Sigma fraternities. Honor societies are represented on campus.

The 152-acre campus is located in a woodland area on the south side of Chicago, just 12 miles from the loop. Chicago's Dan Ryand Rapid Transit, the Illinois Central Railroad, and several bus routes conveniently serve the campus. Two national sororities and one national fraternity have national headquarters in Chicago. These include Alpha Kappa Alpha sorority, Alpha Phi Alpha fraternity, and Sigma Gamma Rho sorority. The Johnson Publishing Company, home of the magazines, *Ebony* and *Jet* is located in Chicago. The city of Chicago is rich in history and offers a wealth of cultural, social, and recreational activities.

Housing Availability

On-campus housing not available.

Handicapped Services

Wheelchair accessibility.

NOTABLE ALUMNI

Margaret Burrough, 1937–Founder/director emeritus, DuSable Museum of African-American History

Edward Gardner–Founder and CEO, SoftSheen Products Co.

Dr. Frank Gardner, 1948–Board of Examiners, Chicago Public Schools

Elizabeth Harris Lawson, 1979–Co-chair, White House Conference on Library & Information Services

KENNEDY-KING COLLEGE

HISTORY

Kennedy-King College is a state-supported, two-year, coed community college affiliated with the City Colleges of Chicago. Founded as Woodrow Wilson Junior College in 1935, the college was initially operated by the Chicago Board of Education until the Illinois State System of Community College Districts took control of it on July 1, 1966.

In honor of Robert F. Kennedy and Martin Luther King, Jr., the name was formally changed to Kennedy-King College in July of 1969. The college is committed to translating the philosophies of these statesmen into an educational mission that includes innovative instructional strategies tailored to the individual needs of each student.

The 18-acre campus houses a multi-level educational complex that received the American Institute of Architect award for its main building.

ACCREDITATION

Kennedy-King College is accredited by the North Central Association of Colleges and Schools (NCACS) to award associate's degrees in four programs: arts, science, applied science, and general studies.

Other Accreditation

Illinois Community College Board

Illinois Office of Education

Department of Adult, Vocational, and Technical Education

Department of Registration and Education of the State of Illinois

COSTS PER YEAR

1992–93 Tuition: $378 (district); $1,178 (in-state); $1,698 (out-state)

Special fees: $125

Books: $350

6800 S. Wentworth Ave.
Chicago, IL 60621-3798
Phone: (312) 602-5000

Total Enrollment:
3,137

Level of Selectivity:
Noncompetitive

Estimated total cost: $853 (district); $1,653 (in-state); $2,173 (out-state)

FINANCIAL AID

1991–92 Institutional Funding

Number of scholarships and grants: 538

Total amount of scholarships and grants: $275,195

Range of scholarships and grants: $512 avg.

Financial Aid Specific to the School

83% of the student body received financial during 1991–92.

Harold Washington Academic Achievement Scholarships are available to students who show academic promise based on their performance in high school or by outstanding GED scores. These scholarships cover the cost of tuition and are renewable based on academic performance.

Air Force ROTC offers a two-year scholarship that pays tuition, fees, books, and other expenses, and provides a monthly stipend of $100. Students must complete advance training at a four-year school to receive a four-year scholarship.

Illinois Veteran Grants are available to students who served in the Armed Forces for at least one year on active duty, were residents of Illinois at the time of enlistment, and after leaving the service, returned to Illinois within six months. This grant includes a tuition waiver and covers the cost of selected fees.

The Illinois Student Assistance Commission Monetary Award Program is available for Illinois residents only; contains waivers for tuition and mandatory fees.

Financial Aid Deadline

August 15 (priority)

Financial Aid Contact

Financial Aid Officer, Kennedy-King College, 6800 S. Wentworth Ave., Chicago, IL 60621-3798; (312) 602-5133.

ADMISSION REQUIREMENTS

Open admissions; SAT or ACT recommended for placement.

Entrance Requirements

Graduation from an accredited high school; if not yet graduated, a transcript from the seventh semester should be forwarded to the Admissions Office. Students not residing in Chicago, Illinois, must pay non-resident tuition in addition to Chicago resident fees.

GED students must meet basic admission requirements.

Transfer students must be in good academic standing as required by Kennedy-King standards.

International Students must submit the I-20 Form on a Student Visa, an affidavit of support, and results of a certified English translation exam.

Early admissions allows academically gifted high school students the opportunity to enroll in college full time before completing high school.

Admission Application Deadline

Rolling admissions provides no specific date for notification of admission so applicant is informed as soon as admission decision is made.

Admission Contact

Mrs. Iver Watson, Clerical Supervisor-Admissions, Kennedy-King College, 6800 South Wentworth Ave., Chicago, IL 60621; (312) 602-5049.

GRADUATION REQUIREMENTS

A minimum of 60 credit hours and completion of core requirements; 2.00 minimum GPA; all courses submitted for credit to graduate must be numbered 101 or above; transfer students must earn at least 15 of the last 60 credits in residence; students must pass exams in Constitution of the United States, Code of the American Flag, and Declaration of Independence or complete and pass Political Science 201. Students planning to transfer to four-year programs must complete specific requirements of the designated four-year school.

Grading System

A-F; I=Incomplete; AUD=Auditor; NSW=No-Show Withdrawal; ADW=Administrative Withdrawal; WTH=Student-Initiated Withdrawal

STUDENT BODY PROFILE

Total enrollment (male/female): 1,067/2,070

From in-state: 3,106

Other regions: 31

Full-time undergraduates (male/female): 515/959

Part-time undergraduates (male/female): 565/1,098

Ethnic/Racial Makeup

African American, 3,043; Hispanic, 31; Asian, 31; International, 31; Other/unclassified, 1.

FACULTY PROFILE

Number of faculty: 163

Student-teacher ratio: 19:1

Full-time faculty: 159

Part-time faculty: 4

Faculty with doctorates or other terminal degrees: 20%

SCHOOL CALENDAR

1992–93: August 24–May 15 (semester hours)

Commencement and conferring of degrees: May

One summer session.

DEGREES OFFERED 1991–92:

Associate of Arts
Art/Fine Arts
Broadcasting
Child Psychology
Commercial Art
Communication Equipment Technology
Home Economics
Humanities
Liberal Arts and General Studies
Modern Languages
Music
Social Work
Theater Arts and Drama

Associate of Arts and Sciences
Automotive Technologies
Child Care
Child and Family Studies
Data Processing
Optometric and Ophthalmic Technologies
Printing Technologies
Radio and Television Studies
Teacher Aide Studies

Associate of Sciences
Accounting
Architectural Technologies
Business Administration
Business Commerce
Business Management
Child Care
Child Development
Dental Services
Early Childhood Education
Education
(Pre)Engineering Sequence
Food Services Management
Heating, Refrigeration, and Air Conditioning
Industrial Engineering Technology

Legal Studies

Marketing, Retailing, and Merchandising

Medical Technology

Mental Health and Rehabilitation
  Counseling

Nursing

Pharmacy and Pharmaceutical Sciences

Physical Education

Recreation and Leisure Services

Secretarial Studies and Office Management

Speech, Rhetoric, Public Address, and
  Debate

Graduates that later obtain higher degrees:
30%

SPECIAL PROGRAMS

Adult/Continuing Education offers six or eight week programs during the days, evenings, and weekends for credit towards a certificate, but credit does not apply to an associate's degree. Categories include adult basic education, agriculture science/horticulture, architecture, biological sciences, business, child development, education, English as a second language, fine arts, foreign language, GED, home economics, humanities, journalism, law, literacy classes, mathematical sciences, medical and office occupations, physical education, physical sciences, social sciences, social work, speech, and trades and industry.

Adult Learning Skills is a program that provides students who have not finished their high school education, five segments to choose from: basic education, English as a second language, GED, literacy, and State Legalization Impact Assistance Grant. This program is offered for the convenience of the student at eight week intervals.

Center for Open Learning offers courses on television and cassette tapes. City Colleges of Chicago owns the public television station, WYCC-TV, which broadcasts the courses on Channel 20. Students who wish to register for these courses, can register on the Kennedy-King campus or directly through the center by mail. Those who register by mail will receive all grades and transcripts from Chicago City-Wide College. Students registering at Kennedy-King will receive grades and transcripts like a normal course.

The College Level Examination Program (CLEP) determines the academic relevance on nontraditional education experiences such as the military, on-the-job experience, or other life experiences through a series of tests and may grant students college credit for these experiences.

College orientation is offered to entering students before classes begin to acquaint them with the college and to prepare them for college life.

Cooperative Air Force ROTC provides training in military science for commission as a second lieutenant in the U.S. Air Force. Two- year scholarships are available.

The Cooperative Education Program alternates formal academic study with related paid work experience. The program provides academic credit and full-time status during co-op placement.

The Cooperative Study-Abroad Program allows students to go to a foreign country for part of their college education.

Credit by Assessment may be granted to adults who have acquired knowledge on the job or through other non-classroom experiences. Adults must assemble a portfolio equating their experiences to specific skills and learning outcomes.

The honors program offers academically talented students a challenging program of study that includes special classes, seminars, colloquia, cultural activities, and special recognition to motivate participants.

Remedial courses are offered to entering students to bring them up to admission standards and to help them adjust for success in college.

ATHLETIC PROGRAMS

Kennedy-King College is a member of the National Junior College Athletic Association (NJCAA).

Intercollegiate sports: men's baseball, basketball, softball, swimming, diving, tennis, and track & field; women's basketball and volleyball.

LIBRARY HOLDINGS

Kennedy-King's Library houses 43,000 bound volumes, 200 microforms, 264 periodical subscriptions, 30,000 audiovisuals, and 60 computers for student use.

STUDENT LIFE

Special Regulations

Orientation required for all incoming students; placement tests required of new, continuing, or former students if SAT or ACT scores are not available.

Campus Services

Health, personal and psychological counseling; career counseling and placement; child care; and transfer center.

Campus Activities

Social and cultural activities include theater, dance, art exhibits, and concerts. Students may get involved in the student-run newspaper. Communication majors or volunteers may work at the student-run radio station, WKKC-FM.

Leadership opportunities are found in the Student Government Association (SGA) or the more than 37 clubs that include the African-American History Club, Communications Arts Guild, Broadcasting Club, Christian Fellowship Club, or Auto Tech Club. Honor societies represented on campus include Phi Theta Kappa International Honor Society and Phi Beta Lambda.

The campus is located in the metropolitan city of Chicago with a population of approximately 3,500,000. Local transportation provides easy access to mass rail and air transportation. Chicago's International O'Hare Airport departs to points all over the world. The city of Chicago offers an array of social and cultural activities including boating, skiing, ice skating, concerts, museums, a zoo, national sports, and shopping. Chicago is home of Johnson Publishing Company, publisher of *Ebony* magazine, and is the headquarters for several national fraternities and sororities.

Handicapped Services

Readers, note-takers, personal care attendants, transcribers, and adaptive treatment.

Kentucky

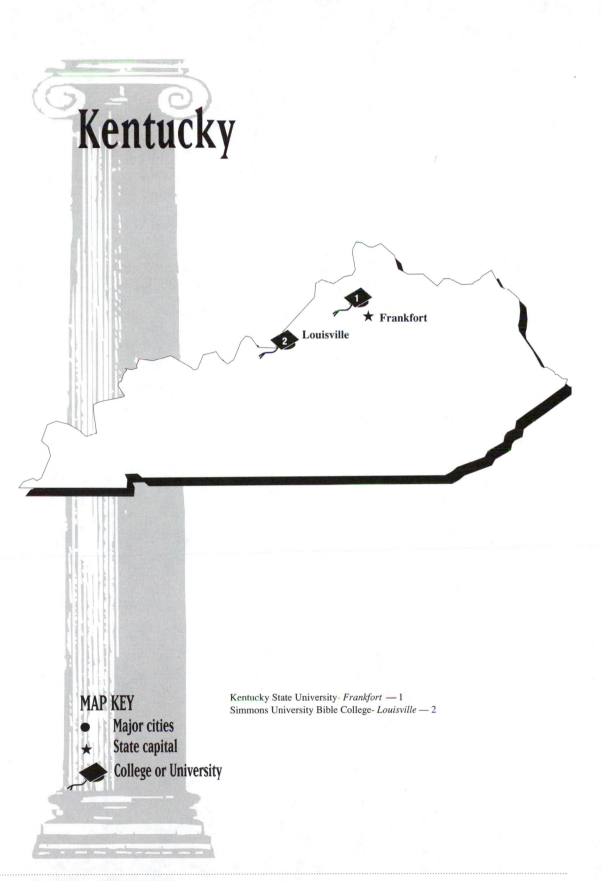

★ Frankfort

1

2 Louisville

MAP KEY
- ● Major cities
- ★ State capital
- ◆ College or University

Kentucky State University- *Frankfort* — 1
Simmons University Bible College- *Louisville* — 2

KENTUCKY STATE UNIVERSITY

E. Main St.
Frankfort, KY, 40601
Phone: (502) 227-6000
Toll-free:
800-325-1716

Total Enrollment:
2,500 students

Level of Selectivity:
Slightly competitive

Motto:
Onward and Upward

HISTORY

Kentucky State University (KSU) is a four-year, state-supported, coed liberal arts university, founded in 1886 as the State Normal School for Colored Persons. The school was established as a normal school for the training of black teachers for black schools. In 1890, the institution became a land grant college, adding several new departments to the school's curriculum.

As the school's programs changed so did the name. In 1902, it became Kentucky Normal and Industrial Institute for Colored Persons. In 1926, "Normal" was dropped from the name. A high school was added in 1930. The name was changed to Kentucky State College for Negroes in 1938. "Negro" was dropped from the name in 1952, and the school became Kentucky State College. After gaining university status, the name was changed to Kentucky State University in 1973.

Current president Mary Smith states that, "education should help students learn skills which help them to analyze and solve problems in life as well as free the mind so that the learner's creativity is unleashed." She contends that each student at Kentucky State is helped to develop these skills.

To emphasize quality and individuality, KSU offers programs such as the Whitney Young Jr.'s Study of the Great Books or the Mentor's Advisement Program, both designed to build small intellectual and social communities.

The 31-building campus continues to grow in size and programs. The school developed a new mission in 1982 aimed at becoming a major repository for the collection of artifacts, books, and records related to its history of educating black citizens. The collection is available to interested students, faculty, and visiting scholars for research and general usage. KSU offers students career opportunities related to state government services and participation in U.S. Department of Agricultural programs, as one of two land grant institutions in the system.

ACCREDITATION

Kentucky State University is accredited by the Southern Association of Colleges and Schools to award the Bachelor of Arts, Bachelor of Science, Associate in Applied Science Technology, Associate of Arts, and Master of Public Administration degrees .

Other Accreditation

Accrediting Commission for Independent Colleges and Schools

American Assembly of Collegiate Schools of Business

American Dietetic Association

Council on Social Work Education

Kentucky Department of Education

National Association of Schools of Music

National Association of Schools of Public Affairs and Administration

National Council for Accreditation of Teacher Education

National League for Nursing

COSTS PER YEAR

1993–94 Tuition: $1,400 (in-state); $4,200 (out-state)

Room and board: $1,226 (room); $1,456 (board)

Special fees: $110

Books: $510

Estimated total cost: $4,702 (in-state); $7,502 (out-state)

FINANCIAL AID

1990–91 Institutional Funding:

Number of scholarships and grants: 863

Total amount of scholarships and grants: $1,274,604

Range of scholarships and grants: $300–$6,500

1991–92 Institutional Funding

Number of scholarships and grants: 1,596

Total amount of scholarships and grants: $1,879,140

Range of scholarships and grants: $100–$2,400

Number of loans: 929

Total amount of loans: $1,273,635

Range of loans: $200–$4,000

Number of work-study: 517

Total amount of work-study: $568,878

Range of work-study: $500–$1,500

Financial Aid Specific to the School

91% of the student body received financial aid during 1991–92.

The Army and Cooperative Air Force ROTC in conjunction with the University of Kentucky offer two-, three- and four-year scholarships that pay tuition, fees, and other expenses, and provide a monthly stipend of $100.

Athletic scholarships are available to students participating in intercollegiate sports.

Coleman Young Scholarships are available to students who participate in the Coleman Young Scholarship Foundation with a high school GPA of 3.0 and an ACT score of 21. Awards pay tuition, activity fees, and insurance.

The deferred payment plan allows students to pay one-half of tuition at registration, one-quarter on the first Friday of October, and one-quarter on the first Friday of November for fall semester; for spring semester, students pay the second two quarters on the first Friday in March and the first Friday in April.

Louisville/Lexington Black Achievers Scholarships are available for participants in the Black Achievers program with high school GPA of 3.0 and an ACT score of 20.

The Micro City Government Scholarships are available for first-time freshmen with a GPA of 3.0 who participate in the Micro City Government program. Awards pay tuition, activity fees, and insurance.

NAFEO District of Columbia Project Scholarships are available for graduates of the District of Columbia public schools. Student must be enrolled as a full-time freshman with a minimum GPA of 3.5 and an ACT composite score of 25. Awards pay tuition, fees, room, board, books, and supplies.

A part-time employment program through the university provides employment for students for up to 30 hours.

Performance grants are available in music, art, athletics, leadership, journalism, and cheerleading. Students must be enrolled full time and meet the criteria for each award.

Pre-engineering programs offer scholarships through a number of local businesses and corporations. Awards range from small stipends to payment of tuition and books.

The Presidential Scholarships are awarded to first-time freshmen with a GPA of 3.0 and an ACT score of 21. Any valedictorian or salutatorian of his/her high school graduating class automatically qualifies for award. Awards pay tuition only to full scholarships.

Service County General Scholarships are available to residents of Anderson, Franklin, Henry, Owen, Scot Shelby, and Woodford Counties. Applicants must be full-time entering freshmen with a GPA of 3.0. Awards pay full scholarships.

South Africa Education Scholars program awards full and partial scholarships to legally disadvantaged residents of South Africa. Scholarships pay tuition, fees, room, board, books, and supplies.

The Thurgood Marshall Black Education Fund provides four-year scholarships to a limited number of entering freshmen with a high school GPA of 3.0 and a SAT score of 1000 or an ACT score of 24 or more. Students must be recommended by high school counselor as exceptional or exemplary in the creative or performing arts. Scholarships pay tuition, fees, room, and board, not to exceed $6,000.

Tuition and fees are waived for war orphans; for survivors of police officers, fire fighters, or volunteer firefighters killed or totally disabled in the line of duty; and for any person 65 years of age or older. Applicants must be residents of the Commonwealth of Kentucky.

Financial Aid Deadline

March 15 (priority); April 15 (spring and fall); February 15 (summer)

Financial Aid Contact

Ms. Carmella Conner, Director of Financial Aid, Kentucky State University, Frankfort, KY 40601; (502) 227-5960.

ADMISSION REQUIREMENTS

ACT: 19 preferred; SAT: 780

Entrance Requirements

An official high school transcript and completion of the precollege curriculum of 20 units to include: 4 English, 3 mathematics, 2 science (one laboratory), 2 social science, and 9 electives. Kentucky residents must rank in upper 40 of class, have an ACT score of 19, or have a 2.75 GPA. Out-of-state residents must be in upper half of class, have a 2.50 GPA, or score at the national average on the ACT. A $15 nonrefundable application fee is required.

GED students must meet the basic admission requirements, submit ACT or SAT scores, and complete the precollege curriculum.

Transfer students must have a GPA of 2.0. Students need official transcripts and must qualify for readmission to the college or university they left.

International students must take the TOEFL exam and submit official transcript, translated in English. Students should apply at least three months in advance of enrollment term. Must submit ACT or SAT scores if a testing center is available. Nigerian students must submit a complete West African School Certificate (WASC) or General Certificate of Education (GCE).

Provisional admission students, deficient in precollege curriculum units, must make up deficiencies within first 24 semester credit hours.

Admission Application Deadline

August 1 (preferred). Rolling admission provides no specific date for notification of admission so applicant is informed as soon as admission decision is made; early admission allows qualified students to enter college full time before completing high school.

Admission Contact

Director of Records, Registration and Admission, Box PG-92, Kentucky State University, Frankfort, KY 40601; (502) 227-6813 or 800-633-9415 (in-state); 800-325-1716 (out-of-state).

GRADUATION REQUIREMENTS

A minimum of 128 credit hours to include 6 foreign language; 3 math; 6 sciences; and 1 computer science (for math, education, business, business administration, chemistry, electronics technology, drafting and design, and criminal justice majors). Student must have a cumulative GPA of 2.0.

A minimum of 64 credit hours is needed for an associate's degree.

Grading System

A-F, P/F = pass/fail

STUDENT BODY PROFILE

Total enrollment (male/female):
 1,050/1,450

From in-state: 1,950

Other regions: 31 states; 13 foreign countries

Full-time undergraduates (male/female):
 609/841

Part-time undergraduates (male/female):
 441/609

Ethnic/Racial Makeup

African American, 1,125; Hispanic, 25; Asian, 25; Caucasian, 1,300; International, 25.

Class of 1995 Profile

Number of applicants: 2,176

Number accepted: 1,219

Number enrolled: 427

Median SAT score: 355V; 415M

FACULTY PROFILE

Number of faculty: 167

Student-teacher ratio: 13:1

Full-time faculty: 130

Part-time faculty: 37

Faculty with doctorates or other terminal
 degrees: 60%

Ethnic/Racial Makeup of Faculty:

African American, 42; Asian, 20; Caucasian, 105.

SCHOOL CALENDAR

1992–93: August 20–May 7 (semesters)

Commencement and conferring of degrees:
   May

One six-week summer session.

DEGREES OFFERED 1991–92:

Bachelor of Arts
Art Education

Business Administration

Child Development and Family Relations

Criminal Justice

Early Elementary Education

English Education

History

History Education

Liberal Studies

Mathematics

Mathematics Education

Physical Education

Political Science

Psychology

Public Administration

Social Studies Education

Social Work

Sociology

Studio Art

Textiles, Clothing, and Merchandising

Bachelor of Science
Applied Mathematics/Engineering

Biology

Biology Education

Chemistry

Computer Science

Medical Technology

Physical Education

Bachelor of Music in Performance
Music Performance

Bachelor of Music Education
Music Education

The Associate in Applied Science Technology Degree
Child Development and Family Relations

Computer Science

Criminal Justice

Drafting and Design Technology

Electronics Technology

Manufacturing Technology

Nursing

Office Administration

Pre-Professional
Community Health

Cytotechnology

Dentistry

Engineering

Law

Medical Technology

Nuclear Medicine Technology

Optometry

Physical Therapy

Veterinay Medicine

Associate of Art
Liberal Studies

Master of Public Administration

SPECIAL PROGRAMS
Three-day college orientation session is provided at no cost; parents may attend.

Academic remediation provides remedial courses for entering students to bring them up to admission standards.

Preparatory programs are offered in the fields of law, engineering, medicine, optometry, veterinary medicine, community health, dentistry, medical technology, cytotechnology, nuclear medicine technology, and physical therapy.

The Whitney M. Young, Jr. Honors College challenges talented students with a special curriculum, including the reading and studying of classical literature.

An academic honor roll and dean's list are published each semester. Those students whose grade point average is 3.2 or above will be included on the honor roll.

Advanced Placement (AP) allows high school students to take various college courses for credit during their junior or senior year.

The College Level Examination Program (CLEP) grants college credits through a series of tests in various subjects for non-traditional educational experiences, such as the military, on-the-job-training, or life experiences.

The Cooperative Education Program alternates or combines academic course work with periods of paid work experience. The program is available in all majors after completion of one full year or 30 hours.

The study abroad program is available in countries such as Britain, Italy, Mexico, Puerto Rico, Scandinavia, and South America. A 3.0 cumulative GPA is necessary and students must fulfill the foreign language portion of KSU's liberal studies requirement.

A Student Exchange Program is available in conjunction with Berea College in south central Kentucky. Berea is recognized for its services to students from the southeastern United States and Appalachian regions.

The Army ROTC provides training in military science for commission as a second lieutenant in the U.S. Armed Forces. The cooperative Air Force ROTC is offered at the University of Kentucky in Lexington, Kentucky. Two-, three- and four-year scholarships are available. All students are required to take several Army ROTC courses.

Three/two dual degree program in engineering in cooperation with the University of Kentucky, Vanderbilt University, the University of Maryland at College Park, and Florida A&M University allows students to get two degrees—one in liberal artrs from home school and one in engineering from cooperating school—by completing three

years at matriculated school and two years at cooperating school.

ATHLETIC PROGRAMS

Kentucky State University is a member of the National Collegiate Athletic Association (NCAA), division II.

Intercollegiate sports: men's basketball, football, golf, tennis, and track & field; women's basketball, golf, tennis, track & field and volleyball.

Intramural sports: archery, badminton, basketball, bowling, softball, flag football, swimming, track, table tennis, tennis, and volleyball.

LIBRARY HOLDINGS

The Paul G. Blazer Library holds 300,000 volumes, 45,000 microforms, 1,250 periodical subscriptions, and 12,500 audiovisuals. Special collections include the African American history and culture collection, the Rufus B. Atwood Papers (KSU president, 1929–1962), and Whitney M. Young, Sr. memorabilia.

STUDENT LIFE

Special Regulations

Freshmen and sophomores must live on campus. Open visitations are from 6 PM–11 PM, Sunday through Thursday; and 12 noon–2 AM, Friday and Saturday.

Campus Services

Health center, personal and psychological counseling, student employment services, and career counseling and placement.

Campus Activities

Cultural and group activities include theater, band, chorale, and dance. Students can get involved in the student-run newspaper (*The Thorobred News*) or the yearbook (*The Thorobred*). Students interested in communications can join the student-run radio station. Special interest clubs are centered around art, music, and literature.

Leadership activities can be found in the Student Government Association or in over 60 other student-run organizations. Three national fraternities and three national sororities are represented on campus, as well as two local fraternities and three local sororities. KSU students have numerous opportunities to participate and get involved in campus life.

Kentucky State is located in the historic city of Frankfort, population approximately 27,500, in the Bluegrass region of Kentucky. The city of Frankfort offers boating, golfing, horseback riding, and water sports. The 485-acre campus is situated 25 miles west of Lexington, 50 miles east of Louisville, and 20 miles from the airport near Lexington. Louisville and Lexington offer horse racing, theater, concerts, and many other social and recreational activities. Bus transportation provides access to these cities.

Housing Availability

887 housing spaces; freshman-housing guaranteed.

Handicapped Services

Include wheelchair accessibility, and services for the visually and hearing impaired.

NOTABLE ALUMNI

Dr. Rufus Barfield, 1952–Vice chancellor, University of Arkansas, Pine Bluff

Ersa H. Poston, 1942–Former president, New York Civil Services Commission

Moneta Sleet Jr., 1947–Photographer, Johnson Publishing Co.

Curtis Sullivan–President, Omni Custom Meats, Inc.

Whitney Young–Executive director, National Urban League

SIMMONS UNIVERSITY BIBLE COLLEGE

1811 Dumesnil St.
Louisville, KY 40210
Phone: (502) 776-1443

Total Enrollment:
103

Level of Selectivity:
Noncompetitive

HISTORY

Simmons University Bible College is a four-year, private, coed, liberal arts institution affiliated with the Baptist Church. Simmons was founded in 1873 to train ministers and Christian educators and remains committed to providing programs in Christian education.

ACCREDITATION

Simmons University Bible College is accredited by the Southern Association of Colleges and Schools to award the Bachelor of Arts and Bachelor of Theology degrees.

COSTS PER YEAR

1991–92 Tuition: $720

Room and board: none

Special fees: $125

Books: $500

Estimated total cost: $1,345

Admission Contact

Charles Price, Director of Admission, Simmons University Bible College, Louisville, KY 40210; (502) 776-1443.

STUDENT BODY PROFILE

Total enrollment: 103

From in-state: 103

Louisiana

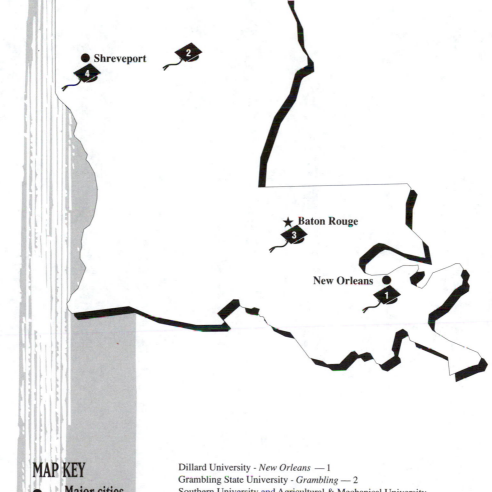

● Shreveport

2

4

★ Baton Rouge

3

New Orleans ●

1

Dillard University - *New Orleans* — 1
Grambling State University - *Grambling* — 2
Southern University and Agricultural & Mechanical University
  at Baton Rouge - *Baton Rouge* — 3
Southern University (New Orleans) - *New Orleans* — 1
Southern University (Shreveport) - *Shreveport* — 4
Xavier University of Louisiana - *New Orleans* — 1

DILLARD UNIVERSITY

2601 Gentilly Blvd.
New Orleans, LA
70122
Phone: (504) 286-4670

Total Enrollment:
1,700

Level of Selectivity:
Slightly competitive

HISTORY

Dillard University is a four-year, private, liberal arts, coeducational school, created in 1930 by the merging of its two parent institutions: Straight University and Union Normal School.

In 1869, Straight University, later renamed Straight College, was established by the Congregational Church. Between 1874 and 1886 Straight operated a law department.

In 1869, Union Normal School was founded by the Methodist Episcopal Church. By the end of the century Union was renamed New Orleans University. The university opened a medical department, including a school of pharmacy and a school of nursing in 1889. The medical college was discontinued in 1911, but the hospital and nursing school continued under the name of Flint-Goodridge Hospital.

On June 6, 1930, Straight College and New Orleans University merged to form Dillard University, which continued to operate the Flint-Goodridge Hospital until 1983.

Dillard University

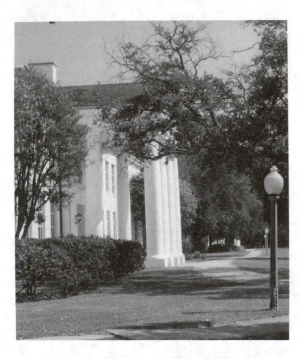

In 1935, Dillard University moved to its present location and began instruction. Dillard had the first speech department in a black university and the first nationally accredited nursing program in Louisiana.

The campus is situated on approximately 48 acres in a lovely residential section of New Orleans. The 19-building campus consists of stately white turn-of-the-century architecture and has been cited as one of the nation's most beautiful campuses. This historically black college is a United Negro College Fund member school.

ACCREDITATION

Dillard is accredited by the Southern Association of Colleges and Schools to award the Bachelor of Arts and Bachelor of Science degrees.

Other Accreditation

Louisiana Department of Education

National Association of Schools of Music

National League of Nursing

COSTS PER YEAR

1992–93 Tuition: $5,800

Room and board: $3,350

Special fees: $165

Books: $500

Estimated total cost: $9,815

FINANCIAL AID

1991–92 Institutional Funding

Number of scholarships and grants: 402

Total amount of scholarships and grants: $604,250

Range of scholarships and grants: $500–$4,200

Number of loans: 294

Total amount of loans: $372,187

Range of loans: $600–$2,500

1991–92 Federal and State Funding

Number of scholarships and grants: 1,218

Total amount of scholarships and grants: $1,439,729

Range of scholarships and grants: $300–$2,900

Number of loans: 632

Total amount of loans: $1,320,559

Range of loans: $300–$2,500

Number of work-study: 264

Total amount of work-study: $334,066

Range of work-study: $800–$2,000

Financial Aid Specific to the School

90% of the student body received financial aid during 1991–92.

Fifteen endowed and ten non-endowed scholarships, awards, and loans are available to Dillard students based on merit and need.

The University Scholars program pays full tuition to freshmen who qualify as university scholars. Qualifying students must have a 3.0 or higher GPA, rank in the top half of their graduating class, and present high SAT or ACT scores. Formal notice is sent to the student and to the high school by the president.

The university awards scholarships to sons and daughters of ministers of the United Methodist Church and United Church of Christ. Scholarships are renewable, but students must re-apply each year.

Tuition waivers are available to full-time Dillard employees and their children for a period of four years. To qualify, employees must be employed for at least two years.

Athletic scholarships are available to students participating in intercollegiate sports.

United Negro College Fund (UNCF) scholarships are awarded to a limited number of students at this school. Qualifying students must have a cumulative grade point average of 2.8 or higher and demonstrate financial need. UNCF scholarships range from $500 to $7,500.

Army ROTC and cooperative Air Force or Navy ROTC programs offer two-, three- and four-year scholarships that pay tuition, fees, books, and other expenses, and provide a monthly stipend of $100.

Financial Aid Deadline
March 31 (fall); (spring)

Financial Aid Contact
Rosie C. Toney, Director Financial Aid, 2601 Gentilly Blvd., New Orleans, LA 70122; (504) 286-4644.

ADMISSION REQUIREMENTS
SAT or ACT required

Entrance Requirements
Graduation from accredited high school with 18 units to include 4 English, 3 mathematics, 3 science (laboratory), 3 social sciences, and 6 electives (foreign language recommended); must be recommended by high school principal or counselor and teacher. A $10 nonrefundable application fee is required.

GED students must meet basic admission requirements.

Transfer students must submit college transcript with a 2.0 GPA, high school transcript, personal essay, and personal recommendations. 60 hours maximum transfer credits accepted.

International students must take the TOEFL examination as well as the SAT or ACT.

Early admissions allows academically gifted high school students to take college credit courses before completing high school. Students should apply before April of their junior year in high school.

Admission Application Deadline
May 30

Admission Contact
Vernese B. O'Neal, Director of Admissions, Dillard University, 2601 Gentilly Blvd., New Orleans, LA 70122; (504) 286-4670.

GRADUATION REQUIREMENTS
127 credit hours and completion of the core requirements to include: 6–9 English, 6–9 mathematics, 8 natural sciences, 6 social sciences, 2 physical education, and 1 computer course. The last 30 hours must be in residence.

Grading System
A–F, I=Incomplete, P=Pass, PR= Progress, W=Withdraw Passing, WF=Withdraw Failing; grades P,I,W and PR are not counted as credits when computing grade point average.

STUDENT BODY PROFILE
Total enrollment (male/female): 442/1,258

From in-state: 680

Other regions: 34 states and 7 foreign countries

Full-time undergraduates (male/female):
433/1,233

Part-time undergraduates (male/female):
9/25

Ethnic/Racial Makeup
African American, 1,615; International, 51; Others/unclassified, 34.

Class of 1995 Profile
Number of applicants: 1,609

Number accepted: 1,207

Number enrolled: 604

Average high school GPA: 2.5

FACULTY PROFILE
Number of faculty: 124

Student-teacher ratio: 15:1

Full-time faculty: 102

Part-time faculty: 22

SCHOOL CALENDAR
1992–93: August 27–May 13 (semester hours)

Commencement and conferring of degrees:
May 17

One summer session.

DEGREES OFFERED 1991–92:

Bachelor of Arts
Accounting

Art

Business Management

Criminal Justice

Economics

Early Childhood Education

Elementary Education

English

Foreign Language

History

Japanese Studies

Mass Communication

Music

Philosophy and Religion

Physical Education and Health

Political Science

Psychology

Secondary Education

Special Education

Social Welfare

Sociology

Speech and Drama

Urban Studies

Bachelor of Science
Biology

Chemistry

Computer Science

Health Education

Mathematics

Nursing

Physics

Pre-Engineering

Pre-Medicine

SPECIAL PROGRAMS
The Accelerated Study Program allows students to complete their undergraduate degree in a shorter period of time than the traditional four-year period.

Advanced Placement (AP) allows high school students to get college credit for scores on the College Board AP tests in various subjects.

College orientation is offered at a cost of $50 to entering students one week before classes begin to orient students to the college and to prepare them for college life; parents may attend.

A cooperative allied health program is offered with Howard University and Tuskegee University.

The Cooperative Education Program alternates formal academic study with practical work experience in major.

A cooperative urban studies program is offered with Columbia University.

The honors program offers academically talented students a challenging program of study that includes special classes, seminars, colloquia, cultural activities, and special recognition to motivate participants.

The part-time degree program allows students to earn an undergraduate degree while attending part time.

Remedial courses are offered to entering students to bring them up to admissions standards and to help them adjust for success in college.

ROTC provides training in military science for commission as a second lieutenant in the Army, Navy, or Air Force. Two-, three- and four-year scholarships are available.

Study Abroad Program allows students to go to France, Germany, or Mexico for a specified period of time for part of their college education.

Three/two dual degree program in engineering is offered in cooperation with Auburn University, Columbia University, or Georgia Institute of Technology. The program allows students to get two degrees—one in liberal arts from home school and one in engineering from cooperating school—by completing three years at matriculated school and two years at cooperating school.

ATHLETIC PROGRAMS

Dillard is a member of the National Association of Intercollegiate Athletics (NAIA).

Intercollegiate sports: men's basketball; women's basketball.

Intramural sports: basketball, bowling, gymnastics, swimming, tennis, track & field, volleyball, and weight lifting.

LIBRARY HOLDINGS

The Will W. Alexander Library holds 139,000 bound volumes, 5,400 microforms, 765 periodical subscriptions, and 1,850 audiovisuals. Fifty computers are available for student use in computer center.

STUDENT LIFE

Special Regulations

Freshmen must attend weekly assembly; class attendance required; cars must be registered to be parked on campus; curfews and quiet hours enforced; college orientation required.

Campus Services

Health center, personal and social counseling, career planning and placement, student employment, chapel and religious services, and religious counseling.

Campus Activities

Social and cultural activities include theater, concerts, chorale, and dances. Students can get involved in the student-run newspaper or yearbook. Communication majors or volunteers may work in the student-run radio or television station. Each year students look forward to participating in the art competition or browsing the art exhibits.

Leadership opportunities are found in the Student Government Association (SGA), class organizations, the debating club, or special interest groups. Greek letter fraternities include Alpha Phi Alpha, Kappa Alpha Psi, Omega Psi Phi, and Phi Beta Sigma; sororities include Alpha Kappa Alpha, Delta Sigma Theta, Sigma Gamma Rho, and Zeta Phi Beta. Six national honor societies are present on campus.

Dillard is located in the metropolitan city of New Orleans, with a population of approximately 1.3 million. Situated on the Mississippi River 50 miles above the Gulf of Mexico, New Orleans is known for its fine foods, entertainment, parks, museums, art galleries, and other attractions. Its famous

Vieux Carre or French Quarter is a living museum. The annual Mardi Gras brings thousands of visitors to the city each year. New Orleans offers opera, a nationally known symphony orchestra, and the Louisiana Superdome, which hosts sports events and attracts famous artists. The campus provides a serious place for study, while the city provides a place for an array of social, cultural, and recreational activities.

Housing Availability

600 spaces available within four resident halls. Freshman-only housing available.

Handicapped Services

Special parking is available for students with disabilities.

NOTABLE ALUMNI

Judge Robert F. Collins, 1951–U.S. district judge, eastern division, Louisiana

Earl Lucas, 1957–Mayor, Mississippi's all black township, Mount Bayou

Dr. William W. Sutton, 1953–President, Mississippi Valley State University

GRAMBLING STATE UNIVERSITY

PO Drawer 607
Grambling, LA 71245
Phone: (318) 274-2000
Toll-free: 800 448-3530

Total Enrollment:
6,485

Level of Selectivity:
Noncompetitive

Motto:
The Place Where
Everyone is Somebody

HISTORY

Grambling State University (GSU) is a four-year, state-supported, coed, liberal arts university founded in 1901 as a relief school for black farmers. A request for assistance from the Farmers' Relief Association of Ruston, Louisiana, prompted Dr. Booker T. Washington to send Charles P. Adams from Tuskeegee Institute to Louisiana. Adams and two faculty members established the Colored Industrial and Agricultural School. The original purpose of the school was to provide all students who were willing to work with a knowledge of how to farm, build houses, and maintain sanitary and wholesome living conditions.

In 1905, Fredelia Jewett donated a large amount of money to the school, which became known as the North Louisiana Agricultural and Industrial Institute. At that time, the school moved two miles west to a 200-acre tract on which it now rests. In 1918, under the direction of the Lincoln Parish School Board, the school was renamed Lincoln Parish Training School. When the school became a junior college in 1928, the name changed to Lincoln Normal and Industrial Institute. In 1940, a four-year program was initiated with the first Bachelor of Science in Elementary Education degrees being awarded in 1944.

The name changed to Grambling College in 1947. A year later, a program in secondary education began, graduating its first teachers in 1953. This was followed the next year by programs in preliminary training for law, medicine, and dentistry. By the 1958–59 school year a full liberal arts curriculum was developed. When Grambling was granted university status in 1974, it adopted its present name.

Grambling remains dedicated to providing a quality education for students from across the country and abroad. The school has a track record of producing leaders in all the professions, including sports. Many of the school's athletes go on to play professional sports, such as Doug Williams, former quarterback for the Washington Redskins. Grambling State's football team and marching band are world renowned.

The campus consists of 75 buildings occupying 360 acres. The basic architectural style is colonial with a blend of red brick and white frame structures.

ACCREDITATION

Grambling State University is accredited by the Southern Association of Colleges and Schools (SACS) to award the Associate of Arts, Bachelor of Science, Master's, and Ed.D. degrees.

Other Accreditation

Accrediting Council on Education in Journalism and Mass Communication

The Council of Social Work Education

The National Association of Schools of Music

National Council for Accreditation of Teacher Education

National League of Nursing

National Recreation and Park Association

COSTS PER YEAR

1992–93 Tuition: $1,800 (in-state); $3,350 (out-state)

Room and board: $1,550 (room); $1,062 (board)

Special fees: $125

Books: $500

Estimated total cost: $5,037 (in-state); $6,587 (out-state)

FINANCIAL AID

1991–92 Institutional Funding

Total amount of scholarships and grants: $895,590

Range of scholarships and grants: $250–$2,500

1991–92 Federal and State Funding

Total amount of scholarships and grants: $1,396,565

Financial Aid Specific to the School

98% of the student body received financial aid during 1991–91.

Army and Air Force ROTC offer two- and four-year scholarships that pay tuition, fees, books, and other expenses, and provide a monthly stipend of $100.

Athletic Awards are available for students who participate in intercollegiate sports.

Cooperative Education Program alternates classroom study with related paid work experience. The program provides academic credit and full-time status during co-op placement.

Creative arts/performance awards are available for students with exceptional talent who participate in choir or band.

Deferred payment plan allows students to pay college costs in two or three installments during the semester.

Louisiana State Scholarships are available to state residents. Student must complete and submit ONEAPP application by March 15. For more information call 800-448-3530.

Scholarships are awarded to academically talented students with a minimum GPA of 3.0 and a minimum ACT score of 16. Application deadline March 1.

Thurgood Marshall Black Education Fund provides a four-year scholarship at this public black college. Qualifying students must have a high school GPA of 3.0 or better and a SAT score of 1,000 or ACT score of 24 or more. Students must be recommended by high school counselor as exceptional or exemplary in the creative or performing arts. Scholarship pays tuition, fees, room, and board, not to exceed $6,000 annually.

Tuition waivers are available to part-time or full-time employees and their children. Waivers are also available to senior citizens.

Financial Aid Deadline

April 15 (fall); November 1 (spring); April 1 (summer)

Financial Aid Contact

Director of Financial Aid, Grambling State University, PO Box 629, Grambling, LA 71245; 800-448-3530 or (318) 247-2334 or 2335.

ADMISSION REQUIREMENTS

ACT or SAT required for placement

Entrance Requirements

Graduation from an accredited high school with the following units: 3 English, 2 mathematics, 2 science, 2.5 social studies, and 7 electives; 1 additional English is recommended. Submit official high school transcript; and provide proof of immunizations against measles, rubella, and mumps. Out-state freshmen given priority with 2.0 or better GPA. A $5 application fee is required.

Transfer students must submit official transcript of all previous college work; be in good standing with last college attended; have a minimum 2.0 GPA.

International students must pass TOEFL examination with a minimum 450 score.

Early admission allows academically gifted high school students the opportunity to enroll in college before completing high school.

Admission Application Deadline

August 15; rolling admission provides no specific date for notification of admission so applicant is informed as soon as admission decision is made.

Admission Contact

Karen C. Lewis, Director of Admissions and Recruitment, Grambling State University, PO Box 864, Grambling, LA 71245; (313) 274-2435.

GRADUATION REQUIREMENTS

A minimum of 128 credit hours; minimum 2.0 GPA; must attend all Lyceum and college sponsored events during freshman and sophomore years; and must pass comprehensive exit exam.

STUDENT BODY PROFILE

Total enrollment (male/female):
2,659/3,826

From in-state: 3,891

Other regions: 41 states, 13 foreign countries

Full-time undergraduates (male/female):
2,148/3,335

Part-time undergraduates (male/female):
169/244

Graduate students (male/female): 241/348

Ethnic/Racial Makeup

African American, 6,226; Hispanic, 65; Asian, 65; International, 129.

Class of 1995 Profile

Number of applicants: 3,201

Number accepted: 2,720

Number enrolled: 1,605

FACULTY PROFILE

Number of faculty: 232

student-teacher ration: 21:1

SCHOOL CALENDAR

1992–93: August–May (semester hours)

Commencement and conferring of degrees: May, July, and December

One summer session.

DEGREES OFFERED 1991–92:

Associate of Arts

Accounting/Bookkeeping

Computer Information System

Electronics Technology

General Clerical

Office Administration

Word Processing

Associate of Science

Child Development

Law Enforcement

Bachelor of Arts

Art

Criminal Justice

English

French

Geography

History

Mass Communication

Music

Philosophy

Political Science

Psychology

Public Administration

Social Science

Sociology

Spanish

Theater

Speech Pathology (non-certified)

Bachelor of Science

Accounting

Art Education

Business Office Education

Computer Information Systems

Early Childhood Education

Economics

English Education

French Education

Health and Physical Education

Home Economics Education

Management

Marketing

Mathematics Education

Music Education

Office Administration

Science Education

Social Science Education

Spanish Education

Special Education

Speech Pathology (certified)

Speech and Theater Education

Therapeutic Recreation

Pre-Professional

Pre-dentistry

Pre-law

Pre-medicine

Master of Arts

Biology Education

Developmental Education

Humanities

Romance Languages

Social Science

Social Work

Sociology

Master of Business Administration

Business Administration

Master of Science

Criminal Justice

Developmental Education

Early Childhood Education

Elementary Education

Sociology Education

Sports Administration

Public Administration

Science

SPECIAL PROGRAMS

Advanced Placement (AP) grants college credit for postsecondary work completed in high school. Students passing AP test will receive credit by examination for each course.

College Level Examination Program (CLEP) determines the academic relevance of nontraditional educational experiences such as the military, on-the-job training, or other life experiences, through a series of tests and may grant students college credit for these experiences.

College orientation is offered to entering students for two days at no cost prior to the beginning of classes to acquaint students with the college and to prepare them for college life.

Cooperative Education Program alternates and combines classroom study with related paid work experience. The program provides academic credit and full-time status during co-op placement for all majors.

Honors program offers academically talented students a challenging program of study that includes special classes, seminars, colloquia, cultural activities, and special recognition to motivate participants.

Remedial courses are offered to entering students to bring them up to admission standards and to help them adjust for success in college.

Study Abroad Program allows students to go to Mexico, India, China, or the Caribbean for a specified period of time for part of their college education. Cooperative study abroad with Japan is also available.

Three/two degree program in engineering in cooperation with Louisiana Technical University allows students to get two degrees—one in liberal arts from home school and one in engineering from cooperating school—by completing three years at matriculated school and two years at cooperating school.

ATHLETIC PROGRAMS

Grambling State is a member of the National Collegiate Athletic Association (NCAA), Division I; football Division I-AA; and the Southwestern Athletic Conference (SWAC).

Intercollegiate sports: men's baseball, basketball, football, golf, tennis, and track & field; women's basketball, golf, tennis, track & field, and volleyball.

Athletic Contact

Phone: (313) 274-2243

LIBRARY HOLDINGS

A. C. Lewis Library holds 250,250 bound volumes, 1,230 periodical subscriptions, 212,300 microforms, and 2,000 audiovisuals.

Special collections include an Afro-American Center Collection of rare and contemporary books, manuscripts, personal papers, and microfilms.

STUDENT LIFE

Special Regulations

Curfews during first week and exam week; quiet hours, and dorm visiting hours 7–11 pm.

Campus Services

Health, career counseling and placement, student employment, learning resource center, tutoring, and religious activities.

Campus Activities

Social and cultural activities include theater, chorale, band, orchestra, and dance. Student travel tours have been made to more than 26 countries and every state in the United States. Students may get involved in *The Gramblinite* (student-run newspaper) or *The Tiger* (yearbook). Communication majors may work at KGRM, the student-run radio station. Grambling strives to provide social and cultural activities that engender a sense of responsibility to the community, state, and nation.

Leadership opportunities are found in the Student Government Association or the numerous other departmental clubs and interest groups on campus. Greek-letter fraternities include Alpha Phi Alpha, Kappa Alpha Psi, Omega Psi Phi, and Phi Beta Sigma; sororities include Alpha Kappa Alpha, Delta Sigma Theta, Sigma Gamma Rho, and Zeta Phi Beta. Honor societies are represented on campus.

GSU is located in the small city of Grambling, Louisiana, with a population of 6,000. The city is five miles west of Ruston, a city of 20,000. The closest metropolitan cities are Monroe, within a 30-minute drive, and Shreveport, within a one-hour drive. Mass bus transportation gives easy access to the campus. The airport is 36 miles away.

The Bayou state offers recreational activities, such as fishing, hunting, and boating.

Housing Availability
3,500 housing spaces

Handicapped Services
Wheelchair accessibility.

NOTABLE ALUMNI
Willie Davis, 1956–Professional football player, Green Bay Packers

James Harris–Professional football player, Los Angeles Rams

Joseph B. Johnson, 1957–President, Talladega

Willis Reed–Ex-professional NBA player

Doug Williams–Retired quarterback, Washington Redskins

SOUTHERN UNIVERSITY AND A&M UNIVERSITY-BATON ROUGE

Baton Rouge, LA
70813
Phone: (504) 771-2011

Total Enrollment:
8,941

Level of Selectivity:
Noncompetitive

Motto:
Southern University a
People's University:
Serving the State, the
Nation and the World

HISTORY

Southern University at Baton Rouge (SUBR) is a four-year, state-supported, coed, liberal arts institution founded in New Orleans in 1880. It was a result of legislation introduced by Pinckney Pinchback, the nations first black governor, and other black politicians to provide an institution for the education of persons of color. The former Hebrew girl's school known as the Israel Sinai Temple Synagogue was originally purchased as the site for Southern University.

When the school opened in 1881, 12 students were in attendance; presently over 8,000 students attend. By 1886 the university had outgrown its facilities and the state appropriated $14,000 to purchase the square at Magazine and Soniat Streets. When an Agricultural and Mechanical Department was added in 1890, the school adopted its present name and within a year the institution became a land grant college under the second Morrill Act. The school awarded its first bachelor's degrees in 1912.

The New Orleans site was closed in 1914 and later that year the Baton Rouge campus opened at Scotlandville. The New Orleans branch reopened in 1959 and the Shreveport branch opened in 1964. The three campuses make up the Southern University system, the only black public university system in the nation. Baton Rouge serves as the main campus. SUBR is part of the Strengthening Historically Black College and University (HBCU) Program designed to enhance the physical plants, academic resources, and student services of HBCU's.

As a land grant institution, Southern University is committed to providing education to students with heterogeneous abilities and varying academic backgrounds. Its purpose is to prepare students to compete in their respective professions and to pursue advanced study in graduate and professional schools.

SUBR consists of 156 buildings and occupies nearly 512 acres in addition to a 372-acre farm. The facilities are an architectural blend of old and modern buildings. Many recently constructed buildings have more than 2,000,000 square feet of floor area. Among the more recently constructed buildings are the Clark Activity Center, J. S. Clark Administration Building, the Music Recital Center, the Cade Library, the School of Nursing, and the New Health Research Wing of Lee Hall.

ACCREDITATION

Southern University is accredited by the Southern Association of Colleges and Schools (SACS) to award the Bachelor of Arts, Bachelor of Science, Master's, and Doctorate degrees.

Other Accreditation

Accreditation Board of Engineering and Technology

American Bar Association

American Chemical Society

American Dietetic Association

Career College Association/Accrediting Commission for Independent Colleges and Schools

Computer Science Accreditation Commission of the Computing Science Accreditation Board

Council for Professional Development of the American Home Economics Association

Council on Social Work Education

National Architectural Accrediting Board

National Association of Schools of Music

National Council for Accreditation of Teacher Education

COSTS PER YEAR

1993-93 Tuition: $1,576 (in-state); $3,098 (out-state)

Room and board: $1,270 (room); $1,276 (board)

Special fees: $125

Books: $500

Estimated total cost: $4,747 (in-state); $6,269 (out-state)

FINANCIAL AID

1990–91 Institutional Funding

Number of scholarships and grants: 1,100

Total amount of scholarships and grants: $1,300,000

Range of scholarships and grants: $100–$5,500

1990–91 Federal and State Funding

Number of scholarships and grants: 6,900

Total amount of scholarships and grants: $13,700,000

Range of scholarships and grants: $100–$2,400

Number of loans: 4,000

Total amount of loans: $12,300,000

Range of loans: $2,655–$7,500

Number of work-study: 743

Total amount of work-study: $180,458

Range of work-study: $425–$5,000

Financial Aid Specific to the School

90% of the student body received financial aid during 1991–92.

Athletic scholarships are available to students participating in intercollegiate sports.

Performance scholarships in music are available for talented students participating in band or choir.

Tuition waivers are offered to members of the Louisiana National Guard and to senior citizens 65 years of age or older on a space available bases.

Deferred payment plan allows students to pay college costs in two or three installments during the semester for a fee of $5.

Cooperative Education Program alternates and combines classroom study with related paid work experience. The program provides academic credit and full-time status during co-op placement.

Thurgood Marshall Black Education Fund provides a four-year scholarship at this public black college. Qualifying students must have a high school GPA of 3.0 or better and a SAT score of 1000 or ACT score of 24 or more. Students must be recommended by high school counselor as exceptional or exemplary in the creative or performing arts. Scholarship pays tuition, fees, room, and board, not to exceed $6,000 annually.

Air Force and Navy ROTC offer two-, three-, and four-year scholarships that pay tuition, fees, books, and other expenses, and provide a monthly stipend of $100.

Financial Aid Deadline

March 15 (priority).

Financial Aid Contact

Cynthia Loeb Tarver, Director of Financial Aid, Southern University, Baton Rouge, LA 70813.

ADMISSION REQUIREMENTS

Open admission. SAT or ACT required for counseling and placement.

Entrance Requirements

Graduation from an accredited high school and completion of the following units: 3 English, 2 mathematics, 2 science, and 2 social science; official high school transcript with at least a 2.0 GPA. A $5 non-refundable application fee is required.

GED students must meed basic admission requirements.

Transfer students must submit official transcripts of all college work, have a minimum 2.0 GPA, and be in good standing at last institution attended. Maximum of 93 semester hours transferred from four-year institution; maximum of 64 semester hours transferred from two-year institution.

International students must submit official transcripts of all secondary schools and colleges attended; students from non-English-speaking countries must take TOEFL examination; must submit scores from SAT/ACT and/or West Africa exam; all documents must be translated into English and certified to be originals; letters of support must be original and notarized, providing proof of ability to pay all college costs. A $10 non-refundable application fee is required.

Early Admission allows academically gifted high school students the opportunity to enroll in college for credit before completing high school.

Admission Application Deadline

July 1 (fall); December 1 (spring); April 1 (summer); July 15 (transfers).

Admission Contact

Henry Bellaire, Jr., Director of Admissions, PO Box 9901, Southern University, Baton Rouge, LA 70813.

GRADUATION REQUIREMENTS

A minimum of 124 semester hours and completion of core requirements to include the following hours: 6 English (composition),

6 mathematics, 9 science, and 6 social science; pass a three-hour course in African American Experience; complete at least 30 hours, one semester, and one summer in residence at SUBR; pass comprehensives in major and various core courses; pass writing proficiency test; and take general section of GRE or professional school entry test (LSAT, MSAT, etc.).

Grading System

A-F; I=Incomplete, W=Withdraw; P= Satisfactory (nontraditional courses and comprehensives); AU=Audit

STUDENT BODY PROFILE

Total enrollment (male/female): 3,776/5,165

From in-state: 6,706

Other regions: 48 states

Full-time undergraduates (male/female): 3,082/4,085

Part-time undergraduates (male/female): 240/388

Graduate students (male/female): 454/692

Ethnic/Racial Makeup

African American, 8,584; Hispanic, 89; Asian, 179; Native American, 89.

Class of 1995 Profile

Number of applicants: 2,786

Number accepted: 2,672

Number enrolled: 1,723

Median ACT score: 15

Transfers enrolled: 894

FACULTY PROFILE

Number of faculty: 623

Student-teacher ratio: 17:1

Full-time faculty: 525

Part-time faculty: 98

Faculty with doctorates or other terminal degrees: 47%

SCHOOL CALENDAR

1992–93: August 17–May 13 (semester hours)

Commencement and conferring of degrees: May 14

One summer session.

DEGREES OFFERED 1991–92:

Accounting

Agriculture

Agriculture Education

Agronomy

Animal Science

Architecture

Art

Art Education

Bacteriology

Biology

Botany

Business Administration/Management/Supervision

Business Education

Chemistry

Child Care

Civil Engineering

Clothing and Textiles

Computer Science

Dietetics

Drama and Speech

Economics

Electrical Engineering

Elementary Education

English

Food and Nutrition Sciences

French

Geography

German

Guidance Counseling Education

Health and Physical Education

Health and Safety

History

Home Economics

Horticulture

Industrial Arts

Industrial Education

Industrial Technology

Law (ABA)

Law Enforcement

Liberal Arts

Library Science

Marketing

Mathematics

Mechanical Engineering

Medical Technology

Microbiology

Music/Education

Nursing

Philosophy

Physics

Plant and Soil Science

Political Science

Psychology

Secondary Education

Sociology

Spanish

Special Education

Speech Pathology and Audiology

Zoology

SPECIAL PROGRAMS

Adult or Continuing Education Program is available for nontraditional students returning to school or working full time.

Advanced Placement (AP) grants college credit for postsecondary work completed in high school. Students scoring 3 or more on the AP test will receive credit by examination for each course and advanced placement.

College Level Examination Program (CLEP) determines the academic relevance of nontraditional educational experiences such as the military, on-the-job training, or other life experiences through a series of tests and may grant college credit for these experiences.

Free college orientation is offered to entering students for one week prior to the beginning of classes to acquaint students with the college and to prepare them for college life; parents may attend.

Cooperative Education Program alternates classroom study with related paid work experience. The program provides academic credit and full-time status during co-op placement.

Cooperative programs in allied health, chemistry and chemical engineering, mechanical and petroleum engineering, public administration, special education, librarianship, nursing and public policy are offered with Louisiana State University.

Cross registration with Louisiana State University allows students to take courses at LSU. Students can register for one course each semester and during the summer.

Honors Program offers academically talented students a challenging program of study that includes special classes, seminars, colloquia, cultural activities, and special recognition to motivate participants.

Individualized Majors allow students to create their own major program(s) of study.

Part-time degree program allows students to earn an undergraduate degree while attending part time.

Remedial courses are offered to entering students to bring them up to admission standards and to help them adjust for success in college.

Study Abroad Program allows students to go to a foreign country for part of their college education.

Three/two dual degree program in chemistry-chemical engineering and public administration in cooperation with Louisiana State allows students to obtain a liberal arts degree from home school and a chemical engineering or public administration degree from cooperating school by completing three years at matriculated school and two years at Louisiana State.

Three/two dual degree program in electrical, mechanical or civil engineering in cooperation with Jackson State University and Xavier University allows students to obtain a liberal arts degree from home school and an engineering degree from cooperating school by completing three years at matriculated school and two years at Jackson State University or Xavier.

Upward Bound program provides academic counseling and cultural enrichment programs to high school students in grades 10, 11, and 12 who are disadvantaged and are in pursuit of a college education. Some credit courses may be offered.

ATHLETIC PROGRAMS

Southern University at Baton Rouge is a member of the National Collegiate Athletic Association (NCAA), Division I; football Division I-AA.

Intercollegiate sports: men's baseball, basketball, cross-country, football, golf, tennis, and track & field; women's basketball, track & field, and volleyball.

Intramural sports: badminton, basketball, bowling, cross-country, softball, table tennis, tennis, volleyball, weight lifting, and wrestling.

Athletic Contact

Marino H. Casem, Director of Athletics, Southern University at Baton Rouge, Baton Rouge, LA 70813; (504)-771-2712.

LIBRARY HOLDINGS

The John B. Cade Library holds 412,790 volumes, 1,989 periodical subscription, 75,644 audiovisuals, and 170,897 government documents. The Computer Center offers 125 computers for student use. Special collections include 562 French classics, a Black Heritage Collection, Rodney G. Higgins Political Science Literature Collection,

the Nursing Collection, and the Art and Architecture Library. Cade library is a partial State and U.S. Government depository. CD-ROM bibliographic databases and on-line searching are available.

STUDENT LIFE

Special Regulations

Freshmen under twenty-one must live on campus.

Campus Services

Health center, personal counseling, career counseling and placement, student employment, legal counseling, remediation, tutoring, and child care.

Campus Activities

Campus activities include theater, concerts, jazz band, marching band, chorale, and dance. Students may get involved in the *Southern University Digest* (student-run newspaper) or the *Jaguar* (yearbook). Communication majors may work at the student-run radio or television station.

Leadership opportunities are found in the Student Government Association or various other departmental clubs, such as the Aquatic Club, The Art Club, National Black Engineers, Jazz Club, and Lacumba Players. General clubs include NAACP, East Coast Connection, Muslim Association, Active Islamic Association, Malaysian Student Organization, Windy City Organization and the Renaissance Organization, to name a few. Religious groups include the Newman Club and clubs representing Baptist, Interdenominational, United Methodist, and Church of God in Christ students.

Greek-letter fraternities include Alpha Phi Alpha, Kappa Alpha Psi, Omega Psi Phi, and Phi Beta Sigma; sororities include Alpha Kappa Alpha, Delta Sigma Theta, Sigma Gamma Rho, and Zeta Phi Beta. Honors groups are represented on campus. The Association of Women Students and the Men's Federation are resident hall support groups. These groups promote community living and provide Thanksgiving and Christmas baskets to city residents yearly.

The Southern University campus is located in the metropolitan capital city of Baton Rouge, with a population of approximately 500,000. Just a two-hour drive from New Orleans, students have access to the rich cultural experience of the Bayou area. Baton Rouge is a major seaport populated with people from French, Spanish, and English backgrounds. Opera, ballet, local theater, recreation centers, and parks are readily accessible in the city.

Housing Availability

3,008 housing spaces; 1,000 freshman-only housing spaces, 2,008 upperclassman spaces; and 34 apartments for families.

NOTABLE ALUMNI

Lou Brock–Major League Baseball's Hall of Fame member; National Black College Alumni Hall of Fame

Felton G. Clark, Ph.D.–Former president, Southern University and A&M University

Willie Davenport, 1970–Olympic gold-medalist, 1968

Cleo Fields–U.S. senator

Edward Honor–Retired lieutenant general

Dolores Margaret Spikes–First female president, Louisiana Public University System; former chancellor, Southern University at New Orleans

Joseph M. Steward, 1965–Senior vice president, Corporate Affairs, Kellogg Food Co.

SOUTHERN UNIVERSITY AT NEW ORLEANS

6400 Press Dr.
New Orleans, LA
70126
Phone: (504) 286-5000

Total Enrollment:
3,734

Level of Selectivity:
Noncompetitive; allied
health and technical
program slightly
competitive

HISTORY

Southern University at New Orleans (SUNO) is a four-year, state-supported, coed, liberal arts institution founded in 1959 for the education of African-American students. SUNO, a branch and extension of Southern University and

A&M University, was created by an act of the state legislature, which later appropriated over one billion dollars for the purchase of property, construction, and furnishings.

In 1959, on a 17-acre plot located in the residential community of Pontchartrain Park, SUNO began classes in one building with 158 students. In 1963, the first class received bachelor's degrees. Ten years later the university was removed from the jurisdiction of the Louisiana State Board of Education and became a branch of Southern University and Agricultural and Mechanical College in Baton Rouge.

As a branch of a land grant institution, SUNO is committed to providing education to students with heterogeneous abilities and varying academic backgrounds. Its purpose is to prepare students to compete in their respective professions or to pursue advanced study.

SUNO is situated on an 17-acre campus, incorporating 10 buildings, including a 300,000-volume library.

ACCREDITATION

Southern University is accredited by the Southern Association of Colleges and Schools (SACS) to award the Associate of Arts, Associate of Science, Bachelor of Arts, Bachelor of Science, and Master's degrees.

Other Accreditation

Council on Social Work Education

Louisiana Department of Education

COSTS PER YEAR

1992–93 Tuition: $1,465 (in-state); $3,035 (out-state)

Room and board: None

Special fees: $125

Books: $500

Estimated total cost: $2,090 (in-state); $3,660

FINANCIAL AID

Financial Aid Specific to the School

80% of the student body received financial aid during 1991–92.

Cooperative Education Program alternates and combines classroom study with related paid work experience. The program provides academic credit and full-time status during co-op placement.

Army and Air Force ROTC in cooperation with Loyola University offer two- and four-year scholarships that pay tuition, fees, books, and other expenses, and provide a monthly stipend of $100.

Financial Aid Deadline

May 1

ADMISSION REQUIREMENTS

Open admission. SAT or ACT (preferred) required for counseling and placement.

Entrance Requirements

Graduate from an accredited high school with completion of the following units: 3 English, 2 mathematics, 2 science, 2 social science; submit official high school transcript; complete physical exam form; and submit letter of recommendation from school counselor or teacher. A $5 nonrefundable application fee is required.

GED students must meet basic admission requirements.

Transfer students must submit official transcript of all college work with a minimum 2.0 GPA.

International students must submit official transcript of all high school and college work; students from non-English-speaking countries must take TOEFL examination; and students must provide proof of ability to pay all college costs.

Early admission allows academically gifted high school students the opportunity to enroll in college for credit before completing high school.

Admission Application Deadline

Rolling admission provides no specific date for notification of admission so applicant is informed as soon as admission decision is made; deferred admission.

Admission Contact

Dr. Melvin Hodges, Director of Admission, Southern University at New Orleans, New Orleans, LA 70126; (504) 286-5314.

GRADUATION REQUIREMENTS

A minimum of 124 semester hours and completion of core requirements to include the following hours: 6 English, 6 mathematics, 6 science, 6 social science, and 2 physical education; complete two semesters in residence at SUNO with a minimum 2.0 GPA.

Grading System

A-F; I=Incomplete, W=Withdraw; P=Satisfactory (nontraditional courses); AU=Audit

STUDENT BODY PROFILE

Total enrollment (male/female): 1,232/2,502

From in-state: 3,659

Other regions: 5 states; 5 foreign countries

Full-time undergraduates (male/female): 832/1,690

Part-time undergraduates (male/female): 334/678

Graduate students (male/female): 66/134

Ethnic/Racial Makeup

African American, 3,487; Hispanic, 16; Asian, 16; Native American, 4; Caucasian, 76; International, 135.

Class of 1995 Profile

Number of applicants: 2,786

Number accepted: 2,676

Number enrolled: 1,670

Median ACT score: 15

FACULTY PROFILE

Number of faculty: 119

Student-teacher ratio: 19:1

Full-time faculty: 90

Part-time faculty: 29

SCHOOL CALENDAR

1992–93: May–August (semester hours)

Commencement and conferring of degrees: May and December

One summer session.

DEGREES OFFERED 1991–92:

Accounting

Biology

Business Administration

Chemistry

Economics

English

History

Music

Philosophy

Political Science

Social Work

SPECIAL PROGRAMS

Advanced Placement (AP) grants college credit for postsecondary work completed in high school. Students scoring 3 on the AP test will receive credit by examination for each course and advanced placement.

College Level Examination Program (CLEP) determines the academic relevance of nontraditional educational experiences such as the military, on-the-job training, or other life experiences, through a series of tests and may grant students college credit for these experiences.

Cooperative Education Program alternates and combines classroom study with related paid work experience. The program provides academic credit and full-time status during co-op placement.

Individualized majors allow students to create their own major program(s) of study.

Internships in various disciplines allow students to apply theory to on-the-job training in industry, business, hospitals, and clinics.

ROTC in cooperation with Loyola University provides training in military science for commission as a second lieutenant in the U.S. Army or Air Force. Two- and four-year scholarships are available.

Study Abroad Program allows students to go to France for part of their college education.

Weekend and evening series provide credit or non-credit activities such as lectures, seminars, and workshops.

ATHLETIC PROGRAMS

Intercollegiate sports: men's basketball and track; women's basketball and track.

LIBRARY HOLDINGS

The library holds 300,000 bound volumes. Special collections include an Afro-American Collection and the Kellogg Business Collection.

STUDENT LIFE

Special Regulations

Cars permitted in designated areas.

Campus Services

Health, personal counseling, career counseling and placement, tutoring, and remediation.

Campus Activities

Social and cultural activities include theater and musicals.

Students may get involved in the student-run newspaper or yearbook.

Leadership opportunities are found in the Student Government Association (SGA) or the various other departmental, social, and service organizations. Fraternities, sororities, and honor societies are represented on campus.

SUNO is located in suburban New Orleans, a metropolitan city of over one million people. The city is accessible by mass bus, air, and passenger rail transportation and by limited water transportation. New Orleans is known for its annual Mardi Gras celebration and its famous French Quarter, featuring quaint shops and cajun cuisine. Students have access to golf, bayou cruises, fishing, horseback riding, college and major league sports. Points of interest include the Musee Conti Wax Museum of Louisiana's Legends, Riverwalk Market Place, New Orleans Museum of Art, and Preservation Hall featuring the finest in jazz each night.

Housing Availability

None

NOTABLE ALUMNI

Norward J. Brooks, 1955–Seattle City comptroller

William J. Jefferson, 1969–Louisiana's first black congressman

SOUTHERN UNIVERSITY AT SHREVEPORT

HISTORY

Southern University at Shreveport (SUS) is a two-year, state-supported, coed, community institution founded in 1964. SUS is a branch campus of Southern University and A&M University - Baton Rouge and part of the Southern University System, the only public black university system in the nation.

As a branch of a land grant institution, SUS is committed to providing education to students with heterogeneous abilities and varying academic backgrounds. Its purpose is to prepare students for technical and semiprofessional careers. Through its liberal arts transfer program students are prepared to continue their education at a four-year institution.

The college consists of five buildings situated on 101 acres in a small town.

ACCREDITATION

Southern University at Shreveport is accredited by the Southern Association of Colleges and Schools (SACS) to award the Associate of Arts, Associate of Science, and Associate of Applied Science degrees.

COSTS PER YEAR

1991–92 Tuition: $830 (in-state); $1,860 (out-state)

Room and board: None

Special fees: $125

Books: $500

Estimated total cost: $1,455 (in-state); $2,485 (out-state)

FINANCIAL AID

Financial Aid Specific to the School

93% of the student body received financial aid during 1991–92.

Martin L. King Jr. Dr.
Shreveport, LA 71107
Phone: (318) 674-3342

Total Enrollment:
1,067

Level of Selectivity:
Noncompetitive

Short-term low-interest loans from the college and external sources range from $50–$400.

Tuition waivers are available to senior citizens age 65 and over on a space available basis.

Deferred Payment Plan allows students to pay college costs in two or three installments during the semester.

Air Force Reserve and National Guard offer financial assistance for active members who demonstrate financial need.

Financial Aid Deadline

July 15 (priority)

ADMISSION REQUIREMENTS

Open admission. ACT required for counseling and placement.

Entrance Requirements

Graduation from an accredited high school; submit official high school transcript.

GED students must meet basic admission requirements.

Transfer students must submit official transcript of last college attended.

International students must submit official transcripts from all high schools and colleges attended; must provide proof of ability to pay all college costs; and students from non-English-speaking countries must take TOEFL examination.

Early admission allows academically gifted high school students the opportunity to enroll in college full time before completing high school.

Admission Application Deadline

Rolling admissions until August 15th. Rolling admission provides no specific date for notification of admission so applicant is informed as soon as admission decision is made.

Admission Contact

Mr. Clifton Jones, Registrar, Southern University at Shreveport–Bossier-City Campus, Shreveport, LA; (318) 674-3342, ext. 545.

GRADUATION REQUIREMENTS

A minimum of 62 semester hours and completion of core requirements.

Grading System

A-F; I=Incomplete, W=Withdraw, P= Satisfactory (nontraditional courses); AU=Audit

STUDENT BODY PROFILE

Total enrollment (male/female): 288/779

From in-state: 1,056

Full-time undergraduates (male/female): 191/515

Part-time undergraduates (male/female): 87/274

Ethnic/Racial Makeup

African American, 962; Hispanic, 1; Native American, 1; Caucasian, 96; International, 7.

Class of 1995 Profile

Number of applicants: 350

Number accepted: 325

Number enrolled: 300

Median ACT score: 12

Average high school GPA: 2.0

Transfer applicants: 150

Transfers accepted: 125

Transfers enrolled: 125

FACULTY PROFILE

Number of faculty: 73

Student-teacher ratio: 17:1

Full-time faculty: 62

Part-time faculty: 11

Tenured faculty: 24

SCHOOL CALENDAR

1992–93: August–May (semester hours)

Commencement and conferring of degrees:
  May

One summer session.

DEGREES OFFERED AND NUMBER CONFERRED 1991–92:

Accounting: 2

Allied Health: 23

Banking and Finance: n/a

Biological Sciences: 4

Business: 8

Chemistry: 2

Computer Science: 1

Day Care: n/a

Early Childhood Education: 5

Electronics Technician: 2

Legal Assistant: 5

Liberal Arts: n/a

Mathematics Education: 2

Medical Lab Technician: n/a

Mental Health/Retardation: 6

Respiratory Therapy: n/a

Secretarial Science: n/a

Small Business Administration: n/a

Social Sciences: n/a

Sociology: 3

Surgical Technician: n/a

Teacher Aide: n/a

Travel and Tourism: n/a

SPECIAL PROGRAMS

College orientation is offered at no cost to entering students for two days prior to the beginning of classes to acquaint students with the college and to prepare them for college life.

Honors Program offers academically talented students a challenging program of study that includes special classes, seminars, colloquia, cultural activities, and special recognition to motivate participants.

Internships in various disciplines allow students to apply theory to on-the-job training in industry and business.

Off-campus study allows students to take courses at Louisiana State University in Shreveport and Bossier Parish Community College for credit if courses are not offered at SUS.

Part-time degree program allows students to earn an undergraduate degree while attending part time.

Remedial courses are offered to entering students to bring them up to admission standards and to help them adjust for success in college.

Upward Bound provides academic counseling and cultural enrichment programs to high school students in grades 10, 11, and 12 who are disadvantaged and are in pursuit of a college education. Some credit courses may be offered.

ATHLETIC PROGRAMS

Southern University at Shreveport is a member of the National Junior College Athletic Association (NJCAA).

Intercollegiate sports: men's basketball.

LIBRARY HOLDINGS

The library holds 38,000 bound volumes, 14,850 microforms, 376 periodical subscriptions, and 880 audiovisuals.

STUDENT LIFE

Campus Services

Health center, personal and psychological counseling, career planning and placement, remediation, and tutoring.

Campus Activities

Social and cultural activities include chorale. Students may get involved in the student-run newspaper or yearbook.

Leadership opportunities are found in the Student Government Association or the various other organizations, including religious organizations, fraternities, sororities, and honor societies.

Shreveport, known for its production of cotton, is one of the larger cities in Louisiana. It is serviced by rail and bus, with the airport approximately 12 miles away. Points of interest include Spring Street Museum, American Rose Center, and the Louisiana Down Racetrack. The city is enriched by libraries, churches, a planetarium, and concert and theater facilities.

Housing Availability

None

XAVIER UNIVERSITY OF LOUISIANA

HISTORY

Xavier University (XU) is a four-year, private, coed, liberal arts institution affiliated with the Catholic Church. It was founded in 1915 by Blessed Katherine Drexel and the Sisters of the Blessed Sacrament. It is the only predominantly black Catholic-affiliated university in the Western Hemisphere and one of only a few historically black institutions with a college of pharmacy.

Beginning as a college preparatory school, Xavier soon developed a normal school curriculum for teachers and, in 1925, established a college of arts and sciences. The college of pharmacy was conceived in 1927, and in 1932 the graduate school was established. In the years to follow, Xavier continued its growth by adding residence halls for men and women, a student center, and a modern library. Its modern and gothic facilities are situated on 27 acres in the heart of New Orleans.

Xavier was established to provide education and training to blacks. It now encourages a pluralistic environment for the ultimate purpose of helping to create a more just and humane society. It continues to be guided by its mission to provide each student with a liberal and professional education.

In 1987, the institution made international history when Pope John Paul II chose Xavier as the site of his address to the presidents of all Catholic colleges in the United States. Xavier has been featured in *Changing Times* magazine as one of the "little known gems in higher education," in *Kipplinger* as "a better educational value than many schools with national reputations," and in *U.S. News and World Report* as an institution that "bucks the odds" in preparing African Americans to excel in math and science.

ACCREDITATION

Xavier University is accredited by the Southern Association of Colleges and Schools to award the Bachelor of Arts, Bachelor of Science, Master's and Doctor of Pharmacy degrees.

Other Accreditation

American Council on Pharmaceutical Education

7325 Palmetto St.
New Orleans, LA
70125
Phone: (504) 483-7511

Motto:
For a Life that Counts

Total Enrollment:
3,330

Level of Selectivity:
Moderately
competitive

COSTS PER YEAR

1993–94 Tuition: $6,500

Room and Board: $3,800

Special Fees: $150

Books: $500

Estimated Total: $10,950

FINANCIAL AID

1991–92 Institutional Funding

Number of scholarships and grants: 144

Total amount of scholarships and grants : $344,268

Range of scholarships and grants : $600–$2,700

1991–92 Federal and State Funding

Number of scholarships and grants: 1,170

Total amount of scholarships and grants total: $1,501,052

Range of scholarships and grants: $600–$2,400

Number of loans: 1,118

Total amount of loans: $2,345,412

Range of Loans: $200–$1,250

Number of work study: 850

Total amount of work study: $850,000

Range of work study: $500–$1,500

Financial Aid Specific to the School

85% of the students received financial aid during 1992–93.

Army and Air Force ROTC with Tulane University and Navy ROTC with Tulane University and Dillard University offer two-, three-, and four-year scholarships that pay tuition, fees, books, and other expenses, and provide a monthly stipend of $100.

Athletic scholarships are available for students participating in basketball.

Carl D. Perkins Scholarships are awarded to students planning a career in teaching at the elementary and secondary level. Scholarships are based on academic achievement. Students must teach for two years for each year of scholarship assistance.

Cooperative Education Program alternates and combines classroom study with related paid work experience. The program provides academic credit and full-time status during co-op placement.

Dana Teaching Apprentices award up to $5,000 to students interested in teaching at the college or university level. Qualifying students must have completed their sophomore year with at least a 3.3 GPA.

General Motors (GM) Scholarships are awarded to minority men and women based on academic ability. Preference given to dependents of GM employees.

Health Professions Loan (HPL) provides loans for students enrolled in the pharmacy program. Students demonstrating financial need are awarded loans first. Contact College of Pharmacy for more information.

Louis Drexel Morrell Scholarships are awarded to worthy young black men who demonstrate financial need.

Performance scholarships are available for talented students participating in art and music.

Sisters of the Blessed Sacrament Teacher Education Grants award $2,500 grants to incoming freshmen majoring in education; grants are renewable for four years. Students must agree to teach in a Catholic school for the number of years of the grant.

State Student Incentive Grants (SSIG) offer $200–$2,000 to students who are residents of Louisiana and demonstrate financial need. Students must be enrolled full time, have a "C" average, have applied for Pell grant, and have a minimum $500 self-help money.

United Negro College Fund (UNCF) scholarships are awarded to a limited number of students at this school who demonstrate financial need. Some scholarships may be based on location and merit. UNCF scholarships range from $500 to $7,500. Qualifying students must have a 3.0 GPA.

Xavier scholarships are awarded to academically talented students based on high school GPA, SAT or ACT scores, extracurricular involvement, and counselor recommendation.

Xavier University Alternative Loans for Students and Parents provide loans from $1,000–$15,000 to families who find that financial need based on need criteria is unavailable or inadequate. Repayment begins with 45 days of loan at a rate of 9%.

Xavier University Awards range from $100–$500 and are based on varying criteria.

Financial Aid Deadline
April 15 (fall); October 15 (spring)

Financial Aid Contact
Mrs. Mildred Higgins, Director of Financial Aid, Xavier University of Louisiana, New Orleans, LA 70125; (504) 483-7517.

ADMISSION REQUIREMENTS
SAT (700) or ACT (18) required

Entrance Requirements
Graduation from an accredited high school with the following 16 units: 4 English, 1 algebra, 1 geometry, 1 natural science, 1 social science, and 8 academic electives; official high school transcript; minimum "C" average; completed physical; and proof of immunizations against measles, mumps, rubella, and tetanus. A $25 nonrefundable application fee is required.

GED students must meet basic admission requirements.

Transfer students must submit official transcript from each previous college attended; if transferring less than 20 credit hours, SAT or ACT results required; must be in good standing with former institution and eligible to return to it; may transfer credit for courses passed with at least a "C" grade.

International students must satisfy general admission requirements; students from non-English-speaking countries must pass the TOEFL examination.

Concurrent admission allows a limited number of academically gifted high school seniors to take 12 hours of credit. For more information contact admissions office.

Admission Application Deadline
March 1 (fall); December 1 (spring)

Admission Contact
Winston D. Brown, Dean of Admissions, Office of Admissions, Xavier University of Louisiana, 7325 Palmetto St., New Orleans, LA 70125; (504) 486-7411.

GRADUATION REQUIREMENTS
A minimum of 128–166 credit hours and completion of core requirements; minimum 2.0 GPA; 2 semesters completed in residence; senior competency examination, GRE, or NTE passed as appropriate.

Grading System
A-F; I = Incomplete; FE = Failure due to excessive absence

STUDENT BODY PROFILE
Total enrollment (male/female):
  1,022/2,308

In-state students: 2,098

From other regions : 24 states and 4 foreign countries

Full-time undergraduates (male/female):
  914/1,966

Part-time undergraduates (male/female):
  61/109

Graduate students (male/female): 73/207

Ethnic/Racial Makeup
African American, 3,011; Hispanic, 13; Caucasian, 213; International, 93.

Class of 1995 Profile
Number of Applicants: 2,687

Number Accepted: 2,074

Number Enrolled: 744

Median SAT score: 409V, 417M

Median ACT score: 17.2

Average High School GPA: 2.78

Transfer Applicants: 472

Transfers Accepted: 256

Transfers Enrolled: 142

FACULTY PROFILE

Total faculty: 230

Student/teacher ratio: 16:1

Full-time faculty (male/female): 126/83

Part-time faculty: 21

Tenured faculty: 52

Faculty with doctorates or other terminal
  degrees: 53%

SCHOOL CALENDAR

1992–93: August 24–May 3 (semesters)

Commencement and conferring of degrees:
  May

One summer session.

DEGREES OFFERED 1991–1992:

Bachelor of Arts

Art

Art Education

Early Childhood Education

Elementary Education

Engineering (dual)

English

English Education

French

German

History

Mass Communication

Music

Philosophy

Physics

Political Science

Social Science Education

Sociology

Spanish

Special Education

Theology

Bachelor of Music

Music

Music Education

Performance

Bachelor of Science

Accounting

Biochemistry

Biology

Biology Education

Business Administration

Chemistry ACS

Chemistry Education

Chemistry - Pre-professional

Computer Information Systems

Computer Science

Economics

Engineering (dual)

Health and Physical Education

Mathematics

Mathematics Education

Microbiology

Physics

Psychology

Speech Pathology

Speech Pathology Education

Statistics

Master of Arts

Administration and Supervision

Curriculum and Instruction

Guidance and Counseling

Theology

Master of Science

Nurse Anesthesiology

Master of Applied Technology

English Teaching

History Teaching

Mathematics Teaching

Doctorate
Pharmacy

SPECIAL PROGRAMS

Adult or Continuing Education Program is available for nontraditional students returning to school or working full time.

Advanced Placement (AP) grants college credit for postsecondary work completed in high school. Students passing the AP test will receive credit by examination for each course and advanced placement.

Candax-McNair Project is a program of seminars and interactive summer research and mentorship for students interested in study toward the doctoral degree.

College Level Examination Program (CLEP) determines the academic relevance of nontraditional educational experiences such as the military, on-the-job training, or other life experiences, through a series of tests and may grant students college credit for these experiences.

College orientation is offered to entering students at no cost prior to the beginning of classes to acquaint students with the college and to prepare them for college life.

Cooperative Education Program alternates classroom study with related paid work experience. The program provides academic credit and full-time status during co-op placement.

Continuing Education offers a number of courses related primarily to education or pharmacy. Continuing Education Units (CEUs) may be earned for participation.

Drexel Center for Extended Learning provides opportunities for self-paced learning through a broad range of programs. Offerings include telecredit, evening and weekend classes, non-degree and certificate programs, workshops, and seminars.

Center for Environmental Programs provides opportunities for students to address environmental issues and careers through training, education, referrals, and guidance in finding needed resources.

Honors Program offers academically talented students a challenging program of study that includes special classes, seminars, colloquia, cultural activities, and special recognition to motivate participants.

New Orleans Consortium allows cross-registration, shared library facilities, and joint cultural activities with Loyola and Notre Dame Universities.

Part-time degree program allows students to earn an undergraduate degree while attending part time.

Pre-law and pre-health curricular programs expose students to courses considered helpful in the pursuit of professional degrees. In some instances, the programs allow accelerated study and combined degree requirements.

Remedial courses are offered to entering students to bring them up to admission standards and to help them adjust for success in college.

ROTC, in cooperation with other colleges and universities, provides training in military science for commission as a second lieutenant in the U.S. Air Force, Army, and Navy. Two- and four-year scholarships are available.

Study Abroad Program allows students to go to cooperating foreign countries for a specified period of time for part of their college education.

Three/two dual degree program in Business Administration allows students to get two degrees—one in liberal arts from home school and one in business administration from Tulane University—by completing three years at matriculated school and two years at cooperating school.

Three/two dual degree program in engineering allows students to get two degrees—one in liberal arts from home school and one in engineering from Tulane University, University of Maryland, University of New Orleans, Georgia Institute of Technology, University of Wisconsin-Madison, Morgan State University, or Southern University and A&M College—by completing three years at matriculated school and two years at cooperating school.

Xavier-Tulane Accelerated MBA Program allows Xavier students in the fourth year of business, marketing, accounting, or economics degree program to take classes at Tulane toward the MBA. As a result, students may complete the BS and the MBA in five years.

In the Xavier-Tulane Accelerated MSPH Program, enrolled seniors may receive joint credit toward the undergraduate degree and the Master of Public Health degree.

ATHLETIC PROGRAMS

Xavier University ia a member of the National Association of Intercollegiate Athletics.

Intercollegiate sports: men's basketball and tennis; women's basketball.

Athletic Director

Felix James, Director of Athletics, Xavier University, 7325 Palmetto St., New Orleans, LA 70125; (504) 486-7411.

LIBRARY HOLDINGS

The library holds 110,000 bound volumes, 100,000 microforms, 10,000 audiovisual materials, 600 periodical subscriptions, and a substantial audiovisual collection. CD-ROM database searching is available; computers are available for student use. Special collections include the Heartman Manuscripts Collection on slavery, Catholic and black collections, and a civil war collection.

STUDENT LIFE

Special Regulations

All freshmen and some transfer students with less than 30 credits must take the freshman orientation seminar. Student cars permitted on campus without restriction. Curfews are in effect; coed visitation allowed once a month.

Campus Services

Health center; personal and psychological counseling; career counseling and placement; speech, language, and hearing services; religious mass; and other services.

Housing Availability

700 housing spaces; freshman housing guaranteed.

NOTABLE ALUMNI

Brenda August–Decennial specialist, U.S. Department of Commerce

Norman C. Francis–President of Xavier

Alexis Herman, 1969–Democratic National Committee chief of staff; named one of 100 outstanding business women in the United States

George McKenna–Superintendent of schools, Inglewood, California

Maryland

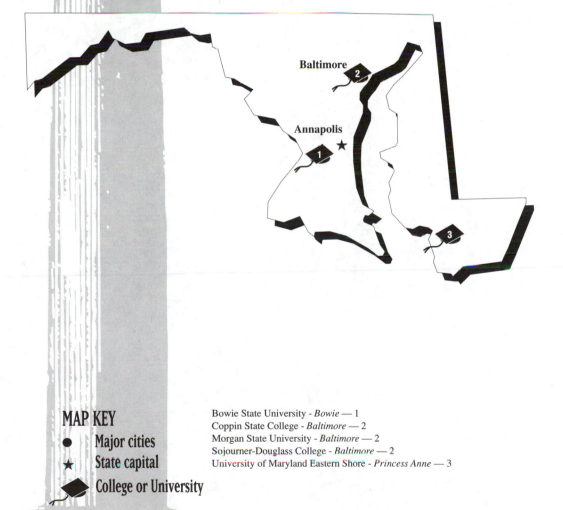

Baltimore

2

Annapolis

★

1

3

MAP KEY

- ● Major cities
- ★ State capital
- ◆ College or University

Bowie State University - *Bowie* — 1
Coppin State College - *Baltimore* — 2
Morgan State University - *Baltimore* — 2
Sojourner-Douglass College - *Baltimore* — 2
University of Maryland Eastern Shore - *Princess Anne* — 3

BOWIE STATE UNIVERSITY

14000 Jericho Pk. Blvd.
Bowie, MD 20715
Phone: (301) 464-3000
Toll-free:
800-464-6510 (in-state)
Fax: (301) 464-9350

Total Enrollment:
4,437

Level of Selectivity:
Slightly competitive

Motto:
Education that works

HISTORY

Bowie State University is a four-year, state-supported, coed, liberal arts university. It was founded in 1865 as the Baltimore Normal School under the auspices of the Baltimore Association for the Moral and Educational Improvement of Colored People. From 1865 to 1988, the school's named changed several times—to Maryland Normal & Industrial School at Bowie in 1914, to Maryland State Teachers College at Bowie in 1935; to Maryland State Teachers College in 1951; to Bowie State College in 1963; and to Bowie State University in 1988.

In 1893, the school changed its focus from a grade and normal school to a teacher-training school for blacks. After receiving state funding status, the school moved from a three-story brick building to a 237-acre tract in Prince George's County, with funds bequeathed for the education of freed negro children by black philanthropist Nelson Wells. Bowie State serves as one of Maryland's four regional comprehensive universities.

ACCREDITATION

Bowie State University is accredited by the Middle States Association of Colleges and Secondary Schools to award the Bachelor of Arts and Bachelor of Science degrees.

Other Accreditation

Adlerian Institute

Council on Social Work Education

Maryland State Department of Education

National Council for the Accreditation of Teacher Education

National League of Nursing

COSTS PER YEAR

1992-93 Tuition: $1,815 (in-state); $3,990 (out-state)

Room and board: $1,085 (room); $845 (board)

Special fees: $350

Books: $500

Estimated total cost: $4,595 in-state; $6,770 out-state

FINANCIAL AID

1991–92 Institutional Funding

Number of scholarships and grants: 95

Total amount of scholarships and grants: $83,328

1991–92 Federal and State Funding

Number of scholarships and grants: 1,881

Total amount of scholarships and grants: $2,065,417

Number of loans: 706

Total amount of loans: $1,503,126

Number of work-study: 532

Total amount of work-study: $598,306

Financial Aid Specific to the School

70% of the student body received financial aid in 1991–92.

Athletic scholarships are available to students participating in intercollegiate sports.

Thurgood Marshall Black Education Fund provides four-year scholarships to entering freshmen who have a high school GPA of 3.0 or better combined with SAT score of 900 or ACT score of 24 or higher. Students must be recommended by high school counselor as an exceptional student. Scholarship pays tuition, fees, room, and board, not to exceed $6,000 annually.

There are approximately 32 alumni or endowed scholarships based mostly on academic achievement.

Tuition waivers are available to BSU employees and their children. College work-study is also available.

Air Force and Army ROTC provides two-year and three-year scholarships that pay tuition, fees, books, and a monthly stipend of $100.

Financial Aid Deadline

April 1 (fall); November 15 (spring)

Financial Aid Contact

Chairperson, Bowie State University Scholarship Committee, Bowie State University, Bowie, Maryland 20715; (301) 464-7110/7111.

ADMISSION REQUIREMENTS

SAT preferred or ACT

Entrance Requirements

A high school diploma with 21 units, including: 4 English; 4 social sciences; 2 sciences (biology and another laboratory science); 3 mathematics; 2 foreign language; and 6 electives. Students must get recommendation of high school officials. A $10 nonrefundable application fee is required.

GED students must meet regular admissions requirements.

Transfer students who enter the university with less than sophomore standing (10-24 transfer credit hours) must submit SAT score results and must take placement examinations in mathematics, reading, and writing to determine whether they have necessary skills or are in need of remediation.

International Students must provide evidence of financial support throughout the period of their studies in the United States. They must submit proof of taking the TOEFL examination. Students are exempt from the TOEFL if the language of instruction in their country is English.

Admission Application Deadline

June 1 (fall); November 1 (spring); early entrance and deferred entrance.

Admissions Contact

Lawrence Walters, Director of Admissions, Bowie State University, 14000 Jericho Pk. Rd., Bowie, Maryland 20715; (301) 464-6563.

GRADUATION REQUIREMENTS

A minimum of 120 credits including completion of the core program with 9 hours of communication skills, 9 hours in humanities, 18 hours in social sciences, 9 hours in science and math, 2 hours in physical education, and one hour in freshman orientation. Must have a cumulative GPA of 2.0 with at least a grade of "C" for major courses, and must pass national standardized exit examinations and departmental comprehensive examinations as appropriate.

Grading System

A-F; I=Incomplete; W=Withdrawal; S=Satisfactory; U=Unsatisfactory, PS=Pass, CR=Credit for Experience.

STUDENT BODY PROFILE

Total enrollment (male/female): 4,437 (1,730/2,707)

From in-state: 3,637

From other regions: 25 states

Full-time undergraduates (male/female): 772/1,207

Part-time undergraduates (male/female): 385/601

Graduate students (male/female): 574/1,472

Ethnic/Racial Makeup

African American, 2,923; Hispanic, 44; Asian, 89; Caucasian, 1,145; International, 89; Other/unclassified, 147.

Class of 1995 Profile

Number of applicants: 1,590

Number accepted: 856

Number Enrolled: 419

Median SAT score: 340V; 385M

Average high school GPA: 2.49

Transfers enrolled: 576

FACULTY PROFILE

Number of faculty: 214

Student-teacher ratio: 20:1

Full-time faculty (male/female): 53/72

Part-time faculty (male/female): 53/36

Faculty with doctorates or other terminal degrees: 44.8%

SCHOOL CALENDAR

1992–93: September 8–May (semesters)

Commencement and conferring of degrees: May

One summer session available.

DEGREES OFFERED 1991–92:

Bachelor of Arts

Art

Communications Media

English

Fine Arts

French

History

International Studies

Journalism

Music

Philosophy & Religion

Political Science

Social Work

Sociology

Bachelor of Science
Accounting

Art Education

Biology/Biology Education

Business Administration

Computer Science

Early Childhood Education

Elementary Education

English Education

French Education

History Education

Mathematics/Mathematics Education

Music Education

Nursing

Physical Education

Psychology Education

Public Administration

Science/Science Education

Social Work

Sociology

Pre-professional
Dentistry

Law

Medicine

Optometry

Pharmacy

Master of Arts
Administrative Management

Counseling Psychology

Human Resource Development

Organizational Communications

Master of Science
Computer Science

Management Information Systems

Nursing

SPECIAL PROGRAMS

Advanced Placement (AP) allows students to get 3 college credits in their junior and senior years of high school for scores of 3 in various subjects on the AP exam.

The College Level Examination Program (CLEP) determines the academic relevance of non-classroom experience and may allow as many as 60 credits for this experience.

Concurrent enrollment is for high school seniors and some juniors who qualify to take up to 6 college credit hours per semester, with a total of 18 semester hours. Acceptance is based upon recommendation of high school counselor and principal.

The Defense Activity for Nontraditional Education Support (DANTES) Program awards college credit for military educational courses and experience evaluated through DANTES.

The honors program offers academically talented students special classes, seminars, cultural activities, and recognition to motivate participants and present them as role models.

Cooperative Education Program combines formal academic study with practical work experience. The program is open to persons who have successfully completed the freshman year with a cumulative GPA of 2.0.

A three/two dual engineering degree program is offered in conjunction with George Washington University. Other pre-professional options are available to students pursuing careers in law, medicine, dentistry, pharmacy, and optometry, through the University of Maryland, George Washington University, Howard University, and University of Baltimore.

The Air Force and Army ROTC programs offer study in military science for a commission in the U.S. Armed Forces. Two- and three-year scholarships are available to qualifying students.

Weekend college opportunities offer programs leading to a Baccalaureate degree for working adult students unable to attend classes during the week.

The remedial program provides remedial courses for entering students to bring them to admissions standards.

ATHLETIC PROGRAMS

Bowie State University is a member of the National Collegiate Athletic Association (NCAA), the National Association of Intercollegiate Athletics (NAIA) and the Central Intercollegiate Athletic Association (CIAA).

Intercollegiate sports: men's baseball, basketball, cross-country, football, and track & field; women's basketball, cross-country, softball, track & field, and volleyball.

Intramural sports: basketball, football, soccer, softball and volleyball.

Athletic Contact

John Organ, Athletic Director, Bowie State University, 14000 Jericho Park Blvd., Bowie, MD 20715; (301) 464-6690.

LIBRARY HOLDINGS

The Thurgood Marshall Library houses 176,000 volumes, 330,000 microforms, 2,500 audiovisual materials, and 1,550 periodical subscriptions. The library has an online catalog system.

STUDENT LIFE

Campus Services

Health, personal counseling, student employment, placement for graduates, and chapel services.

Campus Activities

Social and cultural activities include theater, band, chorale, and dance. Students may get involved in the student newspaper, college radio station, or the college television station.

Leadership opportunities can be found in various student groups on campus, such as the Student Government Association. Greek-letter societies include Alpha Kappa Alpha, Delta Sigma Theta, Sigma Gamma Rho, and Zeta Phi Beta sororities, as well as Alpha Phi Alpha, Kappa Alpha Psi, Omega Psi Phi, and Phi Beta Sigma fraternities.

Bowie State is a suburban campus located approximately 17 miles from Washington, D.C.; 25 miles from Baltimore; and 20 miles from Annapolis, the capital of Maryland. The campus location provides a suburban environment for quiet learning, with close proximity to three cities for an array of social and cultural activities.

Housing Availability

Five resident halls; Goodloe Hall houses 600 students and is reserved for honor students.

Handicapped Services

Wheelchair accessibility; readers and interpreters for the visually and hearing impaired.

NOTABLE ALUMNI

Lawrence Lawson, 1969–Supreme Court judge

Lisa Lee, 1978–Editor, *Essence* magazine

Christa McAuliffe, 1978–Astronaut on
  space shuttle *Challenger*
Beatrice Tignor, 1978–State delegate

COPPIN STATE COLLEGE

2500 W. North Ave.
Baltimore, MD 21216
Phone: (410) 383-3400
Fax: (410) 333-5538

Total Enrollment:
2,816

Level of Selectivity:
Moderately
competitive

HISTORY

Coppin State College (CSC) is a four-year, comprehensive, state-supported, coed, liberal arts university. Coppin's history began in 1900 at Frederick Douglass High School, which was designated by the Baltimore City School Board as a one-year teacher preparatory course for black elementary school teachers. In 1902, the program expanded to a two-year Normal Department within the high school. By 1909, the program was separated administratively from the high school and given its own principal.

In 1926, the teacher program was renamed Fannie Jackson Coppin Normal School in honor of the renowned educator. Several significant changes had taken place by 1938. The curriculum was lengthened to four years; authority was given to grant the bachelor of science degree; and the school's name was changed to Coppin Teacher's College. Coppin struggled for survival for the next twelve years before becoming part of the Maryland higher education system under the State Department of Education. The college's name then changed to Coppin State Teachers College.

Coppin moved to its present location in 1952. In 1963, the Board of Trustees ruled that the college's degree granting authority should no longer be limited to teacher education. The college's name was officially changed to Coppin State College and it conferred its first bachelor of arts degree in 1967. In 1988, Coppin became part of the newly formed University of Maryland System, giving its students access to the libraries and research facilities of fourteen affiliated campuses.

Coppin's mission is to provide quality higher education in the arts and sciences, as well as professional and preprofessional programs. Its focus is on solving the problems, needs, and aspirations of the people of Baltimore's central city.

During the 1970s, Coppin began an aggressive building program, adding research, administrative, classroom, and athletic facilities to the campus. The eleven-building campus has an architectural blend of the 60s, 70s, and 80s. Coppin State College is a traditionally black college.

ACCREDITATION

Coppin State College is accredited by the Middle States Association of Colleges and Secondary Schools to award the Bachelor of Arts, Bachelor of Science, and Master's degrees.

Other Accreditation

Council on Rehabilitation Education

Maryland State Department of Education

National Council for the Accreditation of Teacher Education

National Council on Social Work Education

National League of Nursing

COSTS PER YEAR

1992–93 Tuition: $2,000 (in-state); $3,574 (out-state)

Room and board: $2,270

Special fees: $713

Books: $500

Estimated total cost: $5,483 (in-state); $7,057 (out-state)

FINANCIAL AID

1991–92 Institutional Funding

Number of scholarships and grants: 732

Total amount of scholarships and grants: $2,189,496

Range of scholarships and grants: $955–$1,200

Financial Aid Specific to the School

60% of the student body received financial aid during 1991–92.

Coppin Industrial Cluster prepares students for employment in business, industry, education, and government by working with faculty on curriculum and providing part-time and summer employment or scholarship aid.

Honors scholarships are awarded to honors program participants and include tuition, fees, and book allowance.

Presidential Scholarships are awarded to a limited number of academically gifted entering freshmen and transfer students. The scholarship covers tuition and fees. Contact the Director of the College Honors Program.

Private-Donor Scholarships are awarded to currently enrolled students who have a GPA of 3.0 and to entering students on the basis of academic excellence. Contact Director of the College Honors Program.

Athletic scholarships are available to students participating in intercollegiate sports.

Other Race Grants (ORG) are available to any full-time minority student who demonstrates financial need and is a legal resident of Maryland. Grants range from $200 to $2,200 per semester.

Nursing Student Loans are available to students who are enrolled at least six hours each semester in pursuit of a bachelor's degree in nursing. Student must be a U.S. citizen, demonstrate financial need, and maintain good standing. Loans go up to $2,000 per year. 85% of the loan and interest may be canceled through full-time employment as a nurse.

Deferred payment plan allows students to pay one-third of the total charges at registration and the balance within 45 days of the beginning of the class.

Tuition waivers are available to CSC employees and their children.

Cooperative Education Program alternates or combines classroom study with related paid work experience. The program provides academic credit and full-time status during co-op placement.

Student Emergency Loan Fund (SELF) loans are awarded on the basis of emergency need such as housing, child care, and transportation.

Thurgood Marshall Black Education Fund provides a four-year scholarship at this public black college. Qualifying student must have a high school GPA of 3.0 or better and a SAT score of 1,000 or ACT score of 24 or more. Students must be recommended by high school counselor as exceptional or exemplary in the creative or performing arts. Scholarship pays tuition, fees, room, and board, not to exceed $6,000 annually.

Army ROTC offers two- and four-year scholarships that pay tuition, fees, books, and other expenses, and provide a monthly stipend of $100.

Maryland League for Nursing scholarships are awarded to qualified full-time legal residents of Maryland. Obtain information from Scholarship Board of the Maryland League of Nursing, 1211 Cathedral Street, Baltimore, MD 21201.

Maryland State Scholarships are awarded only to Maryland citizens and include General, State, House of Delegates, Senatorial, Critical Teacher Shortage, and Distinguished Scholarships. Obtain information from high school counselors; Coppin Financial Aid Office; or the State Scholarship Board at 16 Francis St., Jeffery Building, Annapolis, MD 21401.

Financial Aid Deadline

Rolling; April 1 (fall priority); October 15 (spring priority).

Financial Aid Contact

Avon Dennis, Director of Financial Aid, Coppin State College, 2500 W. North Ave., Baltimore, MD 21216; (410) 383-7524.

ADMISSION REQUIREMENTS

SAT (450V; 450M) required

Entrance Requirements

Graduation from an accredited high school with a high school average of at least 80 and completion of the following units: 4 (Carnegie) English, 3 mathematics (algebra I, II, and geometry), 2 science (laboratory-based), 3 social science, 2 foreign language, and 7 electives. Must submit an official transcript. Regular admission projected freshman GPA is 2.5 for 92–93 year. 15% of freshmen whose projected freshman year GPA is less than 2.0 will be accepted. A $15 application fee is required.

Provisional admission is granted to students lacking units with the provision that the courses be completed during the freshman year. Students have three semesters to complete the units (except foreign languages); foreign languages may be completed within four semesters. College-bound students should have a background in oral communication, computers, and fine arts. Students from non-accredited or non-approved high schools will be evaluated on an individual basis.

GED students must meet basic admission requirements.

Transfer students must submit an official transcript of all college work, have a cumulative average of 2.0 from all colleges attended, be in good standing at the last institution attended, and meet the projected freshman average requirement and SAT or ACT requirements. Coppin will accept up to 70 hours of transfer credits from a four-year college. Transfers holding associate's degrees from Maryland community colleges are evaluated by standards set by the Maryland Student Transfer Policy and are given priority.

International Students must submit an official transcript of all secondary and college work, submit results of all national exams such as GCE, pass the TOEFL examination with at least a score of 500, have either a F-1 (Student) Visa or an Exchange Visitor Visa to enter the United States for the purpose of study, and verify that $12,820 is available annually.

Admission Application Deadline

March 15 (priority); July 15 (fall); December 15 (spring)

Admission Contact

Allen Mosley, Director of Admissions, Coppin State College, 2500 W. North Ave., Baltimore, MD 21216; (410) 383-5990.

GRADUATION REQUIREMENTS

A minimum of 120 credit hours and completion of core requirements to include 6 hours of English; 3 hours of mathematics; 4 hours of science; 6 hours of social sciences; and 1 computer course for management, science, or math majors. Students must pass English proficiency exam and take a Standardized Exit Examination which includes the National Teachers Examination, Graduate Record Examination, Graduate Management Admissions Test, Law School College Admissions Test, or the comprehensive nursing examination; the last 30 hours must be in residence at Coppin; all graduates must attend commencement.

Grading System

A–F, PT=Credit by examination, PS= passing grade for developmental programs, CS=non-completion of a developmental program, AU=Audit, I=Incomplete

STUDENT BODY PROFILE

Total enrollment (male/female): 929/1,887

From in-state: 2,591

Other regions: 10 states; 6 foreign countries

Full-time undergraduates (male/female): 551/1,120

Part-time undergraduates (male/female): 284/577

Graduate students (male/female): 94/190

Ethnic/Racial Makeup

African American, 2,563; Hispanic, 29; Asian American, 29; Native American, 29; Caucasian, 84; International, 84.

Class of 1995 Profile

Number of applicants: 1,551

Number accepted: 900

Number enrolled: 414

Median SAT score: 450V; 450M

FACULTY PROFILE

Number of faculty: 153

Student-teacher ratio: 25:1

Full-time faculty: 117

Part-time faculty: 36

Tenured faculty: 88

Faculty with doctorates or other terminal degrees: 60%

SCHOOL CALENDAR

1992–93: August 31–May 16 (semester hours)

Commencement and conferring of degrees: May 16

Two summer sessions.

DEGREES OFFERED 1991–92:

Bachelor of Arts

Criminal Justice

English

Philosophy

Psychology

Social Science

Social Work

Bachelor of Science

Biology

Business Administration/Commerce/ Management

Chemistry

Computer Science

Dentistry (dual degree)

Early Childhood Education

Elementary Education

Engineering (dual degree)

History

Management Sciences

Mathematics

Natural Sciences

Nursing

Pharmacy (dual degree)

Physical Education

Science Education

Secondary Education

Special Education

Master's Degrees

Adult and Continuing Education

Criminal Justice

Rehabilitation Counseling

Special Education

SPECIAL PROGRAMS

Adult/Continuing Education Programs are available for nontraditional students returning to school or working full time.

Advanced Placement (AP) grants college credit for postsecondary work completed in high school. Students passing the AP test will receive credit by examination for each course and advanced placement.

College Level Examination Program (CLEP) determines the academic relevance of nontraditional educational experiences, such as the military, on-the-job training, or other life experiences, through a series of tests and may grant students college credit for these experiences.

Cooperative Education Program alternates and combines classroom study with related paid work experience. The program provides academic credit and full-time status during co-op placement.

Dual degree programs in dentistry, pharmacy, and social work are available with the University of Maryland, Baltimore County. Students receive a liberal arts degree from Coppin and a professional degree from the University of Maryland by completing three years at their home school and the balance at the University of Maryland.

English as a Second Language Program offers courses in English for students whose native language is not English.

Honors program offers academically talented students a challenging program of study that includes special classes, seminars, colloquia, cultural activities, and special recognition to motivate participants.

Internships in various disciplines offer students the opportunity to apply theory and training in actual settings such as business and industry and hospitals and clinics.

Nursing and social work majors may arrange with members of the Cooperative Education Program for off-campus study.

Part-time (day and evening) degree programs allow students to earn undergraduate and graduate degrees while attending part time.

Remedial courses are offered to entering students to bring them up to admission standards and to help them adjust for success in college.

ROTC provides training in military science for commission as a second lieutenant in the U.S. Army. Two- and four-year scholarships are available.

Study Abroad Program allows students to take courses at foreign colleges, institutes, and universities.

Three/two degree program in engineering with the University of Maryland at College Park (UMCP) allows students to get two degrees, one in liberal arts at Coppin and one in engineering at UMCP, by completing three years at matriculated school and two years at cooperating school.

ATHLETIC PROGRAMS

Coppin State College is a member of the National Collegiate Athletic Association (NCAA), Division I, and the Eastern Collegiate Athletic Association (ECAA).

Intercollegiate sports: men's baseball, basketball, tennis, and track; women's basketball, tennis, track, and volleyball.

Intramural sports: basketball, tennis, softball, and volleyball.

Athletic Contact

Ronald DeSouza, Director of Athletics, Coppin State College, Baltimore, MD 21216; (410) 383 5688.

LIBRARY HOLDINGS

The Parlett Longworth Moore Library holds 372,608 volumes, 435,932 microforms, 663 periodical subscriptions, 4,149 audiovisuals. Special collections include the Helen Fuld Collection, the American Civilization Collection, and a juvenile collection.

STUDENT LIFE

Special Regulations

Entering students must take a one-semester orientation course; class attendance is compulsory; graduating students must attend commencement.

Campus Services

Health center, personal and psychological counseling, career counseling and placement, late night escort services, remediation, support for students with disabilities, and off-campus housing.

Campus Activities

Social and cultural activities include theater, chorale, and dance. Students may get involved in the *Coppin Courier* (student-run newspaper) or the *Coppin Eagle* (yearbook). Communication majors or volunteers may work in the student-run radio station or the campus television station.

Leadership opportunities are found in the Student Government Association (SGA) or the more than twenty-five subject clubs or interest groups, which include Coppin Dancers, Coppin Players, Coppin State College Gospel Choir, Inspirational Club, International Studies Club-International Students Association, and National Association of Black Journalists. Greek-letter fraternities include Alpha Phi Alpha, Kappa Alpha Psi, Omega Psi Phi, and Phi Beta Sigma; sororities include Alpha Kappa Alpha, Delta Sigma Theta, Iota Phi Lambda Sorority, Sigma Gamma Rho, and Zeta Phi Beta. Honor societies include Alpha Kappa Mu Honor Society and Pi Gamma Mu Social Sciences Honor Society.

Coppin State is located in the city of Baltimore, population approximately 764,000. Baltimore provides a variety of cultural and social activities including the world renowned Morris A. Mechanic and Lyric Theaters, The Great Blacks in Wax Museum, Hubie Blake National Museum and Cultural Center, and Baltimore Harbor Place. Major league baseball can be enjoyed at the newly completed Oriole Park at Camden Yard (stadium), just twenty minutes from campus by subway. The campus is within an hour of the nation's capital, Washington, D.C., and Howard University. Transportation is available by rail, bus, and air.

Housing Availability

The first on-campus housing opened in 1993, making 300 housing spaces available on a first-come-first-served basis. Students must submit an application and a $150 security deposit by July 31 for fall and December 31 for spring.

Housing Contact

Angel Adams, Director of Housing and Residence, 2500 W. North Ave. Coppin State College, Baltimore, MD 21216; (410) 383-5844.

Handicapped Services

Wheelchair accessibility. Services for the visually and hearing impaired student include readers, note-takers, interpreters, and other special aids if requested six weeks prior to the beginning of class.

NOTABLE ALUMNI

Milton B. Allen, 1938–Retired defense attorney; judge; state attorney for Baltimore, Maryland

St. George Crosse, 1975–Clergyman; attorney; community leader; politician; media personality

Dr. Alice Pinderhughes, 1942–Retired superintendent, Baltimore City Public Schools; chair, Baltimore Urban League Board of Directors

Bishop Robinson, 1973–Secretary for Public Safety and Corrections, State of Maryland

Patricia Schmoke, 1975–Doctor of ophthalmology; wife of Baltimore city (MD) mayor, Kurt Schmoke

MORGAN STATE UNIVERSITY

HISTORY

Morgan State University is a four-year, state-supported, coed university founded in 1867 as Centenary Biblical Institute. The institution's original mission was to prepare black men for Christian ministry. In 1890, the name changed to Morgan College after Dr. Littleton F. Morgan, former chairman of the board of trustees and a generous donor. The school awarded its first baccalaureate degree in 1895.

During its first 50 years Morgan College sustained steady growth marked by the addition of normal and academic curricular offerings, the enrollment of young women, and the establishment of two branch schools. One branch, the Princess Anne Academy (established in 1886) at Olney, Princess Anne, Maryland, exists today as the University of Maryland Eastern Shore. The other, Virginia Collegiate and Industrial Institute at Lynchburg, was destroyed by fire in 1917.

From 1917 to 1919 Morgan College purchased the property on which it is presently located. Morgan became part of the Maryland State College system in 1939, changing its name to Morgan State College. University status was granted to the college in 1975 and its name was changed to Morgan State University.

Located in a northeastern Baltimore city community akin to the suburbs, the institution serves as Maryland's Public Urban University, mandated to provide education to students from urban communities who might not otherwise pursue higher education—part-time adult learners as well as gifted and talented students. This traditionally black college ranks in the top 10% of schools whose students pursue terminal degrees.

The 33-building campus is situated on 122 acres. The School of Engineering, Science Building, and Blount Towers are three new state-of-the-art facilities recently built on campus.

ACCREDITATION

Morgan State University is accredited by the Middle States Association of Colleges and Secondary Schools to

Cold Spring Ln. and
Hillen Rd.
Baltimore, MD 21239
Phone: (410) 319-3000
Toll-free:
800-332-6674
Fax: (410) 319-3107

Total Enrollment:
5,034

Level of Selectivity:
Moderately
competitive

Motto:
A Promise to Keep, a
Legacy to Remember

award the Bachelor of Arts, Bachelor of Science, Master's, and Doctorate degrees.

Other Accreditation

Accreditation Board for Engineering and Technology

American Chemical Society

American Medical Association

Committee on Allied Health Education and Accreditation

Council on Social Work Education

National Association of Schools of Art and Design

National Association of Schools of Music

National Council for Accreditation of Teacher Education

COSTS PER YEAR

1992–1993 Tuition: $2,440 (in-state); $4,880 (out-state)

Room and board: $4,640

Special fees: $600

Books: $600

Estimated total cost: $8,280 (in-state); $10,720 (out-state)

FINANCIAL AID

1990–91 Institutional Funding

Number of scholarships and grants: 1,427

Total amount of scholarships and grants: $2,953,851

1990–1991 Federal and State Funding

Number of scholarships and grants: 2,255

Total amount of scholarships and grants: $4,726,938

Range of scholarships and grants: average $3,562

Number of loans: 1,502

Total amount of loans: $4,258,968

Number of work study: 489

Total amount of work study: $1,143,704

Financial Aid Specific to the School

85% of students received financial aid during 1991–92.

Army ROTC four-year scholarships are available for selected high school seniors who desire to pursue a military career. Scholarships pay for tuition, books, and laboratory fees, and provide a $100 monthly allowance. Three-, two-, and one-year scholarships are awarded on a competitive basis to freshmen, sophomores, and juniors.

Athletic grants are available to selected participants in intercollegiate sports.

Campus Employment Program offers students the opportunity to work on campus. The program is open to international and other students who may not be eligible for work-study programs.

Cooperative Education Program alternates and combines classroom study with related paid work experience. The program provides academic credit and full-time status during co-op placement.

Honor Scholarships are awarded to entering freshmen having high SAT scores and honors high school grade point averages. Awards range up to $8,000. Contact Director of the University Honors Program at Morgan for more information.

Institutional Scholarships are awarded to new and continuing Morgan students and are based on need and academic average. Contact Director of University Honors Program at Morgan for more information.

Maryland State Scholarships are awarded to Maryland residents in several categories that include: General, State, House of Delegates, Senatorial, Critical Teacher Shortage, and Distinguished Scholarships. Contact high school counselors, Morgan's Financial Aid Office, or the State Scholarship Board at 16 Francis St., Jeffery Building, Annapolis, MD 21401.

Other Race Grants are awarded to non-black students who are Maryland residents.

Private scholarships and grants are available to students at different academic levels and in various fields of study.

Thurgood Marshall Black Education Fund provides a four-year scholarship at this public black college. Qualifying students must have a high school GPA of 3.0 or better, and a SAT score of 1,000 or ACT score of 24 or more. Students must be recommended by high school counselor as exceptional or exemplary in the creative or performing arts. Scholarship pays tuition, fees, room, and board, not to exceed $6,000 annually.

Tuition waivers are available to Morgan State employees, spouses, and their children.

Financial Aid Deadline
April 1 (fall priority); November 1 (spring priority); May 1 (summer priority)

Financial Aid Contact
Ernestine Whiting, Director of Financial Aid, Morgan State University, Cold Spring Ln. and Hillen Rd., Baltimore, MD 21239; (410) 444-3170.

ADMISSION REQUIREMENTS
SAT (750) or ACT (17) required.

Entrance Requirements
Graduation from an accredited high school; official high school transcript; "C" high school average; recommendations that assess the ability of the applicant; and completed and returned medical form. Admission of high school students is generally based on seventh semester transcript. A $20 nonrefundable application fee is required.

GED students must pass the GED with a total score of 225 and individual scores of 40 or better.

Transfer students must have a cumulative average of 2.0 from all colleges attended; must be in good standing at the last institution attended; if transferring less than 12 hours, must submit SAT or ACT; and if holding A.A. degree from Maryland community colleges, evaluation is done by standards set by the Maryland Student Transfer Policy.

International students must submit an official transcript from all secondary schools and colleges and results from all national exams such as G.C.E.; must take the TOEFL examination; provide proof of ability to pay first year college cost; have either a F-1 (Student) Visa or an Exchange Visitor Visa to enter the United States for the purpose of study; and submit application package by April 15 for fall and October 15 for spring. A $20 nonrefundable application fee in U.S. dollars paid by money order or certified check is required.

Early admission allows academically gifted high school juniors to take courses for credit before completing high school. Qualifying students must have an 85% high school average and SAT score of 750 or ACT score of 17, plus 3 letters of recommendation. High school must agree to award a diploma after completion of 24 college credits with a 2.0 GPA.

Admission Application Deadline
April 15 (fall priority); December 1 (spring priority); rolling admission provides no specific date for notification of admission so applicant is informed as soon as admission decision is made.

Admission Contact
Chelseia Harold Miller, Director of Admissions, Morgan State University, Baltimore, MD 21239; (410) 444-3000.

GRADUATION REQUIREMENTS
A minimum of 120 credit hours and completion of 46 hours to include the following: 9 language arts, 9 critical thinking skills, 9 humanities and the arts, 9 social and behavioral sciences, 3 African-American studies, 8 biological and physical sciences, 4

mathematics, 3 health and physical education, and 1 hour freshman orientation; minimum 2.0 GPA; last 30 hours completed at Morgan; passing score on both the Speech Proficiency and Writing Proficiency Examinations prior to senior year; completion of the Senior Level Examination.

Grading System

A–F; I=Incomplete; AU=Audit; NR=No grade/no record; PS=Pass; PT=Pass credit for examination; S=Satisfactory completion of course; AW=Administrative withdrawal; W=Official withdrawal

STUDENT BODY PROFILE

Total enrollment (male/female):
2,165/2,869

From in-state: 2,517

Other regions: 42 states; 20 foreign countries

Full-time undergraduates (male/female):
1,627/2,156

Part-time undergraduate (male/female):
265/351

Graduate students (male/female): 273/362

Ethnic/Racial Makeup

African American, 4,631; Caucasian, 201; International, 201.

Class of 1995 Profile

Number of applicants: 4,528

Number accepted: 2,807

Number enrolled: 814

Median SAT score: 396V; 432M

FACULTY PROFILE

Number of faculty: 289

Student-teacher ratio: 18:1

Full-time faculty: 209

Part-time faculty: 80

Tenured faculty: 179

Faculty with doctorate or other terminal degrees: 54%

Ethnic/Racial Makeup

African American, 275; Hispanic, 3; Asian, 3; Native American, 3; International, 6.

SCHOOL CALENDAR

1992–1993: September 1–May 24 (semesters)

Commencement and conferring of degrees: May 23

One summer session.

DEGREES OFFERED 1991–92:

Bachelor of Arts

African-American Studies

African Studies

Economics

English

Fine Arts

French

Geography

History

International Studies

Music

Music Performance

Philosophy

Political Science

Religious Studies

Sociology

Spanish

Speech Communications

Telecommunications

Theater Arts

Bachelor of Science

Accounting

Architecture

Art Education

Biology

Business Administration

Business Education

Chemistry

Chemistry (Pre-Professional)

City and Regional Planning

Civil Engineering

Computer Science

Economics

Electrical Engineering

Elementary Education

Engineering Physics

Food Science/Nutrition

Health Education

Human Ecology

Industrial Engineering

Information Systems

Landscape Architecture

Management

Marketing

Mathematics

Medical Technology

Mental Health

Music Education

Office Administration

Physical Education

Physics

Psychology

Recreation

Science Education

Social Work

Urban Design

Urban Studies

Master of Arts

African American Studies

Economics

English

History

International Studies

Mathematics

Modern Languages

Music Sociology

Master of Business Administration

Accounting

Finance

International Management

Management

Marketing

Master of Science

Educational Administration and
  Supervision

Elementary Education

Middle School Education

Physical Education

Reading

Recreation Administration and Supervision

Science

Transportation

Urban Education

Doctor of Education

Urban Education Leadership

Pre-Professional Programs

Dentistry

Engineering

Law

Medicine

Pharmacy

Graduates That Later Obtain Higher Degrees:
40%

SPECIAL PROGRAMS

Accelerated Study Program allows students to complete their undergraduate degree in a shorter period of time than the traditional four years.

Adult/Continuing Education Programs are available for nontraditional students returning to school or working full time.

Advanced Placement (AP) grants college credit for postsecondary work completed in high school. Students scoring 3 on the AP test will receive credit by examination for each course and advanced placement.

Army ROTC provides training in military science for commission as a second lieutenant in the U.S. Army. Two- and four-year scholarships are available.

College Level Examination Program (CLEP) determines the academic relevance of nontraditional educational experiences, such as the military, on-the-job training, or other life experiences, through a series of tests and may grant students college credit for these experiences.

College orientation is offered for a $100 fee to entering students for one week prior to the beginning of classes to acquaint students with the college and to prepare them for college life; parents may attend.

Cooperative Education Program alternates and combines classroom study with related paid work experience. The program provides academic credit and full-time status during co-op placement.

English as a Second Language Program offers courses in English for students whose native language is not English.

Honors program offers academically talented students a challenging program of study that includes special classes, seminars, colloquia, cultural activities, and special recognition to motivate participants.

Internships in various disciplines offer students the opportunity to apply theory and training in actual settings, such as business and industry and hospitals and clinics.

Off-campus study allows students to take courses at other institutions for credit.

Part-time (day and evening) degree programs allow students to earn undergraduate and graduate degrees while attending part time.

Pre-Law Program prepares students for entry into law schools. Departments having such programs include English and Language Arts, History, Geography, Philosophy and Religious Studies, Political Science and International Studies, Psychology, and Sociology.

Pre-Professional Physical Therapy Program prepares students for admission to a two-year professional program in physical therapy. Morgan's program satisfies the entry requirements for the University of Maryland's program.

Remedial courses are offered to entering students to bring them up to admission standards and to help them adjust for success in college.

ROTC provides training in military science for commission as a second lieutenant in the U.S. Army. Two- and four-year scholarships are available.

Study Abroad Program allows students to take courses at non-American colleges, institutes, and universities.

A three/two dual degree in nursing is offered with the University of Maryland at Baltimore (UMB). Student will attend three years at Morgan and two years at UMB. After the fourth year, students receive a bachelor of science degree and upon completion of the program receive a bachelor of science degree in nursing.

Three/three dual degree in pharmacy with the University of Maryland at Baltimore (UMB) allows students to get two degrees. Student spends three years at Morgan in a pre-professional chemistry track and three years at the University of Maryland School of Pharmacy. The student will earn a bachelor of science in pre-professional chemistry from Morgan after completing a fourth year and a bachelor of science in pharmacy from the University of Maryland School of Pharmacy after completing a sixth year.

Three/four pre-dentistry and pre-medical programs are offered with the University of Maryland Schools of Dentistry and Medicine. Student will attend Morgan for approximately three years and attend UMB at Baltimore for four years. After the successful completion of the first year at UMB, the student will receive a bachelor degree from Morgan. After completion of four years at the University of Maryland, the student will receive either a D.D.S (Doctor of Dental Surgery) or a M.D. (Doctor of Medicine).

ATHLETIC PROGRAMS

Morgan is a member of the National Collegiate Athletic Association (NCAA), Division I; the Eastern College Athletic Conference; and Mid-Eastern Athletic Conference.

Intercollegiate sports: men's basketball, cross-country, football, tennis, track & field, and wrestling; women's basketball, cheerleading, cross-country, tennis, track & field, and volleyball.

Intramural sports: basketball, bowling, cross-country, racquetball, soccer, softball, swimming, table tennis, tennis, track & field, and volleyball.

LIBRARY HOLDINGS

The Soper Library holds 325,044 bound volumes, 2,768 periodicals, 294,748 microforms, 35,095 audiovisual materials, and 106 vertical files. The library is automated, and students have access to five CD-ROM databases. Special collections include the Afro-American History and Life Collection, the Quaker and Slavery Collection, Negro Employment in WWII Collection, and the Mitchell Family Papers. The library is a U.S. Government Documents Depository.

STUDENT LIFE

Special Regulations

Freshmen and transfer students are required to attend orientation; cars must be registered; alcohol prohibited on campus.

Campus Services

Health center, personal and psychological counseling, career counseling and placement, student employment, non-remedial tutoring, remediation, and late night escort.

Campus Activities

Social and cultural activities include theater, band, chorale, dance, and jazz ensemble. Students may get involved in the *Spokesman* (student-run newspaper) or the *Promethean* (yearbook). Communication majors or volunteers may get involved in the student-run radio station, WEAA-FM, or the television production studio.

Leadership opportunities are found in the Student Government Association (SGA) or numerous other clubs and organizations, such as the foreign student groups, honors groups, religious organizations, undergraduate student council, or Evening Student Council. Greek-letter fraternities include Alpha Phi Alpha, Kappa Alpha Psi, Omega Psi Phi, and Phi Beta Sigma; sororities include Alpha Kappa Alpha, Delta Sigma Theta, Sigma Gamma Rho, Zeta Phi Beta, and Iota Phi Lambda. More than 20 honor societies are present on campus including Phi Beta Lambda.

Independent organizations: Alpha Phi Omega, Gama Sigma, Groove Phi Groove Social Fellowship, Iota Phi Theta, National Society of Pershing Angels, National Society of Pershing Rifles, and Tau Alpha Upsilon.

The campus is within an hour of the nation's capital, Washington, D.C., and Howard University. New York City is approximately 3 hours to the north. The city of Baltimore provides a variety of cultural and social activities, including the world renowned Morris A. Mechanic and Lyric Theaters, The Great Blacks in Wax Museum, Hubie Blake National Museum and Cultural Center, and Baltimore Harbor Place. Students enjoy major league baseball at the newly completed Oriole Park at Camden Yards.

Housing Availability

1,500 housing spaces

Handicapped Services

Wheelchair accessibility and services for the speech disabled, and the visually and hearing impaired.

NOTABLE ALUMNI

Wilson W. Goode, 1961–Mayor, Philadelphia, PA

Earl Graves, 1958–Publisher, *Black Enterprise*

Zora Neal Hurston, 1918–Writer

Willie Lanier–Professional football player

Sharon Bell Mathis, 1958–Children's book author

Kweisi Mfume, 1976–U.S. congressman

Parren J.Mitchell, 1950–Former U.S. congressman

SOJOURNER-DOUGLASS COLLEGE

HISTORY

Sojourner-Douglass College (SDC) is a four-year, private, coed college founded in 1972 as Homestead Montebello Center, an off-campus branch of Antioch University in Ohio. In 1980 SDC became independent of Antioch and began operating as a black school. That same year it awarded its first bachelor's degree and adopted its present name.

This neophyte institution was founded by its current president, Dr. Charles W. Simmons, for the purpose of providing higher education to African American adult learners who wanted to pursue higher education. The school, which operates only on weekends and evenings, gives working adults an opportunity to return to school.

Sojourner is unique in that it serves as the college component of an educational complex that includes elementary, middle, and secondary schools. It has a branch school in the Bahamas.

ACCREDITATION

Middle States Association of Colleges and Secondary Schools

COSTS PER YEAR

1992–93 Tuition: $3,305

Room and board: None

Special fees: $125

Books: $500

Estimated total cost: $3,930

FINANCIAL AID

Financial Aid Specific to the School

50% of the student body received financial aid during 1991–92.

Cooperative Education Program combines classroom study with related paid work experience. The program provides academic credit and full-time status during co-op placement.

500 N. Caroline St.
Baltimore, MD 21205
Phone: (410) 276-0306
Fax: (410) 675-1810

Total Enrollment:
441

Level of Selectivity:
Noncompetitive

Motto:
The College Whose
Time Has Come

Deferred Payment Plan allows students to pay college costs in 2 or 3 installments during the semester.

Low-interest, long-term loans are available for students who demonstrate financial need.

Maryland State Scholarships—including general, state, House of Delegates, Senatorial, Critical Teacher Shortage, and Distinguished scholarships—are available to Maryland residents. For more information contact high school counselor, Sojourner's Financial Aid Office, or the State Scholarship Board, 16 Francis T. Jeffery Building, Annapolis, MD 21401.

Tuition waivers (full time or part time) are available to Sojourner employees and their children.

Financial Aid Deadline
August 15 (priority)

Financial Aid Contact
Rita Thompson, Financial Aid Director, Sojourner-Douglass College, 500 N. Caroline St., Baltimore, MD 21205; (301) 276-0306, ext. 48.

ADMISSION REQUIREMENTS
Open admission. SAT or ACT required for placement or counseling.

Entrance Requirements
Graduate from an accredited high school; submit official high school transcript; two recommendations from school officials; personal essay; interview. A $10 nonrefundable application fee required.

GED students must meet basic admission requirements.

Transfer students must submit official transcripts of all college work, minimum 2.0 GPA; personal essay; recommendation from school official; interview; high school transcript recommended.

International students must submit official certificate of high school completion translated into English; take TOEFL examination; and provide proof of ability to pay all college costs.

Admission Application Deadline
Rolling admission provides no specific date for notification of admission so applicant is informed as soon as admission decision is made.

Admission Contact
Clyde Hatcher, Director of Admissions, Sojourner-Douglass College, 500 N. Caroline St., Baltimore, MD 21205; (410) 276-0306, Ext. 42. Fax: (410) 675-1810.

GRADUATION REQUIREMENTS
A minimum of 132 credit hours and completion of core requirements; complete internship; one year in residence.

Grading System
A–F: I=Incomplete; W=Withdrew

STUDENT BODY PROFILE
Total enrollment (male/female): 70/280

From in-state: 347

Full-time undergraduates (male/female): 57/230

Part-time undergraduates (male/female): 13/50

Ethnic/Racial Makeup
African American, 346; Hispanic, 4.

Class of 1995 Profile
Number of applicants: 300

Number accepted: 270

Number enrolled: 189

Transfers enrolled: 63

FACULTY PROFILE
Number of faculty: 51

Student-teacher ratio: 10:1

Full-time faculty: 37

Part-time faculty: 14

Faculty with doctorates or other terminal degrees: 15%

SCHOOL CALENDAR

1992–93: July 25–June 26 (trimester hours)

Commencement & conferring of degrees: June

DEGREES OFFERED 1991–92:

Accounting

Business Administration and Management

Cable Television

Community Organization

Criminal Justice

Early Childhood Education

Economics

Gerontology

Health Care

Hospitality and Tourism

Psychology

Public Administration

Social Work

Sociology

Urban Studies

SPECIAL PROGRAMS

Accelerated Study Program allows students to complete their undergraduate degree in a shorter period of time than the traditional four years.

Adult or Continuing Education Program is available for nontraditional students returning to school or working full time.

Advanced Placement (AP) grants college credit for postsecondary work completed in high school. Students scoring 3 to 5 on the AP test will receive credit by examination for each course and advanced placement.

Cooperative Education Program combines classroom study with related paid work experience. The program provides academic credit and full-time status during co-op placement.

Credit for prior learning allows students to translate up to 42 credit hours for nontraditional educational experiences such as on-the-job training and other life experiences.

Honors Program offers academically talented students a challenging program of study that includes special classes, seminars, colloquia, cultural activities, and special recognition to motivate participants.

Individualized Majors allow students to create their own major program(s) of study.

Internships in various disciplines allow students to apply theory to on-the-job training in industry, business, government, hospitals, and clinics.

Life-Long Learning Module assists students in preparing portfolios for college credit for nontraditional education experiences such as on-the-job training and other life experiences.

Part-time degree program allows students to earn an undergraduate degree part time.

Remedial courses are offered to entering students to bring them up to admission standards and to help them adjust for success in college.

LIBRARY HOLDINGS

The library houses 10,000 bound volumes, 25 periodical subscriptions; 15 computers available for student use in the computer center.

STUDENT LIFE

Campus Services

Health services, personal and psychological counseling, career planning and placement, daycare, and tutoring

Campus Activities

Students may get involved in student-run publications.

Sojourner-Douglass is located in Baltimore, Maryland, home of the world-renowned Morris A. Mechanic and Lyric Theaters, The Great Blacks in Wax Museum, Hubie Blake National Museum and Cultural Center, and Baltimore Harbor Place. Students can enjoy major league baseball at the newly completed Oriole Park at Camden Yards (stadium). The campus is within an hour of Washington, D.C. and Howard University; Morgan State University is located within minutes.

Housing Availability

None

UNIVERSITY OF MARYLAND EASTERN SHORE

HISTORY

The University of Maryland Eastern Shore (UMES) is a four-year, state-supported, coed, liberal arts institution founded in 1886 as Princess Anne College by the Methodist Episcopal Church (MEC) to educate freed blacks. The original site purchased for the school was the historic Onley House, former residence of prominent citizens of Princess Anne. UMES survived a difficult beginning as Princess Anne citizens questioned the fact that freed blacks were allowed to receive an education and that the Onley House was being used for that purpose.

Princess Anne, MD
21853-1299
Phone: (410) 651-2200
Toll-free:
800-232-8637
Fax: (410) 651-2270

Total Enrollment:
2,100

Level of Selectivity:
Slightly competitive
(in-state); Competitive
(out-state)

Having founded the very successful Centenary Biblical Institute (now Morgan State University) in Baltimore in 1867, the Methodist Episcopal Church sought to establish another such school in its Delaware Conference, which included Princess Anne. Since the original purpose of the Centenary Biblical Institute was to educate black men as ministers, tradesmen, and teachers, the conferees thought to establish the new school in Princess Anne for black women. After some discussion and negotiation the school was established as coed.

In 1890, the passage of the Second Morrill Act established that southern states having separate schools for blacks, must provide institutions for them to study agriculture and technology. To that end, UMES became a land grant institution. In 1948, the school was named Maryland State College, a Division of the University of Maryland. On July 1, 1970, Maryland State College became the University of Maryland Eastern Shore, and ten years later UMES became one of the 11 campuses of the newly formed University of Maryland System.

UMES remains committed to providing higher education in the agricultural sciences to blacks. As a land grant institution it has expanded its mission to provide higher education for students from diverse backgrounds, across the state and nation, in a broad range of educational programs.

The campus is situated on 550 acres with Georgian colonial and modern architectural style buildings. Facilities include the Frederick Douglass Library and the Ella Fitzgerald Performing Arts Center, both named for notable African Americans, an art and technology center, a computer center, and a number of laboratories. New facilities include Kiah Hall, Bird Hall, and the Aquaculture Building.

ACCREDITATION

University of Maryland Eastern Shore is accredited by the Middle States Association of Colleges and Secondary Schools (MSACS) to award the Bachelor of Arts, Bachelor of Science, Master's, and Doctorate degrees.

Other Accreditation

Accreditation Board of Engineering and Technology

American Council for Construction Education

American Dietetic Association

American Physical Therapy Association

Career College/Accrediting Commission for Independent College

Committee on Allied Health Education and Accreditation

National Association of Schools of Music

National Council for the Accreditation of Teacher Education

COSTS PER YEAR

1992–93 Tuition: $2,572 (in-state), $5,984 (out-state)

Room and board: $2,080 (room); $1,454 (board)

Special fees: $125

Books: $500

Estimated total cost: $6,731 (in-state); $10,143 (out-state)

FINANCIAL AID

1990–91 Institutional Funding

Number of scholarships and grants: 1,138

Total amount of scholarships and grants: $1,108,891

Range of scholarships and grants: $100–$900

1990–91 Federal and State Funding

Number of scholarships and grants: 1,385

Total amount of scholarships and grants: $1,977,029

Range of scholarships and grants: $250–$4,000

Number of loans: 533

Total amount of loans: $1,849,531

Range of loans: $200–$8,000

Number of work-study: 202

Total amount of work-study: $209,703

Range of work-study: $350–$2,000

Financial Aid Specific to School

90% of the student body received financial aid during 1991–92.

Army ROTC offers two- and four-year scholarships that pay tuition, fee, books, and other expenses as well as provide a monthly stipend of $100. Contact chair of Military Science Department.

Athletic awards are available to students participating in intercollegiate sports.

Cooperative Education Program combines classroom study with related paid work experience. The program provides academic credit and full-time status during co-op placement.

Merit scholarships are awarded by UMES to students based on academic achievement.

Other race scholarships are given to students who are minorities at UMES.

Performance awards are available for students participating in the creative and performing arts.

Thurgood Marshall Black Education Fund provides four-year scholarships that pay tuition, fees, room, and board not to exceed $6,000 to entering freshmen who have high school GPA of 3.0 or higher with SAT score of 900 or ACT score of 24 or more. Students must be recommended by their high school counselor as an exceptional student.

University of Maryland Eastern Shore offers a number of additional grants and assistantships. Contact the Financial Aid Offices for eligibility and amount of awards.

Financial Aid Deadline

April 1

Financial Aid Contact

Dorothy Hardiman, Director of Financial Aid, Financial Aid Office, University of Maryland Eastern Shore, Prince Ann, MD 21853; (410) 651-2200, Ext. 562.

ADMISSION REQUIREMENTS

SAT (750 preferred) or ACT (21 accepted) required

Entrance Requirements

Graduation from an accredited high school and completion of the following units: 4 English, 2 mathematics, 1 science, 3 social sciences, 2 foreign language; submit official high school transcript, minimum "C" average; recommendation from high school counselor, completed medical form by physician. A $25 nonrefundable application fee required (may be waived for some students). Maryland residents given priority by state law.

GED students must meet basic admission requirements and have GED score of 225 and individual scores of 40 or better.

Transfer students submit transcripts from all colleges previously attended; students transferring less than 28 hours must submit official high school transcripts; have a cumulative 2.0 GPA; be in good standing at the last institution attended. Transfers holding A.A. degrees from Maryland community colleges are evaluated by standards set by the Maryland Student Transfer Policy.

International students must submit official certificates of all high school and college work; submit results of the G.C.E.; have a combined SAT score of 800; students from non-English-speaking countries must pass TOEFL examination with a minimum score of 500; have either a F-1 Student Visa or an Exchange Visitor Visa to enter the United States for the purpose of study; must submit financial statement and advanced deposit. A $25 nonrefundable application fee in U.S. dollars is required.

Early admissions allows academically gifted high school students the opportunity to enroll in college for credit before completing high school.

Admission Application Deadline

Rolling admission provides no specific date for notification of admission so applicant is informed as soon as admission decision is made. May 1 (transfer students); April 1 (fall); December 1 (spring)

Admission Contact

Edwina Morse, Director of Admissions, University of Maryland Eastern Shore, Princess Anne, MD 21853; (410) 651-2200, ext. 555; Fax: (410) 651-2270.

GRADUATION REQUIREMENTS

A minimum of 122 credit hours and completion of the core requirements to include 3 credits math, 7 credits science, computer course for some majors; minimum 2.0 GPA; complete 1 credit hour freshman planning; last 30 hours must be in residence at UMES.

Grading System

A-F; I=Incomplete; AU=Audit; NR=No grade/no record; PS=Pass; PT=Pass credit for examination; S=Satisfactory completion of course; AW=Administrative withdrawal; W=Official withdrawal

STUDENT BODY PROFILE

Total enrollment (male/female):
1,029/1,071

From in-state: 1,155

Other regions: 25 states, 15 foreign countries

Full-time undergraduates (male/female):
871/906

Part-time undergraduates: (male/female):
86/90

Graduate students (male/female): 72/75

Ethnic/Racial Makeup

African American, 1,555; Hispanic, 21; Asian, 19; Caucasian, 441; International, 64.

Class of 1995 Profile

Number of applicants: 1,280

Number accepted: 1,203

Number enrolled: 655

Median SAT score: 373V; 348M

Average high school GPA: 2.4

Transfer applicants: 300

Transfers accepted: 150

Transfers enrolled: 170

FACULTY PROFILE

Number of faculty: 157

Student-teacher ratio: 19:1

Full-time faculty: 116

Part-time faculty: 41

Faculty with doctorates or other terminal degrees: 80%

SCHOOL CALENDAR

1992–93: August–May (semester hours)

Commencement and conferring of degrees:
  May

Two summer sessions.

DEGREES OFFERED 1991–1992:

Accounting

Agricultural Education

Agricultural Sciences

Airway Sciences

Art

Art Education

Biology

Business Administration

Business Education

Chemistry

Computer Science

Construction Management Technologies

Criminal Justice

Dietetics

Ecology/Environmental Studies

Economics

Education

Electrical and Electronic Technologies

Electrical Engineering Technology

Elementary Education

Engineering Technology

English

Environmental Sciences

Fashion Merchandising

Food Sciences

Food Services Management

French

General Studies

German

History

Home Economics

Home Economics Education

Hotel and Restaurant Management

Human Ecology

Industrial Arts Education

Liberal Arts/General Education

Marine Estuarine Science

Mathematics

Medical Laboratory Technology

Medical Technology

Music Education

Physical Education

Physical Therapy

Physics

Poultry Management Technology

Psychology

Radiologic Technology

Rehabilitation Therapy

Social Science

Social Work

Sociology

Spanish

Special Education

Pre-professional

Community Planning

Dental Hygiene

Dentistry

Engineering

Law

Medical Technology

Medicine

Nursing

Pharmacy

Physical Therapy

Radiologic Technology

Social Work

Veterinary Medicine

Master's of Education

Applied Computer Science

Counseling

Guidance

Special Education

Master of Science

Agriculture Education

Agriculture Extension

Estuarine Environmental Science

Doctorate

Estuarine Environmental Science

SPECIAL PROGRAMS

Accelerated Study Program allows students to complete their undergraduate degree in a shorter period of time than the traditional four years.

Adult/Continuing Education Programs are available for nontraditional students returning to school or working full time.

Advanced Placement (AP) grants college credit for postsecondary work completed in high school. Students passing the AP test will receive credit by examination for each course and advanced placement.

Army ROTC provides training in military science for commission as a second lieutenant in the United States Army. Two- and four-year scholarships are available.

College Level Examination Program (CLEP) determines the academic relevance of nontraditional educational experiences such as the military, on-the-job training or other life experiences through a series of test, and may grant students college credit for these experiences.

Cooperative Education Program combines classroom study with related paid work experience. The program provides academic credit and full time status during co-op placement.

Cooperative Engineering Program in aerospace, agricultural, chemical, civil, electrical, fire protection, materials, mechanical, and nuclear engineering with the University of Maryland at College Park (UMCP). Students complete two years at UMES, meeting all prerequisites, before transferring to UMCP to complete program.

Dual degree program in sociology and social work in cooperation with Salisbury State University.

English as a Second Language Program offers courses in English for students whose native language is not English.

Honors Program offers academically talented students a challenging program of study that includes special classes, seminars, colloquia, cultural activities, and special recognition to motivate participants. Students must have a "B" average, provide three letters of recommendation, and participate in a special interview with Honors Committee.

Internships in various disciplines offer students the opportunity to apply theory and training in actual settings such as business/industry and hospitals/clinics.

Off-campus study for majors in Nursing, Social Work and Physical Therapy with the six members of the Cooperative Education Consortium.

Part-time (day and evening) Degree Programs allow students to earn undergraduate and graduate degrees on a part-time basis.

Remedial courses are offered to entering students to bring them up to admission standards and to help them adjust for success in college.

Study Abroad Program allows students to go to a foreign country for part of their college education.

ATHLETIC PROGRAMS

University of Maryland Eastern Shore is a member of the National Collegiate Athletic Association, Division I, and the Mid-Eastern Athletic Conference.

Intercollegiate sports: men's baseball, basketball, cross-country, track & field; women's basketball, soccer, softball, track and field and volleyball.

Athletic Contact

Dr. Hallie E. Gregory, Director of Athletics, University of Maryland Eastern Shore, Princess Anne, MD 21853-1299; (410) 651-2200, Ext. 606.

LIBRARY HOLDINGS

The Frederick Douglass Library houses 130,500 volumes, 145,000 microforms, 1,261 periodical subscriptions, 23,900 government documents, and 1,575 audiovisuals. The library is fully automated and online bibliographic database searching is available.

STUDENT LIFE

Special Regulations

Freshman orientation mandated; cars allowed with permits.

Campus Services

Health center, personal and psychological counseling, career counseling and placement, student employment services, remediation and tutoring.

Campus Activities

Social and cultural activities include theater and chorale. Students may get involved in the student-run newspaper and yearbook. Communication majors or volunteers can work on the student-run radio station.

Leadership opportunities can be found in the Student Government Association (SGA) or foreign-student groups, undergraduate student council, Caribbean International Club, Centennial Club, Collegiate Chapter of Future Farmers of America, Engineering Technology Society, Eta Rho Mu, Groove Phi Groove Social Fellowship, Human Ecology Club, Miaka Club, NAACP, National Student Business League, Panhellenic Council, Students for Progressive Action, Accounting Club, Student Construction Association, Wicomico Hall Men's Association. Greek-letter fraternities include Alpha Phi Alpha, Kappa Alpha Psi, Omega Psi Phi, and Phi Beta Sigma; sororities include Alpha Kappa Alpha, Delta Sigma Theta, and Zeta Phi Beta. Honor societies are also represented on campus.

Located on the eastern shore of the Chesapeake Bay in the small town of Princess Anne, UMES is only one hour from Maryland's famed Ocean City resort. The campus is 13 miles south of Salisbury, Maryland for shopping and recreation. The vast cultural offerings in Baltimore, Maryland, and Washington, D.C, can each be reached in 3 hours. The airport is 12 miles away.

Housing Availability

1,000 housing spaces; freshman-only housing.

Handicapped Services

Wheelchair accessibility

NOTABLE ALUMNI

Dr. Warren W. Morgan–President, Paul Quinn College, Waco, Texas

General Emmett H. Paige, Jr., 1972–Army's first black general

Arthur L. Shell, 1968–First black to coach
a modern National Football League team;
member, NFL Hall of Fame

Massachusetts

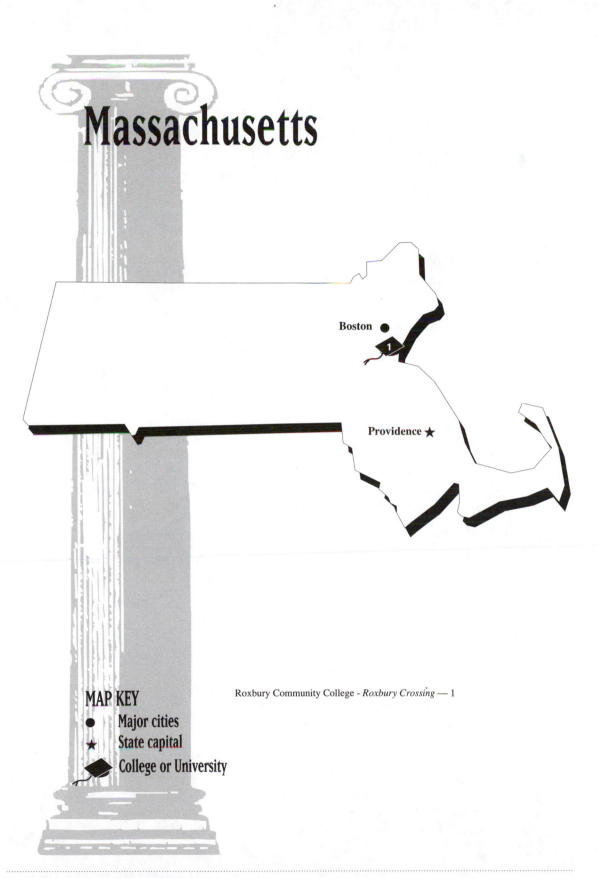

Boston ●

Providence ★

Roxbury Community College - *Roxbury Crossing* — 1

MAP KEY
● Major cities
★ State capital
◆ College or University

ROXBURY COMMUNITY COLLEGE

1234 Columbus Ave.
Roxbury Crossing,
MA 02120-3400
Phone: (617) 427-0060

Total Enrollment:
1,800

Level of Selectivity:
Noncompetitive

HISTORY

Roxbury Community College (RCC) is a two-year, state-supported, coed, liberal arts institution that has the unique distinction of being the only college in New England to serve a primarily minority-based population. RCC has two campuses: the Boston Business School Campus and the Roxbury Crossing Campus.

The Boston Business School (BBS), founded in 1914, originally served as a technical training school for the city of Boston. In 1984, the school merged with RCC. It now offers certificate programs and associate degrees in accounting and office technology. The BBS campus is located on Commonwealth Street, a few blocks from Boston University.

The Roxbury Crossing Campus (RCC) was founded in 1973. After being housed in temporary facilities for almost 15 years, the main campus moved to its present location on Columbus Avenue. Facilities include modern labs, a greenhouse, a media complex, and music studios. RCC offers programs in liberal arts, business administration, health sciences, human service, and the technologies.

The college's mission is to serve the higher education needs of minorities who have been historically deprived of access to higher education and who are newcomers to the Boston area and the United States. Its goal is to adequately prepare its students for a four-year college or for the work place. RCC serves Boston and adjacent cities, concentrating on the inner-city neighborhoods of Roxbury, Mattapan, Dorchester, Jamaica Plain, the South End, Mission Hill, and Chinatown.

RCC's two campuses are located on 12 acres. Facilities include classroom buildings, specialized laboratories, a learning resource center, a learning center, a day-care center, a 500-seat theater, and a music, dance, and art studio.

ACCREDITATION

Roxbury Community College is accredited by the New England Association of Schools and Colleges (NEASC) to award the Associate of Arts and Associate of Science degrees. Certificates are also awarded.

COSTS PER YEAR

1992–93 Tuition: $1,150 (in-state); $4,870 (out-state)

Room and board: none available

Special fees: $430

Books: $500

Estimated total cost: $2,080 (in-state); $5,800 (out-state)

FINANCIAL AID

Financial Aid Specific to the School

85% of the student body received financial during 1991–92.

Graduation Scholarships are awarded to five outstanding students who have completed two-thirds or more of their course work at RCC. Selection is made based on academic achievement and service to the college. Scholarships range from $250–$1,000.

Roxbury Community College awards academic merit scholarships to outstanding students each semester.

Northeastern University offers full-tuition scholarships to students living in Boston Public Housing Units. Other subsidized housing not included. March 1 deadline.

Wentworth Presidents Scholarships are awarded to first-time applicants of Wentworth Institute of Technology. Scholarships are based on academic achievement and participation in extracurricular activities.

Veterans Benefits may be available for anyone who has served in the armed forces. Contact the Registrar's office for more information.

Massachusetts Tuition Waiver Program is a state-supported program through which Roxbury College can waive from two-thirds to the entire cost of the tuition. Only day-school students and Boston Business School students are eligible.

Massachusetts State Scholarships are awarded to needy students who are residents of the state. Priority filing date is May, and the Financial Aid Form (FAF) is used to file an application.

Chancellor's Scholarship for Excellence awards 30 scholarships to Massachusetts residents planning to enter RCC in the fall.

Colgan Fund provides renewable loans averaging $800 to students who are Massachusetts residents attending undergraduate two- and four-year institutions. Colgan loans are repayable when student graduates, at which time interest starts to accrue. April 30 is the fall deadline; October 31 is the spring deadline.

Edwards Scholarships are available for students who have lived in Boston since their junior year in high school and who are part of a two-year associate in arts or four-year undergraduate program.

Financial Aid Deadline

Rolling.

Financial Aid Contact

Angel Urena, Acting Director, Financial Aid Office, Room #201, Administration Building, Roxbury Community College, Roxbury Crossing, MA 02120; (617) 427-0060.

ADMISSION REQUIREMENTS

Open admission.

Entrance Requirements

Graduate from high school, submit official high school transcript, have a minimum 2.0 GPA, provide proof of immunization, and take placement test(s). A $10 application fee for in-state students and a $35 application fee for out-state students is required.

Transfer students must submit official transcripts of all college work; a minimum of "C" (2.0) is required for transfer credit consideration; "P" grades may be accepted as general elective credits; a maximum of 30 transfer credits accepted; courses taken 10 years prior to enrollment at RCC will not be accepted.

International students must have graduated from an equivalent high school program, submit official certified translated transcripts of all high school and college work, and students from non-English-speaking countries must take TOEFL examination. All international students must submit an affidavit of support from a sponsor, a bank letter verifying the sponsor's assets, a letter of verification of sponsor's employment, one semester's tuition, and funds of $10,000 per year if the applicant is self-supporting. A $35 nonrefundable application fee required.

Students from English-speaking commonwealth countries or British system must submit the following: General Certificate of Education Ordinary Level, School Certificate, Royal Society of Arts Stage 2 or 3, London Chamber of Commerce Stage 2 or 3, The Caribbean School Certificate, and Teachers Certificate.

Admission Application Deadline

August 15 (fall); January 15 (spring): rolling admission provides no specific date for notification of admission so applicant is informed as soon as admission decision is made.

Admissions Contact

N. Michael Rice, Director of Admissions, Roxbury Community College, Roxbury Crossing, MA 02120; (617) 427-0060.

GRADUATION REQUIREMENTS

A minimum of 60–69 credit hours and completion of the core requirements to include the following hours: 6 English, 3 mathematics, 8 science (2 labs), 9 social science, and 9 humanities (3 literature); minimum 2.0 GPA; and completion of 30 credit hours at RCC.

Grading System

A-F; S=Satisfactory; U=Unsatisfactory; IP=In Progress; W=Official Withdrawal, WA=Administrative Withdrawal; P=Pass No Credit Course; NP=Did Not Pass No Credit Course.

FACULTY PROFILE

Number of faculty: 101

Student-teacher ratio: 25:1

Full-time faculty: 71

Part-time faculty: 30

Faculty with doctorates or other terminal degrees: 25%

SCHOOL CALENDAR

1994–95 September 1–May 18 (semester hours)

Commencement and conferring of degrees: June 2

DEGREES OFFERED 1991–92:

Associate of Arts Degree

Biological Sciences

Business Administration

English

Liberal Arts

Mathematics

Physical Sciences

Pre-nursing

Social Science

Associate in Science Degree

Accounting

Business Management

Computer Programming

Early Childhood Education

Engineering and Architectural Design/Computer-Assisted Drafting

Executive Secretary/Shorthand

Executive Secretary/Word Processing

Legal Secretary

Medical Secretary

Nursing

Retail Management

Certificates

Bookkeeping

Computer Information Systems/Micro Computer Application

Engineering and Architectural Design and Computer Assisted Drafting

Office Technology Training

Word Processing

SPECIAL PROGRAMS

College Survival Seminar is a 1.5 credit course that provides college readiness skills to help students succeed in college.

Cooperative Education Program and internships allow students to gain work experience related to their academic major.

Continuing Education (CE) allows adults to continue or resume their educational interest on a full- or part-time basis in a variety of credit and non-credit courses. These activities include short courses, seminars, conferences, and workshops.

Dual degree program in social work is available with Boston University (BU) Metropolitan College. Students earn an Associate of Arts degree in liberal arts with concentration in social sciences at RCC and transfer to earn a Bachelor of Science degree in social work at BU.

Dual degree program in early childhood education and social work is offered with Wheelock College. Students earn an Associate of Science degree in early childhood education or an Associate of Arts degree in liberal arts with concentration in social sciences at RCC. Students then transfer to earn a Bachelor of Science degree in early childhood education or social work at wheelock.

English as a Second Language (ESL) provides non-native English and foreign speaking students with English reading, writing, and conversation skills.

Historically Black Colleges and Universities (HBCU) Dual Admission Program facilitates the smooth transfer of RCC graduates in transfer programs to appropriate upper level programs at HBCUs. RCC students must complete their associate's degree with a minimum of 60 credit hours, a 2.0 GPA (over 4.0), and completion of appropriate program requirements. For more information contact RCC's Counseling and Placement Services (CAPS), Room #311, Student Center.

Off-campus study in gerontology at the University of Massachusetts is available to RCC students.

One-year certificate programs offer technical training in specific occupations.

Remedial courses are offered to entering students to bring them up to admission standards and to help them adjust for success in college.

Tuition waiver are available for senior citizens 60 years of age or older on a space available basis. Does not apply to non-credit courses and special programs.

ATHLETIC PROGRAMS

Roxbury Community College is a member of the National Junior College Athletic Association (NJCAA).

Intercollegiate sports: men's basketball, soccer, and track & field; women's basketball and track & field.

Intramural sports: men's basketball, soccer, and volleyball; women's basketball and volleyball.

LIBRARY HOLDINGS

Learning Resource Center houses the library which holds books, periodicals, audiovisuals, and CD-ROM bibliographic indexes. Computers are available for student use in the center.

STUDENT LIFE

Special Regulations

Automobiles must be registered; hazing illegal; smoking allowed in designated areas.

Campus Services

Health, personal counseling (psychological counseling provided by COPE and

Father, Inc.), career counseling and placement, child care, tutoring, and ministry.

Campus Activities

Social and cultural activities include theater, arts, lectures, chorale, and dances. Other activities include karate, tennis, and cheerleading. Students may work on *Unity Speaks* (student-run newspaper). Each year students look forward to International Student Week—a celebration of diversity.

Leadership opportunities are found in the Student Government Association (SGA) or other organizations such as the African, Asian, Caribbean, Hispanic, or Haitian clubs. The Women's Club discusses issues of concern to women at RCC. The Theater Arts Guild is open to students interested in acting. Special interest groups include the Newswriters Club and the Science Club. Alpha Xi Phi Fraternal Organization and Phi Theta Kappa Honor Society are represented on campus.

Located in the historical city of Boston, Roxbury Community College students have a rich variety of places to see. The city is served by mass air, bus, and rail. Students can get around the city on the MBTA local transportation system. Across the Charles River is Cambridge where Harvard and Massachusetts Institute of Technology (MIT) are located. Freedom Trail walking tours may be taken from the Boston City Hall. Other points of interest include the Boston Public Library, Boston Tea Party ship and museum, Bunker Hill Monument, Christian Science Publishing Society, John Hancock Observatory, New England Aquarium, Paul Revere's house, and the USS Constitution. Plymouth is 45 miles away. Nantucket Island is around 80 miles away and can be reached by air or boat. The famous Cape Cod is 100 miles to the southeast.

Housing Availability

None

Michigan

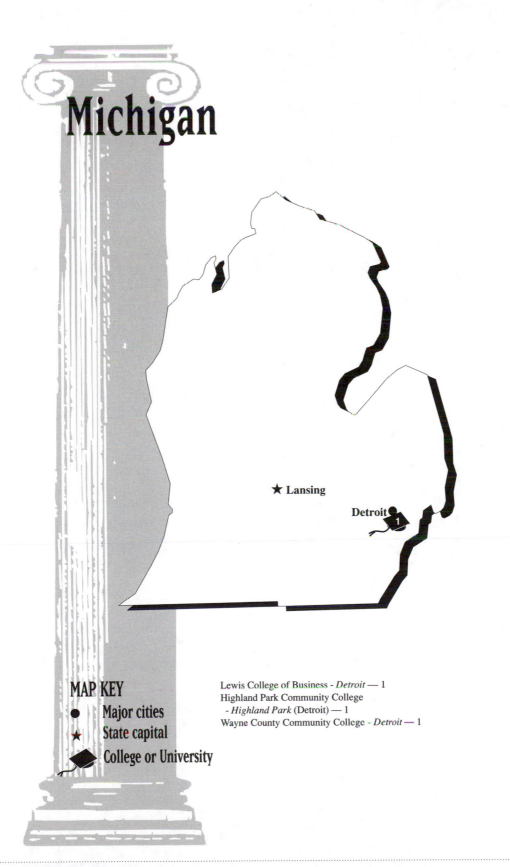

★ Lansing

Detroit ● [1]

MAP KEY

● Major cities
★ State capital
🎓 College or University

Lewis College of Business - *Detroit* — 1
Highland Park Community College
 - *Highland Park* (Detroit) — 1
Wayne County Community College - *Detroit* — 1

HIGHLAND PARK COMMUNITY COLLEGE

Glendale at Third
Avenue
Highland Park, MI
48203
Phone: (313) 252-0475
Fax: (313) 252-0397

Total Enrollment:
2,335

Level of Selectivity:
Noncompetitive
(nursing—slightly
competitive)

HISTORY

Highland Park Community College (HPCC) is a two-year, state-supported, coed liberal arts college founded in 1918. Top rated among community colleges in Michigan and second only to one older institution, Highland Park was established as a junior college. Originally, the college mainly served Highland Park residents, but since World War II, the college has served students from the Detroit metropolitan area, from out-of-state, and from foreign countries.

In 1962, it became a community college, reflecting broader interests and keeping up with the developments in post high school education. Highland Park Community College's mission is to maintain a positive environment in which students develop sound values and judgement, and gather knowledge to effectively take their places in society.

Located on three acres, the college building houses the cafeteria, bookstore, library, and media center.

ACCREDITATION
Highland Park Community College is accredited by the North Central Association of Colleges and Schools to award the Associate of Arts, Associate of Applied Arts and Science, and the Associate of General Studies degrees.

Other Accreditation
Committee on Allied Health Education and Accreditation

COSTS PER YEAR
1992–93 Tuition: $1,270 (in-state); $1,720 (out-state)

Room and board: none

Special fees: $125

Books: $225

Estimated total cost: $1,620 (in-state); $2,070 (out-state)

Financial Aid Specific to the School
90% of the student body received financial aid during 1991–92.

Highland Park Optimist Club offers six scholarships. Three of the scholarships are for residents of Highland Park with a 3.0 or better GPA and relative financial need. The other three scholarships are for Highland Park residents with a 3.0 or better GPA. Stipends cover most college costs.

Highland Park Resident Academic Scholarship Program grants full tuition scholarship to those students who are residents of the state and maintain a 4.0 GPA.

College work-aid is available to students who do not qualify for college work-study.

Deferred payments allow students owing more than $100 to pay one-half of cost at registration and the other half a month later.

Michigan Adult Part-time Grant provides assistance for up to $600 for needy adults enrolled on a part-time basis.

Michigan Educational Opportunity Grant program provides grant assistance up to $1,000 to needy undergraduates enrolled for at least half time.

The Board of Education awards four tuition scholarships to first year students who live in the city of Detroit or the state of Michigan. Qualifying students must be in the upper fourth of their class and demonstrate financial need. Contact high school principal for more information. August 15th deadline date.

Vocational Rehabilitation provides financial assistance to students who have a disability that has interfered with job performance. Contact Vocational Rehabilitation Department of Education, Lansing, MI 48904.

Financial Aid Deadline
Continuous. May 1 (priority)

Financial Aid Contact
Director of Financial Aid, Highland Park Community College, Highland Park, MI 48203; (313) 252-0475.

ADMISSION REQUIREMENTS
Open admission.

Entrance Requirements
Submit high school transcript; personal interviews requested for nursing program. A $15 nonrefundable application fee required.

GED students must meet basic admission requirements.

Transfer students must submit official transcript of all previous college work.

International students from countries not speaking English must take the TOEFL examination; TOEFL examination recommended for students from English speaking countries; provide proof of ability to pay all college costs. A complete certified English translation of the student's record showing the courses taken, grades earned, brief description of the course content, and standing in class is needed.

Early admission allows academically gifted high school students the opportunity to enroll for college credits before completing high school.

Admission Application Deadline

Rolling admission provides no specific date for notification of admission decision so applicant is informed as soon as admission decision is made.

Admission Contact

Ms. Ameenah Omar, Director of Admissions and Registrar, Highland Park Community College, Glendale at Third Avenue, Highland Park, MI 48203; (313) 252-0475, ext. 238; Fax (313) 252-0397.

GRADUATION REQUIREMENTS

A minimum of 60 semester hours and completion of the core requirements to include 8 hours of mathematics, 8 hours of science, 1 computer course for some majors; 2.0 GPA. Transfer students must complete a minimum of 15 hours at Highland Park Community College with an honor point average of 2.0 or more.

Grading System

A–F, E=No Credit, W=Official Withdrawal, I=Incomplete, AW=Administrative Withdrawal.

STUDENT BODY PROFILE

Total enrollment (male/female): 700/1,633

From in-state: 2,286

Full-time undergraduates (male/female): 420/980

Part-time undergraduates (male/female): 280/653

Ethnic/Racial Makeup

African American, 2,100; Hispanic, 23; Asian, 47; Native American, 23; International, 47; Other/unclassified, 93.

FACULTY PROFILE

Number of faculty: 167

Student-teacher ratio: 21:1

Full-time faculty: 124

Part-time faculty: 43

SCHOOL CALENDAR

1992–93: August–May (semester hours)

One summer session.

DEGREES OFFERED 1991–92:

Associate of Arts

Liberal Arts (transfer program)

Associate of Arts and Science

Automotive Technology

Business Technology

Drafting Technology

Electronic/Robotics Technology

Surgical Technology

Associate of Science

Computer Information Technology

Liberal Arts (transfer program)

Medical Assistant

Medical Lab Technician

Nursing

Secretarial

Word Processing

SPECIAL PROGRAMS

Adult or Continuing Education Program is available for nontraditional students returning to school or working full time.

College Level Examination Program (CLEP) determines the academic relevance of nontraditional educational experiences, such as the military, on-the-job training, or other life experiences, through a series of tests and may grant students college credit for these experiences.

College orientation is offered to entering students at no cost prior to the beginning of classes to acquaint students with the college and to prepare them for college life.

Evening/Weekend College Program offers a wide range of courses for students who want to pursue their education.

The honors program offers academically talented students a challenging program of study which includes special classes, seminars, colloquia, cultural activities, and special recognition to motivate participants.

The part-time degree program allows students to earn an undergraduate degree while attending part time.

Remedial courses are offered to entering students to bring them up to admission standards and to help them adjust for success in college.

A two/two automotive, drafting and electronics program is offered with Wayne State University, Western University, University of Dearborn, Eastern Michigan University, University of Detroit, and Detroit College of Business. Students complete two years at Highland Park and receive an Associate's Degree, then transfer to a cooperating school to complete two years and receive a Bachelor of Engineering Technology degree.

A two-year liberal arts transfer program prepares students for transfer to a four-year program.

ATHLETIC PROGRAMS

Highland Park is a member of the National Junior College Athletic Association (NJCAA).

Intercollegiate sports: men's basketball, baseball, cross-country, and bowling (limited schedule); women's basketball.

Intramural sports: basketball, bowling, softball, track, and tennis.

LIBRARY HOLDINGS

The library holds 40,000 volumes, 155 periodical subscriptions, 2,687 audiovisuals; 75 computers are available for student use in the computer center.

STUDENT LIFE

Special Regulations

No smoking in college buildings.

Campus Services

Personal and psychological counseling, career counseling and placement, remediation, student employment, and tutoring.

Campus Activities

Social and cultural activities include theater and *The AMKA* (student newspaper).

Leadership opportunities are found in the Student Government Association and special interest groups. Phi Theta Kappa honor society is represented on campus.

Located in the city of Detroit, Highland Park students have access to a variety of activities such as shopping, dining, concerts, and horseback riding. Points of interest include the Henry Ford Museum, fifteen miles from the campus; the Motown Historical Museum, within five miles; the Detroit Historical Museum and the Detroit Institute of Arts, both within ten miles; and the GM assembly plant, within ten miles. Windsor, Ontario, Canada is between 15 and 20 miles to the east, and Indiana is 60 miles to the south. The state of Michigan is surrounded by four great lakes: Erie, Huron, Michigan, and Superior.

LEWIS COLLEGE OF BUSINESS

17370 Meyers Rd.
Detroit, MI 48235
Phone: (313) 862-6300
Fax: (313) 862-1027

Total Enrollment:
346

Level of Selectivity:
Noncompetitive

HISTORY

Lewis College of Business (LCB), Detroit's first black-owned business school, is a two-year, private, coed business college. LCB began at the onset of the great depression in 1928, when Dr. Violet T. Lewis, an African American woman, began the school in Indianapolis, Indiana. At that time, the segregation laws did not allow African American students the opportunity for postsecondary education.

In 1938, Dr. Lewis was contacted by the Detroit Chamber of Commerce to consider opening a business school in Detroit, Michigan. Finding no vocational schools in Detroit that would accept African American students, she opened a branch of the school in 1939. In 1978, the Indianapolis branch merged with the Detroit branch to form the present school. The Lewis College of Business has since stood firm in the premier objective of providing higher education to African Americans.

Recognizing the institution's historical significance, the Michigan Historical Commission erected a Michigan historical marker in 1987 at the first permanent site of the college in Detroit. That same year, the U.S. Secretary of Education designated Lewis College of Business as an Historically Black College and University (HBCU); LCB is one of four HBCU's in the northeast section of the country.

LCB offers both academic and technical programs that provide entry into the job market or transfer privileges to a senior college. Lewis is committed to serving students in business related professions and meeting the academic, cultural, and vocational needs of students from a wide range of academic preparations and background.

ACCREDITATION

Lewis College of Business is accredited by the North Central Association of Colleges and Schools (NCACS) to award the Associate of Art degree. The school also awards certificates in typing and stenography.

Other Accreditation

Michigan Department of Education

COSTS PER YEAR

1992–93 Tuition: $2,250

Room and board: none

Special fees: $125

Books: $500

Estimated total cost: $2,875

FINANCIAL AID

Financial Aid Specific to the School

87% of the student body received financial aid during 1991–92.

LCB offers several scholarships based on academic merit, financial need, and interests.

Low-interest, long-term loans are available to students.

Cooperative Education Program alternates classroom study with related paid work experience. The program provides academic credit and full-time status during co-op placement.

Financial Aid Deadline

July 15 (priority)

Financial Aid Contact

Violet Ronders-Reese, Director, Financial Aid and Federal Programs, Lewis College of Business, 17370 Meyers Rd., Detroit, MI 48235; (313) 862-6300, ext. 49.

ADMISSION REQUIREMENTS

Open admission

Entrance Requirements

Students must graduate from an accredited high school, submit official high school transcript, and take college placement test.

GED students must meet basic admission requirements.

International students must take the TOEFL examination and provide proof of ability to pay all college costs.

Transfer students must meet basic admission requirements, submit high school and college transcripts, and qualify for readmission to previous college or university attended. Only "C" or better grades may be transferred.

Early admission allows academically gifted high school students the opportunity to enroll in college for credit before completing high school.

Admission Application Deadline

August (fall); January (spring); rolling admission provides no specific date for notification of admission so applicant is informed as soon as admission decision is made.

Admission Contact

Dr. Frank De Shazor, Director of Admissions, Lewis College of Business, 17370 Meyers Rd., Detroit, MI 48235; (313) 862-6300, ext. 31 or 32.

GRADUATION REQUIREMENTS

A minimum of 60 credit hours and completion of the core requirements to include three hours of mathematics, one computer course and minimum 2.0 GPA for the Associate of Arts degree; minimum of 30 credit hours and completion of the core requirements for Certificates.

Grading System

A-E; E=Failure; I=Incomplete; W= Withdrawal.

STUDENT BODY PROFILE

Total enrollment (male/female): 59/287

From in-state: 339

Full-time undergraduates (male/female): 40/188

Part-time undergraduates (male/female): 20/98

Ethnic/Racial Makeup

African American, 343; Asian, 3.

Class of 1995 Profile

Number of applicants: 200

Number accepted: 180

Number enrolled: 180

Transfers enrolled: 12

FACULTY PROFILE

Number of faculty: 35

Student-teacher ratio: 13:1

Full-time faculty (male/female): 11/16

Part-time faculty: 8

Faculty with doctorates or other terminal degrees: 10%

SCHOOL CALENDAR

1991–92: August 30–April 25 (semesters)

Commencement and conferring of degrees: April 30

Two summer sessions.

DEGREES OFFERED 1991–92:

Associate of Arts

Accounting

Business Administration

Computer Information Systems

Computer Management

Computer Programming

General Studies

Information Systems

Secretarial Science

Word Processing

Certificates

Clerk Typist

Stenography

SPECIAL PROGRAMS

Adult or Continuing Education Program is available for nontraditional students returning to school or working full time.

College orientation is offered to entering students for two days at no cost prior to the beginning of classes to acquaint students with the college and to prepare them for college life. Parent participation is welcome.

Cooperative Education Program alternates classroom study with related paid work experience. The program provides academic credit and full-time status during co-op placement.

Independent study provides the opportunity for a limited number of students to earn college credit without the traditional class setting.

Part-time degree program allows students to earn an undergraduate degree while attending part time.

Remedial courses are offered to entering students to bring them up to admission standards and to help them adjust for success in college.

Student Support Services provides developmental courses, counseling, and cultural activities to students who need aid to succeed in college.

ATHLETIC PROGRAMS

Intercollegiate sports: men's basketball

LIBRARY HOLDINGS

2,600 bound volumes, 50 periodical subscriptions, 100 audiovisuals; 60 computers available for student use in computer lab; 35 typewriters in typing lab.

STUDENT LIFE

Special Regulations

Class attendance required.

Campus Services

Personal and psychological counseling, career planning and placement, comprehensive typing lab, and comprehensive computer lab.

Campus Activities

Social activities include chorale. Students may get involved in the student-run newspaper. Special annual events include Founder's Day observance, the Black History Month Observation, and the school's annual parade.

Leadership opportunities are found in the Student Government Association and several sororities, including one national sorority.

Located in northwest Detroit, Lewis Business College is one block north of West McNichols and easily accessible from the John C. Lodge Freeway (US 10). The city of Detroit is served by mass air, bus, and rail, and provides local transportation via the city bus lines. Detroit offers many cultural, recreational, and social activities, such as dance clubs, the Metroparks, boat trips on the Detroit River, and a recognized escape route on the Underground Railroad. It is within minutes of Canada and four hours to Niagara Falls. The Motor City, as it is sometimes called, plays host to major recording artists, the symphony, the orchestra, and major league sports.

Housing Availability

None

WAYNE COUNTY COMMUNITY COLLEGE

801 W. Fort St.
Detroit, MI 48226
Phone: (313) 496-2500

Total Enrollment:
11,123

Level of Selectivity:
Noncompetitive

Motto:
Learning, Service,
Opportunity, and
Community

HISTORY

Wayne County Community College (WCCC) is a two-year, local and state-supported, coed, liberal arts college founded in 1967 by the state legislature to serve the people living in Detroit and the surrounding area.

Initially WCCC students used local school facilities for classrooms because the college had no facilities. Today WCCC has 5 state-of-the-art campuses spread throughout Wayne County, with a combined enrollment of more than 11,000 students of which 80% attend part time.

The Northwest Campus opened in 1975; the Downriver Campus in Taylor opened in 1978; the Downtown Campus opened in 1979; the Western Campus in Van Buren Township opened in 1981; and the Eastern Campus opened in 1982. All campuses provide both liberal arts and career programs.

WCCC's unified mission is to prepare students for the workplace or for transfer to advanced degree programs.

ACCREDITATION

Wayne County Community College is accredited by the North Central Association of Colleges and Schools to award the Associate of Art, Associate of Science, and Associate of Applied Science degrees.

Other Accreditation

American Dental Association

American Dietetic Association

American Veterinary Association

COSTS PER YEAR

1991–92 Tuition: $1,014 (in-state); $1,914 (out-state)

Room and board: None

Special fees: $125

Books: $500

Estimated total cost: $1,639 (in-state); $2,539 (out-state)

FINANCIAL AID

Financial Aid Specific to the School

50% of the student body received financial aid during 1991–92.

Cooperative Education Program alternates and combines classroom study with related paid work experience. The program provides academic credit and full-time status during co-op placement.

Tuition waivers are available to Native Americans and senior citizens who are residents of the state on a space available basis. Fees, books, and supplies are not included.

Financial Aid Deadline

July 1 (priority)

Financial Aid Contact

Director of Financial Aid, Wayne County Community College, 801 W. Fort St., Detroit, MI 48226; (313) 496-2500.

ADMISSION REQUIREMENTS

Open admission. ACT and ASSET used for placement in math and English.

Entrance Requirements

Graduation from high school or a dual enrollment form signed by parent or guardian to enroll in courses not offered at student's high school.

GED students must meet basic admission requirements.

Transfer students must submit official transcript of all previous college work.

International students must take the TOEFL examination.

Early admission allows academically gifted high school students the opportunity to enroll in college for credit before completing high school.

Admission Application Deadline

Rolling admission provides no specific date for notification of admission so applicant is informed as soon as admission decision is made. Deferred entrance.

Admission Contact

Office of Admissions, Wayne County Community College, 1001 W. Fort, Detroit, MI 48225-9975.

GRADUATION REQUIREMENTS

A minimum of 60 credit hours and completion of the core requirements to include the following hours: 6 English, 9 humanities, 8 to 20 science, 9 social science, and 3 American Government; 1 computer course for some majors; complete last 15 hours at WCCC; minimum 2.0 GPA.

Grading System

A-E; CR=Credit by Exam; CRE=Credit for Experience; I=Incomplete; V=Audit; WI-Institutional Withdrawal; WP=Student Withdrawal

STUDENT BODY PROFILE

Total enrollment (male/female):
  4,227/6,896

From in-state: 9,455

Other regions: 30 countries

Full-time undergraduates (male/female):
  830/1,395

Part-time undergraduates (male/female):
  3,381/5,517

Ethnic/Racial Makeup

African American, 8,342; Hispanic, 222; Asian, 111; Native American, 111; Caucasian, 2,226; International, 111.

Class of 1995 Profile

Number of applicants: 4,000

Number accepted: 4,000

Number enrolled: 2,000

FACULTY PROFILE

Number of faculty: 400

Student-teacher ratio: 25:1

Full-time faculty: 150

Part-time faculty: 250

Faculty with doctorates or other terminal
  degrees: 32%

SCHOOL CALENDAR

1992–93: August–May (semester hours)

Commencement and conferring of degrees:
  May

One summer session.

DEGREES OFFERED 1991–92:

Associate of Arts

Business Administration

Dietetic Technology

Mental Health

Nursing

Associate of Science

Dental Hygiene

Hospitality Careers

Associate of Applied Science

Accounting

Administrative Assistant

Automotive Body Repair

Automotive Service Technology

Aviation Mechanic

Business Administration

Child Care

Computer Information Systems

Criminal Justice

Culinary Arts

Dental Assistant

Drafting/Computer Aided Design

Electrical/Electronic Technology

Electromechanical/Robotics

Electronics Engineering Technology

General Office Clerk

Gerontology

Heating, Ventilation, and Air Conditioning

Interior Design

Legal Secretary

Machine Tool Technology

Marketing/Management

Medical Secretary

Mental Health

Numerical Control

Occupational Therapy Assistant

Telecommunication Technology

Veterinary Technology

Video Technology

Welding Technology

Word Processing

Certificates

Automotive Body Repair

Automotive Service Technology

Aviation Mechanic

Child Care

Drafting/Computer Aided Design

Electrical/Electronic Technology

Electromechanical/Robotics

Electronics Engineering Technology

Gerontology

Machine Tool Technology

Mental Health

Small Engine Repair

Substance Abuse Counseling

Telecommunications Technology

Video Technology

Welding Technology

SPECIAL PROGRAMS

Advanced Placement (AP) grants college credit for postsecondary work completed in high school. Students scoring 3 to 5 on the AP test will receive credit by examination for each course and advanced placement.

College Level Examination Program (CLEP) determines the academic relevance of nontraditional educational experiences, such as the military, on-the-job training, or other life experiences, through a series of tests and may grant students college credit for these experiences.

College orientation is offered to entering students at no cost prior to the beginning of classes to acquaint students with the college and to prepare them for college life.

Cooperative Education Program alternates and combines classroom study with related paid work experience. The program provides academic credit and full-time status during co-op placement.

Part-time degree program allows students to earn an undergraduate degree while attending part time.

Remedial courses are offered to entering students to bring them up to admission standards and to help them adjust for success in college.

ATHLETIC PROGRAMS

Intramural sports: baseball, basketball, bowling, soccer, softball, and volleyball.

LIBRARY HOLDINGS

The main library at the downtown campus holds 75,500 bound volumes, 552 audiovisuals, and 125 computers for student use.

STUDENT LIFE

Campus Services

Personal counseling, career planning and placement, student employment, and childcare.

Campus Activities

Social and cultural activities include films, lectures, and performing arts. Students may get involved in the student-run publication or the student leadership retreat held annually.

Leadership opportunities are found in the Student Government Association or the numerous other clubs and organizations, including a national sorority.

Wayne County Community College is located in the metropolitan city of Detroit, providing students with access to a variety of social, cultural, and recreational activities. Detroit is known as the automotive industry capital of the nation. It is also known for its Motown Sound Recordings of such greats as Diana Ross and the Supremes. Detroit plays host to major league sports teams and national conferences. The city offers fine shopping and dining, as well as museums and orchestra. Served by mass bus, air, and rail, the campus is easily accessible by freeways.

Housing Availability

None

Handicapped Services

Available for the hearing and visually impaired. Services include counseling, interpreters, notetakers, readers, tutors, visualtex machines, telecommunication devices, and referrals.

Mississippi

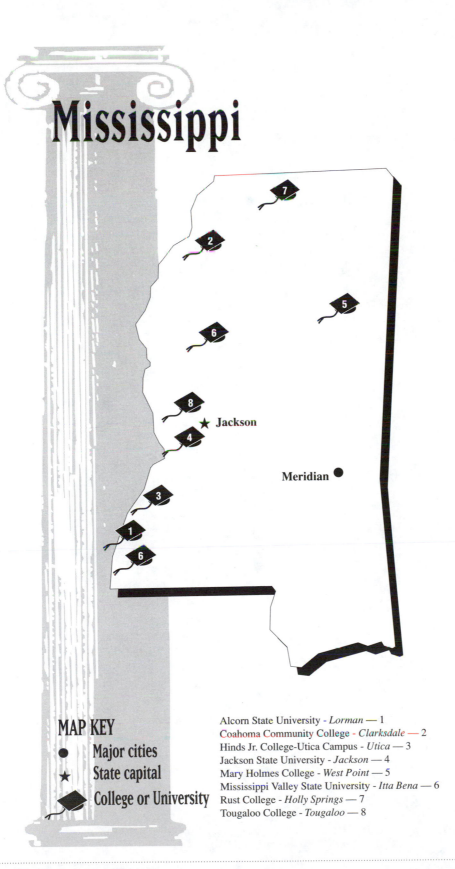

Jackson

Meridian

MAP KEY

- ● Major cities
- ★ State capital
- ◆ College or University

Alcorn State University - *Lorman* — 1
Coahoma Community College - *Clarksdale* — 2
Hinds Jr. College-Utica Campus - *Utica* — 3
Jackson State University - *Jackson* — 4
Mary Holmes College - *West Point* — 5
Mississippi Valley State University - *Itta Bena* — 6
Rust College - *Holly Springs* — 7
Tougaloo College - *Tougaloo* — 8

ALCORN STATE UNIVERSITY

Lorman, MS 39096
Phone: (601) 877-6147
or 877-6148
Toll-free in-state:
800-222-6790
Fax: (601) 877-2975

Total Enrollment:
3,526

Level of Selectivity:
Slightly competitive

Motto:
Serving the People
Since 1871

HISTORY

Alcorn State University (ASU) is a four-year, state-supported, coed college founded in 1871 as Alcorn University. Alcorn is the oldest historically and predominantly black land grant university in the United States. It began as part of Oakland College, established in 1830 for white males. In 1831, the first degree issued in Mississippi was conferred here. During the Civil War, Oakland College closed; the state purchased the school in 1871 as Alcorn University for the education of black males. ASU's first president, Hiram R. Revels, was the first black elected to the U.S. Senate.

Under the 1862 Morrill Land Grant Act, Alcorn became a land grant institution in 1878; subsequently the name was changed to Alcorn A&M College of the State of Mississippi. In 1903, the institution admitted women. The college's name changed to Alcorn State University in 1974. In 1989, President Bush gave the commencement address at Alcorn.

The primary aim of Alcorn is to assume the role of a citadel of learning, where scholars are encouraged to seek new truths and make the proper application of existing knowledge for the betterment of mankind.

Alcorn's 89-building campus includes the famed Oakland Memorial Chapel. The campus is situated on 300 acres with an additional 1,456 adjacent acres devoted to agriculture and research. Older historic campus buildings stand in sharp contrast to the modern, air-conditioned dormitories.

ACCREDITATION

Alcorn State University is accredited by the Southern Association of Colleges and Schools to award the Associate of Science, Bachelor of Arts, Bachelor of Science, Master's, and Educational Specialist degrees.

Other Accreditation

American Dietetic Association

National Association of Industrial Technology

National Association of Schools of Music

National Council for the Accreditation of Teacher Education

National League for Nursing

COSTS PER YEAR

1992–93 Tuition: $1,188 (in-state); $2,167 (out-state)

Room and board: $1,049

Special fees: $125

Books: $400

Estimated total cost: $2,762 (in-state); $3,741 (out-state)

FINANCIAL AID

1991–92 Institutional Funding

Total amount of scholarships and grants: $1,615,521

1991–92 Federal and State Funding

Total amount of scholarships and grants: $3,993,062

Financial Aid Specific to the School

95% of the student body received financial aid in 1991–92.

Alcorn offers general service and special scholarships and university academic excellence scholarships. Scholarships range from $625 to $5,132.

Thirty-six endowed scholarships, awards, and loans are available to qualifying students including the Medgar Evers Scholarship, administered through the Alcorn National Alumni Association for students majoring in critical manpower areas. Medgar Evers awards are at least $500 for the year.

Athletic scholarships are available for students participating in intercollegiate sports.

Performance grants are available for music students who meet the department criteria.

Cooperative Education Program alternates classroom study with related paid work experience. The program provides full-time status during co-op placement and may provide academic credit.

Thurgood Marshall Black Education Fund provides a four-year scholarship at this public black college. Qualifying student must have a high school GPA of 3.0 or better and a SAT score of 1000, or ACT score of 24 or more. Students must be recommended by high school counselor as exceptional or exemplary in the creative or performing arts. Scholarship pays tuition, fees, room, and board, not to exceed $6,000 annually.

Army ROTC program offers two- and four-year scholarships that pay tuition, fees, books, and other expenses, and provide a $1,000 stipend each year.

State Student Incentive Grant (SSIG) awards grants to Mississippi residents who are full-time students and demonstrate financial need. Grants range from $200 to $1,500 an academic year. Several other state assistance programs are available.

Financial Aid Deadline

May (fall); October (spring)

Financial Aid Contact

Office of Financial Aid, Alcorn State

College, Lorman, MS 39096; (601) 877-6190 or 6191.

ADMISSION REQUIREMENTS

ACT score of fifteen (Enhanced ACT: eighteen for out-of-state students) is required or SAT score of 720.

Entrance Requirements

High school diploma is needed with a minimum of 13.5 units to include: 4 English, 3 three mathematics (algebra I and II and geometry), 3 science (biology, advanced biology, chemistry, advanced chemistry, physics, advanced physics), 3.5 social sciences (U.S. history, American government), and 1 elective (foreign language, math beyond algebra II, or an extra science); must submit an official transcript; must provide proof of immunization against measles and rubella.

GED students must meet basic admission requirements.

Transfer students must submit an official transcript and qualify for readmission at previous college or university. Transfer students must have an overall "C" average in the following 24 semester hours: 6 English composition, 3 mathematics, 6 laboratory science, and 9 transferable electives.

International students must take the TOEFL examination, provide proof of ability to pay all college costs, and score 20 or above on ACT or 870 on the SAT.

Early admission allows academically gifted high school students the opportunity to enroll in college full time before completing high school. Students must have an ACT score of 20 or SAT score of 870 and be recommended by high school principal.

Admission Application Deadline

July 15; March (priority)

Admission Contact

Albert Z. Johnson, Director of Admissions, PO Box 300, Alcorn State University, Lorman, MS 39096; (601) 877-6147 or 6148.

GRADUATION REQUIREMENTS

Minimum of 128 semester hours with 6 hours English, 6 hours creative arts, 3 hours oral communications, 12 hours social science, 9 hours natural science, 3 hours mathematics, 4 hours physical education or military science, and 1 hour student adjustment. A 2.0 cumulative GPA is necessary, plus a minimum GPA of 2.0 in the major field of study. Each student must pass the English Proficiency Examination taken at the beginning of the junior year. Each student must complete a departmental examination or written senior project. The last 12 hours of study must be completed at Alcorn State.

Grading System

A–F; I=incomplete; WP=withdrawal passing; WF=withdrawal failing; L=incomplete in a developmental course; P=pass.

STUDENT BODY PROFILE

Total enrollment (male/female): 1,587/1,939

From in-state: 2,996

Other regions: 26 states; 4 foreign countries.

Full-time undergraduates (male/female): 1,395/1,704

Part-time undergraduates (male/female): 95/117

Graduate students (male/female): 97/118

Ethnic/Racial Makeup

African American, 3385; Asian, 353; Native American, 705; International, 353.

Class of 1995 Profile

Number of applicants: 3,020

Number accepted: 2,114

Number enrolled: 1,208

Median ACT score: 18.5

Average high school GPA: 2.495

FACULTY PROFILE

Number of faculty: 189

Student-teacher ratio: 20:1

Faculty with doctorates or other terminal
degrees: 50%

SCHOOL CALENDAR

1991–92: August 29–May 7

Commencement and conferring of degrees:
May 9

Two summer sessions.

DEGREES OFFERED 1991–92:

Associate of Science
Nursing

Bachelor of Arts
Economics
English
History
Music
Political Science
Psychology
Social Science
Social Work
Sociology

Bachelor of Science
Accounting
Agricultural Economics
Agriculture Education
Agronomy
Animal Science
Biology
Business Administration
Business Education
Chemistry
Communications
Computer Science
Criminal Justice

Criminology
Early Childhood Education
Economics
Educational Psychology
Elementary Education
Engineering Technology
Food Sciences/Nutrition
General Agriculture
General Home Economics
Guidance and Counseling
Health, Physical Education, and Recreation
Health Science
Home Economics Education
Industrial Arts
Institutional Management
Journalism
Mathematics
Medical Records
Nursing
Secondary Education
Secretarial Science
Soil Sciences
Special Education
Technical Education
Textiles/Clothing

Bachelor of Music Education
Music

Bachelor of Science in Nursing
Nursing

Master's Degrees
Agriculture
Educational Administration
Elementary Education

Pre-Professional
Dentistry
Education Specialist
Engineering
Law
Medicine

Pharmacy

Veterinarian

SPECIAL PROGRAMS

Accelerated Study Program allows students to complete their undergraduate degree in a shorter period of time than the traditional period of four years.

Advanced placement grants college credit for postsecondary work completed in high school. Students scoring three or above on the AP test will receive credit by examination for each course and advanced placement.

Cooperative Education Program alternates classroom study with related paid work experience. The program provides academic credit and full-time status during the co-op placement.

College Level Examination Program (CLEP) determines the academic relevance of nontraditional education experiences, such as the military, on-the-job training, or other life experiences, through a series of tests and may grant students college credit for these experiences.

College orientation is offered to entering students at no cost prior to the beginning of classes to acquaint students with the college and to prepare them for college life.

Cooperative Study Abroad Program is available for students that qualify.

English as a Second Language offers courses in English for students whose native language is not English.

The honors program offers academically talented students a challenging program of study that includes special classes, seminars, colloquia, cultural activities, and special recognition to motivate participants.

Remedial courses are offered to entering students to bring them up to admission standards and to help them adjust for success in college.

ROTC provides training in military science for commission as a second lieutenant in the U.S. Army. Two- and four-year scholarships are available.

Three/two degree program in engineering in cooperation with Mississippi State University allows students to get two degrees—one in liberal arts from home school and one in engineering from cooperating school—by completing three years at matriculated school and two years at cooperating school.

Upward Bound is a summer residential program and Saturday follow-up program during the academic year to encourage high school youth to pursue higher education.

ATHLETIC PROGRAMS

Alcorn State University is a member of the National Collegiate Athletic Association (NCAA), Division 1-A for basketball, Division 1-AA, Southwestern Athletic Conference.

Intercollegiate sports: men's basketball, baseball, cross-country, football, golf, tennis, indoor track, and track & field; women's basketball, cross-country, tennis, indoor track, volleyball, and track & field.

Intramural sports: basketball, bowling, flag football, softball, and volleyball.

Athletic Contact

Cardell Jones, Director of Intercollegiate Athletics, Alcorn State University, Lorman, MS 39096; (601) 877-6500, 6501, or 6502.

LIBRARY HOLDINGS

The John Dewey Boyd Library has more than 161,232 volumes; 225,667 government documents; 4,581 audiovisuals; 35,904 microforms; and 764 periodicals. Boyd Library is a selective U.S. government depository library. Beginning in 1970, the library has been a complete depository for Mississippi state documents.

STUDENT LIFE

Special Regulations

All students are expected to live in university residence halls, with the exception of those who are within commuting distance.

Campus Services

Health center; personal and psychological counseling; career counseling and placement; and testing services for NTE, ACT, GRE, GMAT, LSAT, GED, MCAT, Miller Analogies test, National Engineering Aptitude Search, Sanford Test of Academic Skills, and English Proficiency Exam.

Campus Activities

Social activities include theater, concert and marching band, wind ensemble, Men's Glee Club, drama, choir, ROTC band and drill team, and Jazz Ensemble. Students may work on *The Alcornite* yearbook or *The Greater Alcorn Herald,* the student newspaper. Broadcasting students can work at WPRL, a public broadcasting radio station run by the university.

Leadership opportunities are found in the student government association (SGA) and other student-run organizations, such as Circle-K, NAACP, Black History Month Society, Campus Union Board, Cheering Squad and Beauté Noir Modeling Squad, Christian organizations, and department and class organizations. Greek-letter fraternities include Alpha Phi Alpha, Kappa Alpha Psi, Omega Psi Phi, and Phi Beta Sigma; sororities include Alpha Kappa Alpha, Delta Sigma Theta, Sigma Gamma Rho, and Zeta Phi Beta. Honorary societies are also represented on campus.

Alcorn is located in Claiborne County, Mississippi, seven miles west of Lorman and 45 miles south of Vicksburg. Not far from Lorman is the Windsor home spared by Grant's torch during the Civil War. The home was built in 1860 by approximately 600 slaves.

Mass bus transportation is seven miles away; air transportation is 35 miles away; and mass rail is approximately ninety miles away in Jackson, Mississippi, the state capital. Convenient transportation is available daily to reach or leave the campus for shopping and other recreational activities in nearby cities.

Housing Availability

Four dormitories for men and four for women totalling 2,000 spaces are available. Separate dorms are designated for freshmen, athletes, and female band members. Students who are not receiving full financial aid are required to pay a deposit for the residence halls.

Handicapped Services

Wheelchair accessibility.

NOTABLE ALUMNI

Del Anderson–President, San Jose City College, California

Alex Haley, 1939–Author; journalist

Moses Leon Howard, 1952–Teacher; author (pseudonym Musa Nagenda)

Burnett Joiner, Ph.D., 1964–President, LeMoyne-Owen College, Memphis, Tennessee

COAHOMA COMMUNITY COLLEGE

Route 1, Box 616
3240 Friars Point Rd.
Clarksdale, MS 38614-9799
Phone: (601) 627-2571
Toll-free in-state:
800-844-1222
Fax: (601) 627-9350

Total Enrollment:
1,373

Level of Selectivity:
Noncompetitive

Motto:
The College That
Cares

HISTORY

Coahoma Community College is a two-year, comprehensive, coed college, founded in 1924 as Coahoma County Agricultural High School. Coahoma was the first county in Mississippi to provide such an institution for African-Americans. In 1949, twenty-five years later, the junior college was added, and the name changed to Coahoma Junior College and Agricultural High School. Two years after adding the junior college, Coahoma became the first public junior college for blacks to receive funding from the Mississippi state government. July of 1989 marked the change of the school's name to Coahoma Community College. In 1992, Coahoma Community College was proud to announce that Dr. Vivian M. Presley would become the eighth president of the institution and Mississippi's first black woman college president.

The 70-acre campus features 25 buildings in an agrarian setting. Most students are from Coahoma, Bolivar, Quitman, and Sunflower counties; however, the college also attracts students from other states and other countries. Coahoma offers associate's degrees that can be transferred to four-year colleges or universities; in addition, certificates are offered in a variety of vocational programs. The mission of the college is to teach, research, and provide community service.

ACCREDITATION

Coahoma Community College is accredited by the Southern Association of Colleges and Schools to award Associate of Arts and Associate of Applied Science degrees.

Other Accreditation
Accrediting Commission of the State of Mississippi

COSTS PER YEAR
1992–93 Tuition: $700 (district); $1,100 (in-state); $2,100 (out-state)

Room and board: $778 (room); $1,034 (board)

Special fees: $200

Books: $250

Estimated total cost: $2,962 (district); $3,362 (in-state); $4,362 (out-state)

FINANCIAL AID

1991–92 Institutional Funding
Total amount of scholarships and grants: $153,108

1991–92 Federal and State Funding
Total amount of scholarships and grants: $2,119,260

Financial Aid Specific to the School
95% of the student body received financial aid during 1991–92.

Twenty-three endowed scholarships and awards are available to Coahoma Community College students.

Presidential scholarships are awarded to entering students from designated Mississippi high schools upon recommendation of high school principals.

Minority Honors scholarships are awarded to minority students majoring in energy-related occupations. Students must have a 3.0 GPA to be eligible.

Music scholarships are available to students in band and choir.

Athletic scholarships are awarded to students participating in intercollegiate sports.

The Alpha Phi Alpha Fraternity Scholarship is awarded to an entering freshmen based on academic merit. Student must have a 3.0 GPA, plan to return to Coahoma for sophomore year, and plan to continue formal education beyond two years of college.

The Fannie Lou Hammer Memorial Scholarship is awarded to a sophomore student each year based on academic merit and good moral character.

Financial Aid Deadline
March 15

Financial Aid Contact
Dr. Edward Vaughn, Director of Financial Aid, Route 1, Box 616, 3240 Friars Point Rd., Clarksdale, MS 38614-9799; (601) 627-2571

ADMISSION REQUIREMENTS
Open admissions. ACT required for students under 21 years of age or for certain programs such as Computer Technology.

Entrance Requirements
Graduation from an accredited high school with completion of 17 high school units to include 4 English, 2 mathematics, 2 science, and 2 social science. Students who have completed 17 units, but have not graduated from high school may be accepted under certain circumstances.

GED students must submit a satisfactory score on the GED and meet basic admission requirements.

Transfer students must submit an official transcript from the institution previously attended. ACT not required for students who have completed seventeen semester credit hours.

Admission Application Deadline
April 1 (fall); November 1 (spring). Rolling admission provides no specific date for notification so applicant is informed as soon as admission decision is made.

Admission Contact
Rita S. Hanfor, Dean of Admissions and Records and Veterans Coordinator, Route 1, Box 616, 3240 Friars Point Rd., Clarksdale, MS 38614-9799; (601) 627-2571, ext. 154

GRADUATION REQUIREMENTS
Minimum of 65 semester hours including 3 hours of algebra and 3 hours of computer science, with a minimum GPA of 2.0;

last 15 semester hours completed at Coahoma Community College. Students planning to transfer to a Mississippi public university must complete the following core requirements with a minimum 2.0 average: 6 semester hours of English composition, 3 semester hours of college algebra, 6 semester hours of laboratory science, and 3 semester hours of humanities and fine arts.

Grading System

A-F; I=Incomplete; N=Non-Attendance; W=Withdrawal

STUDENT BODY PROFILE

Total enrollment (male/female): 439/934

From in-state: 1,277

Other regions: 8 states

Full-time undergraduates (male/female): 224/476

Part-time undergraduates (male/female): 215/458

Ethnic/Racial Makeup

African American, 1,238; Other/unclassified, 137.

Class of 1995 Profile

Number of applicants: 1,986

Number accepted: 1,986

Number enrolled: 993

Transfers enrolled: 27

FACULTY PROFILE

Number of faculty: 80

Student-teacher ratio: 22:1

Full-time faculty: 60

Part-time faculty: 20

Faculty with doctorates or other terminal degrees: 11%

SCHOOL CALENDAR

1991–1992: August 22–May 13 (semester hours)

Commencement and conferring of degrees: May 17

Two summer sessions.

DEGREES OFFERED 1991–92:

Associate in Arts

Accounting

Art

Biology

Chemistry

Computer Science–Business Oriented

Computer Science–Math Oriented

Criminal Justice

Early Childhood Education

Economics

Elementary Education

English

General Business

General Education

Health and Physical Education

Mathematics

Mathematics Education

Medical Technology

Printing and Graphic Management

Radio and Television Broadcasting

Science Education

Social Science

Social Science Education

Social Work

Associate in Applied Science

Administrative Support Services

Agricultural Industry Technology

Computer Maintenance Technology

Computer Programming

Drafting and Design Technology

Electronics Technology

Graphic, Print, and Reprographic Service
  Technology

Graphic and Print Technology

Pre-Professional

Pre-Agriculture

Pre-Dental Hygiene

Pre-Engineering

Pre-Forestry

Pre-Law

Pre-Medical

Pre-Nursing

Pre-Optometry

Pre-Pharmacy

Pre-Physical Therapy

Pre-Veterinary Science

SPECIAL PROGRAMS

All entering freshmen are required to take the Stanford Test of Academic Skills (TASK). Students who do not perform well on the test will be directed to basic developmental courses in reading, mathematics, and English.

The Evening Program is an extension of the junior college program and provides educational opportunities for students who cannot attend regular classes. To be admitted, students must meet regular admission standards.

The off-campus program is designed to carry the continuing education program to working adults in all areas of the community.

Vocational programs are available for students not interested in degree programs. The following vocational programs of study are available: auto body and fender repair; auto mechanics; barbering; carpentry; combination welding; construction masonry; cosmetology; farm tractor and implement mechanics; heat, air conditioning, and refrigeration and wiring; industrial electricity; machine shop; print, graphics, and reprographics; job training partnership act; and single parent/displaced homemakers. College fees are the same as degree programs. A

standardized test may be required of some students.

ATHLETIC PROGRAMS

Coahoma is a member of the National Junior College Athletic Association (NJCAA).

Intercollegiate sports: men's baseball, basketball, football, and track & field; women's basketball.

Intramural sports: basketball, football, baseball, and track.

Athletic Contact

Mr. Roosevelt Ramsey, Dean of Student Affairs and Director of Upward Bound, Route 1, Box 616, 3240 Friars Point Rd., Clarksdale, MS 38614-9799; (601) 627-2571, ext. 171.

LIBRARY HOLDINGS

Dickerson-Johnson Library Center includes a media center, seminar room, alumni room, Delta Heritage room, and a computer center with thirty computers for student use.

STUDENT LIFE

Special Regulations

Class attendance required; permission needed to visit students of opposite sex in dormitories; calling hours.

Campus Services

Personal and psychological counseling; testing; health; career planning, placement, and follow-up; day care; and religious activities.

Campus Activities

Social and cultural activities include theater, chorale, and band. Interested students may get involved in the *Coahoma Tribune* (student newspaper) or *The Coahoma* (yearbook).

Leadership opportunities are found in the Student Government Association (SGA) and other student-run organizations and clubs, such as the Dormitory Council, Education Club, English Club, Students in Free Enterprise (SIFE), Science Symposium, Social Science Forum, Black Literacy Society, Physical Education Majors Club (PEMS), Vocational Industrial Club of America (VICA), Young Men's Progressive Club, and Young Women's Progressive Dormitory Club. Coahoma is home to two fraternities: Phi Beta Lambda, for business students, and Phi Theta Kappa, a national junior college fraternity promoting scholarship, leadership, and the development of character.

Coahoma Community College is located in Clarksdale, Mississippi, a community with a population just under 20,000. Clarksdale is the home of the Delta Blues Museum in the Carnegie Public Library which highlights the work of such local musicians as Muddy Waters and W. C. Handy. Coahoma Community College is 50 miles northwest of Greenwood and about 60 miles south of Memphis, Tennessee. Coahoma's small-town campus provides a quiet environment for study and a close proximity to Memphis, Tennessee, for social and cultural activities.

Housing Availability

Separate men's and women's dormitories are available on campus. Single parent housing, with child care services, is available on campus.

NOTABLE ALUMNI

Ruth Campbell–Associate director, Universities Center, Jackson State University

HINDS COMMUNITY COLLEGE

HISTORY

Hinds Community College is a state-supported, two-year, coed, college founded in 1903 as the Utica Normal and Industrial Institute. Fourteen years later the Hinds County Agricultural High School was founded in Raymond, which in 1922 became Hinds Junior College. In 1958, Utica Normal and Industrial became Utica Junior College as a result of the institution becoming public and joining the Mississippi system of junior colleges. Meanwhile, Hinds Junior College expanded its locations to include the Jackson branch in 1970 and the Vicksburg-Warren County branch in 1975.

Hinds Community College was created by a 1983 merger of Hinds Junior College and the historically black Utica Junior College, as well as the inclusion of the Rankin branch. With the merger and expansion came a new college mission to create an educational system conducive to learning for both the traditional and the nontraditional student.

The Utica Campus is the oldest of seven locations of Hinds Community College. The 236-acre campus with its 26 buildings is 3.5 miles south of Utica, Mississippi. Over 50 academic, cultural, and vocational programs are available at this location. The Hinds County Agricultural High School is located on this campus.

ACCREDITATION

Hinds Community College is accredited by the Southern Association of Colleges and Schools (SACS) to award the Associate in Arts, Associate in Applied Science, and Associate of Applied Science in Occupational Education degrees.

Other Accreditation

American Dental Association

Committee on Allied Health Education and Accreditation

Mississippi Commission on College Accreditation

National League for Nursing

Utica Campus
Utica, MS 39175-9599
Phone: (601) 885-6062
Fax: (601) 885-6062

Total Enrollment:
934

Level of Selectivity:
Noncompetitive

Motto:
The College for All
People

COSTS PER YEAR

1992–93 Tuition: $1,020 (in-state); $3,226 (out-state); $5,932 (international)

Room and board: $924 (room); $948 (board)

Special fees: $125 registration fee

Books: $350

Estimated total cost: $3,367 (in-state); $5,573 (out-state); $8,279 (international)

FINANCIAL AID

1991–92 Institutional Funding:

Total amount of scholarships and grants: $77,250 (Utica Campus only)

Financial Aid Specific to the School

68% of the student body received financial aid during 1991–92.

Dean's Scholarships pay tuition for four consecutive fall/spring semesters. Must be a full-time student, score 25 to 28 on ACT, and be a Mississippi resident. Applications received before February 1 will be given priority.

Faculty Scholarships pay one-half of tuition for up to four consecutive fall/spring semesters. Students must be full time, score 21 to 24 on ACT, maintain 3.0 GPA, and be a Mississippi resident.

Gifted and Talent Scholarships are awarded annually and pay tuition based on academic achievements, student talent, skills, and leadership abilities.

Hinds Community College Development Foundation offers 10 scholarships, 25 endowed scholarships, 12 foundation unrestricted tuition scholarships, and 16 special development foundation scholarships.

Presidential Scholarships pay tuition, room, and board for up to four consecutive fall/spring semesters. Students must be full time, score 29 or above on ACT, maintain 3.0 GPA, and be a Mississippi resident.

Other Race Scholarships pay tuition to full-time students enrolling at the Utica Campus for the first time.

The Trustmark Scholarship pays $200 a semester for four fall/spring consecutive semesters. Student must be a graduate of Hinds, Rankin, or Madison high schools; have a 12 or better ACT score; have a 2.0 GPA; and be free of disciplinary problems. Family combined income must be less than $15,000.

Athletic scholarships are awarded at the Utica Campus in basketball.

The deferred payment plan allows a family to pay tuition in two or three installments during the semester.

The Cooperative Education Program combines classroom study with related paid work experience. The program provides academic credit and full-time status during co-op placement.

State Student Incentive Grants (SSIG) are available for Mississippi residents.

Financial Aid Deadline

April 1 (priority)

Financial Aid Contact

Thurman Mitchell, Director of Financial Aid, Hinds Community College-Utica Campus, Utica, MS 39175-9599; (601) 885-6062 or (601) 354-2327.

ADMISSION REQUIREMENTS

ACT required for students under 21 years of age.

Entrance Requirements

Graduation from an accredited high school and submission of an official transcripts with 17 units; proof of immunizations for measles and rubella.

GED students must meet basic admission requirements.

Transfer students must provide an official transcript and, if under age 21, must submit ACT score.

International students must score 500 or better on TOEFL examination and submit an affidavit of financial support.

Admission Application Deadline

Rolling admission provides no specific date for notification of admission so applicant is informed as soon as admission is made.

Admission Contact

Billy T. Irby, District Director, Admissions and Records, Hinds Community College, Raymond, MS 39154-9799; (601) 857-3212 or (601) 857-3280.

GRADUATION REQUIREMENTS

Minimum of 64 credit hours.

Grading System

A-F; I=Incomplete; AU=Audit; IP=In Progress; W=Withdrawal; NC=No credit

STUDENT BODY PROFILE

Total enrollment: 934

From in-state: 915

Other regions: 16 states and 3 foreign countries

Full-time undergraduates: 710

Part-time undergraduates: 224

Class of 1995 Profile

Transfers enrolled: 75

FACULTY PROFILE

Number of faculty: 82 (Utica Campus)

Student-teacher ratio: 19:1

Faculty with doctorates or other terminal degrees: 10%

SCHOOL CALENDAR

1993–1994: August 23–May 12 (semester hours)

Commencement and conferring of degrees: May 15

Two summer sessions.

DEGREES OFFERED 1991–92:

Associate of Arts

Accounting

Agriculture–Agribusiness

Agriculture–Agricultural Economics

Agriculture–Agronomy

Agriculture–Animal Science

Agriculture–Dairy Science

Agriculture–Entomology

Agriculture–Food Science and Human Nutrition

Agriculture–Horticulture

Agriculture–Landscape Architecture

Agriculture–Plant Pathology and Weed Science

Agriculture–Poultry Science

Anthropology

Architecture

Art

Biochemistry

Biology

Biomedical Science

Broadcast Journalism

Business Administration–Advertising

Business Administration–Finance

Business Administration–General Business

Business Administration–Management

Business Administration–Marketing

Business Education

Chemistry

Child Development

Clothing and Textiles

Coaching and Sports Administration

Commercial Aviation

Communications

Community and Regional Planning

Computer Science

Construction Engineering

Court Reporting

Criminal Justice

Dietetics

Distributive Education

Economics

Education for the Deaf

Education–Elementary

Education–Secondary

Educational Psychology

Engineering–Agricultural

Engineering–Architectural

Engineering–Biological

Engineering–Chemical

Engineering–Civil

Engineering–Computer

Engineering–Electrical

Engineering–Geological

Engineering–Industrial

Engineering–Mechanical

Engineering–Nuclear

Engineering–Petroleum Engineering
  Technology

English

Environmental Health

Environmental Science

Family and Human Development

Family Life Studies

Fashion Merchandising

Foods and Nutrition

Food Science Technology

Foreign Language

Forestry

General Program of Study

Geography

Geology

Health, Physical Education, and Recreation

History

Home Economics

Hotel and Restaurant Administration

Industrial Arts

Industrial Technology

Institutional Management

Interior Design

International Studies

Journalism

Law Enforcement

Liberal Arts

Library Science

Linguistics

Mass Communication

Mathematics

Medical Records Administration

Medical Technology (transfer)

Meteorology

Microbiology

Music–Brass

Music–Guitar

Music–Organ

Music–Percussion

Music–Piano

Music–Strings

Music–Voice

Music–Woodwinds

Nursing (transfer)

Office Administration

Paralegal Studies

Philosophy

Physics and Astronomy

Political Science

Polymer Science

Psychology

Public Administration

Radio, TV, and Film

Reading

Recreation

Religious Studies

Social Science

Social Work

Sociology

Southern Studies

Speech

Theater

Urban Studies

Wildlife and Fisheries

Wood Science and Technology

Zoology

Pre-Professional

Pre-Dentistry

Pre-Law

Pre-Medicine

Pre-Optometry

Pre-Pharmacy

Pre-Physical Therapy

Pre-Veterinary Science

Associate of Applied Science (Utica Campus)

Business and Office Technology–Administrative Support Services Technology Option

Business and Office Technology–Business Management Technology Option

Business and Office Technology–Office Systems Technology

Child Development

Computer Programming

Drafting and Design–Architectural Drafting Option

Drafting and Design–Computer Aided Mapping Option

Drafting and Design–General Drafting Options

Drafting and Design–Mechanical Drafting Option

Electrical and Electronics–Electronics Technology Option

Electrical and Electronics–Telecommunications Options

General Technology

Media Technology

Associate of Applied Science in Occupational Education Degree (Utica Campus)

Automotive Body and Frame Repair

Automotive Mechanics

Barbering

Building Construction–Brick, Block, and Stone Masonry Option

Building Construction–Residential Carpentry Option

Clothing and Textile Services

Cosmetology

Food Production and Management

Welding

SPECIAL PROGRAMS

The British Studies Program includes a residential summer session during July and August in London, England.

College Level Examination Program (CLEP) determines the academic relevance of nontraditional education experiences such as the military, on-the-job training, or other life experiences and through a series of tests may grant students college credit for these experiences.

Advanced Placement (AP) grants college credit for postsecondary work completed in high school. Students scoring 3 or more will receive credit by examination for each course and advanced placement.

The Cooperative Education Program combines classroom study with related paid work experience. The program provides academic credit and full-time status during co-op placement.

Vocational Individualized Development Systems (VIDS) is a program that assists students with deficiencies in basic academic skills that relate to their field of study; VIDS also assists high students with GED preparation.

ATHLETIC PROGRAMS

Hinds Community College is a member of the National Junior College Athletic Association (NJCAA) and the Mississippi Junior College Athletic Association.

Intercollegiate sports (Utica Campus): men's basketball, baseball, and tennis; women's basketball, baseball, and tennis.

Intramural sports: volleyball, basketball, and flag football.

LIBRARY HOLDINGS

The libraries hold 147,000 bound volumes, 900 periodical subscriptions, and 140,000 audiovisuals. Each location has a Learning Resource Center that houses materials that support the college curriculums. The libraries are automated.

STUDENT LIFE

Campus Services

Health, personal counseling, testing, tutoring, and religious activities.

Campus Activities

Social and cultural activities include theater, precision dance team, and chorale.

Interested students may work on the student newspaper or yearbook.

Leadership opportunities are found in the Student Government Association (SGA) or various other groups such as Afro-American Culture Club and Vocational-Industrial Clubs of America (VICA). Honor societies include the Phi Theta Kappa honorary society.

Utica is approximately 25 miles from the city of Jackson, Mississippi. Jackson, the state capital, has a population of approximately 209,000. The city of Jackson has museums, a zoo, art galleries, and shopping. The Hinds College-Jackson campus is within walking distance of downtown.

Housing Availability

288 housing spaces. Separate residence halls for men and women are available.

JACKSON STATE UNIVERSITY

HISTORY

Jackson State University (JSU) is a four-year, state-supported, coed, liberal arts university. It was founded in 1877 as the Natchez Seminary by the American Baptist Home Mission Society in Natchez, Mississippi. The purpose of the seminary was for the moral, religious, and intellectual improvement of Christian leaders of the colored people of Mississippi and the neighboring states. In 1882, the institution moved to Jackson because of its central location in the state, and shortly thereafter the name was changed to Jackson College.

For 63 years the school operated as a private church school. In 1940, the college became a state institution for training rural and elementary school teachers. The first bachelor's degrees were awarded in 1944. In subsequent years, the name changed to Jackson State College. Expansion of the curriculum and facilities elevated the college to university status in 1974; thus, the name changed to Jackson State University.

1400 John R. Lynch St.
Jackson, MS 39217
Phone: (601) 968-2100
Toll-free in-state:
800-682-5390
Toll-free out-state:
800-848-6817

Total Enrollment:
6,203

Level of Selectivity:
Slightly competitive

Motto:
You shall know the truth and the truth shall make you free

In 1979, Jackson State University was officially designated the Urban University of Mississippi, and as such, seeks solutions for urban problems through its programs and activities. The college is pledged to the advancement of a free society and continued progress of democracy.

In 1983, the university completed a $11.2 million capital campaign, which resulted in the renovation and improvement of several campus buildings and provided for expanded programs offered in continuing education.

ACCREDITATION

Jackson State University is accredited by the Southern Association of Colleges and Schools (SACS) to award Bachelor of Arts, Bachelor of Science, Master's, Education Specialist, and Doctor of Education degrees.

Other Accreditation

The Accrediting Council on Education in Journalism and Mass Communications

American Chemical Society

Council on Rehabilitation Education

Council on Social Work Education (baccalaureate level)

National Association of Industrial Technology

National Association of Schools of Art and Design

National Association of Schools of Music

National Association of Schools of Public Affairs and Administration

National Council for the Accreditation of Teacher Education

COSTS PER YEAR

1992–93 Tuition: $2,230 (in-state); $4,190 (out-state)

Room and board: $1,546 (room); $1,220 (board)

Special fees: $125

Books: $500

Estimated total cost: $5,621 (in-state); $7,581 (out-state)

FINANCIAL AID

1991–92 Institutional Funding

Number of scholarships and grants: 341

Total amount of scholarships and grants: $687,145

Range of scholarships and grants: $200–$3,000

1991–92 Federal and State Funding

Number of scholarships and grants: 5,969

Total amount of scholarships and grants: $3,700,000

Range of scholarships and grants: $200–$2,000

Number of loans: 1,207

Total amount of loans: $1,400,000

Range of loans: $100–$3,000

Number of work-study: 1,145

Total amount of work-study: $150,795

Range of work-study: $2,000/yr

Financial Aid Specific to the School

90% of the student body received financial aid during 1991–92.

Performance scholarships are available for students who excel in areas such as drama, music, art, computer science, elementary education, chemistry, and business.

Several endowed scholarships and awards are available for students who demonstrate academic excellence.

Remission of fees is available for JSU employees; tuition waivers are available for employee's children.

National Institute of Health—MARC Honors Program provides eight junior or senior biology or chemistry students with full tuition and a $250 monthly stipend.

The Young Scientists Program supports chemistry students with full tuition, books, supplies, and summer research jobs at sponsor companies.

Junior or community college graduates may be eligible for a limited number of scholarships.

The Hearing & Hess Scholarship provides $5,000 each year to a student majoring in computer science. Student must have a "B" average or better in high school, an ACT score of 24 or more, and demonstrated leadership potential. To maintain scholarship funds, students must maintain a cumulative GPA of 3.25 or higher.

The Charles F. Moore Scholarship is awarded annually to a junior in the school of business with a "B" average or better. The scholarship is renewable.

General Motors (GM) EEOC provides scholarships for GM employees and their spouses and children if the family demonstrates financial need. Scholarships are based on admission test scores and GPA. If no GM employees apply for scholarships then non-GM minorities are eligible.

Athletic scholarships are available to students participating in intercollegiate sports.

Thurgood Marshall Black Education Fund provides a four-year scholarship at this public black college. Qualifying student must have a high school GPA of 3.0 or better and a SAT score of 1000 or ACT score of 24 or more. Students must be recommended by high school counselor as exceptional or exemplary in the creative or performing arts. Scholarship pays tuition, fees, room, and board not to exceed $6,000 annually.

The Cooperative Education Program alternates or combines classroom study with related paid work experience. The program provides academic credit and full-time status during co-op placement.

Army ROTC offers two- and four-year scholarships that pay tuition, fees, books, and other expenses, and provide a monthly stipend of $100. Jackson State will pay room and board for students with four-year ROTC scholarships.

State Student Incentive Grants (SSIG) are available to Mississippi residents.

Financial Aid Deadline
April 1

Financial Aid Contact
Melvin Phillips, Associate Director of Student Financial Aid, B. B. Roberts Hall, Jackson State University, Jackson, MS 39217; (601) 968-2100.

ADMISSION REQUIREMENTS
SAT or ACT required. A minimum score of 15 on the Enhanced ACT is required for Mississippi residents; out-of-state residents must score 16 or above on the Enhanced ACT or 620 on the SAT. Students 21 years of age or older may request a waiver of ACT scores.

Entrance Requirements
Graduation from an accredited high school and submission of an official transcript with 13 1/2 units to include: 4 English; 3 mathematics—algebra I, algebra II, and geometry; 3 science, one of which must have lab–biology, advanced biology, chemistry, advanced chemistry, physics, or advanced physics; 2 1/2 social sciences—U.S. history and American government; and 1 elective—foreign language, additional mathematics, or science. Recommended requirements include 2 units of a single foreign language; mathematics in the senior year; a computer course; and typing proficiency. Proof of immunizations for measles and rubella is required.

GED students must meet basic admission requirements.

Transfer students must submit an official transcript for each college attended with a GPA of 2.00. For those with less than 24 semester hours of credit, a high school transcript and ACT or SAT scores must be submitted. A maximum of 64 semester hours can be accepted for transfer credit.

International students must submit a minimum ACT score of 20 or a minimum SAT score of 840. The minimum score for

TOEFL is 525. Certified and translated transcripts and a certified declaration of financial support are required.

Admission Application Deadline

August 15 (fall); December 15 (spring)

Admission Contact

Mrs. Barbara J. Luckett, Director of Admissions and Recruitment, Jackson State University, 1400 John R. Lynch St., Jackson, MS 39217; (601) 968-2100; 800-682-5390 (in-state); 800-848-6817 (out-state).

GRADUATION REQUIREMENTS

A minimum of 128 credit hours and completion of the core requirements to include: 15 to 21 semester hours in communications, 9 semester hours in natural science, 12 semester hours in social and behavioral science, 2 to 3 semester hours in health and physical education, 2 semester hours in concepts for success, and requirements in major field of study. A 2.0 cumulative GPA and a 2.0 cumulative GPA in all courses in major field of study is needed. Thirty hours of upper-level work in major completed at Jackson State. Pass English proficiency exam.

Grading System

A-F; S=satisfactory progress; U=unsatisfactory progress; P=pass; IP=in progress; R=repeated course; I=incomplete; W=authorized withdrawal; WP=authorized withdrawal, passing; WF=authorized withdrawal, failing; AU=audit.

STUDENT BODY PROFILE

Total enrollment (male/female): 2,667/3,536

From in-state: 4,348

Other regions: 40 states and 6 foreign countries

Full-time undergraduates (male/female): 2,087/2,766

Part-time undergraduates (male/female): 259/344

Graduate students (male/female): 321/426

Ethnic/Racial Makeup

African American, 5,800; Hispanic, 62; Native American, 62;
Caucasian, 186; International, 93.

Class of 1995 Profile

Number of applicants: 2,080

Number accepted: 1,800

Number enrolled: 1,658

Median ACT score: 17

Transfers enrolled: 142

FACULTY PROFILE

Number of faculty: 380

Student-teacher ratio: 16:1

Full-time faculty: 315

Part-time faculty: 65

Tenured faculty: 179

Faculty with doctorates or other terminal degrees: 70%

SCHOOL CALENDAR

1992–93: August 24–May 14 (semester hours)

Commencement and conferring of degrees: May 15

One summer session.

DEGREES OFFERED AND NUMBER CONFERRED 1991–92:

Bachelor of Arts

Art: 3

Art Education–Art Studio: n/a

Art Education–Graphic Arts: n/a

English/English Literature: 24

History: 5

History–African American History: n/a

History–American History: n/a
History–European History: n/a
Political Science: 20
Political Science–American Politics: n/a
Political Science–International Affairs: n/a
Political Science–Pre-Law: n/a
Sociology: 12
Speech: 17
Urban Affairs: 3

Bachelor of Science
Biology: n/a
Biology Education: 48
Chemistry/Chemistry Education: 8
Chemistry–Pre-Chemistry Engineering: n/a
Computer Science: 70
Criminal Justice: 42
Environmental Science: 3
Health, Physical Education, and Recreation: 14
Health, Physical Education, and Recreation–Therapeutic Recreation: n/a
History: n/a
Industrial Technology: 34
Industrial Technology–Airway Science: n/a
Industrial Technology–Drafting Technology: n/a
Industrial Technology–Industrial Computer Technology: n/a
Industrial Technology–Industrial Construction Management: Technology: n/a
Industrial Technology–Industrial Electronic Technology: n/a
Industrial Technology–Industrial Engineering Technology: n/a
Industrial Technology–Industrial Manufacturing Technology: n/a
Mass Communications–Advertising: n/a
Mass Communications–Broadcast Journalism: 29
Mass Communications–News Editorial: n/a
Mass Communications–Public Relations: n/a
Mathematics: n/a

Mathematics–Pre-Engineering: n/a
Meteorology: 1
Physics: n/a
Pre-Dental Hygiene: n/a
Pre-Dentistry: n/a
Pre-Medicine: n/a
Pre-Nursing: n/a
Pre-Optometry: n/a
Pre-Pharmacy: n/a
Pre-Physical Therapy: n/a
Pre-Veterinary Medicine: n/a
Psychology: 35
Rehabilitation Services: 7
Science: 6
Speech: n/a

Bachelor of Science Education
Business Education: 2
Elementary Education: 56
Industrial Arts Education: n/a
Mathematics Education: 26
Secondary Education: 7
Social Science Education: 22
Special Education: 13

Bachelor of Business Administration
Accounting: 44
Business Administration: 96
Economics: 1
Finance: 40
Management: 37
Marketing: 28
Office Administration: 11

Bachelor of Music Education
Music–Music Education: 6
Music–Piano Performance: n/a

Bachelor of Social Work
Social Work: 25

SPECIAL PROGRAMS
Advanced Placement (AP) grants college credit for postsecondary work completed in high school. Students passing the AP

test will receive credit by examination for each course and advanced placement.

College Level Examination Program (CLEP) determines the academic relevance of nontraditional educational experiences such as the military, on-the-job training, or other life experiences through a series of tests and may grant students college credit for these experiences.

College orientation is offered to entering students prior to the beginning of classes to acquaint students with the college and to prepare them for college life; parents may attend.

The Cooperative Education Program alternates and combines classroom study with related paid work experience in six majors. The program provides academic credit and full-time status during co-op placement.

Cooperative study abroad is available to full-time students who meet the qualifications.

Remedial courses are offered to entering students to bring them up to admissions standards and to help them adjust for success in college.

ROTC provides training in military science for commission as a second lieutenant in the U.S. Army. Two- and four-year scholarships are available.

The W. E. B. Du Bois Honors College, National Institute of Health–MARC Honors Program, and Young Scientist Program are available for exceptional students.

ATHLETIC PROGRAMS

Jackson State is a member of the National Collegiate Athletic Association (NCAA), the Southwestern Athletic Conference, Association for Intercollegiate Athletics for Women, and National Association of Women's Sports.

Intercollegiate sports: men's baseball, basketball, cross-country running, football, golf, tennis, and track & field; women's basketball, cross-country running, volleyball, and track & field.

Intramural sports: touch football, cross–country, table tennis, basketball, bowling, volleyball, swimming, badminton, softball, golf, tennis, billiards, track & field, chess, weight lifting, archery, and horseshoes.

Athletic Contact

Dr. Howard Davis, Director of Athletics, Jackson State University, Jackson, MS 39217; (601) 968-2100.

LIBRARY HOLDINGS

The Henry T. Sampson Library holds over 360,400 books, 2,706 periodicals, 437,500 microforms, and audiovisual materials. In addition three satellite libraries–Curriculum Center Library, Music Library, and Information Services Library for demographics, census data, business, and economics–are available. Special collections include the Margaret Walker Alexander Collection, the Bolton C. Price Collection, the Afro-American Collection, and the Mississippi Collection.

STUDENT LIFE

Special Regulations

Class attendance is mandatory. Students must register their car with the Campus Police Office.

Campus Services

Health center, personal and psychological counseling, and career planning and placement.

Campus Activities

Social and cultural activities include theater, musicals, orchestra, chorale, and dance. Interested students may work on the *Blue and White Flash* (student newspaper) or the *Jacksonian* (yearbook).

Leadership opportunities are found in professional and departmental associations or special interest groups such as the chess club, karate club, NAACP, or the *Blue and White Flash,* an independent newspaper on campus. Students with musical, dramatic, or dance talent may join the Orchestra Club, the Dunbar Drama Guild, or JSU Modern Dance Troupe. Greek-letter fraternities include Alpha Phi Alpha, Kappa Alpha Psi, Omega Psi Phi, and Phi Beta Sigma; sororities include Alpha Kappa Alpha, Delta Sigma Theta, Sigma Gamma Rho, and Zeta Phi Beta sororities. Honor societies include four general honor societies–Alpha Chi, Alpha Kappa Mu, Alpha Lambda Delta, Phi Kappa Phi, and fourteen departmental honor societies. The Religious Council consists of seven clubs of various faiths.

Jackson State University is located in the heart of Jackson, the capital of Mississippi, with a population of approximately 396,000. The city features a zoological park, an art museum and gallery, house museums, historic buildings, and a planetarium. Shopping malls are nearby. Annual activities include the Mississippi State Fair, a blues festival, and the Jubilee Jam. The city is served by mass rail and air transportation. New Orleans, Louisiana, is approximately a four-hour drive from the campus.

Housing Availability
2,596 housing spaces; four men's dormitories, an honor's dormitory, and two large women's dormitory complexes. A housing fee of $25 is required to reserve a room.

Handicapped Services
Wheelchair accessibility.

NOTABLE ALUMNI
George Everett Barnes, Ph.D., 1962–President, Hinds Community College

Lem Barney–Former NFL member

Robert G. Clark, 1953–Representative, State of Mississippi District 47

Dr. Elwyn M. Grimes, 1964–Director, Truman Medical Center, Missouri

Sebetha Jenkins, Ed.D.–President, Jarvis Christian College

Walter Payton, 1975–Former NFL all-Pro Chicago Bears Team

Mary Levi Smith, Ed.D., 1957–President, Kentucky State University

Robert M. Walker, 1966–Mayor of Vicksburg, MS

Gladys J. Willis, 1965–Professor of English and department chair, Lincoln University, PA

Mary
Holmes
College

MARY HOLMES COLLEGE

PO Drawer 1257
Highway 50 West
West Point, MS 39773
Phone: (601) 494-6820
Toll-free:
800-634-2744
Fax: (601) 494-5319

Total Enrollment:
745

Level of Selectivity:
Noncompetitive

Motto:
Not to seem,
but to be

HISTORY

Mary Holmes College is a two-year, church-related, coed, liberal arts college. It was founded in 1892 by the Board of Freedmen of the Presbyterian Church (USA). The school's original name was Mary Holmes Seminary, named for a woman who dedicated her life to helping former slaves. The school's original purpose was to provide a Christian education and "to instruct black girls in the domestic sciences." The school moved from Jackson to West Point in 1897 after a fire destroyed the building in Jackson. In 1932, Mary Holmes College became coeducational, created its first college department, and changed its mission to training teachers. Mary Holmes College became a two-year college in 1959.

Mary Holmes College's current mission is to promote students in the pursuit of knowledge, academic achievement, cultivation of religious conviction, and dedication to community service. Most students are the first in their families to attend college, hence the inspiring school motto, "Not to seem, but to be." Mary Holmes serves the community as well as its students. In 1965 it trained volunteers for the Head Start Program in Mississippi. For many years it operated the only rural transportation service in its county and in 1960 it was the location for the start-up projects to develop catfish farming and legal services for the poor.

Situated on 192 acres, the campus is located in West Point, a small rural town with a population of 10,000. Mary Holmes College is 15 miles northwest of Columbus, Mississippi. The campus facilities include classroom buildings, housing for faculty and students, maintenance and support facilities, a student center, a learning resources center, a tennis court, a baseball field, and an intramural sports field.

ACCREDITATION

Mary Holmes College is accredited by the Southern Association of Colleges and Schools to award the Associate of Arts, Associate of Sciences, and Associate of Applied Sciences degrees.

Other Accreditation

Mississippi Department of Education.

Mississippi Commission on College
Accreditation

COSTS PER YEAR

1992–93 Tuition: $4,000

Room and board: $1,800 (room); $2,000
(board)

Special fees: $100

Books: $400

Estimated total cost: $8,300

FINANCIAL AID

1991–92 Institutional Funding

Number of scholarships and grants: 472

Total amount of scholarships and grants:
$1,428,280

Range of scholarships and grants:
$200–$8,500

1991–92 Federal and State Funding

Total amount of scholarships and grants:
$1,448,225

Financial Aid Specific to the School

98% of the students received financial
aid during 1992–93.

Athletic scholarships are available at
this school for students participating in intercollegite sports.

The Cooperative Education Program alternates and combines classroom study with
related paid work experience. The program
provides academic credit and full-time status
during co-op placement.

A deferred payment plan allows students to pay college costs in two or three installments during the semester.

Mary Holmes awards over $1 million in
scholarships each year. Three of its scholarships include the president, dean, and faculty awards given each year for academic
achievement. Mary Holmes scholarships

and grants are awarded to entering freshmen
based on merit.

The Mississippi State Student Incentive
Grant Program (SSIG) is available to Mississippi residents who show substantial financial need. Award ranges are $200–$500
for an academic year.

Performance scholarships are awarded
to students who demonstrate talent in music,
drama, or student leadership.

Trinity Presbyterian Church offers a
monetary award for religious leadership and
service.

Tuition waivers for full- or part-time tuition are available for employees of Mary
Holmes and their children.

Vocational Rehabilitation assistance is
available to qualifying students who are disabled.

Financial Aid Deadline

August 1 (priority)

Financial Aid Contact

Darnell Davidson, Financial Aid Counselor, Mary Holmes College, PO Drawer
1257, Highway 50 West, West Point, MS
39773; (601) 494-6820.

ADMISSION REQUIREMENTS

Open admission. SAT or ACT used for
placement.

Entrance Requirements:

Graduation from an accredited high
school and completion of the following
units: 4 English, 3 mathematics, 2 social science, and 2 science; an official high school
transcript; 3 letters of recommendation.

GED students must meet basic admission requirements.

Transfer students must submit a high
school transcript if less than 15 college credit hours have been completed; official transcript of all college work; and 3 letters of
recommendation.

International students must pass the
TOEFL examination and provide proof of

ability to pay all college costs by completing certificate of finance.

Early admission allows academically gifted high school students the opportunity to enroll for college credits before completing high school.

Admission Application Deadline

Rolling admission provides no specific date for notification of admission so applicant is informed as soon as the admission decision is made.

Admission Contact

Director of Admissions, PO Drawer 1257, Mary Holmes College, West Point, MS 39773; (601) 494-6820, Ext. 470 or toll free 800-634-2749.

GRADUATION REQUIREMENTS

A minimum of 64 credit hours and completion of core requirements to include the following hours: 6 English, 6 mathematics, 6 science, 6 social sciences, 2 physical education, and 1 computer course; minimum 2.0 grade point average with no grade less than a C- in the major field of study; last 15 credit hours completed at Mary Holmes College; recommended by the faculty; and paid $50 graduation fee.

Grading System

A–F; I=Incomplete; W=Withdrew-without penalty; WP=Withdrew-passing, no penalty; WF=Withdrew-failing; AU=Audit; K=Credit by examination.

STUDENT BODY PROFILE

Total enrollment (male/female): 297/448

From in-state: 633

Other regions: 13 states; 4 foreign countries

Full-time undergraduates (male/female): 262/394

Part-time undergraduates (male/female): 36/53

Ethnic/Racial Makeup

African American, 730; International, 15.

Class of 1995 Profile

Number of applicants: 941

Number accepted: 894

Number enrolled: 340

Average high school GPA: 2.495

FACULTY PROFILE

Number of faculty: 37

Student-faculty ratio: 20:1

Full-time faculty: 26

Part-time faculty: 11

Faculty with doctorate or other terminal degrees: 29%

SCHOOL CALENDAR

1993–94: August 18–April 27 (semesters)

Commencement and conferring of degrees: May 1

One summer session.

DEGREES OFFERED 1991–92:

Associate of Science

Accounting

Business Administration

Business Education

Business Management

Chemical Technology

Chemistry

Computer Science

Data Processing

Early Childhood Education

Economics

Elementary Education

Mathematics

Office Administration

Physical Education

Physics

Political Science

Pre-Science/Biological Science

Pre-Science/Medical Technology

Pre-Science/Natural Science

Social Science

Special Education

Associate of Arts

Communications

English

History

Liberal Arts (2 year transfer)

Music

Psychology

Religion

Speech and Drama

Associate of Applied Science

Cosmetology and Salon Management

Pre-Professional Programs

Pre-Dentistry

Pre-Engineering

Pre-Law

Pre-Medicine

Pre-Nursing

Graduates that later obtain higher degrees:
65%

SPECIAL PROGRAMS

Adult or Continuing Education Program is available for nontraditional students returning to school or working full time.

Advanced Placement (AP) grants college credit for postsecondary work completed in high school. Students scoring 3 on the AP test will receive credit by examination for each course.

College Level Examination Program (CLEP) determines the academic relevance of nontraditional educational experiences, such as the military, on-the-job training, or other life experiences, through a series of tests and may grant students college credit for these experiences. A maximum of 30 hours will be accepted.

College orientation is offered at no cost to entering students for two days prior to the beginning of classes to acquaint students with the college and to prepare them for college life.

Certificate programs in Cosmetology, Entrepreneurial Skills, and Child Development Associate are offered.

Honors Colloquium is designed to enhance reading, writing, and critical thinking skills. Qualifying students must have a minimum 3.5 high school or college GPA.

Individualized majors allow students to create their own major program(s) of study.

The part-time degree program allows students to earn an undergraduate degree while attending part time.

Remedial courses are offered to entering students to bring them up to admission standards and to help them adjust for success in college.

ATHLETIC PROGRAMS

Mary Holmes college is a member of the National Junior College Athletic Association (NJCAA).

Intercollegiate sports: men's basketball, cross-country, and soccer; women's basketball, softball, and volleyball.

Intramural sports: Archery, badminton, basketball, cross-country running, football, soccer, table tennis, track & field, volleyball, and weight lifting.

Athletic Contact

James Crawford, Coach, Mary Holmes College, PO Drawer 1257, Highway 50 West, West Point, MS 39773; (601) 494-6820 or toll free 1-800-634-2749.

LIBRARY HOLDINGS

The library holds 23,144 volumes, 1,264 microforms, 106 periodical subscriptions, and 71 audiovisuals; 75 computers are available for student use in the library and elsewhere on campus.

STUDENT LIFE

Special Regulations

Official attendance records are kept and students are required to attend class.

Campus Services

Health center, personal and psychological counseling, career placement counseling, tutoring, and campus ministry program.

Campus Activities

Social and cultural activities include theater, chorale, movies, concerts, dances, guest speakers, talent shows, and skating parties. Assemblies and church services enhance each student's college experience. Students can work on the student-run newspaper or yearbook.

Leadership opportunities are found in the Student Government Association or other student-run groups such as the drama club, service organizations, or special interest groups. Several local fraternities and sororities are represented on campus.

Mary Holmes College is located in the small rural town of West Point, Mississippi with a population of approximately 10,000. The campus is close to downtown West Point for shopping. Mass bus transportation is one mile from campus. The airport is 14 miles away, with limousine service available to West Point.

Housing Availability

642 housing spaces are available, including single-parent housing.

NOTABLE ALUMNI

Evelyn K. Bonner, 1961–Librarian, Sitka, Alaska

Lester Coffee, 1968–CPA, U.S.A. Security Exchange

Ceasar Coleman, 1940–Bishop, Christian Methodist Episcopal Church

Joseph Coleman, 1941–President, Philadelphia city counsel

Doris Gore, 1968–Assistant principal, Patterson, New Jersey public schools

Dr. Pearl Walter Headd, 1935–Professor emeritus, Tuskegee Institute

Dr. Clifton Orr, 1969–Professor of chemistry, University of Arkansas

Charles Thomas, 1970–Vice-President, Yazoo City (Mississippi) State Bank

MISSISSIPPI VALLEY STATE UNIVERSITY

Highway 82 West
Itta Bena, MS 38941
Phone: (601) 254-9041
Fax: (601) 254-6704

Total Enrollment:
1,691

Level of Selectivity:
Slightly competitive

Motto:
Live for Service

HISTORY

Mississippi Valley State University (MVSU) is a state-supported, four-year, coed, liberal arts college. Endorsed by the Mississippi Legislature in 1946, the Mississippi Vocational College opened in the summer of 1950 to train teachers for rural and elementary schools and to provide vocational training. In 1964, the name of the institution was changed to Mississippi Valley State College to reflect the addition of a liberal arts and sciences curriculum. Ten years later, the governor of Mississippi granted university status to the school and hence, the name change to Mississippi Valley State University in 1974.

Mississippi Valley's mission is to serve all students—students who are accelerated, students with adequate college preparation, and students who require remediation. While the student population is from all over the country, the majority of students come from the predominantly black Mississippi Delta region.

The 33-building campus is located on 450 acres, one mile northeast of Itta Bena. In addition to dorms, classrooms, and administrative buildings, 32 faculty homes and 127 modernly designed apartments are on the campus. Many faculty members and their families, as well as the university president, live on campus. This school is one of 104 traditional black colleges and universities.

ACCREDITATION

Mississippi Valley State University is accredited by the Southern Association of College and Schools (SACS) to award the Bachelor of Arts, Bachelor of Science, and Master of Science degrees.

Other Accreditation

Accrediting Commission on Education for Health Services Administration

Council on Social Work Education

National Accreditation Council for Environmental Health Curricula

National Association of Industrial Technology

National Association of Schools of Art and Design

National Association of Schools of Music

National Council for the Accreditation of Teacher Education

State Department of Education of Mississippi

COSTS PER YEAR

1992–93 Tuition: $2,164 (in-state); $4,189 (out-state)

Room and board: $2,025

Special fees: $125

Books: $500

Estimated total cost: $4,814 (in-state); $6,839 (out-state)

FINANCIAL AID

1991–92 Institutional Funding

Total amount of scholarships and grants: $902,276

1991–92 Federal and State Funding

Total amount of scholarships and grants: $3,774,239

Financial Aid Specific to the School

95% of the student body received financial aid during 1991–92.

Athletic grants are available in football, basketball, track, baseball, volleyball, tennis, and golf through the athletic department.

College work aid is available for students not qualifying for work-study to work in various departments on campus.

The Cooperative Education Program alternates classroom study with related paid work experience. The program provides academic credit and full-time status during co-op placement.

The deferred payment plan allows students who live on campus and who receive no financial aid from the university to make three separate payments each semester for a cost of $25.

Music scholarships are available in choir and band through the fine arts department.

State Student Incentive Grants (SSIG) are available for qualifying students.

Front entrance, Mississippi Valley State University

The Thurgood Marshall Black Education Fund provides a four-year scholarship at this public black college. Qualifying students must have a high school GPA of 3.0 or better and a SAT score of 1,000 or ACT score of 24 or more. Students must be recommended by high school counselor as exceptional or exemplary in the creative or performing arts. Scholarship pays tuition, fees, room, and board, not to exceed $6,000 annually.

Financial Aid Deadline
April 1 (priority)

Financial Aid Contact
Director of Financial Aid, Lucille Petry Leon Building, MVSU, Itta Bena, MS 38941; (601) 254-9041, ext. 6540.

ADMISSION REQUIREMENTS
SAT or ACT required. State residents should have a minimum ACT score of 13, although some students with scores between 10 and 12 will be considered for admission. Out-of-state students must have a minimum score of 15 on the ACT or 600 on the SAT. International students must have a minimum ACT score of 20 or SAT score of 780.

Entrance Requirements
Graduation from an accredited high school. Students whose ACT scores are below 20 must have the following high school credits: 4 units English; 3 units mathematics—algebra I and II, and geometry; 3 units science, one of which must include a lab—biology, advanced biology, chemistry, advanced chemistry, physics, or advanced physics; 2 1/2 units social science, including U.S. history and American government; and 1 unit elective—foreign language, mathematics above algebra II, or extra science course. Students must submit proof of immunization for measles and rubella.

Students 21 or over who are not veterans and who do not have an ACT score or who do not meet the minimum requirements are admitted on a temporary basis.

GED students must meet basic admission requirements.

Transfer students are required to have an overall "C" average in the following 24 semester credit hours: 6 English composition; 3 college algebra or above; 6 laboratory science; and 9 transferable electives. Students must be in good standing from previous college attended and provide proof of immunization for measles and rubella.

International students must have a minimum score of 525 on the TOEFL examination, as well as a composite score of 21 on the ACT or 840 on the SAT; must provide proof of immunization for measles and rubella.

Admission Application Deadline
Rolling admission provides no specific date for notification of admission so applicant is informed as soon as admission decision is made.

Admission Contact
Office of Admissions, Lucille Petry Leon Building, MVSU, Itta Bena, MS 38941; (601) 254-9041, ext. 6393 or (601) 254-6435.

GRADUATION REQUIREMENTS

A minimum of 124 credit hours and completion of core requirements to include 12 hours in English, 3 hours in fine arts, 6 hours in social studies, 3 hours in speech, 3 hours in health education, 2 hours in physical education or ROTC, 3 hours in general psychology, 6 hours in science with lab, and 3 hours in college algebra. Students must complete the requirements of the major field of study with a "C" or better in each major course and earn a GPA of not less than 2.0. Students must complete the senior year or its equivalent on campus with a minimum of 30 semester hours completed at MVSU and pass the English Proficiency requirement.

Grading System

A-F; I=Incomplete; L=In Progress; W= Withdrew for class; WP=Withdrew from school; P=Passing.

STUDENT BODY PROFILE

Total enrollment (male/female): 693/998

From in-state: 1,415

Full-time undergraduates (male/female): 451/649

Part-time undergraduates (male/female): 240/345

Graduate students (male/female): 2/4

FACULTY PROFILE

Number of faculty: 127

Student-teacher ratio: 18:1

Faculty with doctorates or other terminal degrees: 42%

SCHOOL CALENDAR

1993–94: August 24–May 13 (semester hours)

Commencement and conferring of degrees: May 14

One summer session.

DEGREES OFFERED 1991–92:

Bachelor of Arts

Art–painting

Art–visual communication

Broadcasting

Communication

English

Journalism

Political Science

Public Relations

Sociology

Speech Communication

Bachelor of Science

Biology

Business Administration–accounting

Business Administration–general business administration

Business Administration–management

Computer Science

Criminal Justice

Elementary Education

Elementary Education–computer science

English Education

Environmental Health

Health, Physical Education and Recreation

Industrial Technology–architectural technology

Industrial Technology–building construction technology

Industrial Technology–electronic technology

Industrial Technology–graphic technology

Industrial Technology–management

Industrial Technology–manufacturing/ robotics technology

Mathematics

Music Education–instrumental

Music Education–vocal

Music Education–keyboard

Office Administration–administrative assistant

Office Administration–office systems

Secondary Education

Social Work

Master of Science
Environmental Health

SPECIAL PROGRAMS

Accelerated study program allows students to complete their undergraduate degree in a shorter period of time than the traditional four years.

Advanced Placement (AP) grants college credit for postsecondary work completed in high school. Students scoring 3 on the AP test will receive credit by examination for each course and advanced placement.

College Level Examination Program (CLEP) determines the academic relevance of nontraditional educational experiences such as the military, on-the-job training, or other life experiences through a series of tests and may grant students college credit for these experiences.

The Cooperative Education Program combines classroom study with related paid work experience. The program provides academic credit and full-time status during co-op placement.

Educational Talent Search identifies talented youth who may have been overlooked, yet have the potential for rewarding careers in trades and professions.

The Honors program offers academically talented students a challenging program of study that includes special classes, seminars, colloquia, cultural activities, and special recognition to motivate participants.

MVSU Writing Project provides professional development opportunities for teachers in all disciplines, kindergarten through college, in the Mississippi Delta region. The program offers credit and non-credit activities generally for 6 hours of graduate credit by special arrangement with Mississippi State University or for continuing education credit.

The nursery/preschool program provides education majors opportunities to gain practical experience teaching children between the ages of 3 and 6.

ROTC provides training in military science for commission as a second lieutenant in the U.S. Army and Air Force. Two- and four-year scholarships are available.

Student support services provides developmental courses and counseling to students who need aid to succeed in college.

ATHLETIC PROGRAMS

Mississippi Valley State University is a member of the National Collegiate Athletic Association (NCAA), Football Div I-AA.

Intercollegiate sports: men's football and track; women's track.

Athletic Contact
Charles J. Prophet, Director of Athletics, Recreation and Assembly Building, Itta Bena, MS 38941; (601) 254-9041, ext. 6370.

LIBRARY HOLDINGS

The James Herbert White Library has 160,000 volumes, 675 periodical subscriptions, 262,000 microforms, and 7,555 audiovisuals. The library has an archives and oral history collection located in the Mississippi Room.

STUDENT LIFE

Special Regulations
Alcohol prohibited on campus.

Campus Services
Health center; career counseling and placement; testing for ACT, SAT, NTE, CLEP, and English Proficiency II; preschool program; and religious activities, including chapel.

Campus Activities
Social activities include theater, orchestra, and band. Students may work on the *Del-*

vian (yearbook) or the *Delta Devil Gazette* (student-run newspaper).

Leadership opportunities are found in the Student Government Association (SGA) or other organizations such as English Club, Future Teachers of America, and Trades and Industries Club.

Itta Bena is located in the heart of the Mississippi Delta region, known for its fish farms and blues music. The campus is approximately 8 miles from Greenwood, which is one of the largest cotton markets in the United States and has a rich American Indian history. To the south, approximately 100 miles, is the city of Jackson, Mississippi—the state capital with a population of approximately 209,000. To the north approximately 120 miles is the city of Memphis, Tennessee. Both cities offer an array of social and cultural activities.

Housing Availability

Five residence halls for men and five residence halls for women.

NOTABLE ALUMNI

Fannye E. Love–Chairperson of teacher education, LeMoyne-Owen College

Hampton Smith–Professor of health and physical education, Albany State College

RUST COLLEGE

HISTORY

Rust College is a private, four-year, coed college, founded in 1866 by the Freedman's Aid Society of the Methodist Episcopal Church. It is the oldest historically black college in Mississippi. Rust began as Shaw School and was chartered in 1870 as Shaw University, in honor of Reverend S. O. Shaw. It originally provided elementary education; later, high school and college courses were added. In 1878, the college graduated its first two students. Shaw University became Rust University in 1892 to eliminate confusion with another school of the same name. In 1915, the name Rust College was adopted to more accurately reflect the scope of programs. The elementary and secondary programs were discontinued in 1930 and 1953 respectively.

As a private, church-related school, Rust College works to heighten each student's moral, spiritual, intellectual, and social growth. Rust's first president, Reverend A. C. McDonald, created the school's motto "By their fruits ye shall know them."

150 Rust Ave.
Holly Springs, MS
38635-2330
Phone: (601) 252-4661
Fax: (601) 252-6107

Total Enrollment:
1,129

Level of Selectivity:
Slightly competitive

Motto:
By their fruits ye shall
know them

Over 30 buildings grace the rural 120-acre campus, including the original 1867 building, Oakview Mansion, which is now a dormitory for women. The Leontyne Price Library, named for the Metropolitan Opera star, was one of eight major building projects completed between 1967 and 1974. An aggressive construction program has continued into the 1990s, with the Ervin "Magic" Johnson Sports Arena completed in 1992.

ACCREDITATION

Rust is accredited by the Southern Association of Colleges and Schools to award the Bachelor of Arts, Bachelor of Science and Associate in Science degrees.

Other Accreditation

Mississippi State Department of Education

University Senate of the United Methodist Church

COSTS PER YEAR

1992–93 Tuition: $3,600

Room and board: $898 (room); $1,050 (board)

Special fees: $552

Books: included in tuition

Estimated total cost: $6,100

FINANCIAL AID

1991–92 Institutional Funding

Number of scholarships and grants: 556

Total amount of scholarships and grants: $629,451

Range of scholarships and grants: $200–$6,100

1991–92 Federal and State Funding

Number of scholarships and grants: 2,150

Total amount of scholarships and grants: $2,395,414

Range of scholarships and grants: $200–$2,400

Number of loans: 646

Total amount of loans: $1,421,458

Range of loans: $500–$4,000

Number of work-study: 512

Total amount of work-study: $326,000

Range of work-study: $200–$550

Financial Aid Specific to the School

During the 1991–92 school year, 98% of the student body received financial aid.

Students not receiving financial assistance who pay their tuition during registration receive a 5% discount.

The deferred payment plan allows students with special permission to pay 50% of money owed at registration, with the balance due in two equal payments. A 5% charge is issued on the unpaid amount.

There are 32 endowed scholarships, several of which have multiple recipients.

The College Grant-In-Aid program awards a limited number of choir and band performance grants ranging from $100–$1,000.

The Honors Track Program awards three types of scholarships to students with a 3.0–3.5 GPA and ACT scores of 17-22. The Honors Track awards full scholarships, the Presidential scholarship awards up to $2,000, and the Academic Dean scholarship awards up to $1,500.

Employees of Rust, and their families, receive a 75% discount on tuition (minimum employment requirement is 2 years). Work-study is also available.

The United Negro College Fund scholarship is available to entering students scoring high on the ACT or ETS exams, or students with a high school GPA of 3.0. Students must maintain a cumulative GPA of 3.0 in college to renew scholarships.

The Army ROTC program offers two-, three-, and four-year scholarships that pay tuition, books, fees, other expenses, and a monthly stipend of $100.

The State Student Incentive Grant (SSIG) is awarded to Mississippi residents with a 2.0 GPA and proof of financial need.

The United Methodist (UM) scholarship is awarded to U.S. citizens who are members of the UM church with a 'B' average or better.

Licensed or ordained ministerial students receive a 10% discount on tuition.

Financial Aid Deadline

May 1 (fall); August 15 (spring)

Financial Aid Contact

Ms. Fannie Lampley, Director of Financial Aid, Rust College, Holly Springs, MS 38635; (601) 252-4852.

ADMISSION REQUIREMENTS

SAT or ACT scores required.

Entrance Requirements

Graduation from an accredited high school and completion of the following units: 16 units: 4 English, 3 social studies, 3 mathematics, 2 natural sciences, 4 electives. Two letters of recommendation are required, with one from the school principal or counselor. A medical exam is required. A $10 non-refundable application fee is required.

GED students must have two letters of recommendation from persons who can certify the student's ability to do college-level work.

Transfer students must meet the same requirements as stated above. Students who have completed a minimum of 15 semester hours at the college level, however, need not submit ACT or SAT scores.

International students must pass the TOEFL examination and provide satisfactory proof of adequate financial resources.

Veterans must meet the general admission requirements and provide a certificate of eligibility for training.

Conditional admission students must satisfy regular academic admission requirements within the first semester.

Admission Application Deadline

Rolling admission provides no specific date for notification of admission so applicant is informed as soon as admission decision is made; early admission allows qualified students to enter college full time before completing high school; early decision provides notification of acceptance early in applicant's 12th year of high school.

Admission Contact

Miss Joan Scott, Director of Admissions, Rust College, Holly Springs, MS 38635; (601) 252-8000, ext. 4068.

GRADUATION REQUIREMENTS

Bachelor's Degree

124 semester hours, including core requirements with a 2.0 minimum GPA; full-time student for at least two semesters; last

30 semester hours completed at Rust College, including one-third of the courses in the major area of study at Rust College.

Associate's Degree

63 semester hours including core requirements with a 2.0 minimum GPA; full-time student for at least one semester; last 15 semester hours completed at Rust College.

Grading System

A-F; I=Incomplete; W=Withdrew.

STUDENT BODY PROFILE

Total enrollment (male/ female): 406/723

From in-state: 751

Other regions: 22 states; 11 foreign countries

Full-time undergraduates (male/female): 304/541

Part-time undergraduates (male/female): 102/182

Ethnic/Racial Makeup

African American, 1062; Caucasian, 25; International, 23; Others/unclassified 19.

Class of 1995 Profile

Number of applicants: 912

Number accepted: 550

Number enrolled: 354

Median ACT score: 16

Average high school GPA: 2.5

Transfer applicants: 86

Transfers accepted: 58

Transfers enrolled: 44

FACULTY PROFILE

Number of faculty: 61

Student-teacher ratio: 18:1

Full-time faculty: 53

Part-time faculty: 14

Tenured faculty: 6

Faculty with doctorates or other terminal degrees: 60%

SCHOOL CALENDAR

1993-94: August 14–April 25 (semesters)

Commencement and conferring of degrees: April

One summer session.

DEGREES OFFERED AND NUMBER CONFERRED 1991–92:

Associate in Science

Business Administration: 0

Early childhood education: 0

Secretarial Science: 0

Bachelor of Arts

Economics: 0

English: 6

English/Journalism: 2

English/Pre-law: 1

History: 0

Mass Communication/Journalism: 1

Mass Communication/Television: 9

Mass Communication/Television/Radio: 3

Music: 1

Music Media: 1

Political Science: 9

Social Work: 12

Sociology: 5

Bachelor of Science

Biology: 7

Business Administration/Accounting: 11

Business Administration/Computer Science: 13

Business Administration/Management: 15

Business Administration/Marketing: 7

Business Education/Administrative Information: 5

Chemistry: 5

Computer Science/Business Administration: 9

Computer Science/Natural Science: 1

Early Childhood Education: 9

Elementary Education: 0

Health-Physical Education and Recreation (non-teaching): 9

Mathematics: 1

Medical Technology (in collaboration with other colleges and universities): 0

Graduates that later obtain higher degrees:

1% enter medical school

2% enter law school

1% enter business school

3% enter arts and sciences

SPECIAL PROGRAMS

Adult of continuing education is available for nontraditional students returning to school or working full time.

A three/two dual degree in engineering is offered in cooperation with Georgia Institute of Technology, Tuskegee Institute, Memphis State University, University of Mississippi, Mississippi State University, or Auburn University. Upon completion of a five-year curriculum, the student receives a Bachelor of Science degree from Rust and an engineering degree from the cooperating institution.

Three/two dual degree in nursing in cooperation with Alcorn State University. Upon completion of a five-year curriculum, the student receives a Bachelor of Science degree from Rust and a nursing degree from Alcorn.

College orientation is offered at no cost to entering students for two days prior to the beginning of class to acquaint student with the college and prepare them for college life. Parents may attend.

Cooperative Medical Technology Program with Meharry Medical College and Tennessee State. The student receives a Bachelor of Science in Medical Technology from Rust and a certificate from Meharry Medical College/Tennessee State University after completing the four-year curriculum.

The Cooperative Education Program combines knowledge gained in the classroom with "hands on" paid work experience.

Many of the baccalaureate programs require 12 semester hours of cooperative education experience. Students are assisted by the college in securing a job placement.

Honors program offers academically talented students a challenging program of study that includes special classes, seminars, colloquia, cultural activities, and special recognition to motivate students.

The two-week Basic Study Skills Program is required for all entering freshmen at no cost. The program acquaints students with the skills necessary to succeed in college.

Remedial courses are offered to entering students to bring them up to admissions standards and to help them adjust for success in college.

ROTC provides training in military science for commission as a second lieutenant in the U.S. Armed Forces. Two-, three- and four-year scholarships are available.

ATHLETIC PROGRAMS

Rust College is a member of the National Association of Intercollegiate Athletics (NAIA), Division III; and the Southern Intercollegiate Athletic Conference (SIAC).

Intercollegiate sports: men's baseball, basketball, cross-country, tennis, and track & field; women's basketball, cross-country, tennis and track & field.

Intramural sports: archery, badminton, basketball, bowling, cross-country, softball, swimming, table tennis, tennis, track & field, and volleyball.

Athletic Contact

Mrs. Fannie Lampley, Athletic Director, Rust College; Holly Springs, MS 38635; (601) 252-8000, ext. 4059.

LIBRARY HOLDINGS

The Leontyne Price Library holds 98,000 volumes, 5,236 microforms, 735 audiovisuals, 402 periodical subscriptions, and 170 computers available for student use. Special collections include the "Black Blues Collection" and the Bishop Edward J. Pendergrass Collection.

STUDENT LIFE

Special Regulations

All students are encouraged to live on campus. Exceptions are made for married students and local students within commuting distance.

Campus Services

Health Center, guidance and counseling, student employment, career placement, testing, remedial assistance, and religious services (including chapel).

Campus Activities

Social and group activities include theater, band, chorale, and dance. Cultural activities on and off campus include music, book reviews, plays, and lectures. Assembly programs offer entertainment and spiritual enrichment. Students may get involved with the student newspaper, the *Rustorian,* or join the *Bearcat* yearbook staff. Communication majors may work in the campus radio station (WURC-FM) or the television station (RC-TV2).

Leadership opportunities can be found in the Student Government Association, the NAACP, the International Students Association, the Honors Council and many other student groups. Greek-letter societies include Alpha Kappa Alpha, Delta Sigma Theta, Sigma Gamma Rho, and Zeta Phi Beta sororities, as well as the Alpha Phi Alpha, Kappa Alpha Psi, Omega Psi Phi and Phi Beta Sigma fraternities. Four honor societies are also represented on campus.

Located in Holly Springs, a small town in northern Mississippi, Rust College is 40 miles southeast of Memphis, Tennessee, and 54 miles northwest of Tupelo, Mississippi. Within an hours drive, students can find a variety of cultural and entertainment activities in these two cities.

Housing Availability

820 housing spaces; 5 dormitories. All students are encouraged to live on campus. Exceptions are made for married students and students within commuting distance.

NOTABLE ALUMNI

David L. Beckley, 1967–President, Wiley College

Amy Bolton-Curley, 1985–Media consultant/executive director

Lonear Heard-Davis, 1964–Corporate executive, James T. Heard Management Corporation, Cerritos, CA

Ida L. Jackson, 1914–First black teacher in Oakland, CA public schools

Dimaggio Nichols, 1973–President, Noble Ford-Mercury, Inc.

Dr. F. C. Richardson, 1960–President, Buffalo State College

Anita Ward, 1977–Pop singer

Ida B. Wells, 1878–Organizer of the NAACP

TOUGALOO COLLEGE

HISTORY

Tougaloo College is a four-year, private, coed, liberal arts college founded in 1869 by the American Missionary Association of New York which purchased 500 acres of a former plantation. Its purpose was to train young people "irrespective of their religious tenets" and to educate with "the most liberal principles for the benefit of our citizens in general." College courses were first offered in 1897, and the first bachelor of arts degree was awarded in 1901. In 1954, the name was changed to Tougaloo Southern Christian Institute, reflecting its merger with the Southern Christian Institute. The school name was changed again to the current Tougaloo College in 1963.

The campus has 19 buildings, including College House, the home to the college president and his family, and several cottages and apartments for faculty wishing to live on campus as well as scholars-in-residence. The Tougaloo Art Collection, housed in Warren Hall, exceeds 1,000 works of art.

300 E. County Line Rd.
Tougaloo, MS 39174
Phone: (601) 977-7711
Fax: (601) 977-7866

Total Enrollment:
1,003

Level of Selectivity:
Slightly competitive

Motto:
Where History Meets
the Future

Tougaloo College is proud that 38% of Mississippi's black physicians and 23% of its black dentists are Tougaloo graduates. The college is a United Negro College Fund school.

ACCREDITATION

Tougaloo College is accredited by the Commission on Colleges of the Southern Association of Colleges and Schools and by the Mississippi Department of Education to award Associate of Arts, Bachelor of Arts, and Bachelor of Science degrees.

Other Accreditation

Council of Higher Education of the United Church of Christ

Council of Protestant Colleges and Universities

Disciples of Christ

COSTS PER YEAR

1991–92 Tuition: $4,190

Room and board: $965 (room); $ 950 (board)

Special fees: $205

Books: $500

Estimated total cost: $6,810

FINANCIAL AID

1991–92 Institutional Funding

Number of scholarships and grants: 218

Total amount of scholarships and grants: $1,162,548

Range of scholarships and grants: $100–$5,637

1990–91 Federal and State Funding

Number of scholarships and grants: 921

Total amount of scholarships and grants: $1,663,311

Range of scholarships and grants: $400–$1,500

Number of loans: 686

Total amount of loans: $1,624,266

Range of loans: $500–$4,000

Number of work-study: 223

Total amount of work-study: $2000,008

Range of work-study: $150–$1,990

Financial Aid Specific to the School

87% of the student body received financial aid in 1991–92.

The Army ROTC offers two- and three-year scholarships that pay tuition, fees, books, and other expenses, as well as provide a monthly stipend of $100.

College work-aid is available to students not qualifying for college work-study to work in various departments of the college.

Fourteen loan funds specific to Tougaloo College make small loans to students for emergencies or short periods of time with no interest charge.

Partial Scholarships are available to freshmen with a minimum 3.0 high school GPA and a score of 18 or above on the Enhanced ACT. Scholarships range from $500 to $1,000. Presidential and Partial Scholarships are highly competitive.

The Presidential Scholarship covers tuition, room, and board and is renewable for four years if the student maintains a minimum average of 3.5. Eligible students must have 3.5 or higher high school GPA and score a minimum of 24 on the Enhanced ACT.

Twenty-three endowed scholarships are available at Tougaloo College. Eligibility for these funds varies by scholarship.

Students who do not receive financial aid from the college may make payments on an annual, semester, or installment basis. A 30 to 60 day deferment may be granted to students with proof of the following guaranteed payments: Guaranteed Student Loan, Plus Loan, Veteran Benefits, Social Security Payment, or Pending Pell Grant.

United Negro College Fund (UNCF) scholarships are available to entering students scoring high on the ACT or ETS, or students with a high school GPA of 3.0 or better. Students must maintain a cumulative GPA of 3.0 in college to renew scholarships.

Financial Aid Deadline
April 15.

Financial Aid Contact
Director of Financial Aid, Tougaloo College, Tougaloo, MS 39174; (601) 977-7769.

ADMISSION REQUIREMENTS
SAT or ACT required.

Entrance Requirements
High school diploma with a minimum "C" average and 16 units: 3 English, 2 history and social science, 2 mathematics, and 2 science. It is strongly urged that the math units comprise algebra and geometry. Two years of natural science (general science, biology, chemistry, or physics) and two years of a foreign language are recommended. An official high school transcript is required.

For GED students, a minimum score of 40 on the GED is required.

Transfer students must provide copies of all previous college transcripts and must have a minimum of a "C" (2.0) average and statement of satisfactory status at previous college attended.

International students must meet entrance qualifications as stated above and prove English language verbal and written proficiency. A score of 500 on the Test of English as a Foreign Language (TOEFL) or a passing grade on the test given by the English Language Institute (ELI) is needed. Proof of sufficient financial resources for tuition, room, and board, is also necessary.

Admission Application Deadline
Rolling admission provides no specific date for notification of admission so applicant is informed as soon as admission decision is made.

Admission Contact
The Student Enrollment Management Center, Tougaloo College, Tougaloo, MS 39174; (601) 977-7770 or 977-7771

GRADUATION REQUIREMENTS
To graduate, students must earn a minimum of a 2.0 average and pass 124 semester hours, including approximately 56 semester hours in general education; at least 27, but not more than 48, semester hours in a discipline major; and electives or professional requirements for certification in special fields. Students must have a minimum grade of 2.0 for all courses in major and pass the English Proficiency Examination. A comprehensive senior paper is required. Some departments may require students to pass a comprehensive examination as well. The final 30 semester hours must be earned from Tougaloo College.

Grading System
A-F; CR=Credit; NC=No credit; I=Incomplete; WP=Withdrew passing; WF=Withdrew failing; W=Withdrawal without penalty.

STUDENT BODY PROFILE
Total enrollment (male/female): 351/652

From in-state: 873

From other regions: 19 states and territories; 2 foreign countries

Full-time undergraduates (male/female): 334/619

Part-time undergraduates (male/female): 17/33

Ethnic/Racial Makeup
African American, 983; Native American, 10; International, 10.

Class of 1995 Profile
Number of applicants: 828

Number accepted: 811

Number enrolled: 316

Average high school GPA: 2.50

Transfers enrolled: 50

FACULTY PROFILE
Number of faculty: 66

Student/teacher ratio: 19:1

Full-time faculty: 44

Faculty with doctorates or other terminal degrees: 62%

SCHOOL CALENDAR

1992–93 August 24–May 14 (semesters)

Commencement: May 16

DEGREES OFFERED 1991–92:

Associate of Arts

Child Development

Early Childhood Education

Bachelor of Arts

Art

Biology

Chemistry

Economics

Economics–Accounting

Economics–Business Administration

Elementary Education

English

English–Journalism

Health, Physical Education, and Recreation

History

Humanities

Mathematics

Mathematics–Computer Science

Music

Physics

Political Science

Psychology

Sociology

Bachelor of Science

Biology

Chemistry

Mathematics

Mathematics–Computer Science

Physics

Graduates that later obtain higher degrees:

50%

SPECIAL PROGRAMS

The Boston University School of Medicine and Tougaloo College offer an early admissions policy for medical school that combines the senior year at Tougaloo with medical school classes at Boston University. Brown University School of Medicine offers a similar program.

The Cooperative Education Program combines formal academic study with practical work experience in major. Schedules may be alternating, parallel, or a combination of both.

The Pre-Engineering and Physical Sciences (PEPS) Program is a three/two program that gives students the opportunity to get two degrees—one in liberal arts from Tougaloo and the other in engineering from one of the following institutions: Brown University, Georgia Institute of Technology, the University of Mississippi, the University of Wisconsin at Madison, Tuskegee University, Howard University, Washington University in St. Louis, or Memphis State University.

The Army, Army Reserves, and Army National Guard ROTC provide training in military science at Jackson State University to Tougaloo students for a commission as a second lieutenant in the U. S. armed forces. The program is offered to all full-time students and offers two- and three-year scholarships.

Advanced Placement (AP) allows high school students to gain college credit for scores on the College Board AP tests in various subjects.

ATHLETIC PROGRAMS

Tougaloo College is a member of the Gulf Coast Athletic Conference and the National Association of Intercollegiate Athletics. The athletic program includes indoor and outdoor track, cross-country, and basketball.

Intramural-extramural sports include basketball, archery, tennis, flag football, soccer, and outdoor track. Teams include faculty, staff, and students.

Athletic Contact

Charles Orr, Director of Athletics, Tougaloo College, 300 E. County Line Rd., Tougaloo, MS 39174.

LIBRARY HOLDINGS

The L. Zenobia Coleman Library holds 91,251 bound volumes, 4,799 microforms, 450 periodical subscriptions, and 3,074 audiovisual materials. Special collections include the Black History Collection, a unique research resource of 3,400 rare and first edition books and 350 recordings.

STUDENT LIFE

Special Regulations

Class attendance required; must have a minimum cumulative grade point average of 2.50 and a 2.50 the previous semester to join Greek-letter organizations.

Campus Services

Academic computing center, counseling center, health center, mathematics center, modern foreign language laboratory, reading study skills and resource center, and writing center.

Campus Activities

Social activities include theater, departmental clubs, dances and other social affairs, convocations, weekly assembly programs, college choir, gospel choir, lectures, concerts,

and religious groups. Students may participate in the student newspaper, *Harambee,* and the Student Government Association. Greek-letter fraternities include Alpha Phi Alpha, Kappa Alpha Psi, Omega Psi Phi, and Phi Beta Sigma; sororities include Alpha Kappa Alpha, Delta Sigma Theta, Sigma Gamma Rho, and Zeta Phi Beta. Honor societies and service organizations include Alpha Kappa Delta, Alpha Kappa Mu Honor Society, Alpha Lambda Delta Honor Society, and Alpha Phi Omega National Service Fraternity.

Tougaloo College is located 3 miles north of Jackson, the largest city in Mississippi and the state capital. Historic Jackson is the home of a natural science museum, art museum, planetarium, botanical garden, zoological park, and several house museums. The city is known for its leading educational and medical centers.

Housing Availability

Men's and women's dormitories are available on campus.

NOTABLE ALUMNI

Reuben Anderson, 1964–Mississippi's first black Supreme Court Justice

Elaine Baker, Ph.D.–Professor of Sociology, Albany State

Dr. Oscar A. Rogers, Jr., 1950–President, Claflin College

Terrecia W. Sweet, 1977–Professor, California State University, Fresno

Walter Washington, 1948–President, Alcorn State University

Missouri

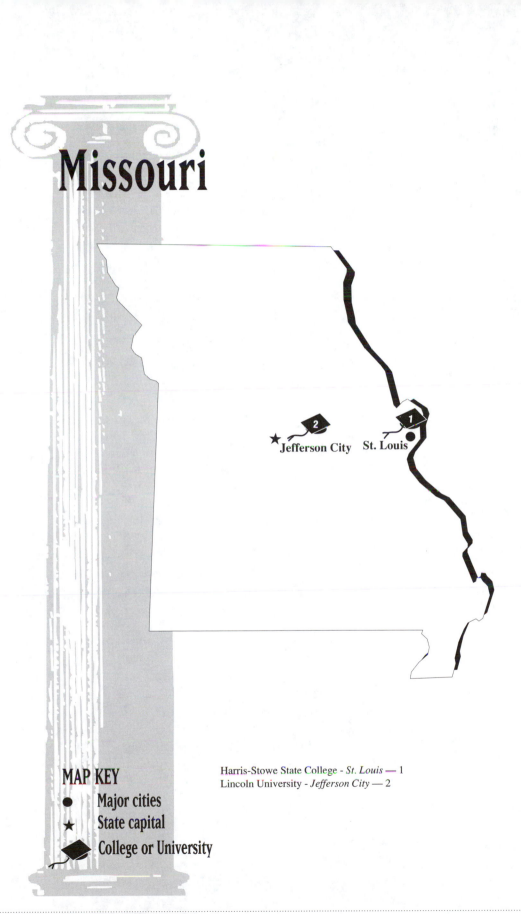

Jefferson City **St. Louis**

MAP KEY

● Major cities

★ State capital

◆ College or University

Harris-Stowe State College - *St. Louis* — 1
Lincoln University - *Jefferson City* — 2

HARRIS-STOWE STATE COLLEGE

3026 LaClede Ave.
St. Louis, MO 63103
Phone: (314) 340-3366
Fax: (314) 340-3322

Total Enrollment:
1,881

Level of Selectivity:
Slightly competitive

HISTORY

Harris-Stowe State College is a four-year, state-supported, coed, teachers' college. Established by the public school system of St. Louis in 1857, Harris Teacher's College was for white students only. In 1890, the public school system established the Sumner Normal School, an extension of Sumner High School, for the education of black teachers of elementary schools. In 1924, Sumner became a four-year degree granting college and five years later changed the institution's name to Stowe Teachers College, in honor of abolitionist and novelist Harriet Beecher Stowe. The current Harris-Stowe State College was created by the St. Louis Board of Education when it merged Harris Teacher's College and Stowe Teacher's College in 1954. The merger of the two teaching colleges was one of the first steps taken by the board of education to integrate the St. Louis public school system. In 1979, Harris-Stowe became a part of the Missouri state system of public higher education.

Harris-Stowe State College is an urban college exclusively dedicated to educating students to become teachers and education specialists. The college was approved for its unique Bachelor of Science in Urban Education degree in 1981. All programs at Harris-Stowe are devoted to professional education development.

ACCREDITATION

Harris-Stowe is accredited by the North Central Association of Colleges and Schools to award the Bachelor of Science degree.

Other Accreditation

Missouri Department of Elementary and
  Secondary Education
National Council for Accreditation of
  Teacher Education

COSTS PER YEAR

1992–93 Tuition: $1,728; (in-state); $3,296
  (out-state)
Special fees: $125
Books: $400
Estimated total cost: $2,253 (in-state);
  $3,821 (out-state)

FINANCIAL AID

1991–92 Institutional Funding

Total amount of scholarships and grants:
  $150,925

1991–92 Federal and State Funding

Total amount of scholarships and grants:
  $638,351

Financial Aid Specific to the School

85% of the student body received financial aid during 1991–92.

Academic scholarships that are based on character and scholastic record are available.

Athletic scholarships range from partial to full tuition scholarships for outstanding student athletes; they may include $100 or $50 for books.

Emergency loans provided by approximately thirteen endowments are available for a short term through the office of financial aid.

College Employment Program (CEP) provides an opportunity for students to work in various departments on campus part time.

A deferred payment plan allows students to pay college costs in four installments during the semester.

Army and Air Force ROTC in conjunction with Park College offer two- and four-year scholarships that pay tuition, fees, books, and other expenses, and provide a monthly stipend of $100.

Missouri residents may be eligible for the Missouri Student Grant Program (MSGP). Students should apply for MSGP by April 20th of each year.

The Scholarship Foundation of St. Louis Loan Program provides interest-free loans to students who are permanent residents of St. Louis; St. Louis County; or the school districts of Fox C-6, Francis Howell, Overland Farm, or St. Charles.

Financial Aid Deadline

April 15

Financial Aid Contact

Sharon Mitchell, Director of Financial Aid, Harris-Stowe State College, 3026 LeClede Ave., St. Louis, MO 63103; (314) 340-3500.

ADMISSION REQUIREMENTS

SAT or ACT required.

Entrance Requirements

Graduation from an accredited high school with a minimum of 14 units to include: 4 English (2 composition), 3 mathematics (1 algebra), 2 science (1 laboratory experience), 2 social studies; the remaining 3 units must be in foreign language, or any of the four areas previously cited. Students must submit an official transcript. A $15 application fee is required.

GED students must meet basic admission requirements.

Transfer students must satisfy all the admission requirements and have a satisfactory GPA.

International students must take the TOEFL examination, provide proof of ability to pay all college costs, and deposit funds at Harris-Stowe to cover tuition and fees for at least two semesters.

Early admission allows academically gifted high school students the opportunity to enroll in college full time before completing high school.

Admission Application Deadline

Rolling admission provides no specific date for notification of admission so applicant is informed as soon as admission decision is made; must apply two weeks prior to enrollment.

Admission Contact

Valerie A. Beeson, Director of Admissions and Advisement, Harris-Stowe State College, St. Louis, MO 63103; (314) 340-3300.

GRADUATION REQUIREMENTS

A minimum of 128 semester hours and completion of the core requirements to include: 9 credit hours humanities, 9 credit hours communication skills, 9 credit hours social and behavioral science, 10 credit hours physical and biological science, 3 credit hours mathematics; a 2.5 cumulative GPA is required. The last 30 semester hours of study must be at Harris-Stowe.

Grading System

A–F; AU=audit; CR=credit; NC=no credit; W=authorized withdrawal during 3rd or 4th week of classes; WN=authorized withdrawal after the 4th week of classes; INC=incomplete; P=pass; WL=withdrawal on re-enrollment of previously failed class; WR=repeat of passing grade less than C.

STUDENT BODY PROFILE

Total enrollment (male/female): 545/1,336

From in-state: 1,832

From other regions: 2 states; 11 foreign countries

Full-time undergraduates (male/female): 302/740

Part-time undergraduates (male/female): 213/596

Ethnic/Racial Makeup

African American, 1,336; Hispanic, 19; Native American, 19; International, 132; Other/unclassified, 375.

FACULTY PROFILE

Number of faculty: 99

Student-teacher ratio: 18:1

Full-time faculty: 37

Part-time faculty: 62

Faculty with doctorates or other terminal degrees: 62%

SCHOOL CALENDAR

1993–94: August 26–May 14 (semester hours)

Commencement and conferring of degrees:
  May 15

Two summer sessions.

DEGREES OFFERED 1991–92:

Bachelor of Science

Early Childhood Education

Elementary Education-art

Elementary Education-biology

Elementary Education-computer science

Elementary Education-early childhood
  education

Elementary Education-educational
  computing

Elementary Education-English

Elementary Education-mathematics

Elementary Education-multi-cultural
  education

Elementary Education-music (vocal)

Elementary Education-natural science

Elementary Education-physical education

Elementary Education-psychology

Elementary Education-social studies

Elementary Education-special education-
  behaviorally disordered

Elementary Education-special education-
  learning disabled

Elementary Education-special education-
  mentally handicapped

Elementary Education-speech and theater

Middle School/Junior High School
  Education-mathematics

Middle School/Junior High School
  Education-natural science

Middle School/Junior High School
  Education-social studies

Urban Education-accounting

Urban Education-business administration

Urban Education-management information
  systems

Urban Education-public administration

Urban Education-urban studies

Certification Program
Reading Specialist

SPECIAL PROGRAMS
Accelerated Study Program allows students to complete their undergraduate degree in a shorter period of time than the traditional period of four years.

College Level Examination Program (CLEP) determines the academic relevance of nontraditional educational experiences, such as the military, on-the-job training, or other life experiences, through a series of tests and may grant students college credit for these experiences.

Cooperative Study Abroad Program allows students to go to a foreign country for a specified period of time for part of their college education.

English as a Second Language is a program that offers courses in English for students whose native language is not English.

Off-campus study at St. Louis University and University of Missouri-St. Louis allows students to take courses for credit at these institutions.

Remedial courses are offered to entering students to bring them up to admission standards and to help them adjust for success in college.

ROTC provides training in military science for commission as a second lieutenant in the U.S. Army and Air Force in cooperation with Park College. Two- and four-year scholarships are available.

Student Support Services/Title IV Program assists low income and first generation students in their freshman and sophomore years with supplemental instruction.

ATHLETIC PROGRAMS
Harris-Stowe is a member of the National Association of Intercollegiate Athletics (NAIA).

Intercollegiate sports: men's baseball, basketball, and soccer; women's track, basketball, and volleyball.

Intramural sports: basketball, volleyball, flag football, floor hockey, softball, and tennis.

Athletic Contact

James Velten, Director of Athletics, Harris-Stowe State College, St. Louis, MO 63103; (314) 533-3366, ext. 305.

LIBRARY HOLDINGS

62,000 bound volumes.

STUDENT LIFE

Campus Services

Career planning and placement; personal guidance and counseling; and testing services for ACT, CAT (California Achievement Test) C-BASE (College Basic Academic Subjects Examination), and the NTE.

Campus Activities

Social and cultural activities include theater and chorale. Students look forward to annual homecoming events and Afro-American history month. Students may work on *The Hornets Nest* (student newspaper), *The Torch* (yearbook), or *The Fringe Benefit* (student art/literature magazine).

Leadership opportunities are found in the Student Government Association and numerous other student-run organizations such Student Ambassadors, Student Association Council for Exceptional Children, Ecology Club, and Student-MSTA (Missouri State Teacher's Association). Honor societies include Alpha Chi, Kappa Delta Pi, and Sigma Tau Delta.

Harris-Stowe is located in the city of St. Louis, population just under 400,000. Cultural and educational activities include the history museum, art museums, science center, zoological park, botanical garden, theater, concerts, and several colleges and universities. Other activities include a helicopter tour of the city, golf, or fine dining. Major league sporting events are held in Busch Stadium. St. Louis is known for the Gateway Arch, Six Flags Over Mid-America amusement park, its towering buildings, and its fine shopping area. The city is served by mass bus, rail, and air.

Handicapped Services

Wheelchair accessibility.

NOTABLE ALUMNI

George Hyran–Vice president emeritus, Harris-Stowe

LINCOLN UNIVERSITY

HISTORY

Lincoln University is a four-year, state-supported, coed university that was founded in 1866 as Lincoln Institute. Lincoln's illustrious history began at the close of the Civil War when soldiers and officers of the Sixty-second United States Colored Infantry contributed $5,000 to create Lincoln Institute to educate the freed blacks of Missouri. Additional funds were supplied by the Sixty-fifth Colored Infantry who contributed $1,324.50. Classes began in September of 1866. Three years later the institute moved to its current location. The following year, Lincoln received state aid for teacher training. In 1877, college level work was added to the curriculum and two years later Lincoln became a state institution. The first bachelor's degrees were awarded in 1891. In 1921, the school became Lincoln University.

Since September of 1954, Lincoln has accepted any qualified student who wished to enroll. Today, Lincoln University prides itself in providing students with a culturally, educationally, and socially diverse learning environment.

820 Chestnut St.
Jefferson City, MO
65101-9880
Phone: (314) 681-5000
Toll-free out-state:
800-521-5052
Fax: (314) 681-6074

Total Enrollment:
4,101

Level of Selectivity:
Noncompetitive

Motto:
Laborare et Studere

Lincoln University's campus is located on approximately 152 acres in the small town of Jefferson City, Missouri. An additional 800 acres is used for a research farm. The 20-building campus includes both historic and modern facilities. Under the second Morrill Act of 1890, Lincoln University of Missouri became a land grant institution.

ACCREDITATION

Lincoln University is accredited by North Central Association of Colleges and Secondary Schools to award the Associate of Arts, Associate of Applied Science, Bachelor of Arts, Bachelor of Science, and Master's degrees.

Other Accreditation

American Assembly of Collegiate Schools of Business

National Association of Schools of Music

National Council for Accreditation of Teacher Education

National League of Nursing

COSTS PER YEAR

1992–93 Tuition: $1,632 (in-state); $3,264 (out-state)

Room and board: $2,728

Special fees: $125

Books: $400

Estimated total cost: $4,885 (in-state); $6,517 (out-state)

FINANCIAL AID

1991–92 Institutional Funding

Number of scholarships and grants: 606

Total amount of scholarships and grants: $1,820,858

Range of scholarships and grants: $100–$6,517

1990–91 Federal and State Funding

Number of scholarships and grants: 1,570

Total amount of scholarships and grants: $2,713,219

Range of scholarships and grants: $200–$2,400

Number of loans: 747

Total amount of loans: $2,168,940

Number of work-study: 276

Total amount of work-study: $239,590

Financial Aid Specific to the School

80% of the student body received financial aid during 1991–92.

Army ROTC offers two- and three-year scholarships that pay tuition, fees, books, and other expenses, and provide a monthly stipend of $100.

Athletic scholarships are awarded to men in basketball, track, baseball, soccer, and golf. Women's athletic scholarships are awarded in basketball, tennis, track, and softball.

College work-aid is available to students not qualifying for college work-study to work in departments of the college.

The Cooperative Education Program combines classroom study with related paid work experience. The program provides academic credit and full-time status during co-op placement.

Curators Scholarships are awarded to Missouri students who rank in the top 10% of their high school class or who have a composite score of 22 on the ACT, and who continue on to college immediately after high school. Curators Scholarships are renewable for students who maintain a 3.25 cumulative GPA

Dean's Scholarships are awarded to high school students who rank in the top 25% of their high school class or who have a composite score of 18 on the ACT, and who continue on to college immediately after high school.

Institutional Scholarships are awarded to high school students who rank in the top 20% of their high school class or who have a composite score of 20 on the ACT, and who continue on to college immediately after high school. Also eligible are transfer or currently enrolled Lincoln students who have a 3.0 cumulative GPA in 30 credit hours of course work. Institutional Scholarships are renewable for students who maintain a 3.0 cumulative GPA

A deferred payment plan allows students to pay college costs in three installments during the semester, with a $26 service charge each semester.

Presidential Scholarships are awarded to high school students who rank in the top 15% of their high school class or who have a composite score of 21 on the ACT, and who continue on to college immediately after high school. Presidential Scholarships are renewable for students who maintain a 3.1 cumulative GPA

Performance grants are available in art, band, communications, drama, journalism, and music.

A Thurgood Marshall Black Education Fund provides a four-year scholarship at this public black college. Qualifying students must have a high school GPA of 3.0 or better and a SAT score of 1,000 or ACT score of 24 or more. Students must be recommended by high school counselor as exceptional or exemplary in the creative or performing arts. Scholarship pays tuition, fees, room, and board, not to exceed $6,000 annually.

Twelve endowed scholarships are awarded with various restrictions to Lincoln students.

Financial Aid Deadline
March 1 (priority)

Financial Aid Contact
Financial aid office: (314) 681-6156.

ADMISSION REQUIREMENTS
Open admission for sate residents. ACT required for counseling and placement.

Entrance Requirements
Graduation from an accredited high school and submission of an official high school transcript with 6 semesters of high school grades; non-residents must have a "C" average; must show proof of a recent physical by the end of the first semester. A $17 non-refundable application fee is required.

GED students must meet basic admission requirements.

Transfer students must submit an official college transcript with a minimum 2.0 GPA and ACT scores if transferring less than 30 semester hours.

International students must take the TOEFL examination with a score of 500 or the Michigan English Test with a score of 80%, submit ACT scores, and provide proof of ability to pay all college costs.

Early admissions allows academically gifted high school students the opportunity to enroll in college full time before completing high school.

Admission Application Deadline
Rolling admission (up to two weeks prior to enrollment) provides no specific date for notification of admission so applicant is informed as soon as admission decision is made; March 1 (priority).

Admission Contact
Office of Admissions; (314) 681-5599 or 800-521-5052.

GRADUATION REQUIREMENTS
Minimum of 124 semester hours with 9 hours in composition and speech; 8 hours in science; 5 hours in mathematics; 12 hours in social science; 6 hours in health and physical education; 6 hours in humanities; 6 hours in interpersonal relations; 13 hours in foreign language for B.A. and B.S. in biology, chemistry, and physics; 1 hour in freshman orientation; 2 hours in military science for male students, some exceptions apply. All students must complete core requirements; the last 30 hours of credit must be obtained at Lincoln University.

Minimum of 64 semester hours for an associate's degree and completion of core requirements to include 6 hours in composition and speech, 3 hours of mathematics, 6 hours in social sciences, and one hour in physical education.

Grading System

A–F; PR=progress-re-enrolled; S=satisfactory; u=unsatisfactory; I=incomplete; X=incomplete-absent from final exam; WP=withdrawal-passing; WF=withdrawal-failing H=hearer

STUDENT BODY PROFILE

Total enrollment (male/female): 1,653/2,448

From in-state: 2,666

Other regions: 27 states; 12 foreign countries

Full-time undergraduates (male/female): 972/1,200

Part-time undergraduates (male/female): 551/975

Graduate students (male/female): 130/273

Ethnic/Racial Makeup

African American, 1,034; Hispanic, 22; Native American, 26; Caucasian, 2,829; International, 120; Other/unclassified, 70.

FACULTY PROFILE

Number of faculty: 249

Student-teacher ratio: 18:1

Full-time faculty: 170

Part-time faculty: 79

Tenured faculty: 65

Faculty with doctorates or other terminal degrees: 40%

SCHOOL CALENDAR

1992–93: August 19–May 14 (semester hours)

Commencement and conferring of degrees: May 15

One summer session.

DEGREES OFFERED 1991–92:

Associate of Arts
Criminal Justice

Secretarial Science

Associate of Arts and Science
Agriculture

Building Science

Computer Science

Drafting Technology

Electronics Technology

Mechanical Technology

Nursing Science

Bachelor of Arts
Broadcasting

Economics

English

French

History

Journalism

Mathematics

Philosophy

Political Science

Psychology

Radio, Television Broadcasting

Sociology

Bachelor of Music Education
Music

Bachelor of Science
Accounting

Agriculture

Art

Biology

Broadcasting

Building Engineering

Business Administration

Chemistry

Computer Information Systems

Criminal Justice

Economics

Fashion Merchandising

Food and Nutrition

General Home Economics

Graphic Art Technology

Journalism

Marketing

Mathematics

Medical Technology

Physics

Psychology

Public Administration

Radio, Television Broadcasting

Secretarial Science

Sociology

Bachelor of Science Education

Art

Biology

Business Education

Chemistry

Elementary Education

English

French

Graphic Arts Technology

Health and Physical Education

Mathematics

Mechanical Technology

Physics

Social Science Education

Special Education

SPECIAL PROGRAMS

Accelerated Study Program allows students to complete their undergraduate degree in a shorter period of time than the traditional four years.

Advanced Placement (AP) grants college credit for postsecondary work completed in high school. Students passing the AP test will receive credit by examination for each course and advanced placement.

College Level Examination Program (CLEP) determines the academic relevance of nontraditional educational experiences, such as the military, on-the-job training, or other life experiences, through a series of tests and may grant students college credit for these experiences.

College orientation is offered to entering students at no cost prior to the beginning of classes to acquaint students with the college and to prepare them for college life; parents may attend.

Cooperative Education Program combines classroom study with related paid work experience. The program provides academic credit with full-time status during co-op placement.

An honors program offers academically talented students a challenging program of study that includes special classes, seminars, colloquia, cultural activities, and special recognition to motivate participants.

Remedial courses are offered to entering students to bring them up to admission standards and to help them adjust for success in college.

ROTC provides training in military science for commission as a second lieutenant in the U.S. Armed Forces. Two- and four-year scholarships are available.

ATHLETIC PROGRAMS

Lincoln University is a member of the National Collegiate Athletic Association (NCAA) and the Missouri Intercollegiate Athletic Association (MIAA).

Intercollegiate sports: men's football, basketball, baseball, cross-country, track, and golf; women's basketball, volleyball, softball, cross-country, track, and tennis.

Intramural sports: basketball, volleyball, baseball, track & field, softball, and table tennis.

Athletic Contact

Ronald E. Coleman, Acting Director of Athletics, Lincoln University, Jefferson City, MO 65101; (314) 681-5000.

LIBRARY HOLDINGS

The Inman E. Page Library holds over 150,000 bound volumes, 600 periodical subscriptions, 95,000 microforms, 2,000 audiovisuals, and 80,000 government documents. It has an extensive black history and culture collection and serves as a United States Depository Library.

STUDENT LIFE

Special Regulations

Class attendance is mandatory for freshmen, international students, students of academic probation, and for all courses numbered 199 and below; students must reside on campus for the first four semesters (exceptions for transfer students, commuter students, veterans, and students 21 years of age or older); students must register their cars with the Office of Safety and Security; ROTC required for one hour for two semesters.

Campus Services

Health center, personal and psychological counseling.

Campus Activities

Social and cultural activities include theater, band, choirs, jazz ensemble, dance troupe, and orchestra. Special events include the cooperative annual Black History Week and the Unity Awards in Media with the Jefferson City Community. Students may work on the biweekly, student newspaper, *The Clarion*. Broadcast students may work at KLUM-FM, a 40,000 watt public radio station, or public access television station JCTV.

Leadership opportunities are found in the Student Government Association (SGA) or numerous other student-run organizations, such as the Shutterbug Club. The ROTC Rangers rifle club competes on a local and state level. Greek-letter fraternities include Alpha Phi Alpha, Kappa Alpha Psi, Omega Psi Phi, and Phi Beta Sigma; sororities include Alpha Kappa Alpha, Delta Sigma Theta, Sigma Gamma Rho, and Zeta Phi Beta. Honor societies include Alpha Kappa Mu and Beta Kappa Chi.

Lincoln University is located in Jefferson City, the capital of Missouri, overlooking the Missouri River. Jefferson City, with a population of 35,500, is served by mass transit bus system; passenger rail is 1 mile from campus and the airport is approximately 5 miles. The city has several museums and historic sites. Columbia, located 33 miles north of Jefferson City, is home to several colleges and hospitals.

Housing Availability

630 housing spaces available; freshman-only housing available. Secured housing is available by paying a $125 deposit.

NOTABLE ALUMNI

Bob Boeckman, 1967–Vice president, Jefferson City's Central Bank

Ronald Copes, 1963–Vice president, Human Resources Division, Massachusetts Mutual Life Insurance Co.

Dwayne Crompton, 1968–Executive director, KCMC Development Corp., Kansas City

Clinita Ford, 1948–Retired professor/administrator, Florida A&M

Henry Givens, Jr., 1954–President, Harris-Stowe State College

Jesse Hill, 1947–Chief executive officer, Atlanta Life Insurance Co.

Dr. Orville E. Kean–President, University of the Virgin Islands, St. Thomas

Bette Spence-Dix, 1951–Administrative assistant, Ford Middle School, St. Louis

New York

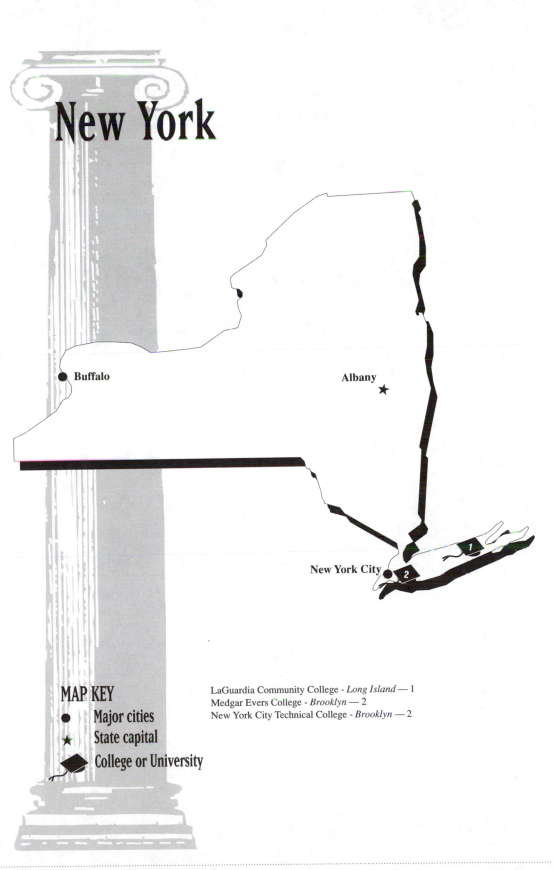

Buffalo

Albany ★

New York City ●

1

2

MAP KEY
- ● Major cities
- ★ State capital
- ◆ College or University

LaGuardia Community College - *Long Island* — 1
Medgar Evers College - *Brooklyn* — 2
New York City Technical College - *Brooklyn* — 2

LAGUARDIA COMMUNITY COLLEGE

31-10 Thompson Ave.
Long Island City, NY
11101
Phone: (718) 482-5000

Total Enrollment:
9,000

Level of Selectivity:
Noncompetitive

Motto:
We have got
news for you

HISTORY

Fiorello H. LaGuardia Community College is a two-year, state-supported, coed college that was founded in 1971. LaGuardia Community College is a branch of the City University of New York (CUNY).

The college supports the principles of open access and equal opportunity. It offers many non-credit Continuing Education (CE) programs both on and off campus. Through its community-based programs, LaGuardia serves over 28,000 CE students by responding to the educational needs of senior citizens, the homeless, recent immigrants, and the unemployed. As LaGuardia moves into its third decade, it continues to provide access to higher education and meaningful employment for the city's historically underserved population.

LaGuardia works to prepare students for a full life of work, service, and personal growth by helping each student acquire the academic, social, and professional knowledge needed to live effectively in an urban environment. The college encourages the dynamic interplay between the classroom and the workplace. It is the only community college that has a mandatory cooperative education program. LaGuardia hosts two high schools on its campus to create educational opportunities for students who are at risk of dropping out.

The one-building campus is housed in a renovated office building in Long Island City.

ACCREDITATION

LaGuardia Community College is accredited by the Middle State Accreditation Association to award the Associate of Arts, Associate of Science, Associate of Applied Science, and Associate in Applied Technology degrees.

Other Accreditation

American Dietetic

American Veterinary Association

COSTS PER YEAR

1992–93 Tuition: $2,100 (in-state); $2,676 (out-state)

Special fees: $204

Books: $400

Estimated total cost: $2,704 (in-state); $3,280 (out-state)

FINANCIAL AID

1991–92 Federal and State Funding

Number of scholarships and grants: 7,939

Total amount of scholarships and grants: $11,806,798

Range of scholarships and grants: $225–$2,400

Number of loans: 244

Total amount of loans: $586,035

Range of loans: $300–$2,625

Number of work-study: 861

Total amount of work-study: $1,055,608

Range of work-study: $600–$2,400

Financial Aid Specific to the School

85% of the student body received financial during 1991–92.

The College Discovery (CD) program offers financial aid to eligible students who are New York City residents, academically and economically disadvantaged, and applying for admission to one of the two-year colleges of City University of New York (CUNY).

Empire State scholarships are awarded to academically talented students who are residents of New York and attend college in the state of New York.

Tuition Assistance Program (TAP) provides financial aid to New York state residents who demonstrate financial need.

Vietnam Veterans Tuition Award provides financial aid to veterans who served in Indochina between 1/63 and 5/75. Full-time awards are $500 per semester or full tuition, whichever is less, and are available for four years or five years in an approved program.

The Child of Veteran Award is a financial aid program for children of veterans who died in the line of duty. Recipients may obtain up to $450 each year for up to four years or five years in special programs.

The Child of Deceased Police Officer/Fire fighter Program is a financial aid program for children of police officers or fire fighters who died in the line of duty. Students may receive up to $450 each year for up to four years.

Financial Aid Deadline

May 2 (spring)

Financial Aid Contact

Ms. Sulema A. Ebrahim, Director of Financial Aid, LaGuardia Community College, 31-10 Thompson Ave., Long Island City, NY 11101; (718)482-5000

ADMISSION REQUIREMENTS

Open admission. SAT or ACT required.

Entrance Requirements

Graduation from an accredited high school; must submit high school transcript; must submit pre-entrance medical record; and must provide proof of immunization against measles, mumps, and rubella. A $35 application fee required.

GED students must meet basic admission requirements.

Transfer students must have a minimum 2.0 GPA or a ``C'' average or better; must submit college or high school transcript or GED; must take the Freshman Skills Assessment Program (FSAP) in reading, writing, and mathematics. Maximum transfer credits are 30 for a degree and ten for a certificate. To receive Associate of Science degree, student must have been matriculated and in good standing at previous college.

International students must take the TOEFL examination.

Early admission allows academically gifted high school students the opportunity to enroll for college credits before completing high school.

Admission Application Deadline

Rolling admission provides no specific date for notification of admission so applicant is informed as soon as admission decision is made.

Admissions Contact

Ms. Linda Tobash, Director of Admissions, Admissions Office, LaGuardia Community College, 31-10 Thompson Ave., Long Island City, NY 11101; (718) 482-7206

GRADUATION REQUIREMENTS

A minimum of 66 credits and completion of the core requirements; 2.0 GPA; demonstrated math competence, and a computer course for some majors; all day-school applicants must complete the cooperative education program and complete last 36 hours in residence.

Grading System

A–F, FIN=Failure from an Incomplete, TCR=Transfer credit, U=Unsatisfactory, W=Official withdrawal, WA=Unofficial withdrawal, Y=Completion of 1 of 2 quarter courses, Z=Temporary Grade.

STUDENT BODY PROFILE

Total enrollment (male/female): 3,150/5,850

From in-state: 8,370

Full-time undergraduates (male/female): 2,495/4,615

Part-time undergraduates (male/female): 661/1,229

Ethnic/Racial Makeup

African American, 2,880; Hispanic, 3,240; Asian, 990; Caucasian, 1,350; Other/unclassified, 540.

Class of 1995 Profile

Number of applicants: 5,225

Number accepted: 5,225

Number Enrolled: 3,448

FACULTY PROFILE

Number of faculty: 646

Student-teacher ratio: 18:1

Full-time faculty: 238

Part-time faculty: 408

Faculty with doctorates or other terminal degrees: 41%

SCHOOL CALENDAR

1992–93: August 31–June 17 (quarter hours)

Commencement and conferring of degrees:
June

One summer session.

DEGREES OFFERED AND NUMBER CONFERRED 1991–92:

Accounting: 200

Business Administration: 143

Business Management: 65

Commercial Food Service Management: 0

Commercial Photography: 7

Computer Operations: 19

Computer Science: 67

Computer Technician: 97

Dietetic Technician: 12

Education Associate: 0

Education Associate (bilingual): 12

Emergency Medical Technology/Paramedic-AAS: 2

Emergency Medical Technology/Paramedic-AS: 6

Human Services: 88

Microcomputer systems and applications: 67

Mortuary Science: 3

Occupational Therapy: 31

Paralegal Studies: 0

Physical Therapist: 92

Pre-Nursing: 56

Programming and Systems: 60

Teacher Education: 0

Travel and Tourism: 71

Veterinary Technology: 12

Associate in Applied Science (Academic)

Accounting: n/a

Biomedical Equipment Technician: n/a

Computer Information Systems: n/a

Criminal Justice: n/a

Electroencephalographic Technician: n/a

Electronic Engineering Technology: n/a

Electronics: n/a

Emergency Medical Technician: n/a

Health Data Processing Technician: n/a

Legal Secretary: n/a

Management and Supervision Technology: n/a

Medical Assistant: n/a

Medical Record Technician: n/a

Medical Secretary: n/a

Multiple Competency Clinical Technician: n/a

Nursing: 56

Occupational Therapy Assistant: 31

Optometric Technician: n/a

Physical Therapist: 92

Radiological Technologist: n/a

Recreational Leadership: n/a

Respiratory Therapist: n/a

Secretarial Science: n/a

Social Worker Technician: n/a

Associate in Applied Science (Technical)

Accounting: 200

Drafting and Design Technology: n/a

Electrical Technology: n/a

Electronics Engineering: n/a

Maintenance Mechanics Technology: n/a

Associate in Arts

English: n/a

General Studies: n/a

Health, Physical Education, and Recreation: n/a

History: n/a

Mathematics: n/a

Political Science: n/a

Pre-Law: n/a

Psychology: n/a

Sociology: n/a

Associate in Science

Business Administration: 143

Business Education: n/a

Business Management: 65

Engineering: n/a

Mathematics: n/a

Music Education: n/a

Science: n/a

Teacher Education: n/a

Certificates (Technology)

Auto Body Technology: n/a

Barbering: n/a

Cabinet Making and Carpentry: n/a

Clerical Technology: n/a

Commercial Foods Preparation: n/a

Commercial Sewing: n/a

Cosmetology: n/a

Drafting and Design Technology: n/a

Electrical Technology: n/a

Electronics Technology: n/a

Masonry: n/a

Maintenance Mechanic: n/a

Plumbing and Pipe Fitting: n/a

Percent of graduates that later obtain higher degrees: 55%

SPECIAL PROGRAMS

The Adult Learning Center provides adult basic education, high school equivalency, and college prep instruction for adults.

Adult or Continuing Education Program is available for nontraditional students returning to school or working full time.

Advanced Placement (AP) allows high school students to get college credit for scores on the College Board AP tests in various subjects.

Certificate Program in Telecommunications is a division of adult education that offers an 180-hour program designed to meet the needs of both entry-level students and professionals in the field. For more information call (718) 482-7244.

College Discovery (CD) program offers a comprehensive program of basic skills courses, tutoring, counseling, and financial aid for eligible students.

College for Children offers low-cost courses in SAT skills, and math and reading classes for ages four to high school. The College for Children also offers martial arts, computer courses, and art classes. For more information call (718) 482-5323.

The College Level Examination Program (CLEP) grants college credit for non-traditional educational experiences, such as the military, work, or other life experiences, by taking the CLEP exam administered by the College Entrance Examination Board.

The Cooperative Education Program alternates formal academic study with practical work experience in all majors.

Cooperative transfer agreement with City University of New York (CUNY) and State University of New York (SUNY) for students who receive a Associate of Arts degree from LaGuardia.

English as a Second Language is a program that offers courses in English for students whose native language is not English.

The honors program offers academically talented students a challenging program of study that includes special classes, seminars, colloquia, cultural activities, and special recognition to motivate participants.

Individualized majors allow students to create their own major program(s) of study.

Off-campus study with Vassar College allows students to take courses for credit.

The part-time degree program allows students to earn an undergraduate degree while attending part time.

Remedial courses are offered to entering students to bring them up to admissions standards and to help them adjust for success in college.

ATHLETIC PROGRAMS

Intramural sports: archery, badminton, basketball, bowling, coed volleyball, softball, indoor soccer, and weight lifting.

LIBRARY HOLDINGS

The library holds 60,000 bound volumes, 550 periodicals subscriptions, and 4,000 audiovisuals. Two hundred and fifty computers are available for student use in the library and computer center. The LaGuardia and Wagner archives which collects, preserves, and makes available historical documents, serves as a research center for scholars.

STUDENT LIFE

Special Regulations

Mandatory new student seminar orientation for all freshman and transfer students; mandatory cooperative education program for full-time students.

Campus Services

Health center, personal and psychological counseling, career development seminar, and remedial services.

Campus Activities

Social activities include theater, clubs and organizations, campus radio station, printing office, video programs, and a student-run newspaper.

Leadership opportunities are found in the Student Government Association. Phi Theta Kappa honor society is represented. Off-campus activities include skiing, ranching, and camping trips. Tournaments and special events, like handball, table tennis, and the Mr. & Mrs. LaGuardia competitions, are scheduled every enhanced semester.

Located in the world famous city of New York, LaGuardia's students have access to a variety of entertainment and cultural experiences. The college is convenient to all major transportation systems. The airport is 20 minutes away. With over 200 miles of subway lines it is easy to go anywhere in New York. Manhattan is 15–20 miles to the Northwest. Central Park, the United Nations Building, the Empire State Building, Lincoln Center for the Performing Arts, New York Public Library, and the Rockefeller Center are all major attractions. Ellis Island, the Statue of Liberty, fine dining and shopping in lower Manhattan are within a half hour's drive by car. Reduced price tickets to Broadway, off-Broadway, and other performing arts in the city are made available for students. The Performing Arts program also sponsors its own talent shows, theatrical events, and film series. New Jersey is 40–50 miles south, and Connecticut is 34 miles to the north.

MEDGAR EVERS COLLEGE OF THE CITY UNIVERSITY OF NEW YORK

1650 Bedford Ave.
and 1150 Carroll St.
Brooklyn, NY 11225
Phone: (718) 270-4900

Total Enrollment:
4,400

Level of Selectivity:
Noncompetitive;
slightly competitive
for nursing program

Motto:
Educating Our
Students for the New
World Order

HISTORY

Medgar Evers College (MEC) is a four-year, state-supported, coed, liberal arts college founded in 1969 in response to the insistence of the community to provide a program of higher for community residents of central Brooklyn. This resulted in the development of a Community Council to serve as an advisor to the college. The council is composed of a representative from community organizations, community residents, faculty, students, and all elected officials.

The school is named for the slain freedom fighter, Medgar Wiley Evers, who tirelessly fought for the civil rights of blacks in the Mississippi Delta area. Evers was only 38 when an assassin quieted his voice. However, founders of the school boast that Evers' quest has not ended, for in the heart of Central Brooklyn stands Medgar Evers College, strong and surviving in the namesake's spirit.

As one of 17 members of the City University of New York (CUNY) Medgar Evers College is mandated to meet the educational and social needs of central Brooklyn. The college's mission is grounded in the belief that education is a right of all individuals in pursuit of self actualization. To this end, the college provides high quality, professional, career-oriented undergraduate degree programs in conjunction with liberal arts, educational, career, and personal goals.

The two-building campus has two locations. The 1650 Bedford facility includes an auditorium, lecture hall, library, learning center, computer lab, classrooms, canteen, several lounges, an amphitheater, and administrative offices. The 1150 Carroll street facility comprises admissions, registrar's office, financial aid, student development, athletics, and college book store as well as classrooms, a science and computer lab, a gymnasium, and a swimming pool.

ACCREDITATION

Medgar Evers College is accredited by the Middle States Association of Colleges and Secondary Schools.

Other Accreditation
National League for Nursing

COSTS PER YEAR
1992–93 Tuition: $1,335 (in-state); $2,025 (out-state)

Room and board: None

Special fees: $125

Books: $500

Estimated total cost: $1,960 (in-state); $2,650 (out-state)

FINANCIAL AID

Financial Aid Specific to the School
75% of the student body received financial aid during 1991–92.

APTS (Aids for Part-time Study) are state awards available to college students who are residents of the state taking between 3–12 credit hours. Combined TAP and APTS award cannot exceed tuition costs.

Athletic scholarships are available to students participating in intercollegiate sports

Cooperative Education Program combines classroom study with related paid work experience. The program provides academic credit and full-time status during co-op placement.

Endowed, corporate, friends, and special interest awards number over 12 and are based on achievement and need.

New York State Regents Scholarships of $250 are awarded to students based on SAT or ACT scores.

STAP (Supplemental Tuition Assistance Program) is awarded to full-time continuing TAP recipients who qualify as educationally disadvantaged and carrying remedial workload.

TAP (Tuition Assistant Program) awards assistance to full-time students who are residents of the state, U.S. citizens, and matriculated in an approved program.

VVTAP pay $500 to full-time students and $250 to part-time students who are residents of the state and are Vietnam Veterans who served in the armed forces of the U.S. in Indochina between January 1, 1963–May 7, 1975. Combined TAP and VVTAP cannot exceed tuition.

Worker Education Program assists student with union-sponsored direct payment tuition and reimbursements plans for working adults pursuing a degree or taking non-degree courses.

Financial Aid Deadline
August 15 (priority)

Financial Aid Contact
Isaac O. Foster, Director of Financial Aid, Medgar Evers College, 1150 Carroll St., Brooklyn, NY 11225; (718) 270-6038.

ADMISSION REQUIREMENTS
SAT or ACT required for counseling and placement.

Entrance Requirements
Graduation from an accredited high school; submit official high school transcript; minimum 2.0 GPA; provide proof of immunizations against measles, mumps and rubella. A $35 application fee is required

GED students must meet basic admission requirements and submit a score of 500.

Transfer students must submit official transcript of all college work; minimum 2.0 GPA. $40 application fee required.

International students must submit certificate of high school completion; take TOEFL examination; provide proof of ability to pay all college costs.

Admission Application Deadline
Rolling admission provides no specific date for notification of admission so applicant is informed as soon as admission decision is made.

Admission Contact

R. Dannenfelser, Director of Admissions, 1150 Carroll St., Medgar Evers College, Brooklyn, NY 11225; (718) 270-6024.

GRADUATION REQUIREMENTS

A minimum of 120 credit hours for a bachelor's degree and completion of core requirements to include the following hours: 6 English, 6–7 mathematics, 3 science (biology), 6 social sciences, and 2–3 physical education; 32 of last 60 hours must be in residence.

A minimum of 64 credit hours for an associate's degree and completion of core requirements to include the following hours: 6 English, 3 mathematics, 2-3 physical education; 3 science (biology); 3 social science; last 18 hours of last 32 hours must be in residence.

Grading System

A–F (plus/minus); PEN=Grade Pending; P=Pass; R=Repeat; NC=No Credit; W=Withdrew; WF=Withdrew Failing; WU=Withdrew Unofficially; P/F=Pass/Fail

STUDENT BODY PROFILE

Total enrollment (male/female):
1,276/3,124

From in-state: 4,180

Other regions: 3 states, 37 foreign countries

Full-time undergraduates (male/female):
740/1,812

Part-time undergraduates (male/female):
536/1,312

Ethnic/Racial Makeup

African American, 4,048; Hispanic, 88; Asian, 88; Native American, 44; International, 132.

Class of 1995 Profile

Number enrolled: 800

Transfers enrolled: 660

FACULTY PROFILE

Number of faculty: 272

Student-teacher ratio: 19:1

Full-time faculty: 115

Part-time faculty: 157

SCHOOL CALENDAR

1992–93: August–May (semester hours)

Commencement and conferring of degrees: May

One summer session.

DEGREES OFFERED 1991–92:

Bachelor of Arts

Liberal Studies

Psychology

Bachelor of Science

Accounting

Biology

Business Administration

Elementary Education

Environmental Science (pending)

Mathematics (pending)

Nursing

Public Administration

Special Education

Associate of Applied Science

Computer Applications

Nursing

Secretarial Science/Executive/Legal

Associate of Arts

Liberal Arts

Teacher Education

Associate of Science

Business Administration

Computer Science

Physical Education (pending)

Public Administration

Science

Certificates
Gerontology

Licensed Practical Nurse (pending)

Word Processing

Pre-professional
Engineering

SPECIAL PROGRAMS

Adult or Continuing Education Program is available for nontraditional students returning to school or working full time.

Africana Resource Center for Elementary Schools (ARCES) sponsors a 12-credit-hour summer institute in July on the topic of Africa and the Diaspora as studied through oral tradition. A 6-credit content course taught by a noted scholar-in-residence is complimented by curriculum workshop courses.

Center for the Study and Resolution of Black and Latino Male Initiatives studies and proposes solutions to the many contemporary issues that contribute to shortage of black and Latino males in higher education. The purpose of the center is to enhance self-esteem and self-worth of MEC male students and to work with males outside the college community who desire to pursue higher education

College Level Examination Program (CLEP) determines the academic relevance of nontraditional educational experiences such as the military, on-the-job training, or other life experiences through a series of tests and may grant students college credit for these experiences.

Cooperative Education Program combines classroom study with related paid work experience. The program provides aca-demic credit and full-time status during co-op placement.

English as a Second Language is a program that offers courses in English for students whose native language is not English.

Honors Program offers academically talented students a challenging program of study that includes special classes, seminars, colloquia, cultural activities, and special recognition to motivate participants.

Off-campus study allows students to take courses for credit at the 16 other colleges in the CUNY system.

Part-time degree program allows students to earn an undergraduate degree part time.

Pre-college science and math programs for disadvantaged high school students encourages pursuit of college science and math programs.

Small Business Development Center provides one-on-one counseling to small business firms in the community

ATHLETIC PROGRAMS

Medgar Evers College is a member of the National Collegiate Athletic Association (NCAA).

Intercollegiate sports: men's basketball, cross-country, soccer, and track & field; women's cross-country, track & field, and volleyball.

Intramural sports: basketball, bowling, swimming, table tennis, tennis, and volleyball.

Athletic Contact
Roy Anderson, Director of Athletics, Medgar Evers College, 1150 Carroll St., Brooklyn, NY 11225; (718) 270-6403.

LIBRARY HOLDINGS
The library houses 75,000 bound volumes, 1,800 microforms, 585 periodical subscriptions; 659 audiovisuals; 150 computers for student use in computer center.

Special collections include the Schomburg Collection on Black Culture on microfilm.

STUDENT LIFE

Campus Services

Career planning and placement, student employment services, legal services, women's center, learning center, and day-care

Campus Activities

Social and cultural activities include theater. The Jackie Robinson Center for Physical Culture provides cultural activities for families and youth of central Brooklyn. Students may get involved in the student-run newspaper. Students can also get involved in the student-run radio station.

Brooklyn is one of five boroughs of New York City with a population of over seven million. Medgar Evers Students are in close proximity to New York's world class shopping, dining, and entertainment including broadway and off-broadway plays. Local transportation provides easy access to Manhattan via the subway, taxis, or bus services. New York City is served by mass air, bus, and passenger rail. Points of interest in Brooklyn include the Brooklyn Museum, Botanical Garden, and Children's Museum. Points of interest in New York City include the Statue of Liberty, Lincoln Center for the Performing Arts, Rockefeller Center, Chinatown, Central Park, and the Empire State Building.

Housing Availability

None

NOTABLE ALUMNI

Betty Shabazz–Professor, Medgar Evers College; wife of Malcolm X

NEW YORK CITY TECHNICAL COLLEGE

HISTORY

New York City Technical College (NYCTC) is a two-year, state-supported, coed, technical college founded in 1946 as the New York State Institution of Applied Arts and Sciences. It became part of the City University of New York (CUNY) in 1964. Voorhees Technical institute was incorporated into the college in 1971 and in 1980 City Technical College was designated as the Technical College of the City University.

The mission of the college is to meet the needs of the city's culturally diverse population for technical and career education. The curricula, varied and rich, integrates technical and liberal arts education. It is committed to quality education, teaching excellence, and access to higher education for all. It offers programs to students that provide marketable, practical, and technical skills, enabling students to advance in their careers.

ACCREDITATION

New York City Technical College is accredited by the Middle States Association of Colleges and Secondary Schools (MSACS) to award the Associate of Applied Science, Associate of Arts, Associate of Science, and Bachelor of Technology degrees.

Other Accreditation

Accreditation Board of Engineering and Technology

American Dental Association

Committee on Allied Health Education and Accreditation

National League for Nursing

New York State Board of Regents

COSTS PER YEAR

1992–93 Tuition: $1,250 (in-state); $2,500 (out-state)

Room and board: none

Special fees: $100

300 Jay St.
Brooklyn, NY 11201
Phone: (718) 260-5500

Total Enrollment:
10,426

Level of Selectivity:
Noncompetitive for associate's degree; slightly competitive for bachelor's degree

Books: $250

Estimated total cost: $1,600 (in-state); $2,850 (out-state)

FINANCIAL AID

Financial Aid Specific to the School

90% of the student body received financial aid during 1991–92.

City University Supplemental Tuition Assistance (CUSTA) is available for students who are full-time matriculated undergraduate students, who are U.S. citizens or eligible non-citizens, and who have not exhausted their Tuition Assistance Program eligibility.

Regents Nursing Scholarships are awarded for full-time study in an undergraduate nursing program based on SAT or ACT scores.

Supplemental Tuition Assistance Program (STAP) is available for students who meet the following criteria: a resident of New York state for at least one year; U.S. citizen or eligible non-citizen; undergraduate student receiving state financial aid; educationally disadvantaged; meet program financial criteria; maintain full-time attendance; and not default on a Stafford loan.

Tuition Assistance Program (TAP) is available for full-time matriculated students who are residents of New York for at least one year or more, are U.S. citizens or eligible non-citizens, and not in default of Stafford loan. Student must be charged at least $2,500 per year and demonstrate financial need. Undergraduates may generally receive TAP money for four years.

Army, Air Force, and Navy ROTC offer two- and four-year scholarships that pay tuition, fees, books, and other expenses, and provide a monthly stipend of $100.

Veterans Administration Educational Benefits are available for eligible applicants and their families.

Vietnam Veteran Tuition Award (VVTA) provides financial assistance to veterans enrolled in undergraduate degree program on full- or part-time basis.

Mayor Scholarships are awarded to New York state residents who are full-time matriculated undergraduate students who demonstrate financial need.

Regents Awards are for children of diseased or disabled veterans who are legal resident of New York state.

Regents College Scholarships are awarded for full-time post-secondary study in New York state based on SAT or ACT scores.

State Aid to Native Americans awards up to $1,100 annually for full-time students or $456 annually for part-time students for undergraduate education up to four years. Applicants must belong to an official New York state tribe and be enrolled in an approved post-secondary program.

Financial Aid Deadline

July 15

Financial Aid Contact

Mr. Ludwig Van Rodriguez, Director of Financial Aid, New York City Technical College, Brooklyn, NY 11202; (718) 260-5700.

ADMISSION REQUIREMENTS

Open admission except bachelor's programs. SAT or ACT required

Entrance Requirements

Graduation from high school; high school transcript; pre-entrance physical including chest x-ray results; and proof of immunizations against measles, mumps, and rubella (students not immunized will have sixty days to obtain immunizations and file proof with college; out-state students have ninety days). A $30 non-refundable application fee is required.

GED students must meet basic admission requirements, submit proof of satisfactory final score, and submit a statement of diploma issuance.

International students must take the TOEFL exam.

Transfer students are required to submit college transcript with a minimum 2.0 GPA. Some cases require high school transcript, minimum 3.0 GPA. Deadline: March 15 (fall); November 1 (spring).

Admission Application Deadline

Rolling admission provides no specific date for notification of admission so applicant is informed as soon as admission decision is made.

Admissions Contact

Mr. Jesse Galin, Director of Admissions, NY City Technical College of the City University of New York, Brooklyn, NY 11201; (718) 260-5510

GRADUATION REQUIREMENTS

A minimum 64 semester hours for an associate's degree and completion of the core requirements to include the following hours: 6 English, 4 mathematics, 4 science, 6 social sciences, 6 or 9 foreign language, 9 humanities, and 1 computer course for all students. At least 34 hours and last semester must be in residence at NYCTC.

A minimum of 128 credits for bachelor's degree and completion of core requirements to include the above-listed.

Grading System

A-F; W=Withdrew Official; I=Incomplete; WU=Withdrew Unofficially; WF=Withdrew Failing; S=Satisfactory; R=Repeat; Y=Course required more than one semester; Z=No grade submitted.

STUDENT BODY PROFILE

Total enrollment (male/female):
  5,213/5,213

From in-state: 10,113

Full-time undergraduates (male/female):
  3,076/3,075

Part-time undergraduates (male/female):
  2,138/2,137

Ethnic/Racial Makeup

African American, 5,734; Hispanic, 2,189; Asian, 834; Native American, 104; Other/unclassified, 1,563.

Class of 1995 Profile

Number of applicants: 4,804

Number accepted: 4,804

Number enrolled: 2,546

FACULTY PROFILE

Number of faculty: 1,074

Student-teacher ratio: 10:1

Full-time faculty: 594

Part-time faculty: 480

SCHOOL CALENDAR

1991–92: August 20–May 21 (semester hours)

Commencement and conferring of degrees: June 14

One summer session

DEGREES OFFERED 1992–93:

Associate Degrees

Accounting

Air Conditioning and Refrigeration/Heating

Architectural Technologies

Automotive Technologies

Chemical Engineering Technology

Civil Engineering Technology

Commercial Art

Construction Technology

Data Processing

Dental Assistant

Drafting and Design

Electrical Engineering Technology

Electromechanical Technology

Engineering Technology

Environmental Engineering Technology

Fashion Merchandising

Gerontology

Human Services

Liberal Arts

Machine and Tool Technology

Marketing

Mechanical Engineering Technology

Medical Laboratory Technician

Nursing

Optometric

Paralegal

Radiology Technician

Secretarial

Bachelor's Degrees
Graphic Arts

Hotel and Restaurant Management

Printing Technology

SPECIAL PROGRAMS

Adult or Continuing Education Program is available for nontraditional students returning to school or working full time.

Advanced Placement (AP) allows high school students to get college credit for scores on the College Board AP tests in various subjects.

College Level Examination Program (CLEP) determines the academic relevance of nontraditional educational experiences, such as the military, on-the-job training, or other life experiences, through a series of tests and may grant students college credit for these experiences.

English as a Second Language program offers courses in English for students whose native language is not English.

Off-campus study allows students to take courses at other branches of the City University of New York (CUNY) system.

Study Abroad Program allows students to go to England, France, or Germany for a specified period of time for part of their college education.

Part-time degree program allow students to earn an undergraduate degree while attending part time.

Remedial program or academic remediation provides remedial courses for entering students to bring them up to admissions standards.

ROTC provides training in military science for commission as a second lieutenant in the U.S. Army, Air Force, or Navy. Two- and four-year scholarships are available.

ATHLETIC PROGRAMS

New York City Technical College is a member of the National Junior College Athletic Association (NJCAA).

Intercollegiate sports: men's basketball, baseball, and soccer; women's basketball, softball, and volleyball.

Intramural sports: basketball and volleyball.

LIBRARY HOLDINGS

The library holds 160,000 bound volumes, 800 periodical subscriptions, 7,350 microforms, 1,954 audiovisuals, and 65,000 items in vertical files.

STUDENT LIFE
Special Regulations
Mandatory orientation for entering students and family; mandatory CUNY Freshman Skills Assessment Tests (CUNY FSAT).

Campus Services
Health clinic, personal and psychological counseling, career counseling and placement, child care, dental and optical care at little or no cost.

Campus Activities

Students may work on the *New Tech Times* (student-run newspaper). The Grace Gallery exhibits painting, sculpture, photographs, graphic design, and advertising arts of faculty, students, alumni, and outside artists.

The more than seventy clubs and organizations on campus, including the Student Government Association, allow students many and varied opportunities to develop self-expression and leadership skills. Theaterworks Acting Groups are available for students interest in expressing themselves through the art of acting.

Located in the city of New York, borough of Brooklyn, the campus is surrounded by world-class shopping, including Bloomingdales, Abram & Strauss, Lord & Taylor, and Macys. The Brooklyn Academy of Music and Brooklyn Botanical Gardens are nearby. Manhattan, which is internationally known for its social and cultural activities, is fifteen miles away. Points of interest include Harlem, Schomburg Arts Center, China Town, Ellis Island, Statue of Liberty, New York Stock Exchange, Central Park, Empire State Building, Lincoln Center, Rockfeller Center, and United Nations Headquarters. The Broadway theater district is world renowned for its on-and off-Broadway productions. Helicopter tours are available to view this metropolitan city, which has a population of over eighteen million.

Housing Availability

None

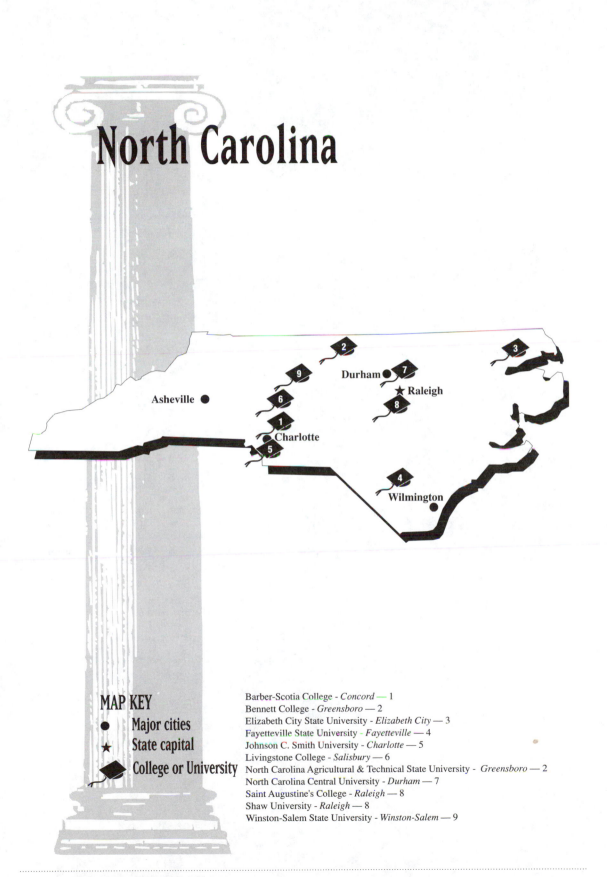

North Carolina

MAP KEY

- ● **Major cities**
- ★ **State capital**
- ◆ **College or University**

Barber-Scotia College - *Concord* — 1
Bennett College - *Greensboro* — 2
Elizabeth City State University - *Elizabeth City* — 3
Fayetteville State University - *Fayetteville* — 4
Johnson C. Smith University - *Charlotte* — 5
Livingstone College - *Salisbury* — 6
North Carolina Agricultural & Technical State University - *Greensboro* — 2
North Carolina Central University - *Durham* — 7
Saint Augustine's College - *Raleigh* — 8
Shaw University - *Raleigh* — 8
Winston-Salem State University - *Winston-Salem* — 9

BARBER-SCOTIA COLLEGE

145 Cabarrus Ave.
Concord, NC 28025
Phone: (704) 786-5171

Total Enrollment:
708

Level of Selectivity:
Noncompetitive

Motto:
*Lumen Veritas et
Utilitas* (Knowledge,
Truth, and Service)

HISTORY:

Barber-Scotia College is a four-year, independent, coed college affiliated with the Presbyterian Church. It was founded in 1867 as Scotia Seminary, training black women as social workers and teachers.

The name of the institution changed to Scotia Women's College in 1916. A merger with Barber Memorial College of Anniston, Alabama in 1930 resulted in the adoption of the present name, Barber-Scotia College, in 1932. The first bachelor's degree was granted in 1945, and in 1946, the North Carolina Board of Education gave the college a four-year rating. In 1954, the school became a coed college, allowing men to enroll.

The 25-building campus includes Bethune Hall, named after one its notable alumni, Mary McLeod Bethune, a 1894 graduate of Barber-Scotia and founder of Bethune-Cookman College. Campus buildings are a placid mix of old and new. Faith Hall, one of the first buildings on the campus, stands in concord to the more modern facilities, such as the

Sage Memorial Learning Resource Center, a multifaceted library.

Barber-Scotia College continues its relationship with the Presbyterian Church, "fulfilling the mission to provide a cadre of educated black leaders." A long way from its beginnings as a training center for teachers and social workers, President Nwagbaraocha states that today the "curriculum relates to the needs directed by the special society of it students, by the world of graduate/professional schools, and by the world of work."

This historically black college is a United Negro College Fund (UNCF) member school.

ACCREDITATION

Barber-Scotia College is accredited by the Southern Association of Colleges and Schools to award the Bachelor of Arts and the Bachelor of Science degrees.

Other Accreditation

North Carolina Department of Public Instruction

COSTS PER YEAR:

1991–92 Tuition: $3,780

Room and board: $1,242 (room); $1,370 (board)

Special fees: $420

Books: $400

Estimated total cost: $7,212

FINANCIAL AID:

1991–92 Institutional Funding:

Number of scholarships and grants: 171

Total amount of scholarships and grants: $146,372

Range of scholarships and grants: $500–$6,487

1991–92 Federal and State Funding:

Number of scholarships and grants: 550

Total amount of scholarships and grants: $2,719,182

Range of scholarships and grants: $100–$2,400

Number of loans: 363

Total amount of loans: $923,364

Range of loans: $500–$4,000

Number of work-study: 296

Total amount of work-study: $139,320

Range of work-study: $200–$800

Financial Aid Specific to the School

90% of the student body received financial aid during 1991–92.

The Mary McLeod Bethune Scholarship is awarded to a student who demonstrates exemplary character, is involved in campus and community activities, and maintains a 3.0 GPA.

The Presidential Scholarship is awarded to an exemplary student leader and role model with a 3.5 GPA or higher. Scholarship ranges from $500 to $3,500. To renew the scholarship the student must maintain 3.5 GPA.

Freshman incentive scholarships are awarded to entering freshmen based on need, high school GPA, SAT scores, and leadership ability.

Approximately 34 endowed scholarships and 15 endowed loan programs are available for students who demonstrate academic achievement and financial need.

Performance scholarships are available in the areas of athletics and music. Students must be enrolled full time, maintaining a GPA of 3.0 for athletics, and 2.5 for music.

The North Carolina Legislators Black Caucus Scholarship is awarded annually to a North Carolina resident majoring in pre-law with a 3.0 GPA or better and competitive SAT or ACT scores. Student must write an essay related to politics and must be active in pre-law activities.

United Negro College Fund (UNCF) scholarships are available to a limited number of entering students scoring high on

ACT or ETS exams, or students with a high school GPA of 3.0. Students must maintain a cumulative GPA of 3.0 in college to renew scholarships.

The Army and Air Force ROTC offers two-year and three-year scholarships that pay tuition, fees, books, and other expenses, and provide a monthly stipend of $100.

Financial Aid Deadline

July (fall); November (spring)

Financial Aid Contact

Mr. Bobby E. Aldrich, Director of Financial

Aid, Barber-Scotia College, Concord, NY 28025; (704) 786-0702.

ADMISSION REQUIREMENTS

Open admission. SAT or ACT is required.

Entrance Requirements

High school diploma with a 2.0 GPA and 16 units: 4 English, 2 mathematics, 2 science (including biology), and 2 social studies (including U.S. history). Three letters of recommendation (one from a high school official), a complete medical exam, a completed dental form, and immunization records are also required.

GED students must meet basic admission requirements and satisfactorily pass the GED exam.

Transfer students must have a 2.0 GPA and an official transcript from each attended institution. A maximum of 65 semester hours may be transferred. A transferring teacher education student may transfer a maximum of 12 general professional semester hours and no semester hours in the area of specialty.

International students must submit certified transcripts of all work at the secondary level, satisfactory completion of the TOEFL esamination, the GED, the EACE (East African Certificate of Education), or the WAEC (West African Examination Council). Also required are an affidavit of support from a sponsor; prepayment of fees and tuition for one full academic year; health, immunization, and dental forms; and three letters of recommendation (one academic).

Admission Application Deadline

August 1 (fall); December 1 (spring). Rolling admission provides no specific date for notification of admission so applicant is informed as soon as admission decision is made.

Admission Contact

Dr. Bruce Smith, Executive Director of Enrollment Management/Registrar, Barber-Scotia College, Concord, NC 28025; (704) 786-5171, ext. 237.

GRADUATION REQUIREMENTS

Minimum of 125 credit hours including the general education core requirements with minimum GPA of 2.0. Teacher education graduation requires a minimum GPA of 2.5. Students must complete the verbal and computational skills assessment examination, and demonstrate computer literacy. Participation in Founders Day and commencement exercises are mandatory.

Grading System

A-F; I=Incomplete

STUDENT BODY PROFILE

Total enrollment (male/female): 354/354

From in-state: 368

Other regions: 18 states; 1 foreign country

Full-time undergraduates (male/female): 342/342

Part-time undergraduates (male/female): 12/12

Ethnic/Racial Makeup

African American, 698; Hispanic, 2; Caucasian, 4; International, 4.

Barber Scotia College

Class of 1995 Profile

Number of applicants: 1,055

Number accepted: 681

Number enrolled: 335

Median SAT score: 350V; 380M

Average high school GPA: 2.5

Transfer applicants: 55

FACULTY PROFILE

Number of faculty: 56

Student-teacher ratio: 12:1

Full-time faculty (male/female): 30/14

Part-time faculty (male/female): 6/6

Faculty with doctorates or other terminal
 degrees: 50%

SCHOOL CALENDAR

1993–94: August 15–May 5 (semesters)

Commencement and conferring of degrees:
 May 8

One six-week summer session.

DEGREES OFFERED AND NUMBER CONFERRED 1991–92:

Bachelor of Arts

Administration of Justice: n/a

Anthropology: n/a

English: n/a

Political Science: n/a

Sociology: 26

Bachelor of Science

Accounting: 3

Banking and Finance: n/a

Biology: 6

Business Administration/Management: n/a

Communication: n/a

Computer/Information Sciences: 4

Early Childhood Education: n/a

Education: n/a

Elementary Education: n/a

Hotel/Restaurant Management: 7

Management Information Systems: n/a

Marketing: 7

Mathematics: 1

Mathematics Education: n/a

Medical Technology: n/a

Physical Education: n/a

Journalism: n/a

Recreation Administration: 1

Pre-Professional

Dentistry: n/a

Engineering: n/a

Law: n/a

Medicine: n/a

Podiatry: n/a

Graduates that later obtain higher degrees:
10%

SPECIAL PROGRAMS

The honors program seeks to challenge
students both academically and creatively.

Entering freshmen are selected based on SAT/ACT scores, high school class rank, creativity, and motivation. Students must maintain a 3.25 GPA or better to remain in honors program.

The college offers a pre-law program in cooperation with St. John's University of New York. Qualified students must have a 3.0 GPA at the end of three years at Barber-Scotia. Students then transfer to St. John's for three years. Successful completion of this program results in the awarding of the Juris Doctorate Degree.

A cooperative pre-engineering program is offered. Students must take three years of basic mathematics at Barber-Scotia and complete an engineering track at a cooperating college with a school of engineering. Students spend three years at Barber-Scotia, then transfer to cooperating college or university to complete engineering degree.

The pre-professional program is for pre-medical students planning to pursue medicine, dentistry, or podiatry. Students should follow a liberal arts degree in biology during undergraduate school.

Advanced Placement (AP) grants college credit for postsecondary work completed oin high school. Students scoring 3 on the AP test will receive advanced placement credit.

The College Level Examination Program (CLEP) grants college credit for nontraditional education such as military experience or work experience through the CLEP exam.

The Charlotte Area Educational Consortium is a cooperative program that allows students to take courses not available on the home campus at any of the twelve member institutions which include Barber-Scotia, Belmont Abbey College, Central Piedmont Community College, Davidson College, Gaston College, Johnson C. Smith University, Limestone College, Queens College, University of North Carolina (UNC) at Charlotte, Wingate College, Winthrop College and York Technical College.

The Army and Air Force ROTC provides training in military sciences for a commission officer as a second lieutenant in the U.S. Armed Forces. This program is offered to students at Barber-Scotia College through cooperative arrangements with Davidson College and UNC at Charlotte.

ATHLETIC PROGRAMS

Barber-Scotia College is a member of the National Association of Intercollegiate Athletics (NAIA) and the Eastern Intercollegiate Athletic Conference (EIAC). Intercollegiate Sports: men's basketball, cross-country, tennis, and track; women's basketball, cross-country, tennis, track, and volleyball.

Intramural Sports: basketball, cross-country, softball, table tennis, tennis, track & field, and volleyball.

Athletic Contact

William Madrey, Athletic Director, Barber-Scotia College, 145 Cabarrus Ave., Concord, NC 28025; (704) 786-5171, ext. 237.

LIBRARY HOLDINGS

The Sage Memorial Learning Resource Center has 80,000 bound volumes, 4,000 microforms, 400 periodical subscriptions, and 70 audiovisuals. In addition, each residential hall has computing and library facilities.

STUDENT LIFE

Special Regulations

Several convocations throughout the year are mandatory. All students must live in the residence halls unless special qualifications as commuter/day students are met. Beepers and pagers must be registered and approved by the campus police office.

Campus Services

Health center, remedial instruction, language laboratory, computer laboratory, counseling services, career planning and placement, and religious services, including chapel.

Campus Activities

Group and cultural activities include theater, chorale, and dance, as well as music groups and departmental clubs. Students can get involved in the student-run newspaper or the yearbook publications.

Leadership opportunities can be found in the Student Government Association or number other student-run organizations. Greek-letter sororities include Alpha Kappa Alpha, Delta Sigma Theta, Sigma Gamma Rho, and Zeta Phi Beta. Fraternities include Alpha Phi Alpha, Kappa Alpha Psi, Omega Psi Phi, and Phi Beta Sigma. Honor societies represented on campus include Alpha Kappa Mu (general) and Beta Kappa Chi (scientific). Alpha Phi Omega service organization is also represented on campus.

The college offers the advantages of a small campus and small–town atmosphere, with the population of Concord around 30,000. It is said that the first gold nugget was found in this little town. The campus is approximately 25 miles from Charlotte, North Carolina's largest city. Charlotte offers theater, concerts, museums, shopping, major league basketball, car racing, and many recreational activities. Charlotte's Douglas International Airport is a transportation hub that provides access to anywhere in the world. The cultural and social resources of the urban area are complemented by easy access to the Atlantic coastal beaches to the east and the Blue Ridge and Great Smoky Mountains to the west.

Housing Availability

645 housing spaces. Freshman-only housing is available. Students are strongly encouraged to live on campus.

Handicapped Services

Wheelchair accessibility.

NOTABLE ALUMNI

Dr. Thelma Adair, 1936–Professor of Education, University of the City of New York; first woman moderator of the United Presbyterian Church USA; and past president of Church Women United in the USA

Vivian Ayer Allen–Director, Adept New America Museum

Mary McLeod Bethune, 1894–Educator and public servant; founder of the National Council of Negro Women and Bethune Cookman College

Dr. Mable McLean, 1941–First woman and first alumnus President of Barber-Scotia College; head of the member institutions of the United Negro College Fund, 1986

Mable Poe Phifer–Owner and director, Black College Satellite Network

BENNETT COLLEGE

900 E. Washington St.
Greensboro, NC
27401-3239
Phone: (919) 273-4431
Toll-free out-state:
800-338-BENN

Total Enrollment:
568

Level of Selectivity:
Slightly competitive

HISTORY

Bennett College is a four-year liberal arts college for women, affiliated with the United Methodist Church. Founded in 1873 as Bennett Seminary, the school was chartered in 1889 as a coeducational college and was renamed Bennett College. Twenty-seven years later, it was reorganized again as a college for women. Bennett College is one of the few remaining four-year liberal arts colleges for women and one of only two historically black colleges for women. Bennett's mission is to provide a unique liberal arts curriculum that produces professionally, socially, and morally responsible women while inspiring women to develop their own identities. Bennett aims to provide quality education for the next generation of world leaders, educators, scientists, and homemakers.

The 55-acre campus houses 25 buildings, including a state-of-the-art telecommunications facility and a children's house with a pre-school laboratory and a single parent/children's program.

ACCREDITATION

Bennett College is accredited by the Southern Association of Colleges and Schools (SACS) to award the Bachelor of Arts and the Bachelor of Science degrees.

Other Accreditation

American Dietetic Association

Council on Social Work Education

University Senate of the United Methodist Church

COSTS PER YEAR

1992–93 Tuition: $5,100

Room and board: $1,300 (room); $1,474 (board)

Special fees: $550

Books: $500

Estimated total cost: $8,924

FINANCIAL AID

1990–91 Institutional Funding

Number of scholarships and grants: 135

Total amount of scholarships and grants: $259,421

Range of scholarships and grants: $400–$7,480

1990–91 Federal and State Funding

Number of scholarships and grants: 683

Total amount of scholarships and grants: $820,770

Range of scholarships and grants: $200–$2,300

Number of loans: 345

Total amount of loans: $819,938

Range of loans: $900–$4,000

Number of work-study: 189

Total amount of work-study: $143,736

Range of work-study: $940–$1,150

Financial Aid Specific to the School

87% of the student body received financial aid during 1991–92.

Tuition waivers are available to Bennett College employees and their children.

Cooperative Education Program alternates and combines classroom study with related paid work experience in five majors. The program provides academic credit and full-time status during co-op placement.

College work-aid is available to students not qualifying for college work-study to work in departments of the college.

Installment plan allows students to pay college costs in smaller installments, usually with some additional cost.

United Negro College Fund (UNCF) scholarships are awarded to a limited number of students at this school who demonstrate financial need. Some scholarships may be based on location and merit. UNCF scholarships range from $500 to $7,500.

Army and Air Force ROTC programs given in cooperation with North Carolina A&T State University offer two- and four-year scholarships that pay for tuition, fees, books, and other expenses, and provide a monthly stipend of $100.

Financial Aid Deadline

May 15

Financial Aid Contact

Miss M. O. Tucker, Director of Student Financial Aid, Bennett College, 900 E.

Washington St., Greensboro, NC 27491-3239; (919) 370-8677 or 800 338-BENN.

ADMISSION REQUIREMENTS

SAT or ACT required.

Entrance Requirements

Graduation from an accredited high school with 16 units to include: 4 English, 2 mathematics, 1 science, and 1 social science. Students must submit official transcript with a minimum 2.0 GPA, a personal essay, and three letters of recommendation; interviews are needed for some prospective students. A $20 non-refundable application fee is required.

GED students must meet basic admission requirements.

Transfer students are required to provide an official transcripts from all previously attended institutions; academic records must show a minimum 2.0 GPA. Transfer students also need to submit an essay, standardized test scores, and recommendations; interviews may be required. Maximum of 64 credit hours may be transferred.

International students must take the TOEFL examination.

Early admission allows academically gifted high school students to enroll in college full time before completing high school.

Admission Application Deadline

Rolling admission provides no specific date for notification of admission so applicant is informed as soon as admission decision is made.

Admission Contact

Ms. Susan Gibson, Director of Admissions, Bennett College, 900 E. Washington St., Greensboro, NC 27401-3239; (919) 370-8624 or 800-338-BENN.

GRADUATION REQUIREMENTS

A minimum of 124 hours and completion of the core requirements to include: 6 hours of mathematics; 6 hours of science, and 1 computer course for some majors.

Grading System

A–F and I=Incomplete.

STUDENT BODY PROFILE

Total enrollment: 568

From in-state: 186

Other regions: 22 states, 2 foreign countries

Full-time undergraduates: 552

Part-time undergraduates: 16

Ethnic/Racial Makeup

African American, 550; International, 18.

Class of 1995 Profile

Number of applicants: 472

Number accepted: 231

Number enrolled: 159

Median SAT score: 368V; 374M

FACULTY PROFILE

Number of faculty: 57

Student-teacher ratio: 10:1

Full-time faculty: 52

Part-time faculty: 5

Faculty with doctorates or other terminal degrees: 58%

SCHOOL CALENDAR

1992–93: August–May (semester)

Commencement and conferring of degrees: May

No summer session.

DEGREES OFFERED 1991–92:

Bachelor of Arts

Art

English

Interdisciplinary Studies

Mass Communications

Political Science

Psychology

Social Work

Sociology

Theater Arts Management

Bachelor of Science

Accounting

Biology

Business Administration

Chemistry

Clothing/Fashion Merchandising

Computer Science

Early Childhood Education

Elementary Education

English Education

Foods/Nutrition/Dietetics

Home Economics

Mathematics

Mathematics/Engineering

Medical Technology

Middle School Education

Music Arts Management

Music Education

Nursing

Special Education

Visual Arts Management

SPECIAL PROGRAMS

Accelerated Study Program allows students to complete their undergraduate degree in a shorter period of time than the traditional four years.

Adult/Continuing Education Program is available for nontraditional students returning to school or working full time.

Advanced Placement (AP) grants college credit for postsecondary work completed in high school. Students passing the AP test will receive credit by examination for each course and advanced placement.

Childcare pre-school laboratory and a single parent/children's program are available.

College orientation is offered at no cost to entering students and their parents for one week prior to the beginning of classes to acquaint students with the college and to prepare them for college life.

Cooperative Education Program alternates and combines classroom study with related paid work experience. The program provides academic credit and full-time status during co-op placement.

Cooperative Program allows students to take college credit toward their degree programs with members of the Greensboro Regional Consortium and the Piedmont Independent College Association. Cooperating schools include Elon College, Greensboro College, Guilford College, High Point College, and Salem Academy and College.

Honors program offers academically talented students a challenging program of study that includes special classes, seminars, colloquia, cultural activities, and special recognition to motivate participants.

Individualized majors allow students to create their own major programs of study.

Part-time degree program allows students to earn an undergraduate degree while attending part time.

Remedial courses are offered to entering students to bring them up to admission standards and to help them adjust for success in college.

ROTC provides training in military science for commission as a second lieutenant in the U. S. Armed Forces. Two- and four-year scholarships are available. Army and Air Force ROTC are offered in cooperation with North Carolina A&T State University.

Student Support Services provide developmental courses, counseling, and cultural activities to students who need aid to succeed in college.

Study Abroad Program allows students to go to a foreign country for a specified period of time for part of their college education.

Three/two degree programs in engineering and nursing allow students to get two degrees—one in liberal arts from home school and one in engineering or nursing from North Carolina Agricultural and Technical

State University—by completing three years at matriculated school and two years at cooperating school.

ATHLETIC PROGRAMS

Bennett College is a member of the National Collegiate Athletic Association (NCAA), Division III.

Intercollegiate sports: women's basketball, softball, tennis, and volleyball.

Intramural sports: basketball, gymnastics, softball, diving, swimming, tennis, volleyball, and track & field.

Athletic Contact

Mr. Leon J. McDougle, Bennett College, 900 E. Washington St., Greensboro, NC 27401-3239; (919) 370-8710.

LIBRARY HOLDINGS

The Thomas F. Holgate Library houses 92,300 volumes, 3,550 microforms, and 259 periodical subscriptions. Eighty-five computers are available for students in the computer center. The library has a special African-American women's collection.

STUDENT LIFE

Campus Services

Health center, personal and psychological counseling, career placement counseling, computer-assisted labs, and women's center.

Campus Activities

Social activities include theater, concerts, chorale, and dances. Annual events include the Belle Festival, Founder's Week, Charter Day, and Recognition Day. Students may work on the student yearbook or the student-run newspaper.

Leadership opportunities are found in the Student Government Association (SGA) or numerous other student-run organizations, including community service organizations and honor societies. Greek-letter societies include Alpha Kappa Alpha, Delta Sigma Theta, Sigma Gamma Rho, and Zeta Phi Beta Sororities. Honor societies are also represented on campus.

Located just one mile from downtown Greensboro, students have access to shopping and dining. Greensboro has a population of 183,500 and is located in the thriving Piedmont Triad, which includes the nearby cities of Winston-Salem and High Point. Approximately one hour away is Raleigh, North Carolina, the state's capital. Served by all major types of mass transportation, students have easy access to the nearby Great Smoky Mountains National Park and the Atlantic Ocean recreational area, which includes the Cape Hatteras and Cape Lookout National Seashores and the Kitty Hawk/Nags Head region.

Housing Availability

Six hundred housing spaces; seven resident halls; freshman-only housing available.

ELIZABETH CITY STATE UNIVERSITY

Parkview Dr.
Elizabeth City, NC
27909
Phone: (919) 335-3400
Toll-free:
800-347-3278
Fax: (919) 335-3615

Total Enrollment:
1,762

Level of Selectivity:
Noncompetitive

Motto:
To Live is to Learn

HISTORY

Elizabeth City State University (ECSU) is a state-supported, coed, four-year college, founded in 1891 as the Elizabeth State Colored Normal School. Secondary level instruction was offered until 1937. The name changed to Elizabeth City State Teachers College in 1939, when it awarded its first baccalaureate degrees. To more accurately reflect the growth in programs, the school's name changed to Elizabeth City State College in 1963 and Elizabeth City State University in 1969. ECSU is one of 16 bodies of higher education that make up the University of North Carolina.

Originally the university's mission was to serve minorities; today the university serves to educate an increasingly multicultural student body. President Jimmie Jenkins states, "that all people who thirst for knowledge have a right in this great democracy of ours, to drink their fill at the academic oasis ECSU provides." The school also endeavors to identify and address the needs of the northeastern region of the state with particular attention to economic development.

The 41-building campus is located on approximately 856 acres, of which approximately 87 acres represent the campus proper; 68 acres comprise the former farm; 639 acres are reserved for educational research; and 35 acres comprise landholding designed for residential or expansion purposes. A golf driving range, a nature trail for outdoor classroom, and tennis courts are located on the campus.

ACCREDITATION

Elizabeth City State University is accredited by the Southern Association of Colleges and Schools (SACS) to award the Bachelor of Arts and the Bachelor of Science degrees.

Other Accreditation

National Association of Industrial Technology

The North Carolina State Board of Education

COSTS PER YEAR

1992–93 Tuition: $590 (in-state); $5,608 (out-state)

Room and board: $1,428 (room); $1,220 (board)

Special fees: $594

Books: $340

Estimated total cost: $4,172 (in-state); $9,190 (out-state)

FINANCIAL AID

1992–93 Federal and State Funding

Number of work-study: 823

Total amount of work-study: $50,500

Financial Aid Specific to the School

90% of the student body received financial aid during 1991–92.

ECSU Incentive Scholarship Program awards scholarships to academically talented students achieving a high school GPA of 3.00 and 850 minimum SAT.

Athletic scholarships are available as well as performance scholarships in band, choir, and the creative arts.

Non-resident Special Talent Waivers are available.

The Cooperative Education Program alternates classroom study with related paid work experience for selected students. The program provides academic credit and full-time status during co-op placement.

The Thurgood Marshall Black Education Fund provides a four-year scholarship at this public black college. Qualifying student must have a high school GPA of 3.0 or better and a SAT score of 1,000 or ACT score of 24 or more. Students must be recommended by high school counselor as exceptional or exemplary in the creative or performing arts. Scholarship pays tuition, fees, room, and board, not to exceed $6,000 annually.

The Army ROTC offers two-year and four-year scholarships that pay tuition, fees, books, and other expenses, and provide a monthly stipend of $100. This program offered at ECSU is in cooperation with Norfolk State University (VA) and North Carolina State University.

North Carolina Student Incentive Grant (NCSIG) is available for full-time North Carolina residents with financial need who show academic progress.

North Carolina Non-Service Scholarships are available to students with at least a 3.0 cumulative GPA and demonstrate financial need.

Minority Presence Grants are available to white residents of North Carolina with financial need who are enrolled in a degree program.

The Freshman Incentive Scholarship Program offers scholarships to academically talented students from high schools in the northeast region of North Carolina.

American Indian Student Legislative Grants award up to $500 to students who es-

Elizabeth City State University

tablish that they are native American and demonstrate financial need.

Vocation Rehabilitation Grants are available to students with any type of physical disability. Contact the vocational rehabilitation counselor at your local health department for determination of eligibility.

Financial Aid Deadline

June 1 (fall); (spring)

Financial Aid Contact

Mr. James E. Swimpson, Director of Financial Aid, Elizabeth City State University, Campus Box 914, Elizabeth City, NC 27909; (919) 335-3305.

ADMISSION REQUIREMENTS

Open admission. SAT or ACT required.

Entrance Requirements

High school graduation with a 2.0 GPA and 12 units including 4 English, 3 mathematics (including geometry, algebra I and algebra II), 2 social studies (including U.S. history, government, and economics), 3 science (including physical science, biology, and 1 laboratory course); 2 years of high school foreign language (recommended); a complete recent physical. A $15 non-refundable application fee required.

GED students must meet basic admission requirements.

Transfer students must have a 2.0 GPA and an official transcript from each college attended. A maximum of 60 semester hours may be transferred from two-year institutions with no limit on transfer hours from four-year institutions, however, 30 hours must be completed in residency to graduate from ECSU. Students with fewer than 24 semester hours of credit must meet both transfer and freshman admission requirements.

International students must provide TOEFL or Michigan Test scores as well as SAT/ACT scores. English translation of all transcripts and proof of financial support are required. Applying at least six months before expected date of entry is strongly suggested.

Early admission allows academically gifted high school students the opportunity to enroll in college full time before completing high school.

Admission Application Deadline

August 1 (fall); December 1 (spring). Rolling admission provides no specific date for notification of admission so applicant is informed as soon as admission decision is made.

Admission Contact

Office of Admissions, Elizabeth City State University, Campus Box 901, Elizabeth City, NC 27909; (919) 335-3305.

GRADUATION REQUIREMENTS

Minimum of 129 semester hours and completion of core courses to include: 1 foreign language, 3 mathematics, 3 science, and 1 computer course for some majors; GPA of 2.0 for all students; and a 30-hour residency requirement. Teacher education students are required to have a 2.50 GPA and to pass the

National Teachers' Examination Core Battery I and II.

Grading System

A-F; I=Incomplete.

STUDENT BODY PROFILE

Total enrollment (male/female): 727/1,292

From in-state: 1,776

Other regions: 25 states and 6 foreign countries

Full-time undergraduates (male/female): 667/1,187

Part-time undergraduates (male/female): 59/106

Ethnic/Racial Makeup

African American, 1,489; Hispanic, 8; Native American, 4; Caucasian, 495; International, 23.

Class of 1995 Profile

Number of applicants: 1,091

Number accepted: 846

Number enrolled: 545

Median SAT score: 376 verbal, 413 math

Average high school GPA: 2.68

Transfer applicants: 224

Transfers accepted: 213

Transfers enrolled: 148

FACULTY PROFILE

Number of faculty: 136

Student-teacher ratio: 15:1

Full-time faculty (male/female): 77/29

Part-time faculty (male/female): 16/14

Tenured faculty: 53

Faculty with doctorates or other terminal degrees: 76%

SCHOOL CALENDAR

1992–93: Fall Semester August–May (semester hours)

Commencement and conferring of degrees: May 9, 1993.

One summer session.

DEGREES OFFERED 1991–92:

Bachelor of Arts

Art Education

Early Childhood Education

English/English Education

French/French Education

History

History Education

Journalism

Middle Grades Education

Music

Philosophy and Religion

Political Science

Political Science Education

Recreation Education

Sociology

Sociology Education

Bachelor of Science

Accounting

Applied Mathematics

Biology/Biology Education

Business Administration

Chemistry/Chemistry Education

Computer and Information Science

Criminal Justice

Elementary Education

Geology

Industrial Technology

Mathematics/Mathematics Education

Music Industry Studies

Physical Education and Health

Physics

Psychology

Special Education

Technology Education

SPECIAL PROGRAMS

Advanced Placement (AP) grants college credit for postsecondary work completed in high school. Students scoring 3 or more on the AP test will receive credit by examination for each course and advanced placement.

College Level Examination Program (CLEP) determines the academic relevance of nontraditional educational experiences such as the military, on-the-job training, or other life experiences through a series of tests and may grant students college credit for these experiences.

College orientation is offered to acquaint entering students with the college and to prepare them for college life.

Continuing Education and Independent (correspondence) Study are offered at Elizabeth City State University.

Cooperative Graduate Programs are offered on the Edgewood campus by the University of North Carolina, Chapel Hill, and by East Carolina University, Greenville.

The Honors program is based upon the colloquium concept, designed to improve oral and written communication skills. The program culminates in a senior project demonstrating the student's research (thesis, literary, or artistic production, etc).

Mathematics and Science Education Network Pre-College Program gives advanced instruction in science and mathematics to average and above average minority and female students.

Off-Campus Study program is available with Howard University.

Remedial courses are offered to entering students to bring them up to admission standards and to help them adjust for success in college.

ROTC provides training in military sciences for a commission as a second lieutenant in the U.S. Armed Forces. Two- and four-year scholarships are available.

Special Student status is available with evidence of the ability to succeed in college course work.

Upward Bound is a program for first-generation college students and/or students from low-income families that offers special academic, cultural, and social activities in the summer during the last two high school years. Upward Bound activities continue during the college experience.

Week-End/Evening Programs offer a curriculum designed for the nontraditional student.

ATHLETIC PROGRAMS

Elizabeth City State University is a member of the National Collegiate Athletic Association (NCAA), Division II, and the Central Intercollegiate Athletic Association (CIAA).

Intercollegiate sports: men's baseball, basketball, football, tennis, track & field, and wrestling; women's cross-country, softball, track & field, and volleyball.

Intramural sports: basketball, flag football, golf, gymnastics, softball, soccer, tennis, and volleyball.

LIBRARY HOLDINGS

The G. R. Little Library houses 136,900 bound volumes, 434,500 microforms, 1,592 periodical subscriptions, 1,220 audiovisuals, and 100 computers for student use in the computer center. The library holdings are computerized. The modern two-story building is completely handicapped accessible. It has a 140-seat auditorium.

STUDENT LIFE

Campus Services

Health center, personal and psychological counseling, testing center, remedial instruction, and religious activities.

Campus Activities

Six honor and recognition societies are active on the ECSU campus.

Four Greek-letter sororities, four Greek-letter fraternities, one service fraternity, one service sorority, and eight social fellowships have chapters on campus.

The Student Government Association offers campus governance involvement and attends to student needs and development.

The United Campus Religious Fellowship (UCRF) is active in promoting non-denominational religious events for the university community.

A number of university publications are available for student participation. A student-run FM radio station is active on campus. Several music organizations, including marching and concert bands, jazz band, university choir, and gospel choir, are available to all enrolled students.

Housing Availability

1,031 housing spaces are available, with 255 designated for

freshmen only. Students are strongly encouraged to live on campus.

Elizabeth City offers a small-town lifestyle with easy access to many recreational and urban resources. Norfolk, Virginia, is 50 miles away and has excellent air, rail, and bus connections. The Atlantic beach resorts and the Outer Banks are also nearby.

NOTABLE ALUMNI

Harold Barnes, Esq., 1977–Attorney, Penny, Barnes, and Rogers, Chesapeake, VA

Clarence Biggs, 1962–Dean of Student Affairs; acting president, Martin Community College, Williamston, NC

Dr. Curtis J. Bryan, 1960–President, Denmark Technical College, Denmark, SC

Dr. Jeanette Hawkins Evans, 1963–Educational specialist, Baltimore City Schools, Baltimore, MD

Wilson Goode, 1966–President, Goode Construction Inc., Chesapeake, VA

Rascoe Hager, 1963–Compliance coordinator, Methods of Administration, Department of North Carolina Community Colleges, Wake Forest, NC

Dr. Jimmy R. Jenkins, Sr., 1965–Chancellor, Elizabeth City State University, Elizabeth City, NC

Jethro Pugh, 1965–Former Dallas Cowboys linebacker, National Football League

Charles C. Rascoe, Jr., 1972–Computer systems analyst, Computer Based Systems, Inc., Fairfax, VA

Dr. Leonard A. Slade, Jr. 1963–Professor and chair, Department of African and Afro-American Studies, State University of New York

Evelyn Dixon Staton, 1965–Former NASA aerospace technologist

Dr. Irene G. Van Travis, 1947–Author, *Networks: Communicating in the World Today*

FAYETTEVILLE STATE UNIVERSITY

HISTORY

Fayetteville State University (FSU) is a four-year, state-supported, comprehensive, liberal arts, coed university. It was founded in 1867 as the Howard School by seven black men who paid $136 for two lots as a site for the education of black children. In 1877, the North Carolina General Assembly selected this institution as a site for teacher training because of its successful record during the previous 10 years. Thus, its name changed to the State Colored Normal School.

Authorized to grant the Bachelor of Science degree in education, the name was changed to Fayetteville State Teachers College in 1939, and the school was granted state and regional accreditation in 1947. The name changed in 1963 to Fayetteville State College and again in 1969 to its present name, Fayetteville State University. FSU became one of the 16 member institutions of the University of North Carolina in 1972.

Although FSU continues to grow its programs and facilities, it remains devoted to educating students in the liberal arts tradition. It is committed to the concept that the mind should be cultivated and nourished for its own sake and for the good of mankind. To this end, FSU's goal is to foster independence of mind, clarity of thought, and depth of spiritual vision that will inspire its students to contribute to the good of society.

Located on 156 acres, the 40-building campus has a mixture of modern and traditional architecture. This traditionally black school is a member of the American Council on Education and the National Association for Equal Opportunity in Higher Education (NAFEO).

ACCREDITATION

Fayetteville State University is accredited by the Southern Association of Colleges and Schools to award the Associate of Arts, Associate of Science, Bachelor of Arts, Bachelor of Science, and Master's degrees.

Newbold Station
1200 Murchison Rd.
Fayetteville, NC
23801-4298
Phone: (910) 486-1111
Toll-free in-state:
800-652-6667
Toll-free out-state:
800-222-2594

Total Enrollment:
3,903

Level of Selectivity:
Slightly competitive

Motto:
Res Non Verba
(Deeds Not Words)

Other Accreditation

The National Council for Accreditation of Teacher Education

The North Carolina State Department of Public Instruction

COSTS PER YEAR

1992–93 Tuition: $1,300 (in-state); $6,400 (out state)

Room and board: $2,300

Special fees: $125

Books: $400

Estimated total cost: $4,125 (in-state); $9,225 (out of state)

FINANCIAL AID

Financial Aid Specific to the School

80% of the student body received financial aid during 1991–92.

Athletic scholarships are awarded in basketball, cross-country, football, golf, tennis, track & field, and volleyball to full-time students who participate in one or more of these sports. Special talent awards are awarded to out-of-state students.

Chancellor's Scholarships are awarded to students who serve as ambassadors to public school students. Qualifying students must serve at least 24 hours a month as mentors and tutors to youth in the public schools.

Performance grants are available in music (band or choir) to full-time students. Awards are granted for a one-year period. Special talent awards are granted to out-of-state students.

College work-aid is available to students not qualifying for college work-study to work in departments of the college for an average of fifteen hours per week. Wages are above minimum wage rate and are used to help students meet educational costs.

Thurgood Marshall Black Education Fund provides a four-year scholarship at this public black college. Qualifying students must have a high school GPA of 3.0 or better, and a SAT score of 1000 or ACT score of 24 or more. Students must be recommended by high school as exceptional or exemplary in the creative or performing arts. Scholarship pays tuition, fees, room, and board, not to exceed $6,000 annually.

Air Force ROTC program offers two- and four-year scholarships that pay tuition, fees, books, and other expenses, and provides a monthly stipend of $100.

North Carolina Student Incentive Grants (NCSIG) are awarded to full-time residents of North Carolina who demonstrate substantial financial need. Grants range from $100 to $1,500.

Minority Presence Grants are available to white residents of North Carolina with financial need who are enrolled in a degree program at minority institutions.

American Indian Student Legislative Grant is made available by the University of North Carolina to qualified American Indian students who maintain cultural identity through tribal membership and are legal residents of North Carolina.

Financial Aid Deadline

April 1 (fall); October 1 (spring); March 1 (summer)

Financial Aid Contact

Mae E. Graves, Director of Financial Aid, Fayetteville State University, 1200 Murchison Rd., Newbold Station, Fayetteville, NC 28301-4298; (910) 486-1325.

ADMISSION REQUIREMENTS

SAT or ACT required.

Entrance Requirements

Graduation from an accredited high school with a minimum of 18 units to include: 4 English, 3 mathematics (algebra I,II and geometry), 3 science (biology, physical science, and lab), 2 social science (U.S. history), 6 electives, and 2 foreign language (strongly recommended); must submit official high school transcript with a minimum 2.0 high school GPA; must have satisfactory combination SAT or ACT score; residents must successfully complete North Carolina Competency Exam; must complete medical exam by July 1 and show proof of immunizations. A $15 non-refundable application fee is required.

GED students must meet basic admission requirements.

Transfer students must qualify for readmission at previous college or university attended and have attained a 2.0 on all previous college courses.

International students must take the TOEFL examination, submit transcripts from all attended institutions, and show satisfactory SAT or ACT scores.

Early admission allows academically gifted high school students the opportunity to enroll in college before completing high school. Qualified students must be seniors and have a SAT score of 900 or more. The early admission dual enrollment program allows seniors to enroll in a college program. Student transcript must reflect that they will meet basic admission requirements when they graduate from high school.

Admission Application Deadline

Rolling admission provides no specific date for notification of admission so applicant is informed as soon as admission decision is made.

Admission Contact

Charles A. Darlington, Director of Admissions, Fayetteville State University, 1200 Murchison Rd., Newbold Station, Fayetteville, NC 28301-4298; (910) 486-1371; in-state: 800-672-6667; Out-of-state: 800-222-2594.

GRADUATION REQUIREMENTS

An Associate of Arts degree requires a minimum of 60 hours of course work and a 2.0 GPA.

A bachelor's degree requires a minimum of 120 hours and completion of core requirements with a cumulative GPA of 2.0 or higher and 2.0 or higher GPA in the major field. One year of study in residence required including 30 hours of course work. Senior year in residence required; special exceptions considered.

Grading System

A–F; I=Incomplete; W=Withdrawal; WN=Withdrawal for non-attendance, WU= Withdrawal from university; R=Academic support courses; S=Satisfactory; U=Unsatisfactory; P=Passing, no grade points; AU= Audit.

STUDENT BODY PROFILE

Total enrollment (male/female):
  1,600/2,303

From in-state: 3,591

Other regions: 35 states; 6 foreign countries

Full-time undergraduates (male/female):
  1,083/2,041

Graduate students (male/female): 231/548

Ethnic/Racial Makeup

African American, 2,459; Hispanic, 78; Asian, 39; Native American, 39; Caucasian, 1,249: Internationals, 39.

Class of 1995 Profile

Average high school GPA: 2.85

Transfers enrolled: 465

FACULTY PROFILE

Number of faculty: 216

Student-teacher ratio: 18:1

Full-time faculty: 185

Part-time faculty: 31

Faculty with doctorates or other terminal
  degrees: 80%

SCHOOL CALENDAR

1993–94: Aug 14–May (semester hours)

Commencement and conferring of degrees:
  May 7

Two summer sessions.

DEGREES OFFERED 1991–92:

Associate of Arts

Biology

Business Administration

Chemistry

Computer Science

Criminal Justice

English

General Studies

Geography

History

Mathematics

Music Education

Police Science

Political Science

Psychology

Public Administration

Sociology

Spanish

Visual Arts

Bachelor of Arts

Chemistry

English Language and Literature

Geography

History

Political Science

Sociology

Spanish

Speech

Visual Arts

Bachelor of Science

Accounting

Biology/Education

Business Administration/Banking/
  Finance/Management/Marketing

Business Education

Chemistry

Computer Science

Criminal Justice

Economics

Elementary Education

Health Education

Marketing Education

Mathematics/Mathematics Education

Medical Technology

Music Education

Nursing (B.S.N.)

Office Administration

Physical Education

Psychology

Social Science Education

Master of Art

Education/Biology/History/Mathematics

Educational Administration and
  Supervision

History

Political Science

Psychology

Sociology

Master of Science

Mathematics

SPECIAL PROGRAMS

Accelerated study program allows students to complete their undergraduate degree in a shorter period of time than the traditional period of four years.

Adult or continuing education program is available for nontraditional students returning to school or working full time.

Advanced Placement (AP) grants college credit for postsecondary work completed in high school. Students scoring 3–5 on the AP test will receive credit by examination for each course and advanced placement.

Air Force ROTC provides training in military science for commission as a second lieutenant in the U. S. Armed Forces. Two- and four-year scholarships are available.

Challenge Exam is a credit by exam program that allows students to receive college credit for passing Challenge tests in the core curriculum area.

College Level Examination Program (CLEP) determines the academic relevance of nontraditional educational experiences, such as the military, on-the-job training, or other life experiences, through a series of tests and may grant students college credit for these experiences.

College orientation is offered to entering students, parents included, at no cost prior to the beginning of classes to acquaint students with the college and to prepare them for college life.

Cooperative Education Program alternates classroom study with related paid work experience. The program provides academic credit and full-time status during co-op placement.

Cooperative Degree Programs allow students to take college credit toward their degree programs at a cooperating institution. Cooperating institutions include The University of North Carolina at Chapel Hill (Medical Technology), Pennsylvania College of Podiatric Medicine, Logan College of Chiropractic Medicine, and Howard University (Pharmacy).

Defense Activity for Nontraditional Education Support (DANTES) is a credit by exam program that allows students to earn college credit toward degrees for work and life experience by passing the DANTES test.

Fort Bragg-Pope Air Force Base Education Program allows military personnel and their dependents to pursue their education while serving in the military. Contact the Director of the Fort Bragg-Pope AFB Center, Box 70156, Fort Bragg, NC 28307.

Honors program offers academically talented students a challenging program of study that includes special classes, seminars, colloquia, cultural activities, and special recognition to motivate participants.

Off-campus study allows students to take courses at other institutions for credit.

The Study Abroad Program allows students to go to a foreign country for a specified period of time for part of their college education.

Part-time degree program allows students to earn an undergraduate degree while attending part time.

Remedial courses are offered to entering students to bring them up to admissions standards and to help them adjust for success in college.

Student Support Services provide developmental courses, counseling, and cultural activities to students who need aid to succeed in college.

University College offers a 45-credit core curriculum, containing all the preparatory courses needed for upper division course work in a supportive academic environment.

Weekend and evening college is available Monday–Friday and Saturday on campus and at Fort Bragg for credit and non-credit activities such as lectures, seminars, and workshops. Students enrolled must take a minimum of three semester hours and a maximum of eighteen hours.

ATHLETIC PROGRAMS

Fayetteville State is a member of the National Collegiate Athletic Association (NCAA), Division II; and the Central Intercollegiate Athletic Association.

Intercollegiate sports: men's basketball, football, cross-country, track & field, tennis, and golf; women's basketball, cross-country, golf, tennis, track & field, and volleyball. Intramural sports: basketball, golf, gymnastics, volleyball, and tennis.

Athletic Contact

Ralph E. Burns, Director of Athletics, Fayetteville State University, 1200 Murchison Rd., Newbold Station, Fayetteville, NC 28301; (919) 486-1314.

LIBRARY HOLDINGS

The Charles Waddell Chestnutt Library holds 175,000 bound volumes, 470,000 microform items, 2,356 periodical subscriptions, and 2,500 audiovisuals; 125 computers are available for student use. The library has a computerized catalog and circulation system. Special collections include the Charles Waddell Chestnut papers, the James Ward Seabrook papers, and material from other individuals who have made noteworthy contributions to southeastern North Carolina.

STUDENT LIFE

Special Regulations

Class attendance is required and absences must be excused by the instructor.

Campus Services

Health center; personal and social counseling; career counseling and placement; remedial instruction; testing service for SAT, GMAT, NTE, DANTES, CLEP, AND GRE; job locator program to help students find part-time work off campus.

Campus Activities

Social activities include theater, concerts, dances, and choir. Students may work on the student-run yearbook or newspaper.

Leadership opportunities are found in the Student Government Association or numerous other student-run organizations. Greek-letter fraternities include Alpha Phi Alpha, Kappa Alpha Psi, Omega Psi Phi, and Phi Beta Sigma; sororities include Alpha Kappa Alpha, Delta Sigma Theta, Sigma Gamma Rho, and Zeta Phi Beta. Honor societies include Alpha Kappa Mu, Phi Beta Sigma, Alpha Kappa Delta, Beta Kappa Chi, Delta Mu Delta, Kappa Delta Pi, Pi Gamma Mu, Pi Omega Pi, and Sigma Tau Delta.

Fayetteville State University is located in Fayetteville, North Carolina's most inland port. This city of 75,000 people on the Cape Fear River has been a prominent business center since its founding. Fort Bragg and the Pope Air Force Base are 30 miles away. Served by all major mass transportation types, Fayetteville is 50 miles away from Raleigh, the nearest large city, and about the same distance from the Atlantic Ocean beaches and attractions around Wilmington, North Carolina. Ideally located, Fayetteville's students are close to the a wide variety of cultural and recreational activities, including the mid-April Dogwood Festival and parade, the Museum of Cape Fear, and the John F. Kennedy Center.

Housing Availability

1,100 housing spaces; 8 residence halls

Handicapped Services

Barrier-free facilities. Disabled students are assisted through the Counseling Center and are provided with opportunities for university recreational and social activities.

JOHNSON C. SMITH UNIVERSITY

HISTORY

Johnson C. Smith University (JCSU) is a four-year, private, coed, liberal arts institution affiliated with the Presbyterian Church. Founded in 1867 as Biddle Memorial Institute, JCSU is one of the oldest historically black institutions in the United States. The first baccalaureate degrees were awarded in 1872, and the name changed to Biddle University in 1876. The present name was given in 1923.

Originally intended as an institute of higher learning for men, it became coeducational in 1941. JCSU's mission is to provide an environment in which men and women may realize their individual potential for intellectual, social, spiritual, emotional, and physical growth and well-being. JCSU carries out this mission by providing exciting, relevant, and future-oriented curriculum and programs. The university also looks backward to celebrate the unique heritage of blacks by instilling racial and ethnic pride as students learn about their history and the unique achievements and contributions of black Americans. JCSU helps its students to understand and adopt a sense of social consciousness and civic responsibility. The school boasts that it is one of the best kept secrets in higher education.

The 85-acre campus houses 46 buildings. Biddle Memorial Hall, an historic landmark with Romanesque Revival architecture, adds a traditional flavor to an eclectic mix of different architectural styles.

ACCREDITATION

Johnson C. Smith University is accredited by the Southern Association of Colleges and Schools (SACS) to award the Bachelor of Science and Bachelor of Arts degrees.

Other Accreditation

Council on Social Work Education

National Council for Accreditation of Teacher Education

100 Beatties Ford Rd.
Charlotte, NC 28216
Phone: (704) 378-1000
Toll-free out-state:
800-782-7303

Total Enrollment:
1,256

Level of Selectivity:
Slightly competitive

Motto:
Sit Lux
(Let There Be Light)

COSTS PER YEAR

1992–93 Tuition: $5,454

Room and board: $1,196 (room); $1,134 (board)

Special fees: $500

Books: $638

Estimated total cost: $8,922

FINANCIAL AID

1990–91 Institutional Funding

Number of scholarships and grants: 308

Total amount of scholarships and grants: $610,990

Range of scholarships and grants: $500–$6,000

1990–91 Federal and State Funding

Number of scholarships and grants: 775

Total amount of scholarships and grants: $1,640,835

Range of scholarships and grants: $200–$2,300

Number of loans: 835

Total amount of loans: $2,195,958

Range of loans: $500–$4,000

Number of work-study: 388

Total amount of work-study: $490,500

Range of work-study: $200–$500

Financial Aid Specific to the School

92% of the student body received financial aid during 1991–92.

Endowed, corporate, friends, private donor scholarships, and university scholarships are available to students based on achievement or areas of interest.

Athletic scholarships are available to students participating in intercollegiate sports.

Performance grants in music are available to talented students in choir or band.

Deferred Payment Plans allow students to pay college costs in two or three installments during the semester at an additional cost of $25. Contact the office of Business & Financial Affairs.

United Negro College Fund (UNCF) scholarships are awarded to a limited number of students at this school who demonstrate financial need. Some scholarships may be based on location and merit. UNCF scholarships range from $500 to $7,500.

Army, Air Force, or Navy ROTC program(s) offer two- and three-year scholarships that pay tuition, fees, books, and other expenses, and provide a monthly stipend of $100.

North Carolina Contractual Grants are available to full-time students who are residents of the state.

North Carolina Legislative Tuition Grants are available for full-time students who are residents of the state and demonstrate financial need.

National Presbyterian College Scholarships are available for students who are members of the Presbyterian denomination. Scholarships are competitive. Contact the National Presbyterian College Scholarship, 100 Witherspoon St., Louisville, KY 40202-1396.

Financial Aid Deadline

April 15

Financial Aid Contact

Director of Financial Aid, Johnson C. Smith University, 100 Beatties Ford Rd., Charlotte, NC 28216; (704) 378-1035.

ADMISSION REQUIREMENTS

SAT or ACT required

Entrance Requirements

Graduation from an accredited high school and completion of the following 16 units: 4 English, 2 mathematics, 2 social sciences, 1 science, and 7 electives. Letters of recommendation are needed. A $20 non-refundable application fee required.

GED students must meet basic admission requirements.

Transfer students must submit official transcripts from each college and high school previously attended, have a "C" average, and qualify for readmission at previous college for advance standing; students transferring from a college approved by a regional association will be admitted as a regular student; transfers with less than a "C" average or less than 10 hours may be admitted under the "Fresh Start" plan or provisional transfer plan.

International students must submit original or certified copy of transcript from secondary schools and/or all colleges attended, take the TOEFL examination and the SAT or ACT, provide statement of financial responsibility, and pay all college costs for one year.

Early admission allows academically gifted high school students the opportunity to enroll in college for credit before completing high school.

Admission Application Deadline

Rolling admission provides no specific date for notification of admission so applicant is informed as soon as admission decision is made; July 1 (fall); December 1 (spring); early decision provides notification of acceptance early in applicant's twelfth year of high school.

Admission Contact

Mr. Marvin Dunlap, Director of Admissions, Johnson C. Smith University, 100 Beatties Ford Rd., Charlotte, NC 28216; (704) 378-1010; Toll-free: 800-782-7303.

GRADUATION REQUIREMENTS

A minimum of 122 hours with a 2.0 GPA and completion of the core requirements to include the following hours: six mathematics, eight science, six foreign language, and one computer course for majors in biology, business, chemistry, and math.

Grading System

A–F; I=Incomplete; W=Withdraw

STUDENT BODY PROFILE

Total enrollment (male/female): 503/753

From in-state: 251

Other regions: 33 states

Full-time undergraduates (male/female): 490/735

Part-time undergraduates (male/female): 15/16

Ethnic/Racial Makeup

African American, 1,243; International, 13.

Class of 1995 Profile

Number of applicants: 1,138

Number accepted: 774

Number enrolled: 379

Median SAT score: 330V; 305M

Transfers enrolled: 38

FACULTY PROFILE

Number of faculty: 96

Student-teacher ratio: 15:1

Full-time faculty: (male/female) 55/29

Part-time faculty: 14

Faculty with doctorates or other terminal degrees: 65%

SCHOOL CALENDAR

1992–93: August–Mid-May (semester hours)

Commencement and conferring of degrees: May

Two summer sessions.

DEGREES OFFERED 1991–92:

Bachelor of Arts

Chemistry

Communication Arts

Economics

English

History

International Studies

Liberal Arts

Music

Political Science

Social Science

Social Work

Sociology

Bachelor of Science

Banking and Finance Education

Biology

Business Administration

Chemistry

Computer Science

Education (Early Childhood and
  Intermediate)

Engineering

General Science

Health Education

Mathematics

Mathematics/Physics

Music/Business

Physical Education

Psychology

Pre-Professional

Pre-Dental

Pre-Law

Pre-Medicine

SPECIAL PROGRAMS

Accelerated study program allows students to complete their undergraduate degree in a shorter period of time than the traditional period of four years.

Advanced placement (AP) grants college credit for postsecondary work completed in high school. Students scoring a certain minimum on the AP test will receive credit by examination for each course.

College orientation is offered for $100 for five days prior to the beginning of classes to acquaint students with the college and to prepare them for college life. Parents may attend.

Cooperative Education Program combines classroom study with related paid work experience. The program provides academic credit and full-time status during co-op placement.

Cooperative Study Abroad Program allows students to take courses toward the degree requirements at an institution in a foreign country.

Honors program offers academically talented students a challenging program of study that includes special classes, seminars, colloquia, cultural activities, and special recognition to motivate participants. Johnson C. Smith University has an Honors College and honors housing.

Joint degree programs exist in pharmacy with Howard University and an international studies program with Davidson College.

Minority Biomedical Research Support Program (MBRS) and the Minority Access to Research Careers Program (MARC) are programs designed to increase the available pool of ethnic minorities in scientific research.

Off-campus study allows students to take courses at other institutions for credit. The ten institutions in the Charlotte Area Educational Consortium are available for this purpose.

Part-time degree program allows students to earn an undergraduate degree while attending part time.

Remedial courses are available to bring students up to admissions standards and to help them adjust for success in college.

ROTC provides training in military science for commission as a second lieutenant in the U. S. Armed Forces. Two- and four-year scholarships are available. Cooperative programs are available in Army ROTC and Air Force ROTC.

Three/two dual degree program in engineering (civil, mechanical, or electrical) allows students to get two degrees—one in liberal arts from Johnson C. Smith University and one in engineering from the University of North Carolina at Charlotte (UNCC)—

by completing three years at Johnson C. Smith University and two years at UNCC.

ATHLETIC PROGRAMS

Johnson C. Smith University is a member of the National Collegiate Athletic Association (NCAA), Division II; and the Central Intercollegiate Athletic Association (CIAA). Intercollegiate sports: men's basketball, cross-country, football, golf, tennis, and track & field; women's basketball, cross-country, softball, track & field, and volleyball.

Intramural sports include badminton, basketball, softball, swimming, tennis, track & field, and volleyball.

The men's and women's basketball teams continue to be at the top of the CIAA. The men's team won its second consecutive Southern Division Champion. In 1992, the centennial of the first intercollegiate football game between black colleges was played between Johnson C. Smith and Livingstone College, with a JCSU victory of 5-0.

Athletic Contact

Director of Athletics, Johnson C. Smith University, 100 Beatties Ford Rd., Charlotte, NC 28216; (704) 378-1072.

LIBRARY HOLDINGS

The James B. Duke Memorial Library has 115,000 bound volumes, 20,000 microform items, 696 periodical subscriptions, and 2,036 audiovisual items; 125 computers are available for students use in the library, computer center, and dormitories. The library is computerized.

STUDENT LIFE

Campus Services

Health clinic, personal and psychological counseling, career counseling and placement, remediation, tutoring, and religious activities.

Campus Activities

Social and cultural activities include theater, art exhibits, concerts, chorale, band, and dance. Chess, film, and photography clubs and activities are available. Interested students may work on the *JCSU Student News* (student newspaper) or *The Bull* (yearbook). Communication majors or volunteers can work at the student-run radio station.

Leadership opportunities are found in the Student Government Association or numerous other student-run organizations, including the Residence Hall Council and the Pan-Hellenic Council. Greek-letter fraternities include Alpha Phi Alpha, Kappa Alpha Psi, Omega Psi Phi, and Phi Beta Sigma; sororities include Alpha Kappa Alpha, Delta Sigma Theta, Sigma Gamma Rho, and Zeta Phi Beta. Honor societies are also represented on campus.

Charlotte, North Carolina, is a thriving city with a population of nearly 400,000. The city is served by all major forms of transportation: bus, rail, and air. The Douglas International Airport is the hub for U.S. Airlines. Just minutes from downtown, students have access to shopping, fine restaurants, and entertainment events. Charlotte offers major league sporting events, museums, concerts, and orchestra. Its location makes easy access to the Smoky Mountains National Park and the Atlantic Ocean beaches and attractions.

Housing Availability

980 housing spaces; eight resident halls; honors housing. Off-campus residence is permitted.

Handicapped Services

Some facilities are wheelchair accessible.

NOTABLE ALUMNI

Freddie (Curly) Neal–Harlem Globetrotter

Tim Newman–Ex-professional player, NFL New York Jets

Pettis Norman–Ex-professional player, NFL Dallas Cowboys

Joachim Weinberg–Ex-professional player, NFL San Diego Chargers

LIVINGSTONE COLLEGE

701 West Monroe St.
Salisbury, NC 28144
Phone: (704) 638-5500
Fax: (704) 638-5502

Total Enrollment:
654

Level of Selectivity:
Slightly competitive

Motto:
Pioneering a New
Century of Academic
Excellence

HISTORY

Livingstone College is a four-year, private, coed, liberal arts college, affiliated with the African Methodist Episcopal (AME) Zion Church. Livingstone was founded in 1879 under the name of Zion Wesley Institute. In 1885, the name changed to Zion Wesley College. It was in 1887 that the college awarded its first baccalaureate degree and adopted its present name.

The AME Zion ministers who founded Livingstone "wished to promote a type of education which would make for self-reliance in their race." These visionary leaders believed through "unswerving faith in self and God they could succeed in establishing an institution to educate blacks." Livingstone college started in the parsonage of the late Bishop C. R. Harris. In 1882, it moved to a one-building, 40-acre site. The campus has increased to 21 buildings on 272 acres, attracting students from the United States, Canada, the Caribbean, and Africa.

Although Livingstone College's programs have expanded, it continues to provide an undergraduate school and seminary to educate men and women in liberal arts and theology. The school offers Baccalaureate and Master's programs in theology. This historically black college is a United Negro College Fund (UNCF) school member.

ACCREDITATION

Livingstone College is accredited by the Southern Association of Colleges and Schools to award the Bachelor of Arts, Bachelor of Science, and Master's of Theology degrees.

Other Accreditation

Council on Social Work Education

Immigration and Naturalization Service for the Training of Alien Students

North Carolina Department of Public Instruction

COSTS PER YEAR

1992–93 Tuition: $4,400

Room and board: $1,400 (room); $2,000 (board)

Special fees: $800

Books: $500

Estimated total cost: $9,100

FINANCIAL AID

Financial Aid Specific to the School

96% of the student body received financial aid during 1991–92.

The Army ROTC offers two- and four-year scholarships that pay for tuition, fees, books, and other expenses, and provide a monthly stipend of $100.

Athletic scholarships are available to students participating in intercollegiate sports.

The Cooperative Education Program parallels academic study with paid related work experience in 15 majors. Students receive academic credit and full-time status during co-op placement.

Full or partial tuition waivers are available to Livingstone employees and their children.

Institution work-aid is provided to a limited number of students not qualifying for work-study. Maximum number of hours received is 40 per month.

Low interest, long-term loans are available through the college fund for students who are from North Carolina.

North Carolina (NC) Legislative Tuition Grants are available to residents of the state attending private colleges and universities in North Carolina.

North Carolina State Grants are based on need and administered through the North Carolina Association of Independent Colleges and Universities.

Student Incentive Grant is administered by the state and given to residents of the state, awarding grants up to $1,500.

Tuition installment payment plans are available.

United Negro College Fund Scholarships are awarded to a limited number of entering students who score high on the ACT or ETS and/or students with high school GPAs of 3.0 or better. To renew awards students must maintain a cumulative GPA of 3.0 in college.

Financial Aid Deadline

July 15 (priority)

Financial Aid Contact

Mrs. Annie L. Pruitt, Director of Financial Aid, Livingstone College, Salisbury, NC 28144; (704) 638-5561.

ADMISSION REQUIREMENTS

SAT or ACT required

Entrance Requirements

Graduation from an accredited high school and completion of the following 16 units; 4 English, 3 math, 2 social studies, 1 science, and 5 electives; a high school GPA of 2.0 or better; a recent physical examination; academic status in top 60% of class; two letters of recommendation from high school; and a $10 application fee with application.

GED scores are accepted in place of high school diploma; must meet basic admission requirements.

Transfer students must submit transcripts from previous institution; no more than 36 credits will be accepted from a two-year college with a 2.0 GPA, and must be in good standing with previous institution.

International students, in addition to meeting the regular requirements, must also take the TOEFL examination.

Admission Application Deadline

Priority. August 1 (fall); December 15 (spring). Rolling admission provides no specific date for notification of admission so applicant is informed as soon as admission decision is made. Early decision provides notification of acceptance early in applicant's 12th year of high school. Advanced placement. Deferred admissions.

Admissions Contact

Mr. Grady Deese, Director of Admissions, Livingstone College, 701 West Monroe St., Salisbury, NC 28144; (704) 638-5500.

GRADUATION REQUIREMENTS

124 semester hours including 53 hours of core requirements to include: 3 freshman English, 3 religion (Old and New Testament), 2 physical education, 8 natural science, 8 mathematics, 9 social science, 6 modern foreign language, and completion of freshman orientation.

Grading System

A-F; Grades of I=Incomplete; AU= Audit; WP=Withdrew Passing; WF=Withdrew Failing, earn no quality points.

Carnegie Library, Livingstone College

STUDENT BODY PROFILE

Total enrollment: 654

From in-state: 348

Other regions:

Full-time undergraduates (male/female): 367/213

Part-time undergraduates (male/female): 12/16

Graduate students (male/female): 30/16

Ethnic/Racial Makeup

African American, 640; Hispanic, 7; Asian American, 7.

Class of 1995 Profile

Number of applicants: 581

Number accepted: 494

Number enrolled: 302

Median SAT score: 320V: 300M

Median ACT score: 12

FACULTY PROFILE

Number of faculty: 63

Student-faculty ratio: 15:1

Full-time faculty: 47

Part-time faculty: 17

Tenured faculty (male/female):

Faculty with doctorates or other terminal
degrees: 43%

SCHOOL CALENDAR

1992–93: August 24–May 7 (semesters)

Commencement and conferring of degrees:
May 11

Two summer sessions.

DEGREES OFFERED 1991–92:

Bachelor's Degrees

Accounting

Biology

Business

Business Administration

Business Management

Chemistry

Computer Information Systems

Computer Science

Early Childhood Education

Education

Elementary Education

Engineering Dual Degree

English

History

Law and History dual degree

Mathematics

Mathematics Education

Music

Music Education

Music Therapy

Pharmacy and Chemistry dual degree

Physical Education

Physical Education/Sports Management

Political Science

Psychology

Recreation Therapy

Science Education

Social Studies Education

Social Work

Sociology

Master's Degree

Theology

Graduates that later obtain higher degrees:
12%

SPECIAL PROGRAMS

The academic remediation program provides remedial courses for entering students to bring them up to admission standards and to help them adjust and succeed in college.

The Advanced Placement Program grants college credit for post-secondary work completed in secondary school. Students scoring 3 or above on the exam will receive credit for each course as well as advance placement in major.

The Army ROTC program provides training in military science for commission as a second lieutenant in the U.S. Armed Forces. Two- and four-year scholarships are available.

The College Level Examination Program (CLEP) grants college credit for nontraditional educational experiences. Students must pass the CLEP exams in various subjects.

The college orientation session for entering freshmen and transfers is free; parents may attend.

The Cooperative Education Program in 15 majors combines academic study and credit with related paid work experience.

Student must be a sophomore and have a 2.0 GPA or better.

Internships provide related work experience and academic credit. Some internships may be paid. Combined cooperative education and intern hours are limited to 12.

A three-three dual degree in chemistry and pharmacy is offered in cooperation with Howard University College of Pharmacy and Pharmacology Sciences. Students complete three years at Livingstone and then three years at Howard. Upon completion of the program the students receive a Bachelor of Science degree in Chemistry from Livingstone and Bachelor of Science degree in Pharmacy from Howard. Students can pursue a Ph.D. in Pharmacy by completing three years at Livingstone and then four years at Howard.

A three-three dual degree in law and history or political science is offered in conjunction with St. John's University Law School. Students attend Livingstone for three years and transfer to St. John's for three years to complete a law degree. Students accepted in the dual degree program will receive a full scholarship and stipend to St. John's Law School.

Three-two dual engineering degree program in conjunction with Georgia Institute of Technology or Clemson University is also available. Student completes three years at Livingston and two years at the cooperating school. Upon completion of the program, students receive a bachelor's degree from Livingstone and an engineering degree from the cooperating school.

ATHLETIC PROGRAMS

Livingstone College is a member of the National Collegiate Athletic Association (NCAA), Division II.

Intercollegiate sports include: men's basketball, football, golf, tennis, track & field and wrestling; women's basketball, tennis, track & field, and volleyball.

Intramural sports: basketball, tennis, track & field, and volleyball.

Athletic Contact

Mr. Delano Tucker, Livingstone College, Salisbury, NC 28144; (704) 638-5660.

LIBRARY HOLDINGS

The Andrew Carnegie Library holds 79,594 volumes; 495 periodical subscriptions; 1,983 audiovisuals; 10,915 microforms; 49 computer terminals for student use. Special collections include a black studies collection.

STUDENT LIFE

Special Regulations

Must take four hours of religion, attend a weekly assembly, attend monthly vespers services, abide by curfews and quiet hours, and follow restricted dorm visitation periods. Seniors must live on campus; all dorm residents must purchase meal tickets.

Campus Services

Health center, personal and psychological counseling, career planning and placement, tutoring, academic remediation, math and writing labs, campus transportation system, religious services. Cars permitted without restrictions.

Campus Activities

Livingstone College offers an array of social and cultural activities for students including a lecture series and concert series with renowned artists, as well as plays and dances. Students may get involved in the college's marching band, concert band, choir, or the Julia B. Duncan Players drama group. Students may get involved in the writing and production of Livingstone's many publications, including its annual publication *(Arts Magazine)*, a literary magazine *(The Bear's Tale)*, a monthly publication *(The Living Stone)*, or the college yearbook *(The Livingstonian)*.

Leadership opportunities can be found in student organizations such as the Student Life Committee. Greek-letter sororities include Alpha Kappa Alpha, Delta Sigma Theta, Sigma Gamma Rho, and Zeta Phi Beta. Three national fraternities are also represented on campus. Honor societies include Alpha Kappa Mu, Beta Kappa Chi, and Psychological Honor Society. Students can choose to get involved in the monthly vesper services where prominent civic, religious, and student groups participate.

Livingstone is located in the small town of Salisbury, North Carolina, population of approximately 23,000. Historic Salisbury offers sites of interest regarding the civil war. Livingstone's campus is within 50 miles of Charlotte and Greensboro, North Carolina. Charlotte's International Douglas Airport is a point of departure to anywhere in the United States and many foreign countries. The cities of Charlotte and Greensboro offer museums, theaters, sports, as well as recreational activities.

Housing Availability

650 spaces available; freshman housing guaranteed; seniors required to live on campus.

Handicapped Services

Include special class scheduling and special parking privileges.

NOTABLE ALUMNI

Alfred Leroy Edwards, 1948–Former deputy assistant, Secretary of Agriculture

Elizabeth Koontz, 1938– Former president, National Education Association; director, Women's Bureau of the Department of Labor

NORTH CAROLINA AGRICULTURAL & TECHNICAL STATE UNIVERSITY

1601 E. Market St.
Greensboro, NC 27411
Phone: (919) 334-7946
Toll-free in-state:
800-443-8964

Total Enrollment:
7,119

Level of Selectivity:
Moderately
competitive

HISTORY

North Carolina A&T State University (NCA&T) is a four-year, state-supported, coed liberal arts institution founded in 1891 as one of two land grant institutions in the state and an annex of Shaw University. NCA&T was originally named A&M College for the Colored Race. The first baccalaureate degrees were awarded in 1896 after the school relocated in Greensboro. It was renamed Agricultural and Technical College of North Carolina in 1915.

The present name was adopted in 1967 and NCA&T was designated a constituent institution of the North Carolina University System in 1972.

As one of the 16 member institutions of the state university system, North Carolina Agricultural and Technical State University offers a diverse and high quality program for an integrated student body. It is committed to providing an intellectual environment where students may find a sense of belonging, responsibility, and achievement that prepares them for roles of leadership and service. To that end the university serves as a laboratory for the development of excellence in teaching research and public service. Its history of quality education is personified in a long list of distinguished graduates.

The school is located on 181 acres with 68 buildings including the H. Clinton Taylor Art Gallery, the African Heritage center, two exceptional museums, and a computer center.

ACCREDITATION

North Carolina Agricultural and Technical State University is accredited by the Southern Association of Colleges and Schools (SACS) to award the Bachelor of Arts, Bachelor of Science, and Master's degrees.

Other Accreditation

Accreditation Board for Engineering and Technology

American Assembly of Collegiate Schools of Business

American Chemical Society

Career College Association/Accrediting Commission for Independent Colleges and Schools

Council on Social Work Education

National Council for Accreditation of Teacher Education

National League for Nursing

COSTS PER YEAR

1992–93 Tuition: $1,228 (in-state); $6,282 (out-state)

Room and board: $1,250 (room); $1,030 (board)

Special fees: $552

Books: $500

Estimated total cost: $4,560 (in-state); $9,614 (out-state)

FINANCIAL AID

1990–91 Institutional Funding

Number of scholarships and grants: 821

Total amount of scholarships and grants: $1,358,141

Range of scholarships and grants: $200–$8,000

1991–92 Federal and State Funding

Number of scholarships and grants: 2,484

Total amount of scholarships and grants: $4,120,987

Range of scholarships and grants: $50–$5,000

Number of loans: 1,712

Total amount of loans: $3,501,637

Range of loans: $100–$4,000

Number of work-study: 535

Total amount of work-study: $536,214

Range of work-study: $400–$3,200

Financial Aid Specific to the School

85% of the student body received financial aid during 1991–92.

Army and Air Force programs offer two- and three-year scholarships that pay tuition, fees, books and other expenses as well as a monthly stipend of $100.

Athletic scholarships are available to students participating in intercollegiate sports.

College work-aid is available to students not qualifying for college work-study to work in departments of the college.

Cooperative Education Program alternates classroom study with related paid work experience. The program provides academic credit and full-time status during co-op placement.

Deferred Payment Plan allows students to pay college costs in two or three installments during the semester.

Insured tuition installment allows students to guarantee payment of college costs by taking out a loan, with interest, from a private loan company.

North Carolina tuition grants are available to students who are residents of the state and demonstrate financial need.

Performance grants are available to students participating in music or art.

Thurgood Marshall Black Education Fund provides a four-year scholarship at this public Black college. Qualifying students must have a high school GPA of 3.0 or better and a SAT score of 1000 or ACT score of 24 or more. Student must be recommended by high school counselor as exceptional or exemplary in the creative or performing arts. Scholarship pays tuition, fees, room, and board not to exceed $6,000 annually.

Tuition waivers available for North Carolina A&T State University employees and their children as well as senior citizens on a space available basis.

Financial Aid Deadline
May 15

Financial Aid Contact
Director of Financial Aid, North Carolina A&T State University, 1601 E. Market St., Greensboro, NC 27411.

ADMISSION REQUIREMENTS
SAT or ACT required (used for counseling & placement)

Entrance Requirements
Graduation from an accredited high school and completion of the following college prep units: 4 English, 3 mathematics, 3 science, 2 social science, 2 physical education and 2 years of foreign language recommended; minimum 2.0 GPA; class rank and recommendation from school. A $25 application fee required.

GED students must meet basic admission requirements.

Transfer students must submit all college transcripts; minimum 2.0 GPA; must meet basic admission requirements.

International students must submit certified high school and college certificates; take the TOEFL examination; provide proof of ability to pay all college costs

Early admission allows academically gifted high school students the opportunity to enroll in college full time before completing high school.

Early decision admits high school students in their junior or senior year to a college of their first choice. Financial aid is determined at time of early decision.

Admission Application Deadline
January 1 (out-state); June 1 (fall); November 1 (spring)

Admission Contact
Mr. John F. Smith, Director of Admissions, North Carolina A&T State University, 1601 E. Market St., Greensboro, NC 27411; (919) 334-7946 or 7947; Toll free 800-443-8964 (in-state).

GRADUATION REQUIREMENTS
A minimum of 124 hours and completion of core requirements to include the following courses: 4 mathematics, 4 science, and 2 courses in one foreign language; satisfy English and math competency tests.

Grading System
A-F; I=Incomplete, W=Withdrew

STUDENT BODY PROFILE
Total enrollment (male/female):
3,630/3,489

From in-state: 4,695

Other regions: 27 states, 13 foreign countries

Full-time undergraduates (male/female): 2,847/2,736

Part-time undergraduates (male/female): 388/373

Graduate students (male/female): 395/380

Ethnic/Racial Makeup

African American, 6,407; Hispanic, 71; Asian, 71; Native American, 71; Caucasian, 356; International, 72; Other/unclassified, 71.

Class of 1995 Profile

Number of applicants: 4,283

Number accepted: 2,698

Number enrolled: 1,484

Transfers enrolled: 498

FACULTY PROFILE

Number of faculty: 424

Student-teacher ratio: 14:1

Full-time faculty: 356

Part-time faculty: 62

Faculty with doctorates or other terminal degrees: 62%

SCHOOL CALENDAR

1992–93: August–May (semester hours)

Commencement and conferring of degrees: May

Two summer sessions.

DEGREES OFFERED 1991–92:

Accounting

Administrative Services

Agricultural Business

Agricultural Economics

Agricultural Education

Agricultural Engineering

Agricultural Science

Agricultural Technology

Art/Design

Art Education

Art/Painting

Biology/Biology Education

Business Administration (Finance, Management, Marketing)

Business Education

Chemical Engineering

Chemistry/Chemistry Education

Child Development

Civil Engineering

Clothing and Textiles

Communications (Broadcasting, Print Journalism, Public Relations)

Computer Science

Early Childhood Education

Economics

Electrical Engineering

Engineering Mathematics

Engineering Physics

English/English Education

Food Administration

Food and Nutrition

Food Science

French/French Education

Health and Physical Education

History/History Education

Home Economics Education

Industrial Arts Education

Industrial Engineering

Industrial Technology

Laboratory Animal Science

Landscape Architecture

Mathematics/Mathematics Education

Mechanical Engineering

Music/Music Education

Nursing

Occupational Safety and Health

Physics/Physics Education

Political Science

Professional Theater

Psychology

Recreation Administration

Safety and Driver Education

Social Science/Social Science Education

Social Services

Social Work

Sociology

Special Education

Speech

Speech and Theater

Transportation

Vocational Education

SPECIAL PROGRAMS

Accelerated Study Program allows students to complete their undergraduate degree in a shorter period of time than the traditional four years.

Adult or continuing education program is available for nontraditional students returning to school or working full time.

Advanced Placement (AP) grants college credit for postsecondary work completed in high school. Students scoring at a certain level on the AP test will receive credit by examination for each course and advanced placement.

College Level Examination Program (CLEP) determines the academic relevance of nontraditional educational experiences such as the military, on-the-job training, or other life experiences through a series of tests, and may grant students college credit for these experiences.

College orientation is offered at no cost to entering students for four days prior to the beginning of classes to acquaint students with the college and to prepare them for college life; parents may attend.

Cooperative Education Program alternates classroom study with related paid work experience. The program provides academic credit and full-time status during co-op placement.

Cooperative Program allows students to take college credit toward their degree programs at a cooperating institution.

English as a Second Language is a program that offers courses in English for students whose native language is not English.

Honors Program offers academically talented students a challenging program of study that includes special classes, seminars, colloquia, cultural activities, and special recognition to motivate participants.

Individualized Majors allow students to create their own major programs of study.

Internships in various disciplines allow students to apply theory to on-the-job training in industry, business, and government.

Off Campus Study allows students to take courses at other institutions for credit. Cooperating institutions include Bennett College, Guilford College, the University of North Carolina at Greensboro, High Point College, and Greensboro College.

Part-time degree program allows students to earn an undergraduate degree part time.

Remedial courses are offered to entering students to bring them up to admission standards and to help them adjust for success in college.

ROTC provides training in military science for commission as a second lieutenant in the U.S. Armed Forces. Two- and four-year scholarships are available. Army and Air Force ROTC have programs at North Carolina A&T State University.

Student Support Services provide developmental courses, counseling, and cultural activities to students who need aid to succeed in college.

Study Abroad Program allows students to go to France for part of their college education.

ATHLETIC PROGRAMS

North Carolina Agricultural and Technical State University is a member of the National Collegiate Athletic Association (NCAA) All Division I with the exception of men's football which is a member of NCAA's Division I-AA.

Intercollegiate sports: men's intercollegiate programs include baseball, basketball, cross-country running, football, swimming and diving, tennis, track & field, and wrestling; women's basketball, softball, swimming and diving, tennis, track & field, and volleyball.

Intramural sports: badminton, basketball, field hockey, bowling, racquetball, soccer, golf, football, table tennis, track & field, weight lifting, swimming and diving, and volleyball.

Athletic Contact

Dr. Willie Burden, North Carolina A&T State University, 1601 E. Market St., Greensboro, NC 27411; (919) 334-7686.

LIBRARY HOLDINGS

The Bluford Library houses 365,288 bound volumes, 1,804 periodical subscriptions, 56,896 microforms, 20,211 audiovisuals, and 175,000 government documents; 250 computers available for student use in computer center. Special collections include a Black Studies collection and teacher education materials. Online and CD-ROM bibliographic database searching available.

STUDENT LIFE

Campus Services

Health center, personal and psychological counseling, career planning and placement, student employment services, remediation, tutoring, and religious activities.

Campus Activities

Social and cultural activities include theater, concerts, dance, drill teams, chorale, and band. Special exhibits of sculpture and painting are on display in the Taylor Art Gallery or the African Heritage Center. Students may work on the *Register* (student-run

newspaper) or the yearbook. The student-staffed educational radio station, WNAA, is an active part of campus life.

Leadership opportunities can be found in the Student Government Association or numerous other special interest or service organizations. Greek-letter fraternities include Alpha Phi Alpha, Kappa Alpha Psi, Omega Psi Phi, and Phi Beta Sigma; sororities include Alpha Kappa Alpha, Delta Sigma Theta, Sigma Gamma Rho, and Zeta Phi Beta. Honor societies include Sigma Xi. In addition, there are local sororities and fraternities.

NCA&T is located in Greensboro, North Carolina, population 183,500. Greensboro is located midway between Raleigh and Winston-Salem creating an urban triangle known as the Piedmont area. Among the many social, cultural, and recreational resources available is the Eastern Music Festival, a six-week series of classical music events attracting world-famous guest artists, held each summer at Guilford College. Served by all major forms of transportation, North Carolina A&T's location provides easy access to the nearby Great Smoky Mountains National Park and the Atlantic Ocean recreational area that includes the Cape Hatteras and Cape Lookout National Seashores and the Kitty Hawk/Nags Head region.

Housing Availability

2,890 housing spaces; freshmen given priority; off-campus living is permitted; honors housing available.

NOTABLE ALUMNI

Rev. Jesse L. Jackson, 1964–Presidential candidate; civil rights activist; founder and president, National Rainbow Coalition

Ann Watts McKinney–Dean, Norfolk State University

Ronald McNair–NASA astronaut and mission specialist

Dr. Willie C. Robinson–President, Florida Memorial College

NORTH CAROLINA CENTRAL UNIVERSITY

1801 Fayetteville St.
Durham, NC 27707
Phone: (919) 560-6100

Total Enrollment:
5,385

Level of Selectivity:
Slightly competitive

Motto:
Truth and Service

HISTORY

North Carolina Central University (NCCU) is a four-year, state-supported, coed, liberal arts institution founded in 1910 as the National Religious Training School and Chautaugua. The school was sold and reorganized in 1915, becoming the National Training School.

Originally chartered as a private school, it became the nation's first state-supported, black, liberal arts college in 1923, changing its name to Durham State Normal School. Three years later the school was named North Carolina College for Negroes. NCCU became one of the 16 member institutions of the North Carolina system in 1972 and is now subject to the control of its board of governors.

North Carolina Central holds to its mission to develop character and to provide sound academic training for real service to the nation. Its programs give students a strong background in general Western culture and African American culture.

The 103-acre campus houses 56 buildings of modern and modified Georgian brick.

ACCREDITATION

North Carolina Central University is accredited by the Southern Association of Colleges and Schools (SACS) to award the Bachelor of Arts, Bachelor of Science, and Master's degrees.

Other Accreditation

American Accreditation for Schools and Colleges of Acupuncture and Oriental Medicine

American Bar Association

American Chemical Society

American Dietetic Association

American Library Association

National Council for the Accreditation of Teacher Education

National League of Nursing

COSTS PER YEAR

1992–93 Tuition: $1,169 (in-state); $5,010 (out-state)

Room and board: $1,568 (room); $1,347 (board)

Special fees: $535

Books: $500

Estimated total cost: $5,119 (in-state); $8,960 (out-state)

FINANCIAL AID

Financial Aid Specific to the School

92% of the student body received financial aid during 1991–92.

American Indian Student Legislative Grant (AISLG) provides funds for a number of needy North Carolina Indian students. Student must be a member of an Indian tribe recognized by the state, federal government, or by another tribal affiliation.

Army, Air Force, and Navy ROTC, in cooperation with Duke University, offer two-, three-, and four-year scholarships that pay tuition, fees, books, and other expenses, and provide a monthly stipend of $100.

Athletic scholarships are awarded to students who participate in intercollegiate sports. Contact Director of Athletics at NCCU.

College work-aid is available to students not qualifying for college work-study to work in departments of the college.

Incentive Scholarships are available for entering students who rank in the top half of their high school graduation class, who have a 2.5 GPA with an associate's degree or a 2.0 GPA with a certificate, and who participate in community service. Scholarships are renewable if students have a 2.0 GPA at end of freshman year, a 2.5 GPA at the end of sophomore year, and 3.0 GPA at end of junior year. Maximum award is $3,000 annually.

Institutional scholarships are awarded to entering students who are enrolled full time and have a SAT score of 900. Scholarships are renewable and range from $1,000 to full payment.

Institutional tuition scholarships are available to continuing students who are residents of North Carolina, demonstrate financial need, and maintain a 2.0 GPA.

Minority Presence Grant provides assistance to qualifying white students who are residents of North Carolina, enrolled in at least 3 hours of degree-credit hours, and demonstrate financial need. The awards depend on student's financial need and availability of funds.

NCCU Grant is awarded for tuition to continuing students who are classified as North Carolina residents and who maintain a cumulative 2.0 GPA. Awards are $1,000 a year for full-time students only.

North Carolina Prospective Teachers Scholarships/Loans are limited to a number of North Carolina residents who plan to teach in North Carolina. Contact the Department of Public Instruction, Scholarship/Loan Branch, Raleigh, NC 27611.

North Carolina Student Incentive Grants (NCSIG) are available to residents of North

Carolina, who are enrolled full time, in good academic standing, and demonstrate substantial financial aid.

North Carolina National Guard Tuition Assistance Program provides $250 tuition assistance for active members of the guard. Contact the Office of Adjutant General, NC National Guard, Attn: AGESO, 4105 Reed Creek Rd., Raleigh, NC 27607; (919) 664-6000.

Performance grants are available to students with special talents who are participating in music, band, or choir.

Special Talent Awards are available to out-of-state students who have a special talent and have a $250 non-federal scholarship. Maximum award is $950 for undergraduates.

Thurgood Marshall Black Education Fund provides a four-year scholarship at this public black college. Qualifying students must have a high school GPA of 3.0 or better and a SAT score of 1000 or ACT score of 24 or more. Students must be recommended by high school counselor as exceptional or exemplary in the creative or performing arts. Scholarship pays tuition, fees, room, and board, not to exceed $6,000 annually.

Veterans Scholarship Awards are available for veterans and dependents of deceased veterans who are enrolled full time for undergraduate classes or for at least nine hours for graduate classes. Contact Veterans Affairs, Albermarle Bldg, Suite 1065, 325 N. Salisbury St., Raleigh, NC 27603; (919) 733-3851.

Vocational Handicapped Scholarships/Awards provide financial aid to students who have suffered a disability that renders them vocationally handicapped. Contact Vocational Rehabilitation Services, 3414 Duke St., Durham, NC; (919) 560-6810.

Financial Aid Deadline

April 1 (priority); March 1 (fall);
  November 1 (spring)

Financial Aid Contact

Ms. Lola T. McKnight, Director of Financial Aid, North Carolina Central University, PO Box 19496, Shepard Station, Durham, NC 27707; (919) 560-6409 or 6202.

ADMISSION REQUIREMENTS

SAT (800) preferred; ACT accepted.

Entrance Requirements

Graduation from an accredited high school and completion of the following units: 4 English (grammar, composition, and literature), 3 mathematics (algebra I & II and geometry), 3 science (biology, chemistry, or physics lab), and 2 social science (U.S. History); 2 units of foreign language also highly recommended. Students must submit an official high school transcript and provide proof of immunizations against measles and rubella. Preference given to North Carolina residents. A $15 non-refundable application fee required.

GED students must meet basic admission requirements.

Transfer students must submit official transcript from high school and all previous colleges, qualify for readmission at previous college or university attended, and provide proof of immunization of measles and rubella. A $15 non-refundable application fee required.

International students must meet basic admission requirements, take the TOEFL examination, provide proof of ability to pay all college costs, and provide proof of accident and hospital insurance.

Admission Application Deadline

March 1 (out-state); June 1 (fall); November 1 (spring)

Admission Contact

Nancy R. Rowland, Director of Undergraduate Admissions, North Carolina Central University, PO Box 19717, Durham, NC 27707; (919) 560-6298 or 6066.

GRADUATION REQUIREMENTS

A minimum of 124–149 hours and completion of the core course requirements to include 4 English, 4 mathematics, 4 science, history, 2 foreign language, and completion of senior seminar in major area of study.

Grading System

A-F; W=Withdraw; I=Incomplete; S= Satisfactory

STUDENT BODY PROFILE

Total enrollment (male/female):
2,100/3,285

From in-state: 4,523

Other regions: 26 states and 11 foreign countries

Full-time undergraduates (male/female):
981/1,535

Part-time undergraduates (male/female):
594/929

Graduate students (male/female): 525/821

Ethnic/Racial Makeup

African American, 4,473; Caucasian, 852; International, 60.

Class of 1995 Profile

Number of applicants: 1,775

Number accepted: 1,331

Number enrolled: 599

Median SAT score: 330V; 340M

Average high school GPA:

Transfers enrolled: 267

FACULTY PROFILE

Number of faculty: 400

Student-teacher ratio: 13.5:1

Full-time faculty: 244

Part-time faculty: 152

Faculty with doctorates or other terminal degrees: 70%

SCHOOL CALENDAR

1993–94: August 19–May 6 (semester hours)

Commencement and conferring of degrees:
May 14

Two summer sessions.

DEGREES OFFERED 1991–92

Bachelor of Arts

Art

Art Education

Dramatic Arts

Dramatic Arts/Secondary Education

Early Childhood Education

Economics

Elementary Education

English

English Education

English/Media Journalism

Fine Arts

French

French Education

History

History Education

Middle Grades Education

Music

Music Education

Philosophy

Political Science

Political Science/Criminal Justice

Political Science/Public Administration

Psychology

Social Sciences

Sociology

Spanish

Spanish Education

Theater Arts Education

Visual Communications

Bachelor of Science

Accounting

Actuarial Science

Banking and Finance

Biology

Biology Education

Business Administration

Business Education

Chemistry
Chemistry Education
Clothing/Textiles
Commerce in Business Education
Community Health Education
Computer Information Sciences
Computer Science
Economics
Food and Nutrition
General Home Economics
Geography
Health Education
Management and Marketing
Mathematics
Mathematics Education
Nursing
Physical Education
Physics
Physics Education
Recreation Administration

Master's Degrees
Business
Education
Library and Information Studies

Pre-Professional Degrees
Dentistry
Law
Medicine

Juris Doctor
Law

SPECIAL PROGRAMS

Adult or continuing education program is available for nontraditional students returning to school or working full time.

Advanced Placement (AP) grants college credit for postsecondary work completed in high school. Students scoring 3 to 5 on the AP test will receive credit by examination for each course and advanced placement.

College Level Examination Program (CLEP) determines the academic relevance of nontraditional educational experiences, such as the military, on-the-job training, or other life experiences, through a series of tests and may grant students college credit for these experiences.

College orientation is offered for $15.00 to entering students and their parents for three days prior to the beginning of classes to acquaint students with the college and to prepare them for college life.

Cooperative Education Program alternates classroom study with related paid work experience. The program provides academic credit and full-time status during co-op placement.

Honors program offers academically talented students a challenging program of study that includes special classes, seminars, colloquia, cultural activities, and special recognition to motivate participants.

Off-campus study allows students to take courses at other institutions for credit. Classes are offered at the University of Wisconsin.

Part-time degree program allows students to earn an undergraduate degree while attending part time.

Pre-professional programs are offered in medicine, law, and dentistry.

Remedial courses are offered to entering students to bring them up to admission standards and to help them adjust for success in college.

ROTC, in cooperation with Duke University, provides training in military science for commission as a second lieutenant in the U.S. Army, Air Force, and Navy. Two-, three-, and four-year scholarships are available.

Student Support Services provides developmental courses, counseling, and cultural activities to students who need aid to succeed in college.

Study Abroad Program allows students to go to a foreign country for part of their college education.

Three/two degree program in engineering allows students to get two degrees—one in physics from North Carolina Central University and one in engineering from Georgia Institute of Technology—by completing three years at matriculated school and two years at cooperating school.

Undergraduate Research Program allows a limited number of undergraduates the opportunity to participate in on-going research projects with faculty mentors.

ATHLETIC PROGRAMS

North Carolina Central University is a member of the National Collegiate Athletic Association (NCAA), Division II and the Central Intercollegiate Athletic Association (CIAA). Intercollegiate sports: men's basketball, cross-country, football, tennis, and track; women's basketball, cross-country, tennis, track, softball, and volleyball.

Intramural sports: basketball, golf, gymnastics, racquetball, tennis, and volleyball.

Athletic Contact

Mr. Christopher Fisher, North Carolina Central University, 1801 Fayetteville St., Durham, NC 27707; (919) 560-6574.

LIBRARY HOLDINGS

The James E. Shepard Memorial Library has approximately 60,000 bound volumes, 70,000 microforms, 4,000 periodical subscriptions, 1,675 audiovisuals, and 117,000 federal and state documents. The library is computerized and has CD-ROM bibliographic database searching.

STUDENT LIFE

Campus Services

Health center, personal and psychological counseling, and career planning and placement.

Campus Activities

Social and cultural activities include theater, concerts, dances, choir, marching band, and jazz ensemble. Students may work on the student-run yearbook or newspaper.

Leadership opportunities are found in the Student Government Association or numerous other student-run organizations. Greek-letter fraternities include Alpha Phi Alpha, Kappa Alpha Psi, Omega Psi Phi, and Phi Beta Sigma; sororities include Alpha Kappa Alpha, Delta Sigma Theta, Sigma Gamma Rho, and Zeta Phi Beta. In addition, there are four local sororities and five local fraternities. Honor societies are also represented on campus.

The campus is one mile from downtown Durham for convenient shopping and dining. This area provides many cultural and recreational resources and is served by all major forms of transportation. The city of Durham is 7 miles from the state's Research Triangle, a center for governmental and industrial research. Three major research universities— Duke, North Carolina University, and North Carolina State University– North Carolina Central University, and a number of additional educational institutions are located in the greater Durham area with a population of 500,000. Durham itself has a population of 136,600 and is known as a center for medicine and research, with 5 major hospitals including Duke University's Medical Center.

Housing Availability

2,000 housing spaces; freshmen given priority; off-campus living permitted.

Handicapped Services

Wheelchair accessibility and services for the visually impaired.

NOTABLE ALUMNI

Daniel T. Blue, Jr.–Speaker of the house, North Carolina

Maynard H. Jackson, JD, 1959–Mayor, Atlanta, Georgia

Robert Massey–Professional football player

S. Dallas Simmons, Ph.D., 1962–President, Virginia Union University

Cleon F. Thompson, Jr., Ph.D., 1954–Chancellor, Winston-Salem State University

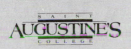

SAINT AUGUSTINE'S COLLEGE

1315 Oakwood Ave.
Raleigh, NC 27611
Phone: (919) 828-4451

Total Enrollment:
1,900

Level of Selectivity:
Slightly competitive

HISTORY

Saint Augustine's College (SAC) is a four-year, private, coed, liberal arts college affiliated with the Episcopal Church. It was founded in 1867 as Saint Augustine's Normal School and Collegiate Institute by the Protestant Episcopal Church and the Episcopal Diocese of North Carolina. The name changed to Saint Augustine's School in 1893 and to Saint Augustine's Junior College in 1919, the first year in which postsecondary level instruction was offered. The school became a four-year institution in 1927 and in 1928 was renamed Saint Augustine College. Baccalaureate degrees were first awarded in 1931.

"AUG," as the school is sometimes referred to, prepares students for graduate school or a professional career through its liberal arts, teacher-education, and career programs.

Saint Augustine's 36-building campus is situated on 125 acres in the northeastern area of Raleigh, North Carolina. This historically black college is a United Negro College Fund Member School.

ACCREDITATION

Saint Augustine College is accredited by the Southern Association of Colleges and Schools (SACS) to award the Bachelor of Arts and the Bachelor of Science degrees.

Other Accreditation

North Carolina Department of Public Instruction

COSTS PER YEAR

1992–93 Tuition: $3,850

Room and board: $3,400

Special fees: $450

Books: $500

Estimated total cost: $8,200

FINANCIAL AID

Financial Aid Specific to the School

93% of the student body received financial aid during 1991–92.

Athletic scholarships are available to students participating in various intercollegiate sports.

Cooperative Education Program alternates classroom study with related paid work experience. The program provides academic credit and full-time status during co-op placement.

Performance grants in music are available to talented students participating in choir or band.

College work-aid is available to students not qualifying for college work-study to work in departments of the college.

United Negro College Fund (UNCF) scholarships are awarded to a limited number of students at this school who demonstrate financial need. Some scholarships may be based on location and merit. UNCF scholarships range from $500 to $7,500.

Army and Air Force ROTC programs offer two- and three-year scholarships that pay tuition, fees, books, and other expenses, and provide a monthly stipend of $100.

Financial Aid Deadline

August 10

Financial Aid Contact

Mrs. Sherri Avent, Director of Financial Aid, Saint Augustine College, 1315 Oakwood Ave., Raleigh, NC 27610; (919) 828-4451, ext. 381.

ADMISSION REQUIREMENTS

SAT or ACT required

Entrance Requirements

Provide proof of graduation from an accredited high school with a minimum of 18 units to include the following: 4 English, 3 mathematics (algebra), 2 science, and 2 social science; submit official high school transcript, essay, and three letters of recommendation on applicant's character, personality, and scholastic abilities; provide medical history and proof of immunizations against measles, rubella, and tetanus-diptheria. A $25 non-refundable application fee is required.

GED students must meet basic admission requirements.

Transfer students must submit SAT or ACT test scores and official transcripts of college work.

International students must take the TOEFL examination. International students with transcripts in languages other than English-speaking or commonwealth countries or British System must submit originals or certified copies of the following academic documents: General Certificate of Education (G.C.E.); school certificate; Royal Society of Arts (RAS) state 2 or 3; The Caribbean School Certificate; Teacher's Certificate. Provide proof of immunization against measles, mumps, rubella, diptheria, and tetanus.

Early decision admits high school students in their junior or senior year to a college of their first choice. Financial aid is determined at time of early decision.

Admission Application Deadline

July 1 (fall); December 1 (spring).

Admission Contact

Mr. Wanzo Hendrix, Director of Admissions, Saint Augustine College, 1315 Oakwood Ave., Raleigh, NC 27610; (919) 828-4451, ext. 207, Fax: (919) 834-6473.

GRADUATION REQUIREMENTS

A minimum of 120 hours; completion of the core requirements; a minimum 2.0 GPA; 30 hours in residence; 2 hours physical education; and passing of exit competency reading and writing examinations. Comprehensive required in individual fields of study as well as 6 to 12 hours of internship in a major.

Grading System

A-F and I for Incomplete.

STUDENT BODY PROFILE

Total enrollment (male/female): 817/1,083

From in-state: 1,159

Other regions: 34 states, 23 foreign countries

Full-time undergraduates (male/female): 768/1,018

Part-time undergraduates (male/female): 49/65

Ethnic/Racial Makeup

African American, 1,604; International, 152; Other/unclassified, 138.

Class of 1995 Profile

Number of applicants: 2,224

Number accepted: 1,579

Number enrolled: 600

Average high school GPA:

Transfers enrolled: 76

FACULTY PROFILE

Number of faculty: 112

Student-teacher ratio: 16:1

Full-time faculty: 96

Part-time faculty: 16

Faculty with doctorates or other terminal degrees: 72%

SCHOOL CALENDAR

1992–93: August–May (semester hours)

Commencement and conferring of degrees: May

One summer session.

DEGREES OFFERED 1991–92:

Bachelor of Arts

Art

Communication Media

Early Childhood Education

Elementary Education

English

French

History and Government

Intermediate Education

Music

Political Science/Pre-Law

Psychology

Social Studies

Sociology

Bachelor of Science

Accounting

Aerospace Engineering

Biological and Agricultural Engineering

Biology

Business Administration

Business Education

Business Management

Chemical Engineering

Chemistry

Civil Engineering

Computer Science

Criminal Justice

Economics

Electrical Engineering

Health and Physical Education

Industrial Engineering

Industrial Hygiene and Safety

Industrial Mathematics

Materials Engineering

Mathematics

Mechanical Engineering

Medical Technology

Office Administration

Physics

Pre-Professional

Pre-Medicine

Pre-Physical Therapy

SPECIAL PROGRAMS

Adult or Continuing Education Program is available for nontraditional students returning to school or working full time.

College Level Examination Program (CLEP) determines the academic relevance of nontraditional educational experiences such as the military, on-the-job training, or other life experiences, through a series of tests and may grant students college credit for these experiences.

College orientation is offered at no cost to entering students for one week prior to the beginning of classes to acquaint students with the college and to prepare them for college life; parents may attend.

Cooperative Education Program alternates classroom study with related paid work experience. The program provides academic credit and full-time status during co-op placement.

Off-campus study allows students from SAC to take courses for credit toward their degree at Cooperating Raleigh Colleges—North Carolina State University, Shaw University, Peace, St. Mary's, and Meredith College. Credits earned are computed in cumulative GPA.

Honors Program offers academically talented students a challenging program of study that includes special classes, seminars, colloquia, cultural activities, and special recognition to motivate participants.

Part-time degree program allows students to earn an undergraduate degree while attending part time.

Remedial courses are offered to entering students to bring them up to admission standards and to help them adjust for success in college.

ROTC provides training in military science for commission as a second lieutenant in the U.S. Air Force and Army. Two- and four-year scholarships are available.

Student Support Services provide developmental courses, counseling, and cultural activities to students who need aid to succeed in college.

Study Abroad Program allows students to go to England and the Bahamas for part of their college education.

Three/two dual degree program in engineering in cooperation with North Carolina State University allows students to obtain a liberal arts degree from Saint Augustine College and an engineering degree from North Carolina State University by completing three years at matriculated school and two years at cooperating school.

ATHLETIC PROGRAMS

Saint Augustine is a member of the Central Intercollegiate Athletic Association (CIAA), all Division II.

Intercollegiate sports: men's baseball, basketball, fencing, golf, soccer, tennis, track, and wrestling; women's basketball, softball, track, and volleyball.

Athletic Contact

Mr. Harvey Heartley, Saint Augustine College, 1315 Oakwood Ave., Raleigh, NC 27611; (919) 828-4451, ext. 315.

LIBRARY HOLDINGS

The Prezell R. Robinson Library houses 135,000 bound volumes, 1,700 microforms,

675 periodical subscriptions, and 685 audio-visuals. One hundred computers are available for student use.

STUDENT LIFE

Campus Services

Health center, personal counseling, remediation, computer laboratory, and religious services, including weekly chapel.

Campus Activities

Social and cultural activities include theater. Students may get involved in the student-run newspaper or yearbook.

Leadership opportunities are found in the Student Government Association (SGA), departmental clubs, and service and social organizations. Greek-letter societies include three national sororities and four national fraternities, as well as several local sororities and fraternities.

Saint Augustine College is located in Raleigh, the capital of North Carolina. Centrally situated in the state, Raleigh provides access to the Great Smoky Mountains and the Atlantic Ocean recreational areas. The most prominent academic and research facilities in North Carolina are nearby, including Research Triangle Park.

Housing Availability

1,459 housing spaces; residents of air-conditioned facilities must pay an additional $50 per semester; residents of the New Dorm must pay a surcharge of $75.

SHAW UNIVERSITY

HISTORY

Shaw University (SU) is a four-year, private, coed, liberal arts institution founded in 1865 by the Baptist Church for the purpose of teaching theology and biblical interpretations to freedmen. It was named the Raleigh Institute in 1866, and the Shaw Collegiate Institute in 1870. Postsecondary instruction began in 1874. The present name, Shaw University, was adopted in 1875 and baccalaureate degrees were awarded in 1878. Shaw continues its affiliation with the Baptist Church.

As a church-related institution, Shaw University is committed to providing educational opportunities for students from all socioeconomic groups. The university offers a wholistic approach to education through its core liberal arts programs. According to President Talbert Shaw, Shaw prepares the student to make moral judgements undergirded by a view of human good. One prominent alumni, William E. Gary, attorney, manifested this view of human good by donating $10 million dollars to the university as a way of repaying a tuition waiver he received during his first year at Shaw.

Situated on 15 acres, the urban campus is composed of 20 buildings. Shaw is a United Negro College Fund (UNCF) member school.

ACCREDITATION

Shaw University is accredited by the Southern Association of Colleges and Schools (SACS) to award the Bachelor of Arts, Bachelor of Science, and Associate of Arts degrees.

COSTS PER YEAR

1992–93 Tuition: $4,872

Room and board: $1,260 (room); $2,114 (board)

Special fees: $400

Books: $500

118 E. South St.
Raleigh, NC 27611
Phone: (919) 546-8275
or 8276
Fax: (919) 546-8301

Total Enrollment:
2,149

Level of Selectivity:
Slightly competitive

Motto:
Why Not the Best?

Estimated total cost: $9,146

FINANCIAL AID

1991–92 Institutional Funding

Number of scholarships and grants: 501

Total amount of scholarships and grants: $955,193

Range of scholarships and grants: $750–$8,000

1991–92 Federal and State Funding

Number of scholarships and grants: 4,664

Total amount of scholarships and grants: $5,345,327

Range of scholarships and grants: $250–$2,400

Number of loans: 1,634

Total amount of loans: $9,993,457

Range of loans: $500–$4,000

Number of work-study: 490

Total amount of work-study: $468,290

Range of work-study: $800–$1,600

Financial Aid Specific to the School

85% of the student body received financial aid during 1991–92.

Army and Air Force cooperative ROTC offer two- and four-year scholarships that pay tuition, fees, books, and other expenses, as well as provide a monthly stipend of $100.

Athletic scholarships are available to students participating in intercollegiate sports.

College work-aid provides part-time employment on and off campus for students not qualifying for college work-study.

Endowed, organization, and friends scholarships number over 15 and are based on varying criteria.

Grant-in-aid is provided by the university to students whose situations warrant special consideration.

Merit scholarships are available to students who are recommended by high school counselors and have a satisfactory SAT score. Scholarship amounts vary and may include full tuition.

North Carolina Contractual Scholarship Fund (NCSCSF) provides grants to students who are residents of the state demonstrating exceptional financial need.

North Carolina Legislative Tuition Grant (NCLTG) provides grants to students who are residents of the state attending private schools full time.

North Carolina Student Incentive Grant (NCSIG) provides grants to legal residents of North Carolina who are full-time students and demonstrate financial need. Deadline is March 15. Direct queries to College Foundation, Inc. of North Carolina at (919)821-4771.

United Negro College Fund (UNCF) scholarships are awarded to a limited number of students at this school who demonstrate financial need. Some scholarships may be based on location and merit. UNCF scholarships range from $500 to $7,500.

Financial Aid Deadline

June 1 (priority)

Financial Aid Contact

Mr. Theodore Hindsman, Director of Financial Aid, Shaw University, 118 E. South St., Raleigh, NC 27611; (919) 546-8240.

ADMISSION REQUIREMENTS

SAT or ACT recommended

Entrance Requirements

Graduation from an accredited high school and completion of the following units: 3 English, 2 mathematics, 2 natural sciences, 2 social sciences; submit official high school transcripts; 3 recommendations; completed medical form by physician; interview required for some applicants; proof of immunizations. A $25 application fee is required.

GED students must meet basic admission requirements.

Transfer students must qualify for readmission at previous college or university attended.

International students from non-English-speaking countries must take the TOEFL examination and provide proof of ability to pay all college costs.

Early admission allows academically gifted high school students the opportunity to enroll in college full time before completing high school.

Early decision admits high school students in their junior or senior year to a college of their first choice. Financial aid is determined at time of early decision.

Admission Application Deadline
August 10

Admission Contact
Mr. Alfonzo Carter, Director of Admissions, Shaw University, 118 E. South St., Raleigh, NC 27611; (919) 546-8275; Fax: (919) 546-8301.

GRADUATION REQUIREMENTS
A minimum of 120 hours and completion of the core requirements to include the following hours: 12 English, 6 mathematics, 6 science, 6 social science, 2 physical education, and a computer course; a minimum 2.0 GPA; complete competency exams in English and Mathematics; last 30 hours must be in residence.

Grading System
A-F; I=Incomplete; NC=No Credit; W=Withdraw; S=Satisfactory (credit by exam); U=Unsatisfactory (credit by exam)

STUDENT BODY PROFILE
Total enrollment: 2,149

From in-state: 1,562

Other regions: 27 states; 10 foreign countries

Full-time undergraduates (male/female): 869/1,121

Part-time undergraduates (male/female): 55/104

Ethnic/Racial Makeup
African American, 1,980; Hispanic, 3; Native American, 18; Caucasian, 129; International, 19.

Class of 1995 Profile
Number of applicants: 791

Number accepted: 772

Number enrolled: 579

Transfers enrolled: 288

FACULTY PROFILE
Number of faculty: 242

Student-teacher ratio: 16:1

Full-time faculty: 80

Part-time faculty: 162

Tenured faculty: 7

Faculty with doctorates or other terminal degrees: 59%

SCHOOL CALENDAR
1992–93: August 15–May 7

Commencement and conferring of degrees: May 8

One summer session.

DEGREES OFFERED AND NUMBER CONFERRED 1991–92:
Bachelor's Degree
Accounting: 13

Adapted Physical Education and Kinesitherapy: 4

Biology/Biology Education: 4

Business: 102

Business Management: n/a

Chemistry Education: 2

Computer and Information Systems: 10

Criminal Justice: 45

Drama/Theater: 4

Early Childhood Education: n/a

Elementary Education: 6

English/English Education/Literature: 2

French/French Education : n/a

History and Government/History
   Education: n/a

International Relations: 3

Journalism/Radio/Television: 14

Liberal Arts: 8

Mathematics/Mathematics Education: 1

Music/Music Education: 1

Philosophy and Religion: 8

Psychology Education: n/a

Public Administration: n/a

Recreation Education: 2

Social Gerontology: n/a

Social Studies: 2

Social Work/Public Administration: 12

Sociology: 37

Special Education: 5

Speech Pathology and Audiology: 4

Associate Degree
Business Management: n/a
Criminal Justice: n/a

SPECIAL PROGRAMS

Adult or continuing education program is available for nontraditional students returning to school or working full time.

Center for Alternative Program in Education (CAPE) is an external degree program for the working adult who, because of job or family situation, and/or military service, is unable to attend college. In addition to regular classes, CAPE students can earn a degree via independent study, internships, seminars, and life experience.

College Level Examination Program (CLEP) determines the academic relevance of nontraditional educational experiences such as the military, on-the-job training, or other life experiences through a series of tests, and may grant students college credit for these experiences.

College orientation is offered to entering students for one week prior to the beginning of classes to acquaint students with the college and to prepare them for college life.

Cooperative Program allows students to take college credit toward their degree programs at a cooperating institution. Authorized institutions are those in the Cooperating Raleigh Colleges (CRC) consortium.

English as a Second Language is a program that offers courses in English for students whose native language is not English.

Honors Program offers academically talented students a challenging program of study that includes special classes, seminars, colloquia, cultural activities, and special recognition to motivate participants.

Part-time degree program allows students to earn an undergraduate degree part time.

Remedial courses are offered to entering students to bring them up to admission standards and to help them adjust for success in college.

ROTC, in cooperation with Saint Augustine College and the North Carolina State University at Raleigh, provides training in military science for commission as a second lieutenant in the U. S. Army and Air Force respectively. Two- and four-year scholarships are available.

Study Abroad allows students to go to a foreign country for part of their college education. Shaw University has study abroad programs in some Middle Eastern countries.

Three/two degree program in engineering allows students to get two degrees—one in liberal arts from Shaw University and one in engineering from North Carolina State University at Raleigh—by completing three years at matriculated school and two years at cooperating school.

ATHLETIC PROGRAMS

Shaw University is a member of the National Collegiate Athletic Association (NCAA) All Division II.

Intercollegiate sports: men's basketball, cross-country, golf, tennis, track & field, and volleyball; women's basketball, cross-country, tennis, track & field, and volleyball.

Intramural sports: weight lifting, track & field, swimming and diving, gymnastics, field hockey, fencing, golf, soccer, tennis, and volleyball.

Athletic Contact

Mr. Keith Smith, Interim Director of Athletics, Shaw University, 118 E. South St., Raleigh, NC 27611; (919) 546-8281.

LIBRARY HOLDINGS

The library houses 88,447 volumes, 445 periodical subscriptions, 3,247 microforms, and 16,050 audiovisuals.

STUDENT LIFE

Special Regulations

Freshmen required to live on campus.

Campus Services

Health center, personal and psychological counseling.

Campus Activities

Social and cultural activities include theater, choir, and band. Students may work on the student-run newspaper or yearbook. Communication majors or volunteers can work at the student-run radio station, WSHA.

Leadership opportunities can be found in the Student Government Association. Greek-letter fraternities include Alpha Phi Alpha, Kappa Alpha Psi, Omega Psi Phi, Phi Beta Sigma, and three national sororities. Honor societies are also represented on campus.

Shaw University is in the heart of Raleigh, North Carolina, the state capital, with a population of 208,000. Raleigh is located close to the educational center of Chapel Hill, Greensboro, and Durham. The Research Triangle, a center for governmental and industrial research, is 15 miles away. Three major research universities, Duke, North Carolina University, and North Carolina State University as well as a number of smaller educational institutions are nearby. Raleigh's location provides access to the Great Smoky Mountain and Atlantic Ocean scenic recreational facilities. The airport is 15 miles away; passenger rail 10 blocks; bus service is within minutes from the campus.

Housing Availability

820 housing spaces, freshmen required to live on campus.

WINSTON-SALEM STATE UNIVERSITY

601 Martin Luther
King Jr. Dr.
Winston-Salem, NC
27110
Phone: (919) 750-2070
Fax: (919) 750-3210

Total Enrollment:
2,655

Level of Selectivity:
Slightly competitive

Motto:
Enter to Learn, Depart
to Serve

HISTORY

Winston-Salem State University (WSSU) is a four-year, state-supported, coed, liberal arts institution founded in 1892 as the Slater Industrial Academy. It was originally housed in a one-room building and had 25 students. Recognized by the State of North Carolina in 1895, it received a charter as the Slater Industrial and State Normal School in 1897.

The school's leadership in quality training of elementary school teachers was rewarded by the General Assembly of North Carolina in 1925 with a new charter and the authority to confer degrees, making it the first black institution in the United States to grant elementary education degrees. A name change to Winston-Salem Teachers College took place at this time.

The Nursing School was added in 1953 and the college was authorized to grant the bachelor of science degree. A charter revision in 1957 expanded the curriculum to include secondary education, and in 1963 the name was changed to Winston-Salem State College.

Legislative action in 1969 changed the name to Winston-Salem State University. The higher education reorganization in North Carolina in 1971 effected a change in school governance. Winston-Salem State University became one of the 16 member institutions of the University of North Carolina on July 1, 1972 and is now subject to the control of the University of North Carolina Board of Governors.

ACCREDITATION

Winston-Salem State University is accredited by the Southern Association of Colleges and Schools (SACS) to award the Bachelor of Arts and Bachelor of Science degrees.

Other Accreditation

National Accrediting Agency for Clinical Laboratory Sciences

National Association of Schools of Music

National Council for Accreditation of Teacher Education

The North Carolina Department of Public Instruction

North Carolina State Board of Nursing and the National League for Nursing

COSTS PER YEAR

1992–93 Tuition: $1,254 (in-state); $6,272 (out-state)

Room and board: $1,342 (room); $1,420 (board)

Special fees: $125

Books: $500

Estimated total cost: $4,641 (in-state); $9,659 (out-state)

FINANCIAL AID

1991–92 Institutional Funding

Number of scholarships and grants: 337

Total amount of scholarships and grants: $2,693,412

Range of scholarships and grants: $250–$2,000

1991–92 Federal and State Funding

Number of scholarships and grants: 687

Total amount of scholarships and grants: $1,223,236

Range of scholarships and grants: $500–$4,000

Number of loans: 402

Total amount of loans: $800,395

Range of loans: $200–$4,000

Number of work-study: 360

Total amount of work-study: $552,244

Range of work-study: $500–$2,500

Financial Aid Specific to the School

85% of the student body received financial aid during 1992–93.

Army ROTC in cooperation with Wake Forest University offers two- and four-year scholarships that pay tuition, fee, books, and other expenses as well as provide a monthly stipend of $100.

Athletic scholarships are available for students participating in intercollegiate sports.

Alumni Scholarship of $1,000 is available annually for qualified freshmen.

Chancellor's Scholarship provides full tuition, books, and fees up to $4,500 annually for four years. Entering freshmen with a 3.5 grade point average and a score of at least 1000 on the SAT or 24 on the ACT are eligible to apply. Recipients must reside on campus during freshman and sophomore years.

Cooperative Education Program combines classroom study with related paid work experience. The program provides academic credit and full-time status during co-op placement.

Deferred Payment Plan allows students to pay college costs in two or three installments during the semester.

North Carolina tuition grants are available to students who are residents of the state and demonstrate financial need.

Performance grants are available for talented students participating in art, drama, or music.

Short-term, low-interest loans averaging $100 are available for students demonstrating financial need.

Thurgood Marshall Black Education Fund provides a four-year scholarship at this public black college. Qualifying students must have a high school GPA of 3.0 or better and a SAT score of 1000 or ACT score of 24 or more. Students must be recommended by high school counselor as exceptional or exemplary in the creative or performing arts. Scholarship pays tuition, fees, room, and board not to exceed $6,000 annually.

Tuition waivers are available for Winston-Salem State University employees and their children as well as senior citizens on a space available basis.

WSSU Incentive Scholarships are available for full-time North Carolina high school graduates who rank in the top half of their graduating class. Qualifying students must also demonstrate financial need and maintain a 2.0 freshman year, a 2.5 by junior year, and 3.0 by senior year.

Financial Aid Deadline

May 1 (priority); May 15 (fall); November 15 (fall)

Financial Aid Contact

Mr. Theodore Hindsman, Director of Financial Aid, Winston-Salem State University, 601 Martin Luther King Jr. Dr., Winston-Salem, NC 27110; (919) 750-3280.

ADMISSION REQUIREMENTS

Open admission. SAT (preferred); ACT (accepted)

Entrance Requirements

Graduation from an accredited high school and completion of the following 12 units: 4 English, 3 mathematics, 3 science, 2 social studies, 2 units of foreign language

recommended; recommendation from high school counselor or teacher. $15 application fee required.

GED students must meet basic admission requirements; cases considered on an individual basis.

Transfer students must have a 2.0 GPA and an official transcript from each attended institution; students transferring less than 30 hours must meet basic admission requirements. A maximum of 96 semester hours from four-year accredited institutions and 64 hours from accredited two-year institutions may be transferred.

International students must submit translated copies of official transcripts; must satisfy all admission requirements; have proficiency in spoken and written English; students from non-English-speaking countries must take TOEFL examination and/or SAT scores; provide documentation of financial ability to pay all college costs.

Early admission allows academically gifted high school students the opportunity to enroll in college full time before completing high school.

Admission Application Deadline

Rolling admission provides no specific date for notification of admission so applicant is informed as soon as admission decision is made.

Admission Contact

Mr. Daniel Lovett, Director of Admissions, Winston-Salem State University, 601 Martin Luther King Jr. Dr., Winston-Salem, NC 27110; (919) 750-2070; Fax: (919) 750-2459.

GRADUATION REQUIREMENTS

A minimum of 127 semester hours and completion of core requirements to include 6 English, 9 mathematics, 9 science, 2 physical education courses, and 1 computer course for some majors; minimum 2.0 GPA; satisfaction of all General Education requirements; completed last 30 hours in residence.

Grading System
A-F; I-Incomplete; P=pass; F=fail

STUDENT BODY PROFILE
Total enrollment (male/female):
1,009/1,646

From in-state: 2,449

Other regions: 22 states, 5 foreign countries

Full-time undergraduates (male/female):
758/1,236

Part-time undergraduates (male/female):
251/410

Ethnic/Racial Makeup
African American, 2,118; Hispanic, 8; Native American, 2; Caucasian, 509; International, 18.

Class of 1995 Profile
Number of applicants: 1,113

Number accepted: 839

Number enrolled: 408

Median SAT score: 371

Average high school GPA: 2.56

Transfer applicants: 574

Transfers accepted: 528

Transfers enrolled: 298

FACULTY PROFILE
Number of faculty: 179

Student-teacher ratio: 15:1

Full-time faculty: 152

Part-time faculty: 27

Tenured faculty: 72

Faculty with doctorates or other terminal degrees: 74%

SCHOOL CALENDAR
1992–93: August–May (semester hours)

Commencement and conferring of degrees:
May 8

Two summer sessions.

DEGREES OFFERED AND NUMBER CONFERRED 1991–92:
Accounting: 29

Applied Science Technologies: 16

Art: 1

Biology: 10

Business Administration: 80

Chemistry/Chemistry Education: 2

Commercial Music: n/a

Computer Science: 16

Economics: n/a

Elementary Education: 35

English: 5

History: 4

Management Information Systems: n/a

Mass Communications: 25

Mathematics: 2

Medical Technology: 9

Middle Grades Education: n/a

Music Education: 3

Nursing: 108

Office Administration: 1

Physical Education: 1

Physical Therapy: n/a

Political Science: 17

Psychology: 13

Sociology: 6

Spanish: 3

Special Education: 3

Sports Management: 4

Therapeutic Recreation: 16

Urban Affairs: 1

SPECIAL PROGRAMS
Accelerated Study Program allows students to complete their undergraduate degree in a shorter period of time than the traditional four years.

Adult or Continuing Education Program is available for nontraditional students returning to school or working full time.

Advanced Placement (AP) grants college credit for postsecondary work completed in high school. Students passing the AP test will receive credit by examination for each course and advanced placement.

College Level Examination Program (CLEP) grants college credit for nontraditional educational experiences such as the military, work, or other life experiences by taking the CLEP exam administered by the College Entrance Examination Board.

College orientation is offered for $25 to entering students for three days prior to the beginning of classes to acquaint students with the college and to prepare them for college life.

Cooperative Education Program combines classroom study with related paid work experience. The program provides academic credit and full-time status during co-op placement.

Health Careers Opportunity Program (HCOP) recruits, counsels, and provides enrichment services and activities to minorities and economically disadvantaged individuals for training and employment in the health professions.

Honors program offers academically talented students a challenging program of study that includes special classes, seminars, colloquia, cultural activities, and special recognition to motivate participation.

Part-time degree program allows students to earn an undergraduate degree part time.

Project Strengthen has been planned to provide research and academic involvement in health or health-related sciences.

Remedial courses are offered to entering students to bring them up to admission standards and to help them adjust for success in college.

ROTC in cooperation with Wake Forest University provides training in military science for commission as a second lieutenant in the U.S. Army. Two- and four-year scholarships are available.

The Study Abroad Program allows students to go to a foreign country for part of their college education.

ATHLETIC PROGRAMS

Winston-Salem State University is a member of the National Collegiate Athletic Association (NCAA) Division II and the Central Intercollegiate Athletic Association (CIAA). Intercollegiate sports: men's basketball, cross-country, football, tennis, and track & field; women's basketball, cross-country, tennis, track & field, softball, and volleyball.

Athletic Contact

Mr. Albert Roseboro, Athletic Director, Winston-Salem State University, 601 Martin Luther King, Jr. Dr., Winston-Salem, NC 27110; (919) 750-2140.

LIBRARY HOLDINGS

The C. G. O'Kelly Library houses 153,000 bound volumes, 1,300 periodical subscriptions; 2,747 audiovisuals; 70 computers are available for student use in the computer center. There is also a large art gallery on the lower level.

STUDENT LIFE

Special Regulations

Class attendance mandatory; freshman orientation required.

Campus Services

Health center, personal and psychological counseling, career planning and placement, student employment services, remediation, and financial counseling.

Campus Activities

Social activities include theater, concerts, band, dances, and choir. Non-majors as well as music majors may join the marching, concert, jazz, or pep bands. Students may work on the *News Argus* (student-run newspaper). Communication majors or volunteers can work at the student-run radio station, WSNC.

Leadership opportunities can be found in the Student Government Association or numerous other student-run organizations such as dormitory councils, departmental organizations, and religious organizations. Greek-letter fraternities include Alpha Phi Alpha, Kappa Alpha Psi, Omega Psi Phi, and Phi Beta Sigma; sororities include Alpha Kappa Alpha, Delta Sigma Theta, Sigma Gamma Rho and Zeta Phi Beta.

Winston-Salem State University is located in the twin city of Winston-Salem North Carolina, population 148,000. The city is served by mass air, passenger rail, and bus transportation systems. Winston-Salem State University is part of the thriving Piedmont Triad that includes the nearby cities of Greensboro and High Point. The historic Piedmont region provides easy access to the nearby Great Smoky Mountains National Park and the Atlantic Ocean recreational area, which includes Cape Hatteras, Cape Lookout National Seashores, and the Kitty Hawk/Nags Head region.

Housing Availability

1,104 housing spaces; freshman-housing guaranteed

Handicapped Services

Wheelchair accessibility and services for the visually impaired

NOTABLE ALUMNI

Calvert H. Smith–President, Morris Brown College

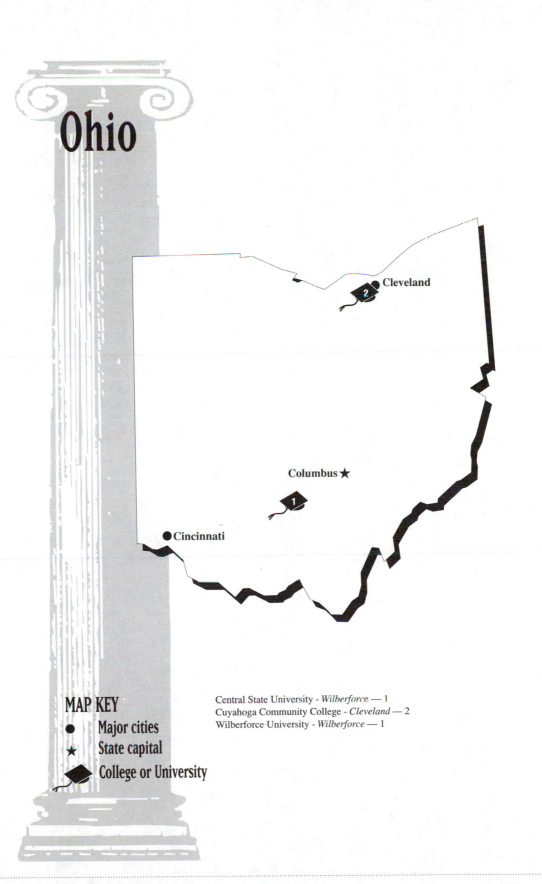

Ohio

Cleveland

●2

Columbus ★

●Cincinnati

MAP KEY
● Major cities
★ State capital
◆ College or University

Central State University - *Wilberforce* — 1
Cuyahoga Community College - *Cleveland* — 2
Wilberforce University - *Wilberforce* — 1

CENTRAL STATE UNIVERSITY

Wilberforce, OH
45384
Phone: (513) 376-6348
Toll-free in-state:
800-832-2222

Total Enrollment:
3,913

Level of Selectivity:
Noncompetitive

Motto:
Right Place, Right
Time

HISTORY

Central State University is a four-year, state-supported, coed university. It was founded in 1887 as the Normal and Industrial Department of Wilberforce University. Although associated with Wilberforce University, the Normal and Industrial Department was considered a separate institution with its own Board of Trustees.

The school became a four-year college in 1941, and the name was changed to College of Education and Industrial Arts. In 1947, the school began operating independently under the name of Wilberforce State College. In 1951, the name was changed to Central State College, and when the school was granted university status in 1965 the name was changed to Central State University.

Central State is Ohio's only predominately black public institution of higher education, and is also one of few black institutions located in the north. President Arthur E. Thomas states that "As the university looks toward the challenges of the 21st century, it has positioned itself to be a leader in higher education that will prepare students for global markets, world economics and managing cultural diversity."

The new Paul Robeson Cultural and Performing Arts Center, the James J. Walker Gymnasium, the Hallie Q. Brown Memorial Library, and the President's home are four of six new buildings standing alongside older buildings. The 60-acre campus is the home of America's largest and most-popular Afro-American Museum and Cultural Center. Located on the east side of the campus is a power plant as well as the university's outdoor education area and natural reserve. Recently the campus gained the distinction of being the only historically black college with a female professor of military science commanding a battalion.

ACCREDITATION

Central State University is accredited by the North Central Association of Colleges and Schools to award the Bachelor of Arts, Bachelor of Science, and Associate degrees.

Other Accreditation

American Chemical Society

National Association of Schools of Music

National Council for Accreditation of Teacher Education

Ohio Department of Education

COSTS PER YEAR

1992–93 Tuition: 2,247 (in-state); $4,788 (out-state)

Room and board: $2,070 (room); $2,223 (board)

Special fees: $388

Books: $565

Estimated total cost: $7,493 (in-state); $10,034 (out-state)

FINANCIAL AID

1991–92 Institutional Funding

Range of scholarships and grants: $500–$2,500

1991–92 Federal and State Funding

Number of scholarships and grants: 1,728

Total amount of scholarships and grants: $576,848

Range of scholarships and grants:

Number of loans: 2,255

Total amount of loans: $9,887,492

Range of loans: $2,625–$4,000

Number of work-study: 546

Total amount of work-study: $552,539

Range of work-study: $1,200–$2,400

Financial Aid Specific to the School

92% of the student body received financial aid during 1991–92.

Approximately 36 endowed and departmental awards are available to students ranging from $100 to $1,500 based on academic achievement.

The Thurgood Marshall Black Education Fund provides four-year scholarships to a limited number of entering freshmen who have a high school GPA of 3.0 or higher, with a SAT score of 900 or an ACT score of 24 or more. Students must be recommended by their high school counselor as exceptional. Scholarships pay tuition, fees, room, and board, not to exceed $6,000 annually.

The Cooperative Education Program allows students to gain paid work experience for one year while gaining full-time credit towards degree program.

The Army ROTC offers two- and four-year scholarships that pay tuition, fees, books, and other expenses, and provide a monthly stipend of $100.

Ohio Instructional Grant (OIG) is awarded to undergraduates who are full-time residents of Ohio and maintain academic standards.

Financial Aid Deadline

April 14 (priority)

Financial Aid Contact

Ms. Sunny Terrell Director of Student Financial Aid, Central State University, Wilberforce, OH 45384; (513) 376-6579.

ADMISSION REQUIREMENTS

ACT scores required. Open admission for state residents.

Entrance Requirements

A copy of an official high school transcript with 15 units: 4 English, 3 mathematics (including Algebra I and II), 3 social studies (including two history), 3 science, 2 foreign language, and 1 visual or performing arts. Out-of-state students must have a cumulative GPA of at least 2.0. Students must present proof of a physical exam within the last 90 days. A non-refundable application fee of $15 is required.

GED students must meet basic admission requirements and have no previous college credit.

Transfer students must submit a copy of an official transcript from previous colleges with a cumulative GPA of 2.0. Students on academic probation from previous school must wait one calendar year for admission to Central State. Students with less than 47 quarter hours must take the ACT.

International students must submit official transcript from high school or colleges attended and must take TOEFL examination if country of origin is non-English-speaking. Students must apply six months in advance

of admission: March 1 (fall); July 1 (winter); October 1 (spring); January 1 (summer).

Admission Application Deadline

June 15 (fall); October 15 (winter); February 15 (spring); April 15 (summer). Rolling admission provides no specific date for notification of admission so applicant is informed as soon as admission decision is made; early admission allows qualified students to enter college full time before completing high school. Advanced Placement is also available.

Admission Contact

The Office of Admissions, Central State University, Wilberforce, OH 45384; (513) 376-6348.

GRADUATION REQUIREMENTS

Bachelor degrees require a minimum of 186 quarter hours with three hours in African American history, fifteen in math, eight in science, five in physical education, one in computer science (business majors), and completion of 71 hours of core requirements. All students must take three hours of university convocation, pass the English Proficiency Exam, and have a cumulative GPA of at least 2.0; education majors must have a 2.3. The last 36 hours must be in residence at Central State. Associate degrees require a minimum of 93 quarter hours.

Grading System

A-F; I=Incomplete; S=Satisfactory; U=Unsatisfactory; CR=Satisfactory Completion; AU=Audit; W=Withdrawal; Z=Failure (non attendance); NC=No Credit.

STUDENT BODY PROFILE

Total enrollment: 3,913

From in-state: 2,091

Other regions: 26 states; 18 foreign countries

Full-time undergraduates (male/female): 1,565/1,696

Part-time undergraduates (male/female): 301/326

Graduate students (male/female): 12/13

Ethnic/Racial Makeup

African American, 3,531; Hispanics, 7; Native American, 6; Caucasian, 209; International, 160.

Class of 1995 Profile

Number of applicants: 2,222

Number accepted: 1,767

Number enrolled: 720

Transfer applicants: 626

Transfers accepted: 626

Transfers enrolled: 626

FACULTY PROFILE

Number of faculty: 147

Student-teacher ratio: 21:1

Full-time faculty: 127

Part-time faculty: 20

Faculty with doctorates or other terminal degrees: 47%

SCHOOL CALENDAR

1991–92: September–July (quarters)

Commencement and conferring of degrees: June

One summer session.

DEGREES OFFERED 1991–92:

Bachelor of Arts

Applied Music

Art

Communications/Radio-Television/Journalism/Speech

Community Recreation

Drawing, Design and Planning

Economics

English Education

English Literature

Foreign Languages

French

Graphic Arts/Printing

Graphic and Commercial Art

History

Jazz Studies

Music

Philosophy and Religion

Political Science

Psychology

Social Work

Sociology and Anthropology

Spanish

Theater

Bachelor of Science

Accounting

Art Education

Business Administration

Computer Information Systems

Computer Technology

Biology

Business Education

Chemistry

Community Health

Computer Science

Earth Science (Geography)

Education

Electronics

Elementary Education

Finance

Geology

Health Education

Industrial Arts Education

Industrial Technology

Management

Marketing

Mathematics and Computer Science

Metal Technology

Music Education

Physical Education

Physics

Public Administration

Secondary Education

Special Education

Water Resources Management

SPECIAL PROGRAMS

A one-week college orientation is offered to help prepare entering students for college life. Cost is $125 and parents may attend.

Three/two dual engineering program is offered in conjunction with Wright State University in Dayton, Ohio. Students must complete three years at Central State and two years at Wright State. Upon completion of program, the student will receive a Bachelor of Science degree and an Engineering degree.

The Army ROTC provides training in military science for commission as a second lieutenant in the U.S. Armed Forces. Two- and four-year scholarship programs are available.

An academic remediation program provides remedial courses for entering students to help them succeed in college.

The Cooperative Education Program alternates academic study with related job experience. The program provides academic credit and full-time student status for one year during co-op placement.

The College Level Examination Program (CLEP) grants college credit for non-traditional educational experiences such as the military or other life experiences. The program is run by the College Entrance Examination Board.

Advanced Placement (AP) allows high school students to take various college courses for credit during their junior and senior year. Students must have passing scores on the College Board AP tests to receive credit.

The honors program places academically gifted students in a special track that develops their professional skills. Students take three two-credit colloquia in their junior year. Students must present and defend a thesis in their major field and must maintain a 3.5 GPA.

Individualized majors allow students to create their own major program of study.

The Institutional Sponsored Study Abroad Program allows students to go to a foreign country for a specified period of time for part of their college education.

CSU-WEST is an off-campus site for the instruction of the university's core curriculum and lower-division evening courses. The program is available for adults who cannot attend classes on campus.

The Center for Studies of Urban Literacy is a network of teachers, professionals, and students working to define and meet the literacy needs of Central State University's predominately urban population. The program assesses, investigates, and develops literacy programs for the university community, public schools, and the community at large.

ATHLETIC PROGRAMS

Central State is a member of the National Association of Intercollegiate Athletics (NAIA), Division I.

Intercollegiate sports: men's football, basketball, indoor/outdoor track, and baseball; women's volleyball, basketball, and indoor/outdoor track.

Intramural sports: basketball, bowling, gymnastics, skiing, softball, swimming, and diving.

Athletic Contact

William Joe, Athletic Director, Central State University, Wilberforce, OH 45384; (513) 376-6319.

LIBRARY HOLDINGS

The Hallie Q Brown Memorial Library houses 149,675 volumes, 529,613 microforms, 877 periodical subscriptions, 390 audiovisuals, and 100 computers for student use.

STUDENT LIFE

Special Regulations

Unmarried freshmen and sophomores must live on campus. Cars are permitted.

Campus Services

Health center; personal and psychological counseling; career planning and placement; tutoring; testing center for GMAT, GRE, LSAT, and GED; remedial instruction; and religious services, including chapel.

Campus Activities

Social and group activities include theater, band, chorale, orchestra, and dance. Students may work on the student newspaper or yearbook. Communication majors can get involved in the campus radio station WCSU-FM (88.9) or the campus television station.

Leadership opportunities can be found in the Student Government Association or numerous other groups. Greek-letter sororities include Alpha Kappa Alpha, Delta Sigma Theta, and Zeta Phi Beta. Fraternities include Alpha Phi Alpha, Kappa Alpha Psi, Omega Psi Phi, and Phi Beta Sigma.

Central State University is located in the small rural town of Wilberforce, Ohio approximately eighteen miles from Dayton. The city of Dayton offers museums, the art institute, and shopping. It is the home of the Wright Brothers and the Oregon Historical District. Outdoor excursions may include skiing, trap shooting, biking, and hiking on the Miami River Corridor. Air and bus transportation are available from Dayton. Both Cincinnati and Columbus are approximately 55 miles from the campus, and provide access to theater, jazz concerts, horse racing, folk festivals, and museums. Columbus, which has earned a reputation as a state-of-the-art city, is home to 150 hi-tech companies.

Housing Availability

1,500 housing spaces. Freshmen required to live on campus.

NOTABLE ALUMNI

Don H. Barden, 1963-64–CEO, Barden Cablevision

Clay Dixon–Mayor, Dayton, Ohio

Leontyne Price, 1949–Opera singer

John W. Shannon, 1955–Assistant secretary of the Army

Joshua Smith, 1963–Founder and CEO, Maxima Corp.

Dr. Arthur E. Thomas–President, Central State University

CUYAHOGA COMMUNITY COLLEGE

Metropolitan Campus
2900 Community
College Ave.
Cleveland, OH 44115
Phone: (216) 987-4000

Total Enrollment:
6,200

Level of Selectivity:
Noncompetitive

HISTORY

Cuyahoga Community College is a two-year, state-supported coed college that began in the 19th-century Brownell School building. Today it spans three campuses and includes the Unified Technologies Center. Founded on September 23, 1963, Cuyahoga Community College immediately made history by having the largest enrollment ever on the first day for a community college.

In 1966, the Western Campus opened for classes in The Parma's Crile Veteran's Hospital. A modern six-building interconnected complex replaced its initial location in 1975, with a design that included a three-story glass-roofed mall.

The Metropolitan Campus was completed in 1969 and is located in the St. Vincent Quadrangle in downtown Cleveland. The modern ten-building complex became Cuyahoga's first permanent facility, and in 1986, it became the home to the Unified Technologies Center.

The Eastern Campus opened in 1971 in Highland Hills. In 1981, a permanent facility was constructed there and brought with it a more informal setting to the educational experience.

All three campuses have a child care center, a computer center, and a library with holdings ranging from 29,000 to 49,000. The modern campuses have outstanding laboratories, theaters, and athletic facilities. Details for the Metropolitan Campus will be described in this guide.

ACCREDITATION

Cuyahoga Community College is accredited by the North Central Association of Colleges and Schools (NCACS) to award the Associate of Arts, Associate of Science, Associate of Applied Science, Associate of Labor Studies, and Associate of Technical Study.

Other Accreditation

American Dental Association Committee on Dental Accreditation

American Dietetic Association

American Medical Association Committee on Allied Health Education and Accreditation

American Occupational Therapy Association Accreditation Committee

Commission on Accreditation of Physical Therapy Education

Commission on Opticianry Accreditation

Committee on Allied Health Education and Accreditation

National Accrediting Agency for Clinical Laboratory Sciences

National League of Nursing

Ohio State Board of Nursing Education and Nurse Registration

COSTS PER YEAR

1992-93 Tuition: $1,382

Special fees: $50

Books: $350

Estimated total cost: $1,782

FINANCIAL AID

Financial Aid Specific to the School

80% of the student body received financial aid during 1991–92.

Cooperative Education Program alternates and combines classroom study with related paid work experience. The program provides academic credit and full-time status during co-op placement.

Air Force ROTC offers two- or four-year scholarships that pay tuition, fees, books, and other expenses, and provide a monthly stipend of $100.

Ohio Instructional Grants (OIG) are available to full-time students who are residents of Ohio. The award provides coverage of all instructional fees and should be applied for directly through the Ohio Board of Regents.

Financial Aid Deadline

April (priority); July 1

Financial Aid Contact

Cuyahoga Community College, Office of Student Financial Aid, Metropolitan Campus, 2900 Community College Ave., Cleveland, OH 44115; (216)987-4000.

ADMISSION REQUIREMENTS

Open Admission. SAT or ACT scores used for counseling and placement.

Entrance Requirements

Graduation from an accredited high school; at least 18 years old; a letter of permission from any other college or university is required only if simultaneous enrollment is desired. A non-refundable $10 application fee is required.

GED students must meet the basic admission requirements.

Transfer students are required to follow the same admission procedures as any other newly entering student; must have a 2.0 GPA. Students entering Cuyahoga with an academic probation will be placed on first probation until 15 or more quarter credits are completed.

International students must submit TOEFL scores and meet special requirements of admission established regarding F-1 visa status. New international students are required to take placement exams for English and mathematics.

Early admission allows qualified students to enter college full time before completing high school.

Admission Application Deadline

Rolling admissions; May 1 (fall); November 1 (spring).

Admission Contact

Mr. Thomas A. Schick, Cuyahoga Community College, Metropolitan Campus, Director of Admissions, 2900 Community College Ave., Cleveland, OH 44115; (216)987-4000.

GRADUATION REQUIREMENTS

Minimum of 93 quarter hours; at least 30 of the last quarter hours completed at Cuyahoga; and maintenance of a 2.0 cumulative GPA. Students who wish to transfer credits to a four-year college must complete the core requirements and maintain a GPA of 2.0. After the student transfers, a major will be decided on to specialize in at the new college.

Grading System

A-F; S=Satisfactory; U=Unsatisfactory; S/U=No grade; AU=Audit; ACE=American Council on Education; AP=Advanced Placement; CLEP=College Level Examination Program; USAF=United Stated Armed Forces; CBE=Credit by Examination; CEU= Continuing Education Unit; I=Incomplete; R=Repeated Course; T=Transfer Credit; W=Withdrawal.

STUDENT BODY PROFILE

Total enrollment (male/female): 2,542/3,658

From in-state: 5,766

Other regions: 50 states and 6 foreign countries

Full-time undergraduates (male/female): 1,068/1,536

Part-time undergraduates (male/female): 1,474/2,122

Ethnic/Racial Makeup

African American, 3,410; Hispanic, 248; Asian, 186; International, 356; Other/unclassified, 2,000.

FACULTY PROFILE

Number of faculty: 445

Student-teacher ratio: 14:1

SCHOOL CALENDAR

1992–93: September 14–June 20 (quarter hours)

Commencement and conferring of degrees: June 19

One eight-week summer session.

DEGREES OFFERED 1991–92:

Accounting

Architectural and Construction Engineering Technology

Automotive Technology

Aviation Technology

Business Management

Cardiovascular Technology

Commercial Art

Community Mental Health Technology

Computer Studies

Court and Conference Reporting

Dental Assisting

Dental Hygiene

Dental Laboratory Technology

Dietetic Technology

Early Childhood Education

Electrical Electronic Engineering Technology

Emergency Medical Technology

Financial Institutions

Fire Technology

Graphic Communications Management and Technology

Great Lakes Maritime Technology

Hospitality Management

Industrial Management

Interior Design Technology

Labor Studies

Law Enforcement

Library/Instructional Media Technology

Manufacturing and Industrial Technology

Marine Technology

Marketing

Mechanical Engineering Technology

Medical Assistant

Medical Laboratory Technology

Medical Records Technology

Nursing

Occupational Therapy Assistant

Office Administration

Ophthalmic Dispensing

Paralegal Studies

Pharmacy Technology

Physical Therapist

Physician Assistant

Plant Science Technology

Production and Inventory Management

Purchasing Management

Radiography

Real Estate

Respiratory Care

Surgeon's Assistant

Transportation Logistics Management

Veterinary Technology

SPECIAL PROGRAMS

Accelerated Study Program allows students to complete their degree in a shorter period of time than the traditional two years.

Adult Learning Center provides training and preparation to potential GED recipients.

Advanced Placement (AP) grants college credit for postsecondary work completed in high school. Students passing the AP test will receive credit by examination for each course and advanced placement.

Business Challenge is a program that offers hands-on training with non-credit workshops and seminars. The program is designed to cover topics such as communication skills, management and supervision, microcomputers, and sales and marketing.

The Center for Applied Gerontology provides training in the area of aging and coordinates the formation of the Senior Adult Education Program.

The Center for Continuing Education for the Health Professional consists of workshops and seminars to enhance area professional's health skills. The program also offers approved units of credit for areas in the health field that require documentation or mandatory continuing education.

College Level Examination Program (CLEP) determines the academic relevance

of nontraditional educational experiences, such as the military, on-the-job training, or other life experiences through a series of tests and may grant students college credit for these experiences.

Continuing and professional education brings credit and non-credit courses to numerous locations in Cuyahoga County for students of all ages.

Cooperative Education alternates classroom study with related paid work experience in major. The program provides academic credit and full-time status during co-op placement.

The Enrollment Options Program is available for junior and senior high school students to earn college credits while still in high school, enhancing their high school experience and providing constructive exposure to the college experience.

The Honors Program offers academically talented students a challenging program of study that includes special classes, seminars, colloquia, cultural activities, and special recognition to motivate participants.

Independent Learning Courses (ILC) are designed to present an alternative to classroom instruction. Self-paced instructional videos and/or audio tapes and in some cases computerized modules, are available to assist everyone enrolled in ILC.

Program Sixty Admission is available to Cuyahoga County residents 60 years of age and above. This program is provided based on open space and is tuition-free. Credit and non-credit courses are available for selection with approval by the instructor.

Remedial courses are provided to entering students to bring them up to admission standards and to help them adjust for success in college.

ROTC provides training in military science for commission as a second lieutenant in the U.S. armed forces. Two- or four-year scholarships are available. In order to become commissioned and complete the program, students must transfer into a four-year college or university.

The Study Abroad Program allows students to go to a foreign country for a specified period of time for part of their college education.

Womenfocus Program offers non-credit courses targeted towards career-minded women who are considering a new career or a change in career.

ATHLETIC PROGRAMS

Cuyahoga Community College is a member of the National Junior College Athletic Association (NJCAA).

Intercollegiate sports: men's baseball, basketball, football, racquetball, soccer, softball, track & field, and volleyball; women's racquetball and volleyball.

Intramural sports: baseball, basketball, bowling, gymnastics, handball, racquetball, softball, tennis, and volleyball.

LIBRARY HOLDINGS

The Metropolitan Campus library holds 49,000 volumes, 10,600 microforms, 400 audiovisuals, and 385 periodical subscriptions. The library is automated.

STUDENT LIFE

Special Regulations

Students must have a CCC ID card; parking fees are charged upon exit to all students; students must prove a twelve-month residency of Ohio/Cuyahoga County in order to avoid paying out-of-state or out-of-county student fees.

Campus Services

Health; personal and psychological counseling, career counseling and placement, assessment, and child care.

Campus Activities

Social and cultural activities include theater, chorale, concerts, recreation and game areas, lectures, dances, interest groups, and jazz bands. Interested students may get involved in the student-run newspaper.

Leadership opportunities are found in the Student Government Association (SGA) or numerous other student groups, such as the Black Student Union, the Latin American Student Organization, and the Nursing Student Association. Thirty other clubs are available, including a religious club, ski club, radio/tv club, and chess club. Honor societies include Phi Theta Kappa honor society and Tau Alpha Pi.

All three campuses are accessed by the Regional Transit Authority buses and also by interstate buses. The Eastern Campus is accessible by interstates 271 and 480; the Metropolitan Campus, by interstates 90, 77, and 71; and the Western Campus, by interstates 71 and 77. The Metropolitan Campus is located in the city of Cleveland, one of the largest cities in Ohio. Cleveland is home to the renowned Cleveland Orchestra and the Cleveland Clinic, which is one the world's most advanced medical treatment facilities. Students have easy access to art exhibits, museums, shopping, and mass rail and air transportation.

Handicapped Services

Wheelchair accessibility as well as services for the learning disabled, and for the visually, hearing, or speech impaired.

WILBERFORCE UNIVERSITY

HISTORY

Wilberforce University (WU) is a four-year, private, independent coeducational liberal arts college, affiliated with the African Methodist Episcopal (AME) Church. Amidst a cry for the end of slavery, Wilberforce was founded in 1856 as Wilberforce University of the Methodist Episcopal Church and named after British abolitionist and philanthropist, William Wilberforce. Wilberforce University was the outcome of a plan by the Cincinnati Conference of the Methodist Episcopal Church to establish an educational institution for blacks in Ohio. Elementary instruction was the work of Wilberforce until 1862 when the school closed. In 1863, Wilberforce reopened as Wilberforce University and was sold to the African Methodist Episcopal Church. The first bachelor's degrees were awarded in 1867.

Distinguished as the first black college and the first college with a black president, Wilberforce played a significant role in the Underground Railroad movement and continues to see itself as a link to liberation through education. The

Wilberforce, OH
45384
Phone: (513) 376-2911
Toll-free in-state:
800-376-8565
Toll-free out-state:
800-367-8568

Total Enrollment:
758

Level of Selectivity:
Slightly competitive

mission of the school is the development of the total person–providing opportunities for spiritual, intellectual, emotional, and physical development.

Wilberforce's long history is evident in its diverse architecture and need for two campuses. The new main campus is located one mile from the original campus. When building the new campus in 1967, care was taken that the heritage and tradition of 136 years would be celebrated and represented. The famous Wilberforce University fountain was transferred from the original campus and reconstructed on the new campus in the fall of 1974.

The old campus, still in use, has seen many changes. A tornado destroyed much, but not all, of this campus in 1974. Shorter Hall (1922), the Charles Leander Hill Gymnasium (1958), and the Carnegie Library (1909) remain standing and in use. The old campus is the site of the National Afro-American Museum and Cultural Center, punctuating its importance in American and Afro-American history. This historically black university is a United Negro College Fund (UNCF) member school.

ACCREDITATION

Wilberforce is accredited by the North Central Association of Colleges and Schools to award the Bachelor of Arts and Bachelor of Science degrees.

Other Accreditation

Ohio Department of Education

COSTS PER YEAR

1992–93 Tuition: $6,346

Room and board: $1,632 (room); $1,760 (board)

Special fees: $600

Books: $500

Estimated total cost: $10,838

FINANCIAL AID

1990–91 Federal and State Funding

Number of scholarships and grants: 724

Total amount of scholarships and grants: $1,007,038

Number of loans: 713

Total amount of loans: $1,617,732

Number of work-study: 789

Total amount of work-study: $1,300,000

Financial Aid Specific to the School

95% of the student body received financial aid during 1991–92.

The mandatory Cooperative Education Program allows for paid work experience to augment classroom theory for all majors.

Installment or deferred tuition payment is available.

Gulf Oil Loan Program is available for juniors and seniors with exceptional financial need. Students must have 2.0 GPA and must repay loan within one year of graduation. Maximum loan amount is $250 a year or $400 for two years.

Full or partial tuition waivers are available for Wilberforce employees or their children.

United Negro College Fund scholarships are awarded for limited number of students who demonstrate financial need. Scholarships may range from $500 to $7,500. Students should contact financial aid office for more information.

Army Loan Repayment Program allows students to repay their Direct Student Loans or Guaranteed Student Loans by enlisting in the Armed Forces. Enlisting three years will repay debt or 1/3 of debt is paid off for each year student enlists.

The cooperative Army ROTC and Air Force ROTC offer two- and three- year scholarships that pay tuition, books, fees, and other expenses, and provide a monthly stipend of $100.

The Ohio Instructional Grant (OIG) is for Ohio residents who demonstrate exceptional financial need. Grants range from $180 to $3,306 per year.

Financial Aid Deadline

April 30 (priority); June 1 (fall); November 15 (spring)

Financial Aid Contact

Ms. Patricia A. Copley, Director of Financial Aid, Wilberforce, OH 45384; (513) 376-2991, ext. 730.

ADMISSION REQUIREMENTS

SAT or ACT required.

Entrance Requirements

High school diploma with 15 units: 4 English; 3 mathematics (including algebra); 3 science (including 1 laboratory science); and 5 electives. Students must have a minimum grade point average of 2.0 and be in the top two-thirds of their graduating class. A $20 application fee is required with application.

GED students must pass General Education Development test and have the minimum admission requirements.

Transfer students must present the same application forms and transcripts as new students. All transfer students are required to meet the university's English proficiency requirement and mandatory cooperative education experience.

International students from non-English-speaking countries must pass the TOEFL exam with a minimum score of 500 and must show proof of ability to pay all college costs.

Admission Application Deadline

June 1 (fall); November 15 (spring). Early admission allows qualified students to enter college full time before completing high school. Transfer six weeks in advance of the semester applied for.

Admission Contact

Ms. Karen Preston, Office of Admissions, Shorter Hall, Wilberforce University, Wilberforce, OH 45384; (513) 376-2911, ext. 789 or toll-free 800-367-8568

GRADUATION REQUIREMENTS

Minimum of 126 credit hours with three in mathematics; two in physical education, and three in computer science; completion of the core requirements; 2.0 minimum GPA; completion of Communications 319 with a grade of at least "C" or writing competency shown by the Junior Level Writing Competency Test; minimum 30 semester hours in residence; minimum of two successful cooperative education experiences; and mandatory graduation ceremony attendance.

Grading System

A-F, I=Incomplete; X=Competency based grade; N=Grades not yet submitted; W=Withdrew prior to drop deadline; WP= Withdrew passing; WF= Withdrew failing; S/U=Satisfactory/Unsatisfactory (cooperative education credit)

STUDENT BODY PROFILE

Total enrollment (male/female): 273/485

From in-state: 323

Other regions: 31 states; 3 foreign countries

Full-time undergraduates (male/female): 262/466

Part-time undergraduates (male/female): 11/19

Ethnic/Racial Makeup

African American, 728; International, 30.

Class of 1995 Profile

Number of applicants: 697

Number accepted: 418

Number enrolled: 226

Average high school GPA: 2.5

FACULTY PROFILE

Student-teacher ratio: 20:1

Full-time faculty: 50

Part-time faculty: 9

Faculty with doctorates or other terminal degrees: 24%

SCHOOL CALENDAR

1992–93: September 26 to May 14 (semesters)

Commencement and conferring of degrees: May 15

No summer sessions.

DEGREES OFFERED 1991–92:

Bachelor of Arts

Chemistry

Fine Arts

Liberal Studies

Literature

Mass Media Communications

Music

Political Science

Psychology

Rehabilitation Services

Sociology

Bachelor of Science

Accounting

Biology

Business Economics

Chemistry

Comprehensive Science

Computer Information Systems

Economics

Finance

Health Services Administration

Management

Marketing

Mathematics

SPECIAL PROGRAMS

A five-day orientation session at no cost is offered before classes begin to acquaint students with the college and prepare them for college life; parents may attend.

An academic remediation program for entering students offers courses to develop study skills and bring students up to admissions requirements.

Air Force and Army ROTC provide military training for commission as a second lieutenant in the U.S. Armed Forces. Two- and three- year scholarships are available.

CLIMB (Credentials for Leadership in Management and Business) is a degree-completion program for the working adult. CLIMB is for students with two years of college credit and experience in the work-force. The program leads to a B.S. in Organizational Management.

Mandatory alternating or combined Cooperative Education Program augments classroom study with paid work experience. Wilberforce is the only black college to require the Cooperative Education Program and it is joined by only one other four-year institution to require Cooperative Education.

Off campus study program allows upperclassmen to cross-register at the following consortium colleges: Air Force Institute of Technology, Antioch University, Capital University-Dayton Center, Central State University, Clark State University, Edison State Community College, General Motors Corporation, Greater Dayton Public Television Inc., Kettering College of Medical Arts, Kettering Foundation, Mead Corporation, Miami-Jacobs Junior College, Monsanto Corporation, NCR Corporation, Sinclair Community College, Southern State Community College, Union for Experimenting Colleges and Universities, United Theological Seminary, University of Dayton, Urbana University, Wilmington College, and Wittenberg University.

A dual computer science degree is offered in conjunction with the University of Dayton and the University of Cincinnati. This program allows a student to earn two bachelor's degrees in five years.

A dual degree in engineering is offered in conjunction with the University of Dayton and the University of Cincinnati; this program allows a student to earn two bachelor's degrees in five years.

The honors program rewards academic excellence and encourages distinguished students. Students have the opportunity to take advanced, specialized courses in this program.

A dual law degree is offered in cooperation with St. John's University. Students attend Wilberforce University for three years with a GPA no less than 3.0 and attend St. John's University, School of Law, Jamaica, New York for an additional three years. After satisfactory completion of the first year of law school, the bachelor's degree will be conferred by Wilberforce, and a jurisprudence degree from St. John's University will be conferred after completion of the program.

Study abroad program allows students to go to a foreign country for a specified period of time for part of their college education.

ATHLETIC PROGRAMS

Wilberforce is a member of the National Association of Intercollegiate Athletics (NAIA).

Intercollegiate sports: men's basketball and track & field; women's basketball, track & field, and volleyball.

Intramural sports: basketball, softball, volleyball, and tennis.

LIBRARY HOLDINGS

Rembert Stokes Learning Resource Center holds 50,000 books, 253 periodical subscriptions, 61 computers, 2,969 microfiche, and 1,890 microfilm. The microfilm collection includes papers of the Martin Luther King, Jr. assassination, Malcolm X, Paul L. Dunbar, and Booker T. Washington, and also includes an Afro-American rare book collection. Other special collections include the Arnett-Coppin & Payne Afro-American History Collection, and scrapbooks, newspaper clippings, handbills, and correspondence of the history the African Methodist Episcopal Church. The library serves as a depository for Ohio government documents.

STUDENT LIFE

Special Regulations

Residence on campus is mandatory for all unmarried, non-commuting students.

Campus Services

Health center, personal and psychological counseling, career counseling and placement, tutoring, and religious activities, including chapel.

Campus Activities

Include theater, chorale, parties, dances, skating, and other socials given by student groups. Students can get involved in the campus newspaper or the join the yearbook staff. Communication majors or student volunteers can get involved in the student-run radio station.

Leadership opportunities are provided through participation in the more than 33 student-run groups including the Student Government Association (SGA). Group leaders are part of the President's council. Greek-letter fraternities include Alpha Phi Alpha, Kappa Alpha Psi, Omega Psi Phi, and Phi Beta Sigma; sororities include Alpha Kappa Alpha, Delta Sigma Theta, Sigma Gamma Rho, and Zeta Phi Beta.

Many opportunities exist for interaction with students at other area colleges and universities. An inter-institutional Cross-Registration Program allows full-time students at a sponsoring institution to take courses as space is available at a host institution. Area colleges and universities include Antioch, Central State University, University of Dayton, Wittenberg University, and Wilmington College.

Wilberforce University is a residential institution stressing the importance of learning interpersonal skills and developing clarification of personal values. Religious life emphasizing religious ideals is an important aspect of Wilberforce University. Students are encouraged to choose their own way of expressing religious faith and service to others and to attend the church of their choice in the surrounding communities.

The rural setting of Wilberforce provides for a safe and quiet environment with easy access to three major metropolitan areas. The campus is 21 miles from Dayton and within an hour's drive from Columbus and Cincinnati, which offer cultural activities and employment opportunities. Wilberforce offers students access to numerous museums, galleries, libraries, sporting events, restaurants, theaters, churches, and concert halls. Three miles from the campus is the city of Xenia, population 25,000.

Housing Availability

725 spaces available. Freshman housing guaranteed. Students must live on campus until their junior year unless they live within commuting distance, are over 25, or are married. Four dormitories, a small group housing complex, and the Wilberforce Student Apartments make up the residential life.

NOTABLE ALUMNI

Hallie Q. Brown, 1873–Educator; elocutionist; civil rights leader and suffragette; president, Ohio State Federation of Women and National Association of Colored Women; founder and chairperson, Scholarship Fund of the National Association of Colored Women

Floyd H. Flake, 1967–Pastor; social worker; politician; first full-term African-American Congressman from the 6th Congressional District; founder, The Allen Christian School

Orchid I. Johnson–Political activist; founder, Freedom Inc.; State Representative, 25th District, Missouri

Bayard Rustin, 1930–32–Activist, Brotherhood of Sleeping Car Porters

Oklahoma

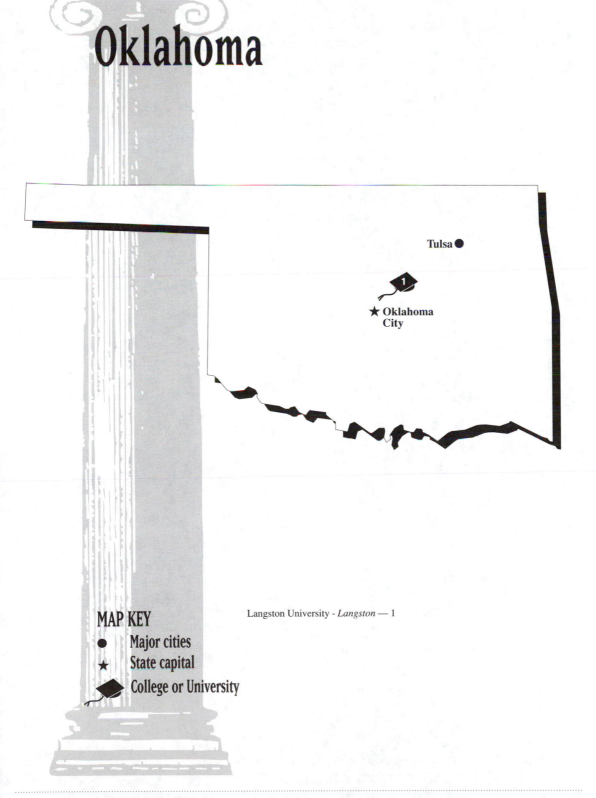

Tulsa ●

★ **Oklahoma
City**

Langston University - *Langston* — 1

MAP KEY
- ● Major cities
- ★ State capital
- ◆ College or University

LANGSTON UNIVERSITY

PO Box 907
Langston, OK 73050
Phone: (405) 466-2231

Total Enrollment:
3,323

Level of Selectivity:
Noncompetitive

Motto:
Education for Service

HISTORY

Langston University (LU) is a four-year, state-supported, coed, liberal arts institution. It was founded in 1897 as the Colored Agricultural and Normal University, for the purpose of instructing men and women of color in the agricultural, mechanical, and industrial arts. Within a year following the territorial act that established the college, black settlers determined to provide higher education for their children raised enough money through auctions, bake sales, and donations to purchase the 40 acres of land on which the school was built. The first bachelor's degree was awarded in 1901. The first president was the son of a former slave, Dr. Inman E. Page. The school adopted its present name, Langston University, in 1941.

After the Civil Rights Act of 1954, many black students in Oklahoma began to attend colleges other than Langston University. President Hale created a ten-year improvement plan to attract both black and white students to the university. Urban centers were instituted in Tulsa and Oklahoma City. These innovations caused an increase in enrollment and a student body that is now approximately 60% black and 50% white, with students coming from 26 states and 18 foreign countries. In 1987, Langston University began to plan its first graduate program.

Langston University is Oklahoma's only historically black college. It serves a double mission as a land grant institution and an urban center for the state. The original mission to carry out agricultural research and cooperative extension continues. Enrollment and programs for urban residents also continue to grow. The university is acclaimed both nationally and internationally for its research projects in the soils, grains, and water of Oklahoma. The American Institute of Goat Research has received international acclaim and has given an added dimension to the cooperative research.

Located on 440 acres of land, the university has plans for a major renovation of several of its buildings including the former president's home (White House); the student union; and the library, the architectural focal point of the campus.

ACCREDITATION

Langston is accredited by the North Central Association of Colleges and Schools to award the Bachelor of Arts, and Bachelor of Science, Associate of Science, and Master's degrees.

Other Accreditation

American Dietetic Association

American Physical Therapy Association

National Council for Accreditation of Teacher Education

National League for Nursing

Oklahoma Board of Nurse Registration and Nursing Education

Oklahoma State Board of Education

Oklahoma State System of Higher Education

COSTS PER YEAR

1992–93 Tuition: $1,090 (in-state); $2,590 (out-state)

Room and board: $1,190 (room); $990 (board)

Special fees: $180

Books: $400

Estimated total cost: $3,850 (in-state); $5,350 (out-state)

FINANCIAL AID

1990–91 Institutional Funding

Number of scholarships and grants: 331

Total amount of scholarships and grants: $754,168

Range of scholarships and grants: $100–$6,379

1990–91 Federal and State Funding

Number of scholarships and grants: 1,384

Total amount of scholarships and grants: $2,553,813

Range of scholarships and grants: $250–$6,535

Number of loans: 700

Total amount of loans: $1,842,941

Range of loans: $175–$7,365

Number of work-study: 252

Total amount of work-study: $392,290

Range of work-study: $50–$2,900

Financial Aid Specific to the School

50% of the student body received financial aid during 1991–92.

Approximately 50 loan funds ranging from $25 to $300 are available for Langston University students. Students interested in loans should contact the Langston University Development Foundation.

Army ROTC offers two- and four-year scholarships that pay tuition, fees, books, and other expenses, and provides a monthly stipend of $100.

Athletic scholarships are available to students participating in intercollegiate sports.

The Bureau of Indian Affairs is a program to enable Native American students to attend college. Students should contact the Bureau of Indian Affairs for more information.

College work-aid is available for those who do not qualify for college work-study.

The Cooperative Education Program combines classroom study with related paid work experience in all majors. The program provides academic credit and full-time status during co-op placement.

Langston University offers three major academic scholarships available for first-time entering freshmen—the McCabe, Regents' and President's scholarships. Selection is based on GPA, ACT or SAT scores, rank in graduating class, and participation in extracurricular activities and community service.

Oklahoma Tuition Aid Grant (OTAG) is available to residents of Oklahoma who demonstrate financial need.

Performance scholarsips are available for students participating in music or drama.

Thurgood Marshall Black Education Fund provides a four-year scholarship at this public black college. Qualifying students must have a high school GPA of 3.0 or better, and a SAT score of 1000 or ACT score of 24 or more. Students must be recommended by high school counselor as exceptional or exemplary in the creative or performing arts. Scholarship pays tuition, fees, room, and board, not to exceed $6,000 annually.

G. Lamar Harrison Library, Langston University

Veterans Administration Benefits provide funds for veterans and/or their dependents to attend college. Contact should be made to the Veterans Affairs Office, which is part of the Financial Aid Office.

Financial Aid Deadline

Rolling. May 1 (priority)

Financial Aid Contact

Ms. Nancy E. Luce, Director of Financial Aid, Langston University, Langston, OK 73050; (405) 466-2231, Ext. 289.

ADMISSION REQUIREMENTS

SAT or ACT required.

Entrance Requirements

Graduation from an accredited high school with the following units: 4 English, 2 science, 3 mathematics, and 2 history.

GED students must meet basic admission requirements

Transfer students from Oklahoma in good standing may apply if they have received a satisfactory GPA to meet the university's retention standards; transfers from out-of-state colleges must submit transcripts from institutions accredited by the North Central

Association or other regional associations; students must be in good standing from prior institution and have a "C" average.

International students should complete the academic program available in their own country; the program should be comparable to a freshman program in content, length, and difficulty. International students need to pass the TOEFL examination with a score of 500 or better, must have financial support from parents or government, and must pay $10,000 to cover the cost of expenses for two semesters.

Early admissions allows academically gifted students to enroll for college credits before completing high school.

Admission Application Deadline

Rolling admission provides no specific date for notification of admission so applicant is informed as soon as admission decision is made.

Admission Contact

Director of Admissions, Langston University, PO Box 728, Langston, OK 73050; (405) 466-3428

GRADUATION REQUIREMENTS

A minimum of 60 semester hours for an associate's degree; a minimum of 124 semester hours for a bachelor's degree and completion of core requirements; at least 45 of total credit hours must be at the senior college level; a minimum of 30 semester hours must be earned at Langston University; a minimum 2.0 GPA is required for graduation; must complete required courses in major and minor with a "C" or better; an internship or field study must be completed; 3 hours in American history and 3 hours in American government are mandated.

Grading System

A–F; I=incomplete; W=withdrawal; P= passing; N=no report; WP=withdrew passing; WF=withdrew failing; S=satisfactory; AU=audit

STUDENT BODY PROFILE

Total enrollment (male/female):
1,387/2,036

Other regions: 26 states, 18 foreign countries

Full-time undergraduates (male/female):
1,187/1,681

Part-time undergraduates (male/female):
188/388

Graduate students (male/female): 12/17

Ethnic/Racial Makeup

African American, 919; Hispanic, 11; Asian, 26; Native American, 27; Caucasian, 2,317; International, 23

FACULTY PROFILE

Number of faculty: 150

Student–teacher ratio: 24:1

Full-time faculty: 100

Part-time faculty: 50

Percent of faculty with doctorates or other terminal degrees: 60%

SCHOOL CALENDAR

1991–92: Aug 18–May 12 (semester hours)

Commencement and conferring of degrees: May 9

One summer session.

DEGREES OFFERED 1991–92:

Associate of Science

Drafting and Design Technology

Electronic Technology

Pre-Architecture

Pre-Engineering

Bachelor of Arts

Broadcast Journalism

English

Gerontology

History

Music

Psychology

Social Science

Sociology

Speech/Drama

Theater Arts

Bachelor of Science

Accounting

Administrative Management

Agricultural Economics

Animal Science

Biology

Business Administration

Business Education

Chemistry

Computer and Information Science

Corrections/Criminal Justice

Early Childhood Development

Economics/Finance

Elementary Education

General Home Economics

Health

Health Care Administration

Industrial Technology

Nutrition and Dietetics

Physical Education and Recreation

Management

Mathematics

Medical Technology

Physical Therapy

Pre-professional Science

Technology Education

Urban Studies

Vocational Home Economics

Master of Education

Bilingual Multicultural Education

Elementary Education

English As a Second Language

Urban Education

SPECIAL PROGRAMS

Accelerated Study Program allows students to complete their undergraduate degree in a shorter period of time than the traditional four years.

Advanced Placement (AP) grants college credit for postsecondary work completed in high school. Students scoring 3 to 5 on the AP test will receive credit by examination for each course and advanced placement.

A cooperative bachelor's degree program in medical technology is offered with approved hospitals.

Cooperative Education Program combines classroom study with related paid work experience. The program provides academic credit and full-time status during co-op placement.

College orientation is offered to entering students prior to the beginning of classes to acquaint students with the college and to prepare them for college life; parents may attend.

The honors program offers academically talented students a challenging program of study that includes special classes, seminars, colloquia, cultural activities, and special recognition to motivate participants.

Pre-professional programs are offered in dentistry, medicine, and veterinary science.

Remedial courses are offered to entering students to bring them up to admission standards and to help them adjust for success in college.

ATHLETIC PROGRAMS

Langston University is a member of the National Association of Intercollegiate Athletics (NAIA).

Intercollegiate sports: men's basketball, football, and track; women's basketball and track.

Intramural sports: basketball, football, soccer, softball, tennis, volleyball, and swimming.

LIBRARY HOLDINGS

The G. Lamar Harrison Library holds 238,000 bound volumes, 1,732 periodical subscriptions, 14,000 microforms, 900 audiovisuals, and 15,000 government documents. Computers are available for student use in computer center. The Melvin B. Tolson Black Heritage Center houses a collection on African history and the African-American experience since 1900. The center houses 15,000 volumes including books, audiovisuals, a rare collection on microforms, and over 80 black newspapers.

STUDENT LIFE

Special Regulations

Cars permitted without restrictions; quiet hours; dorm visitation 6–11 pm.

Campus Services

Health center, personal and psychological counseling, tutoring, and religious services.

Campus Activities

Social and cultural activities include theater, band, dances, movies, and forums. Each year LU brings in renowned artists in serious music, dance, and theater. Students are involved in community service projects. Students may get involved in the *Langston Gazette* (student paper). Communication majors or volunteers may work at the KALU FM Radio Station.

Leadership opportunities are found in the Student Government Association (SGA), departmental clubs, and special interest groups. Greek-letter fraternities include Alpha Phi Alpha, Kappa Alpha Psi, Omega Psi Phi, and Phi Beta Kappa; sororities include Alpha Kappa Alpha, Delta Sigma Theta, Sigma Gamma Rho, and Zeta Phi Beta.

Langston University is located in a small rural community, 40 miles northeast of Oklahoma City, the state capital, and 90 miles west of Tulsa, Oklahoma. Both cities offer cultural and recreational activities including sports events, shopping, dining, concerts, and theater.

Housing Availability

Approximately 1,700 housing spaces.

NOTABLE ALUMNI

James B. Abram, 1959–Department head, Biology, Norfolk State College

Robert DoQui–Entertainer, Los Angeles, CA

Julia Reed Hare, 1964–Director, community affairs, Golden West Broadcasters, KSFO

Dr. Nathan Hare 1954–Chairman, The Black Think Tank, San Francisco, CA

Dr. Henry Ponder, 1951–President, Fisk University

Pennsylvania

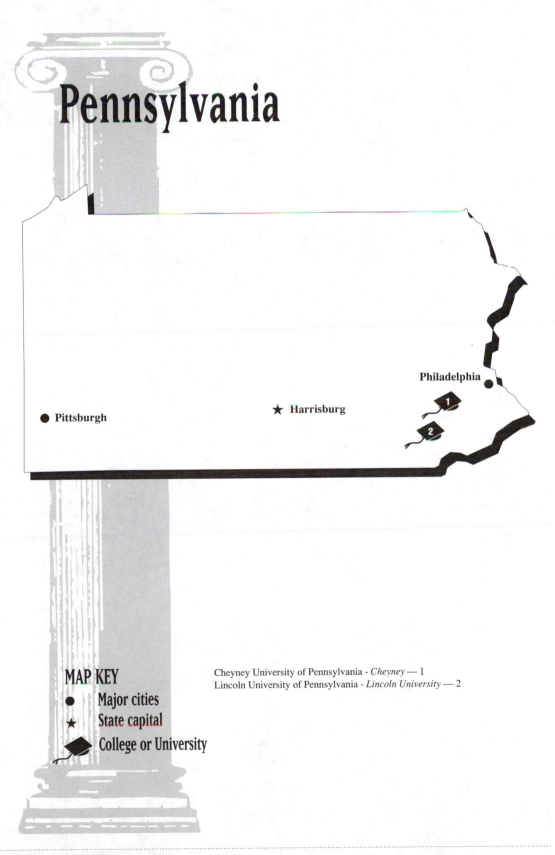

● Pittsburgh

★ Harrisburg

Philadelphia ●

1

2

MAP KEY

● Major cities
★ State capital
College or University

Cheyney University of Pennsylvania - *Cheyney* — 1
Lincoln University of Pennsylvania - *Lincoln University* — 2

CHEYNEY UNIVERSITY OF PENNSYLVANIA

Cheyney, PA 19319
Phone: (215) 399-2000
Toll-free:
800-243-9639

Total Enrollment:
1,607

Level of Selectivity:
Slightly competitive

HISTORY

Cheyney University of Pennsylvania (CUP) is a four-year, state-supported, coed, liberal arts institution founded in 1837 by Philadelphia Quaker Richard Humphreys. The school moved to Cheyney in 1902, began postsecondary instruction in 1931, and awarded its first bachelor's degree in 1932. CUP was originally named Institute for Colored Youth and changed names five times between 1903 and 1959 when it adopted its present name.

Cheyney continues in its original mission to train African-American teachers, but its programs have expanded to include journalism, medicine, business, science, industrial arts, communications, sports, and politics. Cheyney students represent a variety of races, cultures, and nationalities and the university celebrates this diversity by fostering cultural and social experiences and supportive services that will enable individual students to meet the challenges of a dynamic, competitive, technological society.

CUP is situated on 275 acres in a rural area that is steadily becoming more suburban. New facilities include three dormitories, a dining hall, and a student center. A featured campus attraction is the planetarium in the George Washington Carver Center. The university is one of 13 members of the Pennsylvania University System.

ACCREDITATION

Cheyney University is accredited by the Middle States Association of Colleges and Secondary Schools to award the Bachelor of Arts, Bachelor of Science, and Master's degrees.

Other Accreditation

American Dietetic Association

National Council for the Accreditation of Teacher Education

COSTS PER YEAR

1992–93 Tuition: $2,628 (in-state); $4,892 (out-state)

Room and board: $1,770 (room); $1,705 (board)

Special fees: $210

Books: $500

Estimated total cost: $6,813 (in-state); $9,077 (out-state)

FINANCIAL AID

1990–91 Institutional Funding

Number of scholarships and grants: 170

Total amount of scholarships and grants: $173,886

Range of scholarships and grants: $250–$6,000

1990–91 Federal and State Funding

Number of scholarships and grants: 1,708

Total amount of scholarships and grants: $2,172,532

Range of scholarships and grants: $200–$2,000

Number of loans: 1,234

Total amount of loans: $2,827,247

Range of loans: $500–$7,000

Number of work-study: 428

Total amount of work-study: $250,000

Range of work-study: $200–$2,000

Financial Aid Specific to the School

85% of the student body received financial aid during 1991–92.

Army ROTC and cooperative Air Force ROTC offer two- and four-year scholarships that pay tuition, fee, books, and other expenses, as well as provide a monthly stipend of $100.

Athletic scholarships available for students participating in intercollegiate sports.

Connecticut Scholastic Achievement Grant is available to residents of Connecticut. Contact the Connecticut Board of Education, 61 Woodland St., Hartford, CT 06105.

Cooperative Education Program alternates classroom study with related paid work experience. The program provides academic credit and full-time status during co-op placement.

D.C. State Student Incentive Grant (D.C. SSIG) is available to residents of the District who demonstrate substantial financial need. Contact the D.C. Office of Educational Assistance, 1331 H St., NW, Washington, D.C. 20005.

Delaware State Grant Program is available for Delaware residents who demonstrate financial need. Contact the Delaware Post-Secondary Education Commission, Carvel State Office Building, 820 French St., Wilmington, DE 19801.

Endowed, special interest, and alumni scholarships number over 25 and are based on merit and need.

George Sutherland Scholarships sponsored by Men of BACA (Bronze Association for Cultural Advancement) are available for full-time, undergraduate, sophomore, junior, and senior students with a 3.5 GPA. Scholarships of $1,000 are awarded each year. For further information contact the alumni office.

Maryland State Scholarships are available to residents of Maryland. Contact the Maryland State Scholarship Board, 2100 Guilford, Baltimore, MD 21218.

Massachusetts State Scholarships are available to residents of Massachusetts. Contact the Board of Higher Education, 31 St. James Ave., Boston, MA 02116.

Ohio Instructional Grant Program is available to residents of Ohio who demonstrate relative financial need. Contact the Board of Regents, Student Assistant Office, 3600 State Office Tower, 30 E. Broad St., Columbus, OH 4315.

Pennsylvania Higher Education Assistance Agency (PHEAA) Grants are awarded to residents of the state who demonstrate financial need. Application deadline is May 1.

PHEAA-HELP Loans are awarded to Pennsylvania residents attending Pennsylvania schools who need additional financing to pay educational costs. A maximum of $10,000 per academic year may be borrowed by qualified students and their parents. Contact PHEAA, PO Box 2165, Harrisburg, PA, 17105; 800-692-7392.

Presidential Scholarship is a one year grant based on high academic potential.

SICO (Shock Independent Oil Company) Foundation Scholarships are awarded each year to students attending college for the first time. Awards are $4,000 for four years or $1,000 per year. Qualifying students must demonstrate financial need and be residents of the state of Delaware; residents of certain counties in Pennsylvania to include Adams, Berks, Chester, Cumberland, Dauphin, Delaware, Lancaster, and Lebanon; or residents of York or Cecil County in Maryland. Contact high school counselor for more information.

Thurgood Marshall Black Education Fund provides a four-year scholarship at this public black college. Qualifying students must have a high school GPA of 3.0 or better and a SAT score of 1000 or ACT score of 24 or more. Students must be recommended by high school counselor as exceptional or exemplary in the creative or performing arts. Scholarship pays tuition, fees, room, and board not to exceed $6,000 annually.

Tuition waivers (full-time or part time) are available to Cheyney employees and their children.

W. W. Smith Charitable Trust awards $2,000 per year to students whose middle class status makes it difficult to receive financial assistance. Students who qualify are selected by the financial aid office.

West Virginia Higher Education Grant Program is available to residents of the state who attend college full time and demonstrate financial need. Contact the West Virginia Board of Regents, PO Box 4007, Charleston, WV 25304.

Financial Aid Deadline
April 1 (priority)

Financial Aid Contact
Oliver L. Norrell, Director of Financial Aid, Cheyney University of Pennsylvania, Cheyney, PA 19319; (215) 399-2000.

ADMISSION REQUIREMENTS
SAT or ACT required

Entrance Requirements
Graduation from an accredited high school and completion of the following units: 4 English, 3 mathematics, 3 science, 3 social science; some foreign language recommended; submit official high school transcript; minimum 2.0 GPA; recommendation from counselor or teacher; personal essay. A $20 application fee in money order or certified check is required.

Students from Pennsylvania who are motivated and come highly recommended but do not do well on the SAT or ACT will be considered for admission through the Act 101 provision which provides intensive assistance during student's first year.

GED students must meet basic admission requirements.

Transfer students must submit official transcript of all college work; minimum 2.0 GPA; if transferring less than 30 credits must submit high school transcript; minimum "C" average.

International students must submit official certification of high school completion; students from non-English-speaking countries must take TOEFL examination.

Early admission allows academically gifted high school students the opportunity to enroll in college for credit before completing high school.

Admission Application Deadline
Rolling admission provides no specific date for notification of admission so applicant is informed as soon as admission decision is made.

Admission Contact

Earl E. Acker, Director of Admissions, Cheyney University of Pennsylvania, Cheyney, PA 19319; (215) 399-2275 or 800-243-9639 (in-state). Fax: (215) 399-2415

GRADUATION REQUIREMENTS

A minimum of 128 semester hours and completion of core requirements to include 6 English, 3 mathematics, 6 science, 6 social science, 4 physical education, and 1 computer course; minimum 2.0 GPA; 32 hours in residence; graduating students are expected to attend graduation.

Grading System

A–F; WP-Withdraw Passing; P=Passing; I=Incomplete; WF=Withdraw Failing; NGR=No Grade Recorded

STUDENT BODY PROFILE

Total enrollment (male/female): 771/836

From in-state: 900

Other regions: 29 states, 7 foreign countries

Full-time undergraduates (male/female): 597/646

Part-time undergraduates (male/female): 47/50

Graduates (male/female): 128/139

Ethnic/Racial Makeup

African American, 1,543; Hispanic, 16; International, 48.

Class of 1995 Profile

Number of applicants: 916

Number accepted: 678

Number enrolled: 431

Transfers enrolled: 145

FACULTY PROFILE

Number of faculty: 140

Student-teacher ratio: 16:1

Full-time faculty: 99

Part-time faculty: 41

Faculty with doctorates or other terminal degrees: 55%

SCHOOL CALENDAR

1992–93: August–May (semester hours)

Commencement & conferring of degrees: May

Three summer sessions.

DEGREES OFFERED 1991–92:

Bachelor of Arts

Biology

Chemistry

Communication Arts

Computer and Information Sciences

Criminal Justice

English

General Science

Geography

Mathematics

Political Science

Psychology

Social Science

Sociology

Theater Arts

Bachelor of Science

Accounting

Biology Education

Business Administration

Chemistry Education

Clothing and Textiles

Drafting and Design

Early Childhood Education

Electronics

Elementary Education

English Education

Fashion Design

Fashion Merchandising

French Education

Home Economics

Hotel, Restaurant, and Institutional
  Management

Industrial Arts

Industrial Technology

Management

Marketing

Mathematic Education

Office Administration

Recreation

Science Education

Secondary Education

Small Business Administration

Social Science Education

Special Education

Tax Accounting

SPECIAL PROGRAMS

Allied health program is available in co-operation with Jefferson University.

Adult or Continuing Education Program is available for nontraditional students returning to school or working full time.

Advanced Placement (AP) grants college credit for postsecondary work completed in high school. Students passing the AP test will receive credit by examination for each course and advanced placement.

College Level Examination Program (CLEP) determines the academic relevance of nontraditional educational experiences such as the military, on-the-job training or other life experiences through a series of test and may grant students college credit for these experiences.

College orientation is offered at no cost to entering students for two days prior to the beginning of classes to acquaint students with the college and to prepare them for college life.

Cooperative Education Program alternates classroom study with related paid work experience. The program provides academic credit and full-time status during co-op placement.

Cross registration between Cheyney and West Chester University of Pennsylvania allows students to take courses not taught at Cheyney.

Dual degree program is offered in biology and chemistry.

Honors Program offers academically talented students a challenging program of study that includes special classes, seminars, colloquia, cultural activities, and special recognition to motivate participants.

Internships allow students to apply theory to on-the-job training in industry, business, and government.

LEIP (Life Experience Internship Program) provides students with experience in key government offices in the Pennsylvania Capitol.

Off Campus Study allows students to take courses for credit at "cluster" schools, including Lincoln University of Pennsylvania and Temple University.

Part-time degree program allows students to earn an undergraduate degree part time.

Pre-medical and pre-law programs provide liberal arts curriculums that assure entry into medical school or law school.

Remedial courses are offered to entering students to bring them up to admission standards and to help them adjust for success in college.

ROTC provides training in military science for commission as a second lieutenant in the U.S. Army and Air Force. Two-, and four-year scholarships are available.

Study Abroad Program allows students to go to a foreign country for part of their college education.

ATHLETIC PROGRAMS

Cheyney University of Pennsylvania is a member of the National Collegiate Athletic

Association (NCAA), the Pennsylvania Athletic Conference, the Association for Intercollegiate Athletics (AIAW) for Women, and the Eastern College Athletic Conference.

Intercollegiate sports: men's basketball, cross-country, football, tennis, track & field, and wrestling; women's basketball, cross-country, tennis, track & field, and volleyball.

Intramural sports: basketball, karate, softball, swimming, touch football, and volleyball.

Athletic Contact

Andrew Hinston, Athletic Director, Cheyney University of Pennsylvania, Cheyney, PA 19319; (215) 399-2287.

LIBRARY HOLDINGS

The Leslie Pinckney Hill Library houses 233,767 bound volumes, 1,054 periodical subscriptions, 396,743 microforms, 5,217 audiovisuals, 60,444 government documents; 100 computers available for student use. Special collections include the entire Schomburg Collection of African Americans on microfilm.

STUDENT LIFE

Special Regulations

Cars permitted in designated areas; dorm residents must purchase meal plan; mandatory class attendance; freshman dorm visitation is Sunday–Thursday 3–11pm, Friday-Saturday 3pm–midnight; upperclassman visitation is Sunday–Thursday 3pm–midnight and Friday–Saturday 3pm–1am; coed dorm visitation during weekends for upperclassmen; students must have health insurance.

Campus Services

Health center, personal and psychological counseling, career planning and placement, women's center, late-night escort, and religious activities.

Campus Activities

Social and cultural activities include theater, chorale, and band. Students may get involved in the *Cheyney Record* (student-run newspaper); or the *Bacon* (yearbook). Communication majors or volunteers can work at WCUB, the campus radio station.

The World Culture Center exposes students to different international cultures. The Cheyney Wolves have won national competitions in women's and men's basketball and soccer.

Leadership opportunities can be found in the Student Government and Cooperative Association (SGCA) which sponsors speakers and performers. Students can also get involved in the more than 20 campus organizations including pre-medical and pre-law societies, as well as business, and cheerleading clubs. Greek-letter societies include Alpha Phi Alpha, Kappa Alpha Psi, Omega Psi Phi, and Phi Beta Sigma; sororities include Alpha Kappa Alpha, Delta Sigma Theta, Sigma Gamma Rho, and Zeta Phi Beta. Several honor societies are also represented on campus.

Bus service from the Cheyney campus to downtown Cheyney is provided during the academic year. Students also have access to shopping and dining as well as social, cultural, and recreational activities in Wilmington, Delaware (located within 15 miles), and Philadelphia (located 24 miles away).

Housing Availability

1,200 housing spaces; freshmen given priority; freshman-only housing.

NOTABLE ALUMNI

Ed Bradley, 1964–Co-host, "60 Minutes"

Marvin Frazier–Professional football player, Denver Broncos

Andre Waters–Professional football player, Philadelphia Eagles

Robert Woodson, 1962–President, National Center for Neighborhood Enterprise

LINCOLN UNIVERSITY OF PENNSYLVANIA

Lincoln University,
PA 19352
Phone: (215) 932-8300
Fax: (215) 932-8316

Total Enrollment:
1,458

Level of Selectivity:
Moderately
competitive

Motto:
If the sun shall make
you free, ye shall be
free indeed

HISTORY

Lincoln University of Pennsylvania is a four-year, state-affiliated, coed, liberal arts university. It was founded in 1854 as the Ashmun Institute and renamed in 1866 to Lincoln University in honor of Abraham Lincoln.

Lincoln claims to be the oldest college in the United States to have as its original purpose the higher education of youth of African decent. From its inception, Lincoln has attracted an interracial and international enrollment. The university graduated its first class of four black men and two white men in 1868. In 1873, 10 students from Liberia came to study at Lincoln, making the university one of the first, if not the first, U.S. institutions of higher education to accept African students.

In 1945, Dr. Horace Mann Bond became the first black president and the first alumni president at Lincoln. Lincoln's centennial celebration in 1953 marked the acceptance of women applicants. Until 1959 Lincoln had a theological seminary, as well as a college of liberal arts. The university hopes to establish an Institute for International Studies within the next five years.

Lincoln continues its mission to prepare students for the demands of the twenty-first century through study in the liberal arts, balanced with concentrated study in a specialized field. The hallmark of the Lincoln experience is its ability to develop in students the skills and attributes they need to excel in an increasingly complex world.

During the 20s, 30s, and 40s Lincoln graduated several distinguished leaders, including Langston Hughes, Thurgood Marshall, and James L. Usry respectively. This tradition of graduating leaders continues, with Lincoln's alumni having headed 36 colleges and universities. Of the country's black physicians, 20% are graduates of Lincoln; more than 10% of black attorneys are also graduates. Lincoln University trustees control an art collection worth one billion dollars.

Lincoln is located on a 422 acre campus with 27 main buildings and 21 faculty residences, which include historic buildings from the 1860s to modern structures built in the 1990s. Modern facilities include Rivero Hall with an olympic size swimming pool, Dickey Hall, a $5.4 million dollar computer center, and a social science complex. Lincoln University is a traditional black university.

ACCREDITATION

Lincoln University of Pennsylvania is accredited by the Middle States Association of Colleges and Secondary Schools (MSACS) to award the Bachelor of Arts, Bachelor of Science, and Master of Human Services degrees.

Other Accreditation

Accrediting Commission on Education for Health Services Administration

American Chemical Society

American Medical Association (health-related programs)

College and University Council of the State of Pennsylvania

National Council of Rehabilitation Education

National Recreation and Parks Association/American Association for Leisure and Recreation

COSTS PER YEAR

1992–93 Tuition: $3,042 (in-state); $4,362 (out-state)

Room and board: $1,400 (room); $1,300 (board)

Special fees: $460

Books: $500

Estimated total cost: $6,702 (in-state); $8,022 (out-state)

FINANCIAL AID

1990–91 Institutional Funding

Number of scholarships and grants: 795

Total amount of scholarships and grants: $493,612

Range of scholarships and grants: $100–$2,400

1990–91 Federal and State Funding

Number of scholarships and grants: 1,285

Total amount of scholarships and grants: $1,749,306

Range of scholarships and grants: $100–$2,400

Number of loans: 700

Total amount of loans: $1,449,514

Range of loans: $200–$4,000

Number of work-study: 234

Total amount of work-study: $304,302

Range of work-study: $200–$2,600

Financial Aid Specific to the School

95% of the student body received financial aid in 1991–92.

Alumni merit scholarships are awarded to a limited number of incoming students with an SAT score of 950 or higher and a "B" average in high school. Students may receive up to $1,000 per year, and the scholarship is renewable if the student continues to meet Lincoln's standard of excellence. Contact Admissions office for more information.

Athletic scholarships are available to students participating in intercollegiate sports.

Endowed, alumni, friends, and corporate scholarships number approximately twenty-one and are available based on varying criteria of financial need, interest, academic merit, or location.

Founders scholarships are awarded to a limited number of incoming students who have a SAT score of 1,000 or higher and a "B+" average or better. Scholarships pay tuition cost and are renewable for students who continue to meet Lincoln's standards of excellence. Contact the admissions office for more information.

Honors merit scholarship is a need-based scholarship awarded to academically gifted students. The minimum award is $2,500 per year. Contact financial aid office for more information.

Presidential scholarship is a $1,000 incentive grant awarded to incoming freshman students only. Students must have a SAT score of 900 or better with a GPA of 3.0. Scholarship is renewable.

Contact admissions office for more information.

Lincoln University offers many prizes and awards, each based on specific requirements. There are seven general prizes, eight prizes for scholastic standing, 23 prizes for students in the humanities, eleven prizes for students in the natural sciences, and six prizes for students in the social sciences.

LASER (Lincoln Advanced Science and Engineering Reinforcement Program) provides assistance to a limited number of pre-engineering students based on academic merit and financial need. Contact Dr. Willie Williams, Director of LASER Program.

MARC (Minority Access to Research Centers) scholarships provide a limited number of scholarships to students interested in biomedical research. The grant is administered through the National Institute of General Medical Sciences and covers all tuition and fees for the year. Contact Dr. Saligrama C. Subbarao, Director, MARC program.

W. W. Smith Scholarship is a need-based scholarship awarded to academically gifted students. The minimum award is currently $2,500. Contact the financial aid office for more information.

Cooperative Education Program alternates classroom study with related paid work experience. The program provides academic credit and full-time status during co-op placement.

College work-aid is available to students not qualifying for college work-study to work in departments of the college.

Thurgood Marshall Black Education Fund provides a four-year scholarship at this public black college. Qualifying students must have a high school GPA of 3.0 or better and a SAT score of 1000 or ACT score of 24 or more. Students must be recommended by high school counselor as exceptional or exemplary in the creative or performing arts. Scholarship pays tuition, fees, room, and board, not to exceed $6,000 annually.

ROTC provides training in military science for commission as a second lieutenant in the U.S. Air Force in cooperation with the University of Delaware. Two- and four-year scholarships are available.

Pennsylvania residents may be eligible for $100 to $2,000 per year through Pennsylvania Higher Education Assistance Agency (PHEAA) grants. Students must be residents of Pennsylvania and demonstrate financial need.

Financial Aid Deadline
March 15

Financial Aid Contact
Georgia M. Daniel, Director of Financial Aid, Lincoln University of Pennsylvania, Lincoln University, PA 19352; (215) 932-8300 ext. 560.

ADMISSION REQUIREMENTS

SAT (750) required.

Entrance Requirements

Graduation from an accredited high school with a minimum of 22 units including: 4 English, 3 mathematics, 3 social studies, 3 science, 2 arts or humanities, 1 health and physical education, and 6 electives; minimum 2.0 or "C" average; ranked in upper 50% of graduating class; two letters of recommendation; interviews recommended; and reputation of high school considered. A $10 application fee is required.

GED students must meet basic admission requirements.

Transfer students must submit an official transcript, qualify for readmission at previous college, submit a letter from previous institution regarding the student's moral character, and submit a health certificate.

International students must take the TOEFL examination; must submit official transcripts and a General Certificate of Education, a letter of recommendation from the high school principal, and a character recommendation; and must provide proof of ability to pay all college costs.

Early decision admission is for students with a high probability of acceptance and for whom Lincoln University is their first choice. Financial aid is determined at the time of early decision.

Admission Application Deadline

Rolling admission provides no specific date for notification of admission so applicant is informed as soon as admission decision is made; January 1 (fall priority); November 15 (spring priority).

Admission Contact

Jerry Arrington, Director of Admissions, Lincoln Hall, Lincoln University, PA 19352; (215) 932-8300, Ext. 206 or 207.

GRADUATION REQUIREMENTS

A minimum of 64 credit hours for an associate's degree; and a minimum of 120 to 128 credit hours for bachelor's degree with completion of core requirements to include the following hours: 6 English (composition and world literature), 8 humanities, 9 social science, 3–6 foreign language (for certain majors), 6 natural science, 3 mathematics, 2 physical education, and 3 introduction to computer applications; 2 courses with writing emphasis, speaking emphasis, and critical thinking emphasis; a minimum GPA of 2.0; completion of Freshman Assembly Program; completion of a writing proficiency exam; and a major field exit examination.

Grading System

A–F; I=Incomplete; W=Withdrawal; P=Pass; F=Fail

STUDENT BODY PROFILE

Total enrollment (male/female): 598/860

From in-state: 597

From other regions: 31 states; 8 foreign countries

Full-time undergraduates (male/female): 494/712

Part-time undergraduates (male/female): 26/38

Graduate students (male/female): 77/111

Ethnic/Racial Makeup

African American, 1,370; Hispanic, 15; Asian, 15; Caucasian, 29; International, 29.

Class of 1995 Profile

Number of applicants: 1,403

Number accepted: 804

Number enrolled: 407

Median SAT score: 360V; 380M

Average high school GPA: 2.50

FACULTY PROFILE

Number of faculty: 141

Student/teacher ratio: 15:1

Full-time faculty: 81

Part-time faculty: 60

Faculty with doctorates or other terminal
degrees: 65%

SCHOOL CALENDAR

1992–93: August 25–April 23 (semester
hours)

Commencement and conferring of degrees:
May 2

One summer session.

DEGREES OFFERED 1991–92:

Associate of Arts
Business Administration
Computer Science
Early Childhood Education
Recreation Leadership
Spanish

Bachelor of Arts
Accounting
Biology
Business Management
Chemistry
Criminal Justice
Economics
English
Finance
French
General Science
Human Services
Mathematics
Music
Philosophy
Physics
Political Science
Political Science–International Relations
Psychology
Public Affairs–International Relations
Religion
Russian

Sociology
Spanish

Bachelor of Science
Accounting
Actuarial Science
Bilingual Education
Biology
Business Management
Computer Science
Criminal Justice
Early Childhood Education
Economics
Elementary Education
English–Communications
English Education
English–Journalism
Finance
French–Education
Health and Physical Education
Health Science
History
Human Services
Mathematics Education
Music Education
Physics
Political Science
Psychology–Industrial Organization
Psychology–Psychobiology
Secondary Education
Sociology
Spanish–Education
Therapeutic Recreation

Pre-professional Programs
Dentistry
Engineering
Law
Medicine
Nursing
Pharmacy
Veterinary Science

SPECIAL PROGRAMS

Accelerated Study Program allows students to complete their undergraduate degree in a shorter period of time than the traditional four years.

Advanced Placement (AP) grants college credit for postsecondary work completed in high school. Students passing the AP test will receive credit by examination for each course.

College Level Examination Program (CLEP) determines the academic relevance of nontraditional educational experiences, such as the military, on-the-job training, or other life experiences, through a series of tests and may grant students college credit for these experiences. Students must have a sealed score of 55 or higher and must get department approval before taking exam.

College orientation is offered for $30 for a week prior to the beginning of classes to acquaint students with the college and to prepare them for college life; parents may attend.

Cooperative Education Program alternates classroom study with related paid work experience. The program provides academic credit and full-time status during co-op placement.

The foreign language program at Lincoln includes Russian, Chinese, Swahili, Arabic, Japanese, Latin, French, Spanish, and German.

Honors program offers academically talented students a challenging program of study with includes special classes, seminars, colloquia, cultural activities, and special recognition to motivate participants.

Individualized Majors allow students to create their own major program(s) of study.

Remedial courses are offered to entering students to bring them up to admission standards and to help them adjust for success in college.

ROTC provides training in military science for commission as a second lieutenant in the U.S. Air Force in conjunction with the University of Delaware. Two- and four-year scholarships are available.

The Special Program for Enriching Education Development (SPEED) program offers intensive tutorial and counseling assistance for selected students in their freshman and sophomore years.

Study Abroad Program allows students to go to a foreign country for a semester, summer, or longer for part of their college education. Students study in Taiwan, Russia, France, Germany, the Dominican Republic, Mexico, Japan, and Brazil, as well as other countries.

Three/two degree program in engineering in cooperation with Pennsylvania State University, Lafayette College, and New Jersey Institute allows student to get two degrees—a BA from Lincoln and a BS in engineering from cooperating school—by completing three years at Lincoln and two years at cooperating school.

Three/three degree program in engineering in cooperation with Drexel University allows students to get two degrees—one in liberal arts from home school and one in engineering from cooperating school—by completing three years at matriculated school and three years at cooperating school.

Three/two degree program in International Service allows students to get two degrees—a Bachelor of Arts degree from Lincoln and a Master of International Service degree from American University.

The Talent Improvement and Motivational Experience (TIME) program is a voluntary program for students who want to improve their basic writing, reading, and mathematic skills.

ATHLETIC PROGRAMS

Lincoln University is a member of the National Collegiate Athletic Association (NCAA), Eastern College Athletic Association (ECAC), Intercollegiate Association of Amateur Athletes of America (ICAAAA), and EPAC.

Intercollegiate sports: men's baseball, basketball, cross-country, soccer, tennis, and track; women's basketball and volleyball.

Intramural sports: archery, badminton, basketball, bowling, karate, softball, swimming, table tennis, touch football, track, and volleyball.

Athletic Contact

Cyrus D. Jones, Lincoln University, Lincoln University, PA 19352; (215) 932-8300, Ext. 382.

LIBRARY HOLDINGS

Langston Hughes Memorial Library holds 175,000 bound volumes, 675 periodical subscriptions, and 35,000 microforms. Special collections include a collection of Negro and African materials representing all aspects of the black experience, a portion of the Susan Reynolds Underhill Collection, and selections from other collections of African art and artifacts.

STUDENT LIFE

Special Regulations

Freshmen required to live on campus; class attendance is mandatory.

Campus Services

Health center, personal and psychological counseling, career counseling and placement, testing services, reading/writing lab, mathematics laboratory, late night escort, and chapel services.

Campus Activities

Social and cultural activities include theater, chorale, lecture series, jazz band, film festivals, and dance, as well as forums, symposiums, art exhibits, major concerts, coffeehouses, entertainment machines, and tournaments in pool, table tennis, backgammon, and chess. Students may work on *The Lincolnian,* the student newspaper, or *The Lion* yearbook. The university has a student-run FM radio station, WLIU.

Leadership opportunities are found in the Student Government Association or numerous student-run organizations. Student organizations and clubs include Tolson Society, Thurgood Marshall Law Society, and several honor societies. Greek-letter societies include Alpha Kappa Alpha, Delta Sigma Theta, and Zeta Phi Beta sororities; fraternities include Alpha Phi Alpha, Kappa Alpha Psi, Omega Psi Phi, and Phi Beta Sigma.

Lincoln University is located on U.S. Route 1 about 45 miles southwest of Philadelphia; 25 miles west of Wilmington, Delaware; and 55 miles north of Baltimore, Maryland.

Housing Availability

1,100 housing spaces. Eight resident halls for women, five for men. Freshman housing guaranteed. Freshman-only housing available.

NOTABLE ALUMNI

Nnamdi Azikiwe, 1930–First president of Nigeria

Edward Wilmot Blyden III, 1948–International educator and diplomat from Sierra, Leone

Roscoe Lee Browne, 1946–Author and actor

Langston Hughes, 1929–Poet and author

Thurgood Marshall, 1930–First African-American Supreme Court Justice

Kwame Nkrumah, 1939–First prime minister and first president of Ghana

Hildrus A. Poindexter, 1924–International authority on tropical diseases

Wilbert A. Tatum–Publisher, Editor-In-Chief, *Amsterdam News*

Jams L. Usry, 1946–First African-American mayor of Atlantic City

Franklin H. Williams, 1941–Former ambassador to United Nations and Ghana

South Carolina

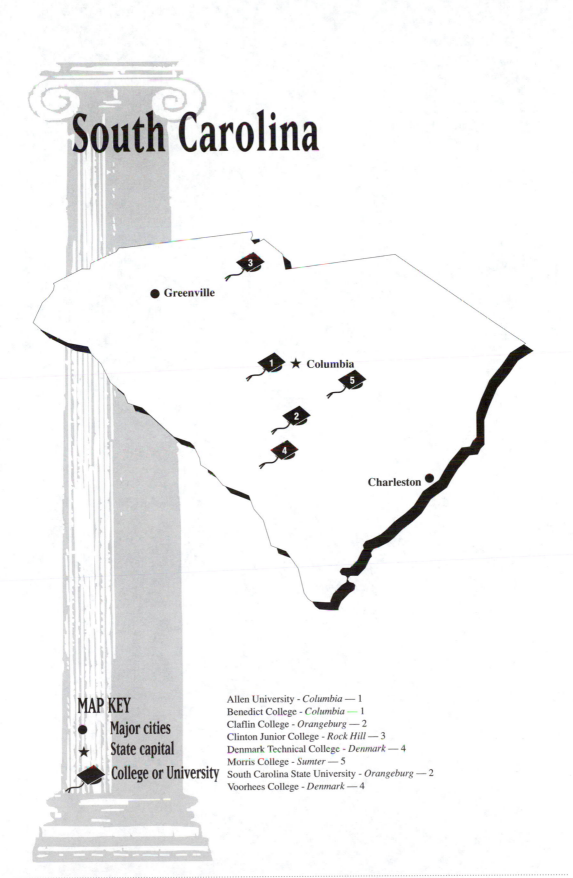

● **Greenville**

3

1 ★ **Columbia**

5

2

4

Charleston ●

Allen University - *Columbia* — 1
Benedict College - *Columbia* — 1
Claflin College - *Orangeburg* — 2
Clinton Junior College - *Rock Hill* — 3
Denmark Technical College - *Denmark* — 4
Morris College - *Sumter* — 5
South Carolina State University - *Orangeburg* — 2
Voorhees College - *Denmark* — 4

ALLEN UNIVERSITY

1530 Harden St.
Columbia, SC 29204
Phone: (803) 254-4165

Total Enrollment:
223

Level of Selectivity:
Noncompetitive

Motto:
We teach the mind
to think, the hands to
work, and the heart
to love

HISTORY

Allen University is a four-year, private, coed, liberal arts institution founded in 1870 as Payne Institute by the African Methodist Episcopal (AME) Church. In 1880, the school reopened under the name Allen University in honor of Richard Allen, founder of the AME Church. The grammar school closed in the mid-1920s and the high school closed in the early 1930s.

Founded to provide higher education in a Christian environment, the development of a wholesome approach to religion is one of the basic objectives of the school. The college provides an undergraduate education, with a strong commitment to teaching, community service, and research. It continues to expand the curricula to meet the demonstrated needs of both society and students. Allen's sound liberal arts program prepares its students to meet the challenges of professional programs and professional careers.

The eight-building campus is located on approximately 23 acres in Columbia, South Carolina. The facilities were built between 1906 and 1950. Five of its buildings were designated "Historic District Status" by the U.S. Department of Interior. Allen, South Carolina's oldest African American college, is a traditionally black institution.

ACCREDITATION

Allen is accredited by the U.S. Department of Education to award the Bachelor of Arts and Bachelor of Science degrees.

Other Accreditation

American Association of College Athletic Directors

American Association of Colleges for Teacher Education

National Business Education Association

COSTS PER YEAR
1992–93 Tuition: $4,500

Room and board: $3,492

Special fees: $410

Books: $500

Estimated total cost: $8,902

FINANCIAL AID

Financial Aid Specific to the School

100% of the student body received financial aid during 1991–92.

The Allen Scholarship or President Scholarship helps freshman students with a $250 award per semester. President scholarships are based on merit.

Budweiser Corporation Scholarship awards $500 to a student in good academic standing who exemplifies high moral standards and good citizenship.

J. T. W. Mims Memorial Scholarship awards $75 to a student who has demonstrated academic achievement and financial need.

John and Amy Northrop Scholarships of $500 are awarded to two needy students with GPAs of 2.0.

E. F. Sweat Scholarship for $100 is available for a student majoring in the social sciences with Afro-American history as part of their core program.

Veterans of Foreign War (VFW) offers a $750 award to assist entering freshmen who demonstrate academic achievement and financial need.

Work assistance (Work-Aid) and (Grant-in-Aid) are available to students not qualifying for work study or other scholarships to work in various departments of the college.

Financial Aid Deadline

March 15

Financial Aid Contact

Office of Financial Aid, Allen University, Chappelle Administration Building, 1530 Harden St., Columbia, SC 29202.

ADMISSION REQUIREMENTS

Open admission. SAT or ACT recommended for counseling and placement.

Entrance Requirements

Graduation from an accredited high school and completion of the following units: 4 English, 2 mathematics, 2 science, and 3 social sciences; an official high school transcript; recommendations from high school counselor and minister (or other character reference); completed health form, including recent immunizations. A $10 application fee is required.

GED students must meet same basic entrance requirements.

Transfer students must submit official transcripts from institutions previously attended at least one month prior to the beginning of the semester. Students with fewer than 30 college credits must also submit high school transcript.

International students must take the TOEFL examination, submit official high school and college transcripts, and deposit a non-refundable fee to cover one year's tuition, fees, room, and board.

Admission Application Deadline

Rolling admission provides no specific date for notification of admission so applicant is informed as soon as admission decision is made; continuous until August 15.

Admission Contact

Rev. Romeo Leonard, Admissions Officer, Allen University, Enrollment Management Programs, 1530 Harden St., Columbia, SC 29204; (803) 376-5716; ext. 115.

GRADUATION REQUIREMENTS

A minimum of 120 semester hours and completion of 62 core requirements to include: 15 English, 9 mathematics, 8 science, 12 social science, and 6 foreign language; minimum 2.0 GPA; minimum of "C" in English 101 and 102; last 30 hours in residence at Allen; student must pass the English Proficiency Exam.

Grading System

A–F; I=Incomplete; to be removed within 6 weeks into new semester. WA=withdraw for excessive absences; WD=withdraw before mid-term exam; WF=withdraw failing; WP=withdraw passing; Aud=auditing class; C=continuing students in need of remediation. Students may withdraw up to end of second week without penalty.

STUDENT BODY PROFILE

Total enrollment (male/female): 132/91

From in-state: 152

Other regions: 17 states; 1 foreign country

Full-time undergraduates (male/female): 116/80

Part-time undergraduates (male/female): 16/11

Ethnic/Racial Makeup

African American, 221; International, 2.

Class of 1995 Profile

Number of applicants: 500

Number accepted: 400

Number enrolled: 124

FACULTY PROFILE

Number of faculty: 40

Student-teacher ratio: 12:1

Full-time faculty: 20

Part-time faculty: 20

SCHOOL CALENDAR

1992–93: August 11–May 7 (semesters)

Commencement and conferring of degrees: May 8

One summer session.

DEGREES OFFERED 1991–92:

Associate of Arts

Secretarial Science

Bachelor of Arts

Art

Economics

English

French

History

Humanities

Sociology

Spanish

Bachelor of Sciences

Biology

Business Administration

Chemistry

Elementary and Secondary Education

Mathematics

Physical Education

SPECIAL PROGRAMS

Accelerated Study Program allows students to complete their undergraduate degree in a shorter period of time than the traditional four years.

College Level Examination Program (CLEP) determines the academic relevance of nontraditional educational experiences, such as the military, on-the-job training, or other life experiences, through a series of tests and may grant students college credit for these experiences.

Directed and Guided Program is an independent study program for juniors and seniors with at least 3.25 GPA.

Honors program offers academically talented students an enriched program of study with options of interdisciplinary focus or independent study. Students who have completed one semester at Allen with a GPA of 3.25 and who demonstrate academic excellence will be invited to participate in the honors program.

Part-time Degree Program allows students to earn a degree while attending classes part time in the daytime or evening.

Remedial courses are offered to entering students to bring them up to admission standards and to help them adjust for success in college.

Senior Citizens Program allows persons 60 and older to attend Allen at the cost of an application fee plus $50 per course.

ATHLETIC PROGRAMS

Allen University is a member of the National Association of Intercollegiate Athletics (NAIA) and the Eastern Intercollegiate Athletic Conference (EIAC).

Intercollegiate sports: men's basketball and track & field; women's basketball and track & field.

Intramural sports: basketball.

Athletic Contact

Mr. Robert Reynolds, Allen University, 1530 Harden St., Columbia, SC 29204; (803) 376-5780, ext. 301.

LIBRARY HOLDINGS

39,000 volumes, 175 periodical subscriptions, 350 audiovisuals; 50 computers available for student use in computer center. Special collections include an Afro-American collection and AME Church materials. The curriculum laboratory supports the teacher education program.

STUDENT LIFE

Special Regulations

New students and transfers must attend college orientation; class attendance mandatory; freshmen/sophomores required to attend weekly assembly programs; all students must attend Opening Convocation, Founder's Day; last 30 hours must be in residence; all vehicles must be registered; off-campus living permitted.

Campus Services

Health services; personal and psychological counseling; grounds patrolled by qualified security; remedial instruction; religious and vesper services.

Campus Activities

Student activities include weekly assemblies that focus on worship. Students may get involved in the student-run newspaper.

Leadership opportunities are found in the Student Government Association (SGA) or other academic, social, and religious clubs. Greek letter fraternities include Alpha Phi Alpha, Kappa Alpha Psi, Omega Psi Phi, and Phi Beta Sigma; sororities include Alpha Kappa Alpha, Delta Sigma Theta, Sigma Gamma Rho, and Zeta Phi Beta. Honor societies are also represented on campus.

Located in the city of Columbia, Allen University is eight blocks from the downtown area. The campus is easily accessible from the highway, railway, and airway systems. Benedict College, a traditional black college, is within minutes of the campus. The city of Columbia, the capital of South Carolina, has a population of approximately 100,000. Points of interest include the Columbia Museum of Art, the Hampton-Presston Mansion and Garden, the Planetarium, the Riverbanks Zoological Park, and the South Carolina State Museum and State House.

Housing Availability

Three dormitories on campus; one for males, two for females; off-campus housing permitted.

NOTABLE ALUMNI

Dr. W. Dean Goldsby, 1959–President, Shorter College

BENEDICT COLLEGE

Harden and
Blanding Streets
Columbia, SC 29204
Phone: (803) 253-5120
Toll-free in-state:
800-868-6958
Fax: (803) 253-5085

Total Enrollment:
1,469

Level of Selectivity:
Slightly competitive

Motto:
The greatest college in
the universe

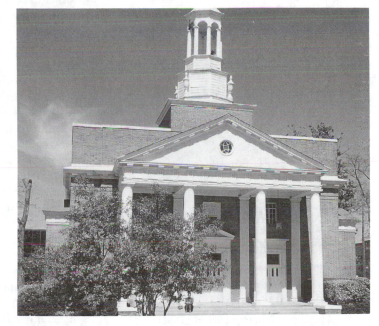

HISTORY

Benedict College is a four-year, private, coed, liberal arts college affiliated with the Baptist Church. Founded in 1870 as Benedict Institute, the college has sought to combine the traditions of the Christian faith with the heritage of African-Americans. Originally instruction was offered at a post-secondary level. The school was chartered in 1889. In 1984, the school awarded its first degree and adopted its present name, Benedict College.

The 25-building campus is situated on 20 acres and includes the Ponders Fine Arts/Humanities Center and a Learning Resource Center that houses the library. There is an architectural blend of newly built facilities and recently renovated historical buildings. This traditionally black college is a UNCF member school.

ACCREDITATION

Benedict College is accredited by the Southern Association of Colleges and Schools (SACS) to award the Bachelor of Arts and Bachelor of Science degrees.

Other Accreditation

Council on Social Work Education

National Recreation and Parks Association

South Carolina Department of Education

COSTS PER YEAR

1991–92 Tuition: $4,584

Room and board: $2,492

Special fees: $300

Books: $400

Estimated total cost: $7,776

FINANCIAL AID

1990–91 Institutional Funding

Number of scholarships and grants: 389

Total amount of scholarships and grants: $1,037,615

Range of scholarships and grants: $100–$7,076

1990–91 Federal and State Funding

Number of scholarships and grants: 2,263

Total amount of scholarships and grants: $3,901,328

Range of scholarships and grants: $100–$4,000

Number of loans: 560

Total amount of loans: $901,823

Range of loans: $250–$4,000

Number of work-study: 980

Total amount of work-study: 814,490

Range of work-study: $400–$1,600

Financial Aid Specific to the School

87% of the student body received financial aid during 1991–92.

Trustee Scholars Program provides a scholarship to high school students who rank in the upper one-fifth of their graduating class and have a 3.4 GPA or above, 950 SAT score or higher, or a minimum ACT score of twenty.

Athletic scholarships are available at this school.

Cooperative Education Program combines classroom study with related paid work experience in eighteen majors. The program provides academic credit and full-time status during co-op placement.

College work aid is available to students who do not qualify for work study.

United Negro College Fund (UNCF) scholarships are awarded to a limited number of students at this school who demonstrate financial need. Some scholarships may be based on location and merit. UNCF scholarships range from $500 to $7,500. The UNCF/Heaf Guarantee Loan Program is available at this school.

Army and cooperative Air Force and Navy ROTC offer two- and three-year scholarships that pay tuition, fees, books, and other expenses, and provide a monthly stipend of $100.

State tuition grants are available to residents of South Carolina who demonstrate financial need. Contact the Higher Education Committee, PO Box 11638, Ledy Street, Columbia, SC 29201 or the Director of Financial Aid at Benedict; out-state students should contact their state committee.

Financial Aid Deadline

February 15

Financial Aid Contact

Mr. Wayne Sumpter, Director of Financial Aid, Benedict College, Columbia, SC 29204; (803) 253-5105

ADMISSION REQUIREMENTS

Open admission. SAT (preferred) or ACT required for placement.

Entrance Requirements

Graduation from an accredited high school and completion of these 18 units: 4

English, 2 mathematics, 2 social sciences, 2 sciences, and 8 electives; foreign language recommended. Must have minimum 2.0 high school GPA, proof of a recent medical exam, 2 letters of recommendation (1 of which should be from an administrator or guidance counselor), and a 1 to 2 page personal essay. A $10 application fee is required.

GED students must meet basic admission requirements and submit minimum scores of 45 on each section of the GED exam.

Transfer students must be in equal standing with Benedict; submit an official transcript from previous college; be in good standing from previous institution; and have maintained a minimum 2.0 GPA. 90 credits may be transferred from an accredited four-year college or up to 65 credits from a two-year institution; a copy of the student's high school transcript and SAT or ACT scores are required.

International students must pass TOEFL examination with a score of at least 500, must provide proof of ability to pay all college costs, and must satisfy all U.S. Immigration and Naturalization requirements. A $60 non-refundable application fee is required.

Early admission allows academically gifted high school students the opportunity to enroll for college credits before completing high school.

Early decision allows students who choose Benedict as their first choice to apply before November 14 and indicate a request for early decision. If credentials are strong, the student will receive a decision by December 1.

Admission Application Deadline

Rolling admission provides no specific date for notification of admission so applicant is informed as soon as admission decision is made.

Admission Contact

Virginia McKee, Director of Admissions and Records, Benedict College, 1600 Harden St., Columbia, SC 29294; (803) 253-5143 or toll-free 800-868-6598.

GRADUATION REQUIREMENTS

A minimum of 125 semester hours and completion of the core requirements to include 7 hours mathematics, 8 hours science, 6 hours foreign language, 1 computer course, a 2.0 GPA, and at least one year in residence at Benedict.

Grading System

A–F; W=Withdraw; I=Incomplete.

STUDENT BODY PROFILE

Total enrollment: 1,469

From in-state: 1,263

Other regions: 13 states; 10 foreign countries

Full-time undergraduates (male/female):
446/905

Part-time undergraduates (male/female):
39/79

Ethnic/Racial Makeup

African American, 1,454; International, 15.

Class of 1995 Profile

Number of applicants: 1,589

Number accepted: 1,208

Number enrolled: 374

Median SAT score: 282V; 311M

FACULTY PROFILE

Number of faculty: 114

Student-teacher ratio: 17:1

Full-time faculty: 101

Part-time faculty: 13

Faculty with doctorates or other terminal degrees: 38%

SCHOOL CALENDAR

1992–93: August 19–May 9 (semester hours)

Commencement and conferring of degrees: May

Two summer sessions.

DEGREES OFFERED AND NUMBER CONFERRED 1991–92:

Biology: 14

Business: 41

Communications: 13

Education: 26

Fine Arts: 3

Health: 11

Mathematics: 13

Public Affairs: 34

Social Science: 11

Theology: 2

SPECIAL PROGRAMS

Adult or Continuing Education Program is available for nontraditional students returning to school or working full time.

Advanced Placement (AP) grants college credit for postsecondary work completed in high school. Students scoring three on the AP test will receive credit by examination for each course.

Armed Forces Teacher Education for Retirees Program (AFTER) permits men and women who are within three years of retirement from the military to enroll in teacher education/certification classes.

Army and cooperative Air Force and Navy ROTC provide training in military science for commission as a second lieutenant in the U.S. Armed Forces. Two- and four-year scholarships are available.

College Level Examination Program (CLEP) determines the academic relevance of nontraditional educational experiences, such as the military, on-the-job training, or other life experiences, through a series of tests and may grant students college credit for these experiences.

College orientation is provided for one week during the summer at no cost to entering students.

Cooperative Study Abroad Program allows students to go to a foreign country for a specified period of time for part of their college education.

Health Careers Opportunity Program (HCOP) helps to prepare students for matriculation in the health professions and public health schools.

Honors program offers academically talented students a challenging program of study that includes special classes, seminars, colloquia, cultural activities, and special recognition to motivate participants.

Individualized majors allow students to create their own major program(s) of study.

An off-campus study center is available for students to pursue their educational goals while working toward their degree from Benedict.

Part-time degree program allow students to earn an undergraduate degree while attending part time.

Minority Access to Teacher Education (MATE) program at Benedict gives encouragement to high school students from rural areas who are academically talented and want to pursue a teaching career.

This program is sponsored in cooperation with the South Carolina Center for Teacher Recruitment housed at Winthrop College. Full financial aid is available for students who qualify.

Minority Access to Research Careers (MARC) program offers honors undergraduate training through a grant from the U.S. Department of Health, Education, and Welfare.

Minority Biomedical Research Support (MBRS) provides qualitative experiences in research related to the student's particular science field.

Remedial courses are offered to entering students to bring them up to admissions standards and to help them adjust for success in college.

South Carolina Criminal Justice Academy in cooperation with Benedict College allows state, county, and municipal employees to achieve recertification to maintain employment or to work toward a bachelor's degree in criminal justice.

Three/two dual degree programs in engineering with Georgia Institute of Technology, Southern College of Technology, Clemson University, and South Carolina State College are available. Student must complete three years at home school and two years at cooperating school. Upon completion of fourth year, student will receive a bachelor of science degree from matriculated school; upon completion of the program student will receive an engineering degree from cooperating school.

ATHLETIC PROGRAMS

Benedict College is a member of the National Collegiate Athletic Association (NCAA), Division II; the National Association of Intercollegiate Athletics (NAIA); and the Eastern Intercollegiate Athletic Conference (EIAC).

Intercollegiate sports: men's baseball, basketball, tennis, cross-country running, and track & field; women's basketball, soccer, volleyball, and tennis.

Intramural sports: basketball, tennis, track & field, and volleyball.

Athletic Contact

Dr. William Gunn, Athletic Director, Benedict College, Columbia, SC 29204; (803) 253-5331.

LIBRARY HOLDINGS

The Benjamin F. Payton Learning Resource Center holds 250,000 bound volumes, 215 microforms, 137 periodical subscriptions, 12,296 audiovisuals, and fifty computers for student use.

STUDENT LIFE

Special Regulations

Only cars with decals are permitted to park on campus.

Campus Services

Health center and personal and psychological counseling.

Campus Activities

Social and cultural activities include theater, band, dances, and the Benedict concert or gospel choir. Students may work on student-run publications or join the writer's club. Communication majors or student volunteers may get involved in the student-run radio station.

Leadership opportunities are found in the many organizations on campus such as the NAACP, the International Council, or the Foreign Language Club. Greek-letter fraternities include Alpha Phi Alpha, Kappa Alpha Psi, Omega Psi Phi, and Phi Beta Kappa; sororities include Alpha Kappa Alpha, Delta Sigma Theta, Sigma Gamma Rho, and Zeta Phi Beta. Honor societies represented on campus include Alpha Chi and Alpha Kappa Mu.

The campus is located within walking distance of downtown Columbia, the capital of South Carolina. Columbia (pop. approximately 98,000) offers social and cultural activities including several museums, an art gallery, and zoological park. Points of interest include Hampton-Preston Mansion and Garden, the South Carolina State Museum, and the State House.

Housing Availability

1,230 housing spaces. Two dormitories for men and four dormitories for women.

NOTABLE ALUMNI

Dr. Jacqueline D. Myers, 1971–Business professor, Alabama State College

Dr. Luns C. Richardson, 1949–President, Morris College.

CLAFLIN COLLEGE

HISTORY

Claflin College is a four-year, private, coed, liberal arts college affiliated with the United Methodist Church. Founded in 1869, the origin of Claflin College may be traced to Baker Biblical Institute, which was founded in 1866. In 1871, the then-named Claflin University and Baker Biblical Institute merged. The College Department of Claflin granted its first diploma in the year 1882. The property on which the present day college stands was formerly where the Orangeburg Female Academy was housed.

In 1872, the South Carolina General Assembly designated the South Carolina Agricultural and Mechanical Institute as a coordinate department of Claflin University. This arrangement remained intact until 1896 when the Act of Separation severed the State Agricultural and Mechanical Institute (SAMI) from Claflin; SAMI later became South Carolina State College.

Claflin's mission is to provide educational opportunities for students who desire a liberal arts education within a

College Ave. NE
Orangeburg, SC 29115
Phone: (803) 534-2710
Toll-free in-state:
800-922-1276

Total Enrollment:
900

Level of Selectivity:
Moderately
competitive

Motto:
A Tradition of Success

Christian environment. The curriculum centers around the Christian ethic, service to humankind, and appreciation of the cultural contributions of all people.

Located on 29 acres, the 17-building campus embraces both historic and modern buildings. This traditionally black college is a United Negro College Fund Member.

ACCREDITATION

Claflin College is accredited by the Southern Association of Colleges and Schools (SACS) to award the Bachelor of Arts and Bachelor of Science degrees.

Other Accreditation

American Medical Association

South Carolina Board of Education

University Senate of the United Methodist Church

COSTS PER YEAR

1992–93 Tuition: $4,230

Room and board: $2,280

Special fees: $250

Books: $500

Estimated total cost: $7,260

FINANCIAL AID

Financial Aid Specific to the School

95% of the student body received financial aid during 1991–92.

Approximately twenty endowed scholarships are available to students based on financial need and merit.

Athletic grant-in-aid scholarships are available to students participating in intercollegiate sports at this college.

Claflin College grant-in-aid is available to students who score 900 or more on the SAT. Grant covers room, board, tuition, and fees.

Performance scholarships are available in art, English, music, religion, and philoso-phy. Recipients must maintain a specific average and exemplify good moral character to retain scholarships.

Vocational Rehabilitation program provides financial assistance for students with mental and physical handicaps.

Cooperative Education Program alternates classroom study with related paid work experience. The program provides academic credit and full-time status during co-op placement. Qualifying students must have completed 45 credit hours at Claflin College.

United Negro College Fund (UNCF) scholarships are awarded to a limited number of students at this school who demonstrate financial need. Some scholarships may be based on location and merit. UNCF scholarships range from $500 to $7,500.

Army and Navy ROTC offer two- and three-year scholarships that pay tuition, fee, books, and other expenses, and provide a monthly stipend of $100.

Veterans Educational Benefits are available to qualifying veterans and their dependents.

South Carolina Tuition Grants are awarded on the basis of financial need and academic merit. Qualifying freshmen must rank in the upper three-fourths of high school class or score 800 or more on SAT. Continuing students must satisfactorily pass twenty-four credit hours. Grants are awarded on a first-come-first-served basis; apply by April 15. Contact the Tuition Grant Agency, 1310 Lady Street, PO Box 12159, Columbia, SC 29211.

United Methodist (UM) Loan is a low interest loan for students who are members of the UM Church. Undergraduate students may borrow between $900–$1,000 per year, but no more than $6,000 during student's educational program.

Financial Aid Deadline

March 31, Jan 1 (priority)

Financial Aid Contact

Mrs. Yvonne C. Clarkson, Director of Financial Aid, Claflin College, College Ave. NE., Orangeburg, SC 29115; (803) 534-2710; toll-free in South Carolina 800-922-1276.

Tingley Administration Building,
Claflin College

International students must submit official high school and college transcripts, take the TOEFL examination if native language is not English, and take SAT or ACT unless students are holders of GCE Level High School certificates. A $10 application fee in U.S dollars as a money order or certified check is required.

Admission Application Deadline

March 1 (fall); August 1 (spring); February 1 (summer)

Admission Contact

Mr. George F. Lee, Director of Admissions, Claflin College, College Ave. NE., Orangeburg, SC 29115; (803) 534-2710, ext 346; or 800-922-1276 (toll-free in state).

ADMISSION REQUIREMENTS

SAT or ACT required.

Entrance Requirements

Graduation from an accredited high school and completion of 16 to 18 units to include: 4 English, 2 mathematics, 2 social studies, 1 science, and 8 electives. Students need recommendation from high school principal, guidance counselor, or homeroom teacher; submit certificate of medical exam; students older than nineteen must pass the Carolina high school certificate examination. A $10 application fee should be submitted with application.

GED students must have a score of not less than 35 on any part of the test and a general average of 45 or more.

Transfer students must submit official transcripts from previous secondary schools or colleges attended showing a 2.0 minimum GPA; must submit SAT scores if less than 60 semester hours earned at a previous educational institution.

GRADUATION REQUIREMENTS

A minimum of 120 semester hours and completion of core requirements to include: 9 hours of English, 5 hours of math, 8 hours of science, 20 hours of humanities, 6 hours of a foreign language, and 1 computer course. Students must complete at least 30 hours and 2 semesters, including senior year, at Claflin.

Grading System

A–F; I=Incomplete; WP=Withdrew-Passing; WF=Withdrew-Failing; X=Absent from Examination; Z=Re-enroll in part of a two part course.

STUDENT BODY PROFILE

Total enrollment (male/female): 360/540

From in-state: 747

Other regions: 21 states, 7 foreign countries

Full-time undergraduates (male/female): 348/522

Part-time undergraduates (male/female): 12/18

Ethnic/Racial Makeup

African American, 882; International, 18.

Class of 1995 Profile

Number of applicants: 624

Number accepted: 393

Number enrolled: 220

Transfers enrolled: 31

FACULTY PROFILE

Number of faculty: 63

Student-teacher ratio: 14:1

Full-time faculty: 54

Part-time faculty: 9

Faculty with doctorates or other terminal degrees: 50%

SCHOOL CALENDAR

1992–93: August 14–May 7 (semester hours)

Commencement and conferring of degrees: May 8

One summer session.

DEGREES OFFERED 1991–92:

Bachelor of Arts

American Studies

Art Education

English

French

History

Music

Music Education

Religion and Philosophy

Sociology

Bachelor of Science

Accounting

Applied Math and Engineering Technology

Biology

Biology Education

Business Administration

Chemistry

Computer Science

Elementary Education

Management

Marketing

Math Education

Mathematics

Science

SPECIAL PROGRAMS

Accelerated Study Program allows students to complete their undergraduate degree in a shorter period of time than the traditional period of four years.

Advanced Placement (AP) grants college credit for postsecondary work completed in high school. Students scoring three to five on the AP test will receive credit by examination for each course and advanced placement.

College orientation is offered at no cost for one week prior to the beginning of classes to acquaint entering students with the college and to prepare them for college life.

Cooperative Education Program alternates classroom study with related paid work experience. The program provides academic credit and full-time status during co-op placement.

Honors program offers academically talented students classes in which instruction is fast paced, student dialogue is encouraged, original writing is required, and reflective thinking is demanded. Seminars are designed to facilitate an understanding of leadership.

Remedial courses are offered to entering students to bring them up to admission standards and to help them adjust for success in college.

ROTC provides training in military science for commission as a second lieutenant in the U.S. Armed Forces. Two- and four-year scholarships are available.

ATHLETIC PROGRAMS

Claflin is a member of the National Association of Intercollegiate Athletics (NAIA) and the Eastern Intercollegiate Athletic Conference (EIAC).

Intercollegiate sports: men's basketball, tennis, and track & field; women's basketball, softball, tennis, track & field, softball, and volleyball.

Intramural sports: basketball, softball, tennis, track & field, and volleyball.

LIBRARY HOLDINGS

The Hubert Vernon Manning Library holds 140,000 volumes, 4,700 microforms, 3,400 audiovisuals, 320 current periodical subscriptions, 441 periodicals on microforms, and 125 computers available for student use in computer center. Special collections include the Wilbur R. Gregg Black Collection and a collection of microfilmed copies of African-American material filmed from the famed Schomburg Collection.

STUDENT LIFE

Campus Regulations

Class attendance required; freshman orientation required; cars must be registered.

Campus Services

Health center, personal counseling, testing service, religious activities, and free use of textbooks the following semester for students earning a 4.0 GPA.

Campus Activities

Social and cultural activities include band and chorale. Interested students may work on *The Panther* (student-run newspaper) or the *Les Memoirs* (yearbook).

Leadership opportunities are found in the Student Government Association (SGA) or the more than thirty-six clubs and organizations, including the Men's and Women's Personnel Council, which monitors the wholesome living of students. Some of the academic organizations are the Earth Science Club, Alpha Rho Tau Art Club, Banneker II Mathematics Club, and Alpha Kappa Mu National Honor Society. The Student Christian Association, Church School, and the Oxford Club are religious organizations. Social and cultural groups include the Off-Campus Panthers, NAACP, Theater Guild, and the National Pre-Alumni Council of the United Negro College Fund. Greek-letter fraternities include Alpha Phi Alpha, Kappa Alpha Psi, Omega Psi Phi, and Phi Beta Sigma; sororities include Alpha Kappa Alpha, Delta Sigma Theta, Sigma Gamma Rho, and Zeta Phi Beta.

Claflin College is located in Orangeburg, South Carolina, within walking distance of downtown. Orangeburg hosts the South Carolina Festival of Roses and the county fair each year. Points of interest include the Edisto Gardens and the National Fish Hatchery. Claflin is forty miles from Columbia, the state capital, where students have access to museums, a zoological garden, churches, the state house, the Woodrow Wilson Boyhood Home, shopping, dining, and recreational activities, such as canoeing, hiking, and fishing.

Housing Availability

559 housing spaces; Asbury, Corson, Dunton, and a temporary dormitory are for women; men are housed in the high rise.

NOTABLE ALUMNI

Robert L. Alford, Ph.D–Director of testing, Norfolk State University

Joseph Bethea–Bishop, SC Conference of United Methodist Church

Ernest A. Finney Jr., 1952–Associate judge, South Carolina Supreme Court

Jonas P. Kennedy, M.D.–Millionaire turkey farmer

Mary Honor Wright–Educator who established several schools in Spartanburg, SC

CLINTON JUNIOR COLLEGE

PO Box 968
Rock Hill, SC 29731
Phone: (803) 327-7402
or (803) 327-5587

Total Enrollment:
200

Level of Selectivity:
Noncompetitive

HISTORY

Clinton Junior College is a two-year, private, coed, liberal arts college affiliated with the American Methodist Episcopal (AME) Church. It was founded in 1894 by the AME Zion Church to eradicate illiteracy among the freedmen of South Carolina. In 1909, the college was incorporated as Clinton Normal and Industrial College. An amended charter changed the name to Clinton Junior College in 1956.

Clinton Junior designs and implements an educational program that helps students lead moral, spiritual, and productive lives. Clinton is committed to both a liberal arts education and vocational training.

Situated on 20 acres, the 7-building campus includes a newly built library.

ACCREDITATION

Clinton Junior College is accredited by the U.S. Department of Education to award the Associate of Arts degree.

COSTS PER YEAR

1992–93 Tuition: $1,250

Room and board: $1,890

Special fees: $320

Books: $250

Estimated total cost: $3,710

FINANCIAL AID

Financial Aid Specific to the School

50% of the student body received financial aid during 1991–92.

College work-aid is available to those students not qualifying for college work-study to work in departments of the college.

Deferred Payment Plan allows students to pay college costs in two to three installments during the semester.

Scholarships are available for students based on merit and financial need.

Veteran's benefits are available for veterans to help defer college costs.

Financial Aid Contact

Financial Aid Committee, Financial Aid Office, Clinton Junior College, Rock Hill, SC 29731; (803) 327-7402 or 5587.

ADMISSION REQUIREMENTS

Open admissions

Entrance Requirements

Graduation from an accredited high school with a minimum of 21 units to include 4 English, 2 science (laboratory science), 2 history, 3 math, 2 units in foreign language, literature, social science, or additional science, and 8 electives; a minimum "C" average; two recommendations; and in some cases interviews. A $10 non-refundable application fee required.

GED students must meet basic admission requirements.

Transfer students must submit official high school transcript with GPA and class rank, official transcripts of all previous college work, and a recommendation from an official at last school attended. Entrance test waived if applicant was a full-time student at previous college; maximum transfer is 30 semester hours.

International students are sought out by Clinton Junior College, but none are presently enrolled.

Admission Application Deadline

Rolling admissions provides no specific date for notification of admission so applicant is informed as soon as admission decision is made.

Admission Contact

Miss Patrice Dixon, Director of Admissions, Clinton Junior College, Rock Hill, SC 29731; (803) 327-5587 or (803) 327-7402.

GRADUATION REQUIREMENTS

A minimum of 64 hours and completion of a core program to include: 12 hours of English, 6 hours of mathematics, 8 hours of science, 12 hours of social studies (government, world geography, and U.S. history), 6 hours of French, 1 hour of freshman orientation, and 2 hours of physical education; minimum 30 semester hours in residence; must attend graduation. $30 graduation fee.

Grading System

A–F; I=Incomplete; W=Withdrawal (by 2/3 of semester); WF=Withdrawal with unsatisfactory work; and FA or NA=Failure or No Credit.

STUDENT BODY PROFILE

Total enrollment (male/female): 80/120

FACULTY PROFILE

Number of faculty: 12

Student-teacher ratio: 17:1

SCHOOL CALENDAR

1992–93: August–May (semester hours)

Commencement and conferring of degrees: May 12

No summer session.

DEGREES OFFERED 1991–92

Business Administration

Business Commerce

Business Education

Business Management

Liberal Arts/General Studies

SPECIAL PROGRAMS

Adult/Continuing Education Program is available for nontraditional students returning to school or employed full time.

College orientation is offered to entering students at no cost prior to the beginning of classes to acquaint students with the college and to prepare them for college life.

Student Support Services provide students with financial planning, health career counseling, and personal and social counseling.

The Probationary Counseling Program exists to address the needs and problems of students with weak academic skills.

ATHLETIC PROGRAMS

Intramural sports: basketball, tennis, track, and volleyball.

LIBRARY HOLDINGS

The library holds 15,000 bound volumes, 68 periodical subscriptions, and 600 pamphlets.

STUDENT LIFE

Special Regulations

New freshmen and transfer students must register in person; freshman orientation mandatory; resident students required to purchase meals in the college dining room; students should attend all classes; no more than 6 of the final 30 hours toward the degree can be taken at another institution.

Campus Services

Health services, personal, social and pastoral counseling, career planning, religious services, financial and probationary counseling.

Campus Activities

Social activities include theater and chorale. Leadership opportunities are found in the Student Government Association (SGA) or the various academic clubs such as history, biology, drama, or French.

Clinton Junior College is located in the heart of the growing, industrial Piedmont area, within the city limits of Rock Hill, South Carolina. Rock Hill has a population of approximately 46,000. Twenty-five miles to the south is Charlotte, North Carolina, a progressively developing city. Columbia, South Carolina, is 72 miles north. Several major highways lend easy access to both Charlotte and Columbia.

Housing Availability

Two hundred housing spaces; freshman housing guaranteed; Cauthen Hall houses female students and Marshall Hall houses male students.

DENMARK TECHNICAL COLLEGE

HISTORY

Denmark Technical College (DTC) is a two-year, state-supported, coed college founded in 1947, after South Carolina's General Assembly authorized the establishment of an institution of higher learning to educate black citizens in a variety of trades. The school opened in 1948 as the Denmark Branch of the South Carolina Trade School System. In 1969, the name changed to Denmark Technical Education Center. After receiving full accreditation from the Southern Association of Colleges in 1979, the school adopted its present name, Denmark Technical College.

Denmark Tech was directed by the State Board of Technical and Comprehensive Education to serve a statewide population because of its uniqueness as the only technical school in the state with resident facilities for students. Denmark Tech serves the broad educational needs of the people of South Carolina by offering a diversity of programs at a cost consistent with the economic status of its constituents. Dr. Douglas W. Brister, the interim president,

Solomon Blatt Blvd.
PO Box 327
Denmark, SC
29042-0327
Phone: (803) 793-3301
Fax: (803) 793-5942

Total Enrollment:
725

Level of Selectivity:
Noncompetitive

relays, "Your community college offers high quality, affordable education; in a friendly, relaxed atmosphere, designed to help you achieve your education or career goals."

Located on 53 acres, the 15-building campus includes modern facilities, a campus park, and picnic shelters for meetings and recreation.

ACCREDITATION

Denmark Technical College is accredited by the Southern Association of Colleges and Schools to award the Associate of Arts and Associate of Science degrees, as well as certificates and diplomas.

COSTS PER YEAR

1992–93 Tuition: $840 (in-state); $1,920 (out-state)

Room and board: $1,198 (room); $1,396 (board)

Special fees: $80

Books: $400

Estimated total cost: $3,914 (in-state); $4,994 (out-state)

FINANCIAL AID

1991–92 Federal and State Funding

Number of scholarships and grants: 1,101

Total amount of scholarships and grants: $1,082,110

Range of scholarships and grants: $100–$2,400

Number of loans: 481

Total amount of loans: $841,118

Range of loans: $200–$2,625

Number of work-study: 243

Total amount of work-study: $187,729

Range of work-study: $300–$1,600

Financial Aid Specific to the School

96% of the student body received financial in 1991–92.

Merit scholarships are available to a limited number students based on academic performance and achievement. Students qualify for awards after they have entered Denmark Technical.

National Guard Tuition Assistance Program provides up to $500 per calendar year for current members of the South Carolina Guard.

Veterans and other persons eligible for VA benefits can receive financial aid to pay for tuition and fees. For full-time students, awards range from $488 per month to $555 per month or more depending on number of dependents. Contact Veterans Affairs Office for more information.

Veterans Educational Assistance Program (VEAP) provides awards ranging from $150–$225 per year for full-time training for veterans who were on active duty in the service.

Financial Aid Deadline

April 15 (priority); May 1 (fall); Nov 1 (spring)

Financial Aid Contact

Mrs. Clara B. Moses, Manager of Student Financial Aid, Denmark Technical College, PO Box 327, Denmark, SC 29042; (803) 793-3301.

ADMISSION REQUIREMENTS

Open admissions. ASSET test required for placement.

Entrance Requirements

Official high school transcript from an accredited high school; must be 18 years of age; resident student must provide proof of required immunizations; student must schedule and take ASSET test by contacting the counseling office; a $5.00 non-refundable application fee is required.

GED students must submit copy of GED certificate with a $5.00 non-refundable application fee; student must schedule to take ASSET test by contacting the counseling office.

Transfer students must submit official transcript from previous school(s) attended and must have at least a "C" or better GPA.

International Students must score 500 or better on the TOEFL examination or submit official report from an English language institute or program within the U.S; must submit financial proof of ability to pay all college cost and pay an advanced deposit of tuition for one full year; must provide proof of health insurance coverage. A $5 non-refundable application fee is required.

Early admission may be granted to high school graduates from the counties of Allendale, Bamberg and Barnwell who are under age 18; must have written approval from the principal and meet basic admission requirements.

Advanced standing transfer credit may be applied for students who attended another accredited post-secondary educational facility; a non-refundable $5.00 application fee must accompany application.

Admission Application Deadline

Rolling admission (fall and spring) provides no specific date for notification of admission so applicant is informed as soon as admission decision is made.

Admission Contact

Mrs. Iris D. Bomar, Director of Enrollment Services, Office of Admissions and Records. Denmark Technical College, PO Box 327, Denmark, SC 29042; (803) 793-3301. Fax: (803) 793-5942.

GRADUATION REQUIREMENTS

A minimum of 102.5 credits with one math course, one computer course for business, accounting, engineering graphics technology, and electronic engineering technology. A minimum cumulative grade point average of 2.0 and at least a "C" in major course of study is needed.

Grading System

A-F; I=Incomplete; W=Withdrawal; S=Satisfactory; SC=Satisfactory Completion; WF=Unofficial Withdrawal; E=Exempt; Au=Audit.

STUDENT BODY PROFILE

Total enrollment (male/female): 326/399

From in-state: 707

Other regions: three states; one foreign country

Full-time undergraduates (male/female): 288/353

Part-time undergraduates (male/female): 36/48

Ethnic/Racial Makeup

African American, 690; Caucasian, 30; international, 5.

Class of 1995 Profile

Number of applicants: 1,507

Number accepted: 744

Number enrolled: 541

Transfer applicants: 35

Transfers accepted: 30

Transfers enrolled: 23

FACULTY PROFILE

Number of faculty: 45

Student-teacher ratio: 16:1

Full-time faculty: 39

Part-time faculty: 6

SCHOOL CALENDAR

1992–93: August 24–May 7 (semesters)

Commencement and conferring of degrees: May 8

One summer session.

DEGREES OFFERED 1991–92:

Associate Degrees

Automotive Technology

Computer Technology

Criminal Justice

Electronics Technology

General Business

General Technology

Human Services

Office Systems Technology

One-Year Diploma Programs

Automated Office

Barbering

Cosmetology

Culinary Arts

Industrial Electricity/Electronics

Machine Tool

Tailoring

Welding

Technical Certificates

Advanced Welding

Automotive Heating/Air Conditioning

Automotive Transmission/Transaxle

Brick Masonry

Carpentry

Computer Operations

Criminal Justice

Culinary Arts (Food Services)

Data Entry

Electrical Systems Repair

Electromechanical Engineering Technology

Electronics Technology

Engine Performance Repair

Industrial Electricity/Electronics

Plumbing

Specialized Welding

Welding

Word Processing

SPECIAL PROGRAMS

The Continuing Education Program offers courses and activities, including occupational upgrading and professional development, and other workshops and one day seminars for community residents.

The Cooperative Education Program in conjunction with Voorhees College allows students at both schools to take courses not available on their own campuses at no additional cost.

The Cooperative Education Program allows students to work in their chosen field while receiving up to four credit hours per semester.

The Cooperative ROTC Program allows students at DTC to take military science training in cooperation with South Carolina State College in Orangeburg. Transportation to the campus is provided free of charge. Tuition allowances can be made for students who elect this ROTC program during their junior and senior years at a four-year institution.

The Transitional Studies Program provides remedial courses for high school students and adults to develop academic skills needed to ensure success in college. Students can also prepare for the GED examination.

Veterans who are eligible under the G.I. Bill may receive training from Denmark Tech. Monthly rates for full-time training currently range from $150–$225 per month which is dependent upon the total amount contributed during active service. The Veterans Educational Assistance Program (VEAP) does not pay benefits for tutorial assistance or dependents.

ATHLETIC PROGRAMS

Intercollegiate sports: men's basketball and baseball; women's basketball and softball.

Intramural Sports: baseball, basketball, football, and volleyball.

LIBRARY HOLDINGS

DTC's Learning Resource Center contains more than 18,585 bound volumes, 192 periodical subscriptions, 35 audiovisuals, and 40 computers for student use.

STUDENT LIFE

Special Regulations

The Residence Agreement contract must be signed by any student for at least a one year residence.

Campus Services

Health center, personal and psychological counseling, tutoring, and testing.

Campus Activities

Social and group activities include choir and theater. Miss Denmark Technical College Coronation and Ball is one of the highlights of the social scene. Students at DTC look forward to Founders Day, Homecoming, and Senior Day. A newsletter is published to keep the student body informed.

Leadership opportunities can be found in the Student Government Association (SGA), the vehicle by which the students share in the administration of the college. Two national Greek-letter fraternities and sororities are active on campus, as well as three local fraternities and sororities. Honor societies include the Kappa Chapter of Alpha Delta Omega National Honor Society. Membership in Phi Theta Kappa, the only national fraternity that recognizes intellectual achievement in American Junior Colleges, is only given to students with 12 semester hours completed with a cumulative grade point ratio of 3.5.

This rural campus is located in a quiet town near the center of the state. Student transportation is provided to a shopping center not far from the campus. Bus service is available for surrounding communities. The campus is 50 miles from Columbia, South Carolina, and Augusta, Georgia, with historic Charleston only 85 miles away.

A variety of social and cultural activities can be found in these nearby cities.

Housing Availability

275 housing spaces. Freshman housing guaranteed.

Handicapped Services

Includes wheelchair accessibility. A counselor is appointed to students with disabilities.

MORRIS COLLEGE

North Main St.
Sumter, SC 29150
Phone: (803) 775-9371
Fax: (803) 773-3687

Total Enrollment:
792

Level of Selectivity:
Noncompetitive

Motto:
Enter to learn; depart
to serve

HISTORY

Morris College (MC) is a four-year, private, coed, liberal arts college affiliated with the Baptist Church. It was founded in 1908 "for the Christian and intellectual training of negro youth." Teacher education and certification were the primary goals. The school was founded by impoverished blacks without any formal education who possessed an unshakable faith in God and a need to provide others with the educational opportunities they did not have. This mission signaled the beginning of a heroic venture in higher education by a group of men and women less than a half century removed from the blight of American slavery.

The original normal program was discontinued in 1929, and the following year the elementary school was no longer in operation. During the next two years, Morris was a junior college only. A full four-year program was resumed in 1933, and the high school level was terminated in 1946.

As the enrollees at Morris College continued striving for Christian and intellectual goals, only African-Americans were in attendance.

It wasn't until 1961 that the doors of Morris College opened to all ethnic groups. Presently, a center for training teachers and ministers, it continues to promote the intellectual and personal develop of each student it admits.

The 16-building, 33-acre campus is a blend of buildings built from the 1920s to the 1980s, including the president's home build in 1986. MC is unique as one of few senior colleges built and operated solely under the auspices of African-Americans.

ACCREDITATION

Morris College is accredited by the Southern Association of Colleges and Schools to award the Bachelor of Arts and Bachelor of Science degrees.

Other Accreditation

South Carolina State Department of Education

COSTS PER YEAR

1992–93 Tuition: $4,026

Room and board: $1,061 (room); $1,373 (board)

Special fees: $210

Books: $500

Estimated total cost: $7,170

FINANCIAL AID

1991–92 Institutional Funding

Number of scholarships and grants: 55

Total amount of scholarships and grants: $52,819

Range of scholarships and grants: $200–$1,000

1991–92 Federal and State Funding

Number of scholarships and grants: 775

Total amount of scholarships and grants: $2,165,108

Range of scholarships and grants: $200–$2,400

Number of loans: 587

Total amount of loans: $1,392,575

Range of loans: $500–$4,000

Number of work-study: 387

Total amount of work-study: $364,941

Range of work-study: $500–$2,000

Financial Aid Specific to the School

98% of the student body received financial aid during 1991–92.

Endowed, friends, and corporation scholarships number over 26 and are based on academic merit, need, and special interest.

Presidential scholarships are available for entering students who have above average high school records, rank in the upper fifth of their graduating class, and apply for the scholarship by April 15. Awards range from $500–$1,500 per year and are renewable each year the student maintains a "B" average. Contact the Office of Admission and Records, Morris College, North Main St., Sumter, SC 29150; (803) 775-9371, ext. 225.

Cooperative Education Program alternates and combines classroom study with related paid work experience. The program provides academic credit and full-time status during co-op placement.

United Negro College Fund (UNCF) scholarships are awarded to a limited number of students at this school who demonstrate financial need. Some scholarships maybe based on location and merit. UNCF scholarships range from $500 to $7,500.

Army ROTC offers two- and four-year scholarships that pay tuition, fees, books, and other expenses, and provides a monthly stipend of $100.

South Carolina Tuition Grants are available to students who are residents of the state and who demonstrate financial need.

South Carolina Teachers Loan Program is available for students who are pursuing a career in teacher education. Repayment of loan can be made by teaching in the South Carolina public school or by repaying the loan with cash at a low interest rate.

Financial Aid Deadline

April 30

Financial Aid Contact

Ms. Sandra S. Gibson, Director of Financial Aid, Morris College, Sumter, SC 29150; (803) 775-9371 ext 238.

ADMISSION REQUIREMENTS

SAT or ACT used for counseling and placement, but is not required.

Entrance Requirements

Graduation from an accredited high school and completion of the following 18 units: 4 English, 2 mathematics, 1 natural science, 2 social sciences, 1 U.S. history, and 7 electives. Must have a health exam by physician and take a placement test in English and mathematics. A $10 non-refundable application fee is required.

GED students must meet basic admission requirements and submit scores from GED tests with GED certificate.

Transfer students must submit an official transcript from previously attended colleges and high school and submit evidence of an honorable release from previous college. Only grades of "C" or above can be transferred.

International students must meet basic admission requirements; students from non-English-speaking countries must pass TOEFL exam and apply at least ninety days prior to expected entrance date.

Admission Application Deadline

Rolling admission provides no specific date for notification of admission so applicant is informed as soon as admission decision is made.

Admission Contact

Mrs. Queen W. Spann, Admissions and Records Officer, Morris College, 100 West College St., Sumter, SC 29150-3599; (803) 775-9371, ext. 225; Fax: (803) 773-3678.

GRADUATION REQUIREMENTS

A minimum of 124 credit hours and completion of core requirements to include six mathematics, and six science credit hours and a 2.0 GPA. Students must pass English and math proficiency test, take written exit exam, complete last thirty hours and senior year in residence at Morris College, and participate in commencement exercises. A $25 graduation fee is required.

Grading System

A-F; U=unsatisfactory; S=satisfactory; I=Incomplete; X=absence from the final exam; WP=Withdraw Passing; WF=Withdraw Failing, and AU=audit.

STUDENT BODY PROFILE

Total enrollment (male/female): 261/531

From in-state: 712

Other regions: 18 states

Full-time undergraduates (male/female): 272/503

Part-time undergraduates (male/female): 8/9

Ethnic/Racial Makeup

African American, 791; Caucasian, 1.

Class of 1995 Profile

Number of applicants: 849

Number accepted: 690

Number enrolled: 295

Transfer applicants: 156

Transfers accepted: 53

Transfers enrolled: 53

FACULTY PROFILE

Number of faculty: 65

Student-teacher ratio: 14:1

Full-time faculty (male/female): 44

Part-time faculty (male/female): 21

Faculty with doctorates or other terminal degrees: 45%

SCHOOL CALENDAR

1992–93: August 17–May 7 (semester hours)

Commencement and conferring of degrees: May 26

Two summer sessions.

DEGREES OFFERED AND NUMBER CONFERRED 1991:

Community Health: n/a

English: n/a

Fine Arts: 6

French: n/a

History: 2

Music: n/a

Philosophy/Religion: 12

Political Science History: 18

Religious Studies: n/a

Social Work: n/a

Sociology: 25

Bachelor of Science

Accounting: n/a

Biology: 2

Business Administration: 41

Chemistry: n/a

Chemistry Education: n/a

Computer Information Science: n/a

Early Childhood Education: 2

Elementary Education: 2

French Education: n/a

Health Science/Community Health: 4

Liberal Studies: 13

Marketing: n/a

Mathematics: n/a

Mathematics Education: 5

Music Education: n/a

Office Administration: n/a

Psychology Education: n/a

Recreation Education: 7

Social Studies: 5

Special Education: n/a

SPECIAL PROGRAMS

Accelerated Study Program allows students to complete their undergraduate degree in a shorter period of time than the traditional period of four years.

College Level Examination Program (CLEP) determines the academic relevance of nontraditional educational experiences, such as the military, on-the-job training or other life experiences, through a series of tests and may grant students college credit for these experiences.

College orientation is offered to entering students for three days at no cost prior to the beginning of classes to acquaint students with the college and to prepare them for college life; parents may attend.

Cooperative Education Program alternates and combines classroom study with related paid work experience. The program provides academic credit and full-time status during co-op placement.

English as a Second Language is a program that offers courses in English for students whose native language is not English.

Honors program offers academically talented students a challenging program of study that includes special classes, seminars, colloquia, cultural activities, and special recognition to motivate participants.

The Minority Science Improvement Program (MSIP) provides the use of computers to support classroom instruction in the areas if mathematics, biology, and physics.

Remedial courses are offered to entering students to bring them up to admission standards and to help them adjust for success in college.

ROTC provides training in military science for commission as a second lieutenant in the U.S. Army. Two- and four-year scholarships are available.

ATHLETIC PROGRAMS

Morris College is a member of the National Association of Intercollegiate Athletics (NAIA).

Intercollegiate sports: men's baseball, basketball, and track; women's basketball, softball, and track.

Intramural sports: basketball, football, tennis, and volleyball.

Athletic Contact

Mr. Clarence Houck, Morris College, North Main St., Sumter, SC 29150; (803) 775-9371, ext. 235.

LIBRARY HOLDINGS

The Carnegie Library, housed in the L. C. Richardson-W. A. Johnson Learning Resource Center, holds 90,800 bound volumes, 117,800 microforms, 591 periodical subscriptions, 1,775 audiovisuals, and 60 computers for student use in the library and science building.

STUDENT LIFE

Special Regulations

Freshmen must live on campus the first year; cars must be registered for a fee; the campus has curfews. Teacher education majors must take the National Teacher Examination (NTE) before assigned to student teaching.

Campus Services

Health center, personal and psychological counseling, career counseling and placement, tutoring, religious services, and activities.

Campus Activities

Social and cultural activities include theater, chorale, and dance. Students may get involved in the *Hornet* (student-run newspaper) or the *Menagerie* (yearbook). Communication majors or volunteers may work at the student radio station or the television station.

Leadership opportunities are found in the Student Government Association or the various other clubs, such as the Chess Club. Greek Letter fraternities include Alpha Phi Alpha, Kappa Alpha Psi, Omega Psi Phi, and Phi Beta Sigma; sororities include Alpha Kappa Alpha, Delta Sigma Theta, Sigma Gamma Rho Sorority, and Zeta Phi Beta. The Alpha Kappa Mu National Honor Society promotes high scholarship and service and is open to junior and senior students who satisfy the academic requirements.

College Assemblies are held every Monday except during Thanksgiving week. Religious activities are an integral part of campus life. During Religious Emphasis Week, the college community has an opportunity to place special emphasis on worship and religious ideals.

Morris College is located in the city of Sumter, South Carolina, with a population of over 40,000. Mass air and rail transportation are approximately 60 miles and 40 miles respectively from the city. Columbia, the capital of South Carolina is thirty miles away. Sumter offers students shopping, dining, a museum, and an art gallery. Whitewater rafting, camping, hiking, canoeing, and horseback riding are nearby at the Sumter National Forest.

Housing Availability

550 housing spaces; freshmen given priority; freshman only housing; three women's dormitories; two men's dormitories.

NOTABLE ALUMNI

Ralph W. Canty, D.D., 1967,70,78–Past president, National Progressive Baptist Convention

Arthenia Bates Millican, Ph.D, 1941–Retired educator; writer

SOUTH CAROLINA STATE UNIVERSITY

South Carolina State College

HISTORY

South Carolina State University (SCSU) is a four-year, state-supported, coed, liberal arts institution founded in 1872 as South Carolina Agricultural and Mechanical Institute. From 1872 to 1895, SCSU existed within the institution of Claflin College. In 1895, the South Carolina General Assembly enacted legislation for the severance of SCSU from Claflin.

SCSU opened independent of Claflin in 1896 as a land grant institution under the name of the Colored Normal Industrial Agricultural and Mechanical College of South Carolina. The name changed to South Carolina State College in 1954. With an expanded mission to provide programs in advanced study, the school received university status in 1992 and thus adopted its present name.

Traditionally, this college has focused on teacher education, research, and service. As a land grant institution, SCSU is committed to providing undergraduate instruction that combines liberal arts with vocational education. SCSU

PO Box 1568
Orangeburg, SC
29117-0001
Phone: (803) 536-7000
or (803) 536-7185
Fax: (803) 536-8622

Total Enrollment:
5,145

Level of Selectivity:
Slightly competitive

Motto:
Knowledge,
Duty, Honor

is also committed to community service, offering programs related to agriculture, as well as adult and continuing education.

The 60-building campus is situated on 160 acres, with a variety of architectural styles. An additional 286 acres are located at Camp Daniel in Elloree, South Carolina. The campus facilities include the Martin Luther King, Jr. Auditorium, Henderson-Davis Theater, Hodge Hall, and Duke Gymnasium and Performing Arts Center, a state-of-the-art facility.

ACCREDITATION

South Carolina State University is accredited by the Southern Association of Colleges and Schools (SACS) to award the Bachelor of Arts, Bachelor of Science, and Master's degrees.

Other Accreditation

Accreditation Board for Engineering and Technology (ABET)

American Dietetics Association

Career College Association/Accrediting Commission for Independent Colleges and Schools

Council for Professional Development of the American Home Economics Association

Council of Rehabilitation Education, Inc.

International Association of Counseling Service, Inc.

National Council for Accreditation of Teacher Education

COSTS PER YEAR

1992–93 Tuition: $1,950 (in-state); $3,980 (out-state)

Room and board: $1,316 (room); $1,420 (board)

Special fees: $125

Books: $600

Estimated total cost: $5,411 (in-state); $7,441 (out-state)

FINANCIAL AID

1991–92 Institutional Funding

Number of scholarships and grants: 327

Total amount of scholarships and grants: $197,458

1991–92 Federal and State Funding

Number of scholarships and grants: 3,230

Total amount of scholarships and grants: $6,058,514

Number of loans: 2,852

Total amount of loans: $8,214,009

Number of work-study: 386

Total amount of work-study: $412,943

Financial Aid Specific to the School

33% of the student body received financial aid during 1991–92.

Endowed, alumni, friends, and corporate scholarships number over 55; they are awarded based on merit, need, and interest. Awards range from $500 to $2,000 yearly.

Performance scholarships in music are available to talented students participating band or choir.

Athletic scholarships are available for students participating in intercollegiate sports.

Cooperative Education Program alternates classroom study with related paid work experience. The program provides academic credit and full-time status during co-op placement.

Thurgood Marshall Black Education Fund provides a four-year scholarship at this public black college. Qualifying students must have a high school GPA of 3.0 or better and a SAT score of 1000 or ACT score of 24 or more. Students must be recommended by high school counselor as exceptional or exemplary in the creative or performing arts. Scholarship pays tuition, fees, room, and board, not to exceed $6,000 annually.

Army and Air Force ROTC offer two- and four-year scholarships that pay tuition, fees, books, and other expenses, and provide a monthly stipend of $100.

Financial Aid Deadline
June 1 (fall); November 1 (spring)

Financial Aid Contact
Mrs. Margaret C. Black, Director of Financial Aid, South Carolina, State College, Wilkinson Hall, PO Box 1886, Orangeburg, SC 29117; (803) 536-7067.

ADMISSION REQUIREMENTS
SAT (700; 750 out-state) or ACT (16 composite)

Entrance Requirements
Graduation from an accredited high school and completion of the following units: 4 English, 2 mathematics, 2 science, 2 social studies, and 2 foreign language; official high school transcript; cumulative "C" average; achievement tests and English composition test for counseling and placement; and a recent physical exam. A $15 non-refundable application fee is required.

GED students must meet basic admission standards and have a cumulative "C" score.

Transfer students must submit college transcript showing a minimum 2.0 GPA from an accredited two-year or four-year institution; submit results of standardized test scores.

International students must take the TOEFL exam and show evidence of ability to pay all college costs.

Admission Application Deadline
July 31; rolling admission provides no specific date for notification of admission so applicant is informed as soon as admission decision is made.

Admission Contact
Mrs. Bennie Mayfield, Dean of Enrollment Management, South Carolina State College, Wilkinson Hall, Orangeburg, SC 29117; (803) 536-7185.

GRADUATION REQUIREMENTS
A minimum of 120 semester hours and completion of core requirements to include the following hours: 6 mathematics, 6 science, and 1 computer course for math, business, engineering, and nursing majors; ROTC or 4 physical education courses; completion of Senior Exit Survey; passing of English Competency Exam; and last 30 hours in residence.

Grading System
A-F; W=Withdraw; S=Satisfactory; U=Unsatisfactory; I=Incomplete;

STUDENT BODY PROFILE
Total enrollment (male/female): 2,109/3,036

From in-state: 4,631

Other regions: 6 states and 8 foreign countries

Full-time undergraduates (male/female): 1,644/2,379

Part-time undergraduates (male/female): 314/453

Graduate students (male/female): 145/210

Ethnic/Racial Makeup
African American, 4,785; Asian, 51; Caucasian, 257; International, 52.

Class of 1995 Profile
Number of applicants: 2,754

Number accepted: 1,928

Number enrolled: 848

Median SAT score: 700 (combined)

Median ACT score: 16

Average high school GPA: 2.50

Transfers enrolled: 515

FACULTY PROFILE
Number of faculty: 241

Student-teacher ratio: 19:1

Full-time faculty: 212

Part-time faculty: 29

Faculty with doctorates or other terminal degrees: 65%

SCHOOL CALENDAR

1992–93: August 17–May 5 (semester hours)

Commencement and conferring of degrees: May 9

Two summer sessions.

DEGREES OFFERED 1991–92:

Bachelor of Arts

Accounting

Agribusiness

Art

Art Education

Art: Printmaking

Biology

Business Economics

Business Education

Chemistry

Civil Engineering Technology

Computer Science

Criminal Justice

Drama

Early Childhood Education

Electrical Engineering Technology

Elementary Education

English

French

Food and Nutrition

Health Education

History

Bachelor of Science

Home Economics in Business

Home Economics Education

Industrial Technology Education

Management

Marketing

Mathematics

Mechanical Engineering Technology

Music

Music Merchandising

Nursing

Office Management and Administration

Physical Education

Physics

Psychology

Sociology

Social Studies

Social Work

Spanish

Special Education

Speech Pathology and Audiology

Pre-Professional Degrees

Agriculture

Dentistry

Medicine

Optometry

Veterinary Medicine

Master's Degrees

Agribusiness

Counselor Education

Elementary Education

Individual and Family Development

Nursing

Rehabilitation Counseling

Secondary Education

Special Education

Speech Pathology and Audiology

SPECIAL PROGRAMS

Accelerated Study Program allows students to complete their undergraduate degree in a shorter period of time than the traditional four years.

Adult or Continuing Education Program is available for nontraditional students returning to school or working full time.

Advanced Placement (AP) grants college credit for postsecondary work completed in high school. Students scoring 3 to 5 on the AP test will receive credit by examination for each course and advanced placement.

SCSU has an articulation agreement with Midlands, Greenville, and Trident technical colleges to provide a sequence of upper division courses leading to a bachelor's degree.

College Level Examination Program (CLEP) determines the academic relevance of nontraditional educational experiences such as the military, on-the-job training, or other life experiences, through a series of tests and may grant students college credit for these experiences.

College orientation is offered for $30 to entering students for two days prior to the beginning of classes to acquaint students with the college and to prepare them for college life; parents may attend.

Cooperative Education Program alternates classroom study with related paid work experience. The program provides academic credit and full-time status during co-op placement.

Cooperative programs in agriculture and nursing with Clemson University and South Carolina State allow students to take credit toward their baccalaureate degrees.

Cross-registration allows students to take advantage of certain courses on the campus of Denmark Technical College that will be credited to their core program at SCSU.

Honors program offers academically talented students a challenging program of study that includes special classes, seminars, colloquia, cultural activities, and special recognition to motivate participants.

Individualized majors allow students to create their own major program(s) of study.

Pre-Professional Programs in agriculture, dentistry, medicine, optometry, and veterinary medicine give students a head start in their pursuit of careers in these fields.

National Student Exchange (NSE) Program allows 100 state-supported schools to exchange students for up to one academic year to broaden academic, social, and cultural awareness.

Off-campus study allows students to take courses at Claflin College for credit toward their degree program.

Part-time degree program allows students to earn an undergraduate degree while attending part time.

Remedial courses are offered to entering students to bring them up to admission standards and to help them adjust for success in college.

ROTC provides training in military science for commission as a second lieutenant in the U.S. Army and Air Force in cooperation with Shaw Air Force Base Center. Two- and four-year scholarships are available.

Study Abroad Program allows students to go to a foreign country for part of their college education.

ATHLETIC PROGRAMS

South Carolina State College is a member of the Mid-Eastern Athletic Conference (MEAC) and the National Collegiate Athletic Association (NCAA), Division I, men's football is Division I-AA. Intercollegiate sports: men's basketball, cross-country, football, golf, tennis, and track & field; women's basketball, tennis, track, and volleyball.

Intramural sports: badminton, basketball, football, handball, racquetball, softball, table tennis, tennis, track & field, and volleyball.

LIBRARY HOLDINGS

The Miller F. Whittaker Library houses 246,764 bound volumes, 375, 569 microforms, 1,036 periodical subscriptions; 181 computers are available for student use. CD-ROM bibliographic database searching and on-line searching services are also available. Special collections include Doctoral Research on the Negro from 1933–1966, Black Studies Dissertation and Master's Thesis, and the South Carolina Historical Collection, emphasizing the history of the college. The library is a partial depository for U.S. Government Documents.

STUDENT LIFE

Special Regulations

All single undergraduates must live on campus unless residing in the city proper no more than 20 miles away; 2.0 GPA needed to participate in one of the various committees of the Student Union Board. Entering students must attend orientation.

Campus Services

Health center, career counseling and placement, tutoring, religious services, and campus post office.

Campus Activities

Social and cultural activities include theater, concerts, art exhibits, band, and religious activities. Students may work on *The Collegian* (student-run newspaper) or *The Bulldog* (yearbook). Communication majors or volunteers may work in the radio station WSSB-FM, which is owned and operated by the college. Timely information is provided about events within Orangeburg, Calhoun, and Bamberg counties.

Leadership opportunities are found in the Student Government Association and numerous other organizations including social, honorary, departmental, service, and religious groups. Greek-letter fraternities include Alpha Phi Alpha, Kappa Alpha Psi, Omega Psi Phi, and Phi Beta Sigma; sororities include Alpha Kappa Alpha, Delta Sigma Theta, Sigma Gamma Rho, and Zeta Phi Beta. Honor societies are also represented on campus.

SCSU is located in Orangeburg, South Carolina, with a population of 13,700. Annual events include the Festival of Roses for the state and the Orangeburg County Fair. Points of interest include the Edisto Gardens and the National Fish Hatchery. The beautiful Cypress Gardens of Charleston and the Atlantic Ocean are within 70 miles away.

Housing Availability

2,194 housing spaces; 8 dorms for women; 4 dorms for men; married student housing available on a first-come, first-served basis.

Handicapped Services

Wheelchair accessibility and services for the hearing impaired and speech disabled.

NOTABLE ALUMNI

Emily M. Chapman–Administrator of the Urban Center, Lincoln University in Pennsylvania

Marianna W. Davis–First woman to serve on South Carolina's Commission on Higher Education

James O. Heyward, 1953–Director of admissions, Alabama A&M University

Veryl Scott, J.D.–Business Department administrator, Norfolk University

Eric M. Westbury–Assistant president, First Union Bank of South Carolina

VOORHEES COLLEGE

HISTORY

Voorhees College (VC) is a four-year, private, coed, liberal arts college affiliated with the Protestant Episcopal Church. The school, originally known as Denmark Industrial School, was founded in 1897 by Elizabeth Evelyn Wright and began with one teacher and 14 students. Presently, the school has 37 instructors and enrolls 600 students.

In 1902 the name changed to Voorhees Industrial School. Between 1922 and 1929 when the school was experiencing financial difficulty, a singing group was developed that toured the country to raise money. In 1929, post-secondary education began and the name changed to Voorhees Normal and Industrial School. The name changed again in 1947, to Voorhees School and Junior College. When the school became a four-year college in 1962, it adopted its present name, Voorhees College.

Voorhees strives to prepare each student for a well-rounded fulfilling future by providing an environment that leads to academic achievement, spiritual enrichment, and

Denmark, SC 29042
Phone: (803) 793-3351

Total Enrollment:
600

Level of Selectivity:
Moderately
competitive

Motto:
A Quantum Leap
Toward Excellence

social development. According to President Leonard Dawson, "the liberal arts emphasis is designed to develop an appreciation and knowledge of the fundamental value of our society and a sense of the common bond that binds man to his fellow."

The 16-building campus is situated on 350 acres, of which 100 are used for growing timber as a cash crop. Facilities are a blend of historic and ultramodern including the Booker T. Washington Hall and the Wrights/Potts Library. Visitors and students are especially impressed by the historic St. Phillips Episcopal Chapel built in 1935 entirely by Voorhees students.

ACCREDITATION

Voorhees College is accredited by the Southern Association of Colleges and Schools to award the Bachelor of Arts, Bachelor of Science, and Associate's degrees.

Other Accreditation

National Council for the Accreditation of
  Teacher Education

COSTS PER YEAR

1991–92 Tuition: $3,470

Room and board: $1,086 (room); $1,447
  (board)

Special fees: $125

Books: $500

Estimated total cost: $6,628

FINANCIAL AID

Financial Aid Specific to the School

95% of the student body received financial aid during 1992–93.

Army ROTC in cooperation with South Carolina State College offers two- and four-year scholarships that pay tuition, fee, books, and other expenses, as well as provide a monthly stipend of $100.

Cooperative Education Program alternates and combines classroom study with related paid work experience. The program

St. Phillip's Chapel, Voorhees College

provides academic credit and full-time status during co-op placement.

Deferred Payment Plan allows students to pay college costs in 2 or 3 installments during the semester.

Endowed, alumni, friends, and special-interest scholarships number more than 15 and are based on academic achievement and good character. Consult catalog or financial aid office for more information.

South Carolina Tuition Grant is awarded to students who are residents of the state based on academic achievement and financial need. Qualifying freshmen must rank in the upper 3/4 of their class or score at least 800 on SAT. Continuing students must pass 24 credit hours during the last full year.

Tuition waivers (part time and full time) are available to Voorhees employees and their children.

United Negro College Fund (UNCF) scholarships are awarded to a limited number of students at this school who demonstrate financial need. Some scholarships may be based on location and merit. UNCF scholarships range from $500 to $7,500.

Veterans Educational Benefits are provided to qualified veterans and their dependents. Contact state or county Veterans Administration (VA) Office or the college VA Director.

Vocational Rehabilitation provides financial assistance to students with physical disabilities or handicapping conditions through the South Carolina Vocational Rehabilitation Office.

Financial Aid Deadline
May 1 (priority)

Financial Aid Contact
Lavenia Freeman, Director of Financial Aid, Voorhees College, Denmark, SC 29042; (803) 793-3351.

ADMISSION REQUIREMENTS
SAT (600) or ACT (16) required

Entrance Requirements
Graduation from an accredited high school and completion of the following units: 4 English, 3 mathematics, 2 science, 3 social sciences, 1 physical education, 7 electives, 2 foreign language recommended; minimum 2.0 GPA; 2 recommendations by counselor or principal and instructor; rank in middle third of high school graduating class; completion of medical form by a physician. A $10 non-refundable application fee required.

GED students must meet basic admission requirements.

Transfer students must submit transcripts of all college work including confidential report from each school; students transferring fewer than 30 hours must also submit high school transcript, class rank, and GPA; SAT or ACT scores must be submitted; minimum 2.0 GPA; personal essay; interview recommended. A $10 non-refundable application fee is required.

International students must meet basic admission requirements; submit official certificate of high school completion; and submit TOEFL scores.

Admission Application Deadline
Rolling admission provides no specific date for notification of admission so applicant is informed as soon as admission decision is made.

Admission Contact
Marion Greene-Thompson, Director of Enrollment Management, Voorhees College, 1411 Voorhees Rd., Denmark, SC 29042; (803) 793-3351, Ext. 7301. Fax: (803) 793-4584.

GRADUATION REQUIREMENTS
A minimum of 122 to 135 credit hours and completion of core requirements to include the following hours: 12 English, 6 mathematics, 6 natural science, 12 social science, 3 computer science, and 12 foreign language for BA degree; must pass English Proficiency Examination; minimum 2.0 GPA; 30 hours in residence; and participate in commencement.

Grading System
A–F; I=Incomplete; WD=Withdrew Without Credit; WP=Withdrew When Passing; WF=Withdrew When Failing; S=Satisfactory; U=Unsatisfactory

STUDENT BODY PROFILE
Total enrollment (male/female): 282/318

From in-state: 438

Other regions: 20 states; 2 foreign countries

Full-time undergraduates: 594

Part-time undergraduates: 6

Ethnic/Racial Makeup
African American, 588; Asian, 6; International, 6.

Class of 1995 Profile
Number of applicants: 1,259

Number accepted: 894

Number enrolled: 206

Median SAT score: 600

Transfers enrolled: 24

FACULTY PROFILE

Number of faculty: 37

Student-teacher ratio: 15:1

Full-time faculty: 32

Part-time faculty: 5

Faculty with doctorates or other terminal
degrees: 35%

SCHOOL CALENDAR

1992–93: August–May

Commencement & conferring of degrees:
May

One summer session.

DEGREES OFFERED 1991–92:

Biology

Business Administration

Computer Science

Criminal Justice

English

Mathematics

Office Management

Political Science

Sociology

Pre-Professional

Engineering

Law

Nursing

Medicine

SPECIAL PROGRAMS

Adult or Continuing Education Program
is available for nontraditional students returning to school or working full time.

Advanced Placement (AP) grants college credit for postsecondary work completed
in high school. Students scoring 3 or more on
the AP test will receive credit by examination
for each course and advanced placement.

College Level Examination Program
(CLEP) determines the academic relevance
of nontraditional educational experiences
such as the military, on-the-job training, or
other life experiences through a series of
tests and may grant students college credit
for these experiences.

College orientation is offered at no cost
to entering students for one week prior to the
beginning of classes to acquaint students
with the college and to prepare them for college life; parents may attend.

Cooperative Education Program alternates and combines classroom study with related paid work experience. The program
provides academic credit and full-time status
during co-op placement.

Honors Program offers academically
talented students a challenging program of
study that includes special classes, seminars,
colloquia, cultural activities, and special
recognition to motivate participants.

Individualized majors allow students to
create their own major program(s) of study.

Internships in various disciplines allow
students to apply theory to on-the-job training in industry, business, and government.

Part-time degree program allows students to earn an undergraduate degree part
time.

Remedial courses are offered to entering students to bring them up to admission
standards and to help them adjust for success
in college.

ROTC in cooperation with South Carolina State College provides training in military science for commission as a second
lieutenant in the U.S. Army. Two- and four-
year scholarships are available.

Study Abroad Program allows students
to go to a foreign country for part of their
college education.

Upward Bound provides academic counseling and cultural enrichment programs to
disadvantaged high school students in grades
10, 11, or 12 who are in pursuit of a college
education. Some credit courses may be offered.

ATHLETIC PROGRAMS

Voorhees College is a member of the
National Athletic Intercollegiate Association.

Intercollegiate sports: men's baseball, basketball, cross-country, indoor track, and track & field; women's basketball, cross-country, softball, track & field.

Intramural sports: basketball, ping-pong, powder puff football, soccer, softball, touchball.

Athletic Contact

Director of Athletics, Voorhees College, Denmark, SC 29042; (803)793-3351

LIBRARY HOLDINGS

The Wright/Potts Library houses 101,000 bound volumes, 25,507 microforms, 450 periodical subscriptions, 697 audiovisuals; 100 computers for student use in computer center. Special collections include American Civilization and Black History collections.

STUDENT LIFE

Special Regulations

Curfew; quiet hours from 7pm–9pm Monday–Thursday; dorm visitation hours from 6pm–11pm Sunday–Thursday; 6–11:30pm Friday–Saturday; required class attendance.

Campus Services

Health center, personal counseling, psychological counseling referred to Brooker Mental Health Center, career planning and placement, student employment services, tutoring, chapel and religious activities.

Campus Activities

Social and cultural activities include theater, chorale, lyceum, and religious activities. Students may get involved in the *Voorhees Vista* (student-run newspaper) or the *Tiger* (yearbook).

The concert choir presents annual Christmas and spring concerts. Black History

Month includes a keynote speaker and a panel discussion focusing on past accomplishments of blacks in America and setting goals for future progress. The Family Life Institute is sponsored annually and focuses attention on the social and psychological problems of the black family.

Leadership opportunities can be found in the Student Government Association (SGA) or the numerous other clubs and organizations which include the NAACP, the GEM literary club, pre-medical, and pre-dental clubs. Greek-letter fraternities include Alpha Phi Alpha, Kappa Alpha Psi, Omega Psi Phi, and Phi Beta Sigma; sororities include Alpha Kappa Alpha, Delta Sigma Theta, Phi Beta Sigma, and Zeta Phi Beta, as well as the Vogue sorority. Honor societies include Alpha Kappa Mu and Alpha Chi.

Voorhees College is located one and one-half miles from the central business district of Denmark, South Carolina, population approximately 4,000.

This rural community offers golf, swimming, boating, fishing, local theater, shopping, and dining. The closest metropolitan city is Columbia, South Carolina, the state capital, which is 45 miles south. Passenger rail service is two miles away; the airport is 50 miles away.

Housing Availability

508 housing spaces; freshman housing guaranteed

NOTABLE ALUMNI

Magdline Davis, 1989–Database administrator, BP Exploration Alaska, Anchorage, Alaska

Prezell Robinson–President, Saint Augustine College

Jerry Screen, 1969–Attorney; chairman of the Board of Trustees, Voorhees College

Lenny Spring, 1968–Vice president, First Union Bank, Charlotte, SC

Tennessee

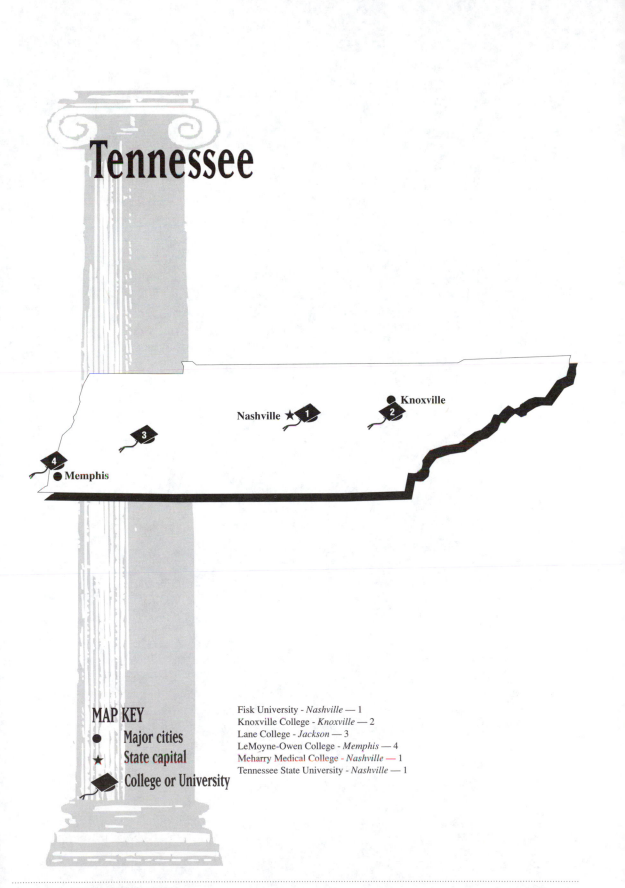

Nashville

Knoxville

Memphis

MAP KEY

- ● Major cities
- ★ State capital
- ◆ College or University

Fisk University - *Nashville* — 1
Knoxville College - *Knoxville* — 2
Lane College - *Jackson* — 3
LeMoyne-Owen College - *Memphis* — 4
Meharry Medical College - *Nashville* — 1
Tennessee State University - *Nashville* — 1

FISK UNIVERSITY

1000 17th Ave. N
Nashville, TN 37203
Phone: (615) 329-8500

Total Enrollment:
867

Level of Selectivity:
Slightly competitive

Motto:
Her Sons and
Daughters Ever on
the Altar

HISTORY

Fisk University is a four-year, private, liberal arts, coed institution affiliated with the United Church of Christ. Fisk was founded in 1866 as Fisk School. In 1871, Fisk began offering instruction at the college level, and in 1875, it offered its first bachelor's degree. In 1967, Fisk became the first black institution to be awarded university status and thus became Fisk University. It was also the first black institution to be accredited by the Southern Association of Colleges and Schools.

Fisk is known for its famous Jubilee Singers who began to perform nationally and internationally in 1876 to bring needed money to the school. The Jubilee Singers have performed at the White House, the World Peace Conference, and before Queen Victoria and Kaiser Wilhelm of Europe. In 1976, Jubilee Hall, the first permanent building of higher education for southern blacks, was designated a national landmark. The Fisk campus was named as a national historic district in 1978 by the U.S. Department of Interior in recognition of its unique place in history, art, and culture.

In the late 1980's, Fisk began to receive large donations from well-known black citizens. Camille and Bill Cosby donated one million dollars to the school in 1988. In 1990, Fisk received more than one million dollars from Michael Jackson's United Negro College Fund contributions.

Fisk's 28-building campus, located on more than 40 acres, has a rich history and has educated such graduates as W. E. B. Dubois, John Hope Franklin, and Aaron Douglas. Fisk's mission is to educate and prepare students so that they are resourceful and skilled to face the challenges of life in a technological society and an increasingly multicultural world.

ACCREDITATION

Fisk University is accredited by the Southern Association of Colleges and Schools to award the Bachelor of Arts and Bachelor of Science degrees.

Other Accreditation

American Chemical Society

National Association of Schools of Music

COSTS PER YEAR

1992-93 Tuition: $5,445

Room and board: $3,420

Special fees: $150

Books: $400

Estimated total cost: $9,415

FINANCIAL AID

1991–92 Institutional Funding

Number of scholarships and grants: 191

Total amount of scholarships and grants: $400,452

Range of scholarships and grants: $100 (average)

1991–92 Federal and State Funding

Number of scholarships and grants: 656

Total amount of scholarships and grants: $1,360,000

Range of scholarships and grants: $500 (average)

Number of loans: 947

Total amount of loans: $3,000,000

Range of loans: $200–$625 (average)

Number of work-study: 228

Total amount of work-study: $222,000

Range of work-study: $200 (average)

Financial Aid Specific to the School

In 1991–92, 72% of the student body received financial aid.

Air Force, Army, and Navy ROTC, in cooperation with Tennessee State University or Vanderbilt University offer scholarships that pay tuition, books, fees, and other expenses, and offer a monthly stipend of $100.

Fisk University National Achievement matching scholarships are available to National Achievement Scholarship Program (NASP) winners who indicate they will attend Fisk University.

A number of Fisk scholarships are available for undergraduates and are awarded on the basis of need. Some scholarships are for students in a particular major; others are funded by foundations or corporations, and have conditions particular to each.

University honor scholarships, based upon exceptional academic potential, are also offered. College work-study and athletic grants and aid are also available.

The United Negro College Fund (UNCF) scholarships are available to entering students scoring high on the ACT or ETS, or students with a high school GPA of 3.0 or better. To renew awards, students must maintain a cumulative GPA of 3.0 or better.

Financial Aid Deadline

April 20 (fall); November 1 (spring)

Financial Aid Contact

Mr. Benjamin D. Cooper, Director of Financial Aid, Fisk University, Nashville, TN 37208; (615) 329-8735

ADMISSION REQUIREMENTS

SAT or ACT strongly recommended.

Entrance Requirements

A high school diploma with 15 units, including 4 English, 1 foreign language, 1 algebra, 1 geometry, 1 history, 1 laboratory science, and 6 academic electives. A written essay, two letters of recommendation, and proof of recent physical are also needed. A non-refundable $25 application fee is required.

GED students must meet the basic admission requirements.

Transfer students must have a 2.0 minimum GPA, high school transcript, college transcript, two letters of recommendation, as well as a written essay. A maximum credit transfer of 60 hours is allowed from a two-year or a four-year institution.

International students must pass the TOEFL examination.

Admission Application Deadline

June 15 (fall); November 1 (spring); rolling admission provides no specific date for notification of admission so applicant is informed as soon as admission decision is made.

Admission Contact

Mr. Harrison F. DeShields, Director of Admissions, 1000 17th Ave. North, Nashville, TN 37208; (615) 329-8665.

GRADUATION REQUIREMENTS

Minimum of 120 credit hours and completion of the core requirements, including 3 foreign language, 2 science and math, and 1 computer course for management majors with a 2.0 GPA. The last 30 hours must be completed in residence. Students must live on campus for the senior year.

Grading System

A-F; Pass-Fail; withdraw (time limit)

STUDENT BODY PROFILE

Total enrollment (male/female): 303/564

From in-state: 185

From other regions: 39 states; 10 foreign countries

Full-time undergraduates (male/female): 294/547

Part-time undergraduates (male/female): 2/4

Graduate students (male/female): 7/13

Ethnic/Racial Makeup

African American, 856; Caucasian, 3; International, 8.

Class of 1995 Profile

Number of applicants: 1,099

Number accepted: 824

Number enrolled: 281

Median SAT score: 900 (combined)

Median ACT score: 22

Transfer applicants: 41

Transfers accepted: 30

Transfers enrolled: 20

FACULTY PROFILE

Number of faculty: 80

Student-teacher ratio: 14:1

Full-time faculty: 62

Part-time faculty: 18

Tenured faculty: 29

Faculty with doctorates or other terminal degrees: 67.7%

Ethnic/Racial Makeup

African American, 78%; Hispanic, 1%; Native American, 1%; International, 11%.

SCHOOL CALENDAR
1992–1993: August 25–May 11 (semesters)
Commencement and conferring of degrees:
May

DEGREES OFFERED AND NUMBER CONFERRED 1991–92:

Bachelor of Arts
Biology: n/a
Chemistry: 17
Dramatics and Speech: n/a
English: 28
French: n/a
History: 7
Mathematics: n/a
Music: n/a
Physics: n/a
Political Science: n/a
Psychology: n/a
Religious and Philosophical Studies: 5
Sociology: 4
Spanish: n/a

Bachelor of Science
Accounting: 5
Art: n/a
Chemistry: n/a
Computer Science: n/a
Economics: n/a
Elementary Education (joint program): n/a
Finance: n/a
International Business Relations: n/a
Management: n/a
Music Education: n/a

Pre-Professional
Dentistry: n/a
Law: n/a
Medicine: n/a
Teacher Preparation: n/a

Jubilee Hall, Fisk University

SPECIAL PROGRAMS

One-week free college orientation for students; parents may attend.

A three/two dual degree program is offered in science and engineering with Vanderbilt, University of Alabama, and Florida A&M University. Student completes three years at Fisk and two years at cooperating school. Upon completion of the program, student receives a liberal arts degree and an engineering degree.

A dual degree program in pharmacy is offered with Howard University. Upon completion of the program, student receives liberal arts degree and a pharmacy degree.

A dual degree is also offered in management with Vanderbilt University. Upon completion of the program, student receives a Bachelor of Science and a Master's in Management.

Cooperative program in Biomedical Sciences allows students to take needed courses at Meharry Medical College.

Cooperative program in Nursing and Medical Technology allows students to take needed courses at Rush Medical in Chicago.

Cooperative Teacher Education program allows students to take courses needed at Peabody College of Vanderbilt University.

Students may receive a Master's degree in Business Administration through a program with the Owen School of Management at Vanderbilt University.

The Army and Navy ROTC, in conjunction with Vanderbilt University, and the Air Force ROTC, in conjunction with Tennessee University, provide training in military science for a commission officer as a second lieutenant in the U.S. Armed Forces. ROTC provides scholarships that pay tuition, fees, books, and other expenses, and provide a monthly stipend of $100 per month.

The Cooperative Study Abroad program is available to students.

The Cooperative Education Program alternates formal academic study with practical work experiences.

The honors program is offered to students who show outstanding academic capability.

Joint program in Elementary Education in cooperation with Peabody College/Vanderbilt University is available to students.

Fisk/UNCF Pre-medical summer institute assists highly motivated minority students to get accepted at medical school.

The Oak Ridge Program is for students interested in science to spend the spring semester of their junior year in residence at the Oak Ridge National Laboratory.

ATHLETIC PROGRAMS

Fisk University is a member of the National Collegiate Athletic Association (NCAA), Division II.

Intercollegiate sports: men's baseball, basketball, cross-country, golf, tennis, and track & field; women's basketball, cross-country, golf, tennis, track & field, and volleyball.

Intramural sports: baseball, basketball, volleyball, softball, tennis, jogging, exercise classes, and weight training.

LIBRARY HOLDINGS

The library houses 200,000 volumes, 5,529 microforms, 3,121 audiovisuals, 149 current periodicals, 3,112 audiovisuals, 312,000 government documents, and an online catalog. Students have access to CD-ROM database searching. Special collections include the Black Oral History Collection; the Negro Collection including the works of W.E.B. DuBois, Langston Hughes, and W.C. Handy, famed blues musician; the notable Aaron Douglas Gallery of African-American Art, and the George Gershwin collection of music.

STUDENT LIFE

Special Regulations

Must attend college orientation program and reside one year on campus. Cars must be registered and display parking permits. Dormitory visitation from 6 p.m. to midnight.

Campus Services

Health services, personal/psychological counseling, career counseling, placement for graduates, and chapel services. Bus transportation is provided between Fisk, Vanderbilt, and Meharry colleges.

Campus Activities

Social and cultural activities include the famous Fisk-Jubilee singers, band, theater, and dance. Students can get involved in the *Fisk Forum* (biweekly student-run newspaper) or *The Dual* (yearbook), or work at the campus radio station (WFSK-FM).

Leadership opportunities can be found in student-run organizations such as the Student Government Association. Greek-letter societies include Alpha Kappa Alpha, Delta Sigma Theta, Sigma Gamma Rho, and Zeta Phi Beta sororities as well as Alpha Phi Alpha, Kappa Alpha Psi, Omega Psi Phi, and Phi Beta Sigma fraternities. Honor societies include Phi Beta Kappa and Sigma Xi.

Located in Nashville, the capital of Tennessee, the campus is situated in a large urban area. The city of Nashville is known for its academic, artistic and musical contributions.

The airport is 11 miles from the campus. Public transportation provides easy access to Memphis and Knoxville. Atlanta and St. Louis are about 250 miles away. Fisk students have access to a variety of entertainment, and social and cultural activities both on campus and in the surrounding cities.

Housing Availability

1,130 housing spaces available; freshman housing guaranteed.

NOTABLE ALUMNI

Hortense Golden Canady, 1947–Civic leader

Wilhelmina Delco, 1950–Texas state representative

Aaron Douglas–Artist of the Harlem Renaissance; taught at Fisk

William Edward Burgharot (W.E.B.) DuBois–Social critic; historian; scholar; educator; founder of Niagara Movement; co-founder, NAACP

John Hope Franklin, 1935–Scholar; history professor, Fisk, Howard University, Cambridge, etc.

Nikki Giovanni, 1967–Poet; writer; lecturer

Alice Hastings, 1957–U.S. representative, Florida

Roland Hayes, 1905-08–Professional singer

John Lewis, 1967–U.S. representative, Atlanta City, Texas

Constance Blake Motley, 1944–First African American female federal judge

Hazel O'Leary–Secretary of Energy

Ron Walters, 1963–Founder, National Black Independent Political Party; former chairman, political science department, Howard University

Margaret James Murray Washington–First Dean of Women at Tuskegee Institute

KNOXVILLE COLLEGE

901 College St.
Knoxville, TN 37921
Phone: (615) 627-3491
Toll-free:
800-743-5669

Total Enrollment:
1,200

Level of Selectivity:
Noncompetitive

Motto:
Success begins here

HISTORY

Knoxville College is a private, four-year, coed, liberal arts college affiliated with the United Presbyterian Church. Founded in 1875 by Presbyterian missionaries, the college had its roots in the McKee School for Negro Youth, which began in 1863. The first postsecondary level instruction was offered in 1877, and the first baccalaureate degree was awarded in 1883.

Knoxville college is dedicated to the development of the first generation college student. Its mission is to provide a stimulating and challenging educational experience to students who have been afforded little advantage in society. To this end, Knoxville College provides programs to prepare students for the jobs of today, while also teaching them skills necessary for the jobs of tomorrow. The college provides an experienced, caring faculty to achieve this goal, and it strongly believes in preserving and disseminating the African-American heritage.

The main campus of Knoxville is located on approximately 39 acres. Its 17-building campus continues to be the primary institution for minority students in east Tennessee. In 1989, Knoxville acquired the two-year Morristown College, which is now named Knoxville College-Morristown. This traditionally black college is a United Negro College Fund member school.

ACCREDITATION

Knoxville College is accredited by the Southern Association of Colleges and Schools (SACS) to award the Bachelor of Arts, Bachelor of Science, and Associate's degrees.

COSTS PER YEAR

1992–93 Tuition: $5,270

Room and board: $1,450 (room); $1,250 (board)

Special fees: $125

Books: $500

Estimated total cost: $8,595

FINANCIAL AID

Financial Aid Specific to the School

95% of the student body received financial aid during 1991–92.

Athletic grants, academic scholarships, university and departmental scholarships, music performance awards, and church scholarships are available.

The Cooperative Education Program combines classroom study with related paid work experience in three majors. The program provides academic credit and full time status during co-op placement.

United Negro College Fund (UNCF) scholarships are awarded to a limited number of students at this school who demonstrate financial need. Some scholarships may be based on location and merit. UNCF scholarships range from $500 to $7,500.

Army and Air Force ROTC offer two- and four-year scholarships that pay for tuition, fee, books, and other expenses, and provide a monthly stipend of $100.

The Douglas Loan Program is a state program that offers loans to students majoring in education.

Tennessee Student Assistance award is available to any Tennessee resident enrolled or accepted for admission as an undergraduate student, and who has demonstrated a need for assistance.

Financial Aid Deadline

June 1 (priority)

Financial Aid Contact

Mrs. Carol Scott, Chief Financial Aid Officer, Knoxville College, Knoxville, TN 37921; (615) 524-6525

ADMISSION REQUIREMENTS

SAT or ACT required

Entrance Requirements

Graduation from an accredited high school in the top half of the graduating class. Submit high school transcription with completion of 15 units including: 3 English; 2 mathematics; 1 natural science; 1 social studies; and 8 electives. "C" average on all high school work or three letters of recommendation, and pre-entrance medical record required. A non-refundable $15 application fee is required.

GED students must meet the basic admission requirements.

Transfer students must submit a transcript of all secondary and college work and be in good standing with the previous institution attended; must have a minimum 2.0 GPA; 68 hours maximum transfer credit from a two-year accredited institution is allowed.

Transfer students from the Morristown two-year campus must complete a minimum of one year before they can be considered for transfer to the main four-year campus; course offerings must be available and personal hardship in attending the two-year campus will be considered; office of Academic Dean must approve transfer.

International Students must pass the TOEFL examination with a score of at least 475; must show proof of financial resources sufficient for at least one full year notarized by the bank.

Admission Application Deadline

Rolling admission provides no specific date for notification of admission so applicant is informed as soon as admission decision is made.

Admission Contact

Mr. Ralph J. Miller, Director of Admissions, Knoxville College, 901 College Street, Knoxville, TN 37921; (615) 524-6525 or 800-627-3491.

GRADUATION REQUIREMENTS

A minimum of 124 semester hours and completion of general education core to include the following hours: 6 English, 6 mathematics, 8 science, 3 computer science, 3 social science, and 6 history. Must have a cumulative average of 2.0, completion of at least 30 semester hours in residence at Knoxville College, and completion of at least 10 semester hours of major courses at Knoxville College. Must prove proficiency in oral and written English expression, reading, and basic mathematics; successful completion of requirements for the senior comprehensive examination.

Grading System

A-F; I=Incomplete; Z=In Progress (student must re-enroll in course); S/U=Satisfactory/Unsatisfactory; W=Withdrawal; WP/WF= Withdrawal Passing/Withdrawal Failing.

STUDENT BODY PROFILE

Total enrollment: 1,200

SCHOOL CALENDAR

1991–92: August 22–May 8 (semester hours)

Commencement and conferring of degrees: May 9

DEGREES OFFERED 1991–92:

Bachelor of Arts

Early Childhood Education

English Communications

Music Education

Political Science

Religion and Philosophy

Sociology

Bachelor of Science

Accounting

Biology

Business

Chemistry

Computer Science

Cooperative Engineering

Early Childhood Education

Elementary Education

Health and Physical Education

Mathematics

Medical Technology

Psychology

Tourism, Food and Lodging Administration

SPECIAL PROGRAMS

College orientation is offered to entering students prior to the beginning of classes to acquaint students with the college and to prepare them for college life.

The Cooperative Education Program combines classroom study with related paid work experience in three majors. The program provides academic credit and full-time status during co-op placement.

In the Cooperative Engineering Program with the University of Tennessee, students complete four years at Knoxville and one year at the University of Tennessee.

The cooperative Tourism, Food and Lodging Administration program is offfered in cooperation with the University of Tennessee.

Internships and work experience programs allow students to apply theory to on-the-job training in industry and business.

Pre-professional programs in law, theology, nursing, dentistry, and medical technology are offered.

Remedial courses are offered to entering students to bring them up to admissions standards and to help them adjust for success in college.

ROTC provides training in military science for commission as a second lieutenant in the U.S. Army and Air Force. Two-, three-, and four- year scholarships are available. Army ROTC is offered in cooperation with the University of Tennessee.

A special program for the culturally disadvantaged enables low-rank students to attend.

Knoxville offers two-year associate degree programs and a one-year post associate program in pre-physical therapy.

ATHLETIC PROGRAMS

Knoxville College is a member of the National Association of Intercollegiate Athletics (NAIA).

Intercollegiate sports: men's basketball, football, tennis, and track & field; women's basketball, tennis, and track & field. Intramural sports: badminton, basketball, softball, table tennis, and volleyball.

LIBRARY HOLDINGS

The library holds 125,000 bound volumes.

STUDENT LIFE

Special Regulations

Cars permitted without restrictions; quiet hours enforced.

Campus Services

Health services; career counseling and placement.

Campus Activities

Social and cultural activities include theater, chorale, band, and dance. Students with musical ability may tour with the Knoxville College Concert Choir or Marching Band throughout the United States and abroad. Interested students may get involved in the student-run newspaper and yearbook.

Leadership opportunities are found in the Student Government Association and departmental clubs. Fraternities, sororities, academic clubs, and honor societies are represented on campus.

Located in Knoxville, the campus is served by a mass transit bus system. The airport is twelve miles away from the campus. Knoxville is the headquarters for the Tennessee Valley Authority. The Tennessee River and the Tennessee Valley Authority lakes offer boating, fishing, swimming, and other water sports. Scenic drives include the famous 100-mile scenic loop trip and the Great Smoky Mountains National Park on the Newfound Gap highway. Some of the historic sites are the Confederate Monument, the Ramsey House, the Governor Blount home, and the Memorial to the 79th NY regiment which took part in the siege of Fort Sanders. Knoxville provides a variety of cultural and entertainment opportunities and is surrounded by many recreation areas. It is minutes from the Oak Ridge National Laboratory, and Atlanta, Georgia is 200 miles or approximately 4 hours away.

Housing Availability

Campus housing available

NOTABLE ALUMNI

Johnny L. Ford, 1964–Mayor, Tuskegee, AL

John E. Reinhardt, 1939–U.S. ambassador to Liberia

Herman Smith–Former chancellor, University of Arkansas at Pine Bluff

LANE COLLEGE

545 Lane Ave.
Jackson, TN 38301
Phone: (901) 426-7500

Total Enrollment:
562

Level of Selectivity:
Slightly competitive

HISTORY

Lane College is a four-year, private, coed, liberal arts college affiliated with the Christian Methodist Episcopal (C.M.E.) Church. Founded in 1882 as the Colored Methodist Episcopal High School, it became Lane Institute in 1883. In 1896, it became Lane College. Lane was chartered in 1884, graduated its first class in 1887, and awarded its first bachelor's degree in 1899.

From the beginning, Lane College has strived to be a source of inspiration for the C.M.E. Church youth. It stands as a symbol of Christian education for students of all colors, creeds, and faiths.

Lane's mission is to prepare students for the future with the knowledge, skills, attitude, and understanding necessary for leadership and participation in a democratic society. Lane offers programs with intellectual experiences that enable students to probe and develop their potential to meet decision-making situations with rational and innovative thinking.

Located on approximately 17 acres, the 7-building campus offers easy access to Jackson's downtown area, business centers, and churches. The newest campus building, the Center for Academic Development, is to be completed by 1993. The campus is located midway between Memphis and Nashville. Both Memphis and Nashville offer a wealth of social and cultural activities. This traditionally black college is a United Negro College Fund member school.

ACCREDITATION

Lane College is accredited by the Southern Association of Colleges and Schools to award the Bachelor of Arts and Bachelor of Science degrees.

COSTS PER YEAR

1991–92 Tuition: $4,087

Room and board: $898 (room); $1,575 (board)

Special fees: $400

Books: $500

Estimated total cost: $7,460

FINANCIAL AID

1990–91 Institutional Funding

Number of scholarships and grants: 75

Total amount of scholarships and grants: $165,800

Range of scholarships and grants: $200–$4,087

1990–91 Federal and State Funding

Number of scholarships and grants: 124

Total amount of scholarships and grants: $173,923

Range of scholarships and grants: $200–$2,500

Number of loans: 200

Total amount of loans: $560,000

Range of loans: $400–$2,500

Number of work-study: 246

Total amount of work-study: $260,562

Range of work-study: $844–$1,260

Financial Aid Specific to the School

97% of the student body received financial aid during 1991–92.

The Dean's Award is given to the student who maintains the highest scholastic average during four years of study at Lane.

Endowed scholarships from alumni, private, and public sources number approximately 35 and are available based on varying criteria.

President's Award is given to the senior student who shows leadership qualities among his/her peers. Student is expected to have strong relationship with the administration and show evidence of mature decision-making.

Teacher Loan/Scholarship program provides loans up to $5,000 a year for Tennessee residents who plan to teach in Tennessee schools. Students must have a 3.0 cumulative GPA, a composite ACT score of 21, two letters of support from existing teachers, and statement of intent to teach in public school in mathematics or science. Deadline for submission of FAF application and ACT score is April 15.

Tennessee Loan Program provides loans to worthy and needy sophomores, juniors, and seniors who are residents and non-residents of Tennessee. Freshmen may be eligible for a loan if judged likely to succeed in college. Repayment of loan begins six months after student leaves school.

United Negro College Fund (UNCF) scholarships are awarded to a limited number of students at this school who demonstrate financial need. Some scholarships may be based on location and merit. UNCF scholarships range from $500 to $7,500. Scholarships are available to students under two categories: restricted and unrestricted. Restricted scholarships specify residence, major field, sex, etc., where as unrestricted do not.

Financial Aid Deadline

April 15 (currently enrolled); May 31 (freshmen and others)

Financial Aid Contact

Mrs. Martha Kizer, Director of Financial Aid, Lane College, 545 Lane Ave., Jackson, TN 38301; (901) 426-7618.

ADMISSION REQUIREMENTS

ACT (13 composite score) or SAT equivalent score required

Entrance Requirements

Graduation from accredited high school and completion of 16 units to include: 4 English, 2 mathematics, 2 natural science, 2 social science, 2 foreign language, and 4 academic electives; official high school transcript with minimum 2.0 GPA; 3 recommendations from counselor, administrator, and a responsible adult; and completed medical form. A non-refundable $10 application fee is required.

GED students must meet basic admission requirements.

Transfer students must submit official transcripts for all previous college work, minimum 2.0 GPA; submit completed health forms; be in good standing at previous school; and submit transfer recommendation from dean of last college attended. A maximum of 96 transfer credit hours allowed from a four-year accredited institution.

International students must take the TOEFL examination and submit a confidential Declaration and Certification of Finance.

Admission Application Deadline

August 1 (fall); December 15 (spring); May 1 (summer)

Admission Contact

Miss E. Ruth Maddox, Director of Admissions, Lane College, Room 103, Administration Building, Jackson, TN 38301; (901) 426-7532.

GRADUATION REQUIREMENTS

Minimum of 128 semester hours and completion of core requirements to include the following hours: 3 mathematics, 8 science, and 1 computer course for science and business majors; minimum 2.0 GPA; last 31 hours completed in residence. Sophomore English Proficiency Exam must be passed, and one-half of the course work in student's major field must be taken at Lane College. All students must attend a minimum of 12 chapel services per semester in order to graduate.

Grading System

A–F; I=Incomplete; IP=In progress for course extended beyond semester; X=Faculty member unable to complete grade because of emergency; W=Withdrew; WP=Withdrew passing; WF=Withdrew failing.

STUDENT BODY PROFILE

Total enrollment (male/female): 272/290

From in-state: 309

Other regions: 21 states and 3 foreign countries

Full-time undergraduates (male/female): 267/276

Part-time undergraduates (male/female): 9/10

Ethnic/Racial Makeup

African American, 556; International, 6

Class of 1995 Profile

Number of applicants: 509

Number accepted: 346

Number enrolled: 173

Median ACT score: 15

Transfers enrolled: 51

FACULTY PROFILE

Number of faculty: 44

Student-teacher ratio: 14:1

Full-time faculty: 39

Part-time faculty: 5

Tenured faculty: 12

Faculty with doctorates or other terminal
degrees: 36%

SCHOOL CALENDAR

1992–1993: August 15–May 1 (semester
hours)

Commencement and conferring of degrees:
May 2

DEGREES OFFERED 1991–92:

Bachelor of Arts

Communication Arts

English

History

Liberal Arts

Music

Religion

Sociology

Bachelor of Science

Biology

Business

Chemistry

Mathematics

Mathematics/Computer Science

Physical Education

Pre-Engineering

SPECIAL PROGRAMS

Advanced Placement (AP) allows high
school students to gain college credit for
scores on the College Board AP tests in various subjects.

The College Level Examination Program (CLEP) grants college credit for non-traditional educational experiences, such as the military, work, or other life experiences, by taking the CLEP exam administered by the College Entrance Examination Board. A minimum score of 50 is necessary on a given examination. A maximum of 32 semester hours are awarded.

College orientation is offered to entering students for three days at no at the beginning of classes to familiarize students with the college and to prepare them for college life; parents may be included.

Cooperative Education Program alternates classroom study with related paid work experience. The program provides academic credit and full-time status during co-op placement.

Dual degree program in Computer Science in cooperation with Jackson State University allows students to get two degrees—one in liberal arts from home school and one in computer science from cooperating school.

Honors program offers academically talented students a challenging program of study that includes special classes, seminars, colloquia, cultural activities, and special recognition to motivate participants.

Off-campus study with Howard University, Jackson State University, and Tennessee State University allows students to take courses at these institutions for credit.

Remedial program or academic remediation provides remedial courses for entering students to bring them up to admission standards.

Student Support Services provides developmental courses, counseling, and cultural activities to students who need aid to succeed in college.

Three/two degree program in engineering allows students to get two degrees—one in liberal arts from home school and one in engineering from the University of Tennessee—by completing three years at matriculated school and two years at cooperating school.

ATHLETIC PROGRAMS

Lane College is a member of the Southern Intercollegiate Athletic Conference (SIAC); and the National Collegiate Athletic Association (NCAA), Division III.

Intercollegiate sports: men's baseball, basketball, cross-country running, football, and tennis; women's basketball, cross-country running, tennis, and volleyball.

Intramural sports: basketball, swimming and diving, track & field, and volleyball.

LIBRARY HOLDINGS

The J. K. Daniels Library holds 36,700 bound volumes, 8,800 microforms, 345 periodical subscriptions, and 1,850 audiovisuals. Special collections include the Negro Heritage Collection, the History of the College, Haitian Art Collection, and personal items of Bishop Isaac Lane. The library has agreements with other West Tennessee College libraries for shared use of their collections.

STUDENT LIFE

Special Regulations

Entering students must attend a three-day college orientation program; last 31 hours must be completed in residence; new students are required to enroll in a "for credit" orientation course for one semester.

Campus Services

Personal counseling, academic remediation, and individual tutoring.

Campus Activities

Social and cultural activities include theater. Students may get involved in the student run publications, *The Lanite* (yearbook) and *The Inquirer* (student-run newspaper).

Leadership opportunities are found in the various departmental clubs. Greek-letter fraternities include Alpha Phi Alpha, Kappa Alpha Psi, Omega Psi Phi, and Phi Beta Sigma; sororities include Alpha Kappa Alpha, Delta Sigma Theta, Sigma Gamma Rho, and Zeta Phi Beta. Honor societies include Beta Kappa Chi, Alpha Kappa Mu, Tau Beta Sigma, Kappa Kappa Psi, Phi Beta Lambda, and Who's Who Among Students in American Universities and Colleges.

A bus system and passenger rail service provide transportation to the campus. Public transportation provides easy access to Memphis and Nashville. Lane students enjoy a variety of entertainment, social, and cultural activities—both on campus and in the surrounding cities.

Housing Availability

Housing spaces total 646; two dormitories for women, two for men; freshmen given priority; freshman-only housing available; off-campus living permitted.

NOTABLE ALUMNI

Otis L. Floyd, Jr.–President, Tennessee State University

David H. Johnson, 1949–Retired educational administrator, Tyler, TX

LEMOYNE-OWEN COLLEGE

HISTORY

LeMoyne-Owen College is a four-year, private, coed, liberal arts college founded in 1968 as the result of a merger between LeMoyne College and Owen College. The merged institutions bring together two religious affiliations, the United Church of Christ and the Tennessee Baptist Missionary and Educational Convention.

LeMoyne College had its beginnings in 1862 when the American Missionary Association started an elementary school named Lincoln School for Negroes. The Lincoln chapel, which housed the school, was destroyed in a fire during the 1866 race riots. The chapel was rebuilt soon and reopened in 1867. In 1871, the school's name changed to LeMoyne Normal and Commercial School after Dr. Francis J. LeMoyne, who had donated a large sum of money when the school was in financial trouble. The college moved to its current site in 1914. Ten years later it became a junior college; in 1934, it became a four-year degree college and the name changed to LeMoyne College.

807 Walker Ave.
Memphis, TN 38126
Phone: (901) 942-7302
Toll-free:
800-737-7778
Fax: (901) 942-7810

Total Enrollment:
1,297

Level of Selectivity:
Noncompetitive;
moderately
competitive for
engineering, teacher
education, and
pre-medicine

Owen College began as S. A. Owen Jr. College in 1954. The school was named after Reverend S. A. Owen, a prominent religious and cultural leader. In 1956, the name changed to Owen College and graduated its first class.

LeMoyne-Owen College boasts that most of Memphis' African American leaders earned their undergraduate degrees from the school, including its first African-American mayor elected in 1991. The school's mission is to prepare students for leadership positions in the community through quality academic and student development programs. It is strongly committed to community outreach service to break the cycle of poverty in the African-American community. One of its community development projects is the adoption of the Garden Housing Development Project, which seeks to provide programs and services to the resident children and their parents. Programs include the Big Brother/Big Sister mentoring program, after school tutoring, a homework center, and a teen pregnancy prevention program for men.

The 9-building campus is situated on 15 acres and includes the Little Theater and a state-of-the-art foreign language lab. The campus facilities comprise both modern and traditional buildings. LeMoyne-Owen is a United Negro College Fund (UNCF) member school.

ACCREDITATION

LeMoyne-Owen College is accredited by the Southern Association of Colleges and Schools (SACS) to award the Bachelor of Arts and Bachelor of Science degrees.

Other Accreditation
Tennessee State Board of Education

COSTS PER YEAR
1992–93 Tuition: $4,200

Room and board: $2,000 (limited number)

Special fees: $125

Books: $500

Estimated total cost: $6,825

FINANCIAL AID

Financial Aid Specific to the School
98% of the student body received financial during 1991–92.

Army ROTC and cooperative Air Force ROTC with Memphis State University offer two- and four-year scholarships that pay tuition, fees, books, and other expenses, and provide a monthly stipend of $100.

Athletic scholarships are available for students with special talents participating in certain intercollegiate sports. Contact the director of athletics for more information.

Cooperative Education Program alternates and combines classroom study with related paid work experience. The program provides academic credit and full-time status during co-op placement.

Endowed, alumni, friends, and corporate scholarships and awards number 48 and are based on varying criteria, including merit, need, or interest.

Tennessee Student Assistance Awards are available to Tennessee residents who are enrolled in eligible Tennessee colleges and universities as undergraduate students.

United Negro College Fund (UNCF) scholarships are awarded to a limited number of students at this school who demonstrate financial need. Some scholarships may be based on location and merit. UNCF scholarships range from $500 to $7,500.

Financial Aid Deadline
April 15 (priority); May 1 (fall); November 1 (spring); April 15 (summer).

Financial Aid Contact
Ms. Stephanie Larry, Director of Financial Aid, LeMoyne-Owen College, Memphis, TN 38126; (901) 774-9090.

ADMISSION REQUIREMENTS
ACT required by July 30

Entrance Requirements
Graduation from an accredited high school with the following 16 units: 4 English, 3 mathematics, 2 science, and 2 social studies; essay required for some; one letter of recommendation; pre-entrance medical record; interview recommended. A $25 non-refundable application fee is required (fee may be waived for applicants with need).

GED students must meet basic admission requirements.

International Students must take the TOEFL examination.

Transfer students should have a 2.0 minimum GPA and submit official transcript of all college work.

Early admission allows academically gifted high school students the opportunity to enroll in college before completing high school

Admission Application Deadline
Rolling admission provides no specific date for notification of admission so applicant is informed as soon as admission decision is made. April 15 (priority); June 15 (fall); November 15 (spring); March 1 (summer); early decision provides notification of acceptance early in applicant's senior year of high school; deferred entrance.

Admission Contact
Mr. Melvin Hughes, Director of Admissions, Brown Lee Hall, LeMoyne-Owen College, 807 Walker Ave., Memphis, TN 38126; (901) 942-7302; Fax (901) 942-7810; Toll free 800-737-7778.

GRADUATION REQUIREMENTS
A minimum of 130 semester hours and completion of core requirements to include 6 mathematics, 6 science, 6 foreign language, and 1 computer course; minimum 2.0 GPA; grade of "C" or better in all core courses; "C" or better in courses counted towards the minimum hours in the major fields; and completion of the required exit interview.

Grading System
A–F; P=Pass; W=Withdraw;

STUDENT BODY PROFILE
Total enrollment (male/female): 384/895

From in-state: 1,215

Other regions: 8 states, 2 foreign countries

Full-time undergraduates (male/female): 317/740

Part-time undergraduates (male/female): 67/155

Ethnic/Racial Makeup
African American, 1,266; International, 13.

Class of 1995 Profile
Number of applicants: 640

Number accepted: 429

Number enrolled: 235

Transfers enrolled: 77

FACULTY PROFILE
Number of faculty: 61

Student-teacher ratio: 18:1

Full-time faculty: 51

Part-time faculty: 10

Tenured faculty: 28

Faculty with doctorates or other terminal degrees: 72%

SCHOOL CALENDAR
1992–1993: August 17–May 7 (semester hours)

Commencement and conferring of degrees: May 16

Two summer sessions.

DEGREES OFFERED 1991–92:

Bachelor of Arts

African-American Studies

Arts/Fine Arts

Commerce/Management

Economics

Education

Elementary Education

English

Government

History

Humanities

Political Science

Secondary Education

Social Sciences

Social Work

Sociology

Bachelor of Science

Accounting

Biology/Biological Sciences

Business Administration

Chemistry

Computer Science

Engineering

Health/Physical Education

Mathematics

Natural Sciences

Pre-professional

Pre-dentistry

Pre-medicine

Graduates That Later Obtain Higher Degrees

5% enter medical school

15% enter business school (MBA programs)

SPECIAL PROGRAMS

Accelerated degree program allows students to earn an undergraduate degree in a three-year period of time rather than the traditional four years.

Adult or Continuing Education program is available for nontraditional students returning to school or working full time.

Advanced Placement (AP) allows high school students to get advanced placement and college credit for scores on the College Board AP tests in various subjects.

College Level Examination Program (CLEP) grants college credit for nontraditional educational experiences, such as the military, work, or other life experiences, by taking the CLEP exam administered by the College Entrance Examination Board.

College orientation is offered to entering students for one week before classes begin at no cost to acquaint students with the college and to prepare them for college life; parents may attend.

Cooperative Education Program combines formal academic study with practical work experience in 21 majors.

Cross registration allows students to register for course credit toward degree requirements with schools in the Greater Memphis Consortium.

ESL (English as a Second Language) program offers courses in English for students whose native language is not English.

Honors program offers academically talented students a challenging program of study, which includes special classes, seminars, colloquia, cultural activities, and special recognition to motivate participants.

Individualized majors allow students to create their own major program(s) of study.

Part-time degree program allows students to earn an undergraduate degree while attending part time.

Pre-medicine, natural science, and mathematics/chemistry programs allow students to take courses toward these programs at Christian Brothers University and the University of Tennessee Medical School.

Remedial program or academic remediation provides remedial courses for entering students to bring them up to admission standards.

ROTC provides training in military science for commission as a second lieutenant in the U.S. Armed Forces. Two-, three-, and four-year scholarships are available through cooperative Army ROTC and cooperative Air Force ROTC.

Study Abroad Program allows students to go to a foreign country for a specified period of time for part of their college education. Countries include France and Mexico.

Summer Bridge Program allows students to participate in pre-college programs and receive credit hours for courses taken.

Three/two degree programs give students the opportunity to get two degrees—one in liberal arts and the other in a professional program or master's program—by completing three years at matriculated school and two years at cooperating school. A three/two degree program in engineering is also available with Christian Brothers University, Tuskegee University, and Tennessee State University.

The Upward Bound Program is a student support program which provides remediation and cultural enrichment services to students in grades 10, 11, and 12 to encourage enrollment in college.

ATHLETIC PROGRAMS

LeMoyne-Owen is a member of the National Collegiate Athletic Association (NCAA), all Division II.

Intercollegiate sports: men's basketball, cross-country running, and track & field; women's basketball.

Intramural sports: badminton, basketball, football, gymnastics, swimming, diving, tennis, and volleyball.

LIBRARY HOLDINGS

The Hollis F. Price Library holds 190,000 bound volumes, 7,000 microforms, 276 periodicals, and 4,800 audiovisuals. Special collections include the Sweeney collection of

books by black authors about black history and culture.

STUDENT LIFE

Special Regulations

Cars permitted in designated areas; $10 fee charged each semester.

Campus Services

Health services, personal and psychological counseling, remediation, tutoring, testing center for ACT, and late night escort.

Campus Activities

Social and cultural activities include theater, chorale, and jazz band. Students may work on *The Magician* (quarterly report), *The Messenger* (weekly newspaper), or the *Columns* (yearbook).

Leadership opportunities are found in the Student Government Association (SGA) or the various other clubs and organizations, such as the NAACP, Pre-alumni Council, Social Work Club, Students In Free Enterprise, and Community Outreach programs. Greek letter fraternities include Alpha Phi Alpha, Kappa Alpha Psi, Omega, Psi Phi, and Phi Beta Sigma; sororities include Alpha Kappa Alpha, Delta Sigma Theta, Sigma Gamma Rho, and Zeta Phi Beta. Honor societies are represented on campus.

LeMoyne-Owen is located in the city of Memphis, the largest city in Tennessee with a population of approximately 80,000, giving students all the benefits of a large metropolitan city. Shopping centers, museums, fine restaurants, theaters, concerts, orchestra, horseback riding, golf, boating, and major league sports are all within easy access of the campus. Local public transportation (MATA) takes students to downtown Memphis; to the international airport, which is 10 miles away; and to the mass rail system, which is five miles away. The city is served by mass bus transportation. Graceland is within 30 minutes from the campus. Memphis was home to two famous singers:

W. C. Handy, known as father of the blues, and Elvis Presley, the king of rock and roll.

Housing Availability

Limited campus housing is available. Off-campus living permitted.

NOTABLE ALUMNI

Marian S. Barry, 1958–Former mayor, Washington, D.C.

Benjamin Lawson Hooks, 1944–Attorney and executive director, NAACP

Eric C. Lincoln, 1947–Educator, Duke University, Durham, NC

MEHARRY MEDICAL COLLEGE

HISTORY

Meharry Medical College is a private, independent professional medical school affiliated with the United Methodist Church. Meharry was founded in 1876 as the Medical Department of Central Tennessee College. Ten years later, the Dental Department was established, and in 1889 a division of Pharmacy was established. In 1900, the name changed to Meharry Medical College of Walden University. After receiving a separate state charter from Walden University in 1915, the school became Meharry Medical College.

Meharry has emerged from the early years, which were marred by discrimination and economic deprivation, to take its place among the leading schools preparing health professionals. Meharry continues a tradition of growth in both programs and facilities. The college includes the Schools of Medicine, Dentistry, Graduate Studies, and Allied Health Professions. It boasts that 40% of all black physicians and dentists are graduates of the school, and it considers all its

1005 D.B. Todd Blvd.
Nashville, TN 37208
Phone: (615) 327-6111
Fax: (615) 327-6228

Total Enrollment:
867

Level of Selectivity:
Competitive

Motto:
Worship of God
through service to man

graduates to be distinguished or notable alumni.

Meharry College is located in the central part of Tennessee with an 18-building campus that includes a 400-bed teaching hospital, a clinical training facility, and a health center. This modern medical school forms a three-institution educational center with Fisk University and Tennessee State University, both within walking distance.

ACCREDITATION

Meharry Medical College is accredited by the Southern Association of Colleges and Secondary Schools to award the Doctor of Philosophy, Doctor of Medicine, Doctor of Dental Surgery, Master of Medical Sciences, and Master of Public Health degrees. Certificates in health professional training are also offered.

Other Accreditation

American Association of Medical Colleges
Liaison Committee of Medical Education
  of the American Medical Association

COSTS PER YEAR

1992–93 Tuition: $13,031

Room: $1,064

Special fees: $1,011

Books: $800

Estimated total cost: $15,906

FINANCIAL AID

1991–92 Institutional Funding:

Number of scholarships and grants: 423

Total amount of scholarships and grants:
  $1,000,000

Range of scholarships and grants:
  $1,000–$2,364

1991–92 Federal and State Funding

Number of scholarships and grants: 423

Total amount of scholarships and grants:
  $2,705,050

Range of scholarships and grants:
  $1,000–$6,395

Total amount of loans: $12,798,190

Total amount of work-study: $156,000

Financial Aid Specific to the School

85% of the student body received financial aid during 1991–92.

The deferred payment plan allows students to pay college costs in two or three monthly installments during the semester at a small cost.

New students in the doctoral or Ph.D. program are automatically considered for scholarships and fellowships that pay full tuition and fees, and provide stipends of $10,000 per year.

A short-term, low-interest loan program is available through the college. The maximum available is $1,000 for a 30 to 60 day loan period.

Tuition Reduction Program for students in the SREB Program grants credit of $900 per year toward college costs.

Tuition Reduction Program for students from New York grants credit of $2,000 per year toward college costs.

Over 50 alumni or endowed scholarships and school awards are available to students based on merit or financial need; some are based on location.

Financial Aid Deadline

April 15

Financial Aid Contact

Mr. George McCarter, Meharry Medical College, 1005 D.B. Todd Blvd., Nashville, TN 37208; (615) 327-6223

ADMISSION REQUIREMENTS

MCAT (Medical College Admission Test) or Dental Aptitude Test required.

Entrance Requirements

Applicants for admission to the medical or dental schools must graduate from an approved secondary school, or its equivalent with at least three full academic years of acceptable college credit earned in a college or institute of technology currently approved by an agency recognized by the Association of American Medical Colleges and by one of the regional Councils on Medical Education of the American Medical Association.

Satisfactory completion of the three years premedical education by September of the year the applicant desires to be admitted is needed, which includes the following semester/quarter hours respectively: 8/12 general biology or zoology with laboratory, 8/12 inorganic chemistry with qualitative analysis including laboratory, 8/12 organic chemistry with laboratory, 8/12 general physics with laboratory, and 6/9 English composition. Recommended electives for medical applicants include general botany, mathematics, economics, history, psychology, sociology, foreign languages, philosophy, fine arts and logic.

Recommended electives for dental applicants include embryology, comparative anatomy, quantitative analysis, mechanical drawing, mathematics, economics, history, psychology, sociology, foreign languages, philosophy, and fine arts. An average grade of at least "C" in each subject field is required. Must meet the specific requirements of the school or division in which admission is sought; must be in upper half of class; must be invited by the admissions committee for a formal interview. Applications should be sent to the American Medical College Application Service (AMCAS). Student should instruct AMCAS to forward files to the Office of Admissions, Meharry Medical College. A non-refundable $25.00 processing fee is due by January 31.

Students applying to the School of Graduate Studies must submit GPA, GRE test scores, and an official transcript from all secondary schools attended; hold a bachelor's, master's or advanced degree from an accredited college or university with an overall "B" average and a "B" average in science courses; submit two letters of recommendation from instructors in the natural sciences; and submit a written essay. Applicants applying to the School of Graduate Studies should apply directly to Meharry Medical College, School of Graduate Studies, Nashville, TN 37208.

With the Early Decision Program, an applicant files an application only to Meharry and is guaranteed prompt notification on or before October 1 of either acceptance or rejection. Official transcripts and all required application materials must be received by AMCAS by August 1. The applicant is responsible for requesting a report of his/her performance on the Medical College Admissions Test which should be submitted to the Office of Admissions and Records. The test should be taken in the spring of the junior year of college.

Advanced standing admission students who have completed no more than two years at other dental schools are eligible for admission. Student must submit official transcripts from each school attended, show evidence of satisfactory scholastic and disciplinary records, and show evidence of honorable dismissal from dean of dental school(s).

International students whose premedical education was done outside the United States must submit all credits earned in a foreign school directly to Meharry; the last two years of prerequisite course work must have been taken at an approved college in the United States; and the Medical College Admission Test (MCAT) must have been taken within the last three years. A proficiency examination may be required in the pre-medical required subjects.

Admission Application Deadline
Dec 15

Admission Contact
Ms. Doris Petway, Director of Admissions, Meharry Medical College, 1005 D.B. Todd Blvd., Nashville, TN 37208; (615) 327-6223.

GRADUATION REQUIREMENTS
For the Doctor of Medicine, students must satisfactorily complete all academic

work required for the M.D. degree as well as the Clinical Clerkship of eight weeks in each of the following: internal medicine, pediatrics, surgery, obstetrics and gynecology, family and preventive medicine, and psychiatry; must have successfully passed Part I and Part II of the National Board of Medical Examiners (NBME); and must be recommended by the faculty to the Board of Trustees of the college as representing a person of good character and of acceptable scholastic attainment. Candidates are required to wear the regalia specified for their degree.

For the Doctor of Dental Surgery (D.D.S.) students must complete all didactic courses, clinical requirements, practical examinations, and Mock State Board Examinations; must pass Part I and II of the National Board Dental Examinations at national level standard; and must maintain regular attendance for minimum of four years of total instruction. Transfers must complete at least two years at Meharry and must demonstrate high standards of moral and ethical conduct.

For a doctoral degree (Ph.D.) in biochemistry, biomedical sciences, microbiology, pharmacology, or physiology, students must complete major requirements as well as core requirements; must pass a comprehensive examination prepared by the committee on instruction; must complete a dissertation approved by the committee on instruction, the department, and graduate dean; must complete an oral examination; and must be in residence for two semesters.

Grading System

A-F; I=Incomplete; E=Conditional; WV=Withdrew Voluntarily; WA=Withdrew Failing.

STUDENT BODY PROFILE

Total enrollment: 867

From in-state: 253

Other regions: 26 states; 12 foreign countries

Graduates: 867

Ethnic/Racial Makeup

African American, 669; Hispanic, 16; Caucasian, 108; International, 74.

Class of 1995 Profile

Number of applicants: 4,225

Number accepted: 315

Number enrolled: 156

Transfer applicants: 10

Transfers enrolled: 1

FACULTY PROFILE

Number of faculty: 192

Student/teacher ratio: 6:1

Tenured faculty: 29

Faculty with doctorates or other terminal degrees: 100%

SCHOOL CALENDAR

1992–93: August–May (semesters)

Commencement and conferring of degrees: May

One summer session.

DEGREES OFFERED AND NUMBER CONFERRED 1991–92:

Dentistry: 18

Life Sciences (Ph.D.): 8

Medicine: 31

N.S.P.H. (Community Health Science): 13

SPECIAL PROGRAMS

The Doctoral Program in the graduate school leads to the interdisciplinary Ph.D. in biomedical sciences with major emphasis in biochemistry, biomedical sciences, microbiology, pharmacology, or physiology. The Ph.D. program is divided into three phases: core, major emphasis, and dissertation. Most students require at least two years to complete the major emphasis phase.

The Dental Hygiene Program has full approval accreditation status from the Commission on Dental Accreditation. Graduates qualify to take the National Board Dental Hygiene Examination, regional examinations, and state board examinations in all states in which the graduates may choose to practice. The program emphasizes courses leading toward certification as a dental hygienist—a licensed professional with specialized clinical and educational skills, who performs preventive and therapeutic services under the supervision of a licensed dentist. This program is under the auspices of the School of Allied Health Professions, jointly supported and administered by Meharry Medical College and Tennessee State University.

The Medical Scholars Program is designed for highly qualified applicants to the School of Medicine. Students identified on the basis of MCAT scores, grade point averages, personal interviews, letters of recommendation, and research interests are recruited as participants in this program which is offered jointly by the Medical School and the School of Graduate Studies. This program is designed to be flexible and individualized. Participants have the option of pursuing a combined course of study leading to a dual M.D./Ph.D. degree. The program begins in the summer before the freshman year of medicine.

The Special Medical Program provides an enriched, 5-year curriculum to students pursuing the M.D. degree. Students selected by the Committee on Admissions must present the same course prerequisites and supporting application credentials as regular applicants. The program begins in June.

The Early Entry Program was begun in the 1990–91 academic year. The primary objective of this program is to reduce the attrition rate by identifying students with potential academic deficiencies, so as to structure appropriate support mechanisms. This uniquely designed program will extend from July through August of each year.

An off-campus clerkship and electives program provides an opportunity for Juniors participating in the Meharry/University of Tennessee program to take 3 months (12 weeks) elective requirements selectively off-campus with the approval of appropriate departments at Meharry.

Combined degree programs will allow students enrolled in the medical school to arrange to earn the Ph.D. with the M.D. Student must be accepted into medical school before applying for the combined doctoral program.

A combined pre-dental and dental curriculum leading to completion of both bachelor's and D.D.S. degrees is available. Student should ascertain from the registrar of the institution in which the three years of pre-dental work was completed whether the first year of dentistry taken at Meharry Medical College will be acceptable as the fourth year toward a bachelor's degree. An official statement to this effect must be presented with application.

LIBRARY HOLDINGS

The library holds over 70,000 volumes, 1,300 current journals/serial titles, a moderate audiovisual collection, and a special archives collection of materials by and about Meharry. A manuscript collection of past Presidents of Meharry and a special collection of books and manuscripts pertinent to role of blacks in medicine, dentistry, nursing, and pharmacy are also available. Students may benefit from bibliographic retrieval through CD-ROM technology, MEDLINE database, Microcomputer Learning Laboratory, Word Perfect software, DIALOG, and NLN databases.

STUDENT LIFE

Special Regulations
Mandatory group health insurance.

Campus Services
Health center, personal and psychological counseling, and career counseling and placement.

Campus Activities

Lectureships provide Meharry students the opportunity to have academic interchange with renowned persons from various health care disciplines in conferences, Grand Rounds, informal discussions, and formal lectures. Table Clinic Day provides an opportunity for first-year dental students to participate in a presentation of an in-depth study on an aspect of dental health.

Greek-letter fraternities include Alpha Phi Alpha, Kappa Alpha Psi, Omega Psi Phi, and Phi Beta Sigma; sororities include Alpha Kappa Alpha, Delta Sigma Theta, and Zeta Phi Beta. Honorary medical societies represented include Omicron Kappa Upsilon Honor Dental Fraternity, Sigma Phi Alpha Dental Hygiene Honor Society, Chi Delta Nu Fraternity, and Kappa Sigma Pi Honorary Dental Fraternity.

Meharry is located in the northern section of the city of Nashville, Tennessee, with a population of approximately 488,400. Taxicab service provides easy access to the bus terminal and airport which is 10 miles away. Nashville, known as the country music capital of the world, provides other cultural and recreational activities such as museums, historic sites, botanical gardens, art centers, swimming, boating, fishing, and spectator baseball and football. Memphis, Tennessee, and Atlanta, Georgia, are within hours of Meharry.

Housing Availability

305 housing spaces available. Women-only housing and family housing are available.

NOTABLE ALUMNI

Dr. James Milton Bell, M.D., 1947–Psychiatrist and clinical director, Berkshire Farm Center & Services for Youth

Dr. Marian Perry Bowers, M.D., 1963–Member of Meharry's Upper Tenth; clinical professor, USC School of Medicine, head & neck surgery

Dr. Alma Rose George–Surgeon and president, Medical Staff, Mercy Hospital, Detroit, Michigan

Dr. Robert D. Miller, Jr., M.D., 1984–President, Arkansas State Board of Health

Dr. Jacob L. Shirley, M.D., 1910–Former director of Health Services, Albany State College

TENNESSEE STATE UNIVERSITY

HISTORY

Tennessee State University (TSU) is a four-year, state-supported, coed, liberal arts university founded in 1912 as a land grant institution. In 1979, TSU merged with the University of Tennessee at Nashville, which was founded in 1971.

The school has evolved from a normal school, to a four-year college in 1922, to a university in 1951. The university became a full-fledged land grant institution in 1958. The center at Nashville met the requirements of accreditation as a four-year degree granting institution in 1971.

TSU has a tri-fold mission as a land grant institution to provide cooperative extension services and programs in the agricultural sciences; as a comprehensive institution to provide programming in agriculture, allied health, arts and sciences, business, education engineering and technology, home economics, human services, and nursing and public administration; and as an urban institution to provide both degree and non-degree programs that are appropriate and accessible to a working population.

Main Campus
3500 John Merritt Blvd.
Nashville, TN
37209-1561
Phone: (615) 320-3131
Avon Williams
(Downtown) Campus
10th and Charlotte
Nashville, TN
37203-3401
Phone: (615) 251-1111

Total Enrollment:
7,500

Level of Selectivity:
Moderately competitive

Motto:
Think, Work, Serve

TSU has two campuses. The main campus is located in a residential area of the city on 450 acres and includes 65 buildings, farmland, and pastures. The downtown campus is located in a large modern building that houses the business and evening programs, a library, a cafeteria, and meeting rooms. A $112 million dollar capital improvement project to be completed by the mid-1990s includes seven new buildings and a completely landscaped campus with courtyards, plazas, and a state-of-the-art utility tunnel.

ACCREDITATION

Tennessee State University is accredited by the Southern Association of Colleges and Schools to award the Bachelor of Arts, Bachelor of Science, Associate's, Master's (Specialist in Education), and Doctoral degrees.

Other Accreditation

Accreditation Board of Engineering and Technology

American Dietetic Association

American Speech-Language Hearing Association

Council on Social Work Education

National Association of Schools of Music

National Council for Accreditation of Teacher Education

National League of Nursing

COSTS PER YEAR

1992–93 Tuition: $1,466 (in-state); $4,830 (out-state)

Room and board: $1,356 (room); $1,186 (board)

Special fees: $125

Books: $500

Estimated total cost: $4,633 (in-state); $7,997 (out-state)

FINANCIAL AID

Financial Aid Specific to the School

85% of the student body received financial aid during 1991–92.

Academic scholarships up to $7,500 may be available to students with a high school GPA of 3.0 or above and ACT score of 21 or above. Tennessee high school students with a minimum ACT score of 19 who are in the top 25% of their graduating class may also qualify.

Departmental and university scholarship programs provide scholarships from business and industry through the various departments of the university.

Minority Student Grants Program provides grants to eligible caucasian undergraduates who have a 2.5 GPA or an ACT score of 19.

Performance scholarships in music are available for students participating in band and choir.

Athletic scholarships are available for students participating in intercollegiate sports.

Presidential scholarships cover tuition, fees, room, and board for black Tennessee high school students with a minimum ACT score of 21 or equivalent SAT and a 3.0 GPA.

Low-interest long-term loans are available from the college funds for students attending TSU.

Thurgood Marshall Black Education Fund provides a four-year scholarship at this public black college. Qualifying students must have a high school GPA of 3.0 or better and a SAT score of 1,000 or ACT score of 24 or more. Students must be recommended by high school counselor as exceptional or exemplary in the creative or performing arts. Scholarship pays tuition, fees, room, and board, not to exceed $6,000 annually.

Air Force ROTC and cooperative Army and Navy ROTC with Vanderbilt University offer two-, three-, and four-year scholarships that pay tuition, fees, books, and other expenses, and provide a monthly stipend of $100.

Tennessee Student Assistance Award provides grants to undergraduate students who are residents of Tennessee.

Financial Aid Deadline

April 1 (priority)

Financial Aid Contact

Mr. Homer R. Wheaton, Chief Financial Aid Officer, Tennessee State University, Avon Williams Campus, 10th and Charlotte Avenues, Nashville, TN 37203-3401; (615) 320-3440.

ADMISSION REQUIREMENTS

SAT (720) or ACT (19) required

Entrance Requirements

Graduation from an accredited high school; pass 13 of 14 State Board of Regents high school unit requirements; in-state students must pass Tennessee proficiency exam and have a minimum 2.25 GPA or an ACT score of 19; out-state students must have a 2.50 GPA or ACT score of 19. A $5 non-refundable application fee required.

GED students must meet the basic admissions requirement.

Transfer students must submit official transcripts of all high school and college work; have a minimum 2.0 GPA; and complete at least 30 hours in residence at TSU.

International students must pass TOEFL exam with a minimum score of 500.

Early admission allows academically gifted high school students the opportunity to enroll in college for credit before completing high school.

Admission Application Deadline

August 1 (fall); December 1 (spring); May 1 (summer)

Admission Contact

Carmelia Taylor, Office of Admissions and Records, Tennessee State University, Main Campus, 3500 John A. Merritt Blvd., Nashville, TN 37209-1561; (615) 320-3420.

GRADUATION REQUIREMENTS

A minimum of 65 hours and completion of core requirements for associate's degree. A minimum of 132 hours and completion of core requirements to include the following hours: 6 English, 3 mathematics; 6 science; 6 social science, 12 foreign language, 2 physical education, and 1 computer course for some majors; minimum cumulative 2.0 GPA for a bachelor's degree.

Grading System

A-F; I=Incomplete, IP=In Progress, NC=I not removed after one year; NG= Given only to special service students for unsatisfactory in credit level course; S=Satisfactory in non-credit course; U=Unsatisfactory in non-credit course; W=Official withdrawal; AU=Audit

STUDENT BODY PROFILE

Total enrollment (male/female):
  3,150/4,350

From in-state: 5,850

Other regions: 38 states, 15 foreign countries

Full-time undergraduates (male/female):
  2,706/3,736

Part-time undergraduates (male/female):
  40/55

Graduate students (male/female): 404/559

Ethnic/Racial Makeup

African American, 4,650; Hispanic, 75; Asian, 150; Native American, 75; Caucasian, 2,235; International, 390.

Class of 1995 Profile

Number of applicants: 6,562

Number accepted: 3,064

Number enrolled: 1,433

Median ACT score: 19

Average high school GPA: 2.5

FACULTY PROFILE

Number of faculty: 430

Student-teacher ratio: 25:1

Full-time faculty (male/female): 324

Part-time faculty (male/female): 106

Faculty with doctorates or other terminal
  degrees: 70%

SCHOOL CALENDAR

1992–93: Aug 22–April 30 (semester hours)

Commencement and conferring of degrees:
  May 1

Two summer sessions.

DEGREES OFFERED 1991–92:

Bachelor of Business Administration

Accounting

Business Administration

Economics and Finance

Office Management

Bachelor of Arts

Arts and Sciences

Biology

English

Foreign Language

History

Mathematics

Physics

Political Science

Psychology

Social Work

Speech Communication and Theater

Bachelor of Science

Aeronautical and Industrial Technology

Agricultural Sciences

Architectural Engineering

Art

Arts and Sciences

Biology

Chemistry

Civil Engineering

Computer Science

Criminal Justice

Dental Hygiene

Early Childhood Education

Electrical Engineering

English

Health Care Administration and Planning

Health, Physical Education, and Recreation

History

Home Economics

Hotel and Restaurant Administration

Mathematics

Mechanical Engineering

Medical Record Administration

Medical Technology

Music

Nursing

Occupational Therapy

Physical Therapy

Physics

Political Science

Psychology

Respiratory Therapy

Social Work

Sociology

Special Education

Speech Communication and Theater

Speech Pathology and Audiology

Urban Planning

Associate of Applied Science

Dental Hygiene

Early Childhood Education

Health Care Administration and Planning

Office Management

Nursing

Master's Degrees

Administration and Supervision

Agricultural Sciences

Biology

Business Administration

Chemistry

Criminal Justice

Curriculum and Instruction

Elementary Education

English

Guidance and Counseling

Health

Home Economics

Mathematical Science

Music Education

Physical Education and Recreation

Psychology

Public Administration

Special Education

Doctoral Degrees

Administration and Supervision

Curriculum and Instruction

Elementary Education

Psychology

SPECIAL PROGRAMS

Accelerated degree program allows students to complete their undergraduate degree in a shorter period of time than the traditional four years.

Adult or Continuing Education Program is available for nontraditional students returning to school or working full time.

Advanced Placement (AP) grants college credit for postsecondary work completed in high school. Students passing the AP test will receive credit by examination for each course and advanced placement.

College Level Examination Program (CLEP) determines the academic relevance of nontraditional educational experiences such as the military, on-the-job training, or other life experiences, through a series of tests and may grant students college credit for these experiences.

College orientation is offered to entering students for two days at no cost prior to the beginning of classes to acquaint students with the college and to prepare them for college life.

Cooperative Education Program alternates and combines classroom study with related paid work experience. The program provides academic credit and full-time status during co-op placement. Student must have a 2.50 GPA and have completed two semesters at TSU.

Cooperative programs with local hospitals are available in clinical training for nursing students. Credits are earned toward degree.

Honors program offers academically talented students a challenging program of study that includes special classes, seminars, colloquia, cultural activities, and special recognition to motivate participants. Qualifying students must have a recommendation from a teacher and have a "B" average.

Joint degree program in allied health with Meharry Medical College (MMC) allows students to take courses at MMC not offered at TSU.

Off-campus study is available in cooperation with Volunteer State Community College and Meharry Medical College.

Part-time degree programs allow students to earn an undergraduate degree while attending part time (daytime, evenings, weekends, and summers).

Remedial courses are offered to entering students to bring them up to admission standards and to help them adjust for success in college.

ROTC provides training in military science for commission as a second lieutenant in the U.S. Air Force, Army, or Navy. Two-, three-, and four-year scholarships are available. Army and Navy ROTC are offered in cooperation with Vanderbilt University.

Upward Bound and Talent Search provide academic counseling and cultural enrichment programs to high school students in grades 10, 11, and 12 who are disadvantaged and are in pursuit of a college education. Some credit courses may be offered.

ATHLETIC PROGRAMS

Tennessee State is a member of the National Collegiate Athletic Association (NCAA), all Division 1, and the Ohio Valley Conference (OVC).

Intercollegiate sports: men's baseball, basketball, cross-country, football, golf, and tennis; women's basketball, cross-country, softball, tennis, track & field, and volleyball.

Intramural sports: baseball, football, softball, track & field, and volleyball.

LIBRARY HOLDINGS

Brown Daniel Memorial (main) Library holds 236,764 volumes, 794 periodical subscriptions, 132,002 microforms, and 33,283 government documents; the downtown library holds 132,295 volumes, 14,857 microforms, and 460 periodical subscriptions.

STUDENT LIFE

Special Regulations

Cars permitted without restrictions; students living in dorms must purchase meal plan.

Campus Services

Health center, personal and psychological counseling, career counseling and placement, international student technical support, and reading center.

Campus Activities

Social activities include drama club, marching club, literary organizations, departmental clubs, student publications, jazz ensemble, international student organization, gospel and concert choirs, and more.

Leadership opportunities are found in the Student Government Association (SGA)

or the various other clubs and organizations. Greek-letter fraternities include Alpha Phi Alpha, Kappa Alpha Psi, Omega Psi Phi, and Phi Beta Sigma; sororities include Alpha Kappa Alpha, Delta Sigma Theta, Sigma Gamma Rho, and Zeta Phi Beta.

TSU is located in Nashville, the capital of Tennessee, with a population of more than 500,000. Nashville offers Broadway plays, concerts, professional dance troupes, and orchestra. Known as the "music city," quality local and national talent entertains both the visitor and resident. Both campuses provide opportunities for shopping and dining. The city is served by mass bus, passenger rail, and airline services.

Housing Availability

1,500 housing spaces; three women's dorms; three men's dorms; freshmen given priority; freshman-only housing; off-campus living permitted; large percent of students live off campus.

NOTABLE ALUMNI

Hazo W. Carter, Jr.–9th President, West Virginia State College

Dick Griffey–CEO Dick Griffey Productions (CA)

Wilma Rudolph–Olympic gold-medalist, Track

Brenda F. Savage–Associate professor, Lincoln University (PA)

Oprah Winfrey–Television star and producer

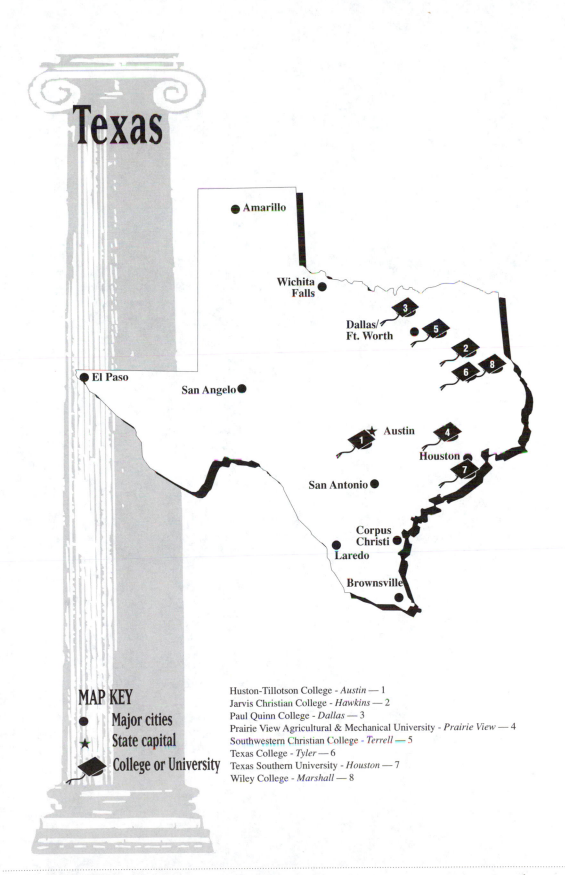

Texas

● Amarillo

Wichita
Falls ●

3

Dallas/
Ft. Worth ● **5**

2

6 **8**

El Paso ●

San Angelo ●

★ Austin **4**

1

Houston ●

San Antonio ● **7**

Corpus
Christi ●

Laredo ●

Brownsville
●

MAP KEY

● **Major cities**

★ **State capital**

◆ **College or University**

Huston-Tillotson College - *Austin* — 1
Jarvis Christian College - *Hawkins* — 2
Paul Quinn College - *Dallas* — 3
Prairie View Agricultural & Mechanical University - *Prairie View* — 4
Southwestern Christian College - *Terrell* — 5
Texas College - *Tyler* — 6
Texas Southern University - *Houston* — 7
Wiley College - *Marshall* — 8

HUSTON-TILLOTSON COLLEGE

1820 E. Eighth St.
Austin, TX 78702
Phone: (512) 505-3000
Fax: (512) 474-0762

Total Enrollment:
536

Level of Selectivity:
Slightly competitive

Motto:
In Union, Strength

HISTORY

Huston-Tillotson College is a four-year, private, independent, coed, liberal arts college affiliated with both the United Church of Christ and the United Methodist Church. The college displays its joint heritage with buildings named after representatives from each denomination. The former Tillotson College was affiliated with the United Church of Christ, while the former Samuel Huston College was affiliated with the United Methodist Church.

Founded as Tillotson College in 1875, the school was chartered as Tillotson Collegiate and Normal Institute in 1877, and then renamed Tillotson College in 1897. Samuel Huston College was founded in 1876. Its name changed to West Texas Conference School in 1878, and then it was renamed Samuel Huston College in 1890. Tillotson College and Samuel Huston College merged in 1952 to form Huston-Tillotson College.

One of the missions of the college is to provide experiences and services to a diverse, multicultural, and international student body. Huston-Tillotson is committed to the historic traditions of its founders and dedicated to providing the necessary skills, knowledge, experiences and attitudes essential for success in the 21st century.

ACCREDITATION

Huston-Tillotson is accredited by the Southern Association of Colleges and Schools (SACS) to award the Bachelor of Arts and Bachelor of Science degrees.

Other Accreditation

Council of Higher Education of the United Church of Christ

Texas Education Agency

University Senate of the United Methodist Church

COSTS PER YEAR

1992–93 Tuition: $3,990

Room and board: $1,484 (room); $1,965 (board)

Special fees: $660

Books: $540

Estimated total cost: $8,639

FINANCIAL AID

1991–92 Institutional Funding

Total amount of scholarships and grants: $83,364

1991–92 Federal and State Funding

Total amount of scholarships and grants: $1,446,814

Range of scholarships and grants: $200–$2,400

Total amount of loans: $1,241,083

Range of loans: $500–$4,000

Total amount of work-study: $158,743

Range of work-study: $200–$4,000

Financial Aid Specific to the School

In 1991–92, 83.9% of the student body received scholarships/grants.

Deferred payment allows students to pay 60% of tuition at registration, with 20% due on October 1 and remaining 20% due November 1 for fall semester; and with 20% due on May 1 and April 1 for spring semester.

Academic Management Services (AMS) and Tuition Management Systems (TMS) administers an installment payment plan that allows students to pay college cost in 10 monthly payments for a service charge of $45.00.

There are approximately 33 endowed scholarships including two geographical scholarships for residents of Austin Independent School District and Fort Bend County residents. Geographical scholarships are $1,000–2,000. Students must have at least a 2.0 GPA for Austin, and a 2.5 GPA for Fort Bend.

The Texas College Work-study program provides employment for Texas residents to work in college departments or non-profit community organizations.

College Work Aid (CWA) provides employment opportunities for students who do not qualify for work-study to work in college departments. Earnings pay educational expenses first.

United Negro College Fund (UNCF) scholarships are available to entering students scoring high on ACT or ETS and having a high school GPA of 3.0 or higher. To renew awards student must maintain a cumulative GPA of 3.0 in college.

The Army ROTC offers two- , three- , and four-year scholarships that pay tuition, fees, books, and other expenses, and provide a monthly stipend of $100.

Tuition Equalization Grants (TEG) are provided to Texas residents who are enrolled at least part-time, have demonstrated financial need, and did not receive an athletic or theological scholarship.

The State Student Incentive Grant (SSIG) is provided in conjunction with TEGs. Only TEG recipients can receive SSIG grants for an amount equal to that of the TEG award.

United Methodist (UM) scholarships are available in varying amounts to students who are members of the UM Church. Entering students must have a "B" average; returning students must maintain a 2.0/3.0 GPA or a 3.0/4.0 GPA.

United Methodist loans are available for students who are UM members. Eligible students may borrow up to $1,000 annually.

Financial Aid Deadline
May 1 (fall); continuous

Financial Aid Contact
Jackie M. Wilson, Director of Financial Aid, Huston-Tillotson College, 1820 East Eighth St., Austin, TX 78702; (512) 505-3030.

ADMISSION REQUIREMENTS
SAT 700 or ACT 15

Entrance Requirements
High school diploma with 18 units: 4 English, 3 mathematics, 2 science, 2 social sciences, 1 physical education, and 6 electives. Student must have a high school GPA of 2.5, an ACT score of 15, a SAT score of 700, and two letters of recommendation from a principal, counselor, or teacher. Complete medical records required. A $15.00 non-refundable application fee required.

GED Students must have an average passing score of 45.

Transfer applicants must have a cumulative GPA of 2.0 or a GPA that meets satisfactory academic progress based on Huston-Tillotson standards.

International students must have a high school diploma, score 15 on ACT, score 700 on SAT, or pass the General Certificate of Examination or the West African Certificate of Examination.

Admission Application Deadline
March 1st (priority); rolling admission provides no specific date for notification of admission so applicant is informed as soon as admission decision is made; early admission allows qualified students to enter college full time before completing high school.

Admission Contact
Mr. Donnie J. Scott, Director of Admissions, Huston-Tillotson College, 1820 East Eighth St., Austin, TX 78702; (512) 505-3027.

GRADUATION REQUIREMENTS
A minimum of 120 credit hours with a GPA of 2.0. One year of course work at Tillotson and the last 30 hours in residence. At least 30 semester hours of concentrated course work must be completed for a major, and at least 18 hours for a minor.

Grading System
A-F; I=Incomplete; IP=In Progress

STUDENT BODY PROFILE
Total enrollment (male/female): 257/279

From in-State: 413

Other regions: two states; one foreign country

Full-time undergraduates (male/female): 223/241

Part-time undergraduates (male/female): 35/37

Ethnic/Racial Makeup
African American, 436; Hispanic, 32;

Caucasian, 8; International, 20; Other/un-classified, 40.

Class of 1995 Profile
Number of applicants: 316
Number accepted: 236
Number enrolled: 157
Median SAT score: 325V; 365M
Median ACT score: 15.3
Average high school GPA: 2.50
Transfers enrolled: 53

FACULTY PROFILE
Number of faculty: 48
Student-teacher ratio: 13:1
Full-time faculty: 40
Part-time faculty: 8
Tenured faculty: 9
Faculty with doctorates or other terminal
   degrees: 44%

SCHOOL CALENDAR
1992–93: 8/31–5/7 (semesters)
Commencement and conferring of degrees:
   May
One summer session.

DEGREES OFFERED AND NUMBER CONFERRED 1991–92:

Bachelor of Arts
English: 1
History and Government: 3
Mass Communication: 7
Music: 2
Physical Education & Recreation: 3
Sociology: 5

Bachelor of Science
Accounting: 4
Biology: 2
Business Administration Education: 18
Chemistry: 3

Computer Science: 7
Education: 5
Finance: 1
Hotel & Restaurant Management: 4
Human Resources Management and
   Industrial Relations: 3
Marketing: 1
Mathematics: 1

SPECIAL PROGRAMS
The Integrated General Studies Program provides students with additional educational opportunities in reading, mathematics, writing, studying, and analytical skills. The program also offers special test-taking seminars and workshops to enhance student ability.

The Continuing Education Program provides nontraditional adult students a special series of workshops, seminars, and non-credit courses in a flexible environment.

The Cooperative Education Program offers students the opportunity to alternate attending class with intervals of related employment, or to simultaneously attend classes and work part time in their related field.

The Army ROTC in cooperation with the University of Texas provides training in military science for a commission as a second lieutenant in the U.S. Armed forces. Two- , three- and four-year scholarships are available.

A mandatory orientation facilitates students in becoming familiar with the college and its regulations.

Project Excel provides academic counseling and tutoring services to students to improve academic skills.

The Upward Bound program provides high school students the opportunity to receive academic support and guidance in an attempt to increase the number of at-risk students attending college.

ATHLETIC PROGRAMS
Huston-Tillotson College is a member of the National Association of Intercollegiate Athletics (NAIA).

Intercollegiate Sports: men's baseball and basketball, and women's basketball, volleyball and track.

Intramural sports: badminton, basketball, soccer, table tennis, and volleyball.

Athletic Contact

James R. Wilson, Athletic Director, Huston-Tillotson College, 1820 East Eighth St., Austin, TX 78702; (512) 505-3052.

LIBRARY HOLDINGS

The Downs-Jones Library houses 78,000 printed volumes, 310 periodical subscriptions, audiovisual materials, and a curriculum library for student teachers. Special collections include a special black history collection.

STUDENT LIFE

Special Regulations

All students are encouraged to live on campus and attend weekly convocations.

Campus Services

Health center, student employment, career planning and placement, and religious services, including chapel.

Campus Activities

Social or group activities include theater, band (including jazz), and chorale. Students may work on the student-run newspaper or yearbook. Communication majors may work in the campus television station.

Leadership opportunities can be found in the Student Government Association (SGA), nine academic clubs, or other student-run organizations. Greek-letter societies include Alpha Kappa Alpha, Delta Sigma Theta, Sigma Gamma Rho, and Zeta Phi Beta sororities, as well as the Alpha Phi Alpha, Kappa Alpha Psi, Omega Psi Phi, and Phi Beta Sigma fraternities. Honors societies include Kappa Xi, Alpha Kappa Mu, Beta Kappa Chi, Phi Beta Lambda, and Sigma Tau Delta.

Huston-Tillotson is located in the eastern part of Austin, the capital of Texas. The campus consists of nine buildings on more than 23 acres. Austin has a population of approximately 536,450. The city is serviced by a mass transit bus system and by passenger rail. San Antonio and Houston, within hours of the campus, offer students an array of social and cultural activities.

Housing Availability

472 housing spaces.

Handicapped Services

Wheelchair accessibility.

NOTABLE ALUMNI

Louie Carrington, 1971–Jazz musician

Ernest Dixon, 1943–United Methodist Bishop

Azie Taylor Morton, 1956–36th U.S. treasurer

Charles Urd, 1956–Mayor Protem, Austin, TX

JARVIS CHRISTIAN COLLEGE

PO Drawer G
Hawkins, TX
75765-9989
Phone: (903) 769-2174
Fax: (903) 769-4842

Total Enrollment:
592

Level of Selectivity:
Noncompetitive

Motto:
Providing an
Education on the
Percept of Christianity,
Service, Knowledge,
and Industry

HISTORY

Jarvis Christian College is a four-year, private, independent, liberal arts, coed college affiliated with the Disciple of Christ Christian Church. Established as Jarvis Christian Institute in 1913, the idea for the school began as early as 1904. In 1914, high school subjects were added to the curriculum and two years later, junior college courses were added. The school was incorporated in 1928. The name changed to Jarvis Christian College in 1937, the year senior college courses were added. Two years later, in 1939, the first bachelor's degrees were awarded.

Jarvis Christian was the brain child of the Negro Disciples of Christ in Texas and the Christian Woman's Board of Missions. The school was named after Major J. J. Jarvis who donated 456 acres of land for the school. The students who attended the school assisted in the construction of the school. This barter and labor concept was the earliest form of a work-study program.

Jarvis College's original mission, "to keep and maintain a school for the elevation and education of the Negro race, to educate the head, heart and hand and to produce useful citizens and earnest Christians" has not changed, although the direction of the educational programs has changed dramatically since its founding. This historically black institution is a member of the United Negro College Fund.

The 15-building campus is situated in an attractive wooded area of about 1,000 acres, which provides adequate room for future expansion. The campus proper covers approximately 243 acres.

ACCREDITATION

Jarvis Texas Christian College is accredited by the Southern Association of Colleges and Schools to award the Bachelor of Arts, Bachelor of Science, and Associate's degrees.

Other Accreditation

Texas Association of Colleges and
 Universities
Texas Education Agency

COSTS PER YEAR

1992–93 Tuition: $3,750

Room and board: $1,510 (room); $1,550
 (board)

Special fees: $285

Books: $300

Estimated total cost: $7,395

FINANCIAL AID

1991–92 Institutional Funding

Number of scholarships and grants: 270

Total amount of scholarships and grants:
 $260,646

Range of scholarships and grants:
 $200–$3,200

1991–92 Institutional Funding

Total amount of scholarships and grants:
 $1,304,442

Range of scholarships and grants:
 $400–$2,400

Number of loans: 484

Total amount of loans: $942,944

Range of loans: $400–$4,000

Number of work-study: 254

Total amount of work-study: $298,113

Range of work-study: $1,400–$1,800

Financial Aid Specific to the School

96% of the student body received financial aid during 1991–92.

United Negro College Fund (UNCF) scholarships are awarded to a limited number of entering students scoring high on ACT or ETS exams, or students with a high school GPA of 3.0 or better. To renew awards students must maintain a cumulative GPA of 3.0.

Tuition Equalization Grants (TEG) are available for Texas residents attending independent colleges and universities. Students must show financial need and not be enrolled in a religious degree program or be a recipient of an athletic scholarship. The average TEG scholarship is $1,200.

State Student Incentive Grants (SSIG) are available for students who qualify for TEG scholarships. SSIG awards up to $1,250 yearly. The Texas Rehabilitation Commission (TRC) provides assistance with tuition and non-refundable fees to students who have disabling conditions. Examples include orthopedic deformities, emotional disorders, diabetes, epilepsy, and heart conditions.

The Hinson-Hazlewood Loan is a Texas Stafford loan available to Texas residents only. The loan is administered through the Texas Coordinating Board.

Texas College Work Study (TCWSP) provides part-time jobs for students attending public or independent colleges. Only Texas residents are eligible for this program.

Financial Aid Deadline

August 10 (priority)

Financial Aid Contact

Mr. Harold Abney, Director of Financial Aid, Jarvis Christian College, Hawkin, TX 75765; (903) 769-5740, ext. 241.

ADMISSION REQUIREMENTS

ACT preferred. SAT accepted.

Entrance Requirements

A high school transcript with 16 units to include: 3 English, 1 science, 3 social sciences, 2 mathematics, and 7 electives. Students must have a physical by a licensed physician that includes verification of immunizations for polio, typhoid, and diphtheria/tetanus. A $15 non-refundable application fee is required.

GED students must meet basic requirements to be accepted.

Transfer students must submit official transcripts from colleges attended and a statement of honorable dismissal from the last institution attended. Full credit from unaccredited institutions will be accepted after completion of twelve hours at Jarvis.

International students must submit an official record verifying graduation from secondary school and must pass TOEFL examination with minimum score of 500; for some, the completion of Level nine of English as a Foreign Language is needed. ACT scores are necessary for students from English-speaking countries, as is proof of the ability to pay all college cost, with a $3,000 deposit to the college before arrival. A medical record and a $15 application fee are also required.

Admission Application Deadline

July 25 (priority). Rolling admission provides no specific date for notification of admission so applicant is informed as soon as admission decision is made.

Admission Contact

Office of Recruitment and Admissions, Jarvis Christian College, Hawkins, TX 75765; (903) 769-5733, ext. 236.

GRADUATION REQUIREMENTS

Minimum of 124 semester hours for a bachelor's degree with a cumulative GPA of 2.0. Last 30 hours must be in residence at Jarvis. Students must complete sophomore comprehensive exam, pass a proficiency test in English and mathematics, and take the Graduate Record Exam (GRE). Two semesters of assembly attendance are also required.

Grading System

A-F; I=Incomplete; W=Withdrew; CR= Credit; NC=No Credit; X=Withdrew Failing.

STUDENT BODY PROFILE

Total enrollment (male/female): 284/308

From in-state: 487

Other regions: 30 states; 7 foreign countries

Full-time undergraduates (male/female): 276/295

Part-time undergraduates (male/female): 8/10

Graduates (male/female): N/A

Ethnic/Racial Makeup

African American, 570; Hispanic, 1; Caucasian, 2; International, 19.

Class of 1995 Profile

Number of applicants: 423

Number accepted: 375

Number enrolled: 130

Median SAT score: 350V; 350M

Median ACT score: 14

Average high school GPA: 2.85

Transfer applicants: 145

Transfers accepted: 99

Transfers enrolled: 46

FACULTY PROFILE

Number of faculty: 49

Student-teacher ratio: 14:1

Full-time faculty (male/female): 22/12

Part-time faculty (male/female): 7/8

Tenured faculty: 1

Faculty with doctorates or other terminal
degrees: 53%

SCHOOL CALENDAR

1992–93: August 25–April 30 (semesters)

Commencement and conferring of degrees:
May 2

One summer session

DEGREES OFFERED AND NUMBER CONFERRED 1991–92:

Bachelor of Arts

English: 2

History: 5

Music: n/a

Religion: 1

Bachelor of Business Administration

Accounting: 5

Computer Science: 4

Management: n/a

Marketing: n/a

Bachelor of Science

Biology/Biology Education: n/a

Business Administration Education: n/a

Chemistry/Chemistry Education: 3

Elementary Education: 2

English Education: n/a

History/History Education: n/a

Human Performance/Human Performance
Education: 2

Mathematics/Mathematics Education: 5

Music/Music Education: n/a

Reading/Reading Education: n/a

Recreation Education: 2

Sociology: 9

Special Education: n/a

Pre-Professional

Law: n/a

Medicine: n/a

Graduates that later obtain higher degrees:
11%

SPECIAL PROGRAMS

The Advanced Summer Enrichment
Program (ASEP) grants six semester hours
and is designed to help students to overcome
difficulties that might interfere with their
academic performance. Students visit on-
site work environments and participate in
cultural events.

The Black Executive Exchange Program (BEEP) in cooperation with the National Urban League is designed to bring
about the merger of work and college. Black
business and professional men and women
serve as visiting professors and role models.

Academic remediation provides remedial courses for entering students to help
them succeed in college and to bring them
up to admission standards.

A joint degree program with St. John's
University School of Law allows a student
to take a minimum of 97 hours at Jarvis for
a bachelor's degree, and upon completion of
St. John's program, the student receives a
law degree. A 3.0 overall average is required
and the LSAT must be taken by end of the
junior year. No specific major is required.

2/3 dual engineering degree is offered in
cooperation with the University of Texas at
Arlington. Students must complete two
years at Jarvis with concentration on mathematics; then students transfer to the cooperating school for three years of engineering

courses. Upon completion of the program, students receive a Bachelor of Science and an Engineering degree.

The College Level Examination Program (CLEP) grants college credit for nontraditional educational experiences such as the military or other life experiences after satisfactory scores on the CLEP examination given by the College Examination Board are achieved.

The individualized major program allows students to create their own major field of study. Three faculty members must sponsor student's major plan.

The honors program places academically gifted students in a special track to motivate them to continue their intellectual development through organized planned research. Honor students present their papers in a seminar and have papers published.

The UNCF-Premedical Summer Program in cooperation with Fisk University is designed to encourage and better prepare minority students to enter medicine. Students must be sophomores or juniors attending UNCF schools.

The Biomedical Science program in cooperation with Meharry Medical College is an intensive eight-week summer program designed to encourage and better prepare minority students to enter medicine, dentistry, and other health professions.

The Brookhaven Semester Program is designed to increase the level of scientific achievement by participating schools. Research opportunities at Brookhaven National Laboratory are provided for students and faculty. Students must be biology, chemistry, or mathematics majors.

ATHLETIC PROGRAMS

Jarvis Christian is a member of the National Association of Intercollegiate Athletics (NAIA) and the Interregional Athletic Conference (IAC). The National Collegiate Athletic Association (NCAA) membership is under study.

Intercollegiate Sports: men's baseball, basketball, track & field, and volleyball; women's basketball, softball, track & field, and volleyball.

LIBRARY HOLDINGS

The Olin Library and Communication Center houses a curriculum library that supports the teacher education program of the college.

STUDENT LIFE

Special Regulations

Assembly attendance required of freshmen and sophomores.

Campus Services

Health, personal counseling, remedial programs, career counseling and placement, and religious services, including chapel.

Campus Activities

Social and group activities include theater, band, chorale, and dance. Students can get involved in the student-run newspaper (The Expression) or the newsletter (The Informer). Other publications include The Bulldog, an annual published by students with faculty guidance, or the Jarvisonian, a quarterly alumni and friends publication. Communication majors may get involved in the student-run radio station.

Leadership opportunities can be found in the Student Government Association (SGA) or the Women's Senate. Professional and academic organizations include pre-law and English clubs, and the National Society of Black Accountants. Greek-letter sororities include Alpha Kappa Alpha, Delta Sigma Theta, Sigma Gamma Rho, and Zeta Phi Beta. Fraternities include Alpha Phi Alpha, Kappa Alpha Psi, Omega Psi Phi, and Pheta Bet Kapa. Honor societies include Alpha Kappa Mu, Beta Kappa Chi, and Sigma Tau Delta.

Jarvis Christian is located on 245 acres in the rural town of Hawkins, Texas. The campus is close to the cities of Tyler and Longview, which both offer airline service to Dallas which is approximately 100 miles to the southeast. Tyler and Longview have populations ranging from 70,000 to 75,000 respectively. Anglers and canoeists can enjoy activities on the Sabine River in Longview. Wildlife enthusiasts and animal lovers can enjoy the wildlife reserve and the zoo. Both cities offer museums and other cultural and recreational activities.

Housing Availability

700 housing spaces available. 200 reserved for freshmen.

Handicapped Services

Include wheelchair accessibility.

NOTABLE ALUMNI

Dr. C. A. Berry–President, Jarvis Christian College

Dr. James O. Perpener–Fifth president, Jarvis Christian College

Dr. E. Wadworth Rand–Seventh president, Jarvis Christian College

PAUL QUINN COLLEGE

HISTORY

Paul Quinn College (PQC) is a four-year, private, coed, liberal arts college affiliated with the African Methodist Episcopal (AME) Church. It was founded in 1872 by a group of black circuit-riding AME ministers. Originally located in Austin, Texas, Paul Quinn moved to Waco in 1887, and to Dallas, Texas in 1990.

The 16-building campus is situated on 120 acres and includes dormitories, a library and a chapel.

ACCREDITATION

Paul Quinn College is accredited by the Southern Association of Colleges and Schools to award the Bachelor of Arts, Bachelor of Science, and Bachelor of Applied Science degrees.

Other Accreditation

Council on Social Work Education

Texas Education Agency

COSTS PER YEAR

1992–93 Tuition: $2,900

Room and board: $2,750

Special fees: $125

Books: $500

Estimated total cost: $6,275

FINANCIAL AID

Financial Aid Specific to the School

98% of the student body received financial aid during 1991–92.

Academic merit scholarships are awarded to students based on test scores, GPA, community service, and extracurricular activities.

3837 Simpson Stuart Rd.
Dallas, TX 75241
Phone: (214) 376-1000

Total Enrollment:
517

Level of Selectivity:
Noncompetitive

Air Force ROTC offers two- and four-year scholarships that pay tuition, fees, books, and other expenses, as well as provide a monthly stipend of $100.

Cooperative Education Program combines classroom study with related paid work experience. The program provides academic credit and full-time status during co-op placement.

Endowed, corporate, friends, and special interest scholarships number over 100 and are based on achievement and need.

Financial Aid Deadline
June 15 (priority)

Financial Aid Contact
Sarah J. Seldon, Director of Financial Aid, Paul Quinn College, Dallas, TX 75241; (214) 376-1000.

ADMISSION REQUIREMENTS
SAT or ACT (preferred) required

Entrance Requirements
Graduation from an accredited high school and completion of the following units: 3 English, 2 mathematics, 2 science, 2 social science, and 6 electives; submit official high school transcript minimum 2.0 GPA. A $10 non-refundable application fee is required.

GED students must meet basic admission requirements.

Transfer students submit official transcripts of all college work, minimum 2.0 GPA.

International students must submit certificate of high school completion; take TOEFL examination; provide proof of ability to pay all college costs.

Admission Application Deadline
Rolling admission provides no specific date for notification of admission so applicant is informed as soon as admission decision is made.

Admission Contact
Marilyn O. Marshall, Director of Admission, Paul Quinn College, Dallas, TX 75241; (241) 376-1000.

GRADUATION REQUIREMENTS
A minimum of 128 hours and completion of core requirements; 30 hours in residence.

Grading System
A–F: I=Incomplete, W=Withdraw

STUDENT BODY PROFILE
Total enrollment (male/female): 207/310

From in-state: 465

Other regions: 5 states, 3 foreign countries

Full-time undergraduates (male/female): 185/278

Part-time undergraduates (male/female): 22/32

Ethnic/Racial Makeup
African American, 439; Hispanic, 26; International, 16; Other/unclassified, 36.

FACULTY PROFILE
Number of faculty: 58

Student-teacher ratio: 12:1

Full-time faculty: 52

Part-time faculty: 6

SCHOOL CALENDAR
1992–93: August 27–May 15

Commencement and conferring of degrees: May

One summer session.

DEGREES OFFERED 1991–92:
Biology

Business

Computer and Information Science

Elementary Education

Fine Art

Health and Physical Education

History

Mathematics

Music

Psychology

Social Work

Sociology

SPECIAL PROGRAMS

College Level Examination Program (CLEP) determines the academic relevance of nontraditional educational experiences such as the military, on-the-job training, or other life experiences through a series of tests and may grant students college credit for these experiences.

Cooperative Education Program combines classroom study with related paid work experience. The program provides academic credit and full-time status during co-op placement.

Cooperative program with Texas State Technical Institute for Associate's degrees in over 20 majors.

Honors Program offers academically talented students a challenging program of study that includes special classes, seminars, colloquia, cultural activities, and special recognition to motivate participants.

Institute of Minority Men Research and Programming gives students an opportunity to study and research issues particular to the African American male.

Remedial courses are offered to entering students to bring them up to admission standards and to help them adjust for success in college.

ROTC provides training in military science for commission as a second lieutenant in the U.S. Air Force. Two-, and four-year scholarships are available.

Study Abroad Program allows students to go to Germany for part of their college education.

ATHLETIC PROGRAMS

Paul Quinn College is a member of the National Association of Intercollegiate Athletics.

Intercollegiate sports: men's baseball, basketball, and track & field; women's basketball, track & field, and volleyball.

Intramural sports: basketball, softball, table tennis, and volleyball.

LIBRARY HOLDINGS

The Sherman Abington Library houses 89,000 bound volumes, 77 periodical subscriptions, 35,000 microforms, and 2,000 government documents. Special collections include a state and regional AME Church Collection and an Ethical Cultural Collection.

STUDENT LIFE

Campus Services

Health services, personal counseling, student employment services, chapel and religious activities.

Campus Activities

Social and cultural activities include theater, chorale, and dance. Students may get involved in the student-run newspaper and yearbook.

Leadership opportunities can be found in the Student Government Association (SGA), organizations, or fraternities and sororities. Honor societies are also represented on campus.

Paul Quinn College is located in Dallas, Texas, population over 2 million. The city is served by mass air, bus, and passenger rail services. The campus is approximately 8 miles from downtown Dallas. Students have access to a variety of social, cultural, and recreational activities including shopping, dining, theater, concerts, fishing, and rodeos. Each New Year's Day the annual Cotton Bowl college football game and parade is held in Dallas. Points of interest include The Sixth Floor; an educational exhibit of President John F. Kennedy; Six Flags

Over Texas Amusement Park; and the Biblical Arts Center.

Housing Availability
262 housing spaces

PRAIRIE VIEW AGRICULTURAL & MECHANICAL UNIVERSITY

PO Box 66
Prairie View, TX
77446-0066
Phone: (409) 857-2626
Toll-free:
800-635-4859 (in-state)
800-334-1807
(out-state)

Total Enrollment:
5,590

Level of Selectivity:
Slightly competitive

Motto:
*Doctrina, servitium,
recercare*

HISTORY

Prairie View A&M University is a four-year, state-supported, coed college founded in 1876 as the Agricultural and Mechanical College of Texas for Colored Youths. Prairie View opened in 1878, with eight black men who were the first blacks to enroll in a state-supported school in Texas. In 1889, the name of the school was changed to Prairie View State Normal and Industrial College. Prairie View State became authorized to offer a four-year degree in 1901. The first bachelor of science degrees were granted in 1903.

The 49th Texas Legislature changed the name of Prairie View Normal and Industrial College to Prairie View University in 1945. The institution's name was again changed, by the 50th Legislature, in 1947 to Prairie View Agricultural and Mechanical College of Texas. To more accurately reflect the scope of its programs, the name was changed to Prairie View A&M University in 1973.

Prairie View is the second oldest institution of higher education in the state of Texas. In 1984, the mission of the university was redefined and Prairie View became one of three Texas universities designated by the Texas constitution as an "institution of first class," with the intention that Prairie View A&M University would become nationally recognized in the areas of education and research. It was also designated as the "state-wide special purpose institution," charged to provide special services to students from diverse ethnic and socio-economic backgrounds.

Prairie View's current president, Julius W. Becton, Jr., states that the university's mission is "to nurture students' academic development and intellectual curiosity by providing stimulating and healthy physical and cultural environments and services."

ACCREDITATION

Prairie View A&M is accredited by the Southern Association of Colleges and Schools (SACS) to award the Bachelor of Arts, Bachelor of Science, and Master's degrees.

Other Accreditation

National Council for Accreditation of Teacher Education

National League of Nursing

COSTS PER YEAR

1992-93 Tuition: $600 (in-state); $4,860 (out-state)

Room and board: $643 (room); $839 (board)

Special fees: $244

Books: $300

Estimated total cost: $2,626 (in-state); $6,886 (out-state)

FINANCIAL AID

1991–92 Institutional Funding

Number of scholarships and grants: 549

Total amount of scholarships and grants: $2,774,483

Range of scholarship and grants: $500–$4,500

1991–92 Federal and State Funding

Number of scholarships and grants: 2,920

Total amount of scholarships and grants: $5,768,587

Range of scholarships and grants: $200–$2,000

Number of loans: 1982

Total amount of loans: $4,445,352

Range of loans: $100–$7500

Number of work-study: 875

Total amount of work-study: $1,174,248

Range of work-study: $500–$10,000

Financial Aid Specific to the School

97.5% of the student body received financial aid during 1991–92.

The fee payment plan allows students to pay 50% of balance before registration, 25% of balance prior to the beginning of the sixth week of class, and remaining 25% of balance prior to the beginning of the 11th week of class.

Approximately 40 institutional or endowed scholarships are granted for academic ability, as well as financial need.

Athletic scholarships are available to students participating in intercollegiate sports.

The Ethnic Recruitment Scholarship is available to a limited number of non-black students who enroll at Prairie View A&M. Grades earned in high school and ACT or SAT scores are taken into consideration.

Tuition waivers are available for employees of Prairie View A&M and for citizens of Texas who were veterans of certain wars and their children. College work-study is also available.

Performance scholarships are available in music, art, and drama.

The Army and Naval ROTC offers two-, three- and four-year scholarships that pay tuition, fees, books, and other expenses, as well as provide a monthly stipend of $100.

The Thurgood Marshall Black Education Fund provides four-year scholarships to entering freshmen attending a land grant institution who have a high school GPA of 3.0 or higher, with a SAT score of 900 or an ACT score of 24 or more. Students must be recommended by high school counselor as exceptional. Scholarships pay tuition, room, and board, not exceeding $6,000 annually.

Texas Public Educational Grant and the Texas Public Educational State Student Incentive Grant are available to Texas residents who demonstrate financial need.

Tuition waivers are available for children and spouses of fire fighters and police officers killed in the line of duty.

Financial Aid Deadline
April 1 (fall); November 1 (spring)

Financial Aid Contact
A. D. James, Jr., Director of Student Financial Aid, Prairie View A&M University, PO Box 2967, Prairie View, TX 77446-2967; (409) 857-2423.

ADMISSION REQUIREMENTS
SAT (700) or ACT (18)

Entrance Requirements
A high school diploma with a 2.0 GPA, SAT score of 700 or ACT score of 18, and graduated in the upper 50% of their class. The following high school units: 4 English, 3 mathematics, 2 social sciences, 2 science, and 4 electives.

GED students need to meet the basic admission requirements.

Transfer applicants can only transfer a maximum of 90 credit hours from a college or university with similar character and content as courses offered at Prairie View A&M University. Transfer students must have a cumulative GPA of at least 2.0.

International students whose main language is not English must score at least 500 on the Test of English as a Foreign Language (TOEFL). A non-refundable $10 application fee is required with application.

Provisional admissions are granted to students who enroll in at least three semester hours each of math and English, and complete each course with a "C" grade or better. A student admitted as a provisional student may carry no more than nine additional credit hours.

Admission Application Deadline
Rolling admission; student should apply at least 10 days before classes begin, 30 days before for international students; applicant is informed as soon as admission decision is made.

Admission Contact
Mrs. Linda Berry, Director of Admissions and Records, Prairie View A&M University, PO Box 2610, Prairie View, TX 77446-2610; (409) 857-2626.

GRADUATION REQUIREMENTS
A minimum of 120 credit hours, including the core curriculum and six credits in American history and six credits in American government; 2.0 minimum GPA; a minimum of 36 hours in residence is required.

Grading System
A-F, I=Incomplete; W=Withdrawal without record; WP=Withdrawal while passing; WF=Withdrawal while failing; AW= Administrative withdrawal.

STUDENT BODY PROFILE
Total enrollment (male/female): 2,701/2,889

From in-state: 4,529

Full-time undergraduates (male/female): 2,124/2,395

Part-time undergraduates (male/female): 313/354

Graduate students (male/female): 190/214

Ethnic/Racial Makeup

African American, 4,771; Hispanic, 77; Native American, 5; Caucasian, 429; Other/unclassified, 308.

Class of 1995 Profile

Number of applicants: 3,107

Number accepted: 2,641

Number enrolled: 1,109

Median SAT score: 700

Median ACT score: 18

Average high school GPA: 2.5

FACULTY PROFILE

Number of faculty: 281

Student-teacher ratio: 20:1

Full-time faculty: 231

Part-time faculty: 50

Tenured faculty: 89

Faculty with doctorate or other terminal degrees: 44%

SCHOOL CALENDAR

1992-93: August 31–May 8 (semesters)

Commencement and conferring of degrees: May

Four summer sessions.

DEGREES OFFERED 1991–92:

Bachelor of Arts

Advertising Art

Applied Music

Art

Communications

Drama

Economics

English

Geography

History

Journalism Communications

Liberal Arts

Music

Political Science (Prelaw)

Radio/Television Communications

Social Work

Sociology

Spanish

Speech Communications

Bachelor of Business Administration

Accounting

Administrative Information Systems

Business Administration

Finance

Management

Marketing

Bachelor of Science

Agricultural Economics

Agricultural Human Resources

Agronomy

Animal Science

Architecture

Biology

Chemical Engineering

Chemistry

Civil Engineering

Computer Engineering Technology

Computer Science

Education

Electrical Engineering Technology

Engineering

Family and Community Services

Health

Human Development and the Family

Human Nutrition and Food

Industrial Technology (CADD)

Interdisciplinary Studies

Law Enforcement

Liberal Arts

Mathematics

Mechanical Engineering Technology

Medical Technology

Merchandising and Design

Nursing

Physics

Psychology

Science (inc. Arts)

Social Work

Sociology

Technology

Master's of Arts

English

History

Music (Applied)

Sociology

Master's of Business Administration

Business Administration

Master's of Education

Agricultural and Human Resources

Master's of Science

Agricultural Economics

Agriculture

Animal Science

Biology

Chemistry

Education

Engineering

Environmental Toxicology

Health and Human Performance

Home Economics

Industrial Education

Liberal Arts

Mathematics

Science

Soil Science

Pre-Professional

Dentistry

Medicine

Veterinary Medicine

Graduates that obtain higher degrees:
27%

SPECIAL PROGRAMS

A three-day college orientation session is provided for students at no cost; parents may attend.

The Alternating Cooperative Education Program allows students to alternate a semester of college course work with a semester of paid on-the-job work experience. Students who have completed 30 credit hours with a minimum GPA of 2.5 are eligible to participate.

The honors program offers academically talented students a challenging program of study that includes special classes, seminars, cultural activities, and special recognition to motivate participants.

The College Level Examination Program (CLEP) is a national testing program that provides credit by examination in accounting, American government, American history, biology, business, chemistry, computer science, economics, English, foreign languages, home economics, mathematics, and sociology.

The Outreach Precollege Program provides a series of two week, on-campus career development workshops for academically superior high school students to enhance their basic academic skills.

The Army and Navy ROTC provides training in military science for commission as a second lieutenant in the U.S. Armed Forces. Two- , three- and four-year scholarships are available.

ATHLETIC PROGRAMS

Prairie View is a member of the National Collegiate Athletic Association (NCAA) and the Southwestern Athletic Conference.

Intercollegiate sports: men's baseball, basketball, cross-country, football, golf, tennis, track & field; women's basketball, cross-country, tennis, track & field, and volleyball.

Intramural sports: basketball, golf, gymnastics, softball, swimming, table tennis, tennis, track & field, and volleyball.

Athletic Contact

Robert Lee Atkins, Health & Human Performance, Prairie View A&M University, PO Box 66, Prairie View, TX 77446-0066; (409) 857-2626.

LIBRARY HOLDINGS

The John B. Coleman Library houses 235,193 printed volumes, 259,823 microforms, 2,078 audiovisuals, 1,600 periodical subscriptions, 15,487 Texas State documents, and 150 computers available for student use. Special collections include an Afro-American Collection, a Master's Thesis collection, and a Prairie View A&M University Archival Collection.

STUDENT LIFE

Special Regulations

All undergraduate students are encouraged to live in the residence halls.

Campus Services

Health center, counseling, remedial programs, student employment, career counseling and placement, and religious services, including chapel.

Campus Activities

Social and group activities include theater, band, chorale, orchestra, and dance. Performing artists and speakers from the public and private sector provide cultural enrichment. Students may get involved in the student-run newspaper or yearbook. Students interested in communications can get involved in the campus radio station (KPVU-FM).

Leadership opportunities can be found in the Student Government Association (SGA) or other student-run organizations.

Greek-letter societies include Alpha Kappa Alpha, Delta Sigma Theta, Sigma Gamma Rho, and Zeta Phi Beta sororities as well as Alpha Phi Alpha, Kappa Alpha Psi, Omega Psi Phi, and Phi Beta Sigma fraternities. Over 30 academic honor societies are represented on campus.

The campus is located on 1,440 acres in the small town of Prairie View, Texas, approximately 40 miles from Houston. This semi-rural campus is approximately one mile from a major highway and 40 miles from the airport. The campus can be accessed by bus. The city of Prairie View offers access to an assortment of restaurants, shopping centers, rodeo events, ethnic festivals, horseback riding, and water sports on the lake. Nearby Houston offers students an array of social and cultural activities.

Housing Availability

3,347 housing spaces; freshman housing guaranteed.

Handicapped Services

Wheelchair accessibility.

NOTABLE ALUMNI

Commanding General Julius W. Becton, Jr., 1960–President, Prairie View A&M University

Jiles P. Daniels, Vice president, Student Affairs of Prairie View A&M University

George Francis, III, 1964–Vice president, Blue Cross/Blue Shield of Michigan

Lois J. Moore, 1957–Chief administrator officer, Harris County Hospital district

Percy E. Sutton, 1969–Retired, Inner City Broadcasting Corp. (NY)

Hobart Taylor, Jr., 1939–Special counsel to President Lyndon B. Johnson

Craig Washington, 1966–U.S. Representative, 18th Congressional District of Texas

SOUTHWESTERN CHRISTIAN COLLEGE

200 Bowser Circle
Terrell, TX 75160
Phone: (214) 524-3341

Total Enrollment:
244

Level of Selectivity:
Noncompetitive

HISTORY

Southwestern Christian College (SWCC) is a four-year, coed, liberal arts institution affiliated with the Church of Christ. It was founded in 1949 as Southern Bible Institute in Fort Worth, Texas. The following year the school moved to Terrell, Texas, occupying the former Texas Military College.

Southwestern strives to provide a wholesome environment for students conducive to the development of Christian character. Its primary purpose is to offer a well-rounded educational program that will motivate students to value academic excellence; to assist educational, culturally and/or economically disadvantaged students in making their transitions from high school to college; to assist students in preparation for varied vocations in life; and to help prepare future leaders of its church constituency.

Among the 15 buildings located on campus is the octagonal Round House Site, one of 20 surviving round houses in the nation. Southwestern Christian also boasts of a recently constructed fine arts building and an ultra-modern learning resources center that houses the library.

ACCREDITATION

Southwestern Christian College is accredited by the Southern Association of Colleges and Schools to award the Bachelor of Arts, Bachelor of Science, and Associate's degrees.

COSTS PER YEAR

1992–93 Tuition: $3,050

Room and board: $1,014 (room); $1,194 (board)

Special fees: $335

Books: $500

Estimated total cost: $6,093

FINANCIAL AID

1991–92 Institutional Funding

Number of scholarships and grants: 94

Total amount of scholarships and grants: $112,563

Range of scholarships and grants: $100–$3,163

1991–92 Federal and State Funding

Number of scholarships and grants: 167

Total amount of scholarships and grants: $193,372

Range of scholarships and grants: $112–$1,200

Number of loans: 95

Total amount of loans: $98,951

Range of loans: $80–$2,000

Number of work-study: 103

Total amount of work-study: $90,803

Range of work-study: $101–$1,440

Financial Aid Specific to the School

90% of the student body received financial aid during 1991–92.

Academic grant-in-aid, which pays tuition, room, board, and books, is available to entering freshmen with a 3.70 GPA (on a 4.0 scale). This grant is renewable annually if student maintains a 3.50 GPA. To apply, student should have high school principal send a recommendation to the Academic Dean stating cumulative GPA on 4.0 scale, class rank, and proposed date of graduation.

Academic grant-in-aid, which pays tuition and books, is available to entering freshmen with a 3.30–3.69 GPA (on a 4.0 scale). This grant is renewable by writing to the Academic Dean. To apply, students should have high school principal send a recommendation to the Academic Dean stating cumulative GPA on 4.0 scale, class rank, and proposed date of graduation. Apply six weeks prior to the start of the semester.

Academic grant-in-aid, which pays up to $750, is available to sophomore students with a cumulative 3.70 GPA, no incompletes, who did not receive an academic grant-in-aid award upon entering SWCC as a freshman.

Athletic scholarships available for students participating in intercollegiate basketball and track.

Endowed, corporate, friends, and special interest scholarships number approximately 18. Consult the school catalog or financial aid office for more information.

Hinson-Hazelwood Loans are provided to Texas residents who attend participating institutions full- or part-time and demonstrate financial need. The maximum loan amount is $2,500. Repayment of at least $30 a month should begin no later than nine months after student completes college or after student ceases to attend at least half-time.

Performance scholarships are available for talented music students.

Presidential Incentive Scholarships of a $300 tuition reduction are offered to students who have attended SWCC for a minimum of one semester and have attained a 3.0 GPA during the semester preceding application of scholarship. Qualifying students must demonstrate financial need and should not qualify for other financial aid.

Tuition Equalization Grant (TEG) provides financial assistance up to $1,900 for Texas residents who attend a private institution full time or half-time and demonstrate financial need. Students receiving an athletic scholarship or who are enrolled in a theological or religious program do not qualify for a TEG.

Financial Aid Deadline

July 15

Financial Aid Contact

Monty Bowden, Director of Financial Aid, Southwestern Christian College, 200 Bowser Circle, Terrell, TX 75160; (214) 524-3341.

ADMISSION REQUIREMENTS

Open admission. SAT or ACT required for counseling and placement.

Entrance Requirements

Graduation from an accredited high school and completion of the following units: 3 English, 12 academic subjects; submit official high school transcript, class rank; recommendation from school official; completed health form by physician; interview recommended. A $10 nonrefundable application fee required.

GED students must meet basic admission requirements.

Transfer students must submit official transcripts of all high school and college work; 2.0 GPA (on 4.0 scale); good standing with previous institution; recommendation from previous institution; transferring from unaccredited institution must meet regular admission requirements.

International students must submit official transcripts of all high school and college work translated in English; submit TOEFL score of 500 or complete level 5 of ESL program; provide proof of ability to pay college costs.

Early admission allows academically gifted high school students the opportunity to enroll in college for credit before completing high school.

Admission Application Deadline

Rolling admission provides no specific date for notification of admission so applicant is informed as soon as admission decision is made.

Admission Contact

Gerald Lee, Director of Admissions, Southwestern Christian College, PO Box 10, Terrell, TX 75160; (214) 524-3341.

GRADUATION REQUIREMENTS

A minimum of 124 credit hours and completion of the core requirements to include the following hours: 10 Bible, 12 English, 6 mathematics, 8 science (A.S. or B.S. degrees); 6 social sciences; 4 physical education; and 32 hours in residence.

Grading System

A–F; W=Withdrew before deadline; WP=Withdrew Passing; WF=Withdrew Failing; UW=Unofficial Withdrawal; I=Incomplete; FA=Failure Due to Absences; IS=Independent Study; AU=Audit; NX=No Credit

STUDENT BODY PROFILE

Total enrollment (male/female): 125/119

From in-state: 142

Other regions: 26 states; 5 foreign countries

Full-time undergraduates (male/female): 110/105

Part-time undergraduates (male/female): 18/11

Ethnic/Racial Makeup

African American, 205; Hispanic, 10; International, 29.

Class of 1995 Profile

Number of applicants: 244

Number accepted: 244

Number enrolled: 207

Transfers enrolled: 12

FACULTY PROFILE

Number of faculty: 25

Student-teacher ratio: 10:1

Full-time faculty: 15

Part-time faculty: 10

Tenured faculty: 12

Faculty with doctorates or other terminal degrees: 20%

SCHOOL CALENDAR

1992–93: August 11–May 6 (semester hours)

Commencement and conferring of degrees: May 9

DEGREES OFFERED 1991–92:

Associate of Arts
Bible Studies

Associate of Science
Religious Education

Bachelor of Arts
Bible Studies

Bachelor of Science
Religious Education

Certificates
Computer Science

Secretarial Science

Pre-professional
Pre-Engineering

SPECIAL PROGRAMS

Advanced Placement (AP) grants college credit for postsecondary work completed in high school. Students passing the AP test will receive credit by examination for each course.

Developmental Studies Program is for students whose high school record and college placement scores indicate a need for additional preparation. Students are admitted to this program until they meet regular admission requirements.

Certificate programs grant certificates in Computer Science and Secretarial Science.

College orientation is offered at no cost to entering students for three days prior to the beginning of classes to acquaint students with the college and to prepare them for college life.

Part-time degree program allows students to earn an undergraduate degree part time.

Remedial courses are offered to entering students to bring them up to admission standards and to help them adjust for success in college.

ATHLETIC PROGRAMS

Southwestern Christian College is a member of the National Junior College Athletic Association.

Intercollegiate sports: men's basketball and track & field; women's basketball and track & field.

Intramural sports: basketball

Athletic Contact

Senca Mangram, Director of Athletics, Southwestern Christian College, 200 Bowser Circle, Terrell, TX 75160; (214) 524-3341, Ext. 121.

LIBRARY HOLDINGS

The library, housed in the Hogan-Steward Learning Center, holds 25,687 bound volumes, 158 periodical subscriptions, 8,645 microforms, 1,014 audiovisuals; 50 computers for student use in the computer center. Special collections include the Bible & Religious Education and Black Studies collections.

STUDENT LIFE

Special Regulations

Bible course required each semester for full-time students; automobiles permitted with permission; daily chapel services required; mid-week religious services encouraged; off-campus living permitted

Campus Services

Health services, remedial instruction

Campus Activities

Social and cultural activities include theater, band, and chorale. A lectureship meeting on religion and current topics is held each year during Thanksgiving week. Students may get involved in the *Ram Beat* (student-run newspaper) or *The Ram* (yearbook).

Leadership opportunities can be found in the student government, Student Senate, or the various other clubs and organizations such as the Sportmen's Club, the International Student Organization, the History Club, or Creative Writing Club. Religious groups include Dorcas Club, Tau Phi Kappa, and the Mission Study Fellowship clubs. National and local fraternities and sororities are represented on campus. Honorary societies are represented on campus.

Southwestern Christian is located in Terrell, Texas, population approximately 16,000, where students have access to shopping, dining, and local theater. Dallas, Texas, is 32 miles to the west.

Housing Availability

304 housing spaces; freshman housing guaranteed; married student housing available.

TEXAS COLLEGE

2404 N. Grand Ave.
Tyler, TX 75702-2404
Phone: (903) 593-8311

Total Enrollment:
400

Level of Selectivity:
Noncompetitive

Motto:
Give the People Light
and They Will Find
Their Way

HISTORY

Texas College (TC) is a four-year, private, coed, liberal arts college affiliated with the Christian Methodist Church (CMC). It was founded in 1894 as a liberal arts college by a group of ministers from the former Colored Methodist Church (now CMC). TC became Phillip University in 1909, and in 1912 returned to its original name, Texas College. From 1946–1966 the school operated a branch of Tyler Junior College on its campus.

TC is a liberal arts and teacher college that upholds its motto to provide light for its students so they can find their way. Its full range of educational and student-life programs encourages students to develop their full potential so they can be leaders in their careers and in service to the area, the state, and the nation.

The college is situated on 66 acres with 15 buildings including a library, computer center, and dormitories.

ACCREDITATION

Texas College is accredited by the Southern Association of Colleges and Schools to award the Bachelor of Arts, Bachelor of Science, and Associate of Arts degrees.

Other Accreditation

Texas Association of Colleges and
  Universities

COSTS PER YEAR

1991–92 Tuition: $3,790

Room and board: $950 (room); $1,530
  (board)

Special fees: 455

Books: $500

Estimated total cost: $7,225

FINANCIAL AID

Financial Aid Specific to the School

97% of the student body received financial aid during 1992–93.

Athletic scholarships available to students participating in intercollegiate sports.

Endowed, special interest, and friends scholarships are available based on merit and need. Some scholarships have multiple recipients.

Merit-based scholarships are awarded by the school based on GPA and standardized test scores.

Performance scholarships are available for students participating in music and the arts.

Tuition Equalization Grant (TEG) is available to students who are residents of the state and demonstrate financial need.

United Negro College Fund (UNCF) scholarships are awarded to a limited number of students at this school who demonstrate financial need. Some scholarships may be based on location and merit. UNCF scholarships range from $500 to $7,500.

Financial Aid Deadline

May 31 (priority)

Financial Aid Contact

J. B. Derrick, Director of Financial Aid, Texas College, Tyler, TX, 75702; (214) 593-8311.

ADMISSION REQUIREMENTS

SAT or ACT required (for counseling and placement)

Entrance Requirements

Graduation from an accredited high school and completion of the following 16 units: 4 English, 2 mathematics, 2 science, 2 history, and 6 electives; official high school transcript; three letters of recommendation; class rank; health record completed by physician. A $5 non-refundable application fee is required.

GED students must meet basic admission requirements.

Transfer students must submit official high school and college transcripts; provide proof of good standing at previous institution; health record completed by physician; 2.0 GPA (on 4.0 scale); maximum of 66 hours transferrable.

International students must submit official transcripts, in English, of all high school and college work; submit TOEFL score of 500 or more; submit GCE (General Certificate of Education) scores of at least 5 at the ordinary level including one English, or the West African School Council Report; statement of financial responsibility and one full year of tuition; 3 letters of recommendation; health certificate completed by physician.

Early admission allows academically gifted high school students the opportunity to enroll in college for credit before completing high school.

Admission Application Deadline

August 15

Admission Contact

Dr. William Ammons, Admissions Office, Texas College, 2404 N. Grand Ave., Tyler, TX 75702; (903) 593-8311.

GRADUATION REQUIREMENTS

A minimum of 124 hours and completion of core requirements to include 12 English, 3 mathematics, 4 science, 9 social sciences, 6 foreign language, 5 physical education, and 3 freshman orientation; minimum 2.0 GPA; and pass senior School & College Ability Test (SCAT).

Grading System

A–F; I=Incomplete; W=Official Withdrawal; WP=Withdrew Passing; WF=Withdrew Failing

STUDENT BODY PROFILE

Total enrollment (male/female): 196/204

From in-state: 188

Other regions: 22 states; 4 foreign countries

Full-time undergraduates (male/female): 172/180

Part-time undergraduates (male/female): 23/25

Ethnic/Racial Makeup

African American, 380; International, 20.

Class of 1995 Profile

Number of applicants: 382

Number accepted: 359

Number enrolled: 122

Transfers enrolled: 24

FACULTY PROFILE

Number of faculty: 35

Student-teacher ratio: 16:1

Full-time faculty: 27

Part-time faculty: 8

Faculty with doctorates or other terminal degrees: 46%

SCHOOL CALENDAR

1992–93: August–May

Commencement & conferring of degrees: May

One summer session.

DEGREES OFFERED 1991–92:

Bachelor of Arts

Art

English

History

Music

Political Science

Studio Art

Bachelor of Science

Art Education

Biology

Business Administration

Business Education

Chemistry

Computer Science

Early Childhood Education

Elementary Education

Mathematics

Music Education

Office Administration

Physical Education

Secondary Education

Social Science

Social Work

Sociology

Pre-Professional

Pre-dentistry

Pre-law

Pre-medicine

Pre-ministry

SPECIAL PROGRAMS

College orientation is offered at no cost to entering students prior to the beginning of classes to acquaint students with the college and to prepare them for college life.

Part-time degree program allows students to earn an undergraduate degree part time.

Remedial courses are offered to entering students to bring them up to admission standards and to help them adjust for success in college.

Study Abroad Program allows students to go to a foreign country for part of their college education.

ATHLETIC PROGRAMS

Texas College is a member of the National Association of Intercollegiate Athletics (NAIA).

Intercollegiate sports: men's baseball, basketball, and track; women's basketball, track, and volleyball.

Intramural sports: basketball, softball, track, and volleyball.

Athletic Contact

Athletic Department, Texas College, Tyler, TX 75702; (214) 593-8311, Ext. 247.

LIBRARY HOLDINGS

The library houses 85,000 bound volumes, 23,500 microforms, 136 periodical subscriptions, 910 audiovisuals; 35 computers available for student use in the library and computer center.

STUDENT LIFE

Special Regulations

Mandatory orientation; freshmen and sophomores must live on campus; cars permitted.

Campus Services

Health center, personal and psychological counseling, career planning and placement, student employment services, remedial instruction, post office and religious activities.

Campus Activities

Social and cultural activities include theater (TC's Little Theater puts on major productions), band, and chorale.

Leadership opportunities can be found in the Student Government Association (SGA) or department and special interest groups. Greek-letter fraternities and sororities include three national fraternities and three national sororities. Alpha Kappa Mu is just one of the honor societies also represented on campus.

Texas College (TC) is located in the city of Tyler, Texas, population approximately 80,000. TC is less than two hours from Dallas and Shreveport providing students with access to a variety of social and cultural activities. Tyler, known for its rose bushes, hosts annual events including the Texas Rose Festival and the Spring Flower Festival. Points of interest include the Municipal Rose Garden, Goodman Museum, and the Caldwell Zoo.

Housing Availability

450 housing spaces; freshmen and sophomores must live in on-campus housing.

Handicapped Services

Wheelchair accessibility

NOTABLE ALUMNI

Jimmie E. Clark, 1950–President, Texas College

E. Grace Payne–Chairperson, Los Angeles Harbor Commission

TEXAS SOUTHERN UNIVERSITY

3100 Cleburne Ave.
Houston, TX 77004
Phone: (713) 527-7011
Fax: (713) 527-7842

Total Enrollment:
10,777

Level of Selectivity:
Slightly competitive

HISTORY

Texas Southern University is a four-year, state-supported, coed, liberal arts university founded in 1947 to serve the black population of Texas. Established as Texas State University, the name was changed to its current name in 1951. In 1973, partially as a result of its metropolitan location, TSU was redesignated as a 'special purpose' institution of higher education for an urban population. Such special programs include projects through the Mickey Leland Center, established in 1989 as a national resource center to study contemporary issues that impact world hunger and peace. The program continues the work of the late Congressman George "Mickey" Leland.

Although the university maintains a selective admissions policy for its graduate and professional programs, TSU maintains an open admissions policy for undergraduates in an effort to attract the diverse ethnic population of its inner city location. As a comprehensive university, TSU offers academic programs in the arts and sciences, business, education, pharmacy, technology, and law. It also provides social services for the campus and the community at large.

TSU is situated on 130 acres with 27 buildings. Facilities include the Terry Library, the Nabrit Science Center, the King Humanities Center, and the Thurgood Marshall Law Library. Contemporary facilities are constructed of Texas Cordova shell stone.

ACCREDITATION

Texas Southern is accredited by the Southern Association of Colleges and Schools to award the Bachelor of Arts, Bachelor of Science, Master's degrees, and Doctoral degrees.

Other Accreditation

American Bar Association

American Chemical Society

American Council of Pharmaceutical Education

American Dietetic Association

Committee on Allied Health Education and Accreditation

Council on Social Work Education

National Association of Industrial Technology

National Council for the Accreditation of Teacher Education

COSTS PER YEAR

1992–93 Tuition: $720 (in-state); $4,860 (out-state)

Room and board: $1,880 (room); $1,560 (board)

Special fees: $225

Books: $600

Estimated total cost: $4,985 (in-state); $9,125 (out-state)

FINANCIAL AID

1991–92 Institutional Funding

Number of scholarships and grants: 1,103

Total amount of scholarships and grants: $8,200,000

Range of scholarships and grants: $900 (average)

1991–92 Federal and State Funding

Number of scholarships and grants: 5,400

Total amount of scholarships and grants: $23,000,000

Range of scholarships and grants: $5,000 (average)

Number of loans: 4,100

Total amount of loans: $14,200,000

Range of loans: $2,500 (average)

Number of work-study: 385

Total amount of work-study: $1,000,000

Range of work-study: $385 (average)

Financial Aid Specific to the School

87% of the student body received financial aid during 1991–92.

Academic scholarships are available to students with 3.0 or better GPA. Contact financial aid office at the school for more information.

Army ROTC, in cooperation with the University of Houston, and Navy ROTC, in cooperation with Rice University, offer two- and three-year scholarships that pay tuition, fees, books, and other expenses, and provide a monthly stipend of $100. For Army ROTC contact University of Houston, (713) 749-4394 or 4395; for Navy ROTC contact Rice University (713) 527-4825.

Athletic awards are available to students participating in intercollegiate sports.

Cooperative Education Program alternates classroom study with related paid work experience. The program provides academic credit and full-time status during co-op placement. Qualifying students must have completed 30 hours and have a 2.0 GPA.

Deferred Payment Plan allows students to pay college costs in two or three installments during the semester.

Health Profession Loans are available for pharmacy students enrolled in a professional sequence in pharmacy. Part of loan may be paid off for two years of service in designated shortage areas.

Hinson-Hazlewood Student Loan is available for Texas residents and students paying resident tuition. Students must attend a pre-loan counseling session and demonstrate financial need.

Texas Public Education State Incentive Grant (TPE-SSIG) awards grants to undergraduate and graduate students who are residents of the state, are enrolled for 12 or more hours, and demonstrate financial need.

The Texas Rehabilitation Commission provides tuition and fee assistance for persons with disabling conditions. It also provides employment readiness assistance.

Thurgood Marshall Black Education Fund provides a four-year scholarship at this public black college. Qualifying students must have a high school GPA of 3.0 or better and a SAT score of 1000 or ACT score of 24 or more. Students must be recommended by high school counselor as exceptional or exemplary in the creative or performing arts. Scholarship pays tuition, fees, room, and board, not to exceed $6,000 annually.

Tuition waivers are available for full-time or part-time minority students.

Financial Aid Deadline

March 15 (fall); August 15 (spring)

Financial Aid Contact

Mr. Yancy Beavers, Director of Financial Aid, Texas Southern University, Houston, TX 77004; (713) 527-7319.

ADMISSION REQUIREMENTS

Open admission. SAT or ACT required for placement

Entrance Requirements

Graduation from an accredited high school and completion of the following 16 units: 4 English, 1 algebra, 1 geometry, 1 natural science, 1 social science, and 8 academic electives; official high school transcript with a minimum "C" average; proof of immunization against diphtheria, rubella, tetanus, polio, and small pox; completion of Texas Academic Skills Program (TASP); and attendance at orientation for new students.

GED students must meet basic admission requirements.

Transfer students must submit official transcript from each college previously attended; have at least a 2.0 GPA; if transferring less than 20 credit hours, submit SAT or ACT results; be in good standing with former institution; transfer maximum of 61 credits; and take TASP unless student has earned three credit hours prior to 1989.

International students must satisfy general admissions requirements; students from non-English-speaking country must pass the TOEFL examination.

Admission Application Deadline

April 1 (priority); August 10

Admission Contact

Mr. Collie Chambers, Coordinator of Recruitment, Texas Southern University, 3100 Cleburne Ave, Houston, TX 77004; (713)527-7070

GRADUATION REQUIREMENTS

A minimum of 124 credits and completion core requirements to include the following hours: 6 freshman English, 6 sophomore English, 6 American history, 6 U.S. and Texas government, 6 math, 8 natural and/or physical science, 3 aesthetics, 2 health education, 2 physical education, and 3 speech; maintain a minimum 2.0 GPA and "B" average in major; last 30 hours and at least 2 semesters must be in residence at TSU.

Grading System

A-F (A-D plus & minus); W=Withdrawn; I=Incomplete (satisfactory); NC=No Grade Submitted; P=Passed; S=Satisfactory; U=Unsatisfactory; R=In Progress

STUDENT BODY PROFILE

Total enrollment: 5,065/5,712

From in-state: 8,864

Other regions: 35 states; 15 foreign countries

Full-time undergraduates (male/female): 2,829/3,168

Part-time undergraduates (male/female): 980/1,354

Graduate students (male/female): 1,150/1,296

Ethnic/Racial Makeup

African American, 8,622; Hispanic, 431; Asian, 108; Native American, 108; Caucasian, 431; International, 1,293.

Class of 1995 Profile

Number of applicants: 4,454

Number accepted: 4,454

Number enrolled: 4,186

Median SAT score: 480V; 460M

Median ACT score: 20

Average high school GPA: 2.5

Transfer applicants: 408

Transfers accepted: 408

Transfers enrolled: 408

FACULTY PROFILE

Number of faculty: 630

Student-teacher ratio: 18:1

Full-time faculty: 535

Part-time faculty: 95

Faculty with doctorates or other terminal degrees: 66%

SCHOOL CALENDAR

1992–93: August 20–May 14 9 (semesters)

Commencement and conferring of degrees: May 15

Two summer sessions.

DEGREES OFFERED 1991–1992:

Bachelor of Arts

Art

Communications

English

Fine Arts

Foreign Language

Geography

History

Interpersonal/Interpersonal Cultural Communication

Journalism

Music

Organizational Communication

Political Science

Psychology

Rhetoric and Public Address

Telecommunications

Theater/Cinema

Bachelor of Business Administration

Accounting

Administrative Management Systems

Banking

Economics

Finance

General Business

Insurance

Management

Marketing

Bachelor of Science

Airway Sciences

Apparel Merchandising

Biology

Biomedical Engineering Technology

Building Construction Management

Chemistry

Child Development

City Planning

Civil Engineering Technology

Communication Disorders

Computer Science

Criminal Justice

Dietetics

Drafting and Design Technology

Electronics Engineering Technology

Elementary and Secondary Education

Engineering Drafting and Design Technology

Engineering and Industrial Technology

Environmental Engineering Technology

Health Care Administration

Home Economics

Interdisciplinary Studies

Mathematics

Medical Record administration

Medical Technology

Photographic Technology

Physical Education

Physics

Public Administration

Respiratory Therapy

Social Work

Sociology

Speech Communication

Telecommunications

First Professional
Law

Pharmacy

Pre-professional
Pre-Dentistry

Pre-Medicine

Master's
Accounting

Administration and Supervision

Administrative Management Systems

Biology

Business Administration

Business Education

Chemistry

City Planning

Communications

Counseling Education

Curriculum and Instruction

Early Childhood Education

Education

Educational Administration

Elementary Education

English

Fine Arts

Foreign Language

Foundations and Higher Education

Health and Physical Education

Higher Education

History

Home Economics

Geography

Guidance and Counseling

Industrial Education

Journalism

Mathematics

Music Speech Communication

Psychology

Public Administration

Reading Education

Secondary Education

Sociology

Special Education

Theater/Cinema

Transportation

Urban Education

Doctorate
Pharmacy

SPECIAL PROGRAMS

Accelerated Study Program allows students to complete their undergraduate degree in a shorter period of time than the traditional four years.

Adult or Continuing Education Program is available for nontraditional students returning to school or working full time.

Advanced Placement (AP) grants college credit for postsecondary work completed in high school. Students passing the AP test will receive credit by examination for each course and advanced placement.

College Level Examination Program (CLEP) determines the academic relevance of nontraditional educational experiences such as the military, on-the-job training, or other life experiences, through a series of tests and may grant students college credit for these experiences.

College orientation is mandatory for entering students for two days at no cost prior to the beginning of classes to acquaint students with the college and to prepare them for college life; parents may attend.

Cooperative Education Program alternates classroom study with related paid work experience. The program provides academic credit and full-time status during co-op placement.

English as a Second Language is a program that offers courses in English for students whose native language is not English.

Honors program offers academically talented students a challenging program of study that includes special classes, seminars, colloquia, cultural activities, and special recognition to motivate participants.

Part-time degree programs allow students to earn an undergraduate degree while attending part time.

Pre-professional programs are available in dentistry, medicine, and interdisciplinary study in public affairs.

Remedial courses are offered to entering students to bring them up to admission standards and to help them adjust for success in college.

ROTC provides training in military science for commission as a second lieutenant in the U.S. Army and Navy. Two- and four-year scholarships are available.

Three/two degree program in engineering allows students to get two degrees—one in liberal arts from home school and one in engineering from cooperating school—by completing three years at matriculated school and two years at cooperating school.

ATHLETIC PROGRAMS

Texas Southern is a member of the National Collegiate Athletic Association (NCAA), all Division I (except football which is Division I-AA); and Southwestern Athletic Conference (SWAC)

Intercollegiate sports: men's basketball, cross-country, football, golf, soccer, tennis, and track & field; women's basketball, cross-country, track & field, and volleyball.

Intramural sports: bowling, soccer, gymnastics, swimming, and diving.

Athletic Contact

Athletic Director, Texas Southern University, 3100 Cleburne Ave., Houston, TX 77004; (713) 527-7011

LIBRARY HOLDINGS

The Robert J. Terry Library holds 255,000 bound volumes, 125 periodical subscriptions, 350 audiovisuals; 400 computers for student use in computer center, dorms, and library. Special collections include the Heartman Black Collection, the Barbara Jordan Archives, and the gallery of traditional African art.

STUDENT LIFE

Special Regulations

Cars must be registered; curfew; guest hours; dorm visitation hours; class attendance mandatory for freshmen, sophomores, and students on probation; graduating students must attend commencement.

Campus Services

Health center; personal and social counseling (psychological counseling provided by community mental health agencies); career counseling and placement; legal; testing center for ACT, MCAT, GMAT, SAT, TOEFL, and GED; tutoring and remediation; and religious activities.

Campus Activities

Social and cultural activities include theater, chorale, band, dance, and lecture series. Students may get involved in the *Herald* (student-run newspaper) or the yearbook. Communications majors or volunteers may work at student-run radio station, KTSU.

Leadership opportunities are found in the Student Government Association or the various other clubs and organizations. United Ministries is a program of interdenominational cooperation that includes the Baptist Student Union, Newman Club, Lutheran Student Organization, and the Wesley Foundation. Greek-letter fraternities include Alpha Phi Alpha, Kappa Alpha Psi, Omega Psi Phi, and Phi Beta Sigma; sororities include Alpha Kappa Alpha, Delta Sigma Theta, Sigma Gamma Rho, and Zeta Phi Beta. Honor societies are also represented on campus.

Texas Southern occupies 130 acres in the heart of Houston, the largest city in Texas, with a population of almost 3 million. The city is served by local mass transit bus, passenger rail, and two major airports—Houston Intercontinental Airport to the north and William P. Hobby Airport to the south. The Houston Astrodome is home to the Houston Astros and Houston Oilers. Points of interest include Astroworld; Anheuser-Busch Brewery; Bayou Bend, a 28-room Latin colonial mansion; and the Lyndon B. Johnson Space Center. The city of Houston offers exquisite shopping at such places as Post Oak, or All American Boots. Theater, concerts, museums, and fine dining are available in the city.

Housing Availability

1,800 housing spaces; 600 freshman-only housing; married student housing; five dormitories.

NOTABLE ALUMNI

Barbara Jordan, Esq., 1956–U.S. representative, 18th district, Texas

George "Mickey" L. Leland–U.S. representative, Texas

Craig Washington–U.S. representative, 18th district, Houston, Texas

WILEY COLLEGE

711 Wiley Ave.
Marshall, TX 75670
Phone: (214) 927-3300

Total Enrollment:
406

Level of Selectivity:
Noncompetitive

Motto:
Artes Scientia Veritas
(New era in quest of
excellence)

HISTORY

Wiley College is a four-year, private, coeducational liberal arts and teaching college affiliated with the United Methodist Church. Named for Bp. Isaac W. Wiley, the college was founded in 1873 as Wiley College and chartered in 1882 by the Freedmen's Aid Society to provide educational opportunities for newly freed men. Wiley was first among black colleges west of the Mississippi River to be granted the "A" rating by the Southern Association of Colleges and Schools.

Wiley's mission is to provide students with a liberal arts and career-oriented education in a close, Christian atmosphere. The college strives to promote excellence, command of language, power of inquiry, development of critical thinking, and search for values, with an emphasis on competition and innovation to enable students to effectively function in a pluralistic society. President David L. Beckley states that, "Wiley is committed to developing the entire student in a church-related environment with all programs geared toward preparing leaders for the future." The college provides educational and cultural activities for the community by presenting concerts, lectures, and athletic events.

The college had its humble beginnings in two frame buildings just south of Marshall before it moved into six buildings in Marshall in 1880. Presently, the 16-building campus spans over 63 acres with a sunken garden that was converted from an old reservoir. Adjoining the sunken garden is a rose arbor that adds to the general beauty of the campus. This historically black college is a United Negro College Fund (UNCF) member school.

ACCREDITATION

Wiley College is accredited by the Southern Association of Colleges and Secondary Schools to award the Bachelor of Arts and Bachelor of Science degrees.

Other Accreditation

The Association of Texas Colleges and Universities

The Texas Education Agency

The University Senate of the Methodist Church

COSTS PER YEAR

1992–93 Tuition: $3,450

Room and board: $1,160 (room); $1,384 (board)

Special fees: $300

Books: $200

Estimated total cost: $6,494

FINANCIAL AID

Financial Aid Specific to the School

95% of the student body received financial aid during 1991–92.

Eighteen endowment scholarships and/or awards, including some from national fraternities and sororities, are available to students based on merit. Awards range from $50 to $500.

The Honors Track Program offers four-year scholarships to 15 entering freshmen who rank in the upper 10% of their high school class and receive a score of 21 on the ACT or 1,000 on the SAT exam. The student must maintain a 3.3 GPA, enroll for 15 semester hours, and pass at least 12 semester hours per semester.

Deferred payment or installment plan allows a family to pay tuition in equal installments. First payment due at registration and up to three additional monthly payments are due on the first of each succeeding month.

40% tuition waivers are available to dependents of United Methodist Church ministers, and children of Wiley College employees.

Performance scholarships are available in athletics, music and drama.

United Negro Scholarship Fund (UNCF) scholarship(s) are available to students who demonstrate financial need. UNCF scholarships range from $500 to $7,500 a year.

Financial Aid Deadline

June 1 (priority); September 1 (fall and spring)

Financial Aid Contact

Kimberly Flanagan, Financial Aid Clerk, Wiley College, 71 Rosborough Springs Rd., Marshall, TX 75670; (214) 927-3210.

ADMISSION REQUIREMENTS

SAT or ACT required (use for counseling). Open admissions.

Entrance Requirements

An official high school transcript including completion of 15 units: 3 English, 2 mathematics, 2 science, 2 social studies, 2 foreign language, and 4 electives; 3 letters of recommendation from high school counselors or teachers; and a mandatory pre-entrance physical.

GED students must meet the basic admission requirements and have a GED test score of forty or above.

Transfer students must have a letter of good standing sent from the last college or university attended; submit official transcript from all colleges/universities attended, high school transcript if college credits are less than 15 semester hours; must be eligible to return to the last college. If last college attended was not a member of a regional accrediting agency, the student is admitted on condition.

International Students must pass the TOEFL exam with a 400 or above if country of origin is not English speaking; must submit a letter of recommendation from churchman or business; must have transcripts from all secondary schools attended; and must submit completed health form.

Admission Application Deadline

September (fall); January (spring); Early admission allows qualified students to enter college full time before completing high school.

Admission Contact

Lee Roberts, Director of Admissions/Recruitment, Wiley College, 71 Rosborough Springs Rd., Marshall, TX 75670; (214) 927-3311.

GRADUATION REQUIREMENTS

A minimum 124 semester hours with a cumulative GPA of 2.0; last 30 semester hours must be completed in residence; at least a "C" in English 131 and 132. Must submit application for graduation by November 15 before beginning last semester; transfer students must complete at least 30 semester hours in residence.

Grading System

A-F; I=Incomplete; X=Satisfactory progress, but failure to master basic skills or achieve 70% on post-test; W=Withdraw.

STUDENT BODY PROFILE

Total enrollment (male/female): 162/244

Full-time undergraduates (male/female): 155/232

Part-time undergraduates (male/female): 8/11

Ethnic/Racial Makeup

African American, 398; Other/unclassified, 8

Class of 1995 Profile

Average high school GPA: 2.49

FACULTY PROFILE

Number of faculty: 50

Student-teacher ratio: 15:1

Full-time faculty: 33

Part-time faculty: 17

Faculty with doctorates or other terminal degrees: 50%

Ethnic/Racial Makeup

African American; Hispanic; Asian American; Native American; Caucasian; International; Other/unclassified.

SCHOOL CALENDAR

1992–93: September 10–April 29 (semesters)

Commencement and conferring of degrees: May 2

One summer session.

DEGREES OFFERED 1991–92:

Bachelor of Arts
Business
English
Music
Religion
Social Sciences

Bachelor of Science
Biological Sciences
Chemistry
Elementary Education
Health
Mathematics
Physical Education

Pre-professional Programs
Pre-dental
Pre-medical
Pre-nursing

Certificate
Gerontology

SPECIAL PROGRAMS

The Basic Skills Program assists students who are below college level in English, math, and reading. It is designed to equip students with the appropriate learning skills to enable them to enter a regular college-level program.

The College Level Examination Program (CLEP) determines the academic relevance of nontraditional educational experiences such as the military, on-the-job training, or other life experiences through a series of tests. A maximum of 24 credit hours may be granted through CLEP.

The Cooperative Education Program combines formal academic study with practical work experience in major. The program provides academic credit during co-op placement.

The cooperative program with Texas Baptist University in Marshall, Texas, allows students to enroll for one course each semester at cooperating institution.

Credit by examination allows students to "test out" of general education courses by taking the course post test. Results of the test must be posted before the last day to drop and add classes. A maximum of 24 credit hours maybe granted through credit by examination.

The Honors Track Program encourages consistent academic achievement from the freshman year through the senior year. It recognizes academic excellence and provides stimulating and challenging activities for high achievers.

Student Support Services provides developmental courses, counseling, and cultural activities to students who need aid to succeed in college.

The Upward Bound Program offers high school students Saturday tutorials and six-week residential summer programs of study.

ATHLETIC PROGRAMS

Intercollegiate sports: men's baseball, basketball, soccer, and track & field; women's baseball, basketball, track & field, and volleyball.

Intramural sports: baseball, basketball, softball, table tennis, tennis, track & field, and volleyball.

LIBRARY HOLDINGS

The Thomas Winston Cole Library holds 80,239 volumes, 2,779 microfilms, and 5,396 Government Document volumes. Special collections include an African American Collection of books by and about blacks.

STUDENT LIFE

Special Regulations

Automobiles must be registered; entering students must take the placement examination; a mandatory lab class requires attendance; courses in American Negro History are required; moderate dress code recommended; must attend a weekly assembly;

non-commuting students must reside in the dormitory.

Campus Services

Health, career counseling and placement, personal and psychological counseling, religious activities, and remediation.

Campus Activities

Social activities include the Acappella Choir, band, dramatics, modern dance group, and piano. Students may work on the college yearbook *(Wiley Reporter)*. Communication majors or student volunteers may get involved in the student-run radio station (KBWC). The Acappella Choir has an annual spring concert tour of the Midwest.

Leadership opportunities can be found in the Student Government Association or the more than forty student-run organizations such as the Oxford Club for students interested in full-time Christian service or the dramatic club for students interested in drama. Greek-letter sororities include Alpha Kappa Alpha, Delta Sigma Theta, Sigma Gamma Rho, and Zeta Phi Beta; fraternities include Alpha Phi Alpha, Kappa Alpha Psi, Omega Psi Phi, and Phi Beta Sigma. Honor societies represented include Alpha Kappa Mu and Beta Kappa Chi.

Located in the city of Marshall, Texas, the community is served by bus lines and rail service. Harrison County Memorial Air-port is three miles away. The campus is approximately 40 miles west of Shreveport, Louisiana, and 150 miles east of Dallas, Texas. The restored Victorian Ginocchio hotel (built in 1896) is the centerpiece of Marshall's three block Ginocchio Historic District. Another legacy that has been preserved is an original section of the Old Stagecoach Road. Local recreation includes fishing, camping, and hunting. Churches of various faiths, hospitals, a public library, and a radio station serve the area.

Housing Availability

594 housing spaces.

Handicapped Services

Includes wheelchair accessibility.

NOTABLE ALUMNI

Thomas W. Cole, Jr., 1961–West Virginia Board of Regents, Chancellor; former West Virginia State President

James Farmer, 1938–Founder, Congress of Racial Equality; former program director, NAACP; assistant secretary, Dept. of Health, Education & Welfare

Walter S. McAfee, 1934–Physicist, AUS elect R & D Commander Fort Monmouth, NJ.

Virgin Islands

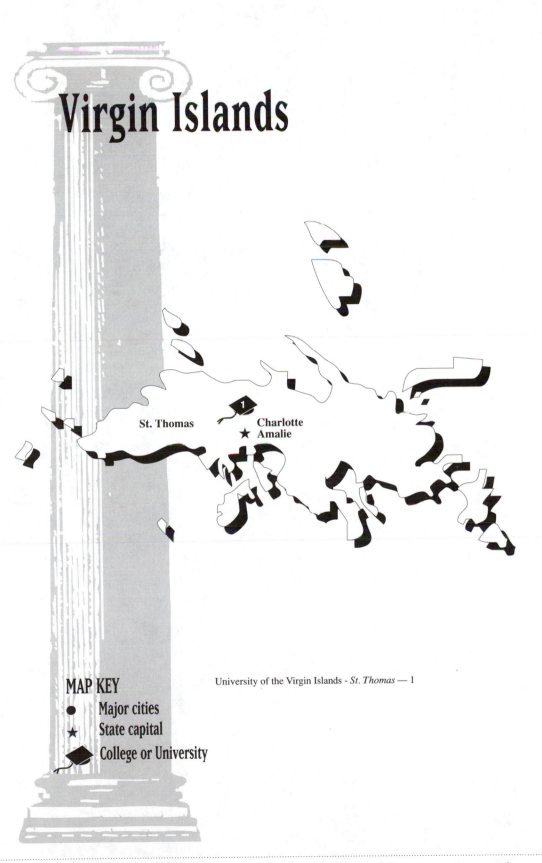

St. Thomas

Charlotte
Amalie

University of the Virgin Islands - *St. Thomas* — 1

MAP KEY

● Major cities

★ State capital

🎓 College or University

UNIVERSITY OF THE VIRGIN ISLANDS

Charlotte Amalie,
St. Thomas
U.S. Virgin Islands
00802
Phone: (809) 776-9200
Fax: (809) 774-2192

RR02–Box 10,000
Kingshill, St. Croix
U.S. Virgin Islands
00851
Phone: (809) 778-1620

Total Enrollment:
2,176

Level of Selectivity:
Slightly competitive

HISTORY

The University of the Virgin Islands (UVI) is a four-year, territory-supported, coed, liberal arts institution. It was founded in 1962 as the College of the Virgin Islands to serve residents of the Virgin Islands and the Caribbean. To more accurately reflect the growth in programs the name changed to the University of the Virgin Islands in 1980. UVI has a main campus in St. Thomas and a branch campus in St. Croix.

The St. Thomas campus occupies 175 acres, overlooking the Caribbean Sea with its own beach, golf course, and tennis courts. The university's role is the same as state colleges and universities on the mainland of the United States. The university was designated a land grant college in 1972.

The St. Croix campus is located 40 miles from the main campus and came into use in 1964, adding 130 acres, the headquarters of the Virgin Islands Extension Service, and the Virgin Islands Agricultural Experiment Station to UVI.

UVI is a territory-supported land grant institution that offers programs of instruction, research, and public service that address the needs of the individual and the region. The university is committed to the advancement of scholarship, excellence, and innovation as it strives to provide intellectual and educational leadership.

ACCREDITATION

The University of the Virgin Islands is accredited by the Middle States Association of Colleges and Secondary Schools to award the Associate of Arts, Associate of Science, Bachelor of Arts, Bachelor of Science, and Master's degrees.

Other Accreditation

National League for Nursing

COSTS PER YEAR

1991–92 Tuition: $1,440 (in-state); $2,025 (out-state)

Room and board: $1,350 (room); $3,000 (board)

Special fees: $125

Books: $500

Estimated total cost: $6,415 (in-state); $7,000 (out-state)

FINANCIAL AID

Financial Aid Specific to the School

Tuition waivers are available for senior citizens 60 years of age or older who have been residents of the Virgin Islands for at least one year.

Financial Aid Deadline
April 15

Financial Aid Contact
Dr. Lynn McConnell, University of the Virgin Islands, St. Thomas, VI 00802; (809) 776-9200, ext. 1222.

ADMISSION REQUIREMENTS
SAT or ACT required

Entrance Requirements
For applicants from the Virgin Islands, United States, and Commonwealth of Puerto Rico, graduation from an accredited high school and completion of the following units: 4 English, 2 mathematics, 2 science, 2 history, 2 physical education, and 1 foreign language recommended; minimum 2.0 GPA; written essay; and completion of U.S. Virgin Islands placement exam. A $20 non-refundable application fee required. Late applications require an additional $10 fee.

GED students must meet basic admission requirements and submit essay.

Transfer students must submit official college transcripts of all previous college work; in some cases high school transcripts may be required; must submit an essay; and must have maintained a minimum 2.0 GPA. Deadline April 15.

International students must submit official high school transcripts; Caribbean applicants must submit official copies of the GCE and CXC exams respectively with a score in the Five "O" Level; British Virgin Islands applicants must submit Grade I Certificates; students from non-English-speaking countries must take TOEFL examination; all students must submit two letters of recommendation from teachers and be prepared to pay all college costs for first year. A $20 non-refundable application fee in U.S. dollars is required.

Early admission allows academically gifted high school students the opportunity to enroll in college full or part time before completing high school.

Admission Application Deadline
April 15

Admission Contact
Judith W. Edwin, Director of Admission, University of Virgin Islands, St. Thomas, U.S. Virgin Islands 00802; (809) 776-9200, ext. 1222; or Student Services Offices, University of the Virgin Island, RR02 Box 10,000 Kingshill, St. Croix, U.S. Virgin Islands 00861; (809) 778-1620.

GRADUATION REQUIREMENTS
A minimum of 62 hours and completion of core requirements for an associate's degree; 120 semester hours and completion of core requirements for bachelor's degree to include the following hours: 6 mathematics, 6 science, 12 foreign language, and a computer course for some majors; satisfactory completion of the English proficiency examination.

Grading System
A-F; W=Withdraw; WP=Withdraw Passing; WF= Withdraw Failing; AW=Administrative Withdrawal; I=Incomplete; AUD=Audit; P=Promoted to Credit Course; NP=Must Continue Skills Course

STUDENT BODY PROFILE
Total enrollment (male/female): 679/2,037

From in-state: 2,010

Other regions: 21 states, 15 foreign countries

Full-time undergraduates (male/female): 231/693

Part-time undergraduates (male/female): 381/1,154

Graduate students (male/female): 63/191

Ethnic/Racial Makeup

African American, 1,820; Hispanic, 81; Asian, 27; Other/unclassified, 788.

Class of 1995 Profile

Number of applicants: 495

Number accepted: 322

Number enrolled: 249

FACULTY PROFILE

Number of faculty: 257

Student-teacher ratio: 15:1

Full-time faculty: 111

Part-time faculty: 146

Faculty with doctorates or other terminal degrees: 60%

SCHOOL CALENDAR

1992–93: August 10–May 17 (semester hours)

Commencement and conferring of degrees: May 30

One summer session.

DEGREES OFFERED 1991–92:

Associate of Arts

Accounting

Agriculture

Business Management

Data Processing

Office Administration

Police Science and Administration

Associate of Science

Nursing

Physics

Bachelor of Arts

Accounting

Biology

Business Administration

Caribbean Studies

Chemistry

Elementary Education

English

Humanities

Marine Biology

Mathematics

Music Education

Psychology

Social Science

Social Work

Spanish

Vocational Education

Bachelor of Science

Biology

Chemistry

Marine Biology

Nursing

Physics

Masters of Arts

Education

Master of Business Administration

Master of Public Administration

SPECIAL PROGRAMS

Advanced Placement (AP) grants college credit for postsecondary work completed in high school. Students scoring 3 on the AP test will receive credit by examination for each course and advanced placement.

College Level Examination Program (CLEP) determines the academic relevance of nontraditional educational experiences such as the military, on-the-job training, or other life experiences, through a series of tests and may grant students college credit for these experiences.

College orientation is offered to entering students for two days at no cost prior to the beginning of classes to acquaint students with the college and to prepare them for college life.

Cooperative medical program with Boston University (BU) allows qualified students to be accepted provisionally into the medical program at BU after their sophomore year. Students spend two summers and senior year at BU and graduate with a Bachelor of Science degree from UVI.

General Certificate of Education from British Education Systems with an "A" level allows students to receive college credit for work completed.

Joint programs in engineering, pre-pharmacy, and pre-medical technology in cooperation with specialized institutions are available to students. Contact chair of Division of Science and Mathematics for more information.

Marine Biology is offered as an undergraduate major at UVI.

National Student Exchange Program allows students to spend either their sophomore or junior year in one of the 107 cooperating institutions on the U.S. mainland. Students return to UVI for completion of degree program.

Upward Bound provides academic counseling and cultural enrichment programs to high school students who are disadvantaged and are in pursuit of a college education. Some credit courses may be offered.

ATHLETIC PROGRAMS

University of the Virgin Islands participates in local amateur leagues and invitational tournaments with teams from other universities in Central America and the Caribbean.

Varsity sports: basketball, cricket, metball, soccer, and volleyball.

Intramural sports: badminton, basketball, golf, gymnastics, swimming, diving, and tennis.

LIBRARY HOLDINGS

The Ralph Paiewonsky Library at the St. Thomas campus holds 81,000 volumes, 771,000 microforms, 1,029 periodical subscriptions, 20,000 audiovisuals, and 15,000 U.S. Government documents. Special collections include the Caribbean civilization, history, and literature collection.

The St. Croix campus library holds 26,000 volumes and 325 periodical subscriptions. Special collections include the Virgin Islands document collection.

STUDENT LIFE

Campus Services

Health, personal counseling, career counseling and placement, and student employment.

Campus Activities

Social and cultural activities include theater group.

The University of the Virgin Islands is divided into two campuses—one on the island of St. Thomas near the town of Charlotte Amalie and one on the island of St. Croix near the town of Christiansted. Both campuses take full advantage of the Caribbean climate with beach facilities, golf courses, and other attractions inviting to students from around the world.

Housing Availability

250 housing spaces (main campus only); off-campus living permitted.

Handicapped Services

Grievances may be raised by handicapped students that relate to academic programs and practices.

Virginia

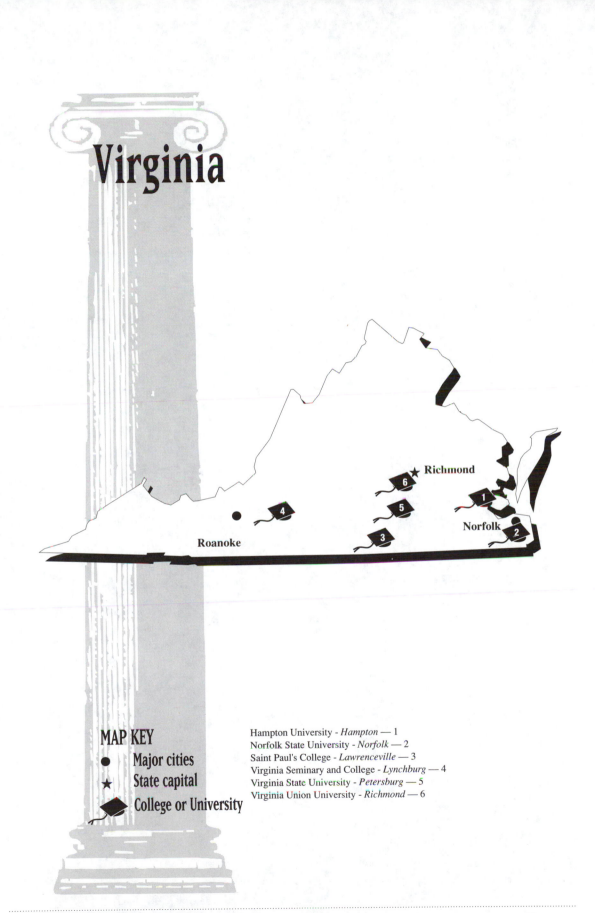

★ Richmond

⬛6

⬛5

⬛4

●

⬛1

Norfolk ⬛2

⬛3

Roanoke

MAP KEY

● Major cities

★ State capital

⬛ College or University

Hampton University - *Hampton* — 1
Norfolk State University - *Norfolk* — 2
Saint Paul's College - *Lawrenceville* — 3
Virginia Seminary and College - *Lynchburg* — 4
Virginia State University - *Petersburg* — 5
Virginia Union University - *Richmond* — 6

HAMPTON UNIVERSITY

Hampton University
Hampton, VA 23668
Phone: (804) 727-5328
or (804) 727-5329
Fax: (804) 727-5084

Total Enrollment:
5,161

Level of Selectivity:
Competitive

Motto:
Learning by Living;
Education for Life

HISTORY

Hampton University (HU) is a four-year, private, coed, liberal arts institution founded in 1868 as Hampton Normal & Agricultural Institute to educate former slaves who had gathered behind the Union line on the Virginia Peninsula. The original purpose was to train selected blacks who would then teach and lead their people. Postsecondary level programs were instituted in 1922; the first bachelor's degree was awarded in 1926; graduate school began in 1928.

In the early years, residence quarters were a problem; the men lived in army tents while the women lived in barracks until the completion of Virginia Hall. Some of the money for this building was raised by the Hampton Singers who toured northern communities.

Hampton University has deep roots in the social history of America and seeks to motivate its students to be responsive to the problems affecting our society. It continues its mission to provide education for the educationally underserved while, increasingly, it seeks promising students from outstanding high schools. While effective teaching and scholarly research play an important role, Hampton places the student at the center of its planning.

The 204-acre campus comprises of approximately 50 main buildings and 75 auxiliary structures. The "Emancipated Oak Tree" stands on the Hampton University campus as a symbol of freedom and education. The Emancipation Proclamation was read to area residents under the tree in 1883; it also served as the first classroom for the new freedmen. The Wigwam building, originally a male residence hall erected in 1878, serves as a reminder of Hampton's role in the education of Native Americans. Five of the buildings are designated National Historic Landmarks including "The Mansion," which predates the founding of the university. Odgen Hall, recognized as having the best acoustics in the state, is home to the Virginia opera and symphony companies.

ACCREDITATION

Hampton University is accredited by the Southern Association of Colleges and Schools to award the Bachelor of Arts, Bachelor of Science, and Master's degrees.

Other Accreditation

American Speech-Language Hearing Association

Computing Science Accreditation Board, Inc.

National Architectural Accrediting Board

National Association of Schools of Music

National Council for Accreditation of Teacher Education

National League of Nursing

Underground Council on Social Work Education

COSTS PER YEAR

1992–93 Tuition: $6,496

Room and board: $ $1,720 (room); $1,400 (board)

Special fees: $510

Books: $500

Estimated total cost: $10,626

FINANCIAL AID

Financial Aid Specific to the School

75% of the student body received financial aid during 1991–92.

Army and Navy ROTC offer two- and three-year scholarships that pay tuition, fee, books, and other expenses, as well as provide monthly stipend of $100.

Athletic awards available to students participating in intercollegiate sports.

Cooperative Education Program alternates and combines classroom study with related paid work experience. The program provides academic credit and full-time status during co-op placement.

Cooperative Work-Study allows Business and Pure & Applied Science majors to work off-campus at industry and business positions.

Deferred Payment Plan allows students to pay college costs in 2 or 3 installments during the semester for an added cost of $20. Deadline is July 1.

Endowed, special interest, and friends scholarships number over 35 and are based on varying criteria.

Merit scholarships are available through the university based on standardized test scores, GPA, character, and community service.

Performance scholarships available for students participating in music and drama.

Tuition waivers (full time or part time) available to Hampton employees and their children.

Financial Aid Deadline

March 31 (priority)

Financial Aid Contact

Veronica Finch, Director of Financial Aid, Hampton University, Hampton, VA, 23668; ((804) 727-5332.

ADMISSION REQUIREMENTS

SAT (800 combined) or ACT (20 English, 20 math) required.

Entrance Requirements

Graduation from an accredited high school and completion of the following Carnegie units: 4 English (grammar, composition, and literature), 3 mathematics (algebra I, II and geometry), 2 natural science (biology and chemistry), 2 social science, and six academic electives; 2 foreign language units recommended; GPA of 2.0 (on 4.0 scale) or "C" average; rank in top half of class; essay; and health certificate completed by a physician. A $15 non-refundable application fee required.

GED students must meet basic admission requirements.

Transfer students must submit official transcripts of all previous college work; students with less than 60 hours must also submit official high school transcript; submit satisfactory SAT or ACT scores; GPA of 2.3; good standing at previous institution; essay; Department of Architecture may request portfolio.

International students must provide evidence of an educational background equal to American high school; recommend translated document or student must pay for translation; submit TOEFL score of 500 and SAT score of 800; African students should submit General Certificate of Education, or West Africa School Certificate at Ordinary Level, and Division II with at least 6 passes to include one English grammar, math, and science; pay first year's fees in full and submit proof of American financial sponsor.

Early admission allows academically gifted high school students the opportunity to enroll in college for credit before completing high school.

Admission Application Deadline
June 1 (fall); Dec 15 (spring)

Admission Contact
Dr. Ollie M. Bowman, Dean of Admission, Hampton University, Hampton, VA 23668; (804) 727-5328 or 5329. Fax: (804) 727-5084.

GRADUATION REQUIREMENTS
A minimum of 120 semester hours and completion of core requirements to include: 6 English; 6 mathematics; 6–8 science; 6 social science; 4 health and physical education; 3 speech; and freshman orientation; minimum 2.0 GPA and last 30 hours in residence.

Grading System
A–E; I=Incomplete; S=Satisfactory; U= Unsatisfactory, Au=Audit

STUDENT BODY PROFILE
Total enrollment (male/female): 1,910/3,251

From in-state: 2,013

Other regions: 38 states; 10 foreign countries

Full-time undergraduates (male/female): 1,681/2,861

Part-time undergraduates (male/female): 95/163

Graduate students (male/female): 134/227

Ethnic/Racial Makeup
African American, 4,694; Hispanic, 55; Asian, 53; Native American, 52; International, 258; Other/unclassified, 49.

Class of 1995 Profile
Number of applicants: 5,974

Number accepted: 2,322

Number enrolled: 1,045

Median SAT score: 400V; 400M

Median ACT score: 20

Average high school GPA: 2.3

Transfers enrolled: 103

FACULTY PROFILE
Number of faculty: 390

Student-teacher ratio: 18:1

Full-time faculty: 307

Part-time faculty: 83

Faculty with doctorates or other terminal degrees: 46%

SCHOOL CALENDAR
1992–93: August 23–May 1

Commencement and conferring of degrees: May 9

Three summer sessions.

DEGREES OFFERED 1991–92:
Accounting

Airway Science

Applied Physics/Engineering

Architecture

Art

Biology

Building Construction Technology

Chemical Engineering

Chemistry

Communicative Sciences and Disorders

Computer Science

Early Childhood Education

Economics

Electrical Engineering

Elementary Education

English

Finance

Foods and Nutrition

General Dietetics

Gerontology

Health and Recreation

History

Interior Design

Management

Marine Science

Marketing

Mass Media Arts

Mathematics

Music

Nursing

Physical Education

Physics

Political Science

Psychology

Social Work

Sociology

Special Education

Speech Communication

Theater Arts

SPECIAL PROGRAMS

Accelerated Study Program allows students to complete their undergraduate degree in a shorter period of time than the traditional four years.

Adult or Continuing Education Program is available for nontraditional students returning to school or working full time.

Advanced Placement (AP) grants college credit for postsecondary work completed in high school. Students scoring 3 on the AP test will receive credit by examination for each course and advanced placement.

College Level Examination Program (CLEP) determines the academic relevance of nontraditional educational experiences such as the military, on-the-job training, or other life experiences through a series of tests and may grant students college credit for these experiences.

College orientation is offered at no cost to entering students for one week prior to the beginning of classes to acquaint students with the college and to prepare them for college life.

Cooperative Education Program alternates and combines classroom study with related paid work experience. The program provides academic credit and full-time status during co-op placement.

Honors Program offers academically talented students a challenging program of study that includes special classes, seminars, colloquia, cultural activities, and special recognition to motivate participants.

Individualized majors allow students to create their own major program(s) of study.

Off-campus study allows students to take enrichment courses not taught at home school at one of the eight member institutions in the Tidewater Consortium.

Part-time degree program allows students to earn an undergraduate degree part time.

Remedial courses are offered to entering students to bring them up to admission standards and to help them adjust for success in college.

ROTC provides training in military science for commission as a second lieutenant in the U.S. Army and Navy. Two-, and four-year scholarships are available.

Study Abroad Program allows students to go to a foreign country for part of their college education.

Talent Search helps targeted, at-risk high school students to complete high school and continue on to college.

Three/two dual degree program in engineering with Old Dominion University allows students to get two degrees—one in liberal arts from home school and one in engineering from Old Dominion—by completing three years at matriculated school and two years at cooperating school.

ATHLETIC PROGRAMS

Hampton University is a member of the National Collegiate Athletic Association (NCAA), All Division II.

Intercollegiate sports: men's basketball, football, golf, softball, tennis, and track; women's basketball, track, and volleyball.

Intramural sports: badminton, basketball, dancing, field hockey, gymnastics, horseshoes, soccer, softball, swimming, table tennis, tennis, track, volleyball, and weight lifting.

Athletic Contact

Dr. Dennis Thomas, Hampton University, Hampton, VA 23668; (804) 727-5642

LIBRARY HOLDINGS

The William R. and Norma B. Harvey Library houses 387,247 bound volumes, 1,477 periodical subscriptions, 39 newspaper subscriptions, 746,000 microforms including 270,000 Eric documents, 500,000 audiovisuals, 72,625 government documents and 50 computers available for student use. Special collections include the Peabody Collection of African American Culture. Online and CD-ROM bibliographic database searching is available for students and staff.

STUDENT LIFE

Special Regulations

Freshman orientation mandatory; freshman cars not permitted; quiet hours; dorm visitation hours enforced.

Campus Services

Health center, personal and psychological counseling, career planning and placement, student employment services, women's resource center, tutoring, remedial instruction, testing for GMAT, GRE, LSAT, PATB, NTE, ACT, ACT-PEP, ACT-ASE, and late-night escort.

Campus Activities

Social and cultural activities include theater, band, chorale, dances, orchestra, movies, art exhibits, lectures. Other activities include open forums, field trips, and athletic contests. Students may get involved in the student-run newspaper or yearbook. Communication major or volunteers can work at the student-run radio station.

The renowned Hampton Jazz Festival originated by the university is an annual event now sponsored jointly with the community. Several other campus-community partnerships give students options for community involvement. The Musical Arts Program brings great artists to the campus in the area of art, dance, drama, media, and music.

Leadership opportunities can be found in the Student Government Association (SGA) or the Student Union Board which plans activities and programs for the university. There are more than 35 other clubs and special interest groups including the radio club, debating society, writer's group, and hobby groups. Greek-letter fraternities include Alpha Phi Alpha, Kappa Alpha Psi, Omega Psi Phi, and Phi Beta Sigma; sororities include Alpha Kappa Alpha, Delta Sigma Theta, Sigma Gamma Rho, and Zeta Phi Beta. Honor societies Alpha Kappa Mu and 13 departmental or special honor societies are also represented.

Hampton University is located in Hampton, Virginia, population approximately 125,000. Points of interest include HU's Museum, Syms-Eaton Museum, and Kecoughtan Indian History Center. The city is served by mass bus transportation; the airport is 10–13 miles away in Norfolk or Newport News; and passenger rail is 10 miles away. The campus is close to Norfolk, Richmond, and Virginia

Beach. Student have access to water sports, fishing, and hiking.

Housing Availability

2,700 housing spaces, freshmen given priority, freshman-only housing.

Handicapped Services

Wheelchair accessibility.

NOTABLE ALUMNI

John L. Henderson, 1955–President, Wilberforce University

William Brown Muse, Jr., 1940–President, Imperial Savings and Loan, Martinville, VA

Booker T. Washington–Founder, Tuskegee University; writer; political leader

NORFOLK STATE UNIVERSITY

2401 Corprew Ave.
Norfolk, VA 23504
Phone: (804) 683-8396

Total Enrollment:
8,624

Level of Selectivity:
Noncompetitive

Motto:
Setting Standards of
Excellence

HISTORY

Norfolk State University (NSU) is a four-year, state-supported, coed, liberal arts institution, founded in 1935 as the Norfolk State Unit of Virginia Union University (VUU). In 1942, the school became independent of VUU and was named Norfolk Polytechnic College. Within two years, by an act of the Virginia Legislature, it became a part of Virginia State College (VSC), granting its first bachelor's degrees in 1956. The college divided from VSC in 1969 and was named Norfolk State College. When granted university status in 1979, the name changed to Norfolk State University.

NSU continues its mission to provide a setting for the youth of the region and the nation to access quality higher education. It maintains its identity as an urban institution, continuing to develop programs specifically related to urban needs.

Eighty-five students attended the first classes held in 1935; today NSU boasts an enrollment of more than 8,600, with students from all sections of the United States and 35 foreign countries. Although a young institution, the university prospers as one of the largest black institutions in the nation. It ranks sixth among schools graduating African Americans with bachelor's degrees.

Located on the former site of the 50-acre Memorial Park Golf Course, which the city of Norfolk sold to the school for one dollar, the campus now encompasses 123 acres of land and 21 buildings. The Joseph G. Echols Memorial Hall is a large health, physical education, and ROTC complex with a seating capacity of 7,500. Other facilities include a television and radio station, and a life science building with a planetarium and labs for animal and cancer research. Norfolk State University is an Historically Black College/University.

ACCREDITATION

Norfolk State University is accredited by the Southern Association of Colleges and Schools (SACS) to award the Associate of Arts, Bachelor of Arts, Bachelor of Science, and Doctor of Philosophy degrees.

Other Accreditation

American Assembly of Collegiate Schools of Business

American Corrective Therapy Association

American Dietetics Association

American Medical Records Association

American Psychological Association

Committee on Allied Health Education and Accreditation

Council on Social Work Education

National Accrediting Agency for Clinical Laboratory Sciences

National Association of Schools of Music

National Council for Accreditation of Teacher Education

National League for Nursing

COSTS PER YEAR

1992–93 Tuition: $2,530 (in-state); $5,760 (out-state)

Room and board: $1,970 (room); $1,430 (board)

Special fees: $225

Books: $500

Estimated total cost: $6,655 (in-state); $9,885 (out-state)

FINANCIAL AID

1991–92 Institutional Funding

Number of scholarships and grants: 1,090

Total amount of scholarships and grants: $2,168,813

Range of scholarships and grants: $200–$5,000

1991–92 Federal and State Funding

Number of scholarships and grants: 3,584

Total amount of scholarships and grants: $5,597,727

Range of scholarships and grants: $200–$2,400

Number of loans: 5,891

Total amount of loans: $10,682,671

Range of loans: $200–$7,500

Number of work-study: 750

Total amount of work-study: $663,560

Range of work-study: $500–$2,000

Financial Aid Specific to the School

95% of the student body received financial aid during 1991–92.

Alumni Merit Scholarship is available to a Virginia resident with a 3.0 GPA. February 28 application deadline.

Army and Navy ROTC offer two- and four-year scholarships that pay tuition, fee, books, and other expenses, and provide a monthly stipend of $100.

Athletic grant-in-aid is available for men and women interested in playing intercollegiate sports. Contact coach of particular sport.

College work-aid provides jobs for students needing financial assistance who do not qualify for college work-study.

Cooperative Education Program alternates classroom study with related paid work experience. The program provides academic credit and full-time status during co-op placement.

Deferred payment plan allows students to pay college costs in two or three installments during the semester.

NSU Cluster Foundation Scholarship aims to attract entering freshmen who graduated in the top 10% of their high school class. March 1 deadline for application.

NSU Foundation Scholarship program aims to attract and retain students who distinguish themselves academically and personally.

Students must maintain a 3.0 GPA. February 28 deadline for application.

Performance scholarship in music is available to talented students participating in band and choir.

Thurgood Marshall Black Education Fund provides a four-year scholarship at this public black college. Qualifying student must have a high school GPA of 3.0 or better and a SAT score of 1,000 or ACT score of 24 or more. Student must be recommended by high school counselor as exceptional or exemplary in the creative or performing arts. Scholarship pays tuition, fees, room, and board, not to exceed $6,000 annually.

Financial Aid Deadline

April 15 (fall); September 15 (spring)

Financial Aid Contact

Mr. Marty L. Miller, Director of Financial Aid, Norfolk State University, 2401 Corprew Ave., Norfolk, VA 23504; (804) 683-8381.

ADMISSION REQUIREMENTS

SAT or ACT required

Entrance Requirements

Graduation from an accredited high school and completion of 16 to 17 academic units to include 4 English, 2 mathematics; 2 social studies, 1 science (2 required for nursing), and 7 to 8 electives (subjects such as art, music, language, and vocational education); submittance of an official high school transcript; two letters of recommendation from counselor and teacher; and completed medical history form by physician. A $15 non-refundable application fee required.

GED students must meet the basic admission requirements.

Transfer students must submit an official transcript from each college attended; provide SAT or ACT scores when transferring less than fifteen semester hours; and provide military information when appropriate. A $15 non-refundable application fee required.

International students must take the TOEFL exam and show their ability to pay for all college expenses.

Admission Application Deadline

August 15 (preferred fall); December 15 (preferred spring); rolling admission provides no specific date for notification of admission so applicant is informed as soon as admission decision is made.

Admission Contact

Dr. Frank W. Cool, Director of Admissions, Norfolk State University, 2401 Corprew Ave., Norfolk, VA 23504; (804) 683-8396.

GRADUATION REQUIREMENTS

A minimum of 126 semester hours and completion of the core requirements to include 6 mathematics, 6 science, and 1 computer course for business administration and mathematic majors; cumulative 2.0 GPA or better; two semesters and 30 credit hours must be in residence at Norfolk State University, including all courses required by the senior year curriculum.

Grading System
A-F

STUDENT BODY PROFILE

Total enrollment (male/female): 3,450/5,174

From in-state: 5,944

Other regions: 39 states and 35 foreign countries

Full-time undergraduates (male/female): 2,690/4,034

Part-time undergraduates (male/female): 402/603

Graduate students (male/female): 358/537

Ethnic/Racial Makeup

African American, 7,675; International, 86; Other/unclassified, 863.

Class of 1995 Profile

Number of applicants: 6,000

Number accepted: 4,800

Number enrolled: 1,600

FACULTY PROFILE

Number of faculty: 451

Student/teacher ratio: 22:1

Full-time faculty: 381

Part-time faculty: 70

Faculty with doctorates or other terminal degrees: 60%

SCHOOL CALENDAR

1992–93: August–May (semester hours)

Commencement and conferring of degrees: May

One summer session.

DEGREES OFFERED 1991–92:

Associate Degrees
Architectural Drafting
Building Construction Technology
Clothing Technology
Industrial Electronics Technology
Library Media
Nursing
Secretarial Science

Bachelor of Arts
Economics
English
Fine Arts
Foreign Languages (French/Spanish)
Graphic Design
History
Interdisciplinary studies
Music Media
Political Science
Psychology
Sociology
Speech Pathology and Audiology
Urban Planning

Bachelor of Science
Accounting
Administrative Services Management
Adult Literacy Development Services
Biology
Building Construction Technology
Chemistry
Child Care Studies
Computer Science
Consumer Services
Corrective Therapy
Design Technology

Early Childhood Education

Electronic Technology

Electronics Engineering

Family Studies

Food and Nutrition

General Business

Health Education

Health Services Management

Home Economics

Home Economics Education

Hotel/Restaurant Management

Industrial Arts Education

Mass Communications

Mathematics

Mathematics Education

Medical Records Administration

Medical Technology

Nursing

Personnel and Industrial Relations

Physical Education

Physics

Public School Music

Recreation Technology Education

Social Work

Special Education

Vocational Industrial Education

Pre-professional

Dentistry

Law

Medicine

Master's Degree

Mass Communication

Music

Psychology

Social Work

Special Education

Urban Affairs

Doctor of Philosophy Degrees

Education

Social Work

SPECIAL PROGRAMS

An accelerated program allows students to complete their undergraduate degree in a shorter period of time than the traditional four years.

Adult or Continuing Education Program is available for nontraditional students returning to school or working full time.

Advanced Placement (AP) grants college credit for postsecondary work completed in high school. Students scoring 3 to 5 on the AP test will receive credit by examination for each course and advanced placement.

College Level Examination Program (CLEP) determines the academic relevance of nontraditional educational experiences, such as the military, on-the-job training, or other life experiences, through a series of tests and may grant students college credit for these experiences.

College orientation held in the spring or summer is mandatory for entering students for one weekend at $25 to acquaint students with the college and to prepare them for college life. Seminars are held for parents. For more information call (804) 883-8024.

Cooperative Education Program alternates classroom study with related paid work experience. The program provides academic credit and full-time status during co-op placement.

Cooperative Study Abroad Program is available to students for credit towards a degree program.

English as a Second Language is a program that offers courses in English for students whose native language is not English.

Honors Program offers academically talented students a challenging program of study that includes special classes, seminars, colloquia, cultural activities, and special recognition to motivate participants.

Off-campus study may be arranged with Old Dominion University, Hampton University, Virginia Wesleyan College, Christopher Newport College, Tidewater Community College, Paul D. Camp Community College, Eastern Shore Community College, or Thomas Nelson Community College.

Part-time degree program allows students to earn an undergraduate degree while attending part time during the daytime, evenings, or summers.

Remedial courses are offered to entering students to bring them up to admission standards and to help them adjust for success in college.

ROTC provides training in military science for commission as a second lieutenant in the U.S. Army and Navy. Two-, and four-year scholarships are available.

ATHLETIC PROGRAMS

Norfolk State University is a member of the Central Intercollegiate Athletic Association (CIAA) and the National Association of Intercollegiate Athletics (NAIA).

Intercollegiate sports: men's baseball, basketball, cross-country, football, track, and wrestling; women's basketball, cross-country, softball, track, and volleyball.

Intramural sports: archery, basketball, billiards, football, softball, tennis, and wrestling.

LIBRARY HOLDINGS

The Lyman Beecher Brooks Library holds 300,000 bound volumes, 1,600 microforms, and 2,600 periodical subscriptions. Tapes are housed in the Audio Lab.

STUDENT LIFE

Special Regulations

Cars must be registered; dorm visitation on Saturdays from noon to 12am and Sunday from noon to 10pm.

Campus Services

Health clinic, personal and psychological counseling, career counseling and placement, remediation, student employment, and tutoring.

Campus Activities

Social and cultural activities include theater, concerts, orchestra, jazz and marching band, chorale, and dance. Other activities include films, art exhibits, recitals, and seminars. Students may get involved in the student-run newspaper or yearbook. Communication majors may work at the student-run radio station, WNSB.

Leadership opportunities are found in the Student Government Association (SGA) or the more than eighty student groups. Greek letter fraternities include Alpha Phi Alpha, Kappa Alpha Psi, and Phi Beta Sigma; sororities include Alpha Kappa Alpha, Delta Sigma Theta, Sigma Gamma Rho, and Zeta Phi Beta. Honor societies are also represented on campus.

NSU's Army ROTC program is the largest non-military school in the state; its Female Cadet Corp is the largest in the United States.

The campus is located within 2 miles of downtown Norfolk and the Military Circle Shopping Mall. The airport is 10 miles away. Norfolk, Virginia, is one of the largest cities in the state and is located in the Tidewater area that includes Hampton, Chesapeake, Portsmouth, Newport News, and Virginia Beach. Points of interest include WaterSide, a new festival marketplace; Polaris Submarines; the largest Naval Base in the world; and the Chrysler Museum. Within an hour are two attractions, historical Colonial Williamsburg and Busch Gardens Amusement Park.

Housing Availability

1,500 housing spaces; freshmen given priority; off-campus housing permitted.

NOTABLE ALUMNI

Alberto Ascercon, 1986–International music lecturer

Bobby Dandridge, 1973–Former professional basketball player

Yvonne Miller, 1954–State senator, 5th district, Virginia

Tim Reid, 1968–Actor/executive producer, Beverly Hill, CA

SAINT PAUL'S COLLEGE

406 Windsor Ave.
Lawrenceville, VA
23868-9988
Phone: (804) 848-3111
Toll-free:
800-678-7071

Total Enrollment:
750

Level of Selectivity:
Slightly competitive

Motto:
An Education for Life

HISTORY

Saint Paul's College (SPC) is a four-year, private, coed, liberal arts institute affiliated with the Episcopal Church. Founded in 1888 as Saint Paul's Normal and Industrial School, the name changed to Saint Paul's Polytechnic Institute in 1941 and authority was granted to offer a four-year program. The first bachelor's degree was awarded in 1944. The present name was adopted in 1957 to more accurately reflect the liberal arts and teacher education curricula.

SPC is a small college that provides a personalized education and an environment that fosters individual strengths and responds to individual needs. Its liberal arts, professional, and pre-professional programs prepare students for careers and graduate programs in humanities, social sciences, education, business, mathematics and natural sciences. It is committed to the development of young Christian men and women who leave capable of taking their place in a multicultural society.

Saint Paul's 11-building campus is situated on 75 acres of green hills. Older buildings were constructed by students and donated by friends of the college.

ACCREDITATION

Saint Paul's College is accredited by the Southern Association of Colleges and Schools (SACS) to award the Bachelor of Arts and Bachelor of Science degrees.

Other Accreditation
Virginia State Board of Education

COSTS PER YEAR
1991–92 Tuition: $5,113

Room and board: $3,380

Special fees: $125

Books: $600

Estimated total cost: $9,218

FINANCIAL AID

1991–92 Institutional Funding

Number of scholarships and grants: 147

Total amount of scholarships and grants: $286,775

Range of scholarships and grants: $1,800–$8,000

1991–92 Federal and State Funding

Number of scholarships and grants: 262

Total amount of scholarships and grants: $241,304

Range of scholarships and grants: $200–$2,400

Number of loans: 347

Total amount of loans: $1,206,996

Range of loans: $500–$4,000

Number of work-study: 219

Total amount of work-study: $302,224

Range of work-study: $1,800–$2,800

Financial Aid Specific to the School

86% of the student body received financial aid during 1991–92.

Army ROTC in cooperation with West Virginia State University offers two- and four-year scholarships that pay tuition, fee, books, and other expenses as well as provide a monthly stipend of $100.

Athletic scholarships are available to students participating in intercollegiate sports.

Cooperative Education Program alternates and combines classroom study with related paid work experience. The program provides academic credit and full-time status during co-op placement.

Endowed, friends, and special interest scholarships number more than 80 and are based on merit and need.

Presidential Scholarships are awarded to students with a GPA of 3.0 or higher who exemplify leadership characteristics.

United Negro College Fund (UNCF) Scholarships are awarded to a limited number of students at this school who demonstrate financial need. Some scholarships may be based on location and merit. UNCF scholarships range from $500 to $7,500.

Virginia Scholarship Assistance and Tuition Assistance Grant Program provides financial assistance to students who are residents of the state and demonstrate financial need.

Financial Aid Deadline

April 1 (priority); June 1

Financial Aid Contact

Barry W. Simmons, Saint Paul's College, 406 Windsor Ave., Lawrenceville, VA 23868; (804) 848-3111, ext 247.

ADMISSION REQUIREMENTS

SAT or ACT required

Entrance Requirements

Graduation from an accredited high school and completion of the following 16 units: 4 English, 2 mathematics, (algebra and geometry), 2 science, 2 social science, 6 electives; submit official high school transcript; complete health form; class rank; and one recommendation. A $15 application fee required.

GED students must meet basic admission requirements.

Transfer students must submit offical high school transcript and transcripts of all college work, minimum 2.0 GPA; complete health form; recommendation from previous college. A $15 application fee required.

International students must meet basic admission requirements; must submit certificate showing completion of high school; take TOEFL examination; and provide proof of ability to pay all college costs.

Admission Application Deadline

Rolling admission provides no specific date for notification of admission so applicant is informed as soon as admission decision is made.

Admission Contact

Larnell R. Parker, Director of Admissions, Saint Paul's College, 406 Windsor

Ave., Lawrenceville, VA 23868; (804) 848-3111, Ext. 233, 241 or (804) 848-3984; or 800-678-7071.

GRADUATION REQUIREMENTS

A minimum of 120 credit hours and completion of core requirements to include 3 mathematics, 4 science, and 1 computer course; minimum 2.0 GPA; last 30 hours in residence.

Grading System

A–F; I=Incomplete; W=Withdraw

STUDENT BODY PROFILE

Total enrollment (male/female): 322/428

From in-state: 570

Other regions: 19 states, 5 foreign countries

Full-time undergraduates (male/female): 307/408

Part-time undergraduates (male/female): 15/20

Ethnic/Racial Makeup

African American, 715: Hispanic, 3; Caucasian, 23; International, 9.

Class of 1995 Profile

Number of applicants: 593

Number accepted: 504

Number enrolled: 280

Transfers enrolled: 23

FACULTY PROFILE

Number of faculty: 44

Student-teacher ratio: 17:1

Full-time faculty: 33

Part-time faculty: 11

Faculty with doctorates or other terminal degrees: 60%

SCHOOL CALENDAR

1992–93: August–May (semester hours)

Commencement and conferring of degrees: May

One summer session.

DEGREES OFFERED 1991–92:

Bachelor of Arts

Criminal Justice

English

General Studies

Political Science

Sociology

Bachelor of Science

Accounting

Biology

Biology Education

Business Administration

Business Education

Business Management

Elementary Education

English Education

Environmental Science

Marketing

Mathematics

Mathematics Education

Middle School Education

Office Management

Pre-school Education

Secondary Education

Social Science Education

SPECIAL PROGRAMS

Adult or Continuing Education Program is available for nontraditional students returning to school or working full time.

Advanced Placement (AP) grants college credit for postsecondary work completed in high school. Students passing the AP test will receive credit by examination for each course and advanced placement.

College Level Examination Program (CLEP) determines the academic relevance of nontraditional educational experiences such as the military, on-the-job training or other life experiences through a series of tests and may grant students college credit for these experiences.

College orientation is offered at no cost to entering students for one week prior to the beginning of classes to acquaint students with the college and to prepare them for college life. Parents may attend.

Cooperative Education Program alternates and combines classroom study with related paid work experience. The program provides academic credit and full-time status during co-op placement.

Honors Program offers academically talented students a challenging program of study that includes special classes, seminars, colloquia, cultural activities, and special recognition to motivate participants.

Internships in various disciplines allow students to apply theory to on-the-job training in industry and business.

Nursing program, in conjunction with Eastern Shore and Tidewater Community Colleges, allows students to use these cooperative schools' resources.

Part-time degree program allows students to earn an undergraduate degree part time.

Remedial courses are offered to entering students to bring them up to admission standards and to help them adjust for success in college.

ROTC, in cooperation with West Virginia State University, provides training in military science for commission as a second lieutenant in the U.S. Army. Two- and four-year scholarships are available.

Study Abroad Program allows students to go to a foreign country for part of their college education.

ATHLETIC PROGRAMS

Saint Paul's College is a member of the National Collegiate Athletic Association (NCAA) and the Central Intercollegiate Athletic Association (CIAA)

Athletic Contact

Jeanette A. Lee, Saint Paul's College, 406 Windsor Ave., Lawrenceville, VA 23868; (804)848-3111

LIBRARY HOLDINGS

The Mes Solomon Russel Memorial Library houses 75,000 bound volumes, 275 periodicals, 3,529 audiovisuals, 32,903 microforms, 12,447 government documents; 50 computers in computer lab. Special collections include a history of St. Paul's College and a West Indies Collection.

STUDENT LIFE

Special Regulations

Freshmen must live on campus unless living with a relative; cars must be registered; designated parking area; physical exam required of each new student by college physician.

Campus Services

Health center, personal and psychological counseling, career planning and placement, remedial instruction, tutoring, chapel, and religious activities.

Campus Activities

Social and cultural activities include theater, jazz combo, lecture and concerts series, films, chorale, dance.

Housing Availability

700 housing spaces; freshmen given priority.

VIRGINIA SEMINARY AND COLLEGE

2058 Garfield Ave.
Lynchburg, VA 24501
Phone: (804) 528-5276.

Total Enrollment:
40

Level of Selectivity:
Noncompetitive

HISTORY

Virginia Seminary and College (VSC) is a four-year, private, coed liberal arts college founded in 1888 to educate blacks for church work. VSC remains committed to providing programs in Christian education.

ACCREDITATION

Virginia Seminary and College is accredited by the Southern Association of Colleges and Schools (SACS) to award Bachelor's degrees.

COSTS PER YEAR

1991–92 Tuition: $2,920 (in-state); $3,320 (out-state)

Room and board: $1,600

Special fees: $125

Books: $500

Estimated total cost: $5,145 (in-state); $5,545

ADMISSION REQUIREMENTS

SAT or ACT required

Admission Contact

James H. Taylor, Jr., Director of Admissions, Virginia Seminary and College, Lynchburg, VA 24501; (804) 524-5070.

STUDENT BODY PROFILE

Total enrollment: 40

DEGREES OFFERED 1991–92:

Business

Mathematics
Social Studies
Theology

NOTABLE ALUMNI
Dr. Ralph Reavis–Church historian,
  Virginia University

VIRGINIA STATE UNIVERSITY

Petersburg, VA 23803
Phone: (804) 524-5000
Fax: (804) 524-6506

Total Enrollment:
4,585

Level of Selectivity:
Noncompetitive

Motto:
A Place to Grow

HISTORY

Virginia State University is a four-year, state-supported, coed university. Founded in 1882 as the Virginia Normal and Collegiate Institute, the school did not open its doors until 1883 because of a hostile lawsuit. The school awarded its first bachelor's degrees in 1889. In 1902, the name changed to Virginia Normal and Industrial Institute. That same year, the legislature revised the charter act to curtail the collegiate program.

Land grant status was moved from Hampton Institute to Virginia State in 1920. Three years later, the college program was restored and in 1930, the name changed to Virginia State College for Negroes. In 1944, the two-year Norfolk branch was added to the college and in 1956, the Norfolk branch became a four-year college gaining its independence as Norfolk State College in 1969. The parent school was renamed Virginia State College in 1946 and adopted its present name Virginia State University in 1979.

From its humble beginnings of 126 students, seven faculty, and one building located on 33 acres, Virginia State has grown to 236 acres with more than 50 buildings, 15 dorms, 16 classroom buildings, and a 416-acre farm. As one of the state's two land grant institutions, Virginia State is dedicated to providing an education that challenges intellect and prepares students to become knowledgeable, perceptive citizens who are secure in their self awareness. This small institution brags of big opportunities, claiming students' possibilities are limited only by their willingness to commit to the task.

ACCREDITATION

The university is accredited by the Southern Association of Colleges and Schools to award the Bachelor of Arts, Bachelor of Science, and Master's degrees.

Other Accreditation
American Dietetic Association

Council on Social Work Education

National Association of Schools of Music

National Council for Accreditation of Teacher Education

Virginia State Board of Education

COSTS PER YEAR

1992–93 Tuition: $2,910 (in-state); $6,310 (out-state)

Room and board: $2,346 (room); $1,781 (board)

Special fees: $1,212

Books: $500

Estimated total cost: $8,749 (in-state); $12,149 (out-state)

FINANCIAL AID

1992–93 Institutional Funding

Number of scholarships and grants: 1,332

Financial Aid Specific to the School

85% of the student body received financial aid during 1991–92.

The Army ROTC offers two- and three-year scholarships that pay tuition, fees, books, and other expenses, and provide a monthly stipend of $100.

Athletic scholarships are available to students participating in intercollegite sports.

The College Work Study (CWS) Deferment Plan allows students to use 75% of their CWS award to finance their fees. Students must sign CWS checks to the university.

The deferred payment plan allows students to pay their college costs in four monthly installments a semester. Entering students must have high school GPA of 2.0 and returning or transfer students must have a GPA of 2.3 to qualify.

Scholarships are granted to entering students or returning students who have a high school or college GPA of 3.0 or better.

Thurgood Marshal Black Education Fund provides a four-year scholarship to an entering freshmen who has a high school GPA of 3.0 or higher with a SAT score of 1,000 or ACT score of 24 or more.

Student must be recommend by high school counselor as an exceptional in the creative or performing arts. Scholarship pays tuition, fees, room, and board, not to exceed $6,000 annually.

The Virginia State University Merit and Board of Visitors scholarships are awarded to students accepted in the Honors College program. To qualify, students must have a high school GPA of at least 3.0 and score at least 900 on the SAT or 21 on the ACT.

The Virginia War Orphans Education Program provides financial assistance to children who have a parent who became permanently disabled or died while in active duty in the military. Eligible students receive a tuition-free education for a maximum of 48 months.

Financial Aid Deadline

March 31 (fall and spring)

Financial Aid Contact

Mr. Henry Debose, Director of Financial Aid, Virginia State University, PO Box 31, Petersburg, VA 23803; (804) 524-5990.

ADMISSION REQUIREMENTS

SAT or ACT required

Entrance Requirements

Must submit an official high school transcript with 15 units including: 4 English, 2 mathematics (including algebra), 2 science (at least one unit with lab of biology, chemistry, or physics), 2 social studies (one unit in U.S. History), 2 foreign language, and 3 electives. Students must have proof of a physical and two letters of recommendation from high school counselor and teacher. A non-refundable application fee of $25.00 is required.

GED students must meet the basic admission requirements.

Transfer students must submit an official transcript from each college previously attended; must have a cumulative average of "C" or a GPA of 2.0 or better and be in good standing with last college attended. Students with less than 24 semester hours must submit high school transcript and SAT or ACT scores. A $25 non-refundable application fee is due with application.

International students from non-English-speaking countries must take the TOEFL examination and verify ability to pay all college costs. All students should apply 12 months prior to term of enrollment.

Admission Application Deadline

May 1 (fall); October 1 (spring)

Admission Contact

Office of Admissions and Recruitment, Virginia State University, PO Box 18, Petersburg, VA 23803; (804) 524-5902.

GRADUATION REQUIREMENTS

A minimum of 120 hours including the core requirements which include 6 hours of mathematics; 3 hours of science; and 3 hours of computer science with at least a 2.0 GPA. Student must earn last 30 hours at Virginia State and must participate in graduation ceremony or submit written notification of absence.

Grading System

A-F; I=Incomplete; E=Allows student 2nd try on a failed examination; P=Students who earned credit hours need to satisfy requirements; S=Satisfactory completion at certain levels; U=Unsatisfactory; AU=Audit; NC=Special services students; NG=No grade received at time grades were processed.

STUDENT BODY PROFILE

Total enrollment: 4,585

From in-state: 2,751

Other regions: 28 states; 12 foreign countries

Full-time undergraduates (male/female): 1,628/2,249

Part-time undergraduates (male/female): 122/261

Graduate students: 325

Ethnic/Racial Makeup

African American, 4,310; International, 46; Other/unclassified, 229.

Class of 1995 Profile

Number of applicants: 3,795

Number accepted: 2,450

Number enrolled: 956

Median SAT score: 385

Median ACT score: 360

FACULTY PROFILE

Number of faculty: 250

Student-teacher ratio: 18:1

Full-time faculty: 194

Part-time faculty: 56

Tenured faculty (male/female):

Faculty with doctorates or other terminal degrees: 60%

SCHOOL CALENDAR

1991–92: August 22–May 9 (semesters)

Commencement and conferring of degrees: May

Two summer sessions.

DEGREES OFFERED 1991–92:

Bachelor of Arts

English

English Education

Fine Arts in Art and Commercial Art and Design

History

International Studies

Political Science

Social Work

Sociology

Bachelor of Science
Accounting
Administrative Systems Management
Agriculture
Biology
Business Administration
Chemistry
Computer Science
Economics
Education
Engineering Technology
Geology
Health and Physical Education and
    Recreation
Home Economics and Business
Humanities and Social Sciences
Industrial Education and Technology
Information Systems
Interdisciplinary Studies
Liberal Studies
Marketing Management
Mathematics
Mathematics Education
Music
Music Education
Physics
Physics Education
Psychology
Public Administrative
Special Education

Master of Arts
Economics (Public Admnistration)
English
History

Master of Science
Administrative Assistant Management
Agricultural Education
Biology
Earth Science
Educational Administration and
    Supervision

Educational Media
Elementary Education
Guidance
Industrial Education
Mathematics
Physics
Psychology
Special Education

Master of Education
Administrative Systems Management
Agricultural Education
Earth Science
Educational Administration and
    Supervision
Educational Media
Elementary Education
Guidance
Industrial Education
Special Education

Pre-professional Programs
Engineering

Certificate of Advanced Graduate Study
Industrial Education
Technical Education
Vocational Education

SPECIAL PROGRAMS
Academic Skills Center is set up for students entering college whose academic skills are under par. The program is designed to help students become more efficient in competitive skills.

Advanced Placement (AP) allows high school seniors to take various college courses for credit during their junior and senior year. Examination scores give students 60 hours maximum college credit. Letter grades are not assigned to AP credits or counted in GPA.

The Advanced Scholars Program allows academically talented high school seniors an opportunity to take college courses during the summer between the junior and senior year and/or during the senior year. Students must have completed junior year with a cumulative average of at least 3.0 and must submit high school transcript with a letter of recommendation from high school counselor. Student can take a maximum of 6 hours each session.

The Army ROTC provides training in military science for commission as a second lieutenant in the U.S. Armed Forces. The program is open to all full-time students and offers two- and three-year scholarships that pay tuition, books, fees, and other expenses, and provide a monthly stipend of $100.

Bachelor of Individualized Studies (BIS) gives working adults an opportunity to earn a bachelor's degree through college course work and examination credit.

The College Level Examination Program (CLEP) determines the academic relevance of nontraditional experiences such as the military, on-the-job training, or other life experiences through the college entrance examination board and may grant college credit for these experiences. Student may be granted a maximum of 48 college credits for a qualifying score of 50 or 500 on the CLEP exam.

Four-day college orientation session is offered for a fee of $60 prior to the beginning of classes to orient students with the college and prepare them for college life; parents may attend.

The Cooperative Education Program combines academic study with paid related work experience.

A three/two engineering degree program is offered in conjunction with Old Dominion University. Three years of liberal arts including math and science are completed at Virginia State and two years of engineering are completed at Old Dominion. Upon completion of the program students receive a Bachelor of Science degree and an engineering degree.

Honors College is a program that provides academically talented students with scholarships and colloquia to improve their oral and written skills, and serves as a forum to expand their horizons with regards to everyday events.

Virginia State University at Fort Lee offers a variety of undergraduate and graduate degree programs through five 8-week sessions each academic year. Six semester hours during a 8-week session qualify students for veterans benefits.

ATHLETIC PROGRAMS

Virginia State College is a member of NCAA, Division II. Intercollegiate sports: men's baseball, basketball, cross country, football, golf, tennis, and wrestling; women's basketball, cross country, golf, tennis, and volleyball.

Intramural sports: basketball, football, tennis, track & field, volleyball, and wrestling.

LIBRARY HOLDINGS

The Johnston Memorial Library holds 245,731 bound volumes, 520,179 titles on microform, 1,303 periodical subscriptions, 3,428 audiovisuals; 125 computers for student use. The library serves as a government documents depository and holds 100,000 federal and state government documents.

STUDENT LIFE

Special Regulations

Registered car permitted.

Campus Services

Health clinic, personal and psychological counseling, remedial services, career counseling and placement, and religious services.

Campus Activities

Student activities include drama or theater groups, band, chorale, and orchestra, as well as a lecture series. Students can get involved in the student-run newspaper and radio station.

Leadership opportunities can be found in the Student Government Association or other student-run organizations. Greek-letter fraternities include Alpha Phi Alpha, Kappa

Alpha Psi, Omega Psi Phi, and Phi Beta Sigma; sororities include Alpha Kappa Alpha, Delta Sigma Theta, Sigma Gamma Rho, and Zeta Phi Beta. Local fraternities and sororities are also represented. Sigma Xi honor society is also present on campus.

Located in historic Petersburg, with a population of approximately 41,000, the campus is only 25 miles north of Richmond, the capital of Virginia; 2 1/2 hours from Washington, D.C. to the north; Virginia Beach rests to the South. Students are surrounded by social and cultural activities, as historic Colonial Williamsburg is within an hour's drive. Historic Petersburg is the site of the first observance of Memorial Day. Students have their choice of museums, shopping, plays, fine dining, major league sports, and the beach in this strategically located area.

Housing Availability

2,082 housing spaces available; freshmen given priority.

Handicapped Services

Include wheelchair accessibility and services for the visually and hearing impaired.

NOTABLE ALUMNI

Luther H. Foster, Ph.D., 1932–Fourth president, Tuskegee University

Reginald F. Lewis, LLB., 1965–President/CEO, TLC Beatrice International Holdings, Inc.

Wesley Cornelious McClure, Ph.D.–17th president, Virginia State University

VIRGINIA UNION UNIVERSITY

1500 N. Lombardy St.
Richmond, VA 23220
Phone: (804) 257-5600
Toll-free in-state:
800-572-2073
Toll-free out-state
800-368-3227

Total Enrollment:
1,511

Level of Selectivity:
Slightly competitive

Motto:
Dominus Providebit
(The Lord Will
Provide)

HISTORY

Virginia Union University (VUU) is a four-year, private, coed, liberal arts college affiliated with the American Baptist Church of the USA. Founded in 1865 as Richmond Theological Institute, Virginia Union is the result of an 1899 merger of the institute and Wayland Seminary in Washington. Later, Hartshorn Memorial College of Richmond and Storer College of Harpers Ferry, West Virginia, merged with VUU to complete the union. The first bachelor's degrees were awarded in 1899.

Located on the site of a former slave jail, VUU is now home to a black institution whose original mission was to "free the mind of the newly emancipated through education in a humanistic environment." Virginia Union can take pride in the fact that the first black governor of the United States, the first black admiral of the U.S. Navy, numerous college presidents, and more than one tenth of all black ministry graduated from the university.

The 72-acre campus has five older granite buildings that have been restored and designated national historic landmarks. The Belgian Friendship Building, which was a gift from the Belgian Government, was on exhibit at the 1939 New York World's Fair and was reconstructed on the campus in 1941. The architectural blend of the 22-building campus embraces the old and the new.

While VUU continues to grow in programs and student diversity, it remains true to its mission to free the minds of blacks through education; its liberal arts and sciences education emphasize both western culture and African American heritage. President Dallas Simmons states that, "we are concentrating on making Virginia Union the flagship of historically black institutions." This historically black college is a member of the United Negro College Fund (UNCF).

ACCREDITATION

Virginia Union University is accredited by the Southern Association of Colleges and Schools to award the Bachelor of Arts, Bachelor of Science, and Master's of Divinity degrees.

Other Accreditation

Association of Theological Schools in the United States and Canada

Council on Social Work Education

Department of Education, Commonwealth of Virginia

COSTS PER YEAR

1992–93 Tuition: $6,131

Room and board: $1,418 (room); $1,744 (board)

Special fees: $359

Books: $500

Estimated total cost: $10,152

FINANCIAL AID

1990–91 Institutional Funding

Number of scholarships and grants: 285

Total amount of scholarships and grants: $808,398

Range of scholarships and grants: $1,800–$2,200

1991–92 Institutional Funding

Number of scholarships and grants: 1,182

Total amount of scholarships and grants: $1,786,103

Range of scholarships and grants: $1,200–$1,500

Number of loans: 804

Total amount of loans: $1,064,610

Range of loans: $1,000–$2,400

Number of work-study: 353

Total amount of work-study: $600,078

Range of work-study: $1,500–$1,800

Financial Aid Specific to the School

97% of the student body received financial aid during 1991–92.

Departmental scholarships are available to students based on academic standards. These include athletic, music, and drama scholarships.

There are approximately 28 endowed and/or alumni scholarships available to students.

The 3/3 dual law degree early entry scholarship pays full tuition, books, and a monthly stipend while students complete the Juris Doctorate at St. John's Law School. Students complete three years at VUU and three years at St. John's Law School. Upon completion of the program the students receive bachelor's and law degrees.

Full or partial tuition waivers are available to VUU employees and their children.

The Cooperative Education Program allows students to receive paid work experience while gaining credits towards their degree program.

United Negro College Fund scholarships are awarded to a limited number of entering students who score high on the ACT or ETS exams or students with a high school GPA of at least 3.0. To renew awards students must maintain a 3.0 cumulative GPA in college.

The Army ROTC program offers two- and three-year scholarships that pay tuition, books, and other expenses, and provide a monthly stipend of $100.

College Scholarship Assistant Programs (CSAP) are state-supported awards granted to Virginia students based on need. The Financial Aid Form (FAF) of the College Scholarship Service must be completed and postmarked no later than March 15th.

Tuition Assistant Grant (TAG) is awarded to Virginia residents attending private colleges and universities in Virginia. Students need to complete application.

Financial Aid Deadline

August 1 (fall and spring); May 1 (priority)

Financial Aid Contact

Mrs. Phenie D. Golatt, Director of Financial Aid, Virginia Union University, Richmond, VA 23220; (804) 257-5882.

ADMISSION REQUIREMENTS

SAT or ACT required.

Entrance Requirements

Graduation from an accredited high school and completion of 16 units: 4 English, 3 mathematics (algebra I and algebra II), 2 foreign language (same language), 2 social sciences (history, government or civics), 2 natural sciences (biology, chemistry or physics), and 3 electives. A copy of student's social security card is required. A $10.00 non-refundable application fee is required.

GED students must meet basic admission requirements.

Transfer students must meet basic admission requirements or must complete during entering year. Transfer students must have a "C" average or better from the former college and be eligible to return to the former college. Students attending community colleges that have transfer agreements with VUU may be admitted upon approval by the registrar's office to junior status.

International students must prove financial ability to pay all college cost and must submit scores from the TOEFL examination.

Admission Application Deadline

June 15 (fall); December 1 (spring); May 1 (summer). Early admission allows qualified students to enter college full time before completing high school. Deferred admission.

Admission Contact

Mr. Gil Powell, Director of Admissions, Virginia Union University, Richmond, VA 23220. (804) 257-5855 or (804) 257-5856; 800-368-3227 (out-state); 800-572-2073 (in-state).

GRADUATION REQUIREMENTS

A minimum of 124 credit hours is required, including the core curriculum with a 2.0 minimum GPA and a "C" or better in each course in major. An essay exam in English must be taken by the junior year. Students must complete freshman orientation and two hours of physical education.

Grading System

A-F; I=Incomplete; W=Withdrawal or neutral grade, zero credits

STUDENT BODY PROFILE

Total enrollment: 695/816

From in-state: 786

Other regions: 31 states; 8 foreign countries

Full-time undergraduate (male/female): 589/692

Part-time undergraduate (male/female): 37/43

Graduate students (male/female): 69/81

Ethnic Racial/Makeup

African American, 1,476; Caucasians, 19; Internationals, 11; Native Americans, 4; Hispanic, 1.

Class of 1995 Profile

Number of applicants: 1,847

Number accepted: 1,610

Number enrolled: 453

Average high school GPA: 2.30

Transfer applicants: 266

Transfers accepted: 150

Transfers enrolled: 63

FACULTY PROFILE

Number of faculty: 115

Student-teacher ratio: 16:1

Full-time faculty: 78

Part-time faculty: 37

Tenured faculty: 24

Faculty with doctorates or other terminal degrees: 41%

SCHOOL CALENDAR

1992–93: August 20–May 7 (semesters)

Commencement and conferring of degrees: May 9

Two summer sessions.

DEGREES OFFERED 1991–92:

Bachelor of Arts

Communications: n/a

English : n/a

French: n/a

History and Government: 7

Journalism: 7

Music: 3

Music Education: n/a

Philosophy and Religion: 1

Political Science : n/a

Psychology : n/a

Social Work: 15

Sociology: 7

Bachelor of Science

Accounting: 10

Biology: 10

Biology Education: 1

Business Administration: 30

Business Education: 1

Chemistry: 1

Chemistry Education: n/a

Computer Science: n/a

Early Childhood Education: 7

Elementary Education: 5

English Education: n/a

French Education: n/a

History Education : n/a

Mathematics: 19

Physics: n/a

Psychology Education: 6

Recreation and Physical Education: 2

Special Education: 3

Pre-Professional

Engineering: n/a

Master's

Theology: n/a

Doctorate

Theology: n/a

SPECIAL PROGRAMS

The mandated freshman college orientation program for all entering freshmen and transfer students is designed to help students adjust to VUU's college environment. A $30 fee is required.

The Work/Life Experience Program awards up to 36 hours for comparable work and life experiences for eligible adults. Written statement with details of experience must be submitted to the vice president for academic affairs.

The National Recognized Kenan Project is designed to prepare high school students for college entry and successful completion of degree requirements. The program is administered by the Center for Teacher Effectiveness.

A three/two dual degree in engineering is offered with Howard University, University of Michigan, and University of Iowa. Three years of math/science must be completed at VUU, and two years of engineering course work must be completed at one of the cooperating institutions. Students receive a Bachelor of Science degree from VUU and a engineering degree from the cooperating school.

A 3/3 dual degree in law with St. John's School of Law is also offered. Students attend VUU for three years and St. John's University in Jamaica, New York, for three years. Students receive a bachelor's degree from VUU after completing the first year at St. John's and a jurisprudence degree from St. John's after completion of the program.

The Army ROTC provides training in military science for commission as a second lieutenant in the U.S. Armed Forces. Two- and three-year scholarships are available.

The Student Exchange Program with Lynchburg College, a predominately white College, provides students from both campuses the opportunity for cultural exchange and diversity.

The Student Early Entrance (SEE) Program allows high school juniors and seniors who qualify to take three to nine credit hours a semester and three courses during the summer. A $10 application fee is required and students should apply one month prior to the entering semester.

The Cooperative Education Program alternates academic course work with career-related work experiences. Each placement is for a semester and a minimum of two placements are required.

Student Support Service provides group activities to assist freshmen and sophomores both academically and personally.

The Special Opportunities Program (SOP) is a six-week intensive program to aid students in English fundamentals, mathematics, developmental reading, and study skills.

The Martin Luther King, Jr. Scholarship Program in conjunction with the Richmond Public Schools trains students through first-hand experience to deal with civil rights problems and solutions.

The School of Theology (STVU) cooperates with Union Theological Seminary in Virginia and the Presbyterian School of Christian Education to form the Richmond Theological Center. Students interested in enrolling in the program should write to the Registrar, School of Theology at VUU.

The Upward Bound Program is designed to motivate pre-college, inner-city students to pursue a college education by developing basic college skills.

Richmond Police Modified Cooperative Education is a partnership between the university and city of Richmond to train specially selected students for a career in law enforcement. The Police Training Academy is housed on the campus.

The Center for Black Enterprise, a free-standing institute headquartered at VUU, is devoted to the history, practice, culture, philosophy, and future of black enterprise in America.

ATHLETIC PROGRAMS

Virginia Union University is a member of the National Collegiate Athletic Association (NCAA) and the Central Collegiate Athletic Association (CCAA). The football team has gone to six consecutive NCAA Division Playoffs.

Intercollegiate sports: men's basketball, cross-country, football, golf, tennis, and track & field; women's basketball, cross-country, softball, track & field and volleyball.

Intramural sports: softball and basketball

Athletic Contact

Mr. Jamie F. Battle, Virginia Union University, Richmond, VA; (804) 257-5890.

LIBRARY HOLDINGS

The campus library holds 139,032 volumes, 348 microforms, 477 records/tapes, 468 periodical subscriptions, and 61 computer terminals available for student use. Special collections include a microfilm collection by and about blacks from the Schomburg Collection in New York City and the L. Douglas Wilder Collection, a collection by and about the current Governor of Virginia.

STUDENT LIFE

Special Regulations

Student automobiles must be registered at a small cost.

Campus Services

Health center, personal and psychological counseling, career planning and placement, stress management and conflict resolution seminars, post office, and religious activities, including chapel.

Campus activities emphasize "total student development and growth" with the more than fifty student organizations available to stimulate interest and develop leadership.

Social and group activities include concert, theater, band, chorale, dance, and a visiting lecture series. Annual activities include homecoming weekend, the president's reception, the Coronation Ball, the Annual Winter Concert and the Fine Arts Festival. Interested students can work on the yearbook (The Panther) or the student newspaper (The VUU Informer). Communication students can get involved in the campus television station.

Leadership opportunities can be found in the more than 45 student organizations including the Student Government Association (SGA). Greek-letter societies include Alpha Kappa Alpha, Delta Sigma Theta, Sigma Gamma Rho, and Zeta Phi Beta sororities; and Alpha Phi Alpha, Kappa Alpha Psi, Omega Psi Phi, and Phi Beta Sigma fraternities. Honor societies include Alpha Kappa Mu and Beta Kappa Chi.

The campus is located in the center of Richmond, the capital of Virginia, with a population of approximately 219,100. It is easily accessible by local transportation to commuting students. The city of Richmond offers museums, theaters, concerts, and professional sports. Sites of interest include the Governor's mansion, the Capitol, and the Federal Reserve Money Museum. The city's mass transit systems provide easy access to historic Colonial Williamsburg, about one hour to the north; Washington, D.C., about two hours to the north; and Virginia Beach, about two hours to the south.

Housing Availability

780 housing spaces. Freshman given priority. About two-thirds of VUU students live on campus.

Handicapped Services

Include wheelchair accessibility.

NOTABLE ALUMNI

Simeon Booker, Jr., 1942–Washington bureau chief, *Jet* magazine

Lucille M. Brown, 1950–Superintendent, Richard Public Schools

Dr. Jean Harris Ellis, 1951–Councilwoman, Eden, Prairie, MN; first black in Virginia's Governor's Cabinet; first black graduate of the Medical College of Virginia

Dr. Walter E. Fauntroy, 1955–Former U.S. congressman, D.C.

Harlow Fullwood, Jr., 1977–Former player, Baltimore Colts

Stu Gardner, 1990–Musical director, "The Bill Cosby Show"

Samuel L. Gravely, 1948–First black Vice Admiral, U.S. Navy (retired)

Charles Oakley–Power forward, New York Knicks

Frank Royal–Director, board of trustees

Kenneth B. Smith, 1953–President, Chicago Theological Seminary

L. Douglas Wilder, 1951–Governor of Virginia (first black governor in United States)

Washington, D.C.

★ Washington

MAP KEY

- ● Major cities
- ★ State capital
- 🎓 College or University

Howard University - *Washington* — 1
Howard University School of Law - *Washington* — 1
University of the District of Columbia - *Washington* — 1

HOWARD UNIVERSITY

2400 Sixth St. NW
Washington, D.C.
20059
Phone: (202) 806-6100
Toll-free out-state:
800-822-6363
Fax: (202) 806-5934

Total Enrollment:
11,222

Level of Selectivity:
Competitive

Motto:
Truth and service;
God and country

HISTORY

Howard University is a four-year, comprehensive, private, coed liberal arts university. It was founded in 1867 to train black teachers and ministers to guide and teach the four million freed slaves and 25,000 free born blacks. The school was first called Howard Normal and Theological Institute for the Education of Teachers and Preachers, named after General Oliver Otis Howard, one of the founding members and commissioner of the Freedmen's Bureau. In 1867, the school was named Howard University in recognition of the much broader educational scope envisioned for the institute. That same year, the university was officially incorporated and chartered. The university's designated departments were normal and preparatory, collegiate, theological, medical, law, and agriculture. In 1872, the first bachelor's degree was awarded.

Integrated since its founding, Howard University's first students were four white girls who were daughters of two of the university's founders. Today, Howard University has an international blend of faculty and students as it continues to embrace and enhance the founders' vision to provide an educational experience of exceptional quality to students of high academic potential, with particular emphasis upon the provision of educational opportunities to promising black students. Now a private institution supported by the federal government, corporations, foundations, and individual contributions, Howard is recognized as the only truly comprehensive predominately black institution of higher education in the world. The 17 schools and colleges incorporate the original intent of the founders with contemporary, relevant topics in 200 subjects.

Howard University has more than 50,000 alumni, and has produced more than 10% of the nation's black doctors, lawyers, business leaders, politicians, social workers, engineers, artists, musicians, and other professionals. The list of distinguished graduates includes Thurgood Marshall, Debbie Allen, Phyllicia Rashad, and New York City's former mayor, David Dinkins. Five national Greek-letter sororities and fraternities were founded and incorporated at Howard University including Alpha Kappa Alpha Sorority (1908), Omega Psi Fraternity (1911), Delta Sigma Theta Sorority (1913), Phi Beta Sigma (1914), and Zeta Phi Beta (1920). Howard students are often in the media spotlight for events such as division championships, demonstrations for improvement of federal financial aid to the campus, or for stopping conservative Lee At-water from becoming a member of the Howard Board of Trustees.

Howard University is located on four campuses in Washington, D.C., and suburban Maryland. The 89-acre main campus houses 65 buildings, which include a theater, a 43 million dollar, 500-bed teaching hospital, and 110-room hotel used for the hotel management program. The newspaper office is located in the house where Charles Drew once lived. The main campus is five minutes from downtown Washington. The hilly 22-acre west campus near Rock Creek Park houses the Howard Law Center. The 108-acre school of life and physical sciences is located in Beltsville, Maryland, and the 22-acre school of divinity is located in northwest Washington.

ACCREDITATION
Howard is accredited by the Middle States Association of Colleges and Secondary Schools (MSACS) to award the Bachelor of Arts, Bachelor of Science, Master's, and Doctorate degrees.

Other Accreditation
Accrediting Board of Engineering and Technology

Accrediting Commission on Education for Health Services Administration

American Assembly of Collegiate Schools of Business

American Bar Association

American Chemical Society

American Council on Education for Journalism and Mass Communications

American Council on Pharmaceutical Education

American Dietetic Association

American Medical Association

American Medical Association Committee on Allied Health Education

American Occupational Therapy Association

American Physical Therapy Association

American Psychological Association

American Society of Hospital Pharmacists

American Speech Language and Hearing Association

Association of American Law Schools

Association of American Medical Colleges (Liaison Committee on Medical Education)

Association of Research Libraries

Association of Theological Schools in the United States and Canada

Commission of Dental Accreditation of the American Dental Association

Computing Science Accreditation Board

Council for Professional Development

Council on Social Work Education

Joint Review Committee on Education in Radiologic Technology

Joint Review Committee on Educational Programs for Physician Assistants

National Accrediting Agency for Clinical Laboratory Sciences

National Architectural Accrediting Board

National Association for Music Therapy

National Association of Schools of Art and Design

National Association of Schools of Music

National Association of Schools of Public Affairs and Administration

National Association of Schools of Theater

National Association of State Directors of Teacher Education and Certification

National League for Nursing

COSTS PER YEAR

1992–93 Tuition: $6,600

Room and board: $1,900 (room); $1,700 (board)

Special fees: $450

Books: $650

Estimated total cost: $11,300

FINANCIAL AID

Financial Aid Specific to the School

68% of the student body received financial aid during 1991–92.

Endowed scholarships and special interest scholarships are available to students based on need and merit.

Athletic scholarships are available at this school for students in intercollegiate sports.

Creative arts awards are available for students who demonstrate special talents in music, drama, and art.

Deferred payment allows students to pay 50% of fall and spring semester at registration and the remaining 50% sixty days after the regularly scheduled last day of registration.

Cooperative Education Program alternates classroom study with related paid work experience. The program provides academic credit and full-time status during co-op placement.

United Negro College Fund (UNCF) scholarships are awarded to a limited number of students at this school who demonstrate financial need. Some scholarships may be based on location and merit. UNCF scholarships range from $500 to $7,500.

Army, Air Force, and cooperative Navy ROTC provide training in military science for commission as second lieutenant in the armed forces. Scholarships pay tuition, fees and books, and provide a monthly stipend of $100.

D.C. Junior Miss Scholarships are available for students based on academic merit and special talents.

LaVerne Noyes Scholarships

Miss Black Teen Age World Scholarships are available for students who demonstrate academic excellence and special talents.

Trustee Scholarships

Financial Aid Deadline

April 1 (fall); November 1 (spring)

Financial Aid Contact

Adrienne W. Price, Director of Financial Aid and Student Employment, Howard

University, 2400 Sixth St., NW, Washington, D.C. 20059; (202) 806-2800.

ADMISSION REQUIREMENTS
SAT or ACT required

Entrance Requirements
Graduation from an accredited high school with the following units: English (grammar, vocabulary development, composition, literature, analytical reading, or oral communication), mathematics (geometry, algebra, trigonometry, statistics, or calculus), social science (history, social studies, economics, geography, psychology, sociology, government, political science, or anthropology), natural or physical science (biology, chemistry, physics, environmental science, botany, or geology); a minimum 2.0 high school GPA; submit an official high school transcript, and one letter of recommendation. A $25 non-refundable application fee is required.

Some colleges or schools at Howard require additional information.

College of allied health requires two letters of recommendation, an autobiographical sketch, and statement of interest. School of education requires three letters of recommendation, an autobiographical sketch, and statement of interest. School of engineering requires College Board ATP Achievement Test in Mathematics. College of fine arts requires audition or tape for music, portfolio for art, two letters of recommendations, a résumé, and a videocassette for drama. College of arts and sciences requires two letters of recommendation, cumulative grade point average, real or estimated class rank, and the Foreign Language Achievement Test for applicants who have studied a foreign language for two years in high school and intend to continue to study that language. College of pharmacy and pharmaceutical sciences requires two letters of recommendation.

Transfer students must have a cumulative GPA of 2.5 from all colleges attended, be in good standing at the last institution attended, meet the predictive average requirement and SAT or ACT requirement for freshman students, and submit two official transcripts from each previous college. 90 credit hours can be transferred from four-year college and 60 credit hours from a two-year college. Individual schools and colleges have varied standards for awarding credit for previous studies.

International Students submit original certificates of all secondary and college work (including mark sheets, syllabi, and official translations) and copies of results on all national examinations such as the GCE. Holders of GCE A-level or comparable certificates are not required to take the SAT (excluding business majors). Students from non-English-speaking countries must take the TOEFL examination and submit a Financial Certification Form verifying how college expenses will be paid while attending the university.

Admission Application Deadline
April 1 (fall); November 1 (spring); March 15 (summer)

Admission Contact
William H. Sherrell, Dean of Admissions and Records, Howard University, 2400 Sixth St. NW, Washington, D.C. 20059; (202) 806-2752 or 800-822-6363.

GRADUATION REQUIREMENTS
A minimum of 127 to 160 credits hours depending on the major and completion of core requirement to include 16 mathematics, 16 science, 14 foreign language, 4 physical education, and 1 computer course for business, economics, mathematics, and engineering majors. The last 30 credits must be taken at Howard; students must have a 2.0 GPA (2.5 in education and social work) and must take a comprehensive examination. Some programs have additional requirements.

Grading System
A–F; I=Incomplete; Aud=Audit (no credit); NR=No grade/no record; W=Withdrawal;R=Repeated (no credit)

STUDENT BODY PROFILE

Total enrollment (male/female):
   4,489/6,733

From in-state: 1,459

Other regions: 45 states, 20 foreign countries

Full-time undergraduates (male/female):
   2,818/4,228

Part-time undergraduates (male/female):
   592/889

Graduate students (male/female):
   1,078/1,617

Ethnic/Racial Makeup

African American, 9,090; Hispanic, 112; Asian, 112; Native American, 112; Caucasian, 224; International, 1,571.

Class of 1995 Profile

Number of applicants: 5,270

Number accepted: 2,684

Number enrolled: 1,250

Median SAT score: 426V; 454M

Median ACT score: 20

FACULTY PROFILE

Number of faculty: 1,877

Student-teacher ratio: 15:1

Full-time faculty: 1,174

Part-time faculty: 703

Faculty with doctorates or other terminal
   degrees: 82%

SCHOOL CALENDAR

1993–94: August 16–May 13 (semester
   hours)

Commencement and conferring of degrees:
   May 14

Four summer sessions.

DEGREES OFFERED 1991–92:

Bachelor of Arts

Anthropology

Art

Art History

Broadcast Management

Broadcast Production

Ceramics

Classics

Communication Arts

Composition

Design

Drama

Early Childhood Education

Economics

English

Experimental Studio

Film Directing

French

Geography

German

Graphic Art

History

Interior Design

International Business

International Development

Jazz Studies

Journalism

Music Education

Music History/Literature

Music Therapy

Musical Theater

Painting

Philosophy

Photography

Political Science

Psychology

Russian

Sculpture

Social Work
Sociology
Spanish
Theater/Speech Education

Bachelor of Science
Accounting
Aerospace Studies
African Studies
Afro-American Study
Astrophysics
Applied Music
Architecture
Art Education
Botany
Chemical Engineering
Chemistry
City Planning
Civil Engineering
Communication Sciences
Computer Information Systems
Computer System Engineering
Dietetics
Electrical Engineering
Elementary Education
Environmental Science
Family Studies
Fashion Fundamentals
Finance
Geology
Hotel/Motel Management
Human Development
Human Nutrition/Foods
Insurance
International Studies in Human Ecology
Macroenvironmental/Population Studies
Management
Marketing
Mathematics

Mechanical Engineering
Medical Technology
Microbiology
Military Science
Nursing
Nutrition
Occupational Therapy
Pharmacy
Physical Education/Recreation
Physical Therapy
Physician's Assistant
Physics
Radiation Therapy Technology
Radiologic Technology
Textiles
Zoology

Certificates
Dental Hygiene
Music Therapy
Physician's Assistantship
Radiation Therapy Technology
Radiography

Doctorate
African Studies
Analytical Chemistry
Anatomy
Applied Biophysics
Clinical Psychology
Communication Disorders
Counseling Psychology
Developmental Psychology
Economics
Educational Psychology
English
Genetics
History
Inorganic Chemistry
Mathematics

Microbiology

Ministry

Organic Chemistry

Pharmacology

Physical Chemistry

Physics

Physiology

Political Science

Psychology

Romance Languages

Social Work

Sociology

Zoology

Master of Arts

African Studies

Art Education

Continuing Education

Counseling Psychology

Early Childhood Education

Economics

Educational Administration

Educational Psychology

English

Guidance and Counseling

History

Human Development

International Developmental Education

Music

Philosophy

Political Science

Public Affairs

Reading

Rehabilitation Counseling

Religious Studies

Research Methodology

School Psychology

Secondary Curriculum and Instruction

Social Work

Special Education

Student Development

Master of Science

Administration of Justice

Analytical Chemistry

Anatomy

Applied Biophysics

Architecture

Botany

Business Administration

Clinical Psychology

Communication Disorders

Developmental Psychology

Genetics

Inorganic Chemistry

Mathematics

Music Education

Nursing

Organic Chemistry

Pharmacology

Physical Chemistry

Physical Education

Physics

Physiology

Psychology

Zoology

Professional

Law

Medicine

Graduates That Later Obtain Higher Degrees: 66%

3% enter medical school

6% enter law school

10% enter business school

47% enter arts and sciences programs

SPECIAL PROGRAMS

Adult/Continuing Education Programs are available for nontraditional students returning to school or working full time.

Advanced Placement (AP) grants college credit for postsecondary work completed in high school. Students scoring three or better on the AP test will receive credit by examination for each course and advanced placement.

Army, Air Force, and cooperative Navy ROTC programs provide training in military science for commission as a second lieutenant in the U.S. armed forces. Two-, three- and four-year scholarships are available.

College orientation is offered at no cost to entering students for four days prior to the beginning of classes to acquaint students with the college and to prepare them for college life.

Cooperative Education Program combines classroom study with related paid work experience. The program provides academic credit and full time status during co-op placement.

English as a Second Language Program offers courses in English for students whose native language is not English.

Howard University Press conducts the Howard University Book Publishing Institute each year. The intensive five-week course offers basic training in publishing and an overview of the requirements and opportunities in publishing. Internships at the press are available for college seniors and graduate students throughout the year in the press's editorial, marketing, design, and production departments.

Honors program offers academically talented students a challenging program of study that includes special classes, seminars, colloquia, cultural activities, and special recognition to motivate participants.

Individualized majors, through the University without Walls Program, allow students to create their own major program(s) of study.

Internships in various disciplines offer students the opportunity to apply theory and training in actual settings such as business and industry, hospitals, and clinics.

Part-time (day and evening) degree programs allow students to earn undergraduate and graduate degrees while attending part time.

Remedial courses are offered to entering students to bring them up to admission standards and to help them adjust for success in college.

Study Abroad Program allows students to take courses at foreign colleges, institutes, and universities.

Student exchange programs are available with Davidson College, Denison University, Duke University, Fisk University, Grinnel College, Miles College, Reed College, Smith College, Stanford University, Swarthmore College, University of Missouri, Vassar College, and Williams College.

ATHLETIC PROGRAMS

Howard University is a member of the National Collegiate Athletic Association (NCAA), Division I; NCAA I-AA for football; and the Mid Eastern Athletic Conference.

Intercollegiate sports: men's baseball, basketball, football, soccer, swimming, tennis, track & field (indoor and outdoor), and wrestling; women's basketball, swimming, tennis, track & field, and volleyball.

Intramural sports: eleven sports available.

Athletic Contact

William P. Moultrie, Director of Intercollegiate Athletics, Howard University, 2400 Sixth St. NW, Washington, D.C. 20059; (202) 806-7140.

LIBRARY HOLDINGS

Howard University Library System includes seven libraries. The Founder's Library is the main library. The library collection includes 1,841,893 bound volumes, 24,966 periodical subscriptions, 2,266,115 microforms, 56,330 audiovisuals, and 110 computers for student use. Special collections include the Moorland-Spingarn Research Center of Afro-American History and Culture, Channing Pollock Theater Collection, Bernard Fall's Southeast Asian Collection and Paul Robeson papers. The library uses a computerized catalog (Sterling) and CD-ROMs.

STUDENT LIFE

Special Regulations

Alcohol prohibited on campus.

Campus Services

Health center, personal and psychological counseling, career planning and placement, and transportation to some off campus housing.

Campus Activities

Social and cultural activities include theater, chorale, concerts, band, jazz ensemble, speaker series, and art displays. A highlight each year is the Spring Festival which includes dance and music concerts, art displays, and picnics. Howard's homecoming and crowning of Miss Howard University are annual events students and alumni look forward to each year. Students may get involved in the award-winning *Hilltop* newspaper (student-run) or the *Bison Yearbook*. Communication majors may work in the student-run radio station, WHUR FM, or the college television station, WHMM-TV, which serves as a training ground for Howard students, transmitting throughout the Washington, D.C. area. WHMM-TV was the nation's first and only black owned and operated public television station.

Leadership opportunities are found in the Student Government Association (SGA) or the more than 150 student organizations, including dance and theater groups, sports clubs, and special interest groups such as the Baptist Student Union, Absalom Jones Student Association, Adventist Community, Methodist Fellowship, Caribbean Student Association, African Cultural Ensemble, and Pan African Association. Greek-letter fraternities include Alpha Phi Alpha and Phi Beta Sigma; sororities include Alpha Kappa Alpha, Delta Sigma Theta, Sigma Gamma Rho, and Zeta Phi Beta. Other Greek-letter organizations recognized that are non Pan Hellenic include Alpha Phi Omega, Iota Phi Theta, Kappa Kappa Psi, Phi Mu Alpha, and Gamma Sigma Sigma. Honor societies include Phi Beta Kappa and Sigma Xi.

Located in one of the most dynamic cities in the world, students have access to a wealth of social, cultural, and recreational activities. Points of interest include the White House, Library of Congress (the world's largest library), Smithsonian Institute, State Treasury, and the Pentagon. Baltimore, Maryland, is within an hour of D.C. The two cities host famous Broadway musicals, renowned music artists, and world class concerts and operas. The city's mass subway system makes it easy to get anywhere in the D.C. area. The airport is six miles away, and mass rail and mass bus transportation are two miles from campus.

Housing Availability

5,000 housing spaces; eight dormitories for women; eight for men, and two coed dorms. A block of freshman housing is reserved on first-come-first-served basis; campus apartments and married student housing available. Contact: (202) 806-6131/6132/6133.

Handicapped Services

Most of the campus is wheelchair accessible. Support services include note taking, reader services for the blind, and special class scheduling.

NOTABLE ALUMNI

Debbie Allen, 1971–Actress; choreographer; dancer; producer/director

David Dinkins, 1950–Manhattan borough president; former mayor, New York City

Thurgood Marshall, 1933, 1947, 1954–Attorney; judge; U.S Supreme Court justice

Phyllicia Rashad, 1970–Actress; singer

HOWARD UNIVERSITY SCHOOL OF LAW

HISTORY

Howard University School of Law (HUSL) is a three-year, private, coed, professional law school founded in 1869 as the law department of Howard University. It became the school of law in 1908.

HUSL's mission is to provide a legal education that trains students to think critically and independently. Its broad-based program encourages students to explore new ideas. Its clinical experiences serve to provide actual courtroom training. Clinical experiences are offered in criminal justice, labor law, equal employment opportunity, and landlord and tenant law. The school boasts that 35% of all black lawyers are Howard graduates.

The law school is located on the west campus along with the Howard University Press and several other institutes. The main campus comprises the graduate school and the university's 17 other schools and colleges. Additionally, 108 acres owned by the university are located in nearby Beltsville, Maryland and are scheduled to be developed as a campus for research in life sciences and training in veterinary medicine.

ACCREDITATION

Howard University School of Medicine is accredited by the American Bar Association (ABA) to award the Juris Doctorate (JD), joint Juris Doctorate and Master in Business Administration (JD/MBA), and Master Comparative Jurisprudence (MCJ) degrees.

Other Accreditation

Association of American Law Schools

COSTS PER YEAR

1992–93 Tuition: $7,725Room and board: $2,250 (room); $1,700 (board)

2900 Van Ness St., NW
Washington, D.C. 20008
Phone: (202) 806-8008

Total Enrollment:
380

Level of Selectivity:
Competitive

Special fees: $555

Books: $500

Estimated total cost: $12,730

FINANCIAL AID

Financial Aid Specific to the School

Merit based scholarships are available to a substantial number of students based on varying criteria of achievement.

Financial Aid Deadline

April 30th

Financial Aid Contact

Phone: (202) 806-8005

ADMISSION REQUIREMENTS

SAT required

Entrance Requirements

Graduation from an accredited four-year undergraduate program; undergraduate GPA and LSAT scores used for admission; submit official transcripts of all college work; letters of recommendation from previous institution; separate application required for the law school and business administration school JD/MBA joint degree program. A $25 application fee is required.

Transfer students must meet basic admission requirements.

International students must meet basic admission requirements.

Admission Application Deadline

Rolling admission provides no specific date for notification of admission so applicant is informed as soon as admission decision is made.

Admission Contact

Ted Miller, Dean of Admissions, Office of Admission, Howard University, 2900 Van Ness St., NW, Washington, D.C. 20008; (202) 806-8008.

GRADUATION REQUIREMENTS

Thesis required for some programs; must be enrolled at Howard during last semester.

STUDENT BODY PROFILE

Total enrollment (male/female): 180/200

Other regions: Throughout U.S. and several foreign countries

Ethnic/Racial Makeup

African American, 279; Asian, 36; Native American, 2; International, 27.

Class of 1995 Profile

Number of applicants: 1,256

Number accepted: 314

Number enrolled: 78

FACULTY PROFILE

Number of faculty: 52

Student-teacher ratio: 8:1

Full-time faculty (male/female): 23/6

Part-time faculty (male/female): 22/1

Faculty with doctorates or other terminal degrees: 90%

SCHOOL CALENDAR

1992–93: August–May (semester hours)

Commencement and conferring of degrees: May

One summer session.

DEGREES OFFERED 1991–92:

Juris Doctorate

Criminal Justice

Equal Employment Opportunity

Labor Law

Landlord and Tenant Law

Juris Doctorate/Master Business Administration (JD/MBA)

Master's of Comparative Jurisprudence (MCJ)

SPECIAL PROGRAMS

Clinical experiences provide actual courtroom training in criminal justice, labor law, equal employment opportunity, and landlord and tenant law.

International Moot Court provides mock courtroom trials where students can apply classroom study with actual courtroom experience in international law.

JD/MBA is a four-year joint degree program offered by the school of law and the school of business administration.

Master of Comparative Jurisprudence (MCJ) degree is offered to graduates of foreign law schools.

Moot Court provides mock courtroom trials where students can apply classroom study with actual courtroom experience.

Project Outreach allows students to provide legal services to community residents who demonstrate financial need.

LIBRARY HOLDINGS

The Allen Mercer Daniel Law Library houses 164,300 bound volumes, 499 periodical subscriptions, 331,626 microforms, 57,944 audiovisuals including 44 motion pictures. LEXIS and WESTLAW citation searching is available online. CD-ROM database searching is also available. Special collections include comprehensive collections on Anglo-American law, government documents, treatises on law-related disciplines, and federal and state constituted statutes. Consortium agreement allows borrowing privileges with member libraries.

STUDENT LIFE

Campus Services

Personal and psychological counseling, career planning and placement, tutoring, low-cost health insurance

Campus Activities

HUSL provides students with lectures, mock trials, and clinical experiences. Student publications include the *Howard Law Journal* and the *Barrister* newspaper.

Leadership opportunities can be found in the Student Bar Association or the numerous other clubs and groups including the Black Law Student Association, Women in Law, the Christian Fellowship, and the International Law Society. Fraternities include Phi Alpha Delta and Phi Delta Phi.

Howard University is located in northwest Washington, D.C., metro population of approximately of over 3 million and a district population of 622,800. The nation's capital provides shopping, dining, concerts, art exhibits, orchestra, opera, and major league sports. Points of interest include the Kennedy Center for Performing Arts, the Library of Congress, National Air and Space Museum, National Art Gallery, National Museum of Women in Art, the Smithsonian Institution, and Washington National Cathedral. The district is served by two airports—the Washington Dulles Airport and the Baltimore Washington International Airport, as well as mass bus and passenger rail.

Housing Availability

Limited housing—rooms and apartments available for single and married students; most students live off campus; deadline for housing application is April 30.

NOTABLE ALUMNI

Thurgood Marshall, 1947, 1954–Supreme Court justice

UNIVERSITY OF THE DISTRICT OF COLUMBIA

4200 Connecticut Ave.
NW
Washington, D.C
20008
Phone: (202) 274-5010

Total Enrollment:
11,153

Level of Selectivity:
Noncompetitive;
moderately
competitive for out-
state and international
students

Motto:
An Invitation to
Success

HISTORY

University of the District of Columbia (UDC) is a four-year, district-supported, liberal arts institution founded in 1976 as a result of a merger between District of Columbia Teachers College (1955), Federal City College (1966), and Washington Technical Institute (1966). Although UDC had its formal founding in 1976, its history began in 1851 with the founding of the Miner Normal School for colored girls, which merged with the Washington Normal School for white girls, which later merged in 1955 to form the District of Columbia Teachers College.

The Federal City College and the Washington Technical Institute were both established in 1966 as a result of the Chase Commission, appointed by John F. Kennedy, which determined the need for a liberal arts and teachers' college in the District. Both schools were given land grant status that same year. After the District of Columbia was granted home rule, a mandate for consolidation of District of Columbia Teachers College, Federal City College, and Washington Technical Institute was issued (1975).

The Cooperative Extension Services Program is one means by which UDC fulfills its land grant mission. Through its outreach program it works directly with District of Columbia residents to solve problems related to improving the quality of life. UDC also operates the District's Agricultural Experiment Station and Water Resource Center.

UDC's three campuses offer students all of the advantages of major universities. Students can easily commute between campuses via public transportation.

The Van Ness campus in upper NW Washington is a modern campus situated on 21 acres that houses the academic facilities for the college of Liberal Arts and Fine Arts, Life Sciences, Physical Sciences, Engineering and Technology. The Mt. Vernon Square campus in the downtown area leases facilities for the College of Business & Public Management and the graduate division. The Georgia Harvard Campus in midtown NW Washington offers the majority of programs in the College of Education and Human Ecology.

ACCREDITATION

University of the District of Columbia is accredited by the Middle States Association of Colleges and Secondary Schools to award the Bachelor of Arts, Bachelor of Science, and Associate's degrees.

Other Accreditation

Accreditation Board for Engineering and Technology

American Chemical Society

American Funeral Service Education Board, Inc.

American Medical Association

American Speech, Language and Hearing Association

Association of Collegiate Schools of Planning

Committee on Allied Health Education and Accreditation, American Medical Association

Council on Social Work Education

District of Columbia Nurses Examining Board

Engineering Accreditation Commission of the Accreditation of Engineering and Technology

Federal Aviation Administration

National Association of Schools of Music

National Association of State Directors of Teacher Education and Certification

National League of Nursing

Planning Accreditation Board of the American Institute of Certified Planners

Technology Accreditation Commission of the Accreditation Board of Engineering and Technology, Inc.

COSTS PER YEAR

1993–94 Tuition: $864 (in-state); $3,456 (out-state)

Room and board: none (estimate $7,000 for off-campus)

Special fees: $125

Books: $600

Estimated total cost: $1,589 (in-state); $4,181 (out-state)

FINANCIAL AID

1990–91 Institutional Funding

Number of scholarships and grants: 343

Total amount of scholarships and grants: $717,578

Range of scholarships and grants: $500–$8,000

1990–91 Federal and State Funding

Number of scholarships and grants: 750

Total amount of scholarships and grants: $1,880,076

Range of scholarships and grants: $200–$2,000

Number of loans: 85

Total amount of loans: $259,999

Range of loans: $500–$7,500

Number of work-study: 113

Total amount of work-study: $239,129

Range of work-study: $600–$2,500

Financial Aid Specific to the School

25% of the student body received financial aid during 1991–92.

Army ROTC and cooperative Air Force ROTC offer two-, three- and four-year scholarships that pay tuition, fee, books, and other expenses, as well as provide a monthly stipend of $100.

Athletic scholarships are available to students participating in intercollegiate sports.

Deferred Payment Plan allows students to pay college costs in 2 or 3 installments during the semester. Phone: (202) 282-7957.

District of Columbia Student Incentive Grants are awarded to students who are residents and demonstrate financial need.

Endowed, special interest, and friends scholarships number more than 25 and are based on merit and financial need.

Performance scholarships are available for students participating in music and drama.

Thurgood Marshall Black Education Fund provides a four-year scholarship at this public black college. Qualifying students must have a high school GPA of 3.0 or better and a SAT score of 1000 or ACT score of 24 or more. Students must be recommended by high school counselor as exceptional or exemplary in the creative or performing arts. Scholarship pays tuition, fees, room, and board not to exceed $6,000 annually.

UDC and it's corporate sponsors list many additional scholarships, awards, and grants. Contact the financial aid office for eligibility and amounts.

Financial Aid Deadline
April 15

Financial Aid Contact
Kenneth Howard, Financial Aid Office, Van Ness Campus, Building 39, Room #101, 4200 Connecticut Ave. NW, Washington, D.C. 20008; (202) 274-5060.

ADMISSION REQUIREMENTS
Open admission. SAT strongly recommended

Entrance Requirements
Graduation from an accredited high school and completion of the following units: 4 English, 2 mathematics (algebra & geometry), 2 lab sciences, 2 social sciences, and 2 foreign language; official high school transcript; provide proof of immunizations against measles, mumps, rubella, tetanus, diphtheria and polio; recent physical by physician; preferential treatment is given to D.C. residents. A $20 application fee required.

GED students must meet basic admission requirements.

Transfer students must submit official transcripts of all previous college work; have a 2.0 GPA ("C" is lowest acceptable grade); 60 credits must be completed at UDC.

International students must submit official high school certificate in English such as WASC or GCE (General Certificate of Education); students from non-English-speaking countries must either submit TOEFL score of at least 500 or have taken two college-level English courses from an accredited American college or university; F-1 student applicants must file affidavit of financial sponsor to pay all education costs. Deadline: March 15 (fall); September 15 (spring); May 1 (summer).

Early admission allows academically gifted high school students the opportunity to enroll in college for credit before completing high school.

Admission Application Deadline
June 14 (fall); November 15 (spring); April 1 (summer)

Admission Contact
Alfred Taylor, Office of Admissions, 4200 Connecticut Ave., NW, Washington, DC 20008; (202) 274-5010.

GRADUATION REQUIREMENTS
A minimum of 120 semester hours and completion of core requirements to include the following hours: 6 English (composition, literature and, advanced writing), 6 mathematics, 6 natural sciences, 6 social science, 3 philosophy, 3 fine arts, and 4 personal and community health; minimum 2.0 GPA; last 30 hours in residence for bachelor's, a minimum of 60 hours and last 15 hours in residence for an associate's degrees.

Grading System
A–F; I=Incomplete; Aud=Audit (no credit); NR=No grade/no record; W=Withdrawal; R=Repeated (no credit)

STUDENT BODY PROFILE
Total enrollment (male/female):
5,584/6,569

From in-state: 8,365

Other regions: 25 states; 37 foreign countries;

Full-time undergraduates (male/female): 1,782/2,091

Part-time undergraduates (male/female): 3,472/4,077

Graduate students (male/female): 330/401

Ethnic/Racial Makeup

African American, 9,844; Hispanic, 486; Asian, 243; Caucasian, 608; International, 972.

Class of 1995 Profile

Number of applicants: 3,100

Number accepted: 2,600

Number enrolled: 1,700

FACULTY PROFILE

Number of faculty: 740

Student-teacher ratio: 10:1

Full-time faculty: 435

Part-time faculty: 305

Faculty with doctorates or other terminal degrees: 44%

SCHOOL CALENDAR

1992–93: August–May

Commencement and conferring of degrees: May

Two summer sessions.

DEGREES OFFERED 1991–92:

Accounting

Administration of Justice

Administration and Supervision

Airway Science

Architecture

Audiology

Biological Science

Building Construction

Business

Chemistry

City Planning

Civil Engineering

Communication

Computer Science

Counseling-Student/Personnel

Criminal Justice

Curriculum and Instruction

Drama

Earth Science

Economics

Education

Engineering

English

Environmental Science

Foreign Language

Geography

Health and Physical Education

Engineering

History

Home Economics

Horticulture

Industrial Arts

Labor Studies

Leisure Studies

Library Science

Mathematics

Mental Health

Music

Nursing

Philosophy

Physics

Political Science

Print Management

Procurement/Public Contact

Public Policy

Reading

Religion

Social Sciences

Spanish

Special Education

Speech and Language Pathology

Urban Planning

Associate of Arts

Advertising Design

Child Development and Nursery School Education

Corrections Administration

Criminology

English

Fashion Buying and Merchandising

History

Law Enforcement

Leisure Studies

Media Library Technology

Music

Philosophy

Public Administration

Urban Studies

Graduates that later obtain higher degrees:

35%

SPECIAL PROGRAMS

Accelerated Study Program allows students to complete their undergraduate degree in a shorter period of time than the traditional four years.

Adult/Continuing Education Programs are available for nontraditional students returning to school or working full time.

College Level Examination Program (CLEP) determines the academic relevance of nontraditional educational experiences such as the military, on-the-job training, or other life experiences through a series of test and may grant students college credit for these experiences.

Cooperative Education Program combines classroom study with related paid work experience. The program provides academic credit and full time status during co-op placement.

English as a Second Language Program offers courses in English for students whose native language is not English.

Honors Program offers academically talented students a challenging program of study that includes special classes, seminars, colloquia, cultural activities and special recognition to motivate participants. Includes study abroad. 90% of honor graduates enter graduate school and receive fellowships and assistantships.

Internships in various disciplines offer students the opportunity to apply theory and training in actual settings such as business/industry and hospitals/clinics.

Off-campus study program provides opportunities for federal and D.C. government employees to enroll in classes at their work; the fire science program is designed to improve fire fighter skills; and the nursing program is available to registered nurses at Walter Reed Army Hospital.

Part-time (day and evening) Degree Programs allow students to earn undergraduate and graduate degrees on a part-time basis.

Remedial courses are offered to entering students to bring them up to admission standards and to help them adjust for success in college.

ROTC provides training in military science for commission as a second lieutenant in the United States Army. Two- and four-year scholarships are available.

Student Development Transcript Program helps students to compile individualized personal transcripts of activities, honor awards, service achievements, and grades. Recommend enrollment in freshman year.

Study Abroad Program allows students to go to a foreign country for part of their college education.

Summer Bridge Program provides free instruction to high school graduates during the summer to improve their skills.

ATHLETIC PROGRAMS

UDC is a member of National Collegiate Athletic Association (NCAA), Division II and Eastern Collegiate Athletic Conference

(ECAC). Intercollegiate sports: men's basketball, cross-country, football, soccer, tennis, and track & field (indoor & outdoor); women's basketball, cross-country, tennis, track & field (indoor & outdoor), and volleyball.

Intramural sports: basketball, flag football, racquetball, swimming, tennis, weight training.

Athletic Contact

Leo Miles, Intercollegiate Athletic Director, Van Ness Campus, Building #47, University of the District of Columbia, Washington, D.C. 20008; (202)-282-7748.

LIBRARY HOLDINGS

The library houses 400,000 volumes, 1,500 periodical subscriptions, 13,331 microforms, 25,000 audiovisuals; 150 computers available for student use in library and computer center. UDC is a member of the Consortium of Universities of the Washington Metropolitan Area giving its students access to the library holdings at American, Catholic, Gallaudet, Georgetown, George Washington, Howard, and Southeastern Universities, Trinity College, and the University of Maryland at College Park.

STUDENT LIFE

Special Regulations

Hazing prohibited; Honor code; freshman orientation is held during the fall semester.

Campus Services

Health center, personal and psychological counseling, career planning and placement, student employment services, remedial instruction, diagnostic testing, testing center.

Campus Activities

Social and cultural activities include theater, band, jazz ensemble, chorale, art exhibits, orchestra, drum and bugle corps, and dance. Annual events include International Day, Cross Cultural Extended Family Program, Family Community Day Picnic, and International Multicultural Recognition Day. In celebration of Black History Month the university hosts exhibits, lecturers, and concerts. Students may get involved in the UDC *Trilogy* (student-run newspaper) or the *Firebird* (yearbook). Communication majors or volunteers can work at the student-run radio station, WDCU-FM 90.1, which features jazz.

Leadership opportunities can be found in the Student Government Association (SGA) which sponsors more than one hundred activities including class mixers; chess and table-tennis tournaments; free movies; popular music groups; and numerous workshops on a variety of subjects. There are three Greek-letter fraternities; sororities include Alpha Kappa Alpha, Delta Sigma Theta, Sigma Gamma Rho, and Zeta Phi Beta. Honor societies are also represented on campus.

The university's location in the nation's capital lets students explore unique intellectual, political, and cultural opportunities.

Students have borrowing privileges at the Library of Congress, access to the famed Smithsonian Institution, and chances to attend concerts, ballet, and opera at the Kennedy Center for Performing Arts. The Washington Metropolitan area is home to professional football, hockey, and basketball teams. Professional baseball is just a half hour train ride away in Baltimore. The University is easily accessible by National, Dulles, and Baltimore-Washington International Airports, Amtrack, and bus services.

Housing Availability

None (off-campus living only)

Handicapped Services

Wheelchair accessibility. Available facilities include elevators, lowered drinking fountains and telephones, specially equipped restrooms, wheelchair ramps, special parking, reader services. Services also available for hearing and visually impaired.

NOTABLE ALUMNI

Marian Johnson-Thompson–Molecular virologist

Joyce F. Leland–Deputy chief of police, Metropolitan Police Department, Washington, D.C.

Floretta Duke McKenzie, 1982–Former Deputy Assistant Secretary, Department of Education; superintendent of D.C. public schools

West Virginia

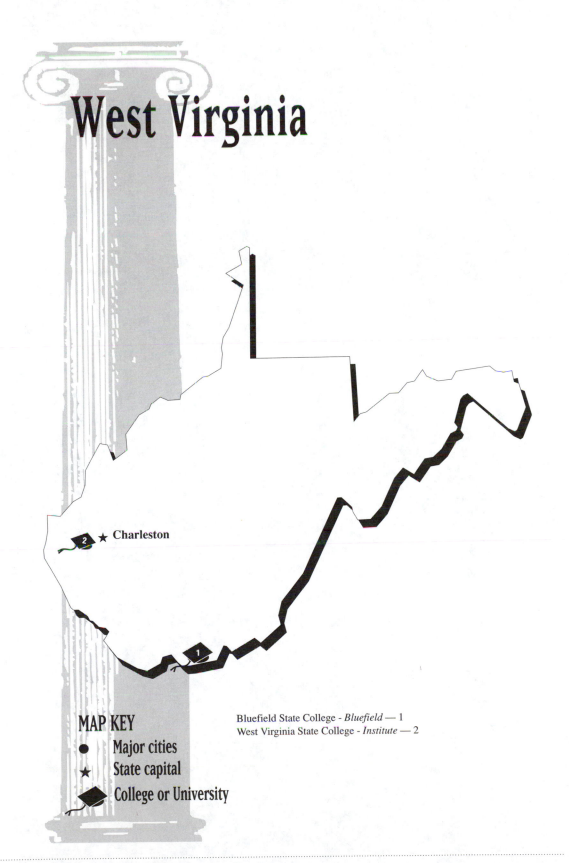

★ Charleston

MAP KEY
- ● Major cities
- ★ State capital
- ◆ College or University

Bluefield State College - *Bluefield* — 1
West Virginia State College - *Institute* — 2

BLUEFIELD STATE COLLEGE

219 Rock St.
Bluefield, WV 24701
Phone: (304) 327-4000
Toll-free in-state:
800-344-8892
Toll-free out-state:
800-654-7798
Fax: (304) 327-7747

Total Enrollment:
2,907

Level of Selectivity:
Noncompetitive

HISTORY

Bluefield State College (BSC) is a four-year, state-supported, coed, liberal arts institution founded in 1865 as Bluefield Colored Institute to train black teachers. Postsecondary education was not offered until 1931 when the name changed to Bluefield State Teachers College. The first bachelor's degree was awarded in 1932, the present named adopted in 1943. Presently, Bluefield offers a comprehensive teacher education program as well as programs in the arts, science, and engineering technology.

Although only 6% of the student population is black, BSC is one of two Historically Black Colleges and Universities in the state. As a state-supported school, BSC's mission is to provide affordable higher education to area residents from all races and cultures. All programs are designed to promote the students' intellectual, personal, ethical, and cultural development. This commuter college serves citizens of south West Virginia at three off-campus sites, including the Greenbrier Community College in Lewisburg, West Virginia, the McDowell Community College in Welch, West Virginia, and the nursing program in Beckley, West Virginia.

ACCREDITATION

Bluefield State College is accredited by the North Central Association of Colleges and Schools to award the Bachelor of Arts, Bachelor of Science, Associate of Arts, and Associate of Applied Science degrees.

Other Accreditation

Accreditation Board of Engineering and Technology

Committee of Allied Health Education and Accreditation

National League of Nursing

West Virginia Department of Education

COSTS PER YEAR

1991–92 Tuition: $1,726 (in-state); $3,996 (out-state)

Room and board: None

Special fees: $125

Books: $500

Estimated total cost: $2,351 (in-state); $4,621 (out-state)

FINANCIAL AID

Financial Aid Specific to the School

72% of the student body received financial aid during 1991–92.

Allied Health scholarships of $750–$950 are awarded through two programs for students majoring in allied health.

Alumni Association Scholarship awards four-year scholarships for in-state tuition and fees based on scholastic achievement and financial need.

Athletic scholarships available for students participating in intercollegiate sports.

Bluefield Regional Medical Center Scholarship Fund for Allied Health Sciences awards from $750–$6,000 to students in the allied health program.

Bluefield State College Foundation Loan Fund offers short-term low-interest loans to assist students in paying tuition and fees until other types of financial aid has been received.

Bluefield State College Undergraduate Scholarships pay tuition costs up to eight semesters for students who demonstrate academic excellence or exceptional talents or skills. Number of scholarships determined by number of full-time students.

Consolidation Coal Company Scholarships are awarded to students with at least a 2.5 GPA who plan a career in mining engineering technology or other engineering technology programs related to the mining industry. Contact financial aid office for information.

Endowed, friends, and special interest scholarships number more than 25 and are awarded based on achievement and financial need.

GTE Scholarships are awarded to entering students interested in any of the degree programs offered at BSC.

Island Creek Coal Company provides unrestricted scholarship funds to be used by the Mining Engineering Technology department. Contact financial aid office for more information.

Laurence E. Tierney Education Foundation assists students based on academic achievement and creative promise. Contact financial aid office for more information.

Job Training Partnership Act (JTPA) provides financial assistance for economically disadvantaged and/or dislocated workers pursuing an Associate's degree.

A. T. Massey Foundation Scholarship provides unrestricted scholarships to students who maintain a "B" average and plan careers in the coal mining areas of southern West Virginia. Contact financial aid office for more information.

Pocahontas Electrical and Mechanical Institute provides scholarships to students maintaining academic standards and majoring in mining, civil, electrical, or mechanical engineering technology.

Princeton Community Hospital Student Loan provides students participating in health-related fields the opportunity to apply for $750 per semester, with an additional $350 stipend for first year students to assist with initial expense of books/supplies. Contact the Human Resources Department, Princeton Community Hospital, PO Box 1369, Princeton, WV 24740; (304) 487-7507.

Tuition waivers (full-time and part time) available to BSC employees and their children.

West Virginia Higher Education Grant Program awards grants that pay a substantial portion of tuition and fees for West Virginia residents who demonstrate financial need.

Financial Aid Deadline
March 15 (priority)

Financial Aid Contact
Audrey C. Clay, Financial Aid Director, Bluefield State College, Bluefield, WV 24701; (304) 327-4022.

ADMISSION REQUIREMENTS

Open admissions. SAT or ACT (preferred) required for placement

Entrance Requirements

Graduation from an accredited high school and completion of the following units: 4 English, 2 mathematics (algebra and higher), 2 lab science, 4 social science (applicants out of high school more than five years exempt from specific units); minimum 2.0 GPA; submit proof of measles and rubella immunizations.

To enter an associate's degree program, student must graduate from an accredited high school; submit official high school transcript; submit ACT or SAT score; submit proof of measles and rubella immunizations.

GED students must meet basic admission requirements.

Transfer students must submit official high school and college transcripts; submit ACT or SAT scores; provide proof of measles and rubella immunizations; maximum 72 hours transferred with associate's degree; maximum 108 quarter hours transferred from junior college accredited by the state.

International students must submit certificate of high school completion; provide proof of ability to pay all college costs; submit TOEFL score of at least 500; submit ACT or SAT score; provide proof of measles and rubella immunizations.

Early admission allows academically gifted high school students the opportunity to enroll in college for credit before completing high school. Qualifying students must have a 3.0 or higher, recommendation from principal, and parental consent.

Admission Application Deadline

Rolling admission provides no specific date for notification of admission so applicant is informed as soon as admission decision is made.

Admission Contact

John C. Cardell, Director of Admissions, Bluefield State College, 219 Rock St., Bluefield, WV 24701; (304) 327-4065. Fax: (304) 327-7747.

GRADUATION REQUIREMENTS

A minimum of 128 credit hours and completion of the core requirements to include 6 mathematics, 8 science, and 1 computer course; minimum 2.0 GPA; 32 hours in residence with last 16 hours at BSC for a bachelor's degree.

A minimum of 64 credit hours and completion of core requirements; last 16 hours in residence with last 8 hours at BSC for an associate's degree.

Grading System

A-F; NGR=No Grade Reported; I=Incomplete; W=Withdraw; WP=Withdraw Passing; WF=Withdraw Failing; X=Audit; FIW+ Failure Due to Irregular Withdrawal; P/F=Pass/Fail (student teaching, continuing education & selected nursing courses); NI=Non-Instructional Credit; S=Satisfactory

STUDENT BODY PROFILE

Total enrollment (male/female):
  1,134/1,773

From in-state: 2,674

Other regions: 12 states; 4 foreign countries

Full-time undergraduates (male/female):
  594/929

Part-time undergraduates (male/female):
  540/844

Ethnic/Racial Makeup

African American, 174; Hispanic, 29; Asian, 29; Native American, 29; Caucasian, 2,616; International, 30.

Class of 1995 Profile

Number of applicants: 1,250

Number accepted: 1,250

Number enrolled: 587

Median ACT score: 16.5

Average high school GPA: 2.5

Transfers enrolled: 233

FACULTY PROFILE

Number of faculty: 186

Student-teacher ratio: 25:1

Full-time faculty: 94

Part-time faculty: 92

Faculty with doctorates or other terminal degrees: 40%

SCHOOL CALENDAR

1992–93: August 20–May 14 (semester hours)

Commencement & conferring of degrees: May 15

Two summer sessions.

DEGREES OFFERED 1991–92:

Accounting

Architectural Technology

Art

Biology

Business Administration

Chemistry

Civil Engineering Technology

Computer Science

Construction Technology

Criminal Justice

Early Childhood Education

Education

Electrical and Electronic Technology

Electrical Engineering Technology

Elementary Education

Engineering Technology

English

History

Liberal Arts

Marketing

Mechanical Engineering Technology

Mining Engineering

Nursing

Physical Education

Police Science

Radiology Technology

Science

Secondary Education

Secretarial Science

Social Science

Special Education

Pre-Professional

Engineering

SPECIAL PROGRAMS

Accelerated Study Program allows students to complete their undergraduate degree in a shorter period of time than the traditional four years.

Adult or Continuing Education Program is available for nontraditional students returning to school or working full time.

Advanced Placement (AP) grants college credit for postsecondary work completed in high school. Students scoring 3 on the AP test will receive credit by examination for each course.

College Level Examination Program (CLEP) determines the academic relevance of nontraditional educational experiences such as the military, on-the-job training, or other life experiences through a series of tests and may grant students college credit for these experiences. Students scoring 22 on ACT English or 17 on ACT reading can take the CLEP English.

College orientation is offered at no cost to entering students prior to the beginning of classes to acquaint students with the college and to prepare them for college life.

English as a Second Language is a program that offers courses in English for students whose native language is not English.

Individualized Majors allows students to create their own major program(s) of study.

Off-campus study in cooperation with Concord College (CC) allows students to take courses at CC not offered at BSC.

Part-time degree program allows students to earn an undergraduate degree part time.

Remedial courses are offered to entering students to bring them up to admission standards and to help them adjust for success in college.

Study Abroad Program in cooperation with China allows students to go to a foreign country for part of their college education.

Two Plus Two degree allows students to apply an occupation associate's degree program to a four-year degree program at a later date.

ATHLETIC PROGRAMS

Bluefield State College is a member of the National Collegiate Athletic Association (NCAA), Division II, the National Associate of Intercollegiate Athletics (NAIA) and West Virginia Intercollegiate Athletic Conference (WVIAC).

Intercollegiate sports: men's baseball, basketball, golf, cross-country, and tennis; women's basketball, cross-country, softball, and tennis.

Intramural sports: backgammon, badminton, basketball, billiards, bowling, chess, darts, flag football, football, free throw, horseshoe, inner tube water polo, racquetball, softball, spades, swimming, table tennis, tennis, and volleyball.

Athletic Contact

Terry W. Brown, Athletic Director, Bluefield State College, Bluefield, WV 24701; (304) 327-4179.

LIBRARY HOLDINGS

The library houses 106,421 bound volumes, 242,231 microforms, 512 periodical subscriptions, 9,043 audiovisuals, 21,000 government documents; 160 computers available for student use in computer center. Library is automated.

STUDENT LIFE

Special Regulations

Cars must be registered.

Campus Services

Health center; personal and psychological counseling; career planning and placement; student employment services; testing for ACT, CLEP, GMAT, GED, PPST, and Nurse's Aide Exam; and tutoring.

Campus Activities

Social and cultural activities include lecturers, jazz band, and chorale. Professional musicians, theater or dance groups, and noon-time shows featuring comedians, coffeehouse entertainers, or novelty shows are sponsored. The annual jazz festival presented by the Bluefield Jazz Ensemble is highlighted each year. Students may get involved in the *Blue Fieldian* (student-run newspaper), *Blue-Literary Magazine,* or *Traces* (a biannual magazine). Communication majors can work at the student-run television station.

Leadership opportunities can be found in the Student Government Association (SGA) or the more than 30 organizations including Minorities on the Move, Thirty Something, USS Yeager Chapter-Star Fleet, International Student Association, and Weight Lifting Club. National Greek-letter fraternities include Alpha Phi Alpha and Kappa Alpha Psi; sororities include Delta Sigma Theta. Also on campus is one local fraternity and three local sororities. Honor societies include Alpha Chi and Phi Eta Sigma.

BSC is located in Bluefield, West Virginia, a coal mining city with a population of approximately 15,300. The city is served by mass bus transportation; passenger rail is one mile from campus; the airport is three miles away. Students have access to shopping at Mercer Mall. Points of interest include the Pocahontas Bituminous Coalfields. Visual and performing arts events, as well as regional craft shows, are held in the Bluefield Arts and Crafts Center. Annual events include the Mountain Festival.

Housing Availability
None

Handicapped Services
Wheelchair accessibility.

"A Living Laboratory of Human Relations"

WEST VIRGINIA STATE COLLEGE

Institute, WV 25112
Phone: (304) 766-3000

Total Enrollment:
4,986

Level of Selectivity:
Slightly competitive

Motto:
Where Excellence is a
Tradition

HISTORY

West Virginia State College (WVSC) is a four-year, state supported, coed college founded in 1891 as West Virginia Colored Institute. WVSC was created after the Second Morrill Act of 1890 stipulated that all land grant institutions could no longer receive federal funds unless provisions were made for the education of black youth. West Virginia University, the state's land grant school, had been in existence for more than two decades for the education of white students. To assure continued federal funds for West Virginia University, the West Virginia Legislature created another school for blacks which is now WVSC.

In 1891, the institution was named West Virginia Colored Institute. The following year a teacher-training curriculum was added which today remains an important part of the school's tradition. In 1915, the name was changed to West Virginia Collegiate Institute to reflect the increase in programs. The first college degrees were awarded in 1919. The school adopted its present name, West Virginia State College in

1929. Because of the leadership of the administration and staff the college was nationally recognized as one of the top institutions in the education of black students.

After the 1954 Supreme Court ruling in Brown vs. Board of Education that segregated schools were unconstitutional, enrollment increased and became racially integrated. The college became a model for successful integration and was nationally known as a "living laboratory for human relations." West Virginia State College's mission is to serve the educational, cultural, and social needs of its students. The college seeks to prepare students to both earn a living and recognize and appreciate a diverse cultural, social, and ethnic society.

In 1978, a community college division was established that offers a variety of associate degrees. West Virginia State College's Reserved Officer Training Corps (ROTC) has been cited as having produced more generals than any other ROTC department of an historically black college.

Situated on 85 acres, the 24-building campus includes an art gallery, music studios, and two theaters. Additional facilities include 16 faculty and staff homes. The educational network uplinks credit courses for the University System and West Virginia's colleges and community college systems. West Virginia State College is the largest institution of higher learning in the Kanawha Valley. This traditionally black college presently has a predominately white student population.

ACCREDITATION

West Virginia State College is accredited by the North Central Association of Colleges and Schools to award the Associate of Arts, Bachelor of Arts, and Bachelor of Science degrees.

Other Accreditation

Accreditation Board of Engineering and Technology

American Chemical Society

Council on Accreditation of the National Recreation and Parks Association

Council of Social Work Education

Joint Review Committee on Educational Programs in Nuclear Medicine Technology of the American Medical Association

National Council for Accreditation of Teacher Education

West Virginia Board of Directors of the State College System.

West Virginia State Department of Education

COSTS PER YEAR

1992–93 Tuition: $856 (in-state); $2,001 (out-state)

Room and Board: $700 (room); $825 (board)

Special fees: $125

Books: $400

Estimated total cost: $2,906 (in-state); $4,051 (out-state)

FINANCIAL AID

1991–92 Institutional Funding

Number of scholarships and grants: 200

Total amount of scholarships and grants: $542,400

1991–92 Federal and State Funding

Number of scholarships and grants: 3,136

Total amount of scholarships and grants: $4,543,514

Number of loans: 1,007

Total amount of loans: $1,832,530

Number of work-study: 352

Total amount of work-study: $492,380

Financial Aid Specific to the School

85% of the student body received financial aid during 1991–92.

Athletic scholarships are available to students participating in intercollegiate sports.

Contributory Educational Assistance Program is available for veterans and service persons who have satisfactorily contributed monthly deductions of $50–$75 (up to $2,700) from military pay to the program. The VA will match the contribution at the rate of $200 for every $1.00 made by participant.

Thirty endowed and alumni scholarships, awards, and loans in varying amounts are available and may be based on merit, need, major, purpose, or resident location.

Performance Scholarships are available to students in art, music, drama, band, and peer tutoring. Awards depend on vacancies. Student must participate in activities in the department. A minimum 2.0 GPA is required. For peer tutoring the student must have a minimum 2.5 GPA and receive at least a "B" in the course.

Union Carbide Corporation Chemical Technology Scholarship is awarded to a Chem Tech student with a 2.5 GPA who is recommended by the Chemistry Department. The award is renewable each semester.

Vocational Rehabilitation benefits are available to physically challenged students by contacting a local vocational rehabilitation center or the center located in Institute, West Virginia.

West Virginia State College Presidential Scholarships are awarded to outstanding academic high school seniors. It is restricted to students who scored in the top ten percent on the ACT exam (minimum of 25 composite score). The award covers tuition and fees for up to 8 semesters in any major for commuting students who maintain a 3.5 GPA. Awards to residential students include room and board.

West Virginia State College Undergraduate Scholarships waive tuition and fees for eligible high school graduates. Student must attend full time and maintain good academic standing. Waivers are renewable for up to 8 semesters.

Cooperative Education combines or alternates formal academic study with practical work experience in major. Qualifying students must have completed 24 hours at the 100 level or above and have a minimum overall GPA of 2.0 and GPA in major of 2.5. Students must commit to two terms and be recommended by faculty co-op coordinator.

Field experiences and internships provide short-term job experiences, in addition to classroom learning. Internships are employer and college supervised work experiences, paid or unpaid, for a specified number of hours.

Off-campus employment is available part time to West Virginia State students in the greater Charleston area. Students apply at the Career Planning and Placement Office.

Workship employment is available to full-time students in good academic standing. Workship may be based on financial need or special skills the student may have.

Army ROTC offers two- and four-year scholarships that pay tuition, fees, books, and other expenses, and provide a monthly stipend of $100.

GI Bill Educational Training is available to veterans who served 180 days on active duty after January 1, 1955, but before January 1, 1977. Certain conditions apply.

West Virginia Higher Education Grant Program is available to full-time students who demonstrate financial need and academic promise. Must be resident of West Virginia at least one year immediately prior to applying.

The Third Congressional District Scholarship is awarded to a student from West Virginia's Third Congressional District with a 2.5 GPA. The award is $500 per semester.

Reduced Tuition for Out-of-State Study is available to West Virginia residents seeking degree programs not offered in the state through the Academic Common Market and contract programs. Students may enter out-of-state schools at reduced tuition rates.

Financial Aid Deadline
April 1 (fall); November 1 (spring)

Financial Aid Contact
Mr. Fred Black, Director of Financial Aid, West Virginia State College, Institute, WV 25211; (304) 766-3131.

ADMISSION REQUIREMENTS
ACT score of 17 or SAT

Entrance Requirements

Graduation from an accredited high school and completion of the following units: 4 English (grammar, composition, and literature); 3 social science (including U.S. history); 2 mathematics (including algebra and higher), and 2 laboratory science (biology, chemistry, or physics). One unit physical education is recommended and 2 units foreign language are highly recommended; submit an official high school transcript; must have a 2.0 or "C" average.

Entrance requirements: Associate degree program requires graduation from a West Virginia school or GED; out-of-state students must have a minimum GPA of 2.0 or 17 on the ACT.

GED students should have a minimum score of 45 on each of the 5 parts, or average score of 55. ACT scores must be submitted.

Transfer students must have an interview, college transcript with a minimum 2.0 GPA, and good academic standing at previous institution. If student has fewer than 30 credit hours, student must submit high school transcript as well as ACT or SAT scores.

International students must submit transcripts with grades equivalent to "C" by U.S. and submit a completed health form. Students from non-English-speaking countries must pass the TOEFL examination and take the ACT.

Early admission allows academically gifted high school seniors to enroll for credit-bearing college courses before completing high school. Qualifying students must have a "B" average and written recommendation of the principal.

Admission Application Deadline
August 10 (fall); November 20 (spring)

Admission Contact

Mr. John L. Fuller, Director of Registration and Admissions, Office of Admissions, Room 106 Ferrell Hall, West Virginia State College, Institute, WV 25112; (304) 766-3221.

GRADUATION REQUIREMENTS

A minimum of 121 credit hours for a bachelor's degree and completion of core requirements to include the following: 6 hours English; 4 mathematics, 8 science, 9 humanities; 9 social sciences; 6 foreign language; 2 physical education; and 1 computer course for all students; recorded scores on the National Teacher Examinations for all teacher education majors; last 30 hours completed at West Virginia State College unless the student has earned a minimum of 64 hours at the college and has permission from the vice president for Academic Affairs and the chairperson of the department to take half of the last 30 hours at another institution; participation in the commencement exercise.

Sixty-one credit hours are needed for an associate's degree; must complete the last 15 hours at West Virginia State College.

Grading System

A–F; I=Incomplete; AUD=Audit; P=Pass; WF=Withdrew/failing at time of withdrawal; WP=Withdrew passing; W=Withdrew; Q=No grade submitted; K=Credit by exam.

STUDENT BODY PROFILE

Total enrollment: 4,986

From in-state: 4,831

Other regions: 25 states, 5 foreign countries

Full-time undergraduates (male/female): 1,267/1,549

Part-time undergraduates (male/female): 976/1,194

Ethnic/Racial Makeup

African American, 583; Hispanic, 14; Native American, 8; Caucasian, 4,346; International, 35.

Class of 1995 Profile
Number of applicants: 4,698

Number accepted: 3,499

Number enrolled: 942

Median ACT score: 18

Average high school GPA: 2.0

Transfer applicants: 374

Transfers accepted: 374

Transfers enrolled: 318

FACULTY PROFILE
Number of faculty: 233

Student-teacher ratio: 21:1

Full-time faculty: 138

Part-time faculty: 95

Tenured faculty: 71

Faculty with doctorates or other terminal degrees: 26%

SCHOOL CALENDAR
1992–93: August 20–May 12 (Semester hours)

Commencement and conferring of degrees: May 16

One summer session.

DEGREES OFFERED AND NUMBER CONFERRED 1991–92:

Bachelor of Arts
Art: 11

Economics: 4

English/English Education: 5

History/History Education: 4

Political Science: 11

Psychology: 13

Regents BA Degree: 102 (nontraditional degree)

Sociology: 2

Bachelor of Science
Biology: 6

Business Administration: 76

Chemistry/Chemistry Education: 8

Communications: 25

Criminal Justice: 26

Elementary Education: 64

Mathematics: 4

Recreation Administration: 5

Secondary Education: 23

Social Work: 7

Associate in Applied Science
Accounting: n/a

Advertising/Sales: n/a

Architectural Drafting Technology: n/a

Banking and Finance: n/a

Chemical Technology: n/a

Communications: n/a

Computer-Aided Drafting and Design: n/a

Computer Science/Information Processing/Programming: n/a

Criminal Justice: n/a

Electronics Engineering Technology: n/a

Fashion Merchandising: n/a

Hospitality Management: n/a

Management: n/a

Medical Assisting: n/a

Nuclear Medicine Technology: n/a

Occupational Development: n/a

Office Administration: n/a

Pre-professional Programs
Dentistry: n/a

Engineering: n/a

Law: n/a

Nursing: n/a

Optometry: n/a

Pharmacy: n/a

Veterinary: n/a

SPECIAL PROGRAMS
Accelerated Study Program allows students to complete their undergraduate degree in a shorter period of time than the traditional four years.

Adult or Continuing Education Program is available for nontraditional students returning to school or working full time.

Advanced Placement (AP) grants college credit for postsecondary work completed in high school. Students scoring 3 on the AP test will receive credit by examination for each course and advanced placement.

Articulation Agreements with area vocational/technical schools are available for students to earn credit toward an associate's degree in an occupational area upon completion of a program at a vocational/technical school.

A one-day college orientation is offered to entering students before classes begin to orient students to the college and to prepare them for college life.

College Level Examination Program (CLEP) determines the academic relevance of nontraditional educational experiences, such as the military, on-the-job training, or other life experiences, through a series of tests and may grant students college credit for these experiences.

Continuing Education/Community Service program allows students to couple classroom instruction with actual experience in major.

Cooperative Study Abroad Program allows students to go to a foreign country for part of their college education.

English as a Second Language is a program that offers courses in English for students whose native language is not English.

Field Experiences Program combines field experience with classroom study.

Internships are supervised field experiences, paid or unpaid, as part of the degree program.

Individualized majors allows students to create their own major program(s) of study.

Job Training Partnership Act (JTPA) is a training/retraining program to ensure West Virginia economically disadvantaged and long-term unemployed an opportunity to train/retrain in a college setting. These educational programs are limited for two-year areas that look promising for job placement upon completion of the program.

Pre-professional programs are available in Dentistry, Engineering, Law, Nursing, Optometry, Pharmacy, and Veterinary Medicine.

Regents Bachelor of Arts degree is available to nontraditional students. Students are awarded credit for work and life experience equivalent to college course work.

ROTC provides training in military science for commission as a second lieutenant in the U.S. Army, Army Reserve, or National Guard. Two- and four-scholarships are available.

Remedial courses are offered to entering students to bring them up to admissions standards and to help them adjust for success in college.

Tech Prep Associate Degree (TPAD) is a college prep parallel course of study that integrates academic and vocational/technical education to prepare students for business and industry technician-level careers. It combines a secondary and postsecondary sequence of courses that emphasizes high level applied mathematics, science and communication skills, integrated with vocational skills, and leading to an associate's degree.

Upward Bound program is designed to prepare low-income high school students for college.

ATHLETIC PROGRAMS

West Virginia State College is a member of the National Association of Intercollegiate Athletics (NAIA) and the West Virginia Intercollegiate Athletic Conference (WVIAC).

Intercollegiate sports: men's baseball, basketball, football, and track; women's basketball, softball, and track.

Intramural sports: basketball, bowling, football, table tennis, and volleyball.

Athletic Contact

Mr. Gregory Smith, Director of Athletics, West Virginia State College, Institute, WV 25112; (304) 766-3164.

LIBRARY HOLDINGS

The library houses 185,043 volumes, 28,295 microforms, 4,560 audiovisuals, 880 periodical subscriptions, 111 computers for student use, and a government depository library; a computerized catalog and circulation system and online searching is available.

STUDENT LIFE

Special regulations: Students must attend college orientation program and reside on campus at least through the junior year unless living with relatives. For membership as a WVSC Ambassador, student must be a sophomore, and maintain a 2.5 GPA.

Campus Services

Health center, personal and psychological counseling, substance abuse prevention program, remedial instruction, peer tutoring, career planning and placement services, college skills tune-up for ACT test, testing services, and religious activities.

Campus Activities

Social and cultural activities include theater, concerts, and art exhibits. Students look forward each year to the Multicultural Awareness Festival, the Higher Education Day, and the Handicap Impact (HI) Day. Students may work on *The Yellow Jacket* (student newspaper) or *The Arch* (yearbook). Students interested in communication can work on the student-run television station.

Leadership opportunities are found in the Student Government Association or numerous other student-run organizations. Greek-letter fraternities include Alpha Phi Alpha, Kappa Alpha Psi, Omega Psi Phi, and Phi Beta Sigma; sororities include Alpha Kappa Alpha, Delta Sigma Theta, Sigma Gamma Rho, and Zeta Phi Beta. Fifteen honor societies are represented including Alpha Kappa Mu and Phi Theta Kappa.

WVSC is located in Institute, West Virginia, which is a suburb of Charleston, the state capital with a population of approximately 60,000. Commuter buses provide service to downtown Charleston, which is only 8 miles away, and to other suburban communities. The city of Charleston offers shopping, museums, and art galleries. Each spring Charleston holds the State Jazz Festival and each fall it hosts the Sternwheel Regatta Festival, which includes fireworks, and tugboat and hot air balloon racing. Points of interest include Coonskin Park for tennis, paddle boat rides, and swimming. A seasonal 12-hour cruise is available.

Housing Availability

Five hundred housing spaces; three residence halls; an apartment complex for married couples and single parents with children; faculty homes on campus.

Handicapped Services

Special services for physically challenged students such as note-takers, books on tape, appliances, motor aids, and personalized educational programs for learning disabled students.

NOTABLE ALUMNI

James Boone, 1981–Men's basketball coach, California University of Pennsylvania

Augusta A. Clark, 1954–Member, Philadelphia City Council

Damon Keith, 1943–Sixth Circuit, U.S. Court of Appeals

Lou Meyers, 1962–Actor, "A Different World"

Georgia F. Morris, 1944–Educator, elementary school named for her in Rialto, CA

L. Eudora Pettigrew, 1950–President, State University of New York (SUNY) at Old Westbury, Long Island, NY

Deborah Phillips, 1974–Member, West Virginia Legislature

Beny Primm, 1950–White House Commission/AIDS

Vincent Reed, 1952–Vice president, Washington Post

MG Chas. C. Rogers, 1951–Congressional Medal/Honor

Leander Shaw, 1952–Chief Justice, Florida State Supreme Court

D. Wayne Smith, 1967–Founder, Friendship Force

Leon H. Sullivan, 1943–Founder, Opportunities Industrialization Centers

Norma Winter, 1961–First female high school administrator in Kanawha County, WV

NOTABLE ALUMNI

NOTABLE ALUMNI	FIELD OF ENDEAVOR	COLLEGE/ UNIVERSITY	YEAR GRADUATED
James B. Abram	Department Head, Biology	Norfolk State University	1959
Thelma Adair	Professor of Education, University of the City of New York (retired); first woman Moderator of the United Presbyterian Church USA; past President, Church Women United in the USA	Barber-Scotia College	1936
Oscar William Adams, Jr.	State Supreme Court Justice	Talladega College	n/a
Nat "Cannonball" Adderly	Jazz Musician	Florida Agricultural and Mechanical University	1951
Robert L. Alford, Ph.D.	Director of Testing, Norfolk State University	Claflin College	n/a
Debbie Allen	Actress; Choreographer; Dancer; Producer/Director	Howard University	1971
Milton B. Allen	Retired Defense Attorney; Judge; States Attorney for Baltimore, Maryland	Coppin State College	1938
Vivian Ayer Allen	Director, Adept New America Museum	Barber-Scotia College	n/a
Del Anderson	President, San Jose City College, California	Alcorn State University	n/a
Reuben Anderson	Mississippi's first black Supreme Court Justice	Tougaloo College	1964
Dr. Thelma D. Anderson	Chairperson, Business Department, Albany State College	Oakwood College	n/a
Richard Arrington, Jr.	Mayor, Birmingham, Alabama	Miles College	1955
Alberto Ascercon	International Music Lecturer	Norfolk State University	1986

NOTABLE ALUMNI

NOTABLE ALUMNI	FIELD OF ENDEAVOR	COLLEGE/ UNIVERSITY	YEAR GRADUATED
Brenda August	Decennial Specialist, U.S. Department of Commerce	Xavier University	n/a
Nnamdi Azikiwe	First President of Nigeria	Lincoln University of Pennsylvania	1930
Elaine Baker, Ph.D.	Professor, Albany State	Tougaloo College	n/a
Don H. Barden	CEO, Barden Cablevision	Central State University	1963–64
Rufus Barfield	Vice Chancellor, University of Arkansas at Pine Bluff	Kentucky State University	1952
George Everett Barnes, Ph.D.	President, Hinds Community College	Jackson State University	1962
Harold Barnes	Attorney, Penny, Barnes, and Rogers, Chesapeake, VA	Elizabeth City State University	1977
Lem Barney	Former NFL member	Jackson State University	n/a
Marian S. Barry	Former Mayor, Washington, D.C.	Lemoyne-Owen College	1958
David L. Beckley	President, Wiley College	Rust College	1967
Julius W. Becton	President, Prairie View A&M University	Prairie View A&M University	1960
Alvertis (Al) Bell	Executive, Barry Gordy Record Company	Philander Smith College	n/a
James Milton Bell, M.D.	Psychiatrist and Clinical Director, Berkshire Farm Center & Services for Youth	Meharry Medical College	1947
Robert Benham	State Supreme Court Justice, Georgia	Tuskegee University	1967
Lerone Bennett, Jr.	Executive Editor, *Ebony* magazine; Author	Morehouse College	1949/1966
Dr. C. A. Berry	President, Jarvis Christian College	Jarvis Christian College	n/a

NOTABLE ALUMNI

NOTABLE ALUMNI	FIELD OF ENDEAVOR	COLLEGE/ UNIVERSITY	YEAR GRADUATED
Joseph Bethea	Bishop, South Carolina Conference of United Methodist Church	Claflin College	n/a
Mary McLeod Bethune	Educator and Public Servant; Founder, National Council of Negro Women; Founder, Bethune-Cookman College	Barber-Scotia College	1894
Clarence Biggs	Dean of Student Affairs/ Acting President, Martin Community College, Williamston, NC	Elizabeth City State University	1962
Billy C. Black	President, Albany State College	Tuskegee University	1960
Joseph Black	Former Vice President, Special Markets, Greyhound	Miles College	1982
Janese M. Bland	Editor and Columnist, *Hollywood Gazette*	University of Arkansas at Pine Bluff	1980
Daniel T. Blue, Jr.	Speaker of the House, North Carolina	North Carolina Central University	n/a
Edward Wilmot Blyden III	International Educator and Diplomat from Sierra, Leone	Lincoln University of Pennsylvania	1948
Dr. Wiley Bolden	Professor Emeritus, Georgia State University	Alabama State University	1939
Evelyn K. Bonner	Librarian, Sitka, Alaska	Mary Holmes College	1961
Simeon Booker, Jr.	Washington Bureau Chief, *Jet* magazine	Virginia Union University	1942
Ina M. Boon	Former Director, NAACP	Oakwood College	n/a
James Boone	Men's Basketball Coach, California University of PA	West Virginia State College	1981
Marian Perry Bowers, M.D.	Member of Meharry's Upper Tenth; Clinical Professor, Head & Neck Surgery, USC School of Medicine	Meharry Medical College	1963

NOTABLE ALUMNI

NOTABLE ALUMNI	FIELD OF ENDEAVOR	COLLEGE/ UNIVERSITY	YEAR GRADUATED
Ed Bradley	Co-Host, "60 Minutes"	Cheyney University of Pennsylvania	1964
Aurelia Brazeal	U.S. Ambassador to Micronesia	Spelman College	n/a
Lou Brock	Major League Baseball's Hall of Fame and National Black College Alumni Hall of Fame	Southern University and A&M University-Baton Rouge	n/a
Oswald P. Bronson, Sr.	President, Bethune-Cookman College	Bethune-Cookman College	1950
Norward J. Brooks	Seattle City Comptroller	Southern University at New Orleans	1955
Aaron Brown	President Emeritus, Albany State College	Talladega College	n/a
Hallie Q. Brown	Educator; Elocutionist; Civil Rights Leader and Suffragette; President, Ohio State Federation of Women and National Association of Colored Women; Founder and Chairperson, Scholarship Fund of the National Association of Colored Women	Wilberforce University	1873
John H. Brown	Professor; Dentist; Founder and Director, Meharry Medical College Hospital of Dentistry	Alabama A&M University	1946
Lucille M. Brown	Superintendent, Richard Public Schools	Virginia Union University	1950
Morgan C. Brown, Ph.D.	Dean, Bridgewater State College (MA)	Paine College	1937
Roscoe Lee Browne	Author and Actor	Lincoln University of Pennsylvania	1946
Dr. Curtis J. Bryan	President, Denmark Technical College, Denmark, SC	Elizabeth City State University	1960

NOTABLE ALUMNI

NOTABLE ALUMNI	FIELD OF ENDEAVOR	COLLEGE/ UNIVERSITY	YEAR GRADUATED
Willie Miles Burns	Vice President, Johnson Publishing Co.	University of Arkansas at Pine Bluff	1939
Margaret Burrough	Founder/Director Emeritus, DuSable Museum of African-American History	Chicago State University	1937
James E. Byrd	President, Byrd's TV/ Curtis Mathes Home Entertainment Center	Denmark Technical College	1958
Dr. Lawrence Callahan	Founder and Manager of five Interdenominational Churches in Florida and the Bahamas	Edward Waters College	n/a
Ruth Campbell	Associate Director, Universities Center, Jackson State University	Coahoma Community College	n/a
Hortense Golden Canady	Civic Leader	Fisk University	1947
Ralph W. Canty, D.D.	Past President, National Progressive Baptist Convention	Morris College	1967, 1970, 1978
Louie Carrington	Jazz Musician	Huston-Tillotson College	1971
Hazo W. Carter, Jr.	Ninth President, West Virginia State College	Tennessee State University	n/a
Emily M. Chapman	Administrator, Urban Center, Lincoln University of Pennsylvania	South Carolina State University	n/a
James Cheek	College President, Shaw and Howard Universities	Shaw University	1955
James Edward Cheek	Former President, Howard University	Tuskegee University	n/a
Augusta A. Clark	Member, Philadelphia City Council	West Virginia State College	1954

NOTABLE ALUMNI

NOTABLE ALUMNI	FIELD OF ENDEAVOR	COLLEGE/ UNIVERSITY	YEAR GRADUATED
Felton G. Clark, Ph.D.	Former President	Southern University and A&M University-Baton Rouge	n/a
Jimmie E. Clark	President, Texas College	Texas College	1950
Robert G. Clark	Representative, State of Mississippi District 47	Jackson State University	1953
Alvin A. Cleveland, Sr.	Religion Professor, Selma University	Selma University	n/a
Jewel Plummer Cobb	Former President, California State University and Fullerton College	Talladega College	n/a
Donnie Cochran	Lieutenant Commander, Blue Angels Pilot	Savannah State College	1976
Lester Coffee	CPA, U.S.A. Security Exchange	Mary Holmes College	1968
Thomas W. Cole, Jr.	Chancellor, West Virginia Board of Regents; former President, West Virginia State	Wiley College	1961
Ceasar Coleman	Bishop, Christian Methodist Episcopal Church	Mary Holmes College	1949
Collie Coleman	President, Allen University	Shaw University	n/a
Joseph Coleman	President, Philadelphia City Council	Mary Holmes College	1941
Daniel A. Collins	Dentist, San Francisco, CA	Paine College	1936
Marva Collins	Founder and Director, Westside Preparatory School, Chicago	Bethune-Cookman College	1957
Robert F. Collins	U.S. District Judge, Eastern Division, Louisiana	Dillard University	1951
Samuel Dubois Cook	President, Dillard University	Morehouse College	1948
Dr. William Cox	President, Ed Cox, Matthews & Associates	Alabama A&M University	1964

NOTABLE ALUMNI

NOTABLE ALUMNI	FIELD OF ENDEAVOR	COLLEGE/ UNIVERSITY	YEAR GRADUATED
St. George Crosse	Clergyman; Attorney; Community Leader; Politician; Media Personality, Maryland	Coppin State College	1975
Bobby Dandridge	Former Professional Basketball Player	Norfolk State University	1973
Jiles P. Daniels	Vice President, Student Affairs, Prairie View A&M University	Prairie View A&M University	n/a
Alice Coachman Davis	First black Olympic Gold Medalist, Women's Track and Field	Albany State College	n/a
Clifton Davis	Actor, TV's "AMEN" (Theology degree from OC)	Oakwood College	n/a
Marianna W. Davis	First Woman to Serve on South Carolina's Commission on Higher Education	South Carolina State University	n/a
Willie Davis	Professional Football Player, Green Bay Packers	Grambling State University	1956
Burnest Webster Dawson	President, Selma University	Selma University	n/a
Leonard E. Dawson	Executive V.P./Director of Special Projects, UNCF	Morris Brown College	1954
William L. Dawson	Musician/Composer/ Conductor; Member, Alabama Music Hall of Fame	Tuskegee University	1955
Wilhelmina Delco	Texas State Representative	Fisk University	1950
David Dinkins	Manhattan Borough President; former Mayor, New York City	Howard University	1950
Clay Dixon	Mayor, Dayton, Ohio	Central State University	n/a
Ernest Dixon	United Methodist Bishop	Huston-Tillotson College	1943
Mattiwilda Dobbs	Opera Diva	Spelman College	1946

NOTABLE ALUMNI

NOTABLE ALUMNI	FIELD OF ENDEAVOR	COLLEGE/ UNIVERSITY	YEAR GRADUATED
Robert DoQui	Entertainer, Los Angeles, CA	Langston University	n/a
Aaron Douglas	Artist of the Harlem Renaissance; taught at Fisk	Fisk University	n/a
Melvin Isadore Douglass	Educator and Clergyman	Tuskegee University	1973
William Edward Burgharot [W.E.B.] DuBois	Social Critic; Historian; Scholar; Educator; Founder, Niagara Movement; Co-founder, NAACP	Fisk University	n/a
Marian Wright Edelman	Founder, Children Defense Fund	Spelman College	1960
Major General Albert J. Edmonds	Assistant Chief of Staff, U.S. Air Force	Morris Brown College	1964
Alfred Leroy Edwards	Former Deputy Assistant, Secretary of Agriculture	Livingstone College	1948
Dr. Jocelyn Elders	United States Surgeon General	Philander Smith College	1952
Ralph Waldo Ellison	Novelist	Tuskegee University	n/a
Dr. Jeanette Hawkins Evans	Educational Specialist, Baltimore City Schools, Baltimore, MD	Elizabeth City State University	1963
James Farmer	Founder, Congress of Racial Equality; former Program Director, NAACP; Assistant Secretary, Dept. of Health, Education & Welfare	Wiley College	1938
Vera King Farris	President, Stockton State College	Tuskegee University	1959
Dr. Walter E. Fauntroy	Former U.S. Congressman, D.C.	Virginia Union University	n/a
Ernest A. Finney, Jr.	Associate Judge, South Carolina Supreme Court	Claflin College	1952

NOTABLE ALUMNI

NOTABLE ALUMNI	FIELD OF ENDEAVOR	COLLEGE/ UNIVERSITY	YEAR GRADUATED
Floyd H. Flake	Pastor; Social Worker; Politician; first full-term African-American Congressman from the 6th Congressional District; Founder, Allen Christian School	Wilberforce University	1967
Charles Fletcher	Finance Planner, IBM	Bethune-Cookman College	1968
Otis L. Floyd, Jr.	President, Tennessee State University	Lane College	n/a
Johnny L. Ford	Mayor, Tuskegee, Alabama	Knoxville College	1964
Luther H. Foster, Ph.D.	Fourth President, Tuskegee University	Virginia State University	1932
George Francis, III	Vice President, Blue Cross/ Blue Shield of Michigan	Prairie View A&M University	1964
Norman C. Francis	President, Xavier University	Xavier University	n/a
John Hope Franklin	Scholar; History Professor: Fisk University, Howard University, Cambridge, etc.	Fisk University	1935
Marvin Frazier	Professional Football Player, Denver Broncos	Cheyney University of Pennsylvania	n/a
Harlow Fullwood, Jr.	Former Football Player, Baltimore Colts	Virginia Union University	1977
Edward Gardner	Founder and CEO, SoftSheen Products Co.	Chicago State University	n/a
Dr. Frank Gardner	Board of Examiners, Chicago Public Schools	Chicago State University	n/a
Stu Gardner	Musical Director, "The Bill Cosby Show"	Virginia Union University	1990
Dr. Alma Rose George	Surgeon and President, Medical Staff Mercy Hospital, Detroit, Michigan	Meharry Medical College	n/a
Althea Gibson	Professional Tennis Player	Florida Agricultural and Mechanical University	1953

NOTABLE ALUMNI

NOTABLE ALUMNI	FIELD OF ENDEAVOR	COLLEGE/ UNIVERSITY	YEAR GRADUATED
Marshall Gilmore	Bishop, Dayton, Ohio	Paine College	1957
Nikki Giovanni	Poet; Writer; Lecturer	Fisk University	1967
W. Dean Goldsby	President, Shorter College	Allen University	1959
Dr. Charles G. Gomillion	Retired Educator, Tuskegee Institute	Paine College	1928
Wilson Goode	President, Goode Construction Inc., Chesapeake, VA	Elizabeth City State University	1966
Wilson W. Goode	Mayor, Philadelphia Pennsylvania	Morgan State University	1961
Doris Gore	Assistant Principal, Paterson, NJ Public Schools	Mary Holmes College	1968
Samuel L. Gravely	First Black Vice Admiral, U.S. Navy (Retired)	Virginia Union University	1948
Earl Graves	Publisher, *Black Enterprise*	Morgan State University	1958
L. C. Greenwood	Former Professional Athlete, Pittsburgh Steelers; Construction Executive	University of Arkansas at Pine Bluff	1969
Dick Griffey	CEO, Dick Griffey Productions, CA	Tennessee State University	n/a
Dr. Elwyn M. Grimes	Director, Truman Medical Center	Jackson State University	1964
Rascoe Hager	Compliance Coordinator, Methods of Administration, Department of North Carolina Community Colleges, Wake Forest, NC	Elizabeth City State University	1963
Alex Haley	Author; Journalist	Alcorn State University	1939
Ruth Simm Hamilton	Professor; Michigan State University Trustee	Talladega College	n/a
Julia Reed Hare	Director, Community Affairs, Golden West Broadcasters, KSFO	Langston University	1964

NOTABLE ALUMNI

NOTABLE ALUMNI	FIELD OF ENDEAVOR	COLLEGE/ UNIVERSITY	YEAR GRADUATED
Nathan Hare	Chairman, The Black Think Tank, San Francisco, CA	Langston University	1954
Dr. Frederick Harper	Publisher; Faculty Member, Howard University	Edward Waters College	n/a
James Harris	Professional Football Player, Los Angeles Rams	Grambling State University	n/a
Jean Ellis Harris	Councilwoman, Eden Prairie, MN; first black in Virginia's Governor's Cabinet; first black Graduate of the Medical College of Virginia	Virginia Union University	1951
Marcelite J. Harris	First black woman Air Force Brigadier General	Spelman College	n/a
Beverly J. Harvard	Deputy Chief of Police, Atlanta, Georgia	Morris Brown College	1972
Dr. William R. Harvey	President, Hampton University	Talladega College	n/a
Alice Hastings	U.S. Representative, Florida	Fisk University	1957
Joseph W. Hatchett	U.S. Circuit Judge, 5th Circuit, Tallahassee, FL	Florida Agricultural and Mechanical University	1954
Roland Hayes	Professional Singer	Fisk University	1905–08
Dr. Pearl Walter Headd	Professor Emeritus, Tuskegee Institute	Mary Holmes College	1935
Lonear Heard-Davis	Corporate Executive, James T. Heard Management Corp.	Rust College	1964
Herbert Helmsley	Founder, Bethune Medical Center	Bethune-Cookman College	1955
John L. Henderson	President, Wilberforce University	Hampton University	1955

NOTABLE ALUMNI

NOTABLE ALUMNI	FIELD OF ENDEAVOR	COLLEGE/ UNIVERSITY	YEAR GRADUATED
Alexis Herman	Democratic National Committee Chief of Staff; named one of 100 Outstanding Business Women in the United States	Xavier University	1969
James O. Heyward	Director of Admissions, Alabama A&M University	South Carolina State University	1953
Dr. James L. Hill	Dean, Albany State College	Fort Valley State College	1963
Jesse Hill	Chief Executive Officer, Atlanta Life Insurance Co.	Lincoln University (MO)	1947
Evelyn A. Hodge	Reading Supervisor, Alabama State College	Albany State College	n/a
Virgil Hall Hodges	Deputy Commissioner, New York State Dept. of Labor	Morris Brown College	1958
Vernette Honeywood	Artist	Spelman College	n/a
Edward Honor	Retired Lieutenant General	Southern University and A&M University-Baton Rouge	n/a
Benjamin Lawson Hooks	Attorney & Executive Director, NAACP	Lemoyne-Owen College	1943–44
William A. Hopkins	Director of Small Business Affairs, Georgia	Albany State College	1968
Fred Horn	U.S. Senator/Congressman	Miles College	1950
Moses Leon Howard	Teacher; Author (pseudonym Musa Nagenda)	Alcorn State University	1952
Langston Hughes	Poet and Author	Lincoln University of Pennsylvania	1929
Frederick S. Humphries	Eighth President, Florida A&M University	Florida Agricultural and Mechanical University	1957
Zora Neal Hurston	Writer	Morgan State University	1918
George Hyran	Vice President Emeritus, Harris-Stowe	Harris-Stowe State College	n/a

NOTABLE ALUMNI

NOTABLE ALUMNI	FIELD OF ENDEAVOR	COLLEGE/ UNIVERSITY	YEAR GRADUATED
Ida L. Jackson	First black teacher in Oakland, CA Public Schools	Rust College	1914
Rev. Jessie L. Jackson	Presidential Candidate; Civil Rights Activist; Founder and President, National Rainbow Coalition	North Carolina A&T State University	1964
Maynard Jackson	Mayor, Atlanta, Georgia	Morehouse College North Carolina Central University	1956 1959
Daniel "Chappie" James	First black Four-Star General in the Armed Forces	Tuskegee University	1942
Herman Delano James	College President, Glassboro State College	Tuskegee University	1965
Mayme S. Jefferies	Director of Assessment, Edward Waters College	Savannah State College	n/a
William J. Jefferson	Louisiana's first black Congressman	Southern University at New Orleans	1969
Dr. Jimmy R. Jenkins, Sr.	Chancellor, Elizabeth City State University, Elizabeth City, NC	Elizabeth City State University	1965
Dr. Julius Jenkins	President, Concordia College	Concordia College	n/a
Sebetha Jenkins, Ed.D.	President, Jarvis Christian College	Jackson State University	n/a
Alberta Helyn Johnson	First African-American woman elected to public office in Wyoming	Talladega College	n/a
Joseph B. Johnson	President of Talladega College	Grambling State University	1957
Orchid I. Johnson	Political Activist; Founder, Freedom Inc.; State Representative, 25th District, Missouri	Wilberforce University	n/a
Robert Johnson	Publisher, *Jet* magazine	Morehouse College	1948
Robert Edward Johnson	Executive Editor, *Jet* magazine	Miles College	1973

NOTABLE ALUMNI

NOTABLE ALUMNI	FIELD OF ENDEAVOR	COLLEGE/ UNIVERSITY	YEAR GRADUATED
William A. Johnson	Vice President of Fiscal Affairs	Albany State College	n/a
Burnett Joiner, Ph.D.	President, LeMoyne Owen College, Memphis, TN	Alcorn State University	1964
Bess E. Jones, M.D., M.P.H.	Public Health Department, DeKalb County, GA	Morehouse School of Medicine	n/a
Barbara Jordan, Esq.	U.S. Representative, 18th district, Texas	Texas Southern University	1956
Damon Keith	Sixth Circuit, U.S. Court of Appeals	West Virginia State College	1943
Jonas P. Kennedy, M.D.	Millionaire Turkey Farmer	Claflin College	n/a
Yvonne Kennedy, Ph.D.	President, Bishop State Community College, 1991–1992; National President of the Delta Sigma Theta Sorority	Alabama State University / Bishop State Community College	1964 / n/a
Rev. Dr. Martin Luther King, Jr.	Nobel Prize Laureate; Civil Rights Leader	Morehouse College	1948
Elizabeth Koontz	Former President of the National Education Association; Director of the Women's Bureau of Department and Labor	Livingstone College	1938
William F. Kornegay	General Motors	Bethune-Cookman College	1954
Willie Lanier	Professional Football Player	Morgan State University	n/a
Elizabeth Harris Lawson	Co-chair, White House Conference on Library and Information Services	Chicago State University	1979
Lawrence Lawson	Supreme Court Judge	Bowie State University	1969
Lisa Lee	Editor, *Essence* magazine	Bowie State University	1978

NOTABLE ALUMNI

NOTABLE ALUMNI	FIELD OF ENDEAVOR	COLLEGE/ UNIVERSITY	YEAR GRADUATED
Spike Lee	Filmmaker	Morehouse College	1979
George "Mickey" L. Leland	U.S. Representative, Texas	Texas Southern University	n/a
Joyce F. Leland	Deputy Chief of Police, Metropolitan Police Department, Washington, DC	University of The District of Columbia	n/a
John Lewis	U.S. Representative, Atlanta City	Fisk University	1967
Reginald F. Lewis	President/CEO TLC Beatrice International Holdings, Inc.	Virginia State University	1965
Eric C. Lincoln	Educator, Duke University	Lemoyne-Owen College	1947
Nathaniel Linsey	Bishop	Paine College	1948
Fred Long	Surgeon	Shaw University	1968
Fannye E. Love	Chairperson, Teacher Education, LeMoyne-Owen College	Mississippi Valley State University	n/a
Earl Lucas	Mayor, Mississippi's all black Township, Mount Bayou	Dillard University	1957
Henry Lucus, D.D.S.	Dentist	Meharry Medical College	n/a
Astrid Mack	Associate Professor, University of Miami's School of Medicine	Bethune-Cookman College	1960
Dr. Dorothy Littlejohn Magett	Deputy Superintendent of Public Instruction, State of Illinois	University of Arkansas at Pine Bluff	1953
Lloyd B. Mallory	Concert Director, Lincoln University (PA)	Oakwood College	n/a
Thurgood Marshall	Atttorney; First African-American Supreme Court Justice	Lincoln University (PA) Howard University Howard University School of Law	1930 1933 1947, 1954

NOTABLE ALUMNI

NOTABLE ALUMNI	FIELD OF ENDEAVOR	COLLEGE/ UNIVERSITY	YEAR GRADUATED
McKinley C. Martin	Retired President of Coahoma Community College	Coahoma Community College	1959
Mahlon Martin	Government Official	Philander Smith College	n/a
Sadye Martin	Mayor, Plant City, Florida	Bethune-Cookman College	n/a
Robert Massey	Professional Football Player	North Carolina Central University	n/a
Sharon Bell Mathis	Children's Book Author	Morgan State University	1958
Helen M. Mayes	Director Emeritus, Albany State College	Savannah State College	1938
Walter S. McAfee	Physicist; AUS Elect R & D Commander Fort Monmouth, NJ	Wiley College	1934
Christa McAuliffe	Astronaut on space shuttle *Challenger*	Bowie State University	1978
Shirley McBay	Educational Leader	Paine College	1954
Wesley Cornelious McClure, Ph.D.	17th President of Virginia State University	Virginia State University	n/a
George McKenna	Superintendent of Schools, Inglewood, California	Xavier University	n/a
Floretta Duke McKenzie	Former Deputy Assistant Secretary, Department of Education; Superintendent of D.C. Public Schools	University of the District of Columbia	1982
Ann Watts McKinney	Dean, Norfolk State University	North Carolina A&T State University	n/a
Dr. Mable McLean	First woman and first alumnus President of Barber-Scotia College; Head of the member institutions of the United Negro College Fund in 1986	Barber-Scotia College	1941
Ronald McNair	NASA Astronaut and Mission Specialist	North Carolina A&T State University	n/a

NOTABLE ALUMNI

NOTABLE ALUMNI	FIELD OF ENDEAVOR	COLLEGE/ UNIVERSITY	YEAR GRADUATED
James Alan McPherson	Writer, Pulitzer Prize Recipient	Morris Brown College	1965
Bryant Melton	State Representative	Stillman College	1965
Lou Meyers	Actor, "A Different World"	West Virginia State College	1962
Kweisi Mfume	U.S. Congressman	Morgan State University	1976
Robert D. Miller, M.D.	President, Arkansas State Board of Health	Meharry Medical College	1984
Yvonne Miller	State Senator, fifth district, Virginia	Norfolk State University	1954
Parren J. Mitchell	Former U.S. Congressman	Morgan State University	1950
Lois J. Moore	Chief Administrative Officer of Harris County Hospital District	Prairie View A&M University	1957
Rev. Florida Morehead	Executive Director, National Society of Black Engineers	University of Arkansas at Pine Bluff	1969
Dr. Warren W. Morgan	President, Paul Quinn College, Waco, TX	University of Maryland	n/a
Azi Taylor Morton	Former 36th U.S. Treasurer	Huston-Tillotson College	1956
Edwin Moses	U.S. Olympic Champion	Morehouse College	1978
Constance Blake Motley	First African-American female Federal Judge	Fisk University	1944
Rev. Cecil Murray	Senior minister, First AME Church, Los Angeles, CA	Florida Agricultural and Mechanical University	n/a
Margaret James Murray-Washington	First Dean of Women at Tuskegee Institute	Fisk University	n/a
William Brown Muse, Jr.	President, Imperial Savings and Loan, Martinville, VA	Hampton University	1940
Dr. Jacqueline D. Myers	Business Professor at Alabama State College	Benedict College	1971

NOTABLE ALUMNI

NOTABLE ALUMNI	FIELD OF ENDEAVOR	COLLEGE/ UNIVERSITY	YEAR GRADUATED
Samuel Nabrit	First black member of Atomic Energy Commission; former Texas Southern University President	Morehouse College	1925
Freddy (Curly) Neal	Harlem Globetrotter	Johnson C. Smith University	n/a
Tim Newman	Ex-professional Player, NFL New York Jets	Johnson C. Smith University	n/a
Dimaggio Nichols	President, Noble Ford-Mercury, Inc.	Rust College	1973
Kwame Nkrumah	First Prime Minister and First President of Ghana	Lincoln University (PA)	1939
Pettis Norman	Ex-professional Player, Dallas Cowboys, NFL	Johnson C. Smith University	n/a
Charles Oakley	Power Forward, New York Knicks	Virginia Union University	n/a
Hazel O'Leary	Secretary of Energy	Fisk University	n/a
Prince B. Oliver, Jr.	Anesthesiologist	Bethune-Cookman College	1958
Dr. Clifton Orr	Professor of Chemistry, University of Arkansas	Mary Holmes College	1969
Gen. Emmett H. Paige, Jr.	Army's first black General	University of Maryland	1972
E. Grace Payne	Los Angeles Harbor Commission	Texas College	n/a
Walter Payton	Former NFL all-pro Chicago Bears	Jackson State University	1975
Patricia Pelham-Harris, M.D.	Family Practice, Ogletree Family Center, Crawford, GA	Morehouse School of Medicine	n/a
Dr. James O. Perpener	5th President of Jarvis Christian College	Jarvis Christian College	n/a
Eudora L. Pettigrew	President, State University of New York (SUNY) at Old Westbury, Long Island, NY	West Virginia State College	1950

NOTABLE ALUMNI

NOTABLE ALUMNI	FIELD OF ENDEAVOR	COLLEGE/ UNIVERSITY	YEAR GRADUATED
Deborah Phillips	Member, West Virginia Legislature	West Virginia State College	1974
Witley A. Phipps	Pastor, Capitol Hill S.D.A. Church, Washington, DC	Oakwood College	n/a
Dr. Alice Pinderhughes	Retired Superintendent, Baltimore City Public Schools	Coppin State College	1942
Hildrus A. Poindexter	International authority on tropical diseases	Lincoln University (PA)	1924
Dr. Henry Ponder	President, Fisk University	Langston University	1951
Ersa H. Poston	Former President, New York Civil Services Commission	Kentucky State College	1942
Leontyne Price	Opera Singer	Central State University	1949
Beny Primm	White House Commission on AIDS	West Virginia State College	1950
Jethro Pugh	Former Dallas Cowboys linebacker, National Football League	Elizabeth City State University	1965
Dr. E. Wadworth Rand	7th President of Jarvis Christian College	Jarvis Christian College	n/a
Charles C. Rascoe, Jr.	Computer Systems Analyst, Computer Based Systems, Inc., Fairfax, VA	Elizabeth City State University	1972
Phyllicia Rashad	Actress, Singer	Howard University	1970
Dr. Benjamin F. Reaves	President of Oakwood College	Oakwood College	1955
Dr. Eddie Reed, MD	Cancer Researcher	Philander Smith College	n/a
Vincent Reed	Vice President, *Washington Post*	West Virginia State College	1952
Willis Reed	Ex-Professional NBA player	Grambling State University	n/a
Tim Reid	Actor/Executive Producer	Norfolk State University	1968

NOTABLE ALUMNI

NOTABLE ALUMNI	FIELD OF ENDEAVOR	COLLEGE/ UNIVERSITY	YEAR GRADUATED
John E. Reinhardt	U.S. Ambassador to Liberia	Knoxville College	1939
F.C. Richardson	President, Buffalo State College	Rust College	n/a
Dr. Luns C. Richardson	President of Morris College	Benedict College	1949
Lionel Brockman Richie, Jr.	Singer, Songwriter, Producer, and Grammy Award winner	Tuskegee University	n/a
William Roberts	Attorney-at-Law, Jacksonville, FL	Edward Waters College	n/a
Bishop Robinson	Secretary for Public Safety and Corrections, State of Maryland	Coppin State College	1973
Jim Robinson	President, Robinson's Marketing Co.	Edward Waters College	n/a
Prezell Robinson	President, Saint Augustine's College	Voorhees College	n/a
Dr. Willie C. Robinson	President, Florida Memorial College	North Carolina A&T State University	n/a
Charles C. Rogers	Congressional Medal of Honor	West Virginia State College	n/a
Dr. Oscar A. Rogers, Jr.	President, Claflin College	Tougaloo College	n/a
Joseph Roulhac	Retired Judge	Stillman College	n/a
Wilma Rudolph	Olympic Gold Medalist, Track	Tennessee State University	n/a
Bayard Rustin	Activist, Brotherhood of Sleeping Car Porters	Wilberforce University	1930–32
Brenda F. Savage	Associate Professor, Lincoln University (PA)	Tennessee State University	n/a
Patricia Schmoke	Doctor of Ophthalmology; Wife of Baltimore City, MD Mayor, Kurt Schmoke	Coppin State College	1975
Veryl Scott, J.D.	Business Department Administrator, Norfolk University	South Carolina State University	n/a

NOTABLE ALUMNI

NOTABLE ALUMNI	FIELD OF ENDEAVOR	COLLEGE/ UNIVERSITY	YEAR GRADUATED
Jerry Screen	Attorney; Chairman of the Board of Trustees, Voorhees College	Voorhees College	n/a
Betty Shabazz	Professor, Medgar Evers College; Wife of Malcolm X	Medgar Evers College	n/a
Lottie Shackleford	First woman Mayor, Largest City in Arkansas	Philander Smith College	1979
John W. Shannon	Assistant Secretary of the Army	Central State University	1955
Leander Shaw	Chief Justice, Florida State Supreme Court	West Virginia State College	1952
Arthur L. Shell	First black to coach a modern national football league team; member of the NFL Hall of Fame	University of Maryland	1968
Dr. Jacob L. Shirley, M.D.	Former Director of Health Services, Albany State College	Meharry Medical College	1910
S. Dallas Simmons, Ph.D.	President, Virginia Union University	North Carolina Central University	1962
Beverly Simons, M.D.	New Lower Richland Medical Center	Morehouse School of Medicine	n/a
Dr. Leonard A. Slade, Jr.	Professor and Chair, Department of African and Afro-American Studies, State University of New York	Elizabeth City State University	1963
Moneta Sleet, Jr.	Photographer, Johnson Publishing Co.	Kentucky State College	n/a
Alfred S. Smith	Assistant Vice President, Alabama State University	Bethune-Cookman College	n/a
Calvert H. Smith	President, Morris Brown College	Winston-Salem State University	n/a

NOTABLE ALUMNI

NOTABLE ALUMNI	FIELD OF ENDEAVOR	COLLEGE/ UNIVERSITY	YEAR GRADUATED
D. Wayne Smith	Founder, Friendship Force	West Virginia State College	1967
Hampton Smith	Professor, Health and Physical Education, Albany State College	Mississippi Valley State University	n/a
Herman Smith	Former Chancellor, University of Arkansas at Pine Bluff	Knoxville College	n/a
Joshua Smith	Founder and CEO, Maxima Corp.	Central State University	1963
Kenneth B. Smith	President, Chicago Theological Seminary	Virginia Union University	1953
Mary Levi Smith, Ed.D.	President, Kentucky State University	Jackson State University	1957
Andrew Sneed, Jr.	Special Program Coordinator, Alabama State University	Miles College	n/a
Dolores Margaret Spikes	First female president, Louisiana Public University; former Chancellor, Southern University at New Orleans	Southern University and A&M University-Baton Rouge	n/a
Lenny Spring	Vice President, First Union Bank, Charlotte, SC	Voorhees College	1968
John Stallworth	President, Madison Research Corp.; former professional football player	Alabama A&M University	1974, 1978
Evelyn Dixon Staton	Former NASA Aerospace Technologist	Elizabeth City State University	1965
Thomas L. Stevens	President, Los Angeles Trade and Technical College, Los Angeles, CA	University of Arkansas at Pine Bluff	1954
Joseph M. Steward	Senior Vice President, Corporate Affairs, Kellogg Food Co.	Southern University and A&M University-Baton Rouge	1965

NOTABLE ALUMNI

NOTABLE ALUMNI	FIELD OF ENDEAVOR	COLLEGE/ UNIVERSITY	YEAR GRADUATED
Ester W. Stokes	Director of Personnel, Jackson State University	Coahoma Community College	n/a
Curtis Sullivan	President, Omni Custom Meats, Inc.	Kentucky State College	n/a
Leon H. Sullivan	Founder, Opportunities Industrial Centers	West Virginia State College	1943
Louis W. Sullivan M.D.	Former Secretary, U.S. Department of Health and Human Services	Morehouse School of Medicine	1954
Ozell Sutton	Past National President, Alpha Phi Alpha Fraternity, Inc.	Philander Smith	1950
Percy E. Sutton	Inner City Broadcasting Corp., New York (Retired)	Prairie View A&M University	1969
Dr. William W. Sutton	President, Mississippi Valley State University	Dillard University	1953
Terricia W. Sweet	Professor, California State University, Fresno	Tougaloo College	1977
Wilbert A. Tatum	Publisher, Editor-In-Chief, *Amsterdam News*	Lincoln University (PA)	n/a
Hobart Taylor, Jr.	Special Counsel to President Lyndon B. Johnson	Prairie View A&M University	1939
Lynette Taylor	President, Taylor Enterprises	Alabama State University	1936
Dr. Arthur E. Thomas	President, Central State University	Central State University	n/a
Charles Thomas	Vice President, Yazoo City State Bank	Mary Holmes College	1970
Cleon F. Thompson, Jr.	Chancellor, Winston-Salem State University	North Carolina Central University	1954
Marian Johnson Thompson	Molecular Virologist	University of the District of Columbia	n/a

NOTABLE ALUMNI

NOTABLE ALUMNI	FIELD OF ENDEAVOR	COLLEGE/ UNIVERSITY	YEAR GRADUATED
Beatrice Tignor	State Delegate	Bowie State University	1978
Myer L. Titus	President, Philander Smith College	Philander Smith College	n/a
Charles Urd	Mayor Protem, Austin, Texas	Huston-Tillotson College	1956
James L. Usry	First African-American Mayor of Atlantic City	Lincoln University (PA)	1946
Dr. Irene G. Van Travis	Author, *Networks: Communicating in the World Today*	Elizabeth City State University	1947
Percy J. Vaughn, Jr.	Dean, College of Business Administration, Morris Brown College	Morris Brown College	1957
Alice Walker	Writer; Pulitzer Prize Recipient	Spelman College	1961, 1963
Robert M. Walker	Mayor, Vicksburg, Mississippi	Jackson State University	1966
Mary Dawson Walters	First black to head one of Ohio State's Library Departments	Savannah State College	n/a
Ron Walters	Founder, National Black Independent Political Party; former Chairman, Political Science Dept., Howard University	Fisk University	1963
Anita Ward	Pop Singer	Rust College	1977
Perry W. Ward	President, Lawson State Community College	Miles College	n/a
Booker T. Washington	Founder, Tuskegee University; Writer; Political Leader	Hampton University	n/a
Craig Washington	U.S. Representative, 18th Congressional District of Texas	Prairie View A&M University	1966
Walter Washington	President, Alcorn State University	Tougaloo College	1948

NOTABLE ALUMNI

NOTABLE ALUMNI	FIELD OF ENDEAVOR	COLLEGE/ UNIVERSITY	YEAR GRADUATED
Andre Waters	Professional Football Player, Philadelphia Eagles	Cheyney University	n/a
Keenan Ivory Wayans	TV Actor/Producer	Tuskegee University	n/a
Joachim Weinberg	Ex-professional Football Player, San Diego Chargers	Johnson C. Smith University	n/a
Ida B. Wells	An organizer of the NAACP (1878)	Rust College	n/a
Eric M. Westbury	Assistant President, First Union Bank of South Carolina	South Carolina State University	n/a
Woodie White	Bishop	Paine College	1958
L. Douglas Wilder	Governor of Virginia (first black governor in U.S.)	Virginia Union University	n/a
Doug Williams	Retired Quarterback, Washington Redskins	Grambling State University	n/a
Franklin H. Williams	Former Ambassador to United Nations and Ghana	Lincoln University (PA)	1941
Luther Steward Williams	Associate Directorate, National Science Foundation	Miles College	1961
Gladys J. Willis	Professor; English Department Chair, Lincoln University (PA)	Jackson State University	1965
Margaret B. Wilson	Assistant Attorney General, Missouri; Civil Rights Leader	Talladega College	n/a
Oprah Winfrey	Television Star and Producer	Tennessee State University	n/a
Norma Winter	First female high school administrator in Kanawha County, West Virginia	West Virginia State College	1961
Carter D. Womack	Executive Vice President, *The Black Collegian*	Alabama A&M University	1973
Dr. Geraldine Pittman Woods	Health Education Consultant	Talladega College	n/a

NOTABLE ALUMNI

NOTABLE ALUMNI	FIELD OF ENDEAVOR	COLLEGE/ UNIVERSITY	YEAR GRADUATED
Robert Woodson	President, National Center for Neighborhood Enterprise	Cheyney University	1962
Mary Honor Wright	Educator who established several schools in Spartanburg, SC	Claflin College	n/a
Dr. Cordell Wynn	President, Stillman College	Fort Valley State College	n/a
Frank Yerby	Author	Paine College	1937
Whitney Young	Executive Director, National Urban League	Kentucky State College	n/a

APPENDIXES

Appendix I
CHURCH-AFFILIATED SCHOOLS

African-Methodist Episcopal (AME)

Allen University   539
Edward Waters College   147
Livingstone College   459
Morris Brown College   204
Paul Quinn College   626
Shorter College   106
Wilberforce University   506

Baptist

Arkansas Baptist College   97
Benedict College   543
Florida Memorial College   160
Morris College   561
Selma University   67
Shaw University   482
Spelman College   223
Virginia Union University   689

Christian Methodist Episcopal

Lane College   589
Miles College   56
Texas College   641

Church of Christ

Southwestern Christian College   636

Congressional Church

Dillard University*   257

Disciple of Christ Christian Church

Jarvis Christian College   620

Episcopal

Saint Augustine's College   477
Saint Paul's College   677
Voorhees College   572

Interdenominational

Interdenominational Theological Seminary
187

Lutheran Church (Missouri Synod)

Concordia College 40

Presbyterian Church

Barber-Scotia College 431
Johnson C. Smith University 454
Knoxville College 585
Mary Holmes Community College 375
Stillman College 71

Roman Catholic Church

Xavier University of Louisiana 284

Seventh-Day Adventist

Oakwood College 61

United Church of Christ

Fisk University 579
Huston-Tillotson College* 615
LeMoyne-Owen College 594
Talladega College 77
Tougaloo College* 392

United Church Missionary Society

Tougaloo College* 392

United Methodist Church

Bennett College 437
Bethune-Cookman College 141
Claflin College 548
Clark Atlanta University 175
Dillard University* 257
Huston-Tillotson College* 615
Meharry Medical College 600
Paine College 211
Philander Smith College 100
Rust College 386
Wiley College 652

Two church affiliations

Appendix II
LAND-GRANT COLLEGES AND UNIVERSITIES

Alabama A&M University 21
Alcorn State University 351
Delaware State University 131
Florida A&M University 152
Fort Valley State College 181
Kentucky State University 247
Langston University 515
Lincoln University (MO) 404
North Carolina A&T State University 465
Prairie View A&M University 630
South Carolina State University 566
Southern University and A&M University-
Baton Rouge 269
Tennessee State University 606
Tuskegee University 86
University of Arkansas at Pine Bluff 110
University of Maryland, Eastern Shore 318
Virginia State University 683

Appendix III
PUBLIC OR STATE-SUPPORTED SCHOOLS

Alabama A&M University 21
Alabama State University 28
Albany State College 169
Alcorn State University 351
Bowie State University* 293
Central State University 495
Cheyney University of Pennsylvania 523
Coppin State College 299
Delaware State University 131
Elizabeth City State University 442
Fayetteville State University 448
Florida A&M University 152
Fort Valley State College 181
Grambling State University 263
Jackson State University 368
Kentucky State University* 247
Langston University 515
Lincoln University (MO) 404
Lincoln University of Pennsylvania 529
Mississippi Valley State University 380
Morgan State University 306
Norfolk State University 671

North Carolina A&T State University   465
North Carolina Central University   471
Prairie View A&M University   630
Savannah State College   217
South Carolina State University*   566
Southern University system*
Tennessee State University   606
Texas Southern University   645
Tuskegee University   86
University of Arkansas at Pine Bluff   110
University of Maryland, Eastern Shore   318
Virginia State University   683
Winston-Salem State University   487

*recently gained university status

Appendix IV
UNITED NEGRO COLLEGE FUND (UNCF) MEMBER SCHOOLS

Barber-Scotia College   431
Benedict College   543
Bennett College   437
Bethune-Cookman College   141
Claflin College   548
Clark Atlanta University   175
Dillard University   257
Edward Waters College   147
Fisk University   579
Florida Memorial College   160
Huston-Tillotson College   615
Interdenominational Theological Center   187
Jarvis Christian College   620
Johnson C. Smith University   454
Knoxville College   585
Lane College   589
LeMoyne-Owen College   594
Livingstone College   459
Miles College   56
Morehouse College   192
Morris Brown College   204
Morris College   561
Oakwood College   61
Paine College   211
Paul Quinn College   626
Philander Smith College   100
Rust College   386
Saint Augustine's College   477
Saint Paul's College   677
Shaw University   482

Spelman College   223
Stillman College   71
Talladega College   77
Texas College   641
Tougaloo College   392
Tuskegee University   86
Virginia Union University   689
Voorhees College   572
Wilberforce University   506
Wiley College   652
Xavier University of Louisiana   284

Appendix V
TWO-YEAR SCHOOLS

Bishop State Community College   35
Clinton Junior College   553
Coahoma Community College   357
Compton Community College   123
Cuyahoga Community College   501
Denmark Technical College   556
Highland Park Community College   337
Hinds Community College   362
J. F. Drake State Technical College   44
Kennedy-King College   240
LaGuardia Community College   413
Lawson State Community College   48
Lewis College of Business   341
Lomax-Hannon Junior College   53
Mary Holmes Community College   375
Medgar Evers College of the City University of New York   419
New York City Technical College   424
Roxbury Community College   329
Shorter College   106
Southern University (Shreveport)   280
Trenholm State Technical College   83
Wayne County Community College   345

Appendix VI
FOUR-YEAR SCHOOLS

Alabama A&M University   21
Alabama State University   28
Albany State College   169
Alcorn State University   351
Allen University   539
Arkansas Baptist College   97
Barber-Scotia College   431
Benedict College   543

Bennett College   437

Bethune-Cookman College   141

Bluefield State College   719

Bowie State University   293

Central State University   495

Cheyney University of Pennsylvania   523

Chicago State University   233

Claflin College   548

Clark Atlanta University   175

Concordia College   40

Coppin State College   299

Delaware State University   131

Dillard University   257

Edward Waters College   147

Elizabeth City State University   442

Fayetteville State University   448

Fisk University   579

Florida A&M University   152

Florida Memorial College   160

Fort Valley State College   181

Grambling State University   263

Hampton University   665

Harris-Stowe State College   399

Howard University   397

Huston-Tillotson College   615

Jackson State University   368

Jarvis Christian College   620

Johnson C. Smith University   454

Kentucky State University   247

Knoxville College   585

Lane College   589

Langston University   515

LeMoyne-Owen College   594

Lincoln University (MO)   404

Lincoln University of Pennsylvania   529

Livingstone College   459

Miles College   56

Mississippi Valley State University   380

Morehouse College   192

Morgan State University   306

Morris Brown College   204

Morris College   561

Norfolk State University   671

North Carolina A&T State University   465

North Carolina Central University   471

Oakwood College   61

Paine College   211

Paul Quinn College   626

Philander Smith College   100

Prairie View A&M University   630

Rust College   386

Saint Augustine's College   477

Saint Paul's College   677

Savannah State College   217

Selma University   67

Shaw University   482

Simmons University Bible College   254

Sojourner-Douglass College   314

South Carolina State University   566

Southern University and A&M University at
Baton Rouge   269

Southern University (New Orleans)   276

Southwestern Christian College   636

Spelman College   223

Stillman College   71

Talladega College   77

Tennessee State University   606

Texas College   641

Texas Southern University   645

Tougaloo College   392

Tuskegee University   86

University of Arkansas at Pine Bluff   110

University of the District of Columbia   709

University of Maryland, Eastern Shore   318

University of the Virgin Islands   659

Virginia Seminary and College   681

Virginia State University   683

Virginia Union University   689

Voorhees College   572

West Virginia State College   725

Wilberforce University   506

Wiley College   652

Winston-Salem State University   487

Xavier University of Louisiana   284

Appendix VII
PROFESSIONAL SCHOOLS

Charles R. Drew University of Medicine &
Science   119

Howard University School of Law   706

Interdenominational Theological Center   187

Meharry Medical College   600

Morehouse School of Medicine   198

Appendix VIII
HISTORICALLY BLACK COLLEGES AND UNIVERSITIES (HBCUs)

Two-Year Schools

Bishop State Community College 35
Clinton Junior College 553
Coahoma Community College 357
Hinds Community College 362
J. F. Drake State Technical College 44
Lawson State Community College 48
Lewis College of Business 341
Lomax-Hannon Junior College 53
Mary Holmes Community College 375
Shorter College 106
Southern University (Shreveport) 280
Trenholm State Technical College 83

Four-Year Schools

Alabama A&M University 21
Alabama State University 28
Albany State College 169
Alcorn State University 351
Allen University 539
Arkansas Baptist College 97
Barber-Scotia College 431
Benedict College 543
Bennett College 437
Bethune-Cookman College 141
Bluefield State College 719
Bowie State University 293
Central State University 495
Cheyney University of Pennsylvania 523
Claflin College 548
Clark Atlanta University 175
Concordia College 40
Coppin State College 299
Delaware State University 131
Denmark Technical College 556
Dillard University 257
Edward Waters College 147
Elizabeth City State University 442
Fayetteville State University 448
Fisk University 579
Florida A&M University 152
Florida Memorial College 160
Fort Valley State College 181
Grambling State University 263
Hampton University 665

Harris-Stowe State College 399
Howard University 397
Huston-Tillotson College 615
Jackson State University 368
Jarvis Christian College 620
Johnson C. Smith University 454
Kentucky State University 247
Knoxville College 585
Lane College 589
Langston University 515
LeMoyne-Owen College 594
Lincoln University (MO) 404
Lincoln University of Pennsylvania 529
Livingstone College 459
Miles College 56
Mississippi Valley State University 380
Morehouse College 192
Morgan State University 306
Morris Brown College 204
Morris College 561
Norfolk State University 671
North Carolina A&T State University 465
North Carolina Central University 471
Oakwood College 61
Paine College 211
Paul Quinn College 626
Philander Smith College 100
Prairie View A&M University 630
Rust College 386
Saint Augustine's College 477
Saint Paul's College 677
Savannah State College 217
Selma University 67
South Carolina State University 566
Southern University and A&M University at Baton Rouge 269
Southern University (New Orleans) 276
Southwestern Christian College 636
Spelman College 223
Stillman College 71
Talladega College 77
Tennessee State University 606
Texas College 641
Texas Southern University 645
Tougaloo College 392
Tuskegee University 86
University of Arkansas at Pine Bluff 110
University of the District of Columbia 709
University of Maryland Eastern Shore 318
University of the Virgin Islands 659

Virginia State University 683
Virginia Union University 689
Voorhees College 572
West Virginia State College 725
Wilberforce University 506
Wiley College 652
Winston-Salem State University 487
Xavier University of Louisiana 284

Professional Schools
Interdenominational Theological Center 187
Meharry Medical College 600
Morehouse School of Medicine 198

Appendix IX
THURGOOD MARSHALL SCHOLARSHIP FUND MEMBER SCHOOLS

Alabama A&M University 21
Alabama State University 28
Albany State College 169
Alcorn State University 351
Bowie State University* 293
Central State University 495
Cheyney University of Pennsylvania 523
Coppin State College 299
Delaware State University 131
Elizabeth City State University 442

Fayetteville State University 448
Florida A&M University 152
Fort Valley State College 181
Grambling State University 263
Jackson State University 368
Kentucky State University* 247
Langston University 515
Lincoln University (MO) 404
Lincoln University of Pennsylvania 529
Mississippi Valley State University 380
Morgan State University 306
Norfolk State University 671
North Carolina A&T State University 465
North Carolina Central University 471
Prairie View A&M University 630
Savannah State College 217
South Carolina State University* 566
Southern University system*
Tennessee State University 606
Texas Southern University 645
Tuskegee University 86
University of Arkansas at Pine Bluff 110
University of the District of Columbia 709
University of Maryland Eastern Shore 318
University of the Virgin Islands 659
Virginia State University 683
Winston-Salem State University 487

*recently gained university status

BIBLIOGRAPHY

Bacate, Clarence A. *The Story of Atlanta University*. Princeton, NJ: Princeton University Press, 1969. **(Clark Atlanta University)**

Biggers, John, Carrol Simms, and Edward Weems. *Black Art in Houston: The Texas Southern University Experience*. College Station, TX: Texas A&M University Press, 1978.

"Bill and Camille Cosby: first family of philanthropy: $20 million gift to Spelman is largest ever in history of Black institutions." *Ebony* 44 (May 1989): 25. **(Spelman College)**

"Bill Cosby, Paul Robeson Jr. highlight Central State's convocation for students." *Jet* 82 (September 21, 1992): 34-35. **(Central State University)**

Billingsley, Andrew, and Julia Elam. *Inside Black Colleges & Universities*. Chicago: Follett Press, 1987.

"Black college enrollment surges." *The Christian Science Monitor*, 20 July 1990, p. 13, col. 5.

"Black colleges at the crossroads." *Ebony* 47 (March 1992): 112.

"As black colleges grow more selective, some worry they are becoming elitist." *The Chronicle of Higher Education* 37 (July 3, 1991): A1.

"Black colleges should recruit and admit more white students." *Chronicle of Higher Education* 37 (March 13, 1991): A2. **(Howard University)**

"Black public colleges and universities: a review of institutional options." *Journal of Black Studies* 22 (June 1992): 494.

Bond, Horace Mann. *Education for Freedom*. Princeton, NJ: Princeton University Press, 1976.

Bryant, Ira B. *Texas Southern University*. Houston: Texas Southern University, 1975. **(Texas Southern University)**

Butler, Addie J. *The Distinctive Black Colleges: Talladega, Tuskegee, & Morehouse*. Metuchen, NJ: Scarecrow Press, Inc., 1977.

Campbell, Clarice, and Oscar Allen Rogers, Jr. *Mississippi: The View From Tougaloo*. Jackson: University Press of Mississippi, 1979. **(Tougaloo College)**

Carter, Wilmoth A. *Shaw's University*. Rockville, MD: D.C. National Publishing, Inc., 1973. **(Shaw University)**

"Central State University gets Paul Robeson's statue as gift from the Cosbys." *Jet* 79 (January 28, 1991): 35. **(Central State University)**

"The class of 1990; Central State grads say knowing where they came from has made them confident about their futures." *Ebony* 45 (August 1990): 76. (**Central State University**)

"Close to 100 percent of Grambling U. students now pass teacher-certification examination, up from 10 percent." *The Chronicle of Higher Education* (November 23, 1988): A23.

"A conversation with Spelman's 'sister president.'" *Black Enterprise* 19 (February 1989): 28. (**Spelman College**)

Conyers, Charline Fay Howard. *A History of Cheyney State Teachers College 1837-1951*. Ann Arbor, MI: University Microfilms International, 1975. (**Cheyney University**)

"Cosby's $20 million gift: a source of funds—and hope." *Black Enterprise* 19 (February 1989): 27. (**Spelman College**)

"Delta blues: Black universities. (Mississippi Valley State University and other Mississippi colleges)." *The Economist* 325 (December 12, 1992): A30. (**Mississippi Valley State University**)

"Division II." *Sports Illustrated* 73 (November 19, 1990): 4-10. (**Morehouse College**)

"Does decision to close black university in Miss. doom state-supported black colleges and universities?" *Jet* 83 (November 30, 1992): 14-17.

Educating Black Doctors: A History of Meharry Medical College. Tuscaloosa, AL: University of Alabama Press, 1983. (**Meharry Medical College**)

"1890 land-grant institutions: their struggle for survival and equality. (The 1890 Land-Grant Colleges: A Centennial View)." *Agricultural History* 65 (spring 1991): 3.

"1st in black degrees. (historically black colleges and universities)." *Black Enterprise* 23 (August 1992): 26.

"Fostering the black campus." *U.S. News & World Report* (November 21, 1988): 16.

"Frustration amidst hope: the land grant mission of Arkansas A&M College, 1873-1972." *Agricultural History* 65 (spring 1991): 115-16. (**Arkansas A&M College**)

"George Foreman makes gift of $100,000 to Texas Southern University." *Jet* 81 (December 2, 1991): 50. (**Texas Southern University**)

Gibbs, Warmoth T. *History of North Carolina Agricultural and Technical College*. Dubuque, Iowa: W. M. C. Brown Book Co., 1966. (**North Carolina A&T State University**)

Gibson, Delois. *A Historical Study of Philander Smith College 1877-1969*. Fayetteville: University of Arkansas, 1972. (**Philander Smith College**)

"A gift to black colleges (from The Links)." *Essence* 15 (November 1984): 62.

Goodwin, Robert K. "Roots and Wings." *Journal of Negro Education* 60 (spring 1991): 126-32.

Halliburton, C. D. *A History of Saint Augustine's College*. Raleigh: Broughton Press, 1937. (**St. Augustine's College**)

Hardin, John. *Onward and Upward, A Centennial History of Kentucky State University, 1866-1986*. Frankfort: Kentucky State University, 1987. (**Kentucky State University**)

Harlon, John. *A History of West Virginia State College*. Dubuque, IA: William C. Brown, 1968. (**West Virginia State College**)

Harris, Ruth M. *Stowe Teachers College and Her Predecessors*. Boston: Christopher Publishing House, 1967. (**Harris-Stowe State College**)

A History of North Carolina College for Negroes. Durham: Duke University Press, 1941. (**North Carolina Central University**)

Hoffman, Carl. "Historic Rust College: Fulfilling a mission." *Appalachia* 22 (summer 1989): 16-21.

"Howard U. to raise admissions standards and close some departments." *The Chronicle of Higher Education* 37 (March 13, 1991): A2. (**Howard University**)

"Howard U. a year after a tense campus sit-in, awaits the arrival of a new president who faces myriad tough, unresolved issues." *The Chronicle of Higher Education* 36 (March 7, 1990): A13. (**Howard University**)

"In tight economy, Tougaloo shows how black institutions can use strategic planning to aid their special missions." *The Chronicle of Higher Education* 38 (October 2, 1991): A1. (**Tougaloo College**)

"Jackson State captures black college golf title, SC State's Roache repeats (National Minority Golf Champion)." *Jet* 82 (June 15, 1992): 47. (**Jackson State University**)

Jones, Edward A. *A Candle in the Dark*. Valley Forge, PA: Judson Press, 1967. (**Morehouse College**)

Jones, Maxine D., and Joe M. Richardson. *Talladega College: The First Century*. Tuscaloosa, AL: University of Alabama Press, 1990.

Jones, Mildred P. *Fayetteville State College*. Fayetteville: Fayetteville State College Print Shop, 1969. (**Fayetteville State University**)

Kearney, Edmund, and E. Maryland Moore. *A History of Chicago State University 1867-1979*. Chicago: Chicago State University, 1979. (**Chicago State University**)

"Lincoln U. controls an art collection worth $1-billion; wealthy collector gave university the right to appoint new trustees." *The Chronicle of Higher Education* 36 (February 14, 1990): A27. (**Lincoln University**)

Logan, Rayford W. *Howard University: The First Hundred Years 1867-1967*. Washington, DC: Howard University Press, 1969. (**Howard University**)

McCulloch, Margaret C. *Fearless Advocate of the Right*. Boston: The Christopher Publishing House, 1941. (**LeMoyne-Owen College**)

McGinnis, Frederick. *A History and an Interpretation of Wilberforce University*. Blanchester, OH: Brown Publishing Co., 1941. (**Wilberforce University**)

"Many black colleges report an increase in admissions this spring: some are up 20 percent or more." *The Chronicle of Higher Education* (July 27, 1988): A20.

"Meharry gets $2.8 million to treat drug-using moms." *Jet* 79 (November 5, 1990): 28. (**Meharry Medical College**)

"Morehouse College renews commitment on 125th anniversary." *Ebony* 47 (June 1992): 26. (**Morehouse College**)

"NASA awards $1/2 million research grants to seven black U.S. universities." *Jet* 81 (March 2, 1992): 21.

Neufeld, Don, ed., *Seventh-day Adventist Encyclopedia*. Washington, DC: Review and Herald, 1976. (**Oakwood College**)

Patterson, Zella J. Black. *Langston University: A History*. Norman, OK: University of Oklahoma Press, 1979. (**Langston University**)

"Paul Quinn College defies odds as it takes over defunct campus (historically black institutions in Dallas, Texas)." *The Chronicle of Higher Education* 37 (May 8, 1991): A3. (**Paul Quinn College**)

Peabody, Francis G. *Education for Life: The Story of Hampton Institute*. Garden City, NY: Doubleday, Page and Co., 1919. (**Hampton University**)

"A postlude to a renaissance." *The Southern Review* 26 (Autumn 1990): 746. (**Fisk University**)

Potts, John F. *The History of South Carolina State College*. Columbia: SC: R. L. Bryant Co., 1978. (**South Carolina State University**)

Read, Florence Matilda. *The Story of Spelman College*. Princeton, NJ: Princeton University Press, 1961. (**Spelman College**)

"Recruits at HBCU's (historically black colleges and universities)." *Black Enterprise* 23 (October 1992): 29.

Rhodes, Lelia Gaston. *Jackson State University: The First Hundred Years 1877-1977*. Jackson: University Press of Mississippi, 1979. (**Jackson State University**)

Richardson, Joe M. *A History of Fisk University 1865-1946*. Tuscaloosa, AL: University of Alabama Press, 1980. (**Fisk University**)

Roman, Charles V. *Meharry Medical College*. 1934. Reprint. Freeport, NY: Books for Libraries Press, 1972.

Roscoe, Wilma J. *Accreditation of Historically & Predominantly Black Colleges & Universities*. Lanham, MD: University Press of America, 1989.

Russell, James Solomon. *Adventures in Faith*. New York: Morehouse Publishers, 1936. (**Saint Paul's College**)

"Selma University gets full academic accreditation." *Jet* 81 (January 13, 1992): 22. **(Selma University)**

"17 colleges get U.S. help." *The New York Times* 142 (October 28, 1992): A16.

Sewell, George. *Morris Brown College: The First One Hundred Years*. Christian, Mass.: Christian Brothers Press, 1981. **(Morris Brown College)**

"Sharp tensions accompany new role for historically black Bowie State U." *The Chronicle of Higher Education* 37 (November 28, 1990): 23. **(Bowie State University)**

"South Carolina State College: a legacy of education and public service." *Agricultural History* 65 (spring 1991): 131. **(South Carolina State College)**

"Spelman receives $37 million, largest gift to a black college." *Jet* 82 (May 25, 1992): 22-23. **(Spelman College)**

"Students at Morgan State end protest over campus conditions." *The Chronicle of Higher Education* 36 (March 28, 1990): B1.

"The Supreme Court must act to preserve and strengthen historically black colleges." *The Chronicle of Higher Education* 38 (October 16, 1991): A60.

"A surge in UNCF enrollments (United Negro College Fund statistics on African American college students)." *Black Enterprise* 22 (July 1992): 45.

Taylor, Clifford. "Jarvis Christian College: Its History and Present Standing in Relationship to the Standards of the Texas State Department of Education and the Southern Association of Colleges and Secondary School." Ph.D. diss., Texas Christian University, 1945. **(Jarvis Christian College)**

"$10 million for Shaw University." *Ebony* (October 1992): 106+. **(Shaw University)**

"Texas Southern gets funds, earmarked for black males." *Jet* 83 (November 2, 1992): 8. **(Texas Southern University)**

"Thanks 10 million (attorney W. Gary makes contribution to Shaw University)." *People Weekly* 37 (April 13, 1992): 65. **(Shaw University)**

Thompson, Daniel C. *A Black Elite: A Profile of Graduates of UNCF Colleges*. Westport, CT: Greenwood Publishing Group, Inc., 1986.

———. *Private Black Colleges at the Crossroads*. Westport, CT: Greenwood Publishing Group, Inc., 1973.

"The Traditionally Black Institutions of Higher Education, 1860 to 1982." *National Center for Education Statistics*. 1984: 132.

Tucker, Samuel J. *Phoenix From the Ashes*. Jacksonville, FL: Convention Press, 1976. **(Edward Waters College)**

"Turning to black colleges," *The Washington Post*, 4 May 1989, p. D3, col 4.

"The Tuskegee Movable School: a unique contribution to national and international agriculture and rural development (The 1890 Land-Grant Colleges: A Centennial View)." *Agricultural History* 65 (spring 1991): 85. **(Tuskegee Institute)**

"USDA scholarship fund gives colleges $2.8 mil. (historically black land grant colleges)." *Jet* 83 (November 23, 1992): 23.

Washington, Booker T. *Up From Slavery*. Rev. ed. New York: Airmont, Inc., 1967. **(Tuskegee University)**

Wells, Jula E. *A History of Morris College*. Sumter: Morris College, 1979. **(Morris College)**

Wilson, Reginald. "Can Black colleges solve the problem of access for Black students?" *American Journal of Education* 98 (August 1990): 443-57.

PHOTO CREDITS

ALABAMA

Alabama Agricultural and Mechanical University. Courtesy Alabama Agricultural and Mechanical University.

Bishop State Community College. Courtesy Bishop State Community College.

Miles College. Courtesy Miles College.

Oakwood College. Courtesy Oakwood College.

Stillman College. Courtesy Stillman College.

Talladega College. Courtesy United Negro College Fund.

Tuskegee University. Courtesy United Negro College Fund.

ARKANSAS

Philander Smith College. Courtesy Philander Smith College.

University of Arkansas at Pine Bluff. Courtesy University of Arkansas at Pine Bluff.

DELAWARE

Delaware State University. Courtesy Delaware State University.

FLORIDA

Bethune-Cookman College. Courtesy Bethune-Cookman College.

Florida Agricultural and Mechanical University. Courtesy Office of Public Black Colleges and Universities.

Florida Memorial College. Courtesy United Negro College Fund.

GEORGIA

Albany State College. Courtesy Albany State College.

Interdenominational Theological Center. Courtesy United Negro College Fund.

Morehouse College. Courtesy Morehouse College.

Morris Brown College. Courtesy Morris Brown College.

Paine College. Courtesy Paine College.

Savannah State College. Courtesy Savannah State College.

Spelman College. Courtesy United Negro College Fund.

Spelman College. Courtesy Spelman College.

ILLINOIS
Chicago State University. Courtesy Chicago State University.

KENTUCKY
Kentucky State University. Courtesy Kentucky State University.

LOUISIANA
Dillard University. Courtesy United Negro College Fund.

Southern University and Agricultural and Mechanical University at Baton Rouge. Courtesy Southern University and Agricultural and Mechanical University at Baton Rouge.

Southern University (New Orleans). Courtesy Southern University.

MARYLAND
Bowie State University. Courtesy Bowie State University.

University of Maryland Eastern Shore. Courtesy of University of Maryland Eastern Shore.

MICHIGAN
Highland Park Community College. Courtesy Kelle Sisung and Peg Bessette.

Lewis College of Business. Courtesy Kelle Sisung and Peg Bessette.

Wayne County Community College. Courtesy Kelle Sisung and Peg Bessette.

MISSISSIPPI
Alcorn State University. Courtesy Office of Public Black Colleges and Universities.

Jackson State University. Courtesy Jackson State University.

Mississippi Valley State University. Courtesy Mississippi Valley State University.

Rust College. Courtesy Rust College.

Tougaloo College. Courtesy United Negro College Fund.

MISSOURI
Harris-Stowe State College. Courtesy Harris-Stowe State College.

Lincoln University (MO). Courtesy Lincoln University (MO).

NEW YORK
LaGuardia Community College. Courtesy LaGuardia Community College.

NORTH CAROLINA
Barber-Scotia College. Courtesy Barber-Scotia College.

Bennett College. Courtesy Bennett College.

Elizabeth City State University. Courtesy Elizabeth City State University.

Livingstone College. Courtesy Livingstone College.

Livingstone College. Courtesy United Negro College Fund.

North Carolina Agricultural and Technical State University. Courtesy North Carolina Agricultural and Technical State.

North Carolina Central University. Courtesy North Carolina Central University.

Saint Augustine's College. Courtesy Saint Augustine's College.

Winston-Salem State University. Courtesy Winston-Salem State University.

OHIO
Central State University. Courtesy Central State University.

Wilberforce University. Courtesy Wilberforce University.

OKLAHOMA

Langston University. Courtesy Langston University.

PENNSYLVANIA

Lincoln University of Pennsylvania. Courtesy Lincoln University of Pennsylvania.

SOUTH CAROLINA

Benedict College. Courtesy United Negro College Fund.

Claflin College. Courtesy Claflin College.

Denmark Technical College. Courtesy Denmark Technical College.

Morris College. Courtesy United Negro College Fund.

South Carolina State University. Courtesy Office of Public Black Colleges and Universities.

Voorhees College. Courtesy United Negro College Fund.

TENNESSEE

Fisk University. Courtesy United Negro College Fund.

Fisk University. Courtesy Fisk University.

Knoxville College. Courtesy Knoxville College.

Lane College. Courtesy United Negro College Fund.

LeMoyne-Owen College. Courtesy LeMoyne-Owen College.

Meharry Medical College. Courtesy Meharry Medical College.

Tennessee State University. Courtesy Tennessee State University.

TEXAS

Huston-Tillotson College. Courtesy Huston-Tillotson College.

Jarvis Christian College. Courtesy Jarvis Christian College.

Prairie View Agricultural and Mechanical University. Courtesy Office of Black Public Colleges and Universities.

Texas College. Courtesy United Negro College Fund.

Wiley College. Courtesy United Negro College Fund.

VIRGINIA

Norfolk State University. Courtesy Norfolk State University.

Virginia Union University. Courtesy United Negro College Fund.

WASHINGTON, DISTRICT OF COLUMBIA

Howard University. Courtesy Howard University.

WEST VIRGINIA

West Virginia State College. Courtesy West Virginia State College.

COMMON ABBREVIATIONS AND DEFINITIONS

A.A. — (Associate in Arts)

A.A.S. — (Associate in Applied Science)

accelerated study program — Student completes an undergraduate degree in a shorter period of time than the traditional four-year period.

accreditation — Approval of the academic standing of a college or university by an impartial accrediting body.

ACT — *See* **American College Testing Program.**

adult or continuing education program — Non-degree or degree programs designed for adults or nontraditional students working full time and returning to school.

Advanced Placement (AP) examinations — Standardized subject area tests available nationally to high school students from the College Entrance Examination Board. Students scoring 3 on the AP test will receive college credit by examination for each course and advanced placement.

American College Testing Program (ACT) — Organizing body that issues the ACT examination used for college admission.

application deadline — Date by which all documents required for the prospective student's admission must be received by the admissions office.

associate's degree — A full-time, two-year degree program that requires 60 to 68 credit hours and completion of major and general education or core requirements. Associate's degrees prepare students for careers at the end of two years of study or prepare students for transfer to a bachelor's degree program at a four-year college or university.

B.A. — (Bachelor of Arts)

bachelor's degree — A full-time, four-year degree program that requires 120 to 128 credit hours and completion of major and general education or core requirements.

B.S. — (Bachelor of Science)

CEEB — (College Entrance Examination Board)

CIAA — (Central Intercollegiate Athletic Association)

CLAST — *See* **College Level Academic Skills Test.**

CLEP — *See* **College Level Examination Program.**

College Level Academic Skills Test (CLAST) — Measures achievement of communication and computation skills that are expected of all students by the time they complete their sophomore year in college.

College Level Examination Program (CLEP) — Standardized subject area test available nationally to students based on nontraditional learning experiences such as on-the-job training or military experience. Students passing test receive college credit by examination.

college prep curriculum — Includes the following high school units: 4 English; 3 mathematics, including Algebra I & II; 3 social sciences, including two units of history; 3 science; and 2 foreign language.

college work study — A federally funded program that provides employment to students with financial need. Students are usually employed by the college or university.

cooperative education program — Integrates classroom learning with alternating or combined periods of paid practical work experience. During alternating periods student works one semester and attends classes one semester. During parallel or combined periods student works half time (approximately 20 hours) and attends school half time. The program provides academic credit and full-time status during co-op placement.

cooperative program — Allows students to take college credit from cooperating institutions other than their own toward their degree programs.

core requirements — *See* **general education requirements.**

CSS — (College Scholarship Service)

DANTES — (Defense Activity for Nontraditional Education Support Program)

deferred payment plan — Students pay college costs in two or three installments during the semester.

early admissions — Gifted high school students enroll full- or part-time for college credit during their senior year in high school. Parental consent may be required.

Ed.D. — (Doctor of Education)

Ed.S. — (Educational Specialist)

EIAC — (Eastern Intercollegiate Athletic Conference)

ESL — *See* **english as a second language.**

english as a second language — Program that offers courses in English to students whose native language is not English.

ETS — (Educational Testing Service)

FAF — (Financial Aid Form)

FAFSA — (Free Application for Federal Student Aid)

field experience — A short-term placement of a student in an appropriate learning setting for the purpose of observation and limited participation.

full-time student — Student taking 12 or more credit hours of college courses.

GCE — *See* **General Certificate of Education.**

GED — (General Education Diploma)

General Certificate of Education (GCE) — A certificate of educational attainment equivalent to a U.S. high school diploma used in countries such as England, Wales, and Canada, as well as some African countries.

general education requirements — A common core of courses that all students must study to receive a bachelor's or associate's degree.

GMAT — (Graduate Management Admissions Test)

GPA — (Grade Point Average)

grants — Gift aid money that students do not repay; usually grants are based on financial need.

GRE — (Graduate Record Examination)

honors program — Academically talented students take a challenging program of study that includes special classes, seminars, colloquia, cultural activities, and special recognition to motivate participants.

individualized majors — Students create their own major program(s) of study.

installment plan — Students pay college costs in agreed-upon installments, usually at a cost.

internship — A supervised work experience in which the student works — under both external professional supervision and college supervision — for a specified number of hours and has a set of objectives to accomplish.

Job Training Partnership Act (JTPA) — A federally funded program designed to give the economically disadvantaged and the long-term unemployed an opportunity to train in a two-year college program in areas that look promising for job placement following completion of the program. JTPA program pays for tuition, fees, and books. Participants are eligible for the Pell Grant and work study. Contact your local state employment services office for more information.

JTPA — *See* **Job Training Partnership Act.**

land-grant institution — State-supported colleges and universities established under the Second Morrill Act of 1890 to promote the study of the agricultural sciences. Most land-grant schools also offer a wide range of non-agricultural subjects.

low-interest loans — Borrowed money that students repay, usually after college. Short-term, low-interest loans must be repaid within the specified loan period, usually six months to a year.

LSAT — (Law School Admission Test)

M.A. — (Master of Art)

major — A sequence of courses taken to give a student an appreciable knowledge and skill in a chosen field. All students are required to complete a major course of study to graduate.

MARC — (Minority Access to Research Centers)

MCAT — (Medical College Admission Test)

MECA — (Mid-Eastern Athletic Conference)

M.Ed. — (Master of Education)

MHSSRA — (Minority High School Research Apprentice)

minor — A sequence of courses taken to give a student some knowledge and skill in a chosen field. A student may elect to complete a minor course of study in addition to the required major.

M.S. — (Master of Science)

MSACS — (Middle States Association of Colleges and Schools)

MSIP — (Minority Science Improvement Program)

NAFEO — (National Association for Equal Opportunity in Higher Education)

NAIA — (National Athletic Intercollegiate Association)

NCAA — (National Collegiate Athletic Association)

NCHS — (National Center for Health Statistics)

NJCAA — (National Junior College Athletic Association)

NTE — (National Teacher Examination)

off-campus study — Students take courses at other institutions for credit.

open admissions — A policy of admitting students to a college regardless of whether the students have the normal entry qualifications. Open admission students must take developmental courses to come up to admission standards.

orientation — A series of meetings designed to acquaint new students with facilities, policies, sources of information and assistance, and the academic and social atmosphere of the campus.

Parent Loans for Undergraduate Students (PLUS) — A loan program for parents to borrow funds to pay educational cost for their children. Repayment of principal and interest begins within 60 days of receipt of the loan.

part-time degree program — Students earn an undergraduate degree while attending college part time.

part-time student — Student taking fewer than 12 credit hours of college courses.

Pell Grants — A federal program that provides grants to college students who demonstrate financial need. Pell Grants do not have to be repaid.

Perkins Loans — A federal loan program for students attending college full time. Repayment of loan begins nine months after student ceases enrollment in college (formerly, National Direct Student Loan).

Ph.D. — (Doctor of Philosophy)

PLUS — (Parent Loans for Undergraduate Students)

pre-professional program — A preparatory curriculum for students who want to pursue a career in professions such as dentistry, engineering, law, medicine, pharmacy, or veterinary medicine.

remedial courses — Classes offered to entering students to bring them up to admissions standards and to help them adjust for success in college.

Reserve Officers' Training Corps (ROTC) — Provides training in military science for commission as a second lieutenant in the U.S. Armed Forces. Two- and four-year scholarships are available.

rolling admissions — High school students may apply to college after completion of their junior year in high school and completion of college entrance requirements. Students are notified of the admission decision when application is completed.

room and board — Cost for room rental and meals in residence hall.

ROTC — *See* **Reserve Officers' Training Corps.**

SAT — *See* **Scholastic Aptitude Test.**

scholarship — Gift aid based on academic merit or talent in a specific area, with some programs also having financial need as a requirement.

Scholarship Aptitude Test (SAT) — Standardized examination used for college admission.

semester — A four-month or sixteen-week period of study at a college or university.

semester hour — A unit of credit in colleges and universities.

SEOG *See* **Supplemental Educational Opportunity Grant.**

SGA — (Student Government Association)

SIAC — (Southern Intercollegiate Athletic Conference)

SSIG — *See* **State Student Incentive Grant.**

Stafford Loan — A bank or other lending institution loan guaranteed by the federal government. Borrowers pay an origination fee and an insurance premium. Repayment begins when student ceases enrollment in college (formerly Guaranteed Student Loan Program [GSL]).

STAP — (Supplemental Tuition Assistance Program [New York])

State Student Incentive Grants (SSIG) — Grants available to students who are residents of a particular state. Grants are base on financial need; some may be based on merit.

student support services — Provides developmental courses, counseling, and cultural activities to students who need aid to succeed in college.

study abroad program — Allows students to study in a foreign country for a specified period of time for part of their college education.

Supplemental Educational Opportunity Grant (SEOG) — A federal program that provides grants to students who demonstrate exceptional financial need via the Financial Aid Form and the Pell Grant. Students do not repay these grants.

talent search — A program that assists at-risk high school students from targeted areas in completing high school and continuing on to college.

Test of English as a Foreign Language (TOEFL) — An internationally administered examination that measures the ability to use the English language for students whose native language is not English. Contact the Test of English as a Foreign Language, Educational Testing Services, Princeton, NJ 18540.

TOEFL — *See* **Test of English as a Foreign Language.**

tuition — Fees for college courses taken.

tuition waiver — Fees for college courses are not charged to the student.

Upward Bound Program — Precollegiate program that provides developmental courses to high school students in grades 10, 11, and 12 who are disadvantaged and are in pursuit of a college education.

VVTA — (Vietnam Veteran Tuition Assistance)

SCHOOL PROFILES INDEX

A

Alabama Agricultural & Mechanical University   21
Alabama State University   28
Albany State College   169
Alcorn State University   351
Allen University   539
Arkansas Baptist College   97

B

Barber-Scotia College   431
Benedict College   543
Bennett College   437
Bethune-Cookman College   141
Bishop State Community College   35
Bluefield State College   719
Bowie State University   293

C

Central State University   495
Charles R. Drew University of Medicine and Science   119
Cheyney University of Pennsylvania   523
Chicago State University   233
Claflin College   548
Clark Atlanta University   175
Clinton Junior College   553
Coahoma Community College   357
Compton Community College   123
Concordia College   40
Coppin State College   299
Cuyahoga Community College   501

D

Delaware State University   131
Denmark Technical College   556
Dillard University   257

E

Edward Waters College   147
Elizabeth City State University   442

F

Fayetteville State University 448
Fisk University 579
Florida Agricultural & Mechanical University 152
Florida Memorial College 160
Fort Valley State College 181

G

Grambling State University 263

H

Hampton University 665
Harris-Stowe State College 399
Highland Park Community College 337
Hinds Community College 362
Howard University 697
Howard University School of Law 706
Huston-Tillotson College 615

I

Interdenominational Theological Center 187

J

Jackson State University 368
Jarvis Christian College 620
J. F. Drake State Technical College 44
Johnson C. Smith University 454

K

Kennedy-King College 240
Kentucky State University 247
Knoxville College 585

L

LaGuardia Community College 413
Lane College 589
Langston University 515
Lawson State Community College 48
LeMoyne-Owen College 594
Lewis College of Business 341
Lincoln University (MO) 404
Lincoln University of Pennsylvania 529
Livingstone College 459
Lomax-Hannon Junior College 53

M

Mary Holmes College 375
Medgar Evers College of the City University of New York 419
Meharry Medical College 600
Miles College 56
Mississippi Valley State University 380
Morehouse College 192
Morehouse School of Medicine 198
Morgan State University 306
Morris Brown College 204
Morris College 561

N

New York City Technical College 424
Norfolk State University 671
North Carolina Agricultural & Technical State University 465
North Carolina Central University 471

O

Oakwood College 61

P

Paine College 211
Paul Quinn College 626
Philander Smith College 100
Prairie View Agricultural and Mechanical University 630

R

Roxbury Community College 329
Rust College 386

S

Saint Augustine's College 477
Saint Paul's College 677
Savannah State College 217
Selma University 67
Shaw University 482
Shorter College 106
Simmons University Bible College 254
Sojourner-Douglass College 314
South Carolina State University 566
Southern University and Agricultural & Mechanical University at Baton Rouge 269
Southern University (New Orleans) 276
Southern University (Shreveport) 280
Southwestern Christian College 636

Spelman College   223
Stillman College   71

T

Talladega College   77
Tennessee State University   606
Texas College   641
Texas Southern University   645
Tougaloo College   392
Trenholm State Technical College   83
Tuskegee University   86

U

University of Arkansas at Pine Bluff   110
University of the District of Columbia   709
University of Maryland Eastern Shore   318
University of the Virgin Islands   659

V

Virginia Seminary and College   681
Virginia State University   683
Virginia Union University   689
Voorhees College   572

W

Wayne County Community College   345
West Virginia State College   725
Wilberforce University   506
Wiley College   652
Winston-Salem State University   487

X

Xavier University of Louisiana   284

MASTER INDEX

A

Aaron Douglas Gallery of African-American Art 583
Abraham Baldwin Agricultural College 173
Accelerated Degree Program 157, 238, 597, 610
Accelerated Study Program 32, 59, 80, 99, 126, 135, 179, 215,
   227, 355, 384, 402, 408, 440, 451, 457, 469, 490, 519, 534, 541,
   551, 569, 649, 668, 713, 722, 729
Accreditation Board of Engineering and Technology 22, 87, 153,
   182, 270, 319, 466, 567, 607, 698, 710, 719, 726
Accrediting Commission of the State of Mississippi 357
Accrediting Commission on Education for Health Services
   Administration 698
Accrediting Council for Graduate Medical Education 199
Accrediting Council on Education in Journalism and Mass
   Communications 153, 369
Active Islamic Association 274
Adams, Charles P. 263
Adams, Lewis 86
Adlerian Institute 294
Adult/Continuing Education Programs 85, 91, 99, 108, 114, 135,
   157, 126, 179, 184, 227, 238, 243, 288, 303, 311, 316, 339, 343,
   378, 408, 417, 422, 427, 440, 451, 480, 491, 527, 554, 546, 569,
   575, 610, 668, 675, 679, 703, 713, 722
Adult Education Program 38, 59, 80, 103, 273, 323, 469, 475, 597,
   649, 730
Adult Learning Center 504
Advanced Placement (AP) 26, 32, 64, 75, 80, 91, 103, 108, 135,
   150, 157, 163, 173, 179, 196, 208, 215, 220, 227, 238, 252, 260,
   266, 273, 278, 288, 302, 311, 316, 323, 348, 355, 366, 372, 378,
   384, 395, 408, 417, 422, 427, 435, 440, 446, 451, 457, 462, 469,
   475, 491, 499, 504, 519, 527, 534, 546, 551, 570, 575, 592, 597,
   610, 628, 639, 649, 661, 668, 675, 679, 686, 703, 722, 730
Advanced Scholars Program 686
Adventist College Abroad (ACA) 65
Adventist Youth Society 66
African American Collection
  Paine College 215
  Savannah State College 221
  Wiley College 655
African Art and Artifacts Collection
   Lincoln University (PA) 535
African Heritage Center 466, 470
African History Collection (Langston University) 520
African Methodist Episcopal (AME) Church 53, 106, 147, 204,
   459, 506, 539, 626
African-American Women's Collection 441
Afro-American Collection (Southern Univ. at New Orleans) 279
Afro-American History Month 403
Afro-American Museum and Cultural Center 496

Agricultural and Mechanical College in Baton Rouge 277

Agricultural and Mechanical College of Texas for Colored Youth 630

Agricultural and Technical College of North Carolina 466

Aid Association for Lutherans 41

Air Force ROTC 29, 51, 57, 59, 75, 88, 142, 154, 177, 193, 206, 224, 241, 248, 259, 264, 271, 277, 281, 384, 400, 402, 449, 451, 455, 457, 466, 469, 472, 475, 483, 485, 502, 531, 534, 567, 568, 583, 586, 588, 595, 598, 607, 699

Airway Science, pre-professional 150

Alabama Agricultural and Mechanical College 22

Alabama Baptist Normal 67

Alabama Board of Nursing 36

Alabama Colored Peoples University 28

Alabama Department of Education 40

Alabama Junior College Conference 42

Alabama Lutheran Academy and College 40

Alabama National Guard Educational Assistance Program 45

Alabama State College 28

Alabama State College Branch (Mobile Center) 35

Alabama State College for Negroes 28

Alabama State Department of Education 22, 29, 40, 48, 53, 57, 72

Alabama State Department of Postsecondary Education 44

Alabama State Missionary Baptist Convention 67

Alabama State University 28

Albany Bible and Manual Training Institute 169

Albany State College 169

Alcorn A&M College of the State of Mississippi 351

Alcorn State University 351

All American Bowl 76

Allen, Debbie 698

Allen, Richard 539

Allen University 539

Allied health program, cooperative 527

Alpha Chi 137, 403, 547, 576, 723

Alpha Kappa Alpha 27, 33, 60, 76, 82, 92, 105, 115, 137, 145, 158, 165, 174, 180, 185, 216, 222, 228, 239, 261, 267, 274, 297, 304, 312, 324, 356, 374, 391, 409, 436, 441, 453, 458, 464, 470, 476, 492, 500, 510, 520, 528, 535, 542, 547, 552, 571, 576, 584, 593, 598, 605, 611, 619, 635, 650, 656, 669, 688, 694, 705, 714, 731

Alpha Kappa Alpha Sorority (1908) 698
  national headquarters 239

Alpha Kappa Mu 60, 76, 105, 137, 174, 216, 222, 304, 436, 464, 547, 552, 576, 593, 619, 644, 656, 731

Alpha Phi Alpha 27, 33, 60, 76, 82, 92, 105, 115, 137, 145, 158, 164, 174, 180, 185, 197, 216, 221, 239, 261, 267, 274, 297, 304, 312, 324, 356, 374, 391, 409, 436, 453, 458, 470, 476,

486, 492, 500, 510, 520, 528, 535, 542, 547, 552, 571, 576, 584, 593, 598, 605, 611, 619, 635, 650, 656, 669, 687, 694, 705, 723, 731

Alpha Phi Alpha Fraternity national headquarters 239

Alpha Phi Sigma 174

Alpha Sigma Mu, veterans' fraternity 174

AME Church Collection 628

AME Zion ministers 459

American Assembly of Collegiate Schools of Business 405, 466, 672, 698

American Association of College Athletic Directors 539

American Association of Colleges for Teacher Education 153, 539

American Association of Colleges of Nursing 153

American Association of Colleges of Pharmacy 153

American Association of Higher Education 153

American Association of Medical Colleges 601

American Baptist Church of the USA 689

American Baptist Home Mission Society 368

American Bar Association 270, 472, 645, 698, 706

American Board of Funeral Service Education, Inc. 36, 710

American Chemical Society 132, 270, 369, 466, 530, 580, 645, 698, 710, 726

American Church Institute 181

American Corrective Therapy Association 672

American Council for Construction Education 319

American Council on Education 72

American Council on Education for Journalism and Mass Communications 698

American Council on Pharmaceutical Education 284, 645, 698

American Dental Association 83, 346
  Committee on Dental Accreditation 501

American Dietetic Association 234, 248, 270, 319, 438, 516, 523, 567, 607, 645, 672, 683, 698

American Home Economics Association 22, 111, 182

American Indian Student Legislative Grant (AISLG) 449, 472

American Institute of Goat Research 516

American Library Association 22, 120, 176, 248, 472

American Medical Association 83, 87, 530, 549, 698
  Committee on Allied Health Education 142, 307, 501, 698, 710

American Medical Records Association 672

American Missionary Association 175, 594

American Occupational Therapy Association 698
  Accreditation Committee 502

American Physical Therapy Association 319, 699

American Planning Association 22

American Psychological Association 672, 699

American Society of Hospital Pharmacists 699

American Speech-Language-Hearing Association 607, 666, 699, 710

American Veterinary Medical Association 87, 182

Amistad Mural 78

Arkansas Agricultural, Mechanical and Normal College 110

Arkansas Baptist College 97

Arkansas Baptist Consolidated Convention 97

Arkansas State Department of Education 101

Armed Forces Teacher Education for Retirees Program (AFTER) 546

Armstrong State College 218

Army ROTC 23, 29, 36, 57, 59, 72, 75, 78, 81, 88, 101, 104, 111, 142, 154, 177, 182, 193, 212, 215, 218, 224, 248, 259, 264, 277, 307, 311, 320, 352, 369, 384, 387, 390, 400, 402, 405, 443, 446, 455, 457, 460, 462, 466, 469, 472, 475, 483, 485, 517, 562, 567, 583, 586, 588, 595, 598, 607, 616, 618, 632, 646, 650, 673, 691, 699, 710, 726

Arnett-Coppin & Payne Afro-American History Collection 510

Art and Architecture Library Collection (Southern Univ. at Baton Rouge) 274

Art scholarships 36, 161, 234, 249, 370, 406, 443, 489, 549, 642, 699, 727

Ashmun Institute 529

Association for Intercollegiate Athletics for Women (AIAW) 528

Association of American Law Schools 699, 706

Association of American Medical Colleges (Liaison Committee on Medical Education) 699

Association of Collegiate Schools of Planning 710

Association of Research Libraries 699

Association of Texas Colleges and Universities 653

Association of Theological Schools in the United States and Canada 188, 690, 699

Athletic Grants-in-Aid 57, 205, 212, 381, 586, 673

Athletic scholarships 23, 29, 36, 41, 49, 68, 78, 88, 101, 107, 111, 123, 132, 154, 161, 170, 176, 182, 193, 234, 249, 258, 264, 271, 285, 307, 320, 352, 358, 363, 376, 400, 405, 420, 432, 443, 449, 455, 466, 472, 478, 483, 488, 524, 544, 549, 568, 580, 595, 607, 637, 642, 646, 653, 666, 678, 699, 710, 720, 726

Atlanta Baptist College 192

Atlanta Baptist Female Academy 223

Atlanta Baptist Seminary 192

Atlanta University 175

Atlanta University Center 175, 188, 192, 202, 224

Augusta Institute 192

B

Bainbridge College 173

Baker Bible Institute 548

Baltimore Association for the Moral and Educational Improvement of Colored People 293

Baltimore Normal School 293

Band scholarships 36, 41, 206, 271, 443, 473, 727

Baptist Church 160, 223, 482, 543

Baptist Institute 97

Baptist Student Union 216

Barbara Jordan Archives 650

Barber-Scotia College 431

Barber Memorial College 431

Beckley, President David L. 653

Becton, Julius W., Jr. 631

Belgian Friendship Building (national historic landmark) 689

BellSouth Foundation 72

Benedict College 543

Bennett College 437

Bernard Fall's Southeast Asian Collection 704

Beta Beta Beta 222

Beta Kappa Chi 105, 222, 436, 464, 593, 619, 656

Bethel University 106

Bethune, Mary McLeod 141, 431

Bethune-Cookman College 141, 431

Bible & Religious Education Special Collection 639

Biddle Memorial Hall 454

Biddle Memorial Institute 454

Biddle University 454

Big Brother/Big Sister mentoring program 595

Biomedical Society 222

Birthright Furniture Collection 75

Bishop Edward J. Pendergrass Collection 391

Bishop State Community College 35

"Black Blues Collection" 391

Black Executive Exchange Program (BEEP) 103

Black Heritage Collection (Southern Univ. at Baton Rouge) 274

Black History Collection (Tougaloo College) 396

Black History Month 104

Black Law Student Association 708

Black newspapers 520

Black settlers 515

Black studies collection
  Livingstone College 463
  North Carolina A&T State Univ. 470
  Talladega College 81

Bluefield Colored Institute 719

Bluefield State College 719

Bolton C. Price Collection 373

Bond, Dr. Horace Mann 529

Booker City 56

Booker T. Washington Collection and Archives 92

Boston Business School 329

Bowie State University 291

Branch Normal College 110

Brown Theological Institute 147

Brown Theological Institution 147

Brown University 147

Brown vs. Board of Education 726
Bureau of Indian Affairs 517
Bush, President George 351

C

Camille Olivia Hanks Cosby Academic Center 224
Campbell, George W. 86
Cape Hatteras 470
Cape Lookout National Seashores 470
Career College Association/Accrediting
  Commission for Independent Colleges and
  Schools 270, 319, 466, 567
Caribbean civilization, history and literature
  collection 662
Carnegie Art Reference Set Collection 180, 190,
  228
Carter Presidential Center and Museum 191
Carver, George Washington 87
Catherine Hughes Art Gallery 175
Catholic Church 284
Centenary Biblical Institute 304
Center for Environmental Programs 288
Center for Studies of Urban Literacy 499
Central Collegiate Athletic Association (CCAA)
  693
Central Intercollegiate Athletic Association
  (CIAA) 297, 446, 452, 458, 476, 480, 491, 676,
  680
Central State University 495
Channing Pollock Theater Collection 704
Charles H. Mason Theological Seminary, Church
  of God in Christ 188
Charles R. Drew Post-Graduate School of
  Medicine (CRDPSOM) 119
Charles R. Drew University of Medicine and
  Science 119
Charles Waddell Chestnut papers 453
Charlotte Area Educational Consortium 435
Chase Commission 709
Cheyney University of Pennsylvania 523
Chicago Normal College 233
Chicago Normal School 233
Chicago State University 233
Chicago Teacher's College 233
Child care pre-school laboratory 440
Choir scholarships 41, 271, 473
Christian Methodist Church (CMC) 641
Christian Methodist Episcopal Church (CME) 56,
  211, 589
Church of Christ 636
Church scholarships 586
City Technical College 424
City University of New York (CUNY) 424
Civil Rights Act of 1954 516
Civil Rights Movement 28, 43
Claflin College 548
Clark Atlanta University 175
Class president scholarships 62

CLIMB (Credentials for Leadership in
  Management and Business) 509
Clinton Junior College 553
Clinton Normal and Industrial College 553
Coahoma Community College 357
Coahoma County Agricultural High School 357
Coahoma Junior College and Agricultural High
  School 357
Cole, Johnnetta 224
Coleman Young Scholarships 249
College and University Council of the State of
  Pennsylvania 530
College Level Examination Program (CLEP) 32,
  38, 55, 59, 65, 75, 91, 103, 114, 135, 163, 173,
  184, 196, 208, 215, 220, 227, 238, 243, 252,
  266, 273, 278, 288, 296, 303, 311, 323, 339,
  348, 355, 366, 373, 378, 402, 408, 417, 422,
  435, 446, 452, 462, 469, 475, 480, 485, 491,
  499, 504, 527, 534, 541, 546, 564, 570, 575,
  592, 597, 610, 624, 628, 634, 649, 655, 661,
  668, 675, 680, 687, 713, 722, 730
College of Education and Industrial Arts 496
College of the Virgin Islands 659
College orientation 26, 32, 38, 55, 69, 91, 108,
  114, 136, 144, 157, 163, 173, 179, 184, 196,
  208, 227, 243, 251, 260, 266, 282, 288, 311,
  340, 343, 348, 355, 373, 378, 395, 408, 427,
  440, 446, 452, 480, 491, 499, 527, 546, 551,
  554, 564, 570, 575, 583, 610, 634, 639, 662,
  668, 675, 680, 687, 692, 704, 722
Colonial Williamsburg 688
Colored (now Christian) Methodist Episcopal
  Church (CME) 56, 211
Colored Agricultural and Normal University 515
Colored Industrial and Agricultural School 263
Colored Methodist Church 641
Colored Methodist Episcopal High School 589
Colored Normal Industrial Agricultural and
  Mechanical College 566
Commission of Dental Accreditation of the
  American Dental Association 699
Commission on Accreditation of Physical
  Therapy Education 502
Commission on Colleges of the Southern
  Association of Colleges 205
Commission on Occupational Education
  Institutions 83
Commission on Opticianry Accreditation 502
Committee on Allied Health Education and
  Accreditation 234, 319, 645, 672, 710, 719
Community and Preventative Medicine Institute
  122
Community Outreach programs 598
Compton Community College 123
Computing Science Accreditation Board, Inc.
  666, 669
Computer Science Accreditation Commission of
  270
Concordia College 40

Continuing Education Program 26, 59, 80, 103, 163, 190, 201, 273, 288, 323, 332, 446, 469, 475, 485, 504, 559, 597, 618, 649, 730

Cook County Normal School 233

Cookman-Collegiate Institute 141

Cooperative Education Program 26, 29, 32, 36, 38, 45, 46, 59, 65, 75, 80, 84, 85, 88, 91, 101, 103, 107, 108, 112, 114, 124, 136, 142, 144, 148, 150, 154, 157, 163, 170, 173, 176, 179, 185, 193, 196, 199, 206, 208, 213, 215, 218, 220, 224, 227, 238, 243, 252, 261, 264, 267, 271, 273, 277, 278, 285, 288, 296, 300, 303, 307, 314, 316, 320, 332, 342, 343, 346, 348, 352, 355, 363, 366, 370, 373, 376, 381, 384, 390, 393, 395, 405, 417, 422, 438, 440, 443, 452, 457, 460, 462, 467, 469, 475, 478, 480, 485, 488, 491, 496, 499, 502, 504, 509, 517, 519, 524, 527, 531, 534, 544, 549, 551, 559, 562, 564, 570, 573, 575, 583, 586, 587, 592, 595, 597, 610, 618, 627, 628, 634, 646, 649, 655, 666, 668, 673, 675, 678, 680, 687, 690, 693, 699, 704, 713, 727

Cooperative Extension Services 709

Cooperative ROTC Program 559

Cooperative student exchange program 75

Cooperative study abroad 46, 243, 373, 395, 402, 675, 730

Coppin State College 299

Coppin State Teachers College 299

Coppin Teacher's College 299

CORK Institute on Black Alcohol and Other Drug Abuse Program 201

Cosby, Bill 224, 580

Cosby, Camille 224, 580

Council for Professional Development 699

Council for Professional Development of the American Home Economics Association 270, 567

Council of Higher Education of the United Church of Christ 616

Council on Accreditation of the National Recreation and Parks Association 726

Council on Rehabilitation Education 300, 369, 567

Council on Social Work Education 22, 62, 78, 87, 132, 176, 218, 248, 264, 270, 277, 307, 369, 381, 438, 454, 460, 466, 544, 607, 626, 646, 666, 672, 683, 690, 699, 710, 726

Councill, William Hooper 21

Creative and performing arts scholarships 321

Cross-registration 26, 150, 196, 510, 527, 570

Cuyahoga Community College 501

D

Darnell, Reverend D.S.S. 141

Dawson, Leonard 573

Daytona Normal and Industrial Institute 141

Defense Activity for Nontraditional Education Support (DANTES) 296

Deferred Payment Plan 88, 154, 176, 194, 225, 249, 264, 405, 601, 631, 666, 699, 710

Delaware State Board of Education 132

Delaware State University 131

Delta Mu Delta 137

Delta Sigma Theta 27, 33, 60, 76, 82, 92, 105, 115, 137, 145, 158, 165, 174, 180, 185, 216, 222, 228, 239, 261, 267, 274, 297, 304, 312, 324, 356, 374, 391, 409, 436, 441, 453, 458, 464, 470, 476, 492, 500, 510, 520, 528, 535, 542, 547, 552, 571, 576, 584, 593, 598, 605, 611, 619, 635, 650, 656, 669, 688, 694, 705, 714, 723, 731

Delta Sigma Theta Sorority (1913) 698

Denmark Branch of the South Carolina Trade School System 556

Denmark Technical College 556

Denmark Technical Education Center 556

Department of Adult, Vocational, and Technical Education 240

Department of Education, Commonwealth of Virginia 690

Department of Registration and Education of the State of Illinois 240

DeWitt Wallace/Spelman College Fund 224

Dexter Avenue Baptist Church 33

"A Different World" 224

Dillard University 257

Dinkins, Mayor David 698

Disciple of Christ Christian Church 620

District of Columbia Nurses Examining Board 710

District of Columbia Teachers College 709

Douglas Wilder Collection 694

Douglas, Aaron 580

Drake, Dr. Joseph Fanning 44

Drama scholarships 36, 101, 154, 193, 370, 376, 489, 653, 666, 699, 711, 727

Drew, Charles 698

Drew/UCLA Medical Education Program 119, 120, 122

Drexel, Blessed Katherine 284

Dubois, W. E. B. 580

Durham State Normal School 471

E

E. D. Nixon's Archival Collection 33

Early admission 24, 30, 37, 49, 63, 79, 88, 98, 102, 107, 113, 124, 145, 177, 183, 194, 219, 225, 241, 259, 265, 271, 277, 281, 321, 339, 342, 346, 353, 377, 388, 394, 401, 406, 415, 439, 444, 450, 467, 484, 502, 518, 545, 558, 596, 608, 642, 654, 667, 711, 721, 728

Early decision 63, 89, 388, 461, 467, 484, 532, 545

East Florida Conference High School 147

Eastern College Athletic Association 303, 534

Eastern College Athletic Conference 311, 528, 713
Eastern Intercollegiate Athletic Conference
    (EIAC) 150, 435, 542, 547, 552
Eastern Music Festival 470
Edisto Gardens 552
Edward Waters College 147
Elizabeth City State College 442
Elizabeth City State Teachers College 442
Elizabeth City State University 442
Elizabeth State Colored Normal School 442
Ella Fitzgerald Performing Arts Center 319
Ellwanger, Dr. Walter H. 41
Emancipated Oak Tree 665
Empire State scholarships 414
Engineering Accreditation Commission of the
    Accreditation of Engineering and Technology
    710
English as a Second Language (ESL) Program 91,
    103, 114, 126, 136, 303, 311, 323, 332, 355,
    402, 427, 485, 597, 704, 713, 722
Episcopal Church 477, 677
Epsilon Delta Epsilon 137
Equal Opportunity Scholarships 235
Ervin "Magic" Johnson Sports Arena 387
Ethical Cultural Collection 628
Ethnic Minority Scholarship 41
Evening programs 55
Exchange Student Program 196, 238
Extended Learning, Drexel Center for 288

F

Family Life Institute (Voorhees College) 576
Fannie Jackson Coppin Normal School 299
Fayetteville State College 448
Fayetteville State Teachers College 448
Fayetteville State University 448
Federal Aviation Administration 710
Federal City College 709
Fisk Jubilee Hall 579
Fisk Jubilee Singers 579
Fisk School 579
Fisk University 579
Fisk/UNCF Pre-medical Summer Institute 583
Flint-Goodridge Hospital 257
Florida Agricultural and Mechanical College 152
Florida Agricultural and Mechanical University
    152
Florida Baptist Institute 160
Florida Memorial College 160
Florida Normal and Industrial Memorial College
    160
Florida Normal and Industrial Memorial Institute
    160
Florida State Board of Nursing 142
Florida State Department of Education for
    Specified Programs 142
Foreign-student grants 176
Fort Valley High and Industrial School 181

Fort Valley State College 181, 217
Franklin, John Hope 580
Frederick Douglass High School 299
Frederick Douglass Library 319
Frederick Douglass Tutorial Institute 197
Freedmen's Aid Society 386, 652
Freedmen's Bureau 175, 698
French Quarters 279
Freshman Accelerated Start-up and Training for
    Retention in the Engineering Curricula
    (FASTREC) 91

G

Gamma Iota Sigma 76
Gammon Theological Seminary, United
    Methodist 188
Garden Housing Development Project 595
Gary, William E. 482
General Chappie James Collection 92
George Gershwin Collection of Music 583
George Washington Carver Museum 93
George Washington Carver Research Foundation
    93
Georgia Department of Education 170
Georgia Institute of Technology 173
Georgia Normal and Agricultural College 169
Georgia Regional Hospital 198
Georgia State Industrial College for Colored
    Youth 217
GI Bill Educational Training 727
GI Dependents' Educational Benefits 22
Goodman, James A. 199
Graceland 598
Grady Memorial Hospital 198
Grambling College 263
Grambling State University 263
Great Blacks in Wax Museum 304
Great Smoky Mountains 481, 486
Great Smoky Mountains National Park 441, 470,
    492
Gulf Coast Athletic Conference 395

H

H. Clinton Taylor Art Gallery 466
Haitian adults, career development program for
    163
Haitian Art Collection 593
Hampton Normal & Agricultural Institute 665
Hampton Singers 665
Hampton University 665
Hampton-Preston Mansion and Garden 542, 547
Handicap Impact (HI) Day 731
Handicapped services 27, 33, 39, 47, 52, 60, 82,
    86, 93, 109, 137, 146, 158, 197, 216, 222, 228,
    244, 253, 262, 268, 312, 314, 324, 348, 356,
    374, 379, 403, 409, 423, 453, 458, 464, 470,

476, 505, 560, 571, 619, 625, 635, 644, 656, 670, 688, 694, 705, 714, 731

Handy, W. C. 599

Harriet Tubman Historical and Cultural Museum 186

Harris Teachers College 399

Harris, Bishop C. R. 459

Harris-Stowe State College 399

Hartshorn Memorial College of Richmond 689

Health Careers Opportunity Program (HCOP) 491, 546

Heartman Black Collection 650

Heartman Manuscripts Collection on Slavery 289

Hebrew girl's school 269

Helen Fuld Collection 303

Henry P. Slaughter and Countee Cullen Memorial Collection 180, 228

Hinds Community College 362

Hinds Junior College 362

Historically Black College/University (HBCU) 78, 211, 270, 386, 454, 516, 653, 690, 726

Historically Black Colleges and Universities (HBCU) Dual Admission Program 332

Holley, Dr. Joseph Winthrop 174

Home Study International 65

Homestead Montebello Center 314

Honor scholarships 300, 307

Honor societies 82, 274, 279, 324, 458, 464, 476, 486, 598, 650

Honors College 687

Honors Colloquium 378

Honors merit scholarship 531

Honors Program 26, 32, 51, 59, 69, 74, 80, 91, 103, 136, 157, 161, 164, 173, 179, 196, 215, 227, 238, 243, 261, 267, 273, 282, 288, 296, 303, 309, 316, 323, 340, 355, 384, 408, 417, 440, 446, 452, 457, 469, 475, 480, 485, 491, 499, 504, 510, 519, 527, 534, 541, 546, 551, 564, 570, 575, 583, 592, 597, 610, 624, 628, 634, 649, 668, 675, 680, 704, 713

Honors Track Program 387, 653

Houston Astrodome 651

Houston Astros 651

Houston Oilers 651

Howard Normal and Theological Institute for the Education of Teachers and Preachers 697

Howard School 448

Howard University 697

Howard University Book Publishing Institute 704

Howard University School of Law 706

Hubie Blake National Museum and Cultural Center 304

Hughes, Langston 530

Huntsville Normal School 21

Huntsville State Vocational Technical School 44

Huston-Tillotson College 615

I

Illinois Community College Board 240

Illinois Office of Education 240

Illinois Teachers College 234

Illinois Veterans Grants 241

Immigration and Naturalization Service for the Training of Alien Students 460

Independent study program 541

Individualized Majors 136, 150, 227, 408, 440, 499, 546, 570, 575, 668, 704, 722

Institute for Colored Youth 523

Institute for International Studies 530

Institute of Food Technologists 22

Institute of Minority Men Research and Programming 628

Intercollegiate Association of Amateur Athletes of America (ICAAAA) 534

Interdenominational Theological Center 187

International Association of Counseling Service, Inc. 111, 567

International Moot Court 708

International programs in Senegal 201

International scholarship 161

Internships 26, 136, 157, 164, 227, 303, 311, 527, 575, 680, 704, 713

Interregional Athletic Conference (IAC) 104, 624

Iron Bowl 76

Israel Sinai Temple Synagogue 269

Itta Bena 385

J

J. B. Watson Collection 115

J. F. Drake State Technical College 44

Jackson College 368

Jackson State College 368

Jackson State University 368

Jackson, Maynard 193

Jackson, Michael 580

James Ward Seabrook papers 453

James, General Daniel "Chappie" 87

Jarvis Christian College 620

Jarvis Christian Institute 620

Jarvis, J. J. 620

Jewett, Fredelia 263

Jimmy Carter Presidential Library 228

Job Training Partnership Act (JTPA) 112, 720

John M. Ross Collection 115

John Paul II, Pope 284

Johnson C. Smith Theological Seminary, Presbyterian USA 188

Johnson C. Smith University 454

Johnson Publishing Co. 239

Joint Enrollment Program 173

Joint Review Committee on Education in Radiologic Technology 699

Joint Review Committee on Educational Programs for Physician Assistants 699

Joint Review Committee on Educational Programs in Nuclear Medicine Technology of the American Medical Association 726
Journalism scholarships 154
Julius Rosenwald Fund 182
Juris Doctorate/Master Business Administration (JD/MBA) 707
Juvenile collection (Harris Library, Philander Smith) 104

K

Kappa Alpha Psi 27, 33, 60, 76, 82, 92, 105, 115, 137, 145, 158, 164, 174, 180, 185, 197, 216, 221, 239, 261, 267, 274, 297, 304, 312, 324, 356, 374, 391, 409, 436, 453, 458, 470, 476, 486, 492, 500, 510, 520, 528, 535, 542, 547, 552, 571, 576, 584, 593, 598, 605, 611, 619, 635, 650, 656, 669, 687, 694, 723, 731
Kappa Delta Pi 137, 174, 222, 403
Kappa Kappa Psi 593
Kappa Xi 619
Keith, Leroy 193
Kellog Business Collection 279
Kennedy Center for Performing Arts 708, 714
Kennedy, President John F. 628, 709
Kennedy-King College 240
Kentucky Department of Education 248
Kentucky Normal and Industrial Institute for Colored Persons 247
Kentucky State College for Negroes 247
Kentucky State University (KSU) 247
King Humanities Center 645
King, Martin Luther, Jr. 33, 193
King/Drew Medical Center 119, 121
Kitty Hawk/Nags Head 470
Knox Nelson Collection 115
Knoxville College 585
Knoxville College Concert Choir 588
Knoxville College-Morristown 586

L

LaGuardia Community College 413
Lane, Bishop Isaac 593
Land Grant Act 217
Land grant institution 21, 87, 110, 131, 153, 182, 247, 269, 277, 351, 404, 465, 516, 566, 606, 631, 659, 683, 709
Lane College 589
Lane Institute 589
Langston Hughes Library Collection 583
Langston University 515
Law Degree Early Entry scholarship 691
Law Enforcement Education Program 29
Lawson State College 48
Lawson, Dr. T. A. 48
Learning disabled students 427, 441

Lee, Spike 193
Leland, George "Mickey" 645
LeMoyne College 594
LeMoyne Normal and Commercial School 594
LeMoyne, Dr. Francis J. 594
Lemoyne-Owen College 594
Leontyne Price Library 387
Lewis College of Business 341
Lewis, Dr. Violet T. 341
Liaison Committee on Medical Education 199, 601
Liberian students 529
Life Experience Internship Program (LEIP) 527
Lilly Endowment 72
Lincoln Chapel 594
Lincoln Institute 404
Lincoln Normal and Industrial Institute 263
Lincoln Normal School 28
Lincoln Parish Training School 263
Lincoln School 594
Lincoln University 404, 529
Lincoln, Abraham 529
Livingstone College 459
Lomax-Hannon Junior College 53
Louis Drexel Morrell Scholarships 285
Louisiana Department of Education 258, 277
Louisiana State Board of Education 277
Lutheran Church Missouri Synod (LCMS) 40
Lyndon B. Johnson Space Center 651

M

Malaysian Student Organization 274
Malcolm X Historical Society 27
Mardi Gras Celebration 279
Margaret Walker Alexander Collection 373
Margaret Washington Collection 92
Marshall, Thurgood 530, 698
Martha L. O'Rourke Afro-American Collection 75
Martin Luther King, Jr. Auditorium 567
Martin Luther King, Jr. Center for Nonviolent Social Change 191, 197, 228
Martin Luther King, Jr. General Hospital 119
Martin Luther King, Jr. International Chapel 193
Martin Luther King, Jr. National Historic Site 191, 197
Martin Luther King, Jr. Scholarship Program 693
Mary Holmes College 375
Mary Holmes Seminary 375
Mary McLeod Bethune Scholarship 432
Maryland Normal & Industrial School at Bowie 293
Maryland State College 319
Maryland State Department of Education 294, 300
Maryland State Teachers College 293
Maryland State Teachers College at Bowie 293
Maryland System 319
McDonald, Rev. A. C. 386
McKee School for Negro Youth 585

McLeod-Bethune Home (historic landmark) 142
Medgar Evers College of the City University of
New York 419
Medgar Evers Scholarship 352
Meharry Medical College 600
Meharry Medical College of Walden University
600
Methodist Episcopal Church (MEC) 318, 386
Methodist Episcopal Church, South 211
Methodist Student Union 216
MIA/POW scholarships 235
Michigan Department of Education 342
Mickey Leland Center 645
Mid-Eastern Athletic Conference (MEAC) 136,
157, 312, 324, 570
Middle State Accreditation Association 414
Middle States Association of Colleges and
Secondary Schools 132, 294, 300, 306, 314,
419, 424, 523, 530, 659, 698, 710
Miles College 56
Miles Memorial College 56
Miles, Bp. William H. 56
Miner Normal School 709
Minister's Institute 97
Ministerial Forum 66
Minority Access to Research Careers Program
(MARC) 122, 221, 457, 546
    Honors Undergraduate Research Training
        Program (MHURT) 80
    scholarships 531
Minority Biomedical Research Support Program
(MBRS) 80, 122, 457, 546
Minority Introduction to Engineering (MITE) 91
Minority Presence Grant 472
Missionary Program 65
Mississippi Commission on College Accreditation
362, 376
Mississippi Delta Region 385
Mississippi Department of Education 376
Mississippi Junior College Athletic Association
366
Mississippi Legislature 380
Mississippi State Department of Education 381, 387
Mississippi State Fair 374
Mississippi Valley State College 381
Mississippi Valley State University 380, 381
Mississippi Vocational College 380
Missouri Department of Elementary and
Secondary Education 400
Mitchell Family Papers 312
Mitchell, Robert 147
Mobile State Junior College 35
Montgomery Bus Boycott 28, 33
Moorland-Spingarn Research Center of Afro-
American History and Culture 704
Moot Court 708
Morehouse College 192
Morehouse School of Medicine 198
Morehouse School of Religion, Baptist 188

Morehouse-Drew-Meharry Cancer Consortium 202
Morgan College 306
Morgan State University 306
Morrill Act 21, 270, 318, 351, 404, 725
Morris Brown College 204
Morris College 561
Morristown College 586
Moses, Edwin 193
Multicultural Awareness Festival 731
Musée Conti Wax Museum 279
Music scholarships 23, 73, 88, 101, 107, 132,
154, 161, 171, 176, 182, 193, 213, 234, 264,
271, 285, 352, 358, 370, 376, 381, 406, 432,
449, 455, 473, 478, 489, 549, 567, 586, 607,
637, 642, 653, 666, 673, 699, 711, 727
Muslim Association 274

N

NAACP 216, 274, 324, 391, 598
NAFEO District of Columbia Project
Scholarships 249
Natchez Seminary 368
National Council on Social Work Education
299
National Accreditation Council for Environmental
Health Curricula 381
National Accrediting Agency for Clinical
Laboratory Sciences 488, 502, 672, 699
National Afro-American Museum and Cultural
Center 507
National Architectural Accrediting Board 87, 153,
270, 666, 699
National Association for Music Therapy 699
National Association for the Accreditation of
Teacher Education 111
National Association of Industrial Technology
352, 369, 381, 443, 646
National Association of Intercollegiate Athletics
(NAIA) 81, 99, 104, 115, 150, 164, 173, 230,
261, 289, 297, 390, 395, 402, 435, 499, 510,
519, 542, 547, 552, 565, 575, 588, 618, 624,
628, 644, 676, 723, 730
National Association of Radio &
Telecommunication Engineers (NARTE) 218
National Association of Schools of Art and
Design 307, 369, 381, 699
National Association of Schools of Music 29,
111, 224, 264, 270, 307, 319, 352, 369, 405,
488, 496, 580, 607, 666, 672, 684, 699, 710
National Association of Schools of Public Affairs
and Administration 369, 699
National Association of Schools of Theater 699
National Association of State Directors of
Teacher Education and Certification 699, 710
National Business Education Association 539
National Collegiate Athletic Association (NCAA)
26, 32, 60, 75, 92, 115, 136, 145, 157, 179, 185,
196, 209, 215, 221, 238, 252, 267, 274, 297,

303, 311, 324, 355, 373, 384, 408, 422, 441, 446, 452, 458, 463, 469, 476, 485, 491, 527, 534, 547, 570, 583, 593, 598, 610, 634, 650, 669, 680, 687, 693, 704, 713, 723

National Council for Accreditation of Teacher Education (NCATE) 22, 29, 62, 142, 170, 182, 224, 234, 264, 270, 294, 299, 307, 321, 352, 369, 381, 400, 405, 449, 454, 466, 472, 488, 496, 516, 523, 567, 573, 607, 631, 646, 666, 672, 684, 726

National Council of Rehabilitation Education 530

National Council on Social Work Education 294

National Guard Tuition Assistance Program 557

National Junior College Athletic Association (NJCAA) 39, 42, 51, 55, 70, 108, 243, 282, 332, 340, 360, 366, 378, 505, 639

National League for Nursing 36, 48, 83, 87, 111, 132, 170, 234, 248, 258, 294, 300, 264, 352, 405, 420, 466, 472, 488, 516, 607, 631, 659, 666, 672, 699, 710, 719

National Presbyterian College Scholarships 455

National Recreation and Parks Association/American Association for Leisure and Education 530, 544

National Religious Training School and Chautauga 471

National Student Exchange (NSE) Program 570, 662

National Training School 471

Navy ROTC 154, 177, 193, 218, 224, 259, 271, 455, 472, 475, 583, 607, 632, 650, 666, 699

Navy ROTC and cooperative Army and Air Force ROTC 206

Negro and African collection 535

Negro Employment in WWII collection 312

Negro Heritage Collection 593

Negro History Collection 619

New England Association of Schools and Colleges (NEASC) 329

New Orleans Museum of Art 279

New Orleans University 257

New York City Technical College 424

New York State Aid to Native Americans 425

New York State Board of Regents 424

New York State Institution of Applied Arts and Sciences 424

Norfolk Polytechnic College 671

Norfolk State College 672, 683

Norfolk State University 671

Normal and Industrial Department of Wilberforce University 495

North Alabama Conference 56

North Carolina A&T State University 465

North Carolina Central University 471

North Carolina College for Negroes 471

North Carolina Department of Public Instruction 432, 460, 478, 488

North Carolina Legislators Black Caucus Scholarship 432

North Carolina National Guard Tuition Assistance Program 473

North Carolina State Board of Education 443

North Carolina State Board of Nursing 488

North Carolina State Department of Public Instruction 449

North Carolina University System 466

North Central Association of College and Schools (NCACS) 97, 106, 110, 234, 240, 342, 346, 400, 405, 496, 501, 507, 719, 726

North Louisiana Agricultural and Industrial Institute 263

Nursing Collection 274

O

Oakland College 351

Oakland Memorial Chapel 352

Oakview Mansion 387

Oakwood College 61

Oakwood Industrial School 61

Oakwood Junior College 61

Oakwood Manual Training School 61

Ohio Department of Education 496, 507

Ohio State Board of Nursing Education and Nurse Registration 502

Oklahoma Board of Nurse Registration and Nursing Education 516

Oklahoma State Board of Education 516

Oklahoma State System of Higher Education 516

Old Stagecoach Road 656

Ollie L. Brown Afro-American Heritage Collection 33

Omega 598

Omega Psi Fraternity (1911) 698

Omega Psi Phi 27, 33, 60, 76, 82, 92, 105, 115, 137, 145, 158, 164, 174, 180, 185, 197, 216, 221, 239, 261, 267, 274, 297, 304, 312, 324, 356, 374, 391, 409, 436, 453, 458, 470, 476, 486, 492, 500, 510, 520, 528, 535, 542, 547, 552, 571, 576, 584, 593, 605, 611, 619, 635, 650, 656, 669, 688, 694, 731

Onley House 318

Open admission 23, 30, 36, 45, 49, 84, 107, 124, 241, 271, 277, 281, 315, 338, 342, 346, 358, 415, 444, 502, 554, 557, 647, 654, 711 (in-state only) 406

Oprah Winfrey scholarships 194

Oral history collection 384

Orangeburg Female Academy 548

Other Race Grants (ORG) 300, 308, 449

Other Race Scholarships 363, 607

Owen College 594

Owen, Reverend S.A. 595

P

Page, Dr. Inman E. 516

Paine College 211

Paine Institute 211

Part-time degree program 32, 38, 42, 51, 70, 85, 91, 99, 108, 115, 126, 136, 157, 164, 173, 179, 185, 208, 227, 261, 282, 288, 303, 311, 316, 343, 348, 378, 408, 417, 422, 427, 440, 452, 491, 527, 541, 546, 570, 575, 610, 668, 676, 680, 704, 713, 723

Paterson, William Burns 28

Patterson, Frederick D. 87

Paul Douglass Teacher Scholarship program 133

Paul Quinn College 626

Paul Robeson Cultural and Performing Arts Center 496

Paul Robeson papers 704

Payne Institute 539

Peabody Collection of African American Collection 669

Peer Tutoring Scholarships 727

Pennsylvania Athletic Conference 528

Pennsylvania University System 523

Phi Alpha Delta 708

Phi Alpha Theta 137, 174

Phi Beta Kappa 105, 115, 193, 216, 520, 705

Phi Beta Lambda 174, 222, 593, 619

Phi Beta Sigma 27, 33, 60, 76, 82, 92, 137, 145, 158, 165, 174, 180, 185, 197, 221, 239, 261, 267, 274, 297, 304, 312, 324, 356, 374, 391, 409, 436, 453, 458, 470, 476, 486, 492, 500, 510, 528, 535, 542, 552, 571, 576, 584, 593, 598, 605, 611, 619, 635, 650, 656, 669, 688, 694, 698, 705, 731

Phi Delta Kappa 93

Phi Delta Phi 708

Phi Eta Sigma 723

Phi Mu Delta 222

Phi Theta Kappa 333, 731

Philander Smith 97, 100

Philander Smith College 100

Phillip University 641

Phillips School of Theology, Christian Methodist Episcopal 188

Physical education scholarship 161

Pi Gamma Mu 222, 304

Piedmont Triad 441

Pinchback, Pinckney 269

Planning Accreditation Board of the American Institute of Certified Planners 710

Police and Firefighters' Educational Assistance 23

Polish exchange student scholarship 161

Pontchartrain Park 277

Porter, James H. 171

Practical Nursing 46

Prairie View A&M University 630

Prairie View Agricultural and Mechanical College of Texas 630

Prairie View State Normal and Industrial College 630

Prairie View University 630

Pre-Matriculant Reinforcement in Medical Education (PRIME) 122

Presbyterian Church 71, 431, 454

Preservation Hall 279

Presley, Dr. Vivian M. 357

Presley, Elvis 599

Princess Anne Academy 306

Princess Anne College 318

Project Outreach legal services 708

Protestant clergy and laymen continuing education for 163

Protestant Episcopal Church 477, 572

Psi Chi 137

Psi Phi 598

Q

Quaker and Slavery Collection 312

R

Raleigh Institute 482

Rashad, Phyllicia 698

Regents' Scholarships 517

Research Triangle 476, 486

Research Triangle Park 481

Reserve Officer Training Corps (ROTC) 726

Revels, Hiram R. 351

Richie, Lionel 87

Richmond Theological Institute 689

Riverwalk Market Place 279

Rockefeller, John D. 223

Rodney G. Higgins Political Science Literature Collection 274

Ronald McNair/Project SPACE Program 196

ROTC 150, 161, 171, 173, 235, 285, 294, 301, 425, 432, 438, 478, 488, 497, 507, 524, 544, 549, 573, 627, 678, 684

Round House Site 636

Roxbury Community College 329

Rufus B. Atwood Papers 252

Rust College 386

Rust University 386

S

S.A. Owen Jr. College 595

S.D. Bishop State Junior College 35

Saint Augustine's College 477

Saint Augustine's Junior College 477

Saint Augustine's Normal School and Collegiate Institute 477

Saint Augustine's School 477

Saint Paul's College 677

Saint Paul's Normal and Industrial School 677

Saint Paul's Polytechnic Institute 677

St. Phillips Episcopal Chapel 573

Samuel Huston College 615, 616
Savannah State College 217
Savery Library 78
Savery, William 77
Schomburg Collection 75, 81, 528, 552, 694
Schomburg Collection on Black Culture on
  microfilm 423
School of Medicine at Morehouse College 198
School Paper Editor Scholarships 62
Scotia Seminary 431
Scotia Women's College 431
Scotlandville 270
Selma University 67
Senior citizens 173, 332, 660
Senior Citizens Program 542
Seventh-day Adventist Black history 65
Seventh-day Adventist Church 61
Shaw Collegiate Institute 482
Shaw, President Talbert 482
Shaw, Reverend S. O. 386
Shaw School 386
Shaw University 386, 465, 482
Short-term loans 182
Short-term, low-interest loans 199, 601
Shorter College 97, 106
Shreveport branch 270
Sigma Delta Chi 222
Sigma Gamma Rho 27, 33, 60, 76, 82, 92, 105,
  115, 137, 145, 158, 165, 174, 180, 185, 216,
  222, 239, 261, 267, 274, 297, 304, 312, 356,
  374, 391, 409, 436, 441, 453, 458, 464, 470,
  476, 492, 510, 520, 528, 542, 547, 552, 571,
  584, 593, 598, 611, 619, 635, 650, 656, 669,
  688, 694, 705, 714, 731
Sigma Gamma Rho Sorority national
  headquarters 239
Sigma Rho Sigma 174
Sigma Tau Delta 222, 403, 619
Sigma Xi 470, 688
Simmons University Bible College 254
Simmons, Dallas 690
Simmons, Dr. Charles W. 314
Sisters of the Blessed Sacrament 284
Slater Industrial Academy 487
Slater Industrial and State Normal School 487
Smith, Adeline 100
Smith, Rev. D. Wayne 732
Smithsonian Institute 714
Sojourner-Douglass College 314
South Carolina State Department of Education 562
South Carolina Agricultural and Mechanical
  Institute 548, 566
South Carolina Board of Education 549
South Carolina Criminal Justice Academy 546
South Carolina Department of Education 544
South Carolina State College 548, 566
South Carolina State Museum 542, 547
South Carolina State University 566
Southern Association of Colleges and Schools
  (SACS) 22, 29, 36, 40, 44, 48, 57, 62, 67, 72,

78, 87, 142, 153, 161, 170, 175, 182, 188, 193,
  199, 212, 218, 224, 248, 254, 258, 264, 270,
  277, 280, 284, 352, 357, 362, 369, 375, 381,
  387, 393, 432, 438, 443, 448, 454, 460, 466,
  472, 478, 482, 488, 544, 549, 557, 562, 567,
  573, 580, 586, 590, 595, 607, 616, 621, 626,
  631, 642, 645, 665, 672, 677, 683, 690
Southern Association of Colleges and Secondary
  Schools (SACS) 601, 653
Southern Athletic Conference 32
Southern Bible Institute 636
Southern California Conferences 127
Southern Christian Institute 392
Southern Intercollegiate Athletic Conference
  (SIAC) 60, 173, 179, 185, 196, 209, 215, 221,
  390, 593
Southern University 276
Southern University and A&M University-Baton
  Rouge 269
Southern University at New Orleans 276
Southern University at Shreveport 280
Southern University system 270
Southwest Hospital and Medical Center 198
Southwestern Athletic Conference (SWAC) 267,
  355, 634, 650
Southwestern Christian College 636
Space research 66
Spelman College 223
Spike Lee scholarships 194
Spring Flower Festival 644
State Agricultural and Mechanical College 21
State Agricultural and Mechanical Institute 21,
  548
State College for Colored Students 131
State Colored Normal School 448
State Jazz festival 731
State Normal and Industrial College for Colored
  Students 152
State Normal and Industrial School at Huntsville
  21
State Normal College for Colored Students 152
State Normal School and University for the
  Education of the Colored Teachers and Students
  28
State Normal School for Colored Persons 247
State Normal School for Colored Students 28
State of Alabama Department of Education 67
State Teachers and Agricultural College 181
State Teachers College 28
Sternwheel Regatta Festival 731
Stillman College 71
Stillman Institute 71
Storer College of Harpers Ferry 689
Stowe Teachers College 400
Straight College 257
Straight University 257
Student Early Entrance (SEE) Program 693
Student Exchange Program 136, 252, 693, 704
Student government scholarships 234

Study abroad program 32, 51, 75, 81, 91, 115,
  126, 150, 157, 173, 179, 185, 196, 215, 221,
  227, 238, 252, 261, 267, 273, 279, 288, 303,
  311, 324, 355, 427, 440, 452, 457, 469, 475,
  480, 485, 491, 499, 505, 527, 534, 546, 570,
  575, 583, 598, 628, 644, 668, 680, 704, 713,
  723
Sudarkasa, Niara 530
Sullivan, Louis 198
Summer Bridge Program 713
Sumner Normal School 399
Surgery (M.D.) 201
Susan Reynolds Underhill Collection 535
Swayne Hall 78
Sweeney collection 598

T

Talent Search Program 610, 699
Talladega Baptist Male High School 78
Talladega College 77
Tarrant, Thomas 77
Tau Alpha Pi 222
Tau Beta Sigma 593
Tau Phi Kappa 640
Taylor Art Gallery 470
Technical College of the City University 424
Technology Accreditation Commission of the
  Accreditation Board of Engineering and
  Technology 218
Tennessee Baptist Missionary and Educational
  Convention 594
Tennessee State Board of Education 595
Tennessee State University 606
Territorial act 515
Texas Association of Colleges and Universities
  621, 642
Texas College 641
Texas Education Agency 616, 621, 626, 653
Texas Military College 636
Texas Rose Festival 644
Texas Southern University 645
Texas State University 645
Thomas, Arthur E. 496
Thurgood Marshall Black Education Fund 29, 88,
  112, 133, 154, 182, 249, 264, 271, 294, 300,
  308, 320, 352, 406, 449, 467, 473, 489, 496,
  517, 525, 531, 568, 607, 632, 646, 673, 684, 711
Thurgood Marshall Law Library 645
Thurgood Marshall Law Society 535
Tillotson College 615, 616
Tillotson Collegiate and Normal Institute 616
Tougaloo College 392
Tougaloo Southern Christian Institute 392
Tougaloo University 392
Trenholm State Technical College 83
Tuition Reduction Program 601
Tuition Waivers 112, 142, 154, 176, 225, 249,
  259, 264, 369, 632, 666, 690

Turner Theological Seminary, African Methodist
  Episcopal 188
Tuscaloosa Institute 71
Tuskegee Institute 87
Tuskegee Normal and Industrial Institute 86
Tuskegee University 86
Tuskegee University (National Historic Site and
  District) 87
Tuskegee University (National Landmark) 87
Tuskegee VA Medical Center 198
Tybee Island 222

U

UNCF Remission Grant 213
UNCF Premedical Summer Program 624
Underground Railroad movement 506
Union Normal School 257
United Church of Christ 77, 579, 594, 615
United Methodist (UM) scholarships 616
United Methodist Church 100, 141, 548, 600,
  615, 652
United Methodist loans 617
United Negro College Fund (UNCF) 72, 161,
  175, 188, 206, 225, 259, 393, 438, 478, 549,
  563, 586, 595, 621, 698
United Negro College Fund (UNCF) scholarships
  58, 62, 72, 79, 88, 101, 148, 176, 188, 193, 194,
  213, 258, 259, 285, 387, 432, 455, 460, 483,
  507, 544, 573, 580, 591, 616, 621, 642, 653,
  678, 690, 699
United Presbyterian Church 585
U.S. Department of Education 539, 553
U.S. Government Documents Depository 312, 611
U.S. News & World Report 224
United States Government Depository Library 355
United States Tennis 435
University of Arkansas at Pine Bluff 110
University of Maryland Eastern Shore 306, 318
University of North Carolina 448, 488
University of Tennessee at Nashville 606
University of the District of Columbia 709
University of the Virgin Islands 659
University Senate of the United Methodist Church
  101, 142, 212, 387, 438, 549, 616, 653
Upward Bound program 51, 70, 104, 274, 282,
  355, 575, 598, 618, 662, 730 610, 655, 693
Usry, James L. 530
Utica Junior College 362
Utica Normal and Industrial Institute 362

V

Victorian Ginocchio Hotel 656
Virgin Islands Agricultural Experiment Station 659
Virgin Islands document collection 662
Virgin Islands Extension Service 659

Virginia Collegiate and Industrial Institute 306
Virginia Normal and Collegiate Institute 683
Virginia Normal and Industrial Institute 683
Virginia Seminary and College 681
Virginia State Board of Education 677, 684
Virginia State College 683
Virginia State College for Negroes 683
Virginia State University 683
Virginia State University at Fort Lee 687
Virginia Union University 689
Vocational Rehabilitation Educational Benefits 182
Vocational Rehabilitation program 549, 574
Voorhees College 572
Voorhees Industrial School 572
Voorhees Normal and Industrial School 572
Voorhees School and Junior College 572
Voorhees Technical institute 424

W

W.E.B. DuBois Honors College 373
W.E.B. DuBois library collection 583
Walden Seminary 100
Washington Normal School 709
Washington Technical Institute 709
Washington, Booker T. 86, 263
Waycross College 173
Wayland Seminary 689
Wayne County Community College 345
Wells, Nelson 293
West Indies Collection 680
West Paces Ferry Hospital 198
West Texas Conference School 616
West Virginia Board of Directors of the State
   College System 726
West Virginia Collegiate Institute 725
West Virginia Colored Institute 725
West Virginia Department of Education 719
West Virginia Intercollegiate Athletic Conference
   (WVIAC) 723, 730
West Virginia State College 725
West Virginia State Department of Education 726
West Virginia University 725
Western Association of Schools and Colleges 123
Western State Conference and the South Coast
   Conference 127

Whitney M. Young, Jr. honors colleges 252
Whitney Young, Jr.'s study of the great books 248
Wilbur R. Gregg Black Collection 552
William Lehman Aviation Center 161
Wigwam Building 665
Wilberforce State College 496
Wilberforce University of the Methodist
   Episcopal Church 506
Wilberforce, William 506
Wiley College 652
Wiley, Bp. Isaac W. 652
William Reese Medical Collection 174
Williams, Doug 263
Wilson, Woodrow
   boyhood home 552
Windsor Home 356
Winfrey, Oprah 193
Winston-Salem State College 487
Winston-Salem State University 487
Winston-Salem Teachers College 487
WISE (Women in Science and Engineering) 227
Woodrow Wilson Junior College 240

X

Xavier University of Louisiana 284

Y

Yearbook Editor Scholarships 62
Young, Andrew 193

Z

Zeta Phi Beta 27, 33, 60, 76, 82, 92, 105, 115,
   137, 145, 158, 165, 174, 180, 185, 216, 222,
   239, 261, 267, 274, 297, 304, 312, 324, 356,
   374, 391, 409, 436, 441, 453, 458, 464, 470,
   476, 492, 500, 510, 520, 528, 535, 542, 547,
   552, 571, 576, 584, 593, 598, 605, 611, 619,
   635, 650, 656, 669, 688, 694, 698, 705, 714,
   731
Zion Wesley College 459
Zion Wesley Institute 459